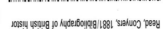

BIBLIOGRAPHY OF
BRITISH HISTORY
TUDOR PERIOD, 1485–1603

Oxford University Press, Amen House, London E.C. 4

GLASGOW NEW YORK TORONTO MELBOURNE WELLINGTON
BOMBAY CALCUTTA MADRAS KARACHI KUALA LUMPUR
CAPE TOWN IBADAN NAIROBI ACCRA

FIRST EDITION 1933
SECOND EDITION 1959

BIBLIOGRAPHY OF
BRITISH HISTORY

TUDOR PERIOD, 1485–1603

ISSUED UNDER THE DIRECTION OF
THE AMERICAN HISTORICAL ASSOCIATION
AND THE ROYAL HISTORICAL SOCIETY
OF GREAT BRITAIN

EDITED BY
CONYERS READ

SECOND EDITION

OXFORD
AT THE CLARENDON PRESS
1959

TO THE MEMORY
OF
CHARLES GROSS
AND
SIR GEORGE PROTHERO

INTRODUCTION

THIS volume is the culmination, at least for the time, of an old project. It might be said to have had its ultimate origin in the presidential address of the late Sir George Prothero before the Royal Historical Society, 19 February 1903, which was an appeal for the preparation and publication of a general bibliography of Modern British History. Five years later, at the meeting of the American Historical Association at Richmond, Virginia, 30 December 1908, the chairman of a conference on research in English History proposed for discussion the production of such a bibliography as one of the most immediate needs of scholars in that field. The proposal awakened a ready response and was discussed at length by Professor R. E. Catterall of Cornell University and Professor A. L. Cross of the University of Michigan, who had been appointed to open up the subject, and by some six or eight others. There was the greatest variety of opinion, some proposing an exhaustive work for the whole modern period, others a practical check list for the sixteenth and seventeenth centuries; some advocating, others deprecating, the proposal to make it a joint enterprise with English scholars, the latter fearing delay and differences of approach to the subject. All agreed that it was high time some such work should be prepared and that it should be in the nature of a continuation of Gross's *Sources and Literature of English History*. It was a time of especially close relations with Great Britain; several of the most active members of the Association had studied much in England, and it was therefore natural that the suggestion should prevail that the work should be a joint one, if possible, carried out by representatives of the American Historical Association and the Royal Historical Society.

In accordance with the recommendations of the conference the Council of the Association appointed a committee, of which the writer of this introduction was made and has remained chairman. The other members of the committee were Professor Cross of the University of Michigan, Professor Merriman of Harvard, Dr. Richardson, librarian of Princeton, and Professor Williston Walker of the Hartford Divinity School. Changes have been made since, as death, loss of interest, or pressure of other duties have made retirement necessary, and others have taken their places, among them Dr. Conyers Read, then of the University of Chicago; Professor Wallace Notestein, then of Cornell University, now of Yale; Dr. Caroline Ware of Vassar College; and Godfrey Davies, then of the University of Chicago, now of the Huntington Library. The Royal Historical Society accepted with readiness an invitation to join in the work and early in 1909 appointed a committee consisting of Sir George Prothero, formerly Professor of History at Edinburgh, and at that time editor of the *London Quarterly Review*, chairman; Sir Charles Firth, then Regius Professor of Modern History at Oxford; Dr. Hubert Hall of the English Public Record Office; Mr. R. H. Tedder, Treasurer of the Royal Historical Society; and Sir Adolphus Ward, Master of Peterhouse. Later Dr. G. P. Gooch,

Hon. J. W. Fortescue, and Mr. H. E. Malden became members of the committee. Numerous conferences were held, some in England, some in America, between the chairmen and other members of the two committees. A plan was worked out, a group of volunteer collaborators was obtained, in addition to the members of the two committees, and a few paid contributors were engaged for special services. In 1912 Sir George Prothero became general editor, and a contract for publication was entered into with Mr. John Murray of London. Funds for current expenses were provided by appropriations from the two societies, by collections from interested donors, and by advance subscriptions.

The plan adopted was an ambitious one. There were to be three volumes, each about the size of Gross; one for the Tudor and Stuart periods, one for the eighteenth and nineteenth centuries, and one for general matter, which should include not only general works, but descriptions of archives, lists of libraries where works in English history could be found, the productions of societies, lists of journals, and such other material. The Tudor part was put in charge of the American, the Stuart, of the English committee; the general volume was to be prepared by the general editor. Both printed and manuscript material as well as contemporary and modern works were to be included. A large amount of correspondence took place and a considerable number of titles was collected and classified and put in the hands of the general editor.

Then came the war. In fact, several packages of title cards from America were in the mails at sea addressed to the general editor when the war broke out. During this period all interests were diverted in other directions. Sir George Prothero was active in war work; at the close of the war he was appointed by the British Government to edit the series of descriptions of the various countries of the world collected by the Foreign Office during the war; before this work was actually completed his health broke down, and his death occurred in July 1922, before he had had time to gather up again the scattered threads of the project.

In the meantime much of the material had become antiquated, the lacunae that had always existed became wider, and the habit of international co-operation had declined. The disability and death of the general editor and the loss of interest and procrastination of many of the collaborators on both sides of the sea made a change of plan desirable. After much consideration and correspondence it was determined early in 1923 to reduce the plan to somewhat more modest dimensions and, for the sake of simplicity, to dissolve the working partnership between the American Historical Association and the Royal Historical Society. The general volume was abandoned, the plan of a volume for the eighteenth and nineteenth centuries was postponed to an indefinite future, and the American and English committees agreed each to prepare and publish independently, the former a volume on the Tudor, the latter a volume on the Stuart period. The latter was completed under the editorship of Mr. Godfrey Davies and published in 1928.

Owing to the causes mentioned above, the wheels of the project slowed down, so far as the Tudor volume was concerned, till it bade fair to come to an entire stop. The plan was galvanized into life by the agreement of Dr. Conyers Read, long a member of the committee and one of the early collaborators on the book, to reorganize the group of contributors, to correlate and reduce to uniformity the old material and the large amount of new that would have to be gathered, and to do the laborious and all-important work of final organization, completion, and the securing of accuracy. To his persistence in enlisting capable and willing collaborators, to his own contributions, and to his scholarship in revision of the whole work, are due the actual appearance of this volume and a large part of such value as it may prove to possess. It is under his editorship that it appears. The original pre-war contract for publication, with Mr. John Murray, was abandoned, and a new contract secured with the Delegates of the Oxford University Press, the publishers also of the Stuart volume, for whose generous and intelligent co-operation acknowledgement must be made.

The original material for this volume has undergone such repeated revisions that it is hard to ascribe much of it to its original authors. The parts done specifically by the editor and the chairman, by the contributing members of the American committee, Professors Cross, Merriman, and Walker, and Dr. Richardson, and by contributing members of the English committee, Sir George Prothero, Sir Julian Corbett, Dr. Hubert Hall, and Mr. H. E. Malden have all been added to and often changed by others. It should, however, be noted that Professor Cross, who originally drafted the chapters on constitutional and legal history over twenty years ago, has assisted in bringing them abreast with the march of more recent scholarship.

Among the new collaborators on the volume since work was resumed in 1924, the most helpful in England has been Professor J. E. Neale of the University of London, in America Dr. Caroline F. Ware of Vassar College. Professor Neale has given valuable help in securing other workers, and has himself read and to some extent corrected the chapters on political, constitutional, legal, and ecclesiastical history. Dr. Ware for the past five years has co-operated closely with the editor in every department of his work. She has herself formulated or reformulated the general introductory chapter, the chapters on political theory, on cultural and social history, on Scotland, Ireland, and Wales. Dr. Mary Hulme Maguire, now of Radcliffe College, has so extensively remodelled the chapter on ecclesiastical history as to make it virtually her own. Professor Charles H. McIlwain of Harvard has done much to improve the chapters on constitutional and legal history and on political theory. Professor Bertha H. Putnam of Mount Holyoke College has added immeasurably to the value of the chapter on legal history by her painstaking and scholarly criticism. Professor R. H. Tawney of the University of London has read and amended the chapter on economic history. The late Robert Dunlop has completely revised the chapter on Ireland. It was perhaps the very last of his many important contributions to a subject in which he was easily pre-eminent. Mr. W. Garmon Jones, librarian of the University of Liverpool, has increased the outstanding indebtedness of students of Welsh history towards him by his very careful revision of the chapter on Wales.

Grateful acknowledgement must also be made to Miss Constantia Maxwell, of Trinity College, Dublin, for her valuable suggestions for the chapter on Ireland; to Dr. Margaret Gay, who contributed the list of printed wage assessments to the chapter on economic history; to Dr. Hubert Hall for the section on prices; and to Dr. John Nef, of the University of Chicago, for the section on coal mining in the same chapter.

To one who assisted at the birth of this bibliographical project as an Anglo-American undertaking, and who assented regretfully to the abandonment of the original plan of close co-operation, it is pleasant to contemplate a list of collaborators in which the names of British and American scholars are so freely intermingled. Evidently the deviation from the original plan has been more formal than actual and the Anglo-American character of the enterprise has persisted to the end.

EDWARD P. CHEYNEY

Chairman of the Committee on a
Bibliography of Modern British History
of the American Historical Association

PREFACE TO THE SECOND EDITION

BIBLIOGRAPHIES begin to be out of date while they are still in press. It is now over twenty-five years since the first edition of this bibliography appeared. During the interval an enormous mass of new material on Tudor England has been published. In the preparation of this edition, some five thousand new titles have been collected and examined. Of these I and my associates have selected about half for publication. We have also reconsidered the entries in the first edition and have discarded those titles which seem to be no longer worthy of attention, though the number of these has not been great.

A comparison of the two editions chapter by chapter reveals the fact that significant contributions to Scottish, Welsh, and particularly Irish history have been relatively more numerous than those to English history. It is somewhat surprising to discover that additions to ecclesiastical history have been relatively more numerous than those to economic history. Among the churches, the history of Roman Catholicism has gained more than that of either the Anglican or the dissenting churches.

The second edition follows the pattern of the first. An exhaustive survey of the material in print has been made to 1 January 1957. Many entries have been made of books and articles appearing since that date, but no complete survey of this more recent literature has been attempted. Like the first edition, this one aims to follow a numerical order in listing titles and an alphabetical order of authors in each section. But later additions and subtractions after the original text and the innumerable cross-references have been printed have sometimes made variations inevitable. Users of the book need not be disturbed if occasionally 2 does not follow 1, or orthodox alphabetical order is not always scrupulously observed.

What is said about the first edition in its preface is equally applicable to the second. For that reason the preface to the first has been reprinted. Professor Cheyney's Introduction to the first edition has also been reprinted because it presents a succinct account of the history of the enterprise. It is sad to reflect that so many of its pioneers are no longer with us. Of the original American group not one survives, and of the English group the most active members, Sir George Prothero, Sir Charles Firth, and Dr. Hubert Hall have all passed away. But what they have planned, though interrupted by two world wars, survives and flourishes. Of the three volumes published since 1928, Davies on the Stuarts, Read on the Tudors, and Pargellis and Medley on the eighteenth century, the first two are a quarter of a century old, and both of them are out of print.

Thanks to the benevolence of the Ford Foundation, money has been provided to finance the preparation of new editions both of Davies and of Read, together with a new edition (the first since 1913) of Gross (*Sources and Literature of English History ... to 1485*), which, though of a different provenience, blazed the trail for all the rest. The present volume is the first fruit of this new enterprise, but editors are at work on new editions both of

Gross and of Davies. These will appear under the names of the new editors, Edgar B. Graves for Gross, Mary Freer Keeler for Davies. Plans are being made for further volumes to continue the work where Pargellis and Medley left off at 1789.

The enterprise, as it was planned in the beginning, still retains in one form or other its Anglo-American character. Certainly this has been true of the present volume. At the outset I asked my old friend Sir John Neale to suggest collaborators from his side the seas, the intention being to secure expert critics for the different sections. Virtually every one of his nominees not only accepted service but rendered it promptly and competently. I have in almost every case accepted their amendments. Though I am responsible for the final text the volume has gained enormously from their contributions. They are, in the order of the chapters they dealt with: Joel Hurstfield, University of London, Chapter II, Political History; Garrett Mattingly, Columbia University, Chapter II, G. Foreign Affairs; S. E. Thorne, Harvard University, Chapter V, Law; T. M. Parker, University College, Oxford, Chapter VI, Ecclesiastical History; T. S. Willen, University of Manchester, Chapter VII, Economic History; Allen Chester, University of Pennsylvania, Chapter X, Literature; Gordon Donaldson, Edinburgh University, Chapter XII, Scotland; R. Dudley Edwards, Dublin University, Chapter XIII, Ireland; A. H. Dodd, University of North Wales, Chapter XIV, Wales. Sir John himself read and improved the whole text.

I have also exploited shamelessly many of my old friends in the profession. I am indebted to Noel Blakiston, Deputy Keeper, Public Record Office; Doris Coates of the National Archives Register; Dorothea Coates, Librarian of Longleat; T. P. O'Neill, Assistant Keeper of Printed Books, National Library of Ireland; Kenneth Setton, Librarian of the University of Pennsylvania, and his staff; Eleanor Campion of the Philadelphia Union Library Catalogue; and to many others.

My good friends, the officers of the Clarendon Press, have seen the volume through the press. The difficulties of printing accurately a book of this sort and of dealing with the innumerable last-minute corrections are well calculated to becloud the sunniest of natures. They have been long suffering and of great goodness. The press work itself is obviously beyond reproach.

My largest debt of gratitude is to my assistant, Marion Ruth Swann. Without her the book could hardly have been produced at all. She collected virtually all the material, arranged it and indexed it with rare diligence and devotion, laying aside important research work of her own in another country and another century. The final decisions of books to be included and the final appraisals of them were mine, but all the laborious preparatory work was hers. While I assume entire responsibility for the book's shortcomings, she deserves the lion's share of credit for its merits.

C. R.

Villa Nova, Pennsylvania, U.S.A.
10 October 1958

PREFACE TO THE FIRST EDITION

THIS book forms the second volume of a series of bibliographies of British history of which Charles Gross, *Sources and Literature of English History . . . to 1485*, forms the first, and Godfrey Davies, *Bibliography of British History . . . 1603 to 1714*, the third. In conjunction with Mr. Davies's volume on the Stuarts it was planned as a continuation of Gross. For that reason the editor has been guided by Gross throughout, and has not hesitated to make cross-references to the titles in his book when economy of space made such procedure desirable.

This bibliography is designed to present a systematic survey of the material in print relative to the history of Tudor England. It includes books and pamphlets, essays and monographs, as well as significant contributions to the subject in journals and in the transactions of learned societies. In all chapters, except those dealing with cultural and local history, it aims to include with something approaching completeness all important collections of printed sources. It does not attempt to consider in detail the great mass of source material in manuscript preserved in the Public Record Office, the British Museum, and elsewhere in England, though the student will find in it all the important calendars, catalogues, and guides to these vast treasuries. It has been prepared primarily for students of history and in the selection and arrangement of titles, as well as in the bibliographical data given in connexion with each title, the aim has been to meet the requirements of the historical student. It will not satisfy the demands of those more concerned with the form than with the content of books.

The editor has undertaken to include everything of importance published before 1 August 1932, when the corrected page proofs went to press, but he speaks with less confidence of completeness for publications which have appeared since 1 January 1930.

This bibliography does not profess to be exhaustive. A very large number of pertinent books are omitted. The basis for the selection of titles varies with the subject. In preparing the chapters on political and ecclesiastical history the problem has been one of selecting the significant contributions from a great mass of printed material, most of which is of no independent value. The titles in these chapters represent in general the survivals of the fittest after a process of rigid elimination. Here, however, as elsewhere, well-known books of indifferent merit have sometimes been included in order to enter a caveat against them. Here also, as elsewhere, and particularly in the chapter on ecclesiastical history, the voluminous controversial literature is dealt with by including books representative of every recognized point of view. In the chapters on constitutional and legal history and on political theory, fields in which the material in print is comparatively scanty, rather scattered, and in general much more scholarly, the problem has been rather one of getting everything in than of leaving anything out. The same thing may be said of the chapter on economic history, except that one has to reckon here with a large number of scholarly studies dealing with economic conditions in particular localities and not confined to the Tudor period. Many of these have found their way into the chapter on local history. It is to be feared that some of them have been missed, though the intention has been to omit none of importance. In the fields of discovery and exploration the intrusion of America and the romantic character of early maritime enterprise have conspired together to produce a great number of textbooks and popular narratives of little or no independent value. All of these have been rigidly excluded. That part of America which is now the United States has received scant attention. It acquires little or no significance so far as English history is concerned before the seventeenth century and has been dealt with at length in Mr. Davies's volume. In the chapters on cultural and local history no attempt at completeness has been made. They are both intended to be rather guides through the voluminous material on these subjects than in themselves adequate bibliographies. There is a real need for a critical bibliography of English local history, a field in which there are so many tares among the wheat, but nothing of the sort has been attempted here.

The chapters on Scotland, Ireland, and Wales are designed to be complete in themselves and to include everything of importance pertinent to the history of those regions during the period under consideration. Thus the history of Scottish law forms part of the chapter on Scotland, not of the general chapter on legal history, and the history of the Irish Church is placed under Ireland, rather than under ecclesiastical history. The editor and his colleagues feel rather apologetic about the chapter on Scotland. It badly needed the winnowing hand of an expert, but none was available, and Scotland in some form or other had to be included. It is hoped that nothing of importance has been left out, though it is feared that much has been included which might wisely have been omitted. The chapters on Ireland and Wales have been more fortunate in their friends. With Robert Dunlop and Miss Maxwell to check the one, and with Mr. W. Garmon Jones to revise the other, it is hardly likely that they can be very far wrong.

The general arrangement under each chapter-heading is indicated in the table of contents. Each subject has been divided and subdivided as far as is practicable, and titles are grouped accordingly. There are, of course, a great number of books which do not fit exactly into any such classification —or rather which fit into it in more than one place. In a very few instances, when a book is of great importance in more than one field, the title has been duplicated, but generally speaking the difficulty is met by cross-references at the head of each section to pertinent material located elsewhere. With the same end in view the subject entries in the index have been carried out in considerable detail. It is suggested that students in search of material upon a particular topic consult first the table of contents and then the index. Dr. Gross's plan of marking important titles with an asterisk has been abandoned, but the short introductory paragraphs to each subdivision generally emphasize the more significant books on the topic under consideration, and the really valuable books are almost always indicated by some individual comment. The arrangement of titles within each section is generally alphabetical, according to authors or catch title, following Gross, rather than chronological, according to the date of publication, following Davies. In one or two instances, however, notably in the section dealing with contemporary writers on political theory, the chronological order has been adopted, since it serves to establish relationships which are of fundamental importance. All such exceptions to the general rule are indicated in the introductory paragraph to the sections to which they apply.

The arrangement of bibliographical data for each individual title is as follows: The author's name is given first, the title (or contracted title) of the book or article second, the editor's name, if any, third, preceded by a 'By'. The place of publication follows and then the date. When, as in the case of collections of documents, catalogues, collections of separate studies, &c., the book is put forth by an editor, not an author, the title of the book is given first and then the editor. When any one of these bibliographical items is definitely known, but not definitely printed in the book itself, it is generally enclosed in square brackets. When any item is conjectured it is enclosed in square brackets with a question mark. Abbreviations are freely used (cf. p. xxvii *infra*) and titles freely contracted. For the sake of brevity, in dealing with the names of authors and editors, all titles of honour and all designations of rank have been omitted except where they are absolutely necessary for purposes of identification. The number of volumes of a book is given, but not the size or the number of pages. This information would be desirable, but in the opinion of the editor not so desirable as to justify the enormous amount of labour involved in making it exact. As for the old conventional classifications, folio, quarto, octavo, &c., they no longer mean enough to warrant even the labour of printing them. In every case the first known edition of a book is given, but subsequent editions only when they differ in some important particular from the first, or when, as in the case of reprints of rare books, they are more readily accessible. When later editions are mentioned they are indicated by a place and a date following the date of the earlier edition and separated from it by a semicolon. If a date only appears in this position the place of publication of the later edition is to be understood to be the same as that of the earlier one.

No definite rule has been followed in making comments on books. Some are remarked upon because they are good, a few because they are bad, many in order to indicate more precisely than their title does the nature of their contents, many in order to give additional bibliographical data. In general it may be said that the comment is such as the book in question seems to call for. The absence of comment should not be construed to mean that the book is negligible or of indifferent merit.

All bibliographies of this sort must be tentative and by reason of the enormous number of separate items involved inevitably faulty. This one has suffered particularly because its editor has no real claim to be regarded as a bibliographer and has been further handicapped by the pressure of other duties. He hopes that all students of Tudor history will regard themselves as collaborators in a later edition, will make corrections, supply omissions, and suggest alterations with the same freedom that they would exercise in a work of their own.

Professor Cheyney, in his introduction, has paid tribute to those scholars on both sides the Atlantic who have given much generous assistance. Perhaps the editor may be permitted a word in closing with reference to his two staunchest friends and coadjutors in these long and painful labours, Dr. Caroline F. Ware and Professor Edward P. Cheyney. Both of these names should properly be associated with his own on the title-page. Without Dr. Ware's loyal co-operation the book could hardly have been completed in any measurable length of time. Professor Cheyney, in his introduction, has with characteristic self-effacement failed even to hint at the extent of his own contributions. He had much to do with setting the whole project on foot in the first place, and he has since nursed it to recovery through more than one critical illness. He has done hard spade work on many of the most important chapters, he has read and revised the whole work both in manuscript and in proof, he has given much wise counsel and has been generously tolerant of the dissenting ideas of one far less learned in Tudor history than himself. If this book falls far short of his own high standards of scholarship, the editor has only himself to blame.

C. R.

Villa Nova, Pennsylvania
1 September 1932

CONTENTS

ABBREVIATIONS

To economize space, cross-references are always made by numbers, usually enclosed in round brackets, to the number of the original entry. Abbreviations are freely used. It is hoped that most of them will be self-explanatory, but the following list may prove useful:

Add. MSS.	= Additional Manuscripts, British Museum.
A.H.R.	= *American Historical Review*; cf. no. 44 *infra*.
app.	= appendix.
Arch.	= *Archaeologia*, London, 1770 ff., or Archaeological.
Arch. Camb.	= *Archaeologia Cambrensis*; cf. no. 4164 *infra*.
Biblio. or Bibliog.	= Bibliographical.
B.M.	= British Museum.
Bull. Inst. Hist. Research	= *Bulletin of the Institute of Historical Research*; cf. no. 45 *infra*.
Cal. S.P.	= *Calendar of State Papers*.
Cambr.	= Cambridge.
Cambr. Hist.	= *Cambridge History of English Literature*; cf. no. 6 *infra*.
Cambr. Mod. Hist.	= *Cambridge Modern History*; cf. no. 20 *infra*.
Cath. Rec. Soc.	= Catholic Record Society.
D.N.B.	= *Dictionary of National Biography*.
Eccles.	= Ecclesiastical.
Econ.	= Economy or Economic.
Edin.	= Edinburgh.
E.E.T.S.	= Early English Text Society, London, 1864 ff.
E.H.R.	= *English Historical Review*; cf. no. 52 *infra*.
Eng.	= English, England.
enl.	= enlarged.
Geo. or Geog.	= Geographical.
Harl.	= Harleian.
Harl. MSS.	= Harleian Manuscripts, British Museum.
Hist.	= History, Historical, Histoire, Historische.
Hist. MSS. Comm.	= Historical Manuscripts Commission.
Hug. Soc.	= Huguenot Society of London.
Ire.	= Ireland, Irish.
Jour.	= Journal.
Jour. Mod. Hist.	= *Journal of Modern History*; cf. no. 58 *infra*.
Lancs.	= Lancashire.
Lib.	= Library.
Lit.	= Literary, Literature.
Lond.	= London.
Misc.	= Miscellany.
Mus.	= Museum.
Nat.	= Natural.
N.C.	= North Carolina, U.S.A.
Oxf.	= Oxford.
Parl. papers	= Parliamentary papers.
Philol.	= Philology.
Philos.	= Philosophical.
Pol.	= Political.

Pol. Sci. Quar.	=	*Political Science Quarterly.*
P.R.O.	=	British Public Record Office, London.
Proc.	=	Proceedings.
Pub.	=	Publications.
Quar.	=	Quarterly.
Q.S.	=	Quarter Sessions.
Rec.	=	Record.
Revue des quest. hist.	=	*Revue des questions historiques*; cf. no. 65 *infra*.
R.H.S.	=	Royal Historical Society.
R.I.A.	=	Royal Irish Academy; cf. no. 5669 *infra*.
R.S.A.I.	=	Royal Society of Antiquaries of Ireland; cf. no. 5670 *infra*.
s.a.	=	No date of publication given.
Scot.	=	Scotland, Scottish.
Shrop.	=	Shropshire.
s.l.	=	No place of publication given.
Soc.	=	Society.
S.T.C.	=	*Short Title Catalogue*; cf. no. 35 *infra*.
Trans.	=	Transactions or translation.
Trans. R.H. Soc.	=	*Transactions of the Royal Historical Society*, London.
Unit. Serv. Mag.	=	*United Service Magazine*, London.
Univ.	=	University.
V.C.H.	=	*Victoria County History*; cf. no. 4203 *infra*.
Yorks.	=	Yorkshire.

I

GENERAL WORKS COVERING THE TUDOR PERIOD

A. BIBLIOGRAPHIES

1. ENGLAND

1 GROSS, CHARLES. The sources and literature of English history from the earliest times to about 1485. Lond. 1900; 1915.

The only adequate bibliography of English history to 1485. Invaluable for the period it covers. Part i, *General authorities*, gives the standard books on historical method, philology, chronology, paleography and diplomatics, sphragistics and heraldry, biography and genealogy, geography and topography, numismatics and archaeology, and art. It contains also serviceable lists of the important historical journals and of the periodic publications by the numerous national and local societies organized for the publication of historical material. Ch. iii on *Archives and libraries*, ch. iv on *Printed collections of sources*, and ch. v on *Modern general histories of England* contain much that is pertinent to the sixteenth century. The 2nd ed., edited after Dr. Gross's death by members of the history department of Harvard University, adds important publications between 1900 and 1910, with some titles as late as 1914. Citations hereafter are to the 2nd ed. There is no adequate bibliography of publications covering the period to 1485 since 1914. A third edition of Gross is in progress.

2 ANNUAL BULLETIN OF HISTORICAL LITERATURE. 1911 ff. Lond. 1912–. Index vols. 1–12, 1911–22, Lond. 1923.

This is published by the *London Historical Association.*

3 BESTERMAN, THEODORE. A world bibliography of bibliographies and of bibliographical catalogues, calendars, abstracts, digests, indexes and the like. 3 vols. and index. Geneva, 3rd ed. 1955–6.

3a BIBLIOGRAPHY OF HISTORICAL WORKS issued in the United Kingdom 1946–1956. By J. C. Lancaster. Lond. 1957.

Compiled for the sixth Anglo-American conference of historians. Published by the *Institute of Historical Research*, Univ. of London. Excellent for the history of particular schools, families, and for local history in general.

4 BRITISH DIARIES: an annotated bibliography of British diaries between 1442 and 1942. By William Matthews. Berkeley, 1950.

This is useful but incomplete.

5 CAMBRIDGE BIBLIOGRAPHY OF ENGLISH LITERATURE. By F. W. Bateson. 4 vols. Cambr. 1941; supplement, ed. George Watson, Camb. 1957.

6 CAMBRIDGE HISTORY OF ENGLISH LITERATURE. By A. W. Ward and A. R. Waller. 15 vols. Cambr. 1907–32.

Vols. iii and iv cover the sixteenth century. Contains valuable bibliographies, cf. particularly vol. iii, ch. xv, *Chroniclers and antiquaries*, with bibliography.

7 COURTNEY, W. P. A register of national bibliography. 3 vols. Lond. 1905–12.

A subject index to bibliographical literature, but only to 1912.

8   DAVIES, GODFREY.   Bibliography of British history, Stuart period, 1603–1714. Oxf. 1928.
The standard bibliography for the period 1603–1714. Contains many general titles, particularly on social history, useful for the Tudor period. A second up-to-date edition is in progress.

9   DICTIONARY OF NATIONAL BIOGRAPHY.   By Leslie Stephen and Sidney Lee. 63 vols. Lond. 1885–1900; 1st supplement, 3 vols., 1901; repr. 22 vols., 1908–9. Index and epitome, 1903.
Invaluable, not only for its biographies but also for its bibliographies. The 1st supplement, printed as vol. xxii of the new ed., deals mainly with the nineteenth century but includes a few sixteenth-century biographies. Corrigenda and addenda are published periodically in the *Bulletin of the Institute of Historical Research* (45).

10   ENGLISH DIARIES OF THE SIXTEENTH, SEVENTEENTH AND EIGHTEENTH CENTURIES. By James Aitken. New York, 1941.

11   [FLAHERTY, W. E.] The annals of England; an epitome of English history. 3 vols. Oxf. 1855–7; 1876.
App. i contains an account of the chronicles, collections of records, publications of societies, &c.; app. ii, an index of statutes. The 2nd ed. (1876) in which Stubbs had a share, is more valuable than the first.

12   FREWER, L. B. Bibliography of historical writings published in Great Britain and Empire, 1940–5. Oxf. 1947.
Published in co-operation with the *International Committee of Historical Sciences* to make available materials published during the war years not yet made available by the *International Bibliography of Historical Sciences* (17).

13   GAIRDNER, JAMES. Early chroniclers of Europe: England. Lond. [1879].
A good popular account of the chroniclers to the latter part of the sixteenth century.

14   GARDINER, S. R., and MULLINGER, J. B. Introduction to the study of English history. Lond. 1881; 1894.
Pt. ii by Mullinger contains a good brief account of the sources and modern literature, but slights record publications.

15   GUIDE TO REFERENCE BOOKS. By Constance Winchell. *Amer. Lib. Assoc.* Chicago, 1951; supplements, 1950–5 (1954–6).

16   HARRISON, H. G. A select bibliography of English genealogy, with brief list for Wales, Scotland and Ireland. Lond. 1937.
Useful for the genealogist, local historian, and record-seeker.

17   INTERNATIONAL BIBLIOGRAPHY OF HISTORICAL SCIENCES. Paris, 1926 ff. (1930–).
Vol. xv, 1940–6, is in preparation. This is published by the *International Committee of Historical Sciences*.

18   WRITINGS ON BRITISH HISTORY, 1934–9. By A. T. Milne. 6 vols. Lond. 1937–54.
A bibliography of books and articles on the history of Great Britain from A.D. 450 to 1914. Deals with the subject year by year. Further volumes in preparation.

19   MACRAY, W. D. A manual of English historians to A.D. 1600. Lond. 1845.
Meagre. Cf. also A. J. Grant, *English historians*, Lond. 1906.

2. CONTINENTAL EUROPE

20 CAMBRIDGE MODERN HISTORY. By A. W. Ward, G. W. Prothero, and Stanley Leathes. 13 vols. and atlas. Cambr. 1902–26; vol. i (revised), Camb. 1957.
Vols. i–iii contain useful but uncritical lists of sources and later works both on England and her neighbours during the sixteenth century.

21 DAHLMANN-WAITZ. Quellenkunde der deutschen Geschichte. 9th ed. By Hermann Haering. Leipzig, 1931; Index, 1932.
The best bibliography of the Holy Roman Empire. It should be supplemented by the periodic bibliographies in *Zeitschrift für Geschichtswissenschaft*. Gives material for Austria-Hungary and the Low Countries as well as Germany.

22 GOSSES, J. H., and JAPIKSE, N. Handboek tot de staatkundige geschiednis van Nederland. The Hague, 1927.
The standard Dutch bibliography. On the Dutch wars of the sixteenth century there is an excellent discussion of the sources in the app. to vol. iii of Blok, *A history of the people of the Netherlands*, trans. R. Putnam, New York, 1900. L. D. Petit, *Repertorium der verhandelingen en bijdragen betreffende de geschiedenis des vaderlands*, 4 vols., Leiden, 1907–33, is a bibiliography of periodical literature dealing with Dutch history. The fifth volume is in progress.

23 HAUSER, HENRI. Les sources de l'histoire de France. Part ii, le seizième siècle (1494–1610). 4 vols. Paris, 1906–15.
The standard bibliography of French history for the period. Useful lists of books are also given in Lavisse, *Histoire de France*, 9 vols. in 18, Paris [1900–11].

24 NIJHOFF, WOUTER, and KRONENBERG, M. E. Nederlandsche bibliographie van 1500 tot 1540. 3 vols., 4 supplements (1925–34). 's-Graven-hage, 1923–51.

25 PIRENNE, HENRI. Bibliographie de l'histoire de Belgique. Ghent, 1893; 1902. Brussels, 1931.
The best bibliography of the Low Countries. It covers all the Low Countries until 1598, Belgium alone thereafter. For more detailed references to minor collections of documents see the *Bulletins de la commission royale d'histoire* (Belgium) which are especially rich in sixteenth-century materials.

26 SÁNCHEZ ALONSO, B. Fuentes de la historia española. Madrid, 1919; 1927; 1952.
The 3rd ed. (1952) has 3 vols. The best general bibliography of Spanish history. R. B. Merriman, *The rise of the Spanish empire* (892), completed to the death of Philip II (1598), contains admirable critical bibliographies attached to each chapter.

B. CATALOGUES

27 AMES, JOSEPH. Typographical antiquities: being an historical account of printing in England . . . 1471–1600 . . . Scotland and Ireland to the same time. Lond. 1749; enlarged by William Herbert, 1790; further enlarged by T. F. Dibdin. 4 vols. Lond. 1810–19.

28 BRITISH MUSEUM, catalogue of printed books. 103 vols. Lond. 1881–1900. Supplement, 16 vols., 1900–5; new ed., 51 vols., 1931–54, still in progress.
Cf. also *Subject index of modern works added to the library of the British Museum 1880–95,*

by G. K. Fortescue, 3 vols., Lond. 1886–97; *of works added in 1881–1900*, 3 vols., 1902–3; *of works added in 1901–25*, 5 vols., 1906–27; *of works added in 1931–5*, 2 vols., 1937; *of works added in 1936–40*, 2 vols., 1944; *of books acquired in 1941–5*, 1 vol., 1953.

29   CATALOGUE OF ENGLISH BROADSIDES. 1505–1897. *Bibliotheca Lindesiana*. s.l. 1898.
Cf. also *Catalogue of a collection of printed broadsides in the possession of the Society of Antiquaries*, by R. Lemon, Lond. 1866.

30   CATALOGUE OF BRITISH FAMILY HISTORIES. By T. R. Thomson. Lond. 1928; 1935.

31   A CENTURY OF THE ENGLISH BOOK TRADE, 1457–1557. By E. G. Duff. Lond. 1905.
A sequel to this is *A Dictionary of printers and booksellers in England, Scotland, and Ireland, and of foreign printers of English books, 1557–1640*, by R. B. McKerrow, Lond. 1910. For London printers cf. *Handlists of books printed by London printers, 1501–56*, by E. G. Duff, W. W. Greg, R. B. McKerrow, H. R. Plomer, A. W. Pollard, R. Proctor, Lond. 1913. All are published by the *Bibliographical Society*.

32   THE ENGLISH CATALOGUE OF BOOKS, 1801 ff. Lond. 1864 ff.

33   HALL, HUBERT. List and index of the publications of the Royal Historical Society, 1871–1924, and of the Camden Society, 1840–1897. Lond. 1925.

35   A SHORT-TITLE CATALOGUE of books printed in England, Scotland, and Ireland, and of English books printed abroad, 1475–1640. By A. W. Pollard, G. R. Redgrave, *et al. Bibliographical Soc.*, 1926. Reprinted, 1946.
Very valuable. Gives libraries and private collections where copies of books may be found. A few checklists and supplements have appeared, e.g. *Huntington library supplement to the Short-title catalogue*, by C. K. Edmonds, *Hunt. Lib. Bull.*, no. iv (1933), 1–152; *English books and books printed in England before 1642 in the Newberry library, a supplement to the record in the Short-title catalogue*, by G. L. Woodward, Chicago, 1939; *A checklist of American copies of Short-title catalogue books*, by W. W. Bishop, Ann Arbor, 2nd ed., 1950; A. F. Johnson, *English books printed abroad*, *Library*, 5th ser., iv (1950), 273–6. The Bibliographical Society of the University of Virginia has published in 1950 an index of printers, publishers, and booksellers in the Short-title catalogue which was compiled by P. G. Morrison. A manuscript copy of additions to the Short-title catalogue can be found at the Folger library.

36   A TRANSCRIPT OF THE REGISTERS of the company of stationers of London, 1554–1640. By E. Arber. 5 vols. Lond. and Birmingham, 1875–94; repr. New York, 1949–50.
Cf. 3678.

C. JOURNALS AND REVIEWS
1. Guides

37   YEAR-BOOK OF THE SCIENTIFIC AND LEARNED SOCIETIES of Great Britain and Ireland. Lond. 1884 ff.
Issued annually. Contains lists of their publications with contents of annual proceedings. Many societies capriciously omitted. Cf. *British Museum catalogue, Academies*.

38   BRITISH UNION—CATALOGUE OF PERIODICALS. A record of periodicals of the world from the seventeenth century to the present day in

British libraries. By J. D. Stewart, M. E. Hammond, and Erwin Saenger. 4 vols. Lond. 1955–8.

39 A GUIDE TO THE HISTORICAL PUBLICATIONS of the societies of England and Wales. Published by the *Institute of Historical Research* (Lond.). Supplements i–xiii, 1929–46.

39a HANDLIST OF RECORD PUBLICATIONS. By R. Somerville. *Br. Rec. Assoc. Pub. Pamphlet*, no. 3. Lond. 1951.
Cf. also *Handlist of Scottish and Welsh record publications*, by P. Gouldesbrough, A. P. Kup, and I. Lewis; *Br. Rec. Assoc. Pub. Pamphlet*, no. 4, Lond. 1954.

40 READERS' GUIDE TO PERIODICAL LITERATURE (Poole's Index). New York, 1882 ff.
Lists only American periodicals. *Supplement, 1907–19*, continued as *International index to periodicals*, 1920 ff., lists English and Scottish historical reviews and some continental historical journals.

41 THE SUBJECT INDEX TO PERIODICALS. Lond. 1915 ff.
The best guide to periodical literature in English history.

2. JOURNALS

42 THE AGRICULTURAL HISTORY REVIEW. Lond. 1953 ff.

42a ARCHAEOLOGIA; or miscellaneous tracts relating to antiquity. *Society of Antiquities of London.* Lond. 1770 ff.

43 ARCHIV FÜR REFORMATIONSGESCHICHTE. Leipzig, 1903 ff.

44 THE AMERICAN HISTORICAL REVIEW. New York, 1895 ff.
Prints quarterly, in the section *Historical news*, a list of important periodical articles on English history.

45 BULLETIN OF THE INSTITUTE OF HISTORICAL RESEARCH. Lond. 1922 ff.
Prints documents, summaries of theses, corrigenda and addenda to *D.N.B.* (9), and a valuable section on the migration of historical documents. Cf. (39).

46 THE CAMBRIDGE HISTORICAL JOURNAL. Cambr. 1923 ff.

47 CHURCH QUARTERLY REVIEW. Lond. 1876 ff.

48 DUBLIN REVIEW. Dublin, 1836 ff.
Deals mainly with church history.

49 ECONOMICA: A journal of the social sciences. Lond. 1921 ff.
Issued by *the London School of Economics and Political Science.*

50 ECONOMIC JOURNAL: the journal of the British Economic Association. Lond. 1891 ff.

51 THE ECONOMIC HISTORY REVIEW. Lond. 1927 ff.
Prints semi-annually a list of publications on English economic history.

52 THE ENGLISH HISTORICAL REVIEW. Lond. 1886 ff.
Prints annually in July a list of pertinent periodical publications.

53 HISTORISCHE ZEITSCHRIFT. Munich, 1859 ff.

54 HISTORY: the quarterly journal of the [English] Historical Association. Lond. 1916 ff.
Publishes quarterly a list of new books on English history, and annually as a separate pamphlet *Annual bulletin of historical literature.*

55 IRISH HISTORICAL STUDIES. Dublin, 1938 ff.
Prints annually a section on writings on Irish history.

56 JOURNAL OF ECCLESIASTICAL HISTORY. Lond. 1950 ff.

57 JOURNAL OF ECONOMIC HISTORY. New York, 1941 ff.

58 JOURNAL OF MODERN HISTORY. Chicago, 1929 ff.
Prints quarterly a useful current bibliography.

59 LAW QUARTERLY REVIEW. Lond. 1885 ff.
For indexes and guides to periodical legal literature cf. Winfield (1489), 40–41.

60 THE MARINER'S MIRROR. Lond. 1911 ff.
Important for naval history.

61 NOTES AND QUERIES. Lond. 1850 ff.

62 QUARTERLY JOURNAL OF ECONOMICS. Boston, 1887 ff.

63 REVUE D'HISTOIRE ECCLÉSIASTIQUE. Louvain, 1900 ff.
Prints valuable current bibliography of new books and articles.

64 REVUE DE SYNTHÈSE HISTORIQUE. Paris, 1900 ff.
Valuable summaries of the progress of historical research.

65 REVUE DES QUESTIONS HISTORIQUE. Paris, 1866 ff.

66 REVUE HISTORIQUE. Paris, 1876 ff.

67 SCOTTISH HISTORICAL REVIEW. Glasgow, 1903–28; 1947 ff.
Discontinued 1928; publication resumed 1947.

68 VIERTELJAHRSSCHRIFT für Sozial- und Wirtschaftsgeschichte. Leipzig, 1903 ff.
Prints articles in English and French as well as in German.

D. SOURCE COLLECTIONS

1. PUBLIC RECORDS

By far the most important repository of unprinted sources for English history is the Public Record Office in London. On the history of this great collection cf. Gross (1), 77–79, with the references there cited, Hall (76) *infra*, and (75).

The contents of the P.R.O. are briefly described in the guides *infra* (74, 82). Detailed inventories, indexes, and descriptive catalogues of some of the records have been published in the *Reports of the deputy keeper of the public records*, especially reports i–x, and in the *P.R.O. lists and indexes.* For a guide to the *Deputy keeper's reports* see Gross (1), no. 491 and app. A, and published indexes, 1865 and 1880. For contents of the *Lists and indexes* consult the current *List of record publications*, published by Her Majesty's Stationery Office, or, to 1914, Gross (1), no. 473.

To many of the records, however, the MS. catalogues found in the P.R.O. are the only detailed guides.

In addition to the following printed calendars cf. for Scottish public records, nos. 4919 ff. *infra*; for Irish public records, 5729 ff. *infra*.

For calendars of material relating to England in foreign archives see chap. ii, sect. G *infra* (pp. 65 ff.)

(a) *Guides*

69 BAXTER, J. H., JOHNSON, CHARLES, and ABRAHAMS, PHYLLIS. Medieval Latin word list from British and Irish sources. Oxf. 1934. Reprinted 1947, 1950.
Prepared under the direction of a committee appointed by the British Academy.

70 A GUIDE TO THE RECORDS IN THE CORPORATION OF LONDON RECORDS OFFICE and the Guildhall library muniment room. By P. E. Jones and Raymond Smith. Lond. 1951.
Detailed description of the two repositories of the Guildhall records.

71 A GUIDE TO THE SEALS IN THE PUBLIC RECORD OFFICE. By Sir Hilary Jenkinson. Lond. 1954.

72 DAVENPORT, F. G. Materials for English diplomatic history, 1509–1783. *Hist. MSS. Comm., 18th report* (1917), 357–402.
An excellent resume to 1917 of materials on diplomatic history in private collections (as revealed by the *Hist. MSS. Comm. reports*) and in the B.M.

73 EDWARDS, A. C. English history from Essex sources, 1550–1750. Chelmsford, 1952.

74 GIUSEPPI, M. S. A guide to the manuscripts preserved in the Public Record Office. 2 vols. Lond. 1923–4.
Vol. i, *Legal records*, &c.; vol. ii, *State papers and records of public departments*. Largely based on 3rd ed. of Scargill-Bird (82), which it supersedes.

75 GUIDE TO THE PUBLIC RECORDS. Pt. i, Introductory. Lond. 1949, repr. 1950.
Intended to supersede Giuseppi. First part deals with historical development of the records office, its functions, activities, problems, &c.

76 HALL, HUBERT. A repertory of British archives, part i, England. Lond. 1920.
A useful survey of the various repositories where public records may be found.

77 HALL, HUBERT. Studies in English official historical documents. Cambr. 1908.
Valuable discussion of types of official records, including a history of the archives.

78 HANDBOOK OF BRITISH CHRONOLOGY. By F. M. Powicke, Charles Johnson, and W. F. Harte. *R.H.S. guides and handbooks*, ii. Lond. 1939.

79 HANDBOOK OF DATES. By C. R. Cheney, *R.H.S. guides and handbooks*, iv. Lond. 1945; rev. 1955.
Particularly valuable for dating days of the week in any year.

80 JENKINSON, HILARY. The later court hands in England: from the fifteenth to the seventeenth century. Oxf. 1927.
With 49 illustrative plates. The standard work on English sixteenth-century handwriting.

81 REPORTS OF THE ROYAL COMMISSION on public records. 3 vols. Lond. 1912–19.
Vol. i, *P.R.O. and central administration*; vol. ii, *Government departments*; vol. iii, *Local records*. Parts i–iii of vol. i published in *Parl. papers*, 1912–13; parts i–iii of vol. ii in *Parl. papers*, 1914; vol. iii in *Parl. papers*, 1919.

82 SCARGILL-BIRD, S. R. Guide to various classes of documents in the Public Record Office. 3rd ed. Lond. 1908.
Superseded by Giuseppi (74).

83 THOMAS, F. S. Notes of materials for the history of public departments. Lond. 1846.
An account of the history of the public records. App. E contains a list of the publications of the various record commissions to 1846.

(b) *Printed Sources*

84 CALENDAR OF DIPLOMATIC DOCUMENTS formerly in the treasury of receipt of the exchequer, . . . 1101–1624. *Deputy keeper's reports*, xlv (1884), app. i, 283–380; xlviii (1887), 561–619.

85 CALENDAR OF STATE PAPERS, COLONIAL SERIES, 1574–1712. By W. N. Sainsbury *et al.* 26 vols. Lond. 1860–1926.
Material before 1603 confined to vol. i (America and West Indies, 1574–1660); vol. ii (East Indies, China, and Japan, 1513–1616); vol. ix (America and West Indies, addenda, 1574–1674). Vol. i based on P.R.O. papers; vol. ii on P.R.O. and B.M. papers much more adequately calendared. Accounts of voyages of discovery not included.

86 CALENDAR OF STATE PAPERS, DOMESTIC. By Robert Lemon (vols. i, ii, 1547–90); M. A. E. Green (vols. iii–vi, 1591–1603, and addenda, and vols. vii, xii, and addenda, 1566–1625). Lond. 1856–72.
Series comprises papers on internal affairs in P.R.O. Vols. edited by Mr. Lemon scarcely more than a catalogue. Vol. ii slightly fuller than vol. i. Those edited by Mrs. Green more fully calendared. Addenda vols. contain chiefly border and Channel Islands documents, unofficial correspondence with people abroad, and other miscellaneous papers previously mislaid. Papers relating to border selected from border collection before *Cal. of Border Papers* (1352) published. Some of addenda papers relating to foreign affairs are reprinted in *Cal. S.P., Foreign*, 1585 ff. (87). Several bundles of supplementary domestic state papers in P.R.O. are not included in these calendars. Cf. Giuseppi (74), ii, 16.

87 CALENDAR OF STATE PAPERS, FOREIGN. Edward VI and Mary. By W. B. Turnbull. 2 vols. Lond. 1861. Elizabeth, by Joseph Stevenson (1558–65); A. J. Crosby (1566–77); A. J. Butler (1577–83); S. C. Lomas (1583–8); S. C. Lomas and A. B. Hinds (1587–8); R. B. Wernham (1588–9). 23 vols. Lond. 1863–1950.

88 FOEDERA, CONVENTIONES, LITTERAE, et cujuscunque generis acta publica inter reges Angliae et alios quosvis imperatores, reges, pontifices, principes, vel communitates. By Thomas Rymer (vols. i–xv) and Robert

Sanderson (vols. xvi–xx). 20 vols. Lond. 1704–35; by George Holmes. 17 vols. Lond. 1727–9; The Hague, 1739–45.

The most complete collection of treaties and other diplomatic documents. T. D. Hardy, *Syllabus of documents in Rymer's Fœdera*, 3 vols., Lond. 1869–85, is a chronological abstract and index of various eds. A general introduction to the *Fœdera* was printed by the Record Commission in 1817, but not published. Cf. also *Acta regia, or an account of the treaties, &c., published in Rymer's Fœdera* (1101–1625), translated from the French (of Paul de Rapin de Thoyras), by Stephen Whatley, 4 vols., Lond. 1726–7; repr., 6 vols., 1731–3.

89 AN INDEX TO BILLS OF PRIVY SIGNET, commonly called signed bills, 1584–96 and 1603–24, with a calendar of writs of privy seal, 1601–3. By W. P. W. Phillimore. *Index Library*, no. 4. Lond. 1890.

90 INDEX OF INQUISITIONS POST MORTEM, 1509–1660. 4 vols. Lond. 1907–9.

P.R.O. Lists and indexes, nos. 23, 26, 31, 33. Vol. i, *Henry VIII to Philip and Mary*; vol. ii, *Elizabeth*.

91 LETTERS AND PAPERS, FOREIGN AND DOMESTIC, of the reign of Henry VIII, 1509–47. By J. S. Brewer (vols. i–iv); James Gairdner (vols. v–xiii with R. H. Brodie, xiv–xxi). 21 vols. in 33 parts. Lond. 1862–1910; by R. H. Brodie, vol. i in 3 parts, Lond. 1920; addenda, vol. i, pts. i, ii. Lond. 1929–32.

Includes letters and other papers in the P.R.O., the B.M., Bodleian, Lambeth, Oxford and Cambridge College libraries. Contains adequate summaries of the French, Scottish, patent, and supplementary rolls, the signed bills and privy seals, the army, ordnance, and wardrobe accounts, and also transcripts made from foreign archives for a new ed. of Rymer's *Fœdera* (88). Material arranged chronologically, well calendared and indexed. Later vols. much fuller than earlier.

2nd ed., vol. i includes much new material, chiefly preserved outside of England, some already calendared in Venetian, Spanish, &c. papers, some resulting from a more thorough combing of sources reviewed in 1st ed. Revises most summaries, rearranges material misplaced chronologically, adds references, and furnishes key to use in connexion with the 1st ed. The addenda volumes include additional miscellaneous material in the P.R.O. 1509–47.

92 STATE PAPERS published under the authority of His Majesty's Commission, King Henry VIII. 11 vols. Lond. 1830–52.

Contains only material in P.R.O. Correspondence printed *in extenso*. Index inadequate. Superseded by *Letters and Papers* (91) except where full text of letter is needed.

2. OTHER PUBLIC COLLECTIONS OF MANUSCRIPTS

There is a good discussion of these in Gross (1), 86–91, with a very serviceable list of printed catalogues.

(a) *General Catalogues*

93 [BERNARD, EDWARD.] Catalogi librorum manuscriptorum Angliae et Hiberniae. Oxf. 1697.

Includes the Bodleian library, the university library at Cambridge, many Oxford and Cambridge college libraries, and some cathedral and private libraries. Incomplete and imperfect, but still useful.

94 EDWARDS, EDWARD. Memoirs of libraries. 2 vols. Lond. 1859.

Contains an account of MSS. in the B.M., the libraries of Oxford and Cambridge, cathedrals, inns of court, Lambeth palace, &c.

(b) *British Museum*

Next to the P.R.O. the most important repository of MSS. in England. A list of MSS. catalogues is published in *British Museum. The catalogues of the MSS. collections*, Lond. 1951. Many of the MSS. in the B.M., particularly those in the *Cotton MSS.* have been microfilmed and are available in the U.S.A. Cf. *Union list of microfilms*; a basic list of holdings in the United States and Canada, Philadelphia, U.S.A., 1942. Supplements 1–5 (1943–7). Rev. enl. ed., J. W. Edwards, Ann Arbor, U.S.A., 1951. This supersedes 1942 ed. and 5 supplements. Rev. enl. supplements, 1949–52, Ann Arbor, 1953; 1952–5 (1957).

The 1951 revised edition lists 25,000 titles in 197 libraries. The basic list does not include the titles of microfilms of books in the *Short-title catalogue*.

(c) *Other London Repositories*

The Inns of Court, the College of Arms, and the Society of Antiquaries all have important MSS. collections (cf. Gross (1), nos. 518–25). Dr. William's library, Gordon Square, London is very rich in MS. material on the history of puritanism, cf. Peel (2407). At the library of the *Institute of Historical Research* (Univ. of London) is a catalogue of unpublished theses, many of them the fruits of the seminars of Professors Pollard, Neale, Bindoff, and others. Some of them valuable contributions to the history of Tudor England.

95   CATALOGUE OF MSS. in the library of Lambeth palace. [By H. J. Todd.] Lond. 1812.

> Cf. also *The MSS. in the library at Lambeth Palace*, by M. R. James, *Cambr. Antiq. Soc.*, 1900; and C. Jenkins, *The historical MSS. at Lambeth*, *Trans. R.H. Soc.*, 3rd ser., xi (1917), 185–98; and *A descriptive catalogue . . . of MSS. at Lambeth Palace*, by M. R. James and Claude Jenkins, pts. i–iii, Cambr. 1930–2.

(d) *Oxford and Cambridge*

The printed catalogues are given in Gross (1), 90–91. The Bodleian library is very rich in MS. material. Cf. H. A. L. Fisher, *Manuscripts in the Bodleian and college libraries in Oxford bearing on English history from 1485 to 1547*, Bull. Inst. Hist. Research, i (1923), 45–48; F. J. Routledge, *Manuscripts at Oxford relating to the later Tudors (1547–1603)*, *Trans. R.H. Soc.*, 3rd ser., viii (1914), 119–59. Cf. also J. G. Milne, *The muniments of Corpus Christi College, Oxford*, Bull. Inst. Hist. Research, x (1932), 105–8.

3. Historical Manuscripts Commission Reports

The *Reports of the Hist. MSS. Comm.* list or calendar, more or less fully, much valuable material in private collections. The early *Reports* are much more cursory in character than the later ones; in many instances collections briefly surveyed at first are calendared more fully later. Each report used to be followed by an app., usually in several parts or vols., which contained abstracts of, or extracts from, documents examined. Since 1899 calendars of MSS. such as were previously published as appendixes in folio, have been issued independently in octavo.

The Commission in its *18th report,* printed an alphabetical list of collections examined to July 1914, with notes of the dates to which they refer and some indications (by F. G. Davenport) of their contents from the point of view of diplomatic history. In its *19th report,* it lists collections, owners and places of deposit to July 1925. An index has been published by the Commission, part I, *Topographical,* Lond. 1912; part II, *Persons,* by Francis Binkley, 2 vols., Lond. 1935-8. On the defects of the index to persons, cf. Neale in *E.H.R.* lii (1937), 723-4, liv (1939), 742-3. For a general account of the work of the Commission, cf. R. A. Roberts, *The reports of the Hist. MSS. Commission,* in *Helps for students of history,* no. 22 (1922).

The collections containing material on the Tudor period are listed below. They are classified under the following headings according to topics: (a) general, including local and ecclesiastical history, (b) Scotland, (c) Ireland, (d) Wales. Under each topic the listing is alphabetical according to the owners of the MSS. It ought to be noted that private collections of MSS. often change hands. This has happened to several of the collections below since they were examined by the Hist. MSS. Comm. Notes on the migration of MSS. are published in the *Bulletin of Historical Research* (45).

The National Register of Archives was set up in 1945 as part of the Hist. MSS. Comm. Its object is to collect, summarize, and index information about all types of archives in England and Wales, except those of the central government. Over 8,000 reports on separate accumulations of archives have now been made or received from various sources. They include family and estate papers, as well as records of local authorities, churches, schools, charities, hospitals, and business firms. There is no limit of date, but in special cases information concerning particular classes of recent records are, at the request of the owners, treated as confidential for the time being.

Indexes of the contents of these reports are being prepared—a topographical index, and selective indexes of persons of national importance and main subjects. These can be consulted by scholars in the Registrar's central office at the P.R.O., Chancery Lane, London, W.C. 2.

The Bulletins of the National Register of Archives have appeared since 1948. They describe the general work of the Register and give valuable information about local collections. They include *Lists of Accessions to Repositories* formerly compiled by the Institute of Historical Research.

(a) *General History, including Local and Ecclesiastical*

96 AILESBURY, MARQUESS OF. *15th report,* 18-21, and app. vii, 152-306.
Calendared.

97 ANCASTER, EARL OF. *13th report,* 31, and app. vi, 203-61, *17th report,* 55-68; and 1 vol. (1907).
Collection chiefly of correspondence of Lord Willoughby de Eresby from the Low Countries, 1585-9.

98 ASHBURNHAM, EARL OF. *8th report,* app. iii, 1-127.
These are Stowe MSS. bought by B.M., 1883. Cf. *Catalogue of Stowe MSS.,* 2 vols., Lond. 1895-6.

99   BAGOT, LORD. *4th report*, xiv, and app., 325–44.
Valuable collection for latter part of Elizabeth's reign, especially Babington plot, Davison's trial, Essex, activities of privy council, and Irish pale. There are also valuable letters of Richard Broughton in parliament. Many of the Essex letters are printed in Devereux (608), and some in *Salusbury Correspondence* (6261), 286–303. Part of this collection is now in the Folger library, Washington, D.C.

100   BATH, MARQUESS OF. *3rd report*, xiii, xiv, and app., 180–202; *4th report*, xi, and app., 227–51; *16th report*, 56–59; vol. i (1904); *17th report*, 35–45, and vol. ii (1907); vol. iii (Prior papers), (1908).
A very rich collection, inadequately reported. For the sixteenth century the valuable collections at Longleat include the Devereux papers, the Dudley papers, the Seymour papers, the Talbot papers, and the Thynne papers. The Seymour papers are in press. There is a transcript of many of the Talbot papers at the P.R.O. Some of the valuable documents in the collection are printed in *Wilts. Arch. Mag.* xiv (1874), 192–216, 237–53; xv (1875), 337–48.

101   BEDFORD, DUKE OF. *2nd report*, ix, and app., 1–4.

102   BEDINGFIELD, SIR HENRY. *3rd report*, xvi, and app., 237–40.
Valuable papers on Elizabeth's life during Mary's reign. Briefly calendared. Many of these printed in 625 and in 633.

103   BERWICK-UPON-TWEED, Corporation of. *3rd report*, xxi, and app., 308, 309; *16th report*, 93. *Various collections*, i, 1–28.
Local history.

104   BEVERLEY, co. York, Corporation of. *16th report*, 91–93, and 1 vol. (1900).
Local history.

105   BOUVERIE, P. P. *10th report*, 22, and app. vi, 82–98.

106   BRAYBROOKE, LORD. *8th report*, xii, and app., 277–96.
Papers on French affairs briefly calendared in *Winwood's Memorials* (832).

107   BRIDGEWATER TRUST OFFICE. *11th report*, 24, and app. vii, 126–67.
Includes catalogue of: (1) Much local material from several counties. (2) Brereton papers: lawsuits in Cheshire, *c.* 1525. (3) Cheyne papers: accounts of sheriffs of Bucks, 1589–90. (4) Derby papers: legal papers relating to Derby estates, at time of Elizabeth–Charles I. (5) Rokeby wills, 1596. (6) Ecclesiastical papers at time of Elizabeth. (7) Exchequer documents, 1593, 1599. Calendars of: (1) Chancery papers of Lord Keeper Egerton, (2) Star Chamber proceedings, 1506–81 (trial of Lord Vaux, 1581, *in extenso*).
Many of these papers (*Ellesmere MSS.*) including a copy of Edmund Dudley's expenditures under Henry VII, have been transferred to the Huntington library, California, U.S.A. They are of great value, particularly for legal history.

108   BRIDPORT, co. Dorset, Corporation of. *6th report*, app. 475–99.
Local records.

109   BRUCE, SIR H. J. L. *Various collections*, vii, 247–96, 389–433.
This collection is at Clifton Hall, Nottingham.

110   BUCCLEUCH AND QUEENSBERRY, DUKE OF. MSS. at Drumlanrig Castle. *15th report*, 43–44, and app. viii (vol. i); *16th report*, 117–22; vol. ii (1903).
Material on Robert, earl of Essex.

111 BUCCLEUCH AND QUEENSBERRY, DUKE OF. MSS. at Montagu House, Whitehall. *16th report*, 29–47; vol. i (1899) and vol. ii, parts of i and ii (1903); *20th report*, 5; vol. iii (1926).
Some of these are printed in Winwood (832).

112 BUXTON, Miss. *16th report*, 105–7. *Various collections*, ii, 227–88.
Fully calendared.

113 CALTHORPE, LORD. *2nd report*, x, and app., 39–46.
A very imperfect catalogue of an important collection previously imperfectly catalogued by Bernard (93) as the *Yelverton MSS*. Contains many papers of Robert Beale, clerk of council to Elizabeth. Very valuable for foreign relations, and Mary Stuart. Some papers printed in Strype, *Annals of Reformation* (2214), one in Pollen (5212), and one in Read (759). Now in B.M. (Add. MSS. 48000–48196), 197 vols. Cf. also B. Schofield, *The Yelverton MSS.*, *Brit. Mus. Quar.* xix (1954), 3–9.

114 CAMPBELL, SIR H. H. *14th report*, 47–49, and app. iii. 56–173.
Papers on Berwick.

115 CANTERBURY, Corporation of. *9th report*, ix, and app. i, 129–77.
Local records.

116 CAREW, COLONEL. *2nd report*, xiii, and app., 74–76; *4th report*, xv, and app., 368–74.
For Walsingham's diary in this collection cf. 637. Cf. also John Bruce's introduction to John Borough's *Notes of the treaty of Ripon*. *Camden Soc*. c (1869).

117 CARLISLE, Dean and Chapter of. *2nd report*, xiii, and app., 123–5.

118 CHESTER, Corporation of. *8th report*, xv, and app., 355–403.
Local records.

119 CHETHAM LIBRARY, MANCHESTER. *2nd report*, app., 156.

120 CHICHESTER, BISHOP OF. *16th report*, 96, 97. *Various collections*, i, 177–86.

121 CLARKE-THORNHILL, T. B. *16th report*, 112–16. *Various collections*, iii, 1–154.

122 COVENTRY, co. Warwick, Corporation of. *1st report*, app., 100–2; *15th report*, 43, and app. x, 101–60.
Local records.

123 COWPER, EARL. *11th report*, 10; *12th report*, 34, 35, and apps. i–iii.
Largely papers collected by Sir John Coke, secretary of state under Charles I. Several papers illustrating the navy under Elizabeth and James I. Correspondence of Coke with Fulke Greville. Some Burghley letters. Calendared fully, several *in extenso*. 1551–1603.

124 DE L'ISLE AND DUDLEY, LORD. *3rd report*, xvi, and app., 227–33; and 1 vol. (1925); *20th report*, 5–6; *21st report*, 13–14; vol. ii (1934), vol. iii, and addenda (1936)
Many of papers listed printed in Collins (629), vol. i deals chiefly with Sir Henry Sidney in Ireland, vol. ii with Sir Robt. Sidney in Flushing, with valuable letters of Rowland White on court news. Financial accounts include those for iron and steel works in Sussex, Kent, Glamorgan, 1541 ff.

125 DEVONSHIRE, DUKE OF. *3rd report*, xiv, xv, and app., 36–45.

126 DOD, WHITEHALL. *3rd report*, xviii, and app., 258–60.

127 DORMER, C. C. *2nd report*, xi, and app., 82–84.

128 DOVASTON, JOHN. *13th report*, app. iv, 247–82.
Material on council of marches of Wales (briefly calendared).

129 DOWNSHIRE, MARQUESS OF, at Easthampstead Park, Berks. 1 vol. (1924).

130 DUNWICH, Suffolk, Corporation (dissolved) of. *Various collections*, vii, 80–113.

131 ESSEX, EARL OF. *Various collections*, vii, 297–350.

132 EXETER, CITY OF. 1 vol., 1916.

133 EWELME ALMSHOUSE, co. Oxford. *8th report*, xiv, and app., 624–32; *9th report*, app. i, 216–22.
Local records.

134 FAVERSHAM, co. Kent, Corporation of. *6th report*, app., 500–11.
Local records.

135 FFARINGTON, Miss. *6th report*, xiii, and app., 426–48.

136 FINCH, A. G. 1 vol. (1913).
Contains correspondence of Sir Thos. Heneage, vice chamberlain *temp.* Elizabeth.

137 FITZHARDINGE, LORD. *4th report*, xiv, and app., 364–7.

138 FOLJAMBE, F. J. S. *15th report*, 35–39, and app. v.
Collection concerning military and naval matters, instructions, musters, commissions, &c., 1557–99 with gaps 1557–71 and 1590–9. Very valuable on military organization, especially in the year 1588. Several extensive extracts here printed with notices of parts already in print.

139 FORTESCUE, G. M. *2nd report*, xiii, and app., 49–63.
Chiefly letters to Walsingham to 1590, and brief summaries, cf. Davies (8), no. 131.

140 FRANK, F. B. *5th report*, x; *6th report*, xiv, and app., 448–65.

141 FRANKLAND-RUSSELL-ASTLEY, Mrs. *16th report*, 86–91; and 1 vol. (1900).
Contains speeches of Sir John Croke, speaker of Commons, 1601.

142 FRERE, G. E. *7th report*, xiv, and app., 518–37.
Contains Paston and Gawdy letters, cf. 143, 292, 612. Collection now in B.M., Add. MS. 36988 and 36989.

143 GAWDY, Family of. *10th report*, 13, 14, and app. ii.
Briefly calendared.

144 GLOUCESTER, Diocese of. *Various collections*, vii, 44–69; *18th report*, 206–11.

145 GURNEY, J. H. *12th report*, 39, and app. ix, 116–64.

146 HASTINGS, R. R. Vols. i–iv (1928–47). Now in Huntington library, California.
Valuable for Council of the north and Elizabethan puritanism. Cf. Summary reports on the Hastings MSS., *Hunt. Lib. Bull.* v (1934), 1–67.

147 HEREFORD, Corporation of. *13th report*, 50, 51, and app. iv, 283–353.
Local records.

148 HODGKIN, J. E. *15th report*, 41, and app. ii.
In extenso.

149 HOME, COL. D. M. *16th report*, 122, and 1 vol. (1902).

150 HOOD, SIR A. A. *5th report*, x; *6th report*, xii, and app., 344–52.

151 HOPKINSON, REV. FRANCIS. *3rd report*, xvi, and app., 261–7.

152 HOUSE OF LORDS MSS. 1450–1625. *3rd report*, xi, and app., 1–36; *4th report*, x, and app., 114–24.
Chiefly drafts of acts and petitions, some not given in *Lord's Journal* (1082), mostly in reign of Elizabeth. Calendared. There is a revised MS. list at the H. of Lords record office.

153 HULTON, W. W. B. *12th report*, 40, and app. ix, 165–78.

154 JERSEY, EARL OF. *8th report*, xi, and app., 92–101.

155 LAMBETH PALACE, MSS. at. *6th report*, xiv, and app., 522–4. Cf. 74.

156 LECONFIELD, LORD. *5th report*, xi; *6th report*, xii, and app., 287–319.

157 LE FLEMING, S. H. *12th report*, 38, 39, and app. vii.

158 LEICESTER, EARL OF. *9th report*, xvi–xx, and app. ii, 340–75; *17th report*, 126–9. *Various collections*, iv, 313–25.

159 LLOYD, S. Z. *10th report*, 20, and app. iv, 444–50.

160 LOWNDES, G. A. *5th report*, xi; *7th report*, xiv, and app., 537–89.
Calendared.

161 MANCHESTER, DUKE OF. *1st report*, x, and app., 12, 13; *8th report*, app. ii, 1–140; re-issued in 1 vol. 1910.
Court of augmentations, *temp.* Henry VIII. Calendared.

162 MAXWELL, SIR J. M. S. *10th report*, 34–37, and app. i, 58–81.
Calendared.

163 MIDDLETON, LORD. 1 vol. (1911).
Sixteenth-century household accounts and inventories *in extenso*. Coal-mining accounts.

164 MILDMAY, CAPTAIN H. G. *7th report*, xiv, and app., 590–6.

165 MOLYNEUX, W. M. *7th report*, xiv, and app., 596–681; *17th report*, 12.
Many papers of Sir Thomas Cawarden, master of the revels under Henry VIII. Sir William More's papers at time of Elizabeth. 214 out of 2240 MSS. in the collection were printed in Kempe, *Losely MSS.* (288). Cf. also *Arch.* xxxvi (1865), 284–310. Valuable on military preparations to meet Armada, on Lady Jane Grey, on operations against Tyrone, and on local government. Many letters *in extenso*, others merely mentioned. There is a good MS. calendar of this collection in P.R.O. Many of these papers now at the Folger library, Washington, D.C.

166 MONEY-KYRLE, MAJOR. *17th report*, 120, 121. *Various collections*, iv, 96–139.
Fully calendared.

167 MONTAGU OF BEAULIEU, LORD. *16th report*, 56–62, and 1 vol. (1900).
Calendared. Much Scottish material.

168 MORDAUNT-HAY, COL. *Various collections*, v, 1–71.

169 MORPETH, Corporation of. *6th report*, app., 526–38.
Local records.

170 MORRISON, ALFRED. *9th report*, xvii, and app. ii, 406–93.
Calendared.

171 NORFOLK, DUKE OF. *16th report*, 108. *Various collections*, ii, 337–47; vii, 153–246.

172 NORTHUMBERLAND, DUKE OF. *3rd report*, xii, and app., 45–125; *5th report*, xi; *6th report*, xi, and app., 221–33.
Much miscellaneous material chiefly on Ireland, military affairs, and the borders, *temp.* Elizabeth. This report gives an inadequate idea of the richness of this collection.

173 PEAKE, FREDERICK. Neville of Holt MSS., *2nd report*, xii, 93–97.
Foreign affairs.

174 PEPYS MSS. preserved at Magdalene College, Cambridge. *18th report*, 21–34, I vol. (1911).
Cf. *Pepys' diary*, 1st ed. (1825), app., for letters on Amy Robsart's death.

175 THE PETYT MSS., INNER TEMPLE, and other collections there. *2nd report*, xv, and app., 151–6; *11th report*, xxxvi, and app. vii, 227–308.
Many valuable papers on Lord Protector Somerset, ecclesiastical affairs under Elizabeth, the Archpriest Blackwell, and trial of Mary Stuart. Some letters printed in *Parker correspondence* (1737). Parts of this collection have been calendared by Inderwick (1619).

176 PHELIPS, W. *1st report*, ix, and app. 57, 58; *3rd report*, xviii, and app., 281–7.
Low Countries, very briefly calendared.

177 PORTLAND, DUKE OF. *13th report*, 13–26, and apps. i and ii; *14th report*, 11–16, and app. ii; *15th report*, 8–16, and app. iv; *16th report*, 14–29, vol. v (1899); vols. vi and vii (1901); *17th report*, 25–28; vol. viii (1907).
Only relevant part *13th report*, app. ii, 521; sixteenth-century royal letters printed *in extenso*.

178 QUEEN'S COLLEGE, OXFORD. *2nd report*, xv, and app., 137–42; *4th report*, xvii, and app., 451–8.

179 RAFFLES, T. S. *6th report*, xvi, and app., 468–75.

180 ROYAL COLLEGE OF PHYSICIANS. *8th report*, xiv, and app., 226–35.

181 RUTLAND, DUKE OF. *1st report*, x, and app., 10–12; *12th report*, 13–23, and app. iv (vol. i) and app. v (vol. ii); *14th report*, 6–11, and app. i (vol. iii); *17th report*, 19–25; vol. iv.
Vols. i and iv contain papers of earls of Rutland as lord wardens of the east and middle marches under Edward VI and as lord presidents of the north under Elizabeth. Valuable. Well calendared except where printed in 294. Nothing on sixteenth century in vols. ii and iii.

182 ST. ALBANS, Corporation of. *5th report*, xviii, and app., 565–8.

183 ST. GERMAINS, EARL OF. *1st report*, x, and app., 41–44.

184 SACKVILLE (KNOLE) MSS. *22nd report*, 10. Vol. i, *Cranfield papers, 1551–1612* (1940).
Knole MSS. were included in earlier reports in MSS. of Earl de la Warr.

185 SALISBURY, MARQUESS OF (Hatfield MSS.) *3rd report*, xii, and app., 147–80; *4th report*, xii, and app., 199–227; *5th report*, vii and app., 261–94; *6th report*, app., 250–77; *7th report*, xiii and app., 182–96; *12th*

report, 23–24; *13th report*, 26–31; *14th report*, 16–23; *15th report*, 21–27; *16th report*, 48–56; *17th report*, 28–34; vol. i, 1306–1571; vol. ii, 1572–82; vol. iii, 1583–9; vol. iv, 1590–4; vol. v, 1594–5; vol. vi, 1596; vol. vii, 1597; vol. viii, 1598; vol. ix, 1599; vol. x, 1600; vol. xi, 1601; vol. xii, 1602; vol. xiii and xiv, addenda and vol. xv (1603).

The most valuable private collection for the reign of Elizabeth, forming an indispensable supplement to the materials in the P.R.O. on both domestic and foreign questions. Papers collected by Lord Burghley and Sir Robert Cecil. Many of these papers have been printed in *Collection of state papers . . . left by William Cecil, Lord Burghley . . .*, by Samuel Haynes and William Murdin, 2 vols., Lond. 1740–59. Some also in Strype, *Annals* (2214); Lodge, *Illustrations of British history* (283); *The secret correspondence of Sir Robert Cecil with James VI* (5322); and *Correspondence of King James VI of Scotland, &c.* (5302).

A microfilm of these papers is now in the B.M. and in the Folger library, Washington, D.C.

This collection should be supplemented by the large and very important collection of Burghley papers in the *Lansdowne MSS.* in the B.M.

186 SALISBURY, Corporation of. *17th report*, 122–4. *Various collections*, iv, 191–254.
Local records.

187 SALISBURY, Dean and Chapter of. *1st report*, app., 90, 91; *16th report*, 102. *Various collections*, i, 338–88.
Sixteenth-century deeds and grants.

188 SAVILE, A. W. *11th report*, 24, and app. vii, 119–26.
Very briefly calendared. Papers on the council of the north.

189 SHIRLEY, E. P. *5th report*, x, and app., 362–9.
Cf. Davies (4) no. 3524.

190 SHREWSBURY PAPERS, the MSS. of Lord Edmund Talbot. *1st report*, app., 50. *Various collections*, ii, 289–336; *16th report*, 107–8.
For other Talbot papers, cf. Lodge (283) and Bath (100).

191 SHREWSBURY, Corporation of. *15th report*, 42, 43, and app. x, 1–65.
Local records.

192 SNEYD, REV. WALTER. *3rd report*, xvii, and app., 287–90.
Papers on Italian relations, cf. 2807a.

193 SOMERSET, DUKE OF. *15th report*, 16–18, and app. vii, 1–151.
Papers on coast defences, fully calendared.

194 SOUTHWARK, MSS. in the custody of the Roman Catholic bishop of *3rd report*, xxi, and app., 233–7.
Roman catholicism.

195 SPENCER, EARL. *2nd report*, ix, and app., 12–20.

196 STEWART, CAPTAIN JAMES. *10th report*, 5, and app. iv, 59–146.

197 STONYHURST COLLEGE. *2nd report*, xiii, and app., 143–6; *3rd report*, xxi, and app., 334–41; *10th report*, 25, and app. iv, 176–99.
Very valuable on Roman catholicism under Elizabeth. Here papers merely listed. Some published by *Catholic Record Society*. These archives have been rearranged since this report of them was drawn up.

198 STRATHMORE AND KINGHORNE, EARL OF. *2nd report*, xviii, and app., 185; *14th report*, 49, and app. iii, 174–90.

199 SUTHERLAND, DUKE OF. *2nd report*, xvi, and app., 177–80; *5th report*, vi, and app., 135–214.

200 TENTERDEN, Corporation of. *6th report*, app., 569–72.
Local records.

201 TOLLEMACHE, JOHN. *1st report*, x, and app., 60, 61.

202 TOWNSHEND, MARQUESS. *11th report*, 13–19, and app. iv.
Selections from the papers of Nathaniel Bacon in this collection are printed in *Stiffkey papers* (1287).

203 VERULAM, EARL OF. *17th report*, 51–54, and 1 vol. (1906).
Calendared. Now deposited in County Record Office at Hertford.

204 WATERFORD, LOUISA, MARCHIONESS OF. *11th report*, 22, and app. vii, 81–90.
Calendared.

205 WENTWORTH, Mrs. *16th report*, 109–10. *Various collections*, ii, 367–432.
Cf. *York Arch. Jour.* xii (1892) 1–35, 159–94.

206 WESTMINSTER ABBEY. *1st report*, app., 94; *4th report*, xi, and app., 171–99.

207 WILLIAMS, REV. DANIEL, LIBRARY. *3rd report*, app., 365–8.
A very important collection on puritanism under Elizabeth, much of it printed in Peel (2407).

208 WILTSHIRE. Records of quarter sessions. *16th report*, 95, 96. *Various collections*, i, 67–176; 283–326.
Local records. Cf. 1305.

209 WINCHESTER, Corporation of. *6th report*, app., 595–605.
Local records.

210 WODEHOUSE, E. R. *13th report*, 48–50, and app. iv, 405–94.

211 WOMBWELL, SIR GEORGE. *16th report*, 103, 104. *Various collections*, ii, 1–226.
Orders of council of the north, *in extenso.*

212 WOOD, F. L., MSS. *Various collections*, viii, 1–195.

213 WORCESTER, Records of the county of. *16th report*, 100, 101. *Various collections*, i, 282–326.
Local records. Cf. 1306.

(b) *Scotland*

An analysis of material relating to Scotland in the *Hist. MSS. Comm. reports* is given in 4904 and 4915. The *Salisbury MSS.* (185) are rich in Scottish material. Cf. also 167.

214 ABERDEEN, Burgh of. *1st report*, xii, and app., 121–3.
Local records.

215 ABERDEEN, EARL OF. *5th report*, xix, and app., 608–10.

216   ADVOCATES' LIBRARY, EDINBURGH. *1st report*, app., 123–5.
A very valuable collection, now (since 1925) the National library of Scotland. For the Balcarres papers in the collection cf. 5132; for the valuable collection of Sir James Balfour of Denmilne cf. 5128 and 5316. Cf. *National library catalogue* (4906).

217   AILSA, MARQUESS OF. *5th report*, xix, and app. 613–17.

218   ARGYLL, DUKE OF. *4th report*, xix, and app., 470–92; *6th report*, xvi, and app., 606–34.
Calendared. Cf. 4946.

219   ATHOLL, DUKE OF. *7th report*, xv, and app., 703–16; *12th report*, 48–51, and app. viii, 1–75.
Calendared.

220   BLAIRS, Roman Catholic college of. *2nd report*, xx, and app., 201–3.
Not much before 1603. Cf. M. V. Hay. *The Blairs papers* (1603–60). Lond. 1929.

221   BUCKIE, Banffshire, MSS. at. *1st report*, app., 120.
Valuable collection for history of Roman Catholics in Scotland from the time of Mary.

222   BUTE, MARQUESS OF. *3rd report*, xiii, xxii, and app., 202–9, 402, 403; *5th report*, xix, and app., 617–20.

223   CAWDOR, EARL OF. *2nd report*, viii, xvii, and app., 31, 193.
Cf. *The book of the thanes of Cawdor, Spalding Club,* 1859, and Cosmo Innes, *Sketches on early Scottish history,* 1861.

224   EDINBURGH, Library of the Roman Catholic bishop of. *1st report*, xii, and app., 120.
Cf. *Rental book of the diocese of Glasgow, 1509–70* (5431).

225   EDINBURGH UNIVERSITY. *1st report*, xii, and app., 121.

226   EDMONSTONE, SIR ARCHIBALD. *3rd report*, xxiii, and app., 407, 408. *Various collections*, v, 72–184.

227   EGLINTON AND WINTON, EARL OF. *10th report*, 30, 31, and app. i, 1–58.

228   ELPHINSTONE, LORD. *9th report*, xviii, and app. ii, 182–229.
Cf. 5179 for published material from this collection.

229   ERSKINE, A. J. *5th report*, xxi, and app., 633–44.
Cf. 4953 for material from this collection.

230   ERSKINE-MURRAY, ISABELLA. *4th report*, xxi, and app., 521–8.

231   FORBES, LORD. *2nd report*, xix, and app., 193–6.

232   GLASGOW, Corporation of. *1st report*, app., 126.
Local records. Cf. 5040–4.

233   GLASGOW, EARL OF. *3rd report*, xxiii, and app., 405; *8th report*, xvii, and app., 304–8.

234   GRAHAM, SIR J. J. *Various collections*, v, 185–275.
Calendared.

235   HAMILTON, DUKE OF. *1st report*, xii, and app., 112–16; *11th report*, 38–42, and app., vi, 1–261; Supplementary report (1932).
Cf. *Hamilton papers* (4926).

236 HOME, EARL OF. *12th report*, 51, and app. viii, 76–185.
Calendared.

237 HOPE-JOHNSTONE, J. J. *15th report*, 45, and app. ix.
Calendared.

238 JAMIESON, G. A. *4th report*, xxii, and app., 511–14.
Cf. Cosmo Innes, *Sketches on early Scottish history*, 1861.

239 KIRKCUDBRIGHT, Burgh of. *4th report*, xxiii, and app., 538–9.
Local records.

240 LAING MSS. preserved in the University of Edinburgh. 1 vol. (1914).
Cf. *Catalogue of the library of David Laing*, Lond. 1879.

241 LOTHIAN, MARQUESS OF. MSS. (a) at Newbattle, *1st report*, x, xii,
and app., 14, 116; (b) at Blickling Hall, 1 vol. (1905).
Calendared. Partly dispersed by sale, 1932.

242 MALET, SIR ALEXANDER. *5th report*, viii and app., 308–21; *7th
report*, xiii, and app., 428–33.
Now in the B.M. Add. MSS. 32091–6.

243 MAR AND KELLIE, EARL OF. *17th report*, 130–8, and 1 vol. (1904);
supp. vol. (1930).

244 MENZIES, SIR ROBERT. *6th report*, xviii, and app., 688–709.

245 MONTROSE, DUKE OF. *2nd report*, xvi, and app., 165–77; *3rd report*,
xxi, and app., 368–402.

246 MORAY, EARL OF. *6th report*, xvii, and app., 634–73.
Valuable on Mary Stuart, Regent Moray, and *temp.* James VI. Calendared, with
many papers *in extenso*.

247 MORAY, CHARLES. *3rd report*, xxiii, and app., 416–29; *10th report*,
37, and app. i, 81–199.

248 MORTON, EARL OF. *2nd report*, xviii, and app., 183–5.
Valuable *temp.* Elizabeth.

249 PERTH, King James's Hospital. *6th report*, xix, and app., 713–15.
Cf. *The blackfriars of Perth*, by R. Milne. Edin. 1893.

250 POWIS, EARL OF. *10th report*, 18, and app. iv, 378–99.
Calendared.

251 RICHMOND, DUKE OF. *1st report*, xiii, and app., 114.
Documents from this collection are printed in 4945, 4954.

252 ROSSLYN, EARL OF. *2nd report*, xviii, and app., 191–2.

253 ROTHES, HENRIETTA, COUNTESS OF. *4th report*, xx, and app.,
492–511.
Calendared. Papers on the murder of Cardinal Beaton.

254 ROXBURGHE, DUKE OF. *14th report*, 46–47, and app. iii, 1–55.

255 ST. ANDREWS UNIVERSITY. *2nd report*, xx, and app., 206–9.
Valuable on ecclesiastical system.

256 SELKIRK, EARL OF. *4th report*, xxiii, and app., 516–18.

257 SOUTHESK, EARL OF. *7th report*, xvi, and app., 716–26.

258 STOPFORD-SACKVILLE, Mrs. *9th report*, xx, xxi, and app. iii, 1–150; *16th report*, 110, 111, and vol. i (1904); vol. ii (1910).
Calendared.

259 TORPHICHEN, LORD. *2nd report*, xix, and app., 196.

260 WEMYSS, R. G. *3rd report*, xxv, and app., 422, 423.

261 WITHAM, Mr. and Mrs. MAXWELL. *5th report*, xx, and app., 650–4.
Documents from this collection are printed in 5463.

(c) *Ireland*

In addition to those given below the following contain important Irish material: 99, 110, 124, 172, 185. Other Irish material in private custody is listed in *Analecta Hibernica* (5646) xv (1944), xx (1958).

262 EGMONT, EARL OF. *7th report*, xiii, and app., 232–49; *17th report*, 143–53, and vol. i (sixteenth and seventeenth centuries) (1905); vol. ii (seventeenth and eighteenth centuries) (1909).
Vol. i contains original entry book of the court of castle chamber, Dubin, 1573–1620.
Calendared.

263 GALWAY, Archives of the town of. *10th report*, 45, and app. v, 380–520.
Calendared.

264 HALIDAY, CHARLES (Acts of the privy council in Ireland, 1556–71). *13th report*, 56; *15th report*, 45, and app. iii, 1–296.
In extenso with table of contents of preceding (lost) council book and lists of contents of two succeeding council books, begun 1571 and 1589.

265 LEINSTER, DUKE OF. *9th report*, xix, and app. ii, 263–93.
Valuable on earls of Kildare.

266 ORMONDE, MSS. of the marquess of, at the castle of Kilkenny. *2nd report*, app., 209–10; *3rd report*, app., 425–30; *4th report*, app., 539–73; *14th report*, app. vii (published separately as vols. i and ii, 1899, with index vol. published 1909). New ser., vol. i (1902).
Chiefly valuable for military organization.

267 ORMSBY-GORE, J. R. *2nd report*, xi, and app., 84–88; *4th report*, xv, and app., 379–97.

268 ROTHE, ROBERT. A register of the antiquities and statutes of the town of Kilkenny. *2nd report*, xxi, and app., 257–62.

269 TABLEY, LORD DE. *1st report*, ix, and app., 46–50.

270 TRINITY COLLEGE, DUBLIN. *4th report*, xxiv, and app., 588–99; *8th report*, xix and app. 572–624.
For a catalogue of this collection cf. 5675.

271 WATERFORD, Corporation of. *1st report*, app., 131, 132; *10th report*, 45, and app. v, 265–339.
Calendared.

(d) *Wales*

In addition to the following, nos. 99, 124, 128, 147, 185 and 191 also contain Welsh material.

272 WELSH LANGUAGE, MSS. in the. *15th report*, 46–49; *16th report*, 132–4; and vol. i. *Lord Mostyn MSS.*; vol. i, parts ii and iii, *Peniarth MSS.*; vol. ii, part i, *Jesus College, Oxford, &c.*; vol. ii, part ii, *Plas Llan Stephan, Free Library, Cardiff*; vol. ii, pt. iii, *Panton, Cwrtmawr*; vol. ii, pt. iv.

4. Miscellaneous Printed Collections of English Sources

For pertinent collections of foreign sources see ch. ii, G *infra* (pp. 65–85).

273 THE BALLAD HISTORY of the reigns of Henry VII and Henry VIII. The ballad history of the reigns of the late Tudors. By C. H. Firth. *Trans. R.H. Soc.*, 3rd ser., ii (1908), 21–50; iii (1909), 51–124.
Cf. A. G. Chester, *The authorship and provenance of a political ballad of the reign of Henry VIII, Notes and Queries*, cxcv (1950), 203–5.

274 CABALA, sive scrinia sacra: mysteries of state and government in letters of illustrious persons ... in the reigns of King Henry the eighth, Queen Elizabeth, King James, and King Charles ... Lond. 1654; 1691.
In 2 parts: pt. i consists of letters, chiefly written in the seventeenth century, arranged in alphabetical order. For Elizabeth's reign there are many valuable letters of Sir Francis Bacon, Sir William Cecil, the earl of Essex, and others, including 78 letters (1568–70) from Cecil to Norris, English ambassador in France; pt. ii contains letters of Lord Buckhurst, Sir Francis Walsingham, and others relative to Leicester's government in the Low Countries. Pt. ii is omitted in the 1st ed.

275 CHRIST CHURCH LETTERS: a volume of medieval letters relating to the affairs of the priory of Christ Church, Canterbury. By J. B. Sheppard. *Camden Soc.*, n.s., xix (1877).
Continues to about the year 1520.

276 A COLLECTION OF HISTORICAL DOCUMENTS illustrative of the reigns of the Tudor and Stuart sovereigns. By E. M. Goldsmid. 2 vols. *Collectanea adamantaea*, xiii. Edin. 1886.

277 DESIDERATA CURIOSA: Or, a collection of divers scarce and curious pieces relating chiefly to matters of English history. . . . By Francis Peck. 2 vols. Lond. 1732–5; by T. Evans, 2 vols., Lond. 1779.
Vol. i and book i of vol. ii deal with Elizabeth's reign. A haphazard collection of material. Includes a valuable contemporary life of Lord Burghley, printed also in A. Collins, *Life of Burghley*, 1732, from original, which has since disappeared, in library of Brownlow, earl of Exeter. Contains also correspondence of Chaderton (1540–1609), bishop of Chester.

278 THE DIARY OF HENRY MACHYN, citizen and merchant-taylor of London, 1550–63. By J. G. Nichols. *Camden Soc.* xlii (1848).
Diary in B.M., Cotton MSS. Author a furnisher of funerals. Throws light on changes of religious observances and on genealogy.

279 AN ENGLISH GARNER. By Edward Arber. 8 vols. Lond. 1877–96; 10 vols. Lond. 1903.
Contains reprints of many rare Tudor tracts.

280 [HARDWICKE STATE PAPERS.] Miscellaneous state papers from 1501 to 1726. . . . [By Philip Yorke, 2nd earl of Hardwicke.] 2 vols. Lond. 1778.

Contains various papers on the reigns of Elizabeth, the originals of which are for the most part in the P.R.O. and the B.M. They include: letters to and from Sir Nicholas Throgmorton in France (1560–1), letters between Mary Stuart and the duke of Norfolk (1569–70), letters to and from Sir E. Stafford in France (1583–8), and an important summary of the evidence against Mary Stuart in the year 1586.

281 THE HARLEIAN MISCELLANY: a collection of scarce, curious, and entertaining pamphlets and tracts . . . found in the late earl of Oxford's library. . . . By William Oldys. 8 vols. Lond. 1744–6; by J. Malham, 12 vols., Lond. 1808–11; standard ed. by T. Park, 10 vols., Lond. 1808–13. Index, 1885.
The 12th vol. of Malham's ed. contains a full index of the whole set. The 1st 2 vols. of the later eds. contain material on the Tudor period, particularly the reign of Elizabeth.

282 HILLS, WILLIAM P. Richard Hill of Hillend and Balliol MS. 354. *Notes and Queries*, cxxvii (1939), 542–56.

283 ILLUSTRATIONS OF BRITISH HISTORY, biography and manners, in the reigns of Henry VIII, Edward VI, Mary, Elizabeth and James I, exhibited in . . . original papers . . . from the MSS. . . . of Howard, Talbot, and Cecil. . . . By E. Lodge, 3 vols. Lond. 1791; best ed. 1838.
Vols. i and ii cover the period from Henry VIII to the death of Elizabeth. The most valuable papers are those from the family archives of the duke of Norfolk, and those from the Talbot papers, preserved at the Herald's College of Arms. Those from the Cecil papers are calendared in 185. The ed. of 1838 contains, in an app. to vol. iii, a list of the Talbot papers still unpublished at the Herald's College of Arms.
  Cf. *The records and collections of the College of Arms*, by A. R. Wagner, Lond. 1952.

284 LETTERS AND PAPERS OF THE VERNEY FAMILY down to the end of the year 1639. By John Bruce. *Camden Soc.* lvi (1853).
Valuable for the life of Sir Ralph Verney, chamberlain to Princess Margaret under Henry VII, and for Dudley's conspiracy under Philip and Mary.

285 LETTERS OF ROYAL AND ILLUSTRIOUS LADIES of Great Britain, from the commencement of the twelfth century to the close of the reign of Queen Mary. By M. A. E. Wood (afterwards Green). 3 vols. Lond. 1846.

286 LETTERS OF STEPHEN GARDINER. By J. A. Muller. Camb. 1933.
Less than 200, well edited.

287 LETTERS OF THE KINGS OF ENGLAND. By J. O. Halliwell. 2 vols. Lond. 1846–8.
Prints *in extenso* many letters of Henry VII–VIII, Edward VI, and James I.

288 THE LOSELEY MANUSCRIPTS . . . illustrative of . . . English history . . . from the reign of Henry VIII to . . . James I, preserved . . . at Loseley House, in Surrey. By A. J. Kempe. Lond. 1835.
Consists chiefly of the papers of Sir Wm. More (1520–1600), sometime sheriff of Surrey. Includes some letters of Queen Elizabeth while princess. Cf. 165.

289 NUGAE ANTIQUAE; being a miscellaneous collection of original papers . . . written during the reigns of Henry VIII, Edward VI, Queen Mary, Elizabeth, and King James, by Sir John Harington . . . and others. . . . By Henry Harington. 2 vols. Lond. 1769; by Thomas Park, 2 vols. Lond. 1804.
Park's is the best ed. but omits a few documents printed in the 1st ed. Contains, for the reign of Elizabeth, several speeches by the queen, papers concerning Stubbs, the puritan pamphleteer, letters from court, 1597 ff., papers on Ireland, 1599 ff., *et al.* Cf. also *The letters and epigrams of Sir John Harington*, by N. E. McClure, Philada. 1930, and Ian Grimble, *The Harington Family*. Lond. 1958.

290 ORIGINAL LETTERS, illustrative of English history . . . from autographs in the B.M. and . . . other collections. By Henry Ellis. 11 vols. Lond. 1824; 1827; 1846.

These letters were published in 3 ser. 1st ser., 3 vols., 2nd and 3rd ser., 4 vols. each. Printed in chronological order, selected haphazard. Chiefly valuable for the reigns of Henry VIII and Elizabeth.

291 ORIGINAL LETTERS OF EMINENT LITERARY MEN of the sixteenth, seventeenth, and eighteenth centuries. By Henry Ellis. *Camden Soc.* xxiii (1843).

Miscellaneous letters, 26 from sixteenth century *in extenso*, include: Roger Ascham, miscellaneous to Burghley, John Dee, Whitgift, Muscovy Company, Sir John Smythe.

292 THE PASTON LETTERS, 1422–1509. By James Gairdner. 3 vols. Lond. 1872–5; 6 vols. Lond. 1904.

The earliest ed. of these letters (by Fenn, 1787) contained no material later than 1485. Upwards of 400 hitherto unpublished letters were added in Gairdner's 1st ed. of 1872–5, and others in the later eds. Cf. 142.

293 PLUMPTON CORRESPONDENCE: a series of letters written in the reigns of Edward IV, Richard III, Henry VII, and Henry VIII. By Thomas Stapleton. *Camden Soc.* iv (1839).

The private letters of a Yorkshire family.

294 RUTLAND PAPERS: original documents illustrative of the courts and times of Henry VII and Henry VIII. By William Jerdan. *Camden Soc.* xxi (1842).

Papers relate chiefly to Field of Cloth of Gold, to Charles V's visit to England and to Henry VIII's household. Cf. 181.

295 SELECT PAPERS. Chiefly relating to English antiquities. By John Ives. Lond. 1773.

An annual of which 3 numbers appeared, 1773–4–5. The 1st number contains, with other tracts, accounts of coronations, Henry VII–Elizabeth.

296 [SOMERS TRACTS.] A collection of scarce and valuable tracts, selected from an infinite number in print and manuscript, in the Royal, Cotton, Sion, and other public, as well as private, libraries, particularly that of the late Lord Somers. 16 vols. Lond. 1748–52; standard ed. by Walter Scott, 13 vols., Lond. 1809–15.

Scott's ed. assembles all the tracts relating to the Tudor period in vol. i.

297 SYLLOGE EPISTOLARUM a variis angliae principibus scriptarum. By Thomas Hearne. Oxf. 1716.

Published as an app. to Hearne's ed. of *Titi Livii Foro-Juliensis Vita Henrici Quinti.* Most of the letters are of the Tudor period.

298 TEN SCARCE BOOKS IN ENGLISH LITERATURE. By E. M. Goldsmid. Edin. 1886.

Contains several documents of the period, among them a contemporary account of the earl of Hertford's expedition into Scotland in 1544 (5135), Henry VIII's instructions for the visitation of the monasteries (2042), and letters from Katharine of Aragon, Anne Boleyn, and Mary Tudor to Henry VIII.

299 TREVELYAN PAPERS. By J. P. Collier. 3 vols. *Camden Soc.* lxvii, lxxxiv, cv (1857, 1863, 1872).

Family papers, particularly significant for early Tudors. The 3rd vol. contains a valuable introduction.

300 TUDOR TRACTS, 1532–1588. By A. F. Pollard. Lond. 1903.

E. CHRONICLES

Of the chronicles listed the following are of independent historical value: 'The Great Chronicle' (310) for the reigns of Henry VII and VIII; Polydore Vergil (320) for the reign of Henry VII; Hall (312) for the reign of Henry VIII; Camden (302), Holinshed (314), and Stow (317) for the reign of Elizabeth.

301 ARNOLD, RICHARD. [Chronicle.] In this book is conteyned the names of ye baylifs custos maires a. sherefs of Lōdon. [Antwerp, 1503]; [Southwark, 1521]; standard ed. by Francis Douce. Lond. 1811.

Published without title but generally known as *Arnold's chronicle* or, by Douce, *The customs of London*. For the conjectural dates and place of publication of the earliest 2 eds. cf. *D.N.B.* (9), art. Arnold, and *S.T.C.* (35) nos. 782–3. A commonplace book dealing with London antiquities of little historical value. Cf. Busch (406) 401. Contains earliest known version of the *Ballade of ye Nottebrowne Mayde*.

302 CAMDEN, WILLIAM. Annales rerum anglicarum et hibernicarum regnante Elizabetha. Lond. 1615; Leyden, 1625; standard ed. by Thomas Hearne, 3 vols., Lond. 1717.

The ed. of 1615 covered Elizabeth's reign to 1588; the ed. of 1625 completed the history of the reign. The 2nd part appeared separately in London in 1627.

English translations: (a) By A. Darcie, to end of 1588. Lond. 1625. (From a French trans. by Paul de Bellegent.) (b) By Thomas Browne, 1589–1603. Lond. 1629. (c) By H. Norton, 1558–1603. Lond. 1635. (d) Lond. 1688. (e) In White Kennett's *Complete history*, Lond. 1706.

The best English version is (d). Camden, though he writes his history in the form of annals, is far in advance of other Elizabethan chroniclers, both in form and in critical acumen. He undertook the task at the prompting of Lord Burghley and had access to Burghley's papers which he used judiciously and discriminately. He reveals much greater insight than other contemporary historians in political matters and a far greater knowledge of foreign affairs. There is no evidence that he 'smoothed down his original account' to please King James. Excepting a few extracts from Stow (317) he does not seem to have borrowed from contemporary chroniclers. Historically the most valuable of contemporary accounts of Elizabeth's reign.

303 THE CHRONICLE OF QUEEN JANE, and of two years of Queen Mary and especially of the rebellion of Sir Thomas Wyat, written by a resident in the Tower of London. By J. G. Nichols. *Camden Soc.* xlviii (1850).

A diary, July 1553–Oct. 1554. Author probably one of officers of royal mint. Valuable app. of documents, including will of Edward VI and documents on the accession of Queen Jane and of Queen Mary, Wyatt's rebellion and the arrival and marriage of Philip II.

304 CHRONICLES OF LONDON. By C. L. Kingsford. Oxf. 1905.

A scholarly ed. of 3 London chronicles, the last one of which extends down to the year 1516, and is sometimes known as the *London City chronicle*. Cf. 305.

305   FABYAN, ROBERT. Fabyan's cronycle newly prynted with the cronycle, actes and dedes done in the tyme of . . . Henry VII. . . . Lond. 1516; 1533; 1542; 1559; by Henry Ellis, Lond. 1811.

The title above is taken from the 2nd ed. The 1st ed. ends with the battle of Bosworth; the 2nd contains a continuation reaching to the death of Henry VII probably also by Fabyan; the 3rd ed. was amended to suit the reformers; the 4th ed. has a continuation in another hand to the accession of Elizabeth. The account of Henry VII's reign, the so-called *City chronicle* (304) and the *Great chronicle* (310) also partially attributed to Fabyan are extracts from a larger London chronicle called by Kingsford 'The Main City Chronicle'. Cf. Kingsford (3612a), 70–112. Cf. Busch (406), 402–15 and Kingsford (304), pp. xxix–xxxi.

306   GRAFTON, RICHARD.

Began his career as a chronicler by printing *The chronicle of John Hardynge from the first begynnyng of Englāde*, Lond. 1543. To this he added a continuation from the beginning of Edward IV's reign, where Hardynge stopped, to 1543. This continuation was reprinted by Henry Ellis, Lond. 1812. It is a very meagre record and has no independent historical value.

In 1547 Grafton issued an edition of *Hall's chronicle* (312) which went as far as the end of the reign of Edward IV; this was reissued with a continuation of the *Chronicle* to the death of Henry VIII in 1548.

Cf. Graham Pollard, *The bibliographical history of Hall's chronicle*, Bull. Inst. Hist. Research, x (1932), 12–17.

For John Stow's criticism of both these performances cf. Kingsford's ed. of Stow's *London* (4591) i, pp. lxxvii ff. Cf. also Kingsford (3612a), 146–8, 186–8, 265.

307   GRAFTON, RICHARD. An abridgement of the chronicles of England. Lond. 1562; 1563; 1564; 1570; 1572.

The last ed. covers the period to 1572.

308   GRAFTON, RICHARD. A manuell of the chronicles of England to this yere 1565. Lond. [1565].

A summary of 307 which he explains in his preface had been impudently plagiarized. Cf. Kingsford's ed. of Stow's *London* (4591) i, pp. xlviii–liii.

309   GRAFTON, RICHARD. A chronicle at large and meere history of the affayres of England . . . to the first yeere . . . of Queen Elizabeth. [Lond.] 1568; 1569; standard ed. by Henry Ellis, Lond. 1809.

Grafton's tables of the bailiffs, sheriffs, and mayors of London from 1189 to 1558 is appended to ed. of 1809. His work is based upon that of Hall and others and has little or no independent historical value.

310   THE GREAT CHRONICLE OF LONDON. By A. H. Thomas and I. D. Thornley. Lond. 1938.

The *Chronicle* is divided into two parts, the first 1189–1439 is written by a mid-fifteenth-century hand, the second, 1439–1512, by a hand of the late fifteenth or early sixteenth century, probably Fabyan. It is based upon the 'Main City Chronicle'. The *Chronicle* is of independent value for the period 1503–12.

The introduction is valuable, noting the relations of this *Chronicle* to parallel compilations. Cf. also Kingsford (3612a), 70–81, 100–1.

For the historical background of the *Chronicle* cf. also A. F. Pollard, *The Great Chronicle of London. Essays of the Year, 1933–4*, Lond. 1934, 263–72.

311   GREY FRIARS OF LONDON CHRONICLE. By J. G. Nichols. Camden Soc. liii (1852).

A repetition of *Arnold's chronicle* (301) up to 1502; after that an independent source of some value down to its close in 1556. There is a somewhat better ed. of this same chronicle in the *Monumenta Franciscana*, Rolls Ser., 1858–82, ii, 143–260.

312 HALL, EDWARD. The union of the two noble and illustre famelies York and Lancaster. . . . Lond. 1542; by R. Grafton, Lond. 1548; standard ed. by Henry Ellis, Lond. 1809; by Charles Whibley, 2 vols., Lond. 1904.

A panegyric of the house of Tudor, especially of Henry VIII, to whose reign the bulk of the work is devoted. The 1542 ed. is probably fictitious, cf. A. F. Pollard, *The bibliographical history of Hall's Chronicle, Bull. Inst. Hist. Research*, x (1932), 12–17. The first ed. undoubtedly did not appear until 1548. Whibley's ed. begins with Henry VIII's accession. The earlier part is practically a trans. of Polydore Vergil (320). Hall finished his chronicle to the year 1532. The remainder of the work put together by Grafton from Hall's notes. Cf. Busch (406), 398–400. Hall's earlier work differs in some particulars from Polydore, cf. Tillyard (3646), 40–50. The best contemporary history of the reign of Henry VIII. Used extensively by Grafton (306), Stow (317), Holinshed (314). Cf. *E. Hall's will and chronicle, Bull. Inst. Hist. Research*, ix (1932), 171–7, also ibid. xi (1933), 31–33; cf. also Edwin Wolf, *Edward Halle's 'The union of the two noble and illustre families of Lancastre and Yorks' and its place among English Americana, Papers Bibliog. Soc. Amer.* xxxiii (1940), 40–54; W. G. Zeeveld, *The influence of Hall on Shakespeare's English historical plays; A portion of 'Edward Hall: a study of sixteenth century historiography in England'*, Baltimore, 1937, pp. i–vi, 317–55.

313 HAYWARD, JOHN. Annals of the first four years of the reign of Elizabeth. By John Bruce. *Camden Soc.* vii, 1840.

Written in 1612 when the author was 52 years old. Printed in part as an app. to the 1636 ed. of Hayward's *Edward VI* (562). A colourful picture of young Elizabeth by a contemporary.

314 HOLINSHED, RAPHAEL. Chronicles, &c. 2 vols., Lond. 1577; by John Hooker *et al.*, 3 vols., Lond. 1587; by Henry Ellis, 6 vols., Lond. 1807–8.

A composite work carrying the history of England, Ireland, and Scotland to the end of the year 1586 (2nd ed.). Holinshed compiled most of the 1st ed., with the exception of Wm. Harrison's *Description of England* (frequently reprinted, cf. (615)), and the Irish history which was for the most part the work of Richard Stanihurst (cf. 5823). In the 1st ed. a few passages in the history of Ireland (pp. 74–78 and 90–91) offended Elizabeth and were deleted in some copies. The 2nd ed. appeared after Holinshed's death and was edited by John Hooker (*alias* Vowell), John Stow, Francis Thynne (*alias* Botevile), and Abraham Fleming. It continued the narrative to the end of the year 1586, and contained also a discourse by Hooker *On the order and usage how to keep a parliament in England in these days*, and a brief history of the chancellors, dukes, lord treasurers, protectors, and cardinals of England, &c., &c., by Thynne. In the 2nd ed. John Stow continued the history of England from 1575 to 1586. He included in it reprints of a number of contemporary pamphlets (cf. 644, 645, 2244).

Extensive castrations from the 2nd ed. were ordered by the government immediately after publication. These dealt chiefly with Anglo-Scottish relations, the Babington plot, and Leicester's expedition to the Low Countries. These castrated passages were published separately in Lond., 1725, and have been included in the ed. of 1807–8. Cf. on this subject *The Bardon papers* (5201), 97.

Holinshed was a conscientious compiler but laid small claim to originality. The only part of his chronicle of independent historical value is the part dealing with the reign of Elizabeth. He drew largely upon Stow (317) for the earlier part of Elizabeth's reign and Stow himself wrote the later part. Indeed, it is fair to say, that excepting Harrison's notable description, the valuable part of Holinshed is Stow's work.

315 LONDON CHRONICLE during the reigns of Henry VII and Henry VIII. By Clarence Hopper. *Camden Soc. Misc.* iv (1859).

Brief.

316 SPEED, JOHN. The history of Great Britaine under the conquests of

ye Romans, Saxons, Danes and Normans . . . with the lives . . . of the English monarchs from Julius Caesar to . . . King James. Lond. 1611.

Speed's history was originally intended as a continuation of his *Theatre of the empire of Great Britaine*, a collection of 54 maps of England and Wales, published, with accompanying descriptions, in 1611. For the history of England before the Tudors he draws upon the same material as Holinshed. André's *Historia* (388) is his chief source for the reign of Henry VII. The charge that his account of Henry VII was taken bodily from Bacon (403) is baseless (cf. *D.N.B.* (9), art. Speed). Hall was his chief source for Henry VIII; Grafton and Stow for Edward VI and Mary. For Elizabeth, he drew freely upon both Stow and Holinshed, usually with acknowledgements. He made use both of Buchanan (4972) and Leslie (4983) for his passages on Scotland, and of Camden's *Britannia* (4190) for Ireland. Speed is one of the most readable of the Elizabethan chroniclers, but his work has little or no independent historical value.

317   STOW, JOHN. Chronicles, &c.

The numerous eds. of Stow's *English chronicles* fall into 3 groups: (a) The summary. First published under the title: *A summarie of Englyshe chronicles, conteyning the true accompt of yeres, wherein every kyng of this realme of England began theyr reigne, how long they reigned, and what notable thyngs have beene done durynge theyr reygnes . . .*, Lond. 1565. Subsequent eds. appeared in 1566, 1570, 1574, [1575], 1590. The later eds., with some slight changes in the original text, carried the story forward to the date of publication. (b) The summary abridged. First published under the title: *The summarie of Englyshe chronicles. Lately collected and published, nowe abridged and continued tyl this present moneth of Marche . . . 1566*, by I. S., Lond. 1566. Subsequent eds. appeared in 1567, 1573, [1579], 1584, [1587], 1598, 1604, 1607, 1611, 1618. These simply carried the abridgement up to date. They condense the summary into a form 'such as may both ease the purse and the carriage'. (c) The chronicles and annals. First published under the title: *The chronicles of England, from Brute unto this present yeare of Christ, 1580*, Lond. [1580]. 2nd ed. published under the title: *The annals of England faithfully collected out of the most authenticall authors, records and other monuments of antiquitie, from the first inhabitation untill this present yeare 1592*, Lond. 1592. Subsequent eds. appeared in [1600], [1601], 1605, 1614, 1615, 1631. The ed. of 1580 is little more than an expansion of the *Summary* of 1575. The wording of the *Summary* is, in general, preserved, some corrections are made and some additional matter inserted. Stow made extensive use of the 1st ed. of Holinshed in preparing his *Chronicle* of 1580, sometimes using Holinshed's exact wording, but without acknowledgement. The *Annals* of 1592, with the subsequent eds. of 1601 and 1605, are based upon the *Chronicle* of 1580 with some slight additions to the original text. The portions of the *Annals* dealing with the period from Nov. 1576 to Sept. 1586 are made up of passages extracted almost verbatim from the additions which Stow wrote for the 2nd ed. of Holinshed (314). There is a list of sources given in ed. 1601 of the *Annals*. The best ed. of the *Annals* is that of 1605. Subsequent eds., edited by Edmond Howes, contain matter interpolated by him in the original text. Probably some of these interpolations were made from Stow's notes. Stow was painstaking and his chronicles give a fairly accurate record of facts in chronological order. They lack proportion and make no attempt to trace historical development. Cf. Kingsford's *Stow* (4591), i, pp. lxxxii–xciii; Busch (406), 408–10, and no. 319 *infra*. Cf. *The great chronicle* (310), Introduction; J. A. Bryant, *John Stow's continuator and the defence of Brute, Mod. Lang. Rev.* xlv (1950), 352–4; *John Stow commemoration addresses* by C. W. F. Goss, *Trans. Lond. and Middx. Arch. Soc.*, n.s., vii (1937), 452–63; by J. E. Neale, ibid. x (1951), 276–9; by C. J. Sisson, ibid. xi (1952), 79–81; J. F. Nichols, ibid. viii (1938), 75–80.

318   [TURPYN, RICHARD.] The chronicle of Calais in the reigns of Henry VII and Henry VIII to the year 1540. By J. G. Nichols. *Camden Soc.* xxxv (1846).

A number of valuable contemporary documents dealing with related subjects are printed in appendixes.

319 TWO LONDON CHRONICLES from the collections of John Stow. By
C. L. Kingsford. *Camden Soc. Misc.* xii (1910).
The earlier chronicle covers the period 1523–40, the later 1548–55. The earlier one
was Stow's chief source in the 1st eds. of his summary of *English chronicles* (317).
Through Stow, the earlier chronicle is several times quoted by Holinshed. Stow made
only slight use of the later chronicle.

320 VIRGILIUS, POLYDORUS, or Polydore Vergil. Historiae Anglicae
libri viginti septem (Libri xxvi in 1st ed.). Basel, 1534; by Antonius Thysius,
Basel, 1546; Leyden, 1651.
On the various eds. and value of the last 2 books of this work, cf. Busch (406), 395–8.
The first two editions carry the story down to 1509; later eds. to 1538. An invaluable
source for the reign of Henry VII. Cf. also the translation and edition by Denys Hay,
Camden Soc., 3rd ser., lxxiv (1950). For the life of Virgil cf. Denys Hay, *Polydore
Vergil; Renaissance historian and man of letters.* Oxf. 1952. Cf. also Gasquet, *Some
materials for a new ed. of Polydore Vergils's history, Trans. R.H. Soc.*, 2nd ser., xvi
(1902), 1–17; Whitney and Cram, *Polydore Vergil's will, Trans. R.H. Soc.*, 4th ser., xi
(1928), 117–38.

321 WRIOTHESLEY, CHARLES. A Chronicle of England. By W. D.
Hamilton. 2 vols. *Camden Soc.*, n.s., xi, pts. i and ii (1875–7).
An extract from *Arnold's chronicle* (301) to 1521, when that work ends; continued, how-
ever, to 1559. The extract fills only 12 out of the 333 pp. in Hamilton's edition.
Wriothesley was Windsor Herald after 1534. Cf. Busch (406), 401.
   Cf. Flower, Robin, *The Wriothesley MSS., Brit. Mus. Quar.* xii (1938), 82–85, on
English heraldry, largely fifteenth and sixteenth centuries. The MSS. are in B.M.,
Add. MSS. 45131–3.

F. LATER WORKS

The best general books on the political history of the Tudor period are Fisher
(339) and Mackie (354) for the period 1485–1547, Pollard (363) and Black (671)
for the period 1547–1603. Lingard (353) presents the old-fashioned moderate
Roman Catholic viewpoint. Froude (340), despite many mistakes in detail and
a pronounced anti-catholic bias, is still invaluable.

322 ACTON, LORD. Lectures on modern history. Lond. 1906.
Contains essays on: Calvin and Henry VIII, Philip II, Mary Stuart, and Elizabeth.

323 ASCOLI, G. La Grande Bretagne devant l'opinion française. . . . Paris,
1927.
Scholarly. Covers period from 1450 to 1600. Chiefly devoted to expressions of French
opinion on English questions in contemporary French literature.

324 AUBREY, JOHN. Brief lives. Lond. 1813; best ed. from Aubrey's MSS.
by O. L. Dick. Lond. 1949.

325 BINDOFF, S. T. Tudor England. Lond. 1950.
Excellent. Sound scholarship.

326 BROSCH, MORITZ. Geschichte von England, vols. vi and vii. 1509–
1688. Gotha, 1890–2.
A continuation of Lappenberg and Pauli's *Geschichte Englands* which stops with vol. v
in 1509.

327 BURKE'S GENEALOGICAL AND HERALDIC HISTORY OF THE
LANDED GENTRY. 17th ed. By L. G. Pine. Lond. 1952.

328   BURKE, S. H. Historical portraits of the Tudor dynasty and the reformation period. 4 vols. Lond. 1879–83.

329   CAM, HELEN. England before Elizabeth. Lond. 1950.

330   CAMPBELL, L. B. Tudor conceptions of history and tragedy in 'A Mirror for Magistrates'. Berkeley, U.S.A. 1936.

331   CHETTLE, H. F. The burgesses for Calais, 1536–1558. *E.H.R.* l (1935), 492–501.

332   COLLINS, ARTHUR. The peerage of England. Lond. 1709; best ed. by S. E. Brydges, 9 vols., Lond. 1812.
Probably the best peerage for historical purposes. G. E. Cokayne, *Complete peerage of England, Scotland, Ireland, etc., extant, extinct, or dormant,* 8 vols., Exeter, 1887–98; rev. ed., by V. Gibbs, 13 vols., Lond. 1910–49, is the most comprehensive. For other peerages, cf. Gross (1), 54 ff. and Davies (8), no. 785.

333   DAUMET, GEORGES. Calais sous la domination anglaise. Arras, 1902.

334   DILLON, H. A. Calais and the Pale. *Arch.* liii (1893), 289–388.

335   ELTON, G. R. England under the Tudors. Lond. 1956.
This replaces Innes, in the *History of England series,* iv. Useful chiefly for administrative reforms under Henry VIII. Thin on foreign affairs and on the period following 1588.

336   EUROPEAN CIVILIZATION: its origins and development. By Edward Eyre. Vol. iv: the Reformation. New York, 1936.
Cf. especially the chapters by F. M. Powicke on the *Reformation in England,* pp. 349–488; by W. E. Brown, on the *Reformation in Scotland,* pp. 489–560; by M. V. Ronan, on the *Reformation in Ireland,* pp. 561–629.

337   FELLOWES, E. H. The Knights of the Garter, 1348–1939. Lond. 1940.

338   FULLER, THOMAS. The Worthies of England. Lond. 1662; by John Freeman, Lond. 1952.
Cf. also ibid., *The Holy and profane state,* Lond. 1642; ed. J. Nichols, 1841.

339   FISHER, H. A. L. The history of England, from the accession of Henry VII to the death of Henry VIII. Lond. 1906.
Vol. v of the *Political history of England,* by William Hunt and R. L. Poole. The best modern work on this field. Contains a useful bibliography.

340   FROUDE, J. A. History of England from the fall of Wolsey to the defeat of the Spanish Armada. 12 vols. Lond. 1856–70; rev. ed., 12 vols., 1862–70; later eds. 1881–2; 1893; 1912 (5 vols. *Reign of Elizabeth. Everyman's library*).
The classic for the period from the fall of Wolsey to the defeat of the Armada and one of the great masterpieces of English historical literature. Based upon very wide research in English and continental archives. Not accurate in detail and coloured throughout by a strong anti-catholic bias, but invaluable. For the virulent and unmerited attack of Freeman and others upon Froude, cf. Herbert Paul's *Life of Froude,* Lond. 1905.

341   GAIRDNER, JAMES, and SPEDDING, JAMES. Studies in English history. Edin. 1881.
Contains articles by Gairdner on Anglo-Spanish negotiations in the fifteenth century, and on Katharine of Aragon's second marriage.

342 GODWIN, FRANCIS (bishop of Hereford). Rerum Anglicarum Henrico VIII, Edwardo VI et Maria . . . regnantibus annales. Lond. 1616; 1628; 1653.
Written from a rather puritan standpoint. English translations were published in 1630 and in 1676; a French one (at Paris) in 1647.

343 GREEN, J. R. Short history of the English people. Lond. 1874; 1892–4. Many later eds. and reprs.
A brilliant essay, pays particular attention to social conditions. Contains notable character sketches of Tudor monarchs and statesmen.

344 GREEN, M. A. E. W. The lives of the princesses of England, from the Norman Conquest [to Charles I]. 6 vols. Lond. 1849–55.
Of uneven value, but contains good biographies of Henry VII's daughters.

345 HALE, J. R. England and the Italian Renaissance. Lond. 1954.
A survey of influence of Italian Renaissance upon England up to the nineteenth century.

346 HARRISON, DAVID. Tudor England. Lond. 1953.
Excellent illustrations, otherwise of little value.

347 HAY, DENYS. The historiographers royal in England and Scotland. *Scot. Hist. Rev.* xxx (1951), 15–29.

348 HILL, R. H. Tales of the jesters. Lond. 1934.

349 HUME, M. A. S. Two English queens, Mary and Elizabeth, and Philip. Lond. 1908.
Useful for the personal side of Anglo-Spanish relations.

350 HUME, M. A. S. The year after the Armada, and other historical studies. Lond. 1896.

352 LLOYD, DAVID. The statesmen and favourites of England since the Reformation. Lond. 1765; by Charles Whitworth. 2 vols. Lond. 1766.

353 LINGARD, JOHN. A history of England from the first invasion by the Romans to the revolution in 1688. 8 vols. Lond. 1819–30; enl. ed., 10 vols., 1849 (the last revised by the author). Many later eds. continued and abridged.
Lingard presents the old-fashioned moderate Roman Catholic attitude towards the religious controversies of the sixteenth century, though even from this point of view he needs to be checked by the later researches of Roman Catholic scholars, particularly those of Gasquet for Henry VIII and of Pollen for Elizabeth.

354 MACKIE, J. D. The earlier Tudors, 1485–1558. Oxf. 1952.
Useful, though thin on Edward and Mary. Valuable chiefly on foreign affairs.

355 MATHEW, DAVID. The Celtic peoples and Renaissance Europe. Lond. 1933.
Valuable for Ireland and Wales, particularly for Welsh connexions in the Essex rising of 1601.

356 MAURENBRECHER, WILHELM. England im Reformationszeitalter, vier Vorträge. Düsseldorf, 1866.
The first two of these lectures deal with Henry VIII, Edward VI, and Mary; the last two with Elizabeth and Mary Stuart.

357   MORRIS, CHRISTOPHER. The Tudors. Lond. 1955.

358   MULLER, J. A. Stephen Gardiner and the Tudor reaction. New York, 1926.
Scholarly. Contains a useful list of Gardiner's printed and unprinted works. Cf. Dunstan Pontifex, *Stephen Gardiner, Downside Rev.* lii (1934), 506–19; G. Scott Thomson, *Background for a bishop,* in *Studies presented to Sir Hilary Jenkinson,* Oxf. 1957, 414–22.

359   NOBBS, DOUGLAS. England and Scotland, 1560–1707. Lond. 1952.
Essay on reciprocal interaction of events and forces in England and Scotland.

360   NOTESTEIN, WALLACE. Four worthies: Ann Clifford, John Chamberlain, John Taylor, Oliver Heywood. Lond. 1956.

361   NOTESTEIN, WALLACE. The English People on the eve of colonization. New York, 1956.
A good picture of social, political and religious England at death of Elizabeth.

362   POLLARD, A. F. Factors in modern history. Lond. 1907.
A collection of suggestive essays, chiefly on the Tudor period.

363   POLLARD, A. F. The history of England from the accession of Edward VI to the death of Elizabeth. Lond. 1913.
Vol. vi of the *Political history of England,* by William Hunt and R. L. Poole. The best general account of the period considered. Contains a useful bibliography.

364   POLLARD, A. F. New Year's day and Leap year in English history. *E.H.R.* lv (1940), 177–93.

365   POLLARD, A. F. Tudor gleanings. *Bull. Inst. Hist. Research,* vii (1929), 1–12, 85–97.

366   RANKE, LEOPOLD VON. Englische Geschichte, vornehmlich im sechzehnten und siebzehnten Jahrhuhndert. 7 vols. Berlin, 1859–68; trans. G. W. Kitchen, C. W. Boase, *et al.,* 6 vols., Oxf. 1875.
Books ii and iii in vol. i of trans. constitute a brilliant essay on English sixteenth-century history.

367   READ, CONYERS. The Tudors: personalities and practical politics in sixteenth century England. New York, 1936.

368   ROGERS, W. H. H. The strife of the roses and days of the Tudors in the west. Exeter and Lond. 1890.

369   ROUND, J. R. Studies in peerage and family history. Lond. 1901.

370   ROUND, J. H. Peerage and pedigree; studies in peerage law and family history. 2 vols. Lond. 1910.

371   ROUND, J. H. Family origins and other studies. Lond. 1930.
369–71 make mature and substantial contributions to Tudor social history.

372   SANDEMAN, G. A. C. Calais under English rule. Oxf. 1908.

373   SCOTT-GILES, C. W. The Romance of heraldry. Lond. 1929; rep. 1951.

374   SCOTT-GILES, C. W. Civic heraldry of England and Wales. Lond. 1933.

375 SEELEY, J. R. Growth of British policy. 2 vols. Cambr. 1895.
A brilliant, though not altogether accurate, sketch of English foreign policy under Elizabeth and her successors.

375a SINGER, C., HOLMYARD, E. J., HALL, A. R., and WILLIAMS, T. I. A history of technology; vol. iii. From the Renaissance to the Industrial Revolution. Oxf. 1957.

376 STRICKLAND, AGNES. Lives of the Tudor princesses, including Lady Jane Grey and her sisters. Lond. 1868.
Useful, but antiquated.

377 STRICKLAND, AGNES. Lives of the queens of England. 12 vols. Lond. 1840–8; revised eds. 8 vols. 1851–2.
Useful, but uncritical and antiquated.

378 STUBBS, WILLIAM. Seventeen lectures on medieval and modern history and kindred subjects, delivered . . . in 1867–84. Oxf. 1886; 1887.
The following are pertinent: xi, *The reign of Henry VIII*; xii, *Parliament under Henry VIII*; xiii–xiv, *The history of the canon law in England*; xv–xvi, *The reign of Henry VII*.

379 TUDOR STUDIES. By R. W. Seton-Watson. Lond. 1924.
Contains: C. A. J. Skeel, *Wales under Henry VII*; Claude Jenkins, *Cardinal Morton's register*; E. R. Adair, *William Thomas: a forgotten clerk of the privy council*; I. D. Thornley, *The destruction of sanctuary*; A. P. Newton, *Tudor reforms in the royal household*; R. R. Reid, *The political influence of the 'North parts' under the later Tudors*; J. E. Neale, *The Commons' privilege of free speech in parliament*; E. Jeffries Davis, *The transformation of London*.

380 WAGNER, A. R. Heralds and heraldry in the Middle Ages. Lond. 1939; 1956.
Especially interesting for the Tudor period.

381 WHITE, BEATRICE. Royal nonesuch: a Tudor tapestry. Lond. 1933.
A vivid picture of Tudor court life.

382 WIFFEN, J. H. Historical memoirs of the house of Russell. . . . 2 vols. Lond. 1833.
Cf. also G. Scott Thomson, *Two centuries of family history*, Lond. 1930.

383 WILLIAMS, C. H. The making of Tudor despotism. Lond. 1928; 1935.

384 WILLIAMS, DAVID. The Welsh Tudors. *History today*, iv (1954), 77–84.

385 WILLIAMSON, J. A. The Tudor Age. Lond. 1953.

386 WOOD, A. C. The Holles family. *Trans. R.H. Soc.*, 4th ser., xix (1936), 145–65.

II

POLITICAL HISTORY, 1485–1603

A. HENRY VII

I. SOURCES

An excellent general discussion of the sources for this reign is in Busch (406). Fisher's (339) bibliography is good. Polydore Vergil (320) and André (388) are the most important of contemporary chroniclers. Gairdner (396, 398) and Campbell (397) print most of the available manuscript material. The *Statutes of the realm* (1016) and the *Proclamations* (1017) should not be ignored. For foreign sources, cf. sect. G *infra* (pp. 65 ff.).

387 ALIA EJUSDEM HISTORIAE croylandensis continuatio. By William Fulman. Oxf. 1684.
In vol. i of *Rerum anglicarum scriptores* (cf. Gross (1), no. 579). The *alia continuatio* covers the years 1485 and 1486.

388 ANDRÉ or ANDREAS, BERNARD. De vita atque gestis Henrici septimi: annales Henrici septimi. By James Gairdner. Lond. 1858.
In *Memorials of King Henry the Seventh* (398). The *Vita* goès only to 1497. The *Annales* cover the years 1504–5, 1507–8. On the value of these works, cf. Busch (406), 393–5.

389 CALENDAR OF THE CLOSE ROLLS, Henry VII, i, 1485–1500. Lond. 1953.

390 CALENDAR OF THE INQUISITIONS POST MORTEM, Henry VII. 3 vols. Lond. 1898–1956.
Especially useful for biographical purposes. Well calendared and indexed.

391 CALENDAR OF PATENT ROLLS, Henry VII, i, 1485–94; ii, 1494–1509. 2 vols. Lond. 1914–16.
Useful for information as to personnel of Henry VII's administration. Index not reliable.

392 CARMELIANUS, PETRUS, solennes ceremoniae et triumphi or The solempnities & triumphs doon & made at the spouselles and mariage of the kynges daughter, the ladye Marye to the prynce of Castile, archeduke of Austrige. Lond. 1508; by Henry Ellis, *Roxburghe Club*, 1818; by James Gairdner, *Camden Soc. Misc.* ix (1893).
Probably written by Henry VII's Latin secretary.

393 CONSPIRACY AGAINST HENRY VII. *Reports of the deputy keeper of pub. rec.* liii (1892), app. ii.
A description of certain documents relating to Perkin Warbeck's conspiracy. The originals have been added to the series of pouches known as the *Baga de secretis* in the P.R.O. (1646).

394 DOCUMENTS RELATING TO PERKIN WARBECK with remarks on his history. By Frederick Madden. *Arch.* xxvii (1838), 153–210.

395 FISHER, JOHN, bp. of Rochester. Hereafter foloweth a mornynge remembraunce had at the moneth mynde of Margarete, countesse of Rychmonde. Lond. [1509]; by Thomas Baker, Lond. 1708; by J. E. B. Mayor (in *Fisher's English works*), *E.E.T.S.* xxvii (1878).

396 LETTERS AND PAPERS ILLUSTRATIVE of the reigns of Richard III and Henry VII. By James Gairdner. 2 vols. *Rolls ser.* Lond. 1861–3.
Important.

397 MATERIALS FOR A HISTORY of the reign of Henry VII. By William Campbell. 2 vols. *Rolls ser.* Lond. 1873.
Contains important documents for the years 1485–90.

398 MEMORIALS OF KING HENRY THE SEVENTH. By James Gairdner. *Rolls ser.* Lond. 1858.
Contains all the works of Bernard André (388) and the journals of Roger Machado (875) and other ambassadors.

399 MORE, THOMAS. The history of King Richard the third. By William Rastell. Lond. 1557; by S. W. Singer, Lond. 1821; by J. R. Lumby, Cambr. 1883.
Lancastrian in tone: valuable for the early life of Henry VII. First appeared in an incorrect version in Grafton's continuation of *Hardynge's chronicle* (306) and was largely used by Edward Hall. There is also a Latin version. Cf. *D.N.B.*, art. T. More and More (450).

400 THE REIGN OF HENRY VII from contemporary sources. By A. F. Pollard. 3 vols. *Univ. of London historical ser.* no. 1. Lond. 1913–14.
A very useful collection. Vol. i, narratives; vol. ii, constitutional, social, economic; vol. iii, diplomacy, church, Ireland.

401 SIR WILLIAM STANLEY AND PERKIN WARBECK. By W. A. J. Archbold. *E.H.R.* xiv (1899), 529–34.
MS. copies of the reports of the trials of Stanley and Warbeck, omitted from *Baga de secretis* (1646).

402 THE WILL OF KING HENRY VII. By Thomas Astle. Lond. 1775.

2. LATER WORKS

The best accounts of the reign are in Fisher (339) and Busch (406), the latter being particularly good on economic questions. Gairdner (411) and Temperley (427) are excellent short biographies. Bacon's life (403) is still valuable. Gairdner (412) gives the authoritative account of Perkin Warbeck. Green (344) gives good biographies of Henry VII's daughters, Margaret and Mary. For Henry's relations with Scotland and Ireland, cf. 5151.

403 BACON, FRANCIS. Historie of the raigne of King Henry the seventh. Lond. 1622; by J. R. Lumby, Cambr. 1885.
On the importance and critical value of this work, cf. Busch (406), 416–23.

404 BRODIE, D. M. Edmund Dudley: minister of Henry VII. *Trans. R.H. Soc.*, 4th ser., xv (1932), 133–61.

405 BROWN, M. C. Mary Tudor, queen of France. Lond. 1911.

406 BUSCH, WILHELM. England unter den Tudors, Band 1, König Heinrich VII. Stuttgart, 1892; Eng. trans. A. M. Todd, Lond. 1895.
A most valuable work with an excellent bibliographical note which is especially useful on the chronicles of the reign. References to this work herein are to the English trans.

407 CHASTELAIN, J. D. L'imposture de Perkin Warbeck. Brussels, 1955.

408 COOPER, C. H. Memoir of Margaret [Beaufort], countess of Richmond and Derby. By J. E. B. Mayor. Cambr. 1874.
Scholarly.

409 CUSSANS, J. E. Notes on the Perkin Warbeck insurrection. *Trans. R.H. Soc.* i (1875), 61–77.

410 GAIRDNER, JAMES. A supposed conspiracy against Henry VII. *Trans. R.H. Soc.*, 2nd ser., xviii (1904), 157–94.

411 GAIRDNER, JAMES. Henry the seventh. Lond. 1889.
The standard English life.

412 GAIRDNER, JAMES. History of the life and reign of Richard the third. Lond. 1878; rev. Cambr. 1898.
A valuable essay on Perkin Warbeck is appended to this work. The ed. of 1898 is considerably revised in the light of later researches and contains a contemporary portrait of Warbeck.

413 GAIRDNER, JAMES. The battle of Bosworth. *Arch.* lv (1896), 159–78.

414 HALSTED, C. A. Life of Margaret Beaufort ... mother of King Henry the seventh. Lond. 1839; 1845.

415 HENES, EDWIN, Jr., and BRINER, G. C. A historical sketch of Perkin Warbeck, pretender to the crown of England. New York, 1902.
Slight.

416 HUTTON, WILLIAM. The battle of Bosworth Field . . . to which is prefixed a history of . . . [Henry VII's] life till he assumed the regal power. Birmingham, 1788; 2nd ed., with additions by J. Nichols, Lond. 1813.

418 KIRBY, J. L. Blackheath, and the Cornish rising of 1497. *Trans. Greenwich and Lewisham Antiq. Soc.* iv (1937), 29–36.

419 LEADAM, I. S. An unknown conspiracy against King Henry VII. *Trans. R.H. Soc.*, 2nd ser., xvi (1902), 133–51.

420 LEGG, J. W. The gift of the papal cap and sword to Henry VII. *Arch. Jour.* lvii (1900), 183–203.

421 MARKHAM, C. R. Richard III; his life and character. Lond. 1906.
Apologetic; believes that Henry VII murdered the princes. Cf. *E.H.R.* vi (1891), 250–83, 444–64; xxii (1907), 576–81.

422 POLLARD, A. F. The *de facto* act of Henry VII. *Bull. Inst. Hist. Research*, vii (1930), 1–12.

423 ROTH, CECIL. Perkin Warbeck and his Jewish master. *Trans. Jew. Hist. Soc. of Eng.* ix (1918–20), 143–62.

424 ROUTH, E. M. G. Lady Margaret mother of Henry VII. Lond. 1925.
An interesting memoir, contributing nothing new.

425 SMITH, J. H. The will of Henry VII. *Church Quar. Rev.* cxvi (1933), 244-51.

426 STEVENSON, JOSEPH. Perkin Warbeck. *The Month,* lxxv (1892), 508-19.

427 TEMPERLEY, GLADYS. Henry VII. Lond. 1914; 1918.

428 W., G. Richard, duke of York, and Perkin Warbeck. *Notes and Queries,* clxviii (1935), 309-11.

429 WILBY, N. M. A noble friendship: Blessed John Fisher and Lady Margaret Beaufort. *The Month,* clxv (1935), 233-41.

430 WILLIAMS, C. H. The rebellion of Humphrey Stafford in 1486. *E.H.R.* xliii (1928), 181-90.

431 WOODHOUSE, R. I. The life of John Morton, archbishop of Canterbury. Lond. 1895.

432 WORMALD, FRANCIS. An Italian poet at the court of Henry VII. *Jour. Warburg and Court. Inst.* xiv (1951), 118-19.
Nagonius Based on B.M. Add. MSS. 45131.

B. HENRY VIII

1. Sources

The greater part of the materials for the reign of Henry VIII is assembled in *Letters and papers* (91). Merriman (520) prints *in extenso* almost all the extant letters of Cromwell. The *Cal. S.P., Spanish* (867), *Venetian* (992), and *Milan* (990) should also be consulted. Materials on the ecclesiastical aspects of the reign are given in ch. vi, sect. 4, *infra* (pp. 170 ff.). Those printed by Strype (1849) are noteworthy. The contemporary controversial literature on the divorce case is too voluminous to mention. It will be found listed in the B.M. catalogues, title Henry VIII, king of England, Divorce. The most useful of the chronicles for this reign is Hall (312).

433 CAVENDISH, GEORGE. The life of Cardinal Wolsey, Lond. 1641; standard ed. by S. W. Singer, 2 vols., Lond. 1827; by H. Morley, Lond. 1885.
A simple but too laudatory account by Wolsey's gentleman usher. Circulated widely in MS. in sixteenth century and utilized by Stow in his *Annals* (317). First printed in garbled ed. in 1641. For later eds. and their value, cf. *D.N.B.* (5), art. Geo. Cavendish. Cf. also Hilary Steurt, *Cavendish's life of Cardinal Wolsey, Downside Rev.* lvii (1939), 23-45.

434 CHRONICLE OF KING HENRY VIII OF ENGLAND. By M. A. S. Hume. Lond. 1889.
The Spanish *Chronica del rey Enrico Ottavo de Inglaterra,* of which this is a slovenly translation, was written by a contemporary and published in Madrid, 1874.

435 THE DRAFT DISPENSATION FOR HENRY VIII's marriage with Anne Boleyn. By James Gairdner. *E.H.R.* v (1890), 544-50.

436   FORREST, WILLIAM. The history of Grisild the second: a narrative, in verse, of the divorce of Katharine of Aragon. By W. D. Macray. *Roxburghe Club*, 1875.

Edited from the author's MS. in Bodleian library. Forrest was chaplain to Queen Mary, and finished his work 25 June 1558.

437   GIUSTINIAN, SEBASTIAN. Four years at the court of Henry VIII. By Rawdon Brown. 2 vols. Lond. 1854.

A trans. of selected dispatches of a contemporary Venetian ambassador to the Signory between 1515 and 1519.

438   A GLASSE OF THE TRUTHE, [an argument by way of dialogue, between a lawyer and a divine; that the marriage of Henry VIII with Catharine of Aragon was unlawful, and that the cause ought to be heard and ordered within the realm]. Lond. [1530]; 1531.

439   HARPSFIELD, NICHOLAS. The life and death of Sr Thomas Moore, knight, sometymes lord high chancellor of England, written in the tyme of Queene Marie by Nicholas Harpsfield. By E. V. Hitchcock and R. W. Chambers. *E.E.T.S.* clxxxvi (1932).

440   HARPSFIELD, NICHOLAS. A treatise on the pretended divorce between Henry VIII and Catharine of Aragon. By Nicholas Pocock. *Camden Soc.*, 2nd ser., xxi (1878).

Harpsfield was archdeacon of Canterbury and wrote in 1556. His work is conscientious and valuable.

441   HENRY VIII'S LOVE LETTERS TO ANNE BOLEYN. By Thomas Hearne. Oxf. 1720; by W. Gunn, *Pamphleteer*, xxi (1813), 346–8, xxii, 114–23; by G. A. Crapelet, Paris, 1826; Boston, 1906; by H. W. Trovillion, Lond. 1933, 1936, 1945.

Hearne's ed. is in app. to his *Robert of Avesbury* (Gross (1), no. 1716); Gunn's ed. contains other valuable contemporary documents; Crapelet's ed. contains a contemporary French poem on the life of Anne Boleyn written a fortnight after her execution.

442   HENRY VIII. Miscellaneous writings of Henry the eighth. By F. Macnamara. Lond. 1924.

Editing unscholarly.

443   INEDITED DOCUMENTS relating to the imprisonment and condemnation of Sir Thomas More. By John Bruce. *Arch.* xxvii (1838), 361–74.

444   KING HENRY VIII. The will of King Henry VIII, from an authentic copy in the hands of an attorney. Lond. 1793.

The will is also printed in Rymer (88) and elsewhere.

445   LETTERE DI XIII HUOMINI ILLUSTRI, alle quali . . . ne sono state aggiunte molte da T. Porcacchi. By Tomasso Porcacchi. Venice, 1565; [1580?].

Contains valuable letters for the period of Henry VIII.

446   LETTERE DI PRINCIPI, le quali o si scrivono da principi o a principi. By Girolamo Ruscelli. Book i, Venice, 1562; books ii and iii, 1564–77. French trans. by F. de Belle-forest, Paris, 1572; 1574.

A miscellaneous collection of diplomatic correspondence, some from the Vatican archives. Contains valuable documents relating to England, *temp.* Henry VIII.

447 ELTON, G. R. Two unpublished letters of Thomas Cromwell. *Bull. Inst. Hist. Research*, xxii (1949), 35–38.

448 THE MANER OF THE TRYUMPHE AT CALEYS AND BUL-LEYN and the noble tryumphaunt coronacyon of Quene Anne. Lond. [1532–3]; repr. in *Harl. Misc.* (279) ii, 33–52; by E. M. Goldsmid, *Biblioteca curiosa*, xx (1884–5).
Two tracts originally printed separately.

449 MILLER, THOMAS. An account of the insurrection in the county of York in 1536. By Edmund Lodge. *Arch.* xvi. (1812), 330–4.

450 MORE, SIR THOMAS. The English works of. By Wm. Rastell. Lond. 1557; by W. E. Campbell and A. W. Reed, Lond. 1927–31 (in progress).
The 1st ed. was carefully edited by More's nephew. Campbell's ed., of which 2 vols. have appeared, includes a facsimile reprint of the 1557 ed. Five more vols. of this ed. were originally contemplated.

451 THE CORRESPONDENCE OF SIR THOMAS MORE. By E. F. Rogers. Lond. 1947.
218 letters in Latin and English—*verbatim et literatim*. A model of careful scholarship.

452 NINE HISTORICAL LETTERS of the reign of Henry VIII, written by Reginald Pole, Thomas Cromwell, &c. By J. P. Collier. Lond. 1871.

453 LE PREMIER DIVORCE DE HENRI VIII et le schisme d'Angleterre. By Charles Bémont. Paris, 1917.
Latin text and French trans. of an anonymous MS. chronicle in the Bibliothèque nationale, Paris. Valuable notes and introduction. Probably written by Dr. Nicholas Harpsfield. Much of it embodied in 440.

454 THE PILGRIMAGE OF GRACE, and Aske's examination. By Mary Bateson. *E.H.R.* v (1890), 330–45, 550–73.
Contemporary documents on the rebellion and the examination of the rebels. Cf. also *New records of the Pilgrimage of Grace, Yorks. Arch. Jour.* xxxiii (1937), 298–308, and *Royal pardons for the Pilgrimage of Grace*, ibid. 397–417, both edited by A. G. Dickens.

455 RECORDS OF THE REFORMATION, the divorce 1527–1533. By Nicholas Pocock. 2 vols. Oxf. 1870.
Contains valuable contemporary documents.

456 ROY, WILLIAM. Rede me and be nott wrothe. Worms, 1526; [Strassburg], 1528; Lond. 1546; 1845; by Edward Arber, Lond. 1871.
D.N.B. (9), art. Roy, gives 1526 as 1st ed., but *S.T.C.* (35) no. 21427 shows none earlier than 1528. A satire against Wolsey.

457 RÖMISCHE DOKUMENTE ZUR GESCHICHTE der Ehescheidung Heinrichs VIII. von England, 1527–1534. By Stefan Ehses. Paderborn, 1893.
Published by the *Görres-Gesellschaft*. Important. Ehses' conclusions are well summarized in Gairdner (503).

458 RO: BA: The lyfe of Syr Thomas More, some tymes lord chancellor of England. By E. V. Hitchcock and P. E. Hallett. *E.E.T.S.* ccxxii (1950).

459 ROPER, WILLIAM. The life, arraignement and death of . . . Syr Thomas More. Paris, 1626; best ed. by E. V. Hitchcock, *E.E.T.S.*, orig. ser., cxcvii (1935).

Written by More's son-in-law and the original source of all information as to More's personal history. On the other early lives of More, cf. *D.N.B.* (9), art. T. More, and R. W. Chambers, *The saga and the myth of Sir Thos. More*, Brit. Acad. Lit. Lect., Lond. 1927.

460 SCHOECK, R. J. Another renaissance biography of Sir Thomas More. *Eng. Studies*, xxxiv (1953), 115–17.

461 SKELTON, JOHN. Works. By Alexander Dyce. 2 vols. Lond. 1843.

Skelton's poems: *Colyn Cloute; Why come ye not to court*; and *Speke Parrot* are virulent attacks upon Wolsey. Cf. also William Nelson, *Skelton's quarrel with Wolsey*, *P.M.L.A* li (1936), 377–98.

462 STAPLETON, THOMAS. Vita Thomae Mori, in *Tres Thomas*. Douai, 1588.

Eng. trans. by P. E. Hallet, Lond. 1928.

463 THOMAS, WILLIAM. The pilgrim: a dialogue on the life and actions of King Henry the Eighth. 1st ed. in Italian trans. under title *Il pelligrino inglese ne 'l quale si defende . . . Henrico Ottavo*. s.l. 1552. 1st English version by A. d'Aubant, *Works of William Thomas*, Lond. 1774; by J. A. Froude, Lond. 1861.

D'Aubant's version is from a sixteenth-century MS. Thomas was clerk of council under Edward VI. He presents the popular view of Henry VIII's character. Cf. Adair (379).

464 VETERUM SCRIPTORUM ET MONUMENTORUM amplissima collectio. By Edmond Martène and Ursin Durand. 9 vols. Paris, 1724–33.

A collection of Wolsey's letters to Silvestro Gigli (1516–20) is printed in vol. iii.

465 THE YORKSHIRE SUBMISSIONS TO HENRY VIII, 1541. By A. G. Dickens. *E.H.R.* liii (1938), 267–75.

466 THE YOUTH OF HENRY VIII, a narrative in contemporary letters. By F. A. Mumby. Boston, 1913.

Many of these letters are taken from untrustworthy sources, and they are by no means always accurately transcribed. The book contains no new information.

2. LATER WORKS

The best general history of the reign is in Fisher (339). Pollard (531) is the best life of the king. For Wolsey, cf. nos. 473, 476–7, 532. Merriman (520) is the standard life of Cromwell. Of Henry's unfortunate queens there are no scholarly biographies, except Friedmann's *Anne Boleyn* (499), which is of first-rate importance. On the divorce case Busch (477), Ehses (491), and Gairdner (501–3) are noteworthy. Dodds (489) is excellent on the Pilgrimage of Grace. For the foreign affairs of the reign, cf. sect. G *infra* (pp. 65 ff.); for ecclesiastical affairs, ch. vi *infra* (pp. 170 ff.).

467 ACTON, LORD. Wolsey and the divorce of Henry VIII. *Quar. Rev.* cxliii (1876), 1–51.

A review of *Letters and papers* (91) vol. iv. Repr. in Acton, *Historical essays and studies*, by J. N. Figgis and R. V. Lawrence, Lond. 1907.

468 BAPST, EDMOND. Deux gentils hommes-poètes de la cour de Henri VIII. Paris, 1891.
Biographies of George Boleyn, Viscount Rochford, and of Henry Howard, earl of Surrey. Valuable on the fall of the Howards and on literary life at court.

469 BARCLAY, D. B. Henry Parker, Lord Morley, 1476–1556. *Trans. Essex Arch. Soc.*, n.s., xxiii (1945), 273–9.

470 BECK, HELENE. Englische Vermittlungspolitik in den Jahren 1526–9 Würzburg, 1934.

471 BEHRENS, BETTY. A note on Henry VIII's divorce project of 1514. *Bull. Inst. Hist. Research*, xi (1934), 163–4.

472 BREEN, QUIRINUS. Celcio Calcagnini (1479–1541). *Church Hist.* xxi (1952), 225–38.
A humanist involved in Henry's divorce.

473 BREWER, J. S. The reign of Henry VIII from his accession to the death of Wolsey. By James Gairdner. 2 vols. Lond. 1884.
The fullest account of the subject. Practically identical with the introductions to the vols. of the *Letters and papers* (91) which cover this period.

474 BRIDGETT, T. E. Life and writings of Thomas More. Lond. 1891.
Scholarly though unsatisfactory in its treatment of More's attitude toward the Lutherans.

475 BROWN, J. M. Henry VIII's book, 'Assertio septem sacramentorum', and the royal title of 'Defender of the faith'. *Trans. R.H. Soc.* viii (1880), 242–61.

476 BUSCH, WILHELM. Der Sturz des Cardinals Wolsey im Scheidungs-handel König Heinrichs VIII von England. *Hist. Taschenbuch*, 6th ser., ix (1890), 39–114.

477 BUSCH, WILHELM. Der Ursprung der Ehescheidung König Heinrichs VIII von England. *Hist. Taschenbuch*, 6th ser., viii (1889), 273–327.

478 CAMPBELL, W. E. Erasmus, Tyndale and More. Lond. 1949.
Contains an account of the death of Erasmus based upon R. G. Villoslada, *La muerte de Erasmo in Miscellanea Giovanni Mercati*, Rome, 1946.

479 CARDINAL, E. V. Cardinal Lorenzo Campeggio, legate to the courts of Henry VIII and Charles V. Boston, U.S.A., 1935.

480 CASADY, E. R. Henry Howard, earl of Surrey. *Mod. Lang. Assoc. Revolving fund*, viii. New York, 1938.

481 CHAMBERS, R. W. Thomas More. Lond. 1935, 1949.
Scholarly, but partisan. Cf. G. G. Coulton, *The faith of Sir Thomas More, Quar. Rev.* cclxv (1935), 327–43.

482 CHENEY, A. D. The holy maid of Kent. *Trans. R.H. Soc.*, 2nd ser., xviii (1904), 107–30.

483 CHILDE-PEMBERTON, W. S. Elizabeth Blount and Henry VIII, with some account of her surroundings. Lond. 1913.

484 CONSTANT, G. The schism of Henry VIII: some questions of evidence. *Clergy Rev.* x (1935), 429–37.

485 CREIGHTON, MANDELL. Cardinal Wolsey. Lond. 1898.
Able, but over eulogistic. On Wolsey's early life, cf. T. W. Cameron in *E.H.R.* iii (1888), 458–77. Cf. 532.

486 DICKENS, A. G. Sedition and conspiracy in Yorkshire during the later years of Henry VIII. *Yorks. Arch. Jour.* xxxiv (1939), 379–98.

487 THE DIVORCE OF CATHERINE OF ARAGON. *Edin. Review*, clii (1880), 258–80; clx (1884), 89–115.
These articles are based on documents first brought to light in vols. iv, vi, and vii of the *Letters and papers* (91).

488 DIXON, W. H. History of two queens, (1) Catharine of Aragon, (2) Anne Boleyn. 6 vols. in 3. Leipzig, 1841; 4 vols. Lond. 1873–4.
Not always trustworthy.

489 DODDS, M. H., and RUTH. The pilgrimage of grace, 1536–7, and the Exeter conspiracy, 1538. 2 vols. Cambr. 1915.
Impartial, wealth of detail, co-ordination of material, but little new in conclusions. Valuable.

490 DU BOYS, ALBERT. Catherine d'Aragon et les origines du schisme anglican. *Société générale de librairie catholique*, 1880.
An English trans. of this work was published, with notes, by C. M. Yonge, 2 vols., Lond. 1881.

491 EHSES, STEFAN. Papst Klemens VII in dem Scheidungsprozesse Heinrichs VII. *Historisches Jahrbuch*, xiii (1892), 470–88.

493 ELTON, G. R. King or minister? The man behind the Henrican reformation. *History*, xxxix (1954), 216–32.

494 ELTON, G. R. The political creed of Thomas Cromwell. *Trans. R.H. Soc.*, 5th ser., vi (1956), 69–92.

495 ELTON, G. R. Thomas Cromwell's decline and fall. *Cambr. Hist. Jour.* x (1951), 150–85.

496 FATTA, CORRADO. Il regno di Enrico VIII d'Inghilterra, secondo i documenti contemporanei. 2 vols. Florence, 1938.

497 FERET, PIERRE. Le premier divorce de Henri VIII. *Revue des quest. hist.* lxiv (1898), 53–89.

498 FIDDES, RICHARD. The life of Cardinal Wolsey. Lond. 1724; 1726.
Valuable documents in app.

499 FRIEDMANN, PAUL. Anne Boleyn, a chapter of English history, 1527–1536. 2 vols. Lond. 1884.
The most important contribution to the history of this subject.

500 FROUDE, J. A. The divorce of Catherine of Aragon, the story as told by the imperial ambassadors resident at the court of Henry VIII. Lond. 1891; 1897.

501 GAIRDNER, JAMES. The fall of Cardinal Wolsey. *Trans. R.H. Soc.*, 2nd ser., xiii (1899), 75–102.

502   GAIRDNER, JAMES. Mary and Anne Boleyn. *E.H.R.* viii (1893),
53–60.
Cf. also *E.H.R.* x (1895), 104.

503   GAIRDNER, JAMES. New light on the divorce of Henry VIII. *E.H.R.*
xi (1896), 673–702; xii (1897), 1–16, 237–53.
Based largely on Ehses (457).

504   GALEA, JOSEPH. Henry VIII and the Order of St. John. *Jour. Brit.
Arch. Assoc.*, 3rd ser., xii (1949), 59–69.

505   GORDON, M. A. Life of Queen Katherine Parr. Kendal, 1952.

506   GREYERZ, H. von. Über Thomas Morus. Zur Erstherausgabe seines
Briefwechsels und zur deutschen Übersetzung der Morusbiographie von
R. W. Chambers. *Schweizer Beiträge zur allgemeinen Gesch.* vii (1949), 160–80.

507   HARRIER, R. C. Notes on Wyatt and Anne Boleyn. *Jour. of Eng. and
German Philol.* liii (1954), 581–4.

508   HARRISON, ERIC. Henry the eighth's gangster: the affair of Ludovico
da L'Armi. *Jour. Mod. Hist.* xv (1943), 265–74.

509   HARTSHORNE, C. H. The obsequies of Katharine of Aragon at Peterborough. *Arch. Jour.* xi (1854), 353–67.

510   HERBERT, LORD EDWARD (of Cherbury). The life and raigne of
King Henry the eighth. Lond. 1649; 1672; 1682; 1741.
Also published in vol. ii of Hughes and White Kennett's *Complete history of England,*
1706.
Apologetic. Contains much information derived from authentic papers.

511   HOGREFE, PEARL. Sir Thomas More's connections with the Roper
family. *P.M.L.A.* xlviii (1933), 523–33.

512   HUGHES, PHILIP. The Pilgrimage of Grace: 1536–1936. *Clergy Rev.*
xii (1936), 261–79.

513   HUME, M. A. S. The wives of Henry the eighth, and the parts they
played in history. Lond. 1905.

514   LE GRAND, JOACHIM. Histoire du divorce de Henri VIII. 3 vols.
Paris, 1688.
Prints part of correspondence of French ambassadors at London and Rome. A refuta-
tion of Burnet (1767). An English trans. with Burnet's answer published in Lond. (?)
1690 (?). To this Le Grand replied in 1691 in *Lettres de M. Le Grand à M. Burnet,*
Paris, 1691.

515   MACKIE, J. D. Henry VIII and Scotland. *Trans. R.H. Soc.*, 4th ser.,
xxix (1947), 93–114.

516   MCNALTY, A. S. Henry VIII, a difficult patient. Lond. 1952.

517   MATTINGLY, GARRETT. Catherine of Aragon. Boston, U.S.A., 1941.
The standard life.

518   MAYNARD, THEODORE. Henry the eighth. Milwaukee, 1949.

519   MAYNARD, THEODORE. Humanist as hero. New York, 1947.
A charming appraisal of More by a devout Roman Catholic.

520   MERRIMAN, R. B. The life and letters of Thomas Cromwell. 2 vols. Oxf. 1902.

The standard book on the subject. Vol. ii contains nearly all of Cromwell's extant letters *in extenso.* Cf. also A. Galton, *The character and times of Thomas Cromwell,* Birmingham, 1887, and Van Dyke (547) and Elton (1023).

521   [MORE, CRESACRE.] The life and death of Sir Thomas More. [St. Omer or Douai, 1631]. By J. Hunter. Lond. 1828.

Written by More's great grandson, based on Roper (459) and Stapleton, but adds some new details. Long erroneously ascribed to Cresacre's brother Thomas.

522   NELSON, WILLIAM. Thomas More, Grammarian and Orator. *P.M.L.A.* lviii (1943), 337–52.

523   NELSON, WILLIAM. John Skelton, laureate. *Columbia Univ. Studies in Eng. and Compar. Lit.* cxxxix. New York, 1939.

524   OGLE, ARTHUR. The tragedy of the Lollards Tower. Oxf. 1949.

Deals with the case of Richard Hunne.

525   OMAN, C. W. C. The personality of Henry the eighth. *Quar. Rev.* cclxix (1937), 88–144.

526   PARKER, T. M. Was Thomas Cromwell a Machiavellian? *Jour. Eccles. Hist.* i (1950), 61–75.

527   PARSONS, W. L. E. Some notes on the Boleyn family. *Norfolk Arch.* xxv (1935), 386–407.

528   PAULI, REINHOLD. Aufsätze zur englischen Geschichte. 2 vols. Leipzig, 1869–83.

Contains several useful essays on the period of Henry VIII.

529   PAULI, REINHOLD. Heinrich VIII und seine neuesten Beurtheiler. *Hist. Zeit.* iii (1860), 97–132.

Criticizes Froude (340).

530   PAULI, REINHOLD. Kardinal Wolsey und das Parlament vom Jahre 1523. *Hist. Zeit.* xxi (1869), 28–64.

531   POLLARD, A. F. Henry VIII. Lond. 1902; 1905; 1913.

The best modern life of Henry VIII. Footnote references were added to the 1905 ed. and the repr. of it in 1913. The 1st ed., in the *Goupil ser.,* is handsomely illustrated.

532   POLLARD, A. F. Wolsey. Lond. 1929; 1953.

An illuminating analysis of Wolsey's policies. Cf. also *Wolsey and the great seal,* by A. F. Pollard, in *Bull. Inst. Hist. Research,* vii (1929), 85–97.

533   REUMONT, ALFRED. Il Cardinale Wolsey e la Santa Sede. *Archivio Storico Italiano,* ix (1853), app., 117–63.

534   RONCAGLIA, CARLO. La questione matrimoniale di Enrico VIII e due umanisti contemporanei. *Giorn. Stor. Lit. Italiana,* cx (1937), 106–19.

Reference in the writings of Francesco Maria Molza and Celcio Calcagnini.

535   ROUND, J. H. The early life of Anne Boleyn, a critical essay. Lond. 1886.

Cf. Gairdner (502).

536   ROUTH, E. M. G. Sir Thomas More and his friends, 1477–1535. Oxf. 1934.

537   SCARISBRICK, J. The pardon of the clergy, 1531. *Cambr. Hist. Jour.* xii (1956), 22–39.

538   SCHNEIDER, REINHOLD. Katharina von Aragon. *Hochland*, xxxiii, bd. ii, heft xii (1936), 497–511.
Roman Catholic viewpoint.

539   SERGEANT, P. W. Anne Boleyn: a study. Lond. 1923; 1934.

540   SHREWSBURY, J. F. D. Henry VIII; a medical study. *Jour. Hist. Med. and Allied Sciences*, vii (1952), 141–85.

541   SMITH, H. M. Henry VIII and the Reformation. Lond. 1948.

542   SMITH, PRESERVED. German opinion of the divorce of Henry VIII. *E.H.R.* xxvii (1912), 671–81.

543   STONE, LAWRENCE. The political programme of Thomas Cromwell. *Bull. Inst. Hist. Research*, xxiv (1951), 1–18.

544   STORER, THOMAS. The life and death of Thomas Wolsey, cardinal. Lond. 1599; repr. Oxf. 1826.
A poem based upon Cavendish (433) and Holinshed (314).

545   TAUNTON, E. L. Thomas Wolsey, legate and reformer. Lond. 1902.

546   VALLANCE, AYMER. Hollingbourne manor and the Culpepers. *Arch. Cant.* xlix (1938), 189–94.
Particularly Thomas Culpeper and Queen Catherine Howard.

547   VAN DYKE, PAUL. Renascence portraits. New York, 1905.
Contains a valuable essay on Thomas Cromwell, and an app. concerning Cardinal Pole's account of him in the *Apologia ad Carolum Quintum*. The latter first appeared in the *A.H.R.* ix (1904), 696–724.

548   VOCHT, HENRY DE. Acta Thomae Mori. History of the reports of his trial and death with an unedited contemporary narrative. *Humanistica Lovaniensia*, vii. Louvain, 1947.

549   WEEKS, W. S. Albert Paslew and the Pilgrimage of Grace. *Trans. Lancs. and Ches. Antiq. Soc.* xlviii (1932), 199–223.

550   WEGG, JERVIS. Richard Pace; a Tudor diplomatist. Lond. 1932.

551   WHATMORE, L. E. William Somers, Henry VIII's jester. *Biog. Studies*, i (1951), 128–30.

552   ZEEVELD, W. G. Foundations of Tudor policy. Lond. 1948.
Deals chiefly with Starkey, Morison, and Ponet and their propagandist writings.

C. EDWARD VI

i. SOURCES

Pollard (567) contains a valuable essay on the sources for the history of the reign under Somerset. Cf. also *Cambr. Mod. Hist.* (20) ii, 795 ff.

The *Cal. S.P., Domestic* (86) gives brief summaries of the comparatively scanty collection in the P.R.O. The *Acts of privy council* (1152), the *Proclamations* (1017), and the *Statutes of the realm* (1016) should be consulted.

Of the contemporary chronicles Wriothesley's (321) is the only one of much independent value. The *Petyt MSS.* (175) and the *Salisbury MSS.* (185) are the richest for material on the reign among private collections. Edward's *Literary remains* (555) is the most valuable source in print. Tytler (554) prints many important documents. For the foreign policy of the reign, cf. sect. G *infra* (pp. 65 ff.), particularly nos. 825 and 867, and *Cal. S.P., Foreign* (87).

553 CALENDAR OF THE PATENT ROLLS preserved in the P.R.O., Edward VI, 1547–1553. By R. H. Brodie. 5 vols. and index. Lond. 1924–9.
Competent calendar, omitting surrenders of church lands to crown, appurtenances of manors, conventional clauses.

554 ENGLAND UNDER THE REIGNS OF EDWARD VI AND MARY, illustrated in a series of original letters never before printed with historical introductions and biographical and critical notes. By P. F. Tytler. 2 vols. Lond. 1839.
Valuable source material *in extenso*.

555 LITERARY REMAINS OF KING EDWARD VI. By J. G. Nichols. 2 vols. *Roxburghe Club*, 1857.
Contains Edward's *Journal*, also printed in Burnet (1767), and other writings. The introduction collects practically all that is known about the young king. On Edward's supposed existence after 1553, cf. *E.H.R.* xxiii (1908), 286–90. Edward's *Journal* was also printed by *Clarendon Hist. Soc.*, n.s., i, 1884.

556 THE SECOND PATENT appointing Edward duke of Somerset protector, *temp*. King Edward the sixth; introduced by an historical review of the various measures connected therewith. By J. G. Nichols. *Arch.* xxx (1844), 463–89.

557 TROUBLES CONNECTED WITH THE PRAYER-BOOK of 1549. By Nicholas Pocock. *Camden Soc.* xxxvii. Lond. (1884).
Important. For errors in this vol. cf. Rose-Troup (568), app. F.

558 NEVILLE, ALEXANDER. De furoribus Norfolcensium, Ketto duce. Lond. 1575.
Cf. Pollard (363), 34.

2. Later Works

The best general account of the reign is in Pollard (363). Pollard's *Somerset* (567) is also of first-rate importance. There is no good biography of Northumberland. Russell (569) is a valuable monograph on *Kett's rebellion*. Nichols (557) in his introduction gives all the known facts about the young king. On foreign policy, cf. sect. G *infra* (pp. 65 ff.), particularly no. 974.

559 CLAYTON, JOSEPH. Robert Kett and the Norfolk rising. Lond. 1912.
Slight.

560 CORNFORD, M. E. A legend concerning Edward VI. *E.H.R.* xxiii (1908), 286–90.

561 HURSTFIELD, JOEL. Corruption and reform under Edward VI and Mary: the example of wardship. *E.H.R.* lxviii (1953), 22–36.

562 HAYWARD, JOHN. The life and raigne of King Edward the sixth. Lond. 1630; 1636.
Repr. in White Kennett's *History of England*, ii.

563 JACKSON, J. E. Wulfhall and the Seymours. *Wilts. Arch. and Nat. Hist. Mag.* xv (1875), 140–207.

563a LINDSAY, PHILIP. The queenmaker: a portrait of John Dudley, Viscount Lisle, earl of Warwick, and duke of Northumberland, 1502–1553. Lond. 1951.
Inadequate.

564 MACLEAN, JOHN. Life of Sir Thomas Seymour. Lond. 1869.
Based on contemporary sources; prints letters.

565 MALKIEWICZ, A. J. A. An eye-witness' account of the coup d'etat of October 1549. *E.H.R.* lxx (1955), 600–9.

566 MARKHAM, C. R. King Edward VI, an appreciation. Lond. 1907.
Slight and biased. Cf. *E.H.R.* xxiii (1908), 199.

567 POLLARD, A. F. England under Protector Somerset. Lond. 1900.
The best modern work on the first part of Edward VI's reign. Frankly favourable to Somerset. The essay on the sources at the close of the vol. is valuable.

568 ROSE-TROUP, FRANCES. The western rebellion of 1549, an account of the insurrections in Devonshire and Cornwall against religious innovations in the reign of Edward VI. Lond. 1913.
Scholarly, but badly composed. Prints many documents and reprints a rare tract, *La Responce du peuple anglois à leur roy Edouard*. Cf. idem, *Lead from the dissolved religious houses in Devon in 1549*, Devon and Cornwall Notes and Queries, xix (1936), 122–6. Cf. also no. 4322 *infra*.

569 RUSSELL, F. W. Kett's rebellion in Norfolk. Lond. 1859.
Founded on Sotherton's *Commoyson in Norfolk*, 1549 (*Harl. MS.* 1576, ff. 564 ff.), and Neville (558). Prints many documents. The standard account. Cf. also S. T. Bindoff, *Ket's rebellion, 1549*, Hist. Assoc., General ser., g. xii (1949); J. W. M. Vyse, *The evidence for Ket's rebellion*, Norfolk Arch. xxvi, pt. ii (1937), 183–91.

570 STRYPE, JOHN. The life of the learned Sir T. Smith.... Lond. 1698; standard ed., Oxf. 1820.

571 STRYPE, JOHN. The life of the learned Sir J. Cheke.... Lond. 1705; standard ed., Oxf. 1821.
Ed. of 1821 contains author's notes and corrections.

D. LADY JANE GREY

1. Sources

The *Literary remains of Lady Jane* are given in Nicolas (573). The *Chronicle of Queene Jane* (303) is a valuable source and contains in an app. many important documents. *Grey Friars' chronicle* (311) is also of value. Rosso (575) is important and there is material of moment in the Spanish (867) and the Venetian calendars (992).

571a FLORIO, M. A. Historia de la vita e de la morte de l'illustrissima Signora Giovanni Graia.... s.l. 1607.
Rare. Contains Italian translations of most of the letters and works attributed to Lady Jane Grey.

572 LETTERS ILLUSTRATING THE REIGN OF QUEEN JANE. By Joseph Burtt. *Arch. Jour.* xxx (1873), 273–9.

572a THE LETTERS OF LADY JANE GREY. By Douglas Geary. Ilfracombe, 1951.

573 THE LITERARY REMAINS OF LADY JANE GREY, with a memoir. By N. H. Nicolas. Lond. 1825.

575 ROSSO, G. R. I successi d'Inghilterra . . . (1553–4). . . . Ferrara, 1560; by Alberto Lollio, Ferrara, 1591.
Rosso was sent by the duke of Ferrara to England in 1554 to congratulate Philip and Mary on their marriage. A pirated ed. of his work was put forth, under the title *Historia delle cose occorse nel regno d'Inghilterra . . . dopo la morte di Odoardo VI*, by the Accademia Venetiana in 1558, and is really a compilation from dispatches of Giovanni Michele, Venetian ambassador to England 1554–7, and of Federigo Badoaro, Venetian ambassador to Charles V. Valuable on Lady Jane Grey and on the accession of Mary,

2. LATER WORKS

The best general accounts are in Pollard (363) and in Froude (340). Of the several lives of Lady Jane, Davey (576) is the best.

576 DAVEY, R. P. B. The nine days' queen, Lady Jane Grey, and her times. By M. A. S. Hume. Lond. 1909.

577 DAVEY, R. P. B. The sisters of Lady Jane Grey, and their wicked grandfather. Lond. 1911.
Popular and unscholarly.

578 THE LIFE, DEATH AND ACTIONS of . . . Lady Jane Grey—containing foure principall discourses written with her owne hands. Lond. 1615; 1829.

579 SIDNEY, PHILIP. Jane the quene. Lond. 1900.

580 TAYLOR, I. A. Lady Jane Grey and her times. Lond. 1908.

E. MARY

1. SOURCES

The *Cal. S.P., Domestic* (86) contains brief summaries of the Domestic papers for the reign in the P.R.O. The Spanish (867) and Venetian (992) calendars are serviceable, as are the *Mémoires* of Noailles (824) and the *Papiers d'État* of Granville (910). Many of Mary's letters are printed in Stone (596) and in Hearne (287). The *Acts of privy council* (1152), the *Proclamations* (1017), and the *Statutes of the realm* (1016) should be consulted. For Mary's relations to her sister, cf. 625. The most valuable contemporary chronicles are Wriothesley's (321), the *Chronicle of Queen Jane and Queen Mary* (303), the *Grey Friars' chronicle* (311), and Quirini's ed. of Pole's correspondence (1739). Cf. also 554 and 575. For the foreign policy of the reign, cf. sect. G *infra* (pp. 65 ff.).

580a The accession, coronation and marriage of Mary Tudor . . . from four MSS. of the Escorial. Trans. by C. V. Malfatti. Barcelona, 1956.

581 CALENDAR OF PATENT ROLLS, Philip and Mary. 4 vols. Lond. 1936–9.

582 GUARAS, ANTONIO DI. Relación muy verdadera . . . como dona Maria fue proclamada por reyna y de todos obedescida y de su coronación. Medina del Campo, 1554; by Richard Garnett, Lond. 1892.
The ed. of 1892 contains an introduction, an English trans., and an app. of documents.

583 POLE, Cardinal REGINALD. Copia d'una lettera d'Inghilterra nella quale narra l'entrata del Rever. Card. Polo. Milan, 1584; [Paris, 1860 (?)].

584 PROCTOR, JOHN. The historie of Wyate's rebellion, with the order and means of resisting the same. Lond. 1554; by Francis Grose, *Antiquarian reportory*, iii (1808), 65–115. Cf. Robin Flower, *The Wyatts of Allington Castle, Brit. Mus. Quar.* ix (1930), 117–18, and Agnes Conway, *The Wyatt MSS., Bull. Inst. Hist. Research*, i (1924), 73–76.

585 LES REVOLUTIONS D'ANGLETERRE en 1553 et 1554, racontés par un fourrier de l'Empereur Charles Quint. By Charles Bémont. *Revue historique*, cix (1912), 60–76.
Part of a chronicle of Charles V. Slight.

2. LATER WORKS

Pollard (363) and Lingard (353) are the best general accounts of the reign. Madan's introduction (1247) contains much good material for her earlier years. Prescott (595) is the best biography. Friedmann's introduction to 994 is valuable. There is a useful account of the Spanish marriage negotiations in 789. Forneron (882) is the best biography of Philip II. On foreign policy, cf. sect. G *infra* (pp. 65 ff.); on ecclesiastical affairs, ch. vi *infra* (pp. 179 ff.).

586 BARRINGTON, MICHAEL. Queen Mary (Tudor). *Notes and Queries*, cxcv (1950), 4–7.
Cf. M. C. Byrne, ibid., 173.

587 CONSTANT, G. Le commencement de la restauration catholique en Angleterre par Marie Tudor (1553). *Revue historique*, cxii (1913), 1–27.
Cf. also ibid., *Le mariage de Marie Tudor et de Philippe II*, in *Revue d'histoire diplomatique*, xxvi (1912), 23–73, 224–74.

588 FRIEDMANN, PAUL. Some new facts in the history of Queen Mary of England. *Macmillan's Mag.* xix (1868), 1–12.
Drawn from Venetian archives.

589 GAMMON, S. R. Mary Tudor's tragedy of conscience. *Emory Univ. Quar.* ix (1953), 39–47.

590 HARBISON, E. H. Rival ambassadors at the court of Queen Mary Lond. 1940.
Scholarly, important.

591 HAY, DENYS. The 'Narratio Historica' of P. Vincentius, 1553. *E.H.R.* lxiii (1948), 350–6.

592 HILTON, RONALD. The marriage of Queen Mary and Philip of Spain. *Hants. Arch. Soc. Proc.* xiv, pt. i (1938), 46–62.

593 PFANDL, LUDWIG. Das England-Erlebnis der Spanier in den Jahren 1554–1558. *Gesch. Aufsätze zur Kulturgeschichte Spaniens*, bd. vii (1938), 207–32.

594 PHILIP, I. G. Queen Mary Tudor's benefaction to the university. *Bodleian Lib. Rec.* v (1954), 27–37.

595 PRESCOTT, H. F. M. A Spanish Tudor: the life of 'Bloody Mary'. New York, 1940; 1953.
The best life of Mary.

596 STONE, J. M. The history of Mary I, queen of England. Lond. 1901.
A Catholic account of Mary's life, based largely on contemporary documents.

597 WARTON, THOMAS. Life of Sir Thomas Pope. Lond. 1772; 1780.
Contains numerous extracts from valuable historical MSS., but is also based in part on manifest forgeries. Serious and in some cases intentional inaccuracies disfigure the book. Cf. *E.H.R.* xi (1896), 282.

598 WHITE, B. M. I. Mary Tudor. Lond. 1935.

599 ZIMMERMANN, ATHANASIUS. Maria die Katholische. Freiburg, 1890.
Heft 48 in Ergänzungsband xii to the *Stimmen aus Maria-Laach katholische Blätter.*

F. ELIZABETH

1. SOURCES

(a) *General*

The most important documentary collections are the *Cal. S.P., Domestic* (86) and *Foreign* (87) based on material in the P.R.O. The B.M. is very rich in material which has never been systematically edited. Among private collections of documents, by far the most important are the *Salisbury MSS.* (185), though there are numerous other collections of value. The correspondence of foreign ambassadors resident in England, notably those of Spain (868) and France (813, 801), is very important. The *Proclamations* (1017), the *Statutes of the realm* (1016), and the *Acts of privy council* (1153) should all be consulted as well for general as for constitutional history. Of the miscellaneous collections of sources, Strype's *Annals* (2214), Lodge (283), *Cabala* (274), *Hardwicke papers* (280), *Desiderata curiosa* (277) and *Nugae Antiquae* (289) contain much Elizabethan material. Birch (601) and Wright (626) are the most useful of the collections cited below.

The chief chronicles of the reign are Camden (302), Holinshed (314), Stow (317), and Hayward (313), of which Camden and Holinshed are the best.

Many contemporary pamphlets are printed in *Eng. Garner* (279), the *Harleian Misc.* (281), and *Somers Tracts* (287). For foreign policy, cf. pp. 65 ff.

600 BACON, FRANCIS. Collected works. By J. Spedding, R. L. Ellis, D. D. Heath. 14 vols. Lond. 1857–74.
For a flattering, but suggestive, sketch of Elizabeth's character, cf. xi, 285, 291–318.

601 BIRCH, THOMAS. Memoirs of the reign of Queen Elizabeth, from the year 1581 till her death, from the original papers of . . . Antony Bacon, esquire. . . . 2 vols. Lond. 1754.
Composed chiefly of selections from the Bacon MSS. in Lambeth palace library, connected by a running commentary. Many, but not all, of the MSS. printed are given *in extenso.* Particularly valuable for the conduct of Robert, earl of Essex.

602 CALENDAR OF PATENT ROLLS, Elizabeth, i, 1558–60; ii, 1560–3. Lond. 1939–48.

603 CARY, ROBERT. Memoirs of the life of . . . written by himself. . . . By John Boyle, earl of Cork and Orrery. Lond. 1759; best ed. by Sir W. Scott, Edin. 1808.
Covers the period 1577–1626. Over three-fourths of the space devoted to the reign of Elizabeth. Valuable for affairs of the Scottish border and particularly for the death of Queen Elizabeth and the accession of James I.

604 CHALONER, THOMAS. De republica Anglorum instauranda libri decem. Lond. 1579.

605 THE LETTERS OF JOHN CHAMBERLAIN. By N. E. McClure. *Amer. Philos. Soc. Memoirs*, xii, pts. i–ii. 2 vols. Philadelphia, 1939.
Scholarly. Important. Displaces earlier editions of Chamberlain's letters, for which cf. ibid. i, pt. v.

606 CLAPHAM, JOHN. Elizabeth of England: certain observations concerning the life and reign of Queen Elizabeth. By E. P. Read and Conyers Read. Philadelphia, 1951.
Particularly valuable for Elizabeth's death. Clapham was a member of Lord Burghley's household.

607 COLLINS, D. C. A handlist of news pamphlets, 1590–1610. Lond. 1943.

608 DEVEREUX, W. B. Lives and letters of the Devereux, earls of Essex, in the reigns of Elizabeth, James I, and Charles I, 1540–1646. 2 vols. Lond. 1853.
Vol. i and vol. ii, 1–218, treat of the lives of Walter and Robert, the first two earls of Essex, who fall within Elizabeth's reign. Consist of correspondence printed generally in full from the originals in the B.M., the P.R.O., and elsewhere, with a running commentary. Particularly valuable for Irish affairs and for the Essex conspiracy. *The Devereux papers . . . 1575–1601*, by H. E. Malden, *Camden Soc. Misc.* xiii (1923), are mostly personal and add little political information. Cf. also H. J. Collins, *The death-warrant of Robert, earl of Essex, Brit. Mus. Quar.* xvi (1951), 37–38. For a forged document about Robert, second earl, cf. Sydney Race, *John Payne Collier and his Essex papers, Notes and Queries*, cci (1956), 218–19.
The original of many of Robert, 2nd earl's, letters are in B.M., Add. MSS. 46188–9 (Hulton collection).

609 EDWARDS, EDWARD. The life of Sir Walter Ralegh, based on contemporary documents . . . together with his letters. 2 vols. Lond. 1868.
Vol. i, the life, has been supplanted by later biographies; vol. ii, the letters, contains nearly all of Ralegh's extant letters.

610 THE EGERTON PAPERS, a collection of public and private documents . . . of the times of Elizabeth and James I, from the original manuscripts . . . of . . . Lord Francis Egerton. . . . By J. P. Collier. *Camden Soc.* xii (1840).
Contains important letters and papers written by different members of Elizabeth's privy council, particularly concerning the queen's marriage.

611 A FULL VIEW OF THE PUBLIC TRANSACTIONS in the reign of Elizabeth. By Patrick Forbes. 2 vols. Lond. 1740–1.
A general collection of state papers, largely on Anglo-French relations and chiefly 1558–63.

612   GAWDY, PHILIP, of West Harling, Norfolk, letters of, 1579–1616. . . .
By I. H. Jeayes. *Roxburghe Club*, 1906.
Interesting court gossip. Cf. 142.

613   GOODMAN, GODFREY. The court of James the first. . . . By J. S.
Brewer. 2 vols. Lond. 1839.
Vol. ii, 1–56, contains some original letters illustrative of court life under Elizabeth.

614   GREVILLE, FULKE. The life of the renowned Sir Philip Sidney . . .
Together with a short account of the maxims and policies used by Queen
Elizabeth. Lond. 1652; best ed. by Nowell Smith, Oxf. 1907.
Greville, Sidney's close friend, wrote *c.* 1612.

615   HARRISON, WILLIAM. An historicall description of the iland of
Britaine. . . . Lond. 1577; 1587; 4 vols. Lond. 1908; 1 vol. Lond. s.a.
Eds. of 1577 and 1587 published as introductions to Holinshed's *Chronicle* (314).
Ed. of 1908 is of 3rd and 4th books only, pub. by *New Shakespeare Society*, with valuable
editorial matter. 4th ed. (London, s.a.) in the *Camelot ser.*, is of selections only.
    A work of great interest and value.

616   HATTON, CHRISTOPHER, K.G. . . . Memoirs of the life and times
of. By N. H. Nicolas. Lond. 1847.
Consists of the correspondence of Hatton arranged in chronological order with a
running commentary. The most important letters fall between 1578 and 1587. Based
chiefly upon Hatton's letter book in B.M., Add. MS. 15891. Valuable, but inadequate.

617   JEWELS AND PLATE OF QUEEN ELIZABETH I. The inventory
of 1574. By A. J. Collins. Lond. 1956.
Edited from Harley MS. 1650 and Stowe MS. 555 in B.M.

618   JONSON, BEN. Conversations with William Drummond of Hawthorn-
den, 1619. By David Laing. *Shakespeare Soc.* xvii (1842); by R. F. Patterson,
Lond. 1923.
Interesting comments on Elizabeth.

619   LETTERS OF QUEEN ELIZABETH. By G. B. Harrison. Lond. 1935.
180 letters reprinted. Many omissions.

620   [LEYCESTER'S COMMONWEALTH.] The copie of a leter, retten by
a master of arte of Cambridge . . . concerning . . . the erle of Leycester and his
friends in England. [Antwerp?], 1584; [Lond.] 1641; by F. J. Burgoyne,
Lond. 1904.
A contemporary attack upon the character of Robert, earl of Leicester. Wrongly
ascribed to Robert Parsons, the Jesuit. Ascribed by Walsingham to Thos. Morgan, by
Pollen, in *Cath. Encycl.*, to Charles Arundell; cf. Leslie Hotson and Leo Hicks in *The
Listener*, xliii (1950), 481–3, 567, 659, 745. The more familiar title, given in brackets,
appeared first in the ed. of 1641 of which ed. 1904 is a repr. Absolutely untrustworthy
as to facts, but valuable as an expression of contemporary opinion. For Sir Philip
Sidney's answer to this diatribe, cf. Feuillerat (630), iii, 61–71.

621   MANNINGHAM, Diary of John . . . 1602–3. By John Bruce. *Camden
Soc.* xcix (1868).
Notes on contemporary events by a London law student. Valuable for Elizabeth's death
and the events immediately following.

622   THE JOURNAL OF LEVINIUS MUNCK. By H. V. Jones. *E.H.R.*
lxviii (1953), 234–58.

623 NICCOLS, RICHARD. Expicedium: a funeral sermon upon Queen Elizabeth. By B. B. Trawick. New York, 1944.

624 NICHOLS, JOHN. The progresses and public processions of Queen Elizabeth, illustrated with historical notes. . . . 4 vols. Lond. 1788–1821; 3 vols. 1823.
Based upon unpublished MSS. and contemporary pamphlets, many of which are printed in full. Valuable.

625 QUEEN ELIZABETH, THE GIRLHOOD OF, a narrative in contemporary letters. By F. A. Mumbey. Lond. 1909.
These letters cover the period from 1533 to 1559. All but a very few have been printed before (102, 633).

626 QUEEN ELIZABETH AND HER TIMES. . . . By Thomas Wright. 2 vols. Lond. 1838.
A series of letters from the correspondence of Burghley, Leicester, Walsingham, Hatton, &c. Valuable.

627 REBELLION OF 1569, DEPOSITIONS RESPECTING THE. Witchcraft and other ecclesiastical proceedings, from the court of Durham. By James Raine. *Surtees Soc.* xxi (1846).
Interesting material on rebellion of 1569.

628 REBELLION OF 1569, MEMORIALS OF THE. By Cuthbert Sharp. Lond. 1840.
A collection of important documents upon the rebellion of 1569, chiefly from the *Bowes MSS.* at Streatlam Castle, with others from the P.R.O. and the B.M. For survey of forfeited estates of rebels, cf. *P.R.O. Misc. Bks. Exchequer K.R.* xxxvii–viii. Cf. also B.M., *Cotton MSS., Caligula,* B ix, f. 6.

629 [SIDNEY PAPERS;] letters and memorials of state . . . written and collected by Sir Henry Sidney . . . Sir Philip Sidney and his brother Sir Robert Sidney . . . transcribed from the originals at Penshurst Place in Kent . . . and his Majesty's office of papers and records. By Arthur Collins. 2 vols. Lond. 1746.
This collection of state papers contains, *inter alia*: Irish papers of Sir Henry Sidney, 1559–80; correspondence concerning English relations with the Low Countries; letters from Rowland White full of Elizabethan court gossip. Vol. i also contains a long memoir on the Sidney family. Cf. 124.

630 SIDNEY, SIR PHILIP. Works. By A. Feuillerat. *Cambr. Eng. Classics.* 4 vols. Cambr. 1922–6.

631 THE CORRESPONDENCE OF SIR PHILIP SIDNEY AND H. LANGUET, now first collected and translated from the Latin. By S. A. Pears. Lond. 1845; by W. A. Bradley, Boston, U.S.A., 1912.

632 SLINGSBY, SIR HENRY. The diary of. By David Parsons. Lond. 1836.
Relates to seventeenth century (cf. Davies (8), no. 1111), but contains some correspondence for Elizabeth's reign.

633 STATE PAPERS relating to the custody of the Princess Elizabeth at Woodstock in 1554; being letters between Queen Mary and her privy council, and Sir Henry Bedingfield. . . . *Norfolk Arch.* iv (1855).
Many of these repr. in Mumby (625).

634　STRADLING CORRESPONDENCE, a series of letters written in the reign of Queen Elizabeth. By J. M. Traherne. Lond. 1840.

635　SIR NICHOLAS THROCKMORTON'S ADVICE to Queen Elizabeth on her accession to the throne. By J. E. Neale. *E.H.R.* lxv (1950), 91–98.

636　VOWELL alias HOOKER, JOHN. The dyscourse and dyscoverye of the lyffe of Sir Peter Carew. . . . By John Maclean. Lond. 1857.
Admirably edited with full notes and an introduction containing all other available information, including documents. Printed also in *Arch.* xxviii (1840), 96–151, and in *Cal. Carew MSS.* (5733), i, pp. lxvii–cxxiii.

637　WALSINGHAM, SIR FRANCIS, Journal of, from December 1570 to April 1583. By C. T. Martin. *Camden Soc. Misc.* vi (1871).
'Consists of notices of Walsingham's movements and occasionally of other events of interest, with memoranda for each day of . . . letters sent and received.' There are four breaks in the entries. Useful but inaccurate and incomplete.

638　WILBRAHAM, SIR ROGER, Solicitor-General in Ireland and Master of Requests, Journal of, for the years 1593–1616. By H. S. Scott. *Camden Soc. Misc.* x (1902).
Parliamentary and legal gossip during the last 10 years of Elizabeth's reign.

639　WILSON, THOMAS. A treatise of England's perils, 1578. By A. J. Schmidt. *Archiv. für Reformations Gesch.* xlvi (1955), 243–9.
Written by Elizabeth's principal secretary.

640　WILSON, THOMAS. The state of England anno. dom. 1600. By F. J. Fisher. *Camden Misc.* xvi, 3rd ser., lii (1936), 1–47.
The author was a nephew of Sir Thomas Wilson, Elizabeth's principal secretary. Valuable.

(b) *Contemporary Pamphlets*

Contemporary pamphlets on almost every conceivable public question appeared in abundance during Elizabeth's reign. Most of them related to the religious controversies of the times; many of them were about naval and military affairs, a few on economic and social questions. Several are reprinted in *Eng. Garner* (279), in the *Harleian Misc.* (281), and in *Somers Tracts* (296). No attempt is made to list them all, but the more important ones are given under the appropriate sections. Those listed immediately below, not otherwise readily classifiable, were most of them officially inspired and were put forth with the object of justifying the government procedure in cases of high treason. They are interesting examples of Elizabeth's use of the press for propaganda purposes. The arrangement is chronological.

641　DISCOURS DES TROUBLES NOUVELLEMENT ADVENUZ au royaume d'Angleterre, au moys d'octobre 1569. Avec une declaration faicte par le comte de Northumberland. . . . Paris, 1570; Lyons, 1570; Rouen, 1587.

642　A TREATISE OF TREASONS AGAINST QUEEN ELIZABETH and the crowne of England, divided into two partes. . . . [Antwerp], 1572.
About the Norfolk plot.

643 A DISCOVERIE OF THE TREASONS practised by F. Throckmorton. . . . Lond. 1584; repr. in *Harl. Misc* (281), i, 522–37.
The official account of the Throckmorton plot. Another English and Latin version of this pamphlet appeared in 1584 and a Dutch version the next year.

644 A . . . REPORT OF THE DECLARATION of some part of the earl of Northumberland's treasons . . . together with the examinations . . . of sundry persons touching the manner of his . . . murder. [Lond. 1585.]
A tract, published by authority, in defence of the condemnation of Northumberland. Repr. in Holinshed (314), 2nd ed., iii, 1404; in *Somers Tracts* (296), i, 212–24.

645 A TRUE AND PLAINE DECLARATION of the horrible treasons practised by W. Parry, the traitor, against the Queenes Majestie. . . . Lond. [1585]; 1679.
The official account of the Parry plot. A Dutch trans. appeared in 1585. Printed also in Holinshed (314), 2nd ed., iii, 1382 ff.

646 THE COPY OF A LETTER sent out of England to Don B. Mendoza. Lond. 1588; repr. Lond. 1746; *Harl. Misc.* ii (1809), 60–85. Ascribed in the *S.T.C.* (15412) to Richard Leigh.
Relevant to preparations to meet the Armada. Written by Lord Burghley.

647 A DECLARATION OF THE TRUE CAUSES of the great troubles, presupposed to be intended against the realme of England. . . . [Cologne (?)], 1592.

648 A TRUE REPORT OF SUNDRY HORRIBLE CONSPIRACIES of late time detected to have . . . taken away the life of the Queenes most excellent Majestie. . . . Lond. 1594; French trans., Paris, 1595.

649 A DECLARATION OF THE PRACTICES and treasons attempted and committed by Robert, late earle of Essex, and his complices. . . . Lond. 1601.
Has been attributed to Robert Barker and also to Sir Francis Bacon.

650 THE ORDER AND PROCEEDING AT THE FUNERALE of . . . Elizabeth, queene of England. . . . By Henry Chettle, 1603; repr. in *Somers Tracts* (296), i, 248–50.

651 PRICKET, ROBERT. Honors fame in triumph riding, or the life and death of the late honourable earle of Essex. Lond. 1604; by A. B. Grosart, Manchester, 1881.
Poem by a soldier who had served with Essex.

652 HISTOIRES MEMORABLES. *s.l.,* 1607.
Contains: (1) *La mort du Comte d'Essex*; (2) A discourse by the queen to the duc de Biron on the subject.

2. LATER WORKS

Neale (743) is the best short life of Elizabeth. Froude (340) gives the most elaborate account of her reign to 1588. Black (671) is the best general account. For Elizabeth's foreign policy, cf. sect. G *infra* (pp. 65 ff.). Seeley's brilliant essay (375) is not always sound. Read (759, 760) deals in detail with foreign relations (1558–98). Cheyney (690) contains the best account of Elizabethan political institutions. The vast literature on Mary Stuart is dealt with in ch. xii *infra* (pp. 435); the religious controversies of the reign in ch. vi *infra* (pp. 183 ff.). There is no good biography of Leicester.

653 ABBOTT, E. A. Bacon and Essex, a sketch of Bacon's earlier life. Lond. 1877.
Holds that Bacon's *Declaration of the treasons of Essex* was a 'pestilent' libel, and that Spedding's estimate of Bacon is open to question.

654 ADLARD, GEORGE. Amye Robsart and the earl of Leycester; a critical inquiry . . . with a vindication of the earl by Sir Philip Sidney, and a history of Kenilworth castle. . . . Lond. 1870.
A careful study. Cf. also J. Gairdner, *The death of Amy Robsart, E.H.R.* i (1885), 235–59, xiii (1897), 83–90; I. Hermann, *Amy Robsart und Graf Leicester*, 1882; A. Lang, *Scandal about Queen Elizabeth, Blackwood's Mag.* cliii (1893), 209–18; W. Rye, *The murder of Amy Robsart*, Lond. 1885; P. Sidney, *Who killed Amy Robsart?* Lond. 1901; Ian Aird, *The death of Amy Robsart, E.H.R.* lxxi (1956), 69–79.

655 AIKIN, LUCY. Memoirs of the court of Queen Elizabeth. 2 vols. Lond. 1818.
Thoroughly unreliable.

656 ALVENSLEBEN, K.VON. Königin Elizabeth von England. By W. von Buelow, 1900.
Bd. v in von Bülow's *Das Weiberregiment an den Hofen Europas.*

657 ANTHEUNIS, LOUIS. La maladie et la mort de la reine Élisabeth d'Angleterre. *Rev. Hist. Eccles.* xliii (1948), 148–78.
Based largely on a Venetian report. Ignores important evidence in 606.

658 ASHE, GEOFFREY. An Elizabethan adventurer: the career of Sir Antony Standen. *The Month*, n.s., viii (1952), 81–92; 218–29.
Standen, under the name Pellegrini, was an English spy in Spain, 1588.

659 AUERBACH, ERNA. An early portrait drawing of Queen Elizabeth. *Connoisseur*, cxxvii (1951), 18–20.

660 AUERBACH, ERNA. Portraits of Elizabeth I. *Burlington Mag.* xcv (1953), 197–205.

661 BARNARD, E. A. B. The Hobys of Evesham (Worcester) and of Bisham, Berks. *Trans. Worcs. Arch. Soc.*, n.s., xii (1936), 18–29.

662 BARRINGTON, MICHAEL. 'The mercury of peace, the Mars of war.' Robert Devereux, second earl of Essex. *Essex Rev.* lix (1950), 165–81; lx (1951), 7–11, 76–80, 116–23, 169–78; lxi (1952), 1–10.

663 BAUGHAN, D. E. Sidney's *Defense of the Earl of Leicester* and the revised *Arcadia. Jour. Eng. and German. Philol.* li (1952), 35–41.

664 BAYNE, C. G. The coronation of Queen Elizabeth. *E.H.R.* xxii (1907), 650–73.
Cf. the criticism by H. A. Wilson in *E.H.R.* xxiii (1908), 87–91; a further note by G. L. Ross, ibid., 533; and the corrections made by Bayne in *E.H.R.* xxiv (1909), 322–3.

665 BEESLEY, E. S. Queen Elizabeth. Lond. 1892.
Slight.

666 BEKKER, ERNST. Beiträge zur englischen Geschichte im Zeitalter Elizabeths. 2 vols. *Giessener Studien aus dem Gebiet der Geschichte*, iv, x, 1887, 1899.
Vol. i contains 5 essays dealing with Anglo-Scottish relations, 1558–60, and 1 on Elizabeth's relations to the German market for mercenary troops; vol. ii, essays upon (a) German industries in England under Elizabeth; (b) *Bildungsreise* of Sir Thos. Cecil; (c) English trade relations with Africa and the commercial war with Portugal under Elizabeth.

667 BEKKER, ERNST. Elizabeth und Leicester. Beiträge zur Geschichte Englands in den Jahren 1560 bis 1562. *Giessener Studien aus dem Gebiet der Geschichte*, v, 1890.
Discusses the relations of Elizabeth and Leicester from 1560 to 1562. Valuable.

668 BELLOC, HILAIRE. Elizabeth, creature of circumstance. New York, 1942.
Roman Catholic view-point.

669 BENNETT, J. W. Churchyard's description of the queen's entertainment at Woodstock in 1592. *Mod. Lang. Notes*, lv (1940), 391–3.

670 BERTIE, GEORGINA. Five generations of a loyal house. Lond. 1845.
Pt. i (no more published) contains lives of Richard Bertie and his son, Peregrine, Lord Willoughby. Prints extracts of Willoughby's letters from the Low Countries.

671 BLACK, J. B. The reign of Elizabeth, 1558–1603. *Oxford Hist. of England Series*, ed. by G. N. Clark. Oxf. 1936.
The best political history of the reign.

672 BOAS, F. S. Queen Elizabeth in drama and related studies. Lond. 1950.
Among the related studies are the Revels' Office, Ovid and the Elizabethans, Sir Thomas Bodley and the Soldier in Elizabethan drama.

673 BOWEN, C. D. The Lion and the Throne. Boston, U.S.A. 1957.
The most recent and best life of Sir Edward Coke. Based entirely upon material in print.

674 BRADFORD, C. A. Helena, marchioness of Northampton. Lond. 1936.
3rd wife (1565) of Wm. Parr, marquis of Northants.

675 BRADFORD, C. A. Blanche Parry, Queen Elizabeth's gentlewoman. Lond. 1935.
Chief gentlewoman of Queen Elizabeth's privy chamber and keeper of her jewels.

676 BRADFORD, C. A. Nicasius Yetsweirt, secretary for the French tongue. s.l. 1934.

677 BRADLEY [SMITH], EMILY. The life of Arabella Stewart. 2 vols. Lond. 1889.
Contains also a collection of her letters. For other lives cf. Davies (8), no. 983. A good new life of Arabella by P. M. Handover has just been published, Lond. 1957.

678 BRETT, S. R. Queen Elizabeth I's legacy to the Stuarts. *Quar. Rev.* ccxcii (1954), 202–14.

679 BROOKE, C. F. TUCKER. Queen Elizabeth's prayers. *Hunt. Lib. Quar.* ii (1938), 69–77.

680   BROOKS, E. St. J.   Sir Christopher Hatton; Queen Elizabeth's favorite. Lond. 1946.
Inadequate.

681   BROWNE, A. L.   Sir John Throckmorton of Feckenham. *Trans. and Proc. Birm. Arch. Soc.* lix (1938), 123–42.

682   BUSHBY, FRANCES.   Three men of the Tudor Time. Lond. 1911.
Biographies of 1st and 2nd Lord North and Sir Thomas North.

683   CAMPBELL, L. B.   Shakespeare's 'histories': mirrors of Elizabethan policy. San Marino, Cal. 1947.

684   CAMPBELL, L. B.   The use of historical patterns in the reign of Elizabeth. *Hunt. Lib. Quar.* i (1938), 135–67.
Illustrated from political writings.

685   CAMPBELL, L. B.   Richard Tarlton and the earthquake of 1580. *Hunt. Lib. Quar.* iv (1941), 293–301.

686   CECIL, A.   A life of Robert Cecil, first earl of Salisbury. Lond. 1915.
The only complete biography. An excellent short appraisal by Joel Hurtstfield is in *History Today*, vii (1957), 279–84. Cf. also 783.

688   CHAMBERS, E. K.   Sir Henry Lee: an Elizabethan portrait. Oxf. 1936.
Cf. Clifford Leech, *Sir Henry Lee's entertainment of Elizabeth in 1592. Mod. Lang. Rev.* xxx (1935), 52–55 and Chamber's reply, ibid. 218. Also F. G. Roe, *The last of Sir Henry Lee, Connoisseur*, cx (1942), 3–12.

689   CHASTENET, JACQUES.   Élisabeth Ière, reine d'Angleterre. *Grandes études historiques*. Paris, 1953.
Psychological interpretation. Well documented.

690   CHEYNEY, E. P.   A history of England, from the defeat of the Armada to the death of Elizabeth. 2 vols. New York, 1914–26; 1948; ed. W. E. Lingelbach.
The best account of Elizabethan political institutions. Discusses foreign affairs, the Essex conspiracy, economic and social questions. Omits religious affairs. Cf. J. E. Neale's review, *E.H.R.* xlii (1927), 430–3. Cf. also *Portrait of an historian, E. P. Cheyney*, Philadelphia, 1935.

691   CHEYNEY, E. P.   England and Denmark in the later days of Queen Elizabeth. *Jour. Mod. Hist.* i (1929), 9–39.

692   COKE, DOROTHEA.   The last Elizabethan: Sir John Coke, 1563–1644. Lond. 1937.

693   CREIGHTON, MANDELL.   Queen Elisabeth. Lond. 1896; 1899.
The 1st ed. in the *Goupil ser.* is handsomely illustrated.

694   DEVLIN, CHRISTOPHER.   The earl and the alchemist. *The Month,* n.s., ix (1953), 23–38, 92–104, 153–66.
Relevant to Richard Hesketh plot.

695   DIMOCK, ARTHUR.   The conspiracy of Dr. Lopez. *E.H.R.* ix (1893), 440–72.

696 DORMER, E. W. Lettice Knollys, countess of Leicester. *Berks. Arch. Jour.*, n.s., xxxix (1935), 82–92.
Cf. also E. V. Hall, *Lettice, countess of Leicester*, Notes and Queries, clxviii (1935), 27–28; P. D. Hicks in *Notes and Queries*, clxvi (1934), 435–8.

697 EGERTON, F. H. A compilation of various authentic evidences and historical authorities tending to illustrate the life and character of Thomas Egerton. Kippis's *Biographia Brittannica*. Lond. 1793; enlarged ed. 1798; best ed. 1816.
The ed. of 1816 contains many documents. Cf. V. B. Heltzel, *Sir Thomas Egerton and William Lambard*, Hunt. Lib. Quar. xi (1948), 201–3.

698 FOX BOURNE, H. R. Sir Philip Sidney. Lond. 1862; rev. 1891.
The standard life; cf. also M. W. Wallace, *Sir P. Sidney*, Cambr. 1915; Mona Wilson, *Sir Philip Sidney*, New York, 1932; John Buxton, *Sir Philip Sidney and the English Renaissance*, Lond. 1954; F. S. Boas, *Sir Philip Sidney*, Lond. 1955.

699 GREW, J. H. Élisabeth d'Angleterre, la reine vierge dans la littérature française. Paris, 1934.

701 HALL, HUBERT. The imperial policy of Elizabeth, from the state papers, foreign and domestic. *Trans. R.H. Soc.*, 2nd ser., iii (1886), 205–41.
Maintains that Elizabeth's policy was 'futile abroad and mischievous at home.'

702 HARRISON, G. B. The life and death of Robert Devereux, earl of Essex. Lond. 1937.

703 HEFFNER, RAY. Essex, the ideal courtier, *Eng. Lit. Hist.* i (1934), 7–36.

704 HEYWOOD, THOMAS. If you know not me, you know nobody. (The troubles of Quenne Elizabeth, 1605). By M. Doran and W. W. Greg. Oxf. 1935.
Cf. also, M. F. Martin, *Library*, 4th ser., xiii (1932), 272–81.

705 HICKS, LEO. Elizabethan royal supremacy and contemporary writers. *The Month*, clxxxiii (1947), 170–7; clxxxiv (1948), 216–28.

706 HICKS, LEO. The strange case of Dr. William Parry. *Studies*, xxxvii (1948), 343–62.

707 HUGHES, M. Y. England's Eliza and Spenser's Medina. *Jour. Eng. and German. Philol.* xliii (1944), 1–15.

708 HUGHEY, R. Note on Queen Elizabeth's Godly Mediation. *Library*, 4th ser., xv (1934), 237–40.

709 HUME, M. A. S. The courtships of Queen Elizabeth. . . . Lond. 1896; 1904.
Uncritical. The ed. of 1904 contains 2 supplementary chapters on Elizabeth's virginity.

710 HUME, M. A. S. The great Lord Burghley; a study in Elizabethan statecraft. Lond. 1898.
Inadequate.

711 HUME, M. A. S. Treason and plot. Struggles for Catholic supremacy in the last years of Queen Elizabeth. Lond. 1901.
Covers the period from 1590 to 1603. Based mainly upon Spanish sources. Badly constructed and inaccurate in details. Cf. *E.H.R.* xvii (1901), 163.

712 IZARD, T. C. George Whetstone: mid-Elizabethan gentleman of letters. *Columbia Univ. Stud. in Eng. and Compar. Lit.* clviii. New York, 1942.

713 JACKSON, W. A. The funeral procession of Queen Elizabeth. *Library*, 4th ser., xxvi (1946), 262–71.

714 [JEBB, SAMUEL]. The life of Robert Dudley, earl of Leicester. Lond. 1727.
Largely based on 620. Unreliable.

715 JENKINS, GLADYS. Ways and means in Elizabethan propaganda. *History*, xxvi (1941), 105–14.

716 JESSOPP, AUGUSTUS, *et al.* William Cecil, Lord Burghley. Lond. 1904.
Genealogical details valuable, remainder of vol. uneven.

717 JOHN, L. C. Roger Manners, Elizabethan courtier. *Hunt. Lib. Quar.* xii (1948), 57–84.

718 KELLY, FRANCIS. Queen Elizabeth and her dresses. *Connoisseur*, cxiii (1944), 71–79.

720 KRETZSCHMAR, JOHANNES. Die Invasionsprojekte der katholischen Mächte gegen England zur zeit Elizabeths. Leipzig, 1892.
Deals with the subject between 1568 and 1584, particularly with the years 1578–84. Original documents from the Vatican archives in the app. Valuable.

721 LA FERRIÈRE-PERCY, Hector de. Les projets de mariage de la reine Elizabeth. Paris, 1882.
Good on Elizabeth's French courtships.

722 LANGSTON, BEACH. Essex and the art of dying. *Hunt. Lib. Quar.* xiii (1950), 109–29.

724 LEE, SIDNEY. Rodrigo Lopez, the original of Shylock. *Gent. Mag.* ccxlvi (1880), 185–200.

725 LETI, GREGORIO. Historia o vero vita di Elizabetta, regina d'Inghilterra, detta per sopranome la Comediante Politica. 2 pts. Amsterdam, 1692; French trans., 2 pts., Amsterdam, 1694.
The Italian original suppressed. Thoroughly unreliable. Leti seems to have invented some of his so-called sources.

726 LOWERS, J. K. Mirrors for rebels: a study of polemical literature relating to the Northern Rebellion, 1569. *Univ. of California, Eng. Studies*, vi. Berkeley, 1953.

727 LYLY, JOHN. Queen Elizabeth's entertainment at Mitchum: poet, painter, and musician. By Leslie Hotson. New Haven, 1952.
Contemporary records of Elizabeth's visits to Mitchum and Chiswick in 1598, ascribed to Lyly.

728   McCALL, H. B. Executions after the northern rebellion. *York. Arch. Jour.* xviii (1887).

729   McDONALD, D. Sir John Harington, Queen Elizabeth's godson. *History Today,* vi (1956), 759–64.

730   McLANE, P. E. The death of a queen: Spenser's Dido as Elizabeth. *Hunt. Lib. Quar.* xviii (1954), 1–11.

732   MAITLAND, F. W. The Anglican settlement and the Scottish reformation. *Cambr. Mod. Hist.* (10) ii, 550–98.
A brilliant interpretation.

733   MARCKS, ERICH. Königin Elizabeth von England und ihre Zeit. Leipzig, 1897.
Suggestive, excellent illustrations.

734   MAYNARD, THEODORE. Queen Elizabeth. Milwaukee, 1940.
Roman Catholic viewpoint.

735   MOMIGLIANO, E. Elisabetta d'Inghilterra, Milan, 1931.

736   MENMUIR, C. The rebellion of the earls of Northumberland and Westmorland, 1569. Newcastle, 1907.

737   MOSSE, G. L. The struggle for sovereignty in England from the reign of Queen Elizabeth to the Petition of Right. East Lansing, 1950.

738   MOUNTS, C. E. The Raleigh-Essex rivalry and *Mother Hubberds Tale. Mod. Lang. Notes,* lxv (1950), 509–13.

739   NARES, EDWARD. Memoirs of the life and administration of . . . Lord Burghley . . . containing an historical view of the times in which he lived . . . with extracts from his private and official correspondence. 3 vols. Lond. 1828–31.
The last 2 vols. cover Burghley's career under Elizabeth. Biased on religious questions and inaccurate on foreign affairs. Made no use of materials from foreign archives. Cf. Lord Macaulay's notable review in the *Edin. Rev.* lv (1832), 27–96.

740   NAUNTON, ROBERT. Fragmenta regalia: or observations on the late Queen Elizabeth, her times and favorites. [Lond.], 1641; 1653; by Edward Arber, Lond. 1895.
A valuable account of the chief courtiers of Queen Elizabeth, embodying many interesting reminiscences. Written about 1630. Arber's ed. is a repr. of the ed. of 1653.

741   NEALE, J. E. The accession of Queen Elizabeth I. *History Today,* iii (1953), 293–300.

741a   NEALE, J. E. The Elizabethan age. *Creighton lecture in history, 1950.* Lond. 1951.

742   NEALE, J. E. The Elizabethan political scene. *Proc. Brit. Acad.* xxxiv (1948), 97–117.

743   NEALE, J. E. Queen Elizabeth. Lond. 1934.
The best life of Elizabeth.

744 NEALE, J. E. The sayings of Queen Elizabeth. *History,* x (1925), 212–33.
An attempt to establish a canon and apocrypha of stories, in a caustic review of Chamberlin, *The sayings of Queen Elizabeth*, Lond. 1923. Scholarly.

745 NICOLL, A. The Elizabethans introduced. A picture-document history. Lond. 1956.

746 NICOLAS, N. H. Life of William Davison, secretary of state and privy councillor to Queen Elizabeth. Lond. 1823.
Contains many of Davison's letters, printed in full, and in an app. four versions of his apology with other papers relating to his trial. Cf. also 785–6.

747 NORSWORTHY, L. L. The Lady of Bleeding Heart Yard, Lady Elizabeth Hatton, 1578–1646. Lond. 1935.
Lady Hatton was Lord Burghley's granddaughter and the 2nd wife of Sir Edward Coke.

748 OSBORNE, FRANCIS. Historical memoires on the reigns of Queen Elizabeth and King James. Lond. 1658; repr. in *Works*, 1673; 1722; and in W. Scott, *Secret history of James I*, Edin. 1811.
Said to be based on contemporary sources of information.

749 PHILIPPSON, MARTIN. Westeuropa im Zeitalter von Philip ii, Elizabeth und Heinrich iv. Oncken, *Allgemeine Geschichte*, iii, pt. 2, Berlin, 1882.
Useful for English foreign relations under Elizabeth.

750 PIKE, C. E. The intrigue to deprive the earl of Essex of the lord lieutenancy of Ireland. *Trans. R.H. Soc.*, 3rd ser., v (1911), 89–104.

751 POLLEN, J. H. The accession of King James I. *The Month,* ci (1903), 572–85.
Deals with negotiations conducted at Rome and elsewhere regarding the succession of James I to the English throne. Makes use of unpublished material in the archives of Naples.

752 POLLEN, J. H. The question of Elizabeth's successor. *The Month,* ci (1903), 517–32.
Utilizes unpublished material in the Vatican archives and elsewhere.

753 PROUTY, C. T. George Gascoigne, Elizabethan courtier, soldier and poet. New York, 1942.

754 RAUMER, F. L. G. VON. Beiträge zur neueren Geschichte aus dem britischen Museum und Reichsarchiven. 5 parts. Leipzig, 1836–9.
Pt. i deals with Elizabeth and Mary Stuart. An English trans. of this work appeared in 2 vols., Lond. 1837, in which the 1st vol. deals with Elizabeth and Mary Stuart.

755 RAWSON, M. S. Bess of Hardwick and her circle. Lond. 1910.

756 RAWSON, M. S. Penelope Rich and her circle. Lond. 1910.

757 READ, CONYERS. Good Queen Bess. *A.H.R.* xxxi (1926), 647–61.
A brief analysis of Elizabeth's character.

758 READ, CONYERS. A letter from Robert, earl of Leicester, to a lady. *Hunt. Lib. Quar.* ix (1936), 15–26.
Relevant to Leicester's affair with Douglas Sheffield.

759   READ, CONYERS. Mr. Secretary Walsingham and the policy of Queen Elizabeth. 3 vols. Oxf. 1925.
Particularly useful on foreign affairs, 1570–90. Contains a critical bibliography and documents in appendixes. Cf. J. E. Neale's review in *E.H.R.* xlii (1927), 127–34.

760   READ, CONYERS. Mr. Secretary Cecil and Queen Elizabeth. Lond. 1955.
Deals with Cecil before his elevation to the peerage as Lord Burghley (1571). A 2nd vol. on his career as Lord Burghley is in preparation.

761   REID, R. R. The rebellion of the earls, 1569. *Trans. R.H. Soc.*, 2nd ser., xx (1906), 171–203.
Good upon local conditions in north England and their bearing upon the rebellion.

762   RICHARDSON, AUBREY. The lover of Queen Elizabeth, being the life and character of Robert Dudley, earl of Leicester, 1533–88. Lond. 1907.
Popular and of little value. There is no scholarly life of Leicester.

763   RIDDEHOUGH, G. B. Queen Elizabeth's translation of Boethius' *De Consolatione Philosophiae. Jour. Eng. and German Philol.* xv (1946), 88–94.

765   ROWSE, A. L. The England of Elizabeth. Lond. 1950.
Deals mainly with the structure of society. Brilliant but strongly coloured by the author's social and religious attitudes.

766   ROWSE, A. L. The expansion of Elizabethan England. Lond. 1955.
Deals with expansion in Wales and Ireland as well as overseas.

767   ROWSE, A. L. Queen Elizabeth and the historians. *History Today*, iii (1953), 630–41.

768   RUTTON, W. L. Three branches of the family of Wentworth. . . . Lond. 1891.
Useful on the careers of Paul and Peter Wentworth.

769   SARGENT, R. M. At the court of Queen Elizabeth: the life and lyrics of Sir Edward Dyer. Oxf. 1935.

770   SCARFE, NORMAN. Sir John Hayward, an Elizabethan historian, his life and disappointments. *Proc. Suffolk Inst. of Arch. and Nat. Hist.* xxv (1950), 79–97.

771   SCHARF, GEORGE. Queen Elizabeth's procession in a litter to celebrate the marriage of Anne Russell at Blackfriars, June 16, 1600. *Arch. Jour.* xxiii (1866), 131–59.
Discusses the well-known picture.

772   SCHMIDT, A. J. Thomas Wilson, Tudor scholar and statesman. *Hunt. Lib. Quar.* xx (1957), 206–18.

773   SMITH, L. P. The life and letters of Sir Henry Wotton. 2 vols. Oxf. 1907.
Vol. i, 227–317, contains letters written during reign of Elizabeth.

774   STÄHLIN, KARL. Sir Francis Walsingham und seine Zeit. Vol. i (no more issued). Heidelberg, 1908.
Covers the life and times of Walsingham to the year 1573. Valuable on Anglo-French relations, 1570–3.

775 STAFFORD, H. G. James VI of Scotland and the throne of England. New York, 1940.
Important for controversies over succession, *temp.* Elizabeth.

776 STONE, LAWRENCE. An Elizabethan: Sir Horatio Palavicino. New York, 1956.
Valuable for financial history.

777 STRACHEY, LYTTON. Elizabeth and Essex. Lond. 1928.
Suggestive.

778 STRICKLAND, AGNES. The life of Queen Elizabeth. Lond. 1840–8.
Originally published in the *Lives of the queens of England.* Has been often republished separately. Useful, but places too much confidence in discredited sources such as Leti (725).

779 TAPP, W. H. Anne Boleyn and Elizabeth at the Royal Manor of Hanworth. Lond. 1953.

780 TENISON, E. M. Elizabethan England. 9 vols. Leamington, 1932–51.
Valuable for the illustrations.

781 TILLYARD, E. M. W. The Elizabethan World picture. Lond. 1943.
Significant.

782 TRESCHOW, CHR. DE. Contributions to the history of Queen Elizabeth, derived from documents in the Danish state archives. Lond. 1871.
Slight, 36 pp.

783 TRESSLER, V. G. A. Die politische Entwickelung Sir Robert Cecils bis zum Tode Burleighs. Leipzig, 1901.
Good.

784 WALDMAN, MILTON. Elizabeth and Leicester. Boston, U.S.A. 1945.

785 WARD, B. M. Queen Elizabeth and William Davison. *E.H.R.* xliv (1929), 104–6.

786 WARD, B. M. The seventeenth earl of Oxford, 1550–1604. Lond. 1928.
Prints many letters. Cf. Dorothy and Charlton Ogburn, *This star of England,* New York, 1952, which identifies Oxford and Shakespeare; Percy Allen, *Anne Cecil, Elizabeth and Oxford,* Lond. 1934; Eggar, K. E. *The seventeenth earl of Oxford, as musician, poet and controller of the queen's revels, Proc. of Music Assoc.* (1935), 39–60.

787 WELPLY, W. H. John, Baron Lumley, 1534?–1609. *Notes and Queries,* clxxxi (1941), 86–88.

788 WERNHAM, R. B. The disgrace of William Davison. *E.H.R.* xlvi (1931), 632–6.

789 WIESENER, LOUIS. La Jeunesse d'Élisabeth d'Angleterre, 1533–58. Paris, 1878; trans. C. M. Yonge, 2 vols., Lond. 1879.
Valuable for Queen Mary's Spanish marriage.

790 WILLIAMS, F. B. Jr. Leicester's Ghost. *Harvard Studies and Notes in Philology,* xviii (1935), 271–85.
Narrative poem about Robert, earl of Leicester. Williams identifies the author of the poem with Thomas Rogers of Bryanston in *ibid.* xvi (1934), 253–67.

791 WILLIAMS, N. J. The coronation of Queen Elizabeth I. *Quar. Rev.* ccxci (1953), 397–410.

792 WILSON, E. C. England's Eliza. *Harvard Studies in Eng.* xx. Cambr., U.S.A. 1939.

793 WILSON, V. A. Queen Elizabeth's maids of honour. Lond. 1922.
Popular, good illustrations. Cf. also Cecilie Goff, *A woman of the Tudor age* (Katharine, duchess of Suffolk), Lond. 1930.

794 WOLF, LUCIEN. The Jews in Elizabethan England. *Trans. Jew. hist. soc. of Eng.* xi (1924-7).
Deals with the political activities of Lopez, Nuñez, and others.

795 YATES, F. A. Queen Elizabeth as Astraea. *Jour. of Warburg and Court. Inst.* x (1947), 27-82.

G. FOREIGN AFFAIRS

1. GENERAL

(a) *Sources*

Most of the treaties are printed in Rymer (88); one or two missing there are in Dumont (808). The foreign correspondence of the government for Henry VIII is in *Letters and papers* (91); after Henry VIII, in the foreign calendars (87), which are, however, confined to the foreign papers in the P.R.O. A great deal of unprinted foreign correspondence, Edward VI and Elizabeth, is in the B.M. There is much material also in foreign affairs in private collections, notably in the *Salisbury MSS.* (185). For an excellent résumé of materials on diplomatic history in private collections and in the B.M., cf. Davenport (72).

Among privately printed collections of documents, Ellis (290) contains scattered letters on foreign affairs in general; the *Lettere de Principi* (446) and Cromwell's letters (520), for the reign of Henry VIII; *Cabala* (274), *Hardwicke papers* (280), Wright (626), and Birch (601), for Elizabeth. Other pertinent private collections are mentioned below under the appropriate heading.

The dispatches of foreign ambassadors in England are very important. These are listed below under the several countries. The Venetian and the Spanish dispatches have been calendared (992, 867-8). Transcripts of many of the French dispatches are in the P.R.O. Many have been privately printed; cf. sect. 2 *infra*.

(b) *Later Works*

For the period between 1529 and 1588 Froude (340) gives the most complete account. The best modern accounts are in Fisher (339), in Pollard (363) and in Mackie (354). For Henry VII's foreign policy, Busch (406) should be consulted; for Henry VIII's, Brewer (473), Pollard (531-2), and Merriman (520); for Edward VI and Mary, Pollard (363) and Harbison (590); for Elizabeth, Seeley (375), Pollard (363), Read (759-60), Cheyney (690) and Black (671). The introductions to the foreign calendars (87) are valuable for Elizabeth's reign, particularly those by Butler, Lomas, and Wernham. On the relations between England and Denmark in the last decade of Elizabeth's reign, cf. 691. On international law, cf. pp. 139-41.

2. FRANCE

(a) *Sources*

Pertinent material in the *Hist. MSS. Comm. reports* and in the B.M. is briefly indicated by Davenport (72). An admirable analysis of the sources on Anglo-French relations, 1558–1603, by F. J. Weaver, is printed in *Bull. Inst. Hist. Research*, iv (1926), 73–86; v (1927), 13–22; vi (1928), 1–9; vii (1929), 13–26.

The correspondence to and from English ambassadors in France can be followed for Henry VIII in *Letters and Papers* (91); for Edward VI–Elizabeth (to 1589) in *Cal. S.P., Foreign* (87).

Among private collections, the *Salisbury MSS.* (185), the *duke of Buccleuch and Queensberry MSS.* (111), and the *Braybrooke MSS.* (106) are important.

Much Anglo-French correspondence for the decade 1558–70 is printed in *Cabala* (274) and in Forbes (611); for the decade 1570–80, in *Compleat ambassador* (803) and Poulet (827); for the decade 1580–90, in *Hardwicke papers* (280), and for the last ten years of the century, in Unton (830), Birch (601), the *Edmondes papers* (810), and Winwood (832).

For the correspondence of French ambassadors in England, cf. in general Hauser (23) and Baschet (797), and for particular embassies, du Bellay (806), Castillon (804), Odet de Selve (825), Noailles (824), La Mothe Fénélon (813), Castelnau (801), De Maisse (817), Boissise and Harlay (853). The correspondence of French ambassadors to England on Scottish affairs is printed in part in Teulet (4929). On the duke of Alençon, cf. 905.

796   BASCHET, ARMAND. List of the French ambassadors in England. *Reports of the deputy keeper of the public records*, xxxvii (1876), app. i, 180–94.

797   BASCHET, ARMAND. List of despatches of ambassadors from France to England, 1509–1714. *Reports of the deputy keeper of the public records*, xxxix (1878), app. i, 573–826.
Baschet's transcripts of French dispatches in P.R.O. include many dispatches not listed in *report* xxxix.

798   BREVE INEDITO DI GIULIO II per la investitura del regno di Francia ad Enrico VIII d'Inghilterra. *Archivio della R. Società Romana di Storia Patria*, xix (1896), 425–41.

799   BIRCH, THOMAS. An historical view of the negotiations between the courts of England, France and Brussels, from the year 1592 to 1617, extracted chiefly from the MS. state papers of Sir Thomas Edmondes ... and Antony Bacon. Lond. 1749.
Many of the papers used are printed *in extenso*. Cf. *Edmondes papers* (810).

800   BOUILLON ET DE SANCY EN ANGLETERRE en 1596 ... Négociations de MM. de. By [G. H.] Gaillard.
In *Notices et extraits des manuscrits de la bibliothèque du roi*, pub. by *L'académie royale des inscriptions et belles-lettres*, ii (1789), 114 ff. Cf. Hauser (23), iv, 187. Cf. also *Les Œuvres de Messire Juillaume du Vair*, rev. ed. Paris, 1625.

801   CASTELNAU, MICHEL DE, seigneur de la Mauvissière. Mémoires. By Jacques Castelnau. Paris, 1621; by J. Le Laboureur, 3 vols., Paris, 1731.
These *Mémoires* were written in England between 1581 and 1585. The author was ambassador to England, 1575–85. Cover the period 1559–70 of French history. Excel-

lent upon English participation in early French religious wars. The ed. of 1731 contains, in the *Additions* scattered through the 3 vols., important documents bearing upon Anglo-French and Anglo-Scottish relations. Of particular value are the extracts from the correspondence of La Mothe-Fénélon while ambassador to England and of Castelnau when he occupied the same position. An English trans. of the *Mémoires* (without the *Additions*) was published anonymously in London in 1724. Cf. Hauser, *Les sources de l'histoire de France* (23), iii, 39–40; cf. also no. 3252 *infra*.

802 CATHERINE DE MÉDICIS. Lettres. By Hector de la Ferrière-Percy, and by Comte Baguenault de Puchesse. 10 vols. Paris, 1880–1909.
Extremely valuable source on Anglo-French relations, 1558–88. In the collection of *Documents inédits sur l'histoire de France*.

803 THE COMPLEAT AMBASSADOR: or two treaties of the intended marriage of Queen Elizabeth . . . comprised in letters of . . . Sir Francis Walsingham . . . together with the answers of the Lord Burghley, the earl of Leicester, Sir Tho: Smith and others. By Sir Dudley Digges. Lond. 1655.
This correspondence covers the period of Walsingham's service as English ambassador in France (1570–3) and of his subsequent embassy to France in 1581. Most of the original letters are among the *Cotton MSS.* in the B.M. and in the P.R.O. A few are missing. The book is carelessly printed and some of the letters are wrongly dated. A French trans. appeared in Amsterdam in 1700 and again in 1717 under the title, *Mémoires et instructions pour les ambassadeurs ou lettres et negotiations de Walsingham*. . . .

804 DE CASTILLON ET DE MARILLAC. Correspondance politique. By J. Kaulek. Paris, 1885.
French ambassadors to England, 1537–41.

805 A DECLARATION OF THE QUENES MAIESTIE. . . . Lond. 1562.
Elizabeth's official explanation for her action in assisting the French Huguenots in 1562. A Latin and a French version appeared the same year. Printed in *Harl. Misc.* (281), i, 374–9.

806 DU BELLAY, JEAN. Ambassades en Angleterre. La première ambassade (Sept. 1527–Feb. 1529). By V. L. Bourrilly and Pierre de Vaissière. Paris, 1905.
In *Archives de l'histoire religieuse de la France*. Prints text of diplomatic correspondence with an admirable introduction.

807 DU BELLAY, MARTIN. Mémoires . . . de plusieurs choses advenues au royaume de France depuis MDXIII jusques au trépas du roy François premier. . . . Paris, 1569; standard ed. (*Soc. de l'histoire de France*), by V. L. Bourrilly, 4 vols., Paris, 1908–19.
Also published in Petitot, *Collection des mémoires*, ser. i, vols. xvii–xix; and in the *Nouvelle collection des mémoires* of Michaud and Poujoulat, er. i, 5. Important for England, because Jean du Bellay, brother of the author, was ambassador in London during the period of the Divorce.

808 DUMONT, J. Corps universel diplomatique. 8 vols. The Hague, 1725.
Contains texts of many treaties.

809 DU PLESSIS-MORNAY, PHILIPPE. Mémoires. Vol. i, s.l.; vol. ii, La Forest, 1624–5; vol. iii, Amsterdam, 1662; by C. R. Auguis and A. D. de la Fontenelle de Vaudoré. 12 vols. Paris, 1824; best ed. by Henriette (Guizot) de Witt, 2 vols., Paris, 1868–9; trans. by Lucy Crump, *A Huguenot family in the sixteenth century*, Lond. 1924.
Papers, official and unofficial, rather than memoirs. Cf. Hauser (23), iii, 59.

810 THE EDMONDES PAPERS. By G. G. Butler. *Roxburghe Club*, 1913.
Cover 1592–9. Largely on relations with France.

811 HENRI IV. Recueil des lettres missives. By Jules Berger de Xivrey and J. Guadet. 9 vols. Paris, 1843–76.
Far from complete.

812 LA HUGUERYE, MICHEL DE. Mémoires inédites. By J. E. A. de Ruble. 3 vols. Paris, 1877–80.
Compiled 1604–6. Useful but unreliable for relations of Elizabeth with French Huguenots.

813 LA MOTHE-FÉNÉLON, B. de S. de. Correspondance diplomatique. By A. Teulet. 7 vols. Paris et Lond. 1838–40; *Bannatyne Club*, no. 67 (1840).
French ambassador to England, 1568–75. Invaluable for Anglo-French relations, and for internal affairs in England during this period. Part of La Mothe-Fénélon's correspondence is printed in the *Additions* to Castelnau's *Mémoires* (801).

814 LETTRES DE ROIS, reines et autres personnages des cours de France et d'Angleterre. By J. J. Champollion-Figeac. 2 vols. Paris, 1845–7.
In the *Collection de documents inédits sur l'histoire de France*. The latter part of vol. ii contains valuable documents for the reigns of Henry VII, and of Henry VIII to 1515.

815 LETTRES DU ROY LOUIS XII et du Cardinal Georges d'Amboise, avec plusieurs autres lettres, mémoires et instructions (1504–14). 4 vols. Brussels, 1712.

816 LETTRES ET MÉMOIRES D'ESTAT DES ROYS, princes et ambassadeurs, sous les règnes de François I et Henri II et François II, 1537–59. By G. Ribier. 2 vols. Paris, 1666.
Valuable collection, well edited from originals in Musée Condé.

817 MAISSE, ANDRÉ HURAULT, sieur de. Journal, 1597. Trans. by G. B. Harrison and R. A. Jones. Lond. 1931.
Maisse's jour. of his abortive mission from Henry IV to Elizabeth in 1597. Trans. from a MS. in the Bibliothèque nationale. Cf. 859.

818 MARGUERITE DE VALOIS. Mémoires. By Auger de Mauléon. Paris, 1628; by François Guessard, Paris, 1842.
Useful for Alençon's intrigues in the Low Countries.

819 MOLINET, JEAN. Chroniques (1474–1506). By J. A. Buchon. 5 vols. Paris, 1827–8.
Valuable for Anglo-French affairs up to 1506.

820 NÉGOCIATIONS DIPLOMATIQUES entre la France et l'Autriche durant les trente premières années du XVIe siècle. By A. J. G. Le Glay. 2 vols. Paris, 1845.
In the *Collection de documents inédits sur l'histoire de France*. Useful for England's foreign relations during the period covered.

821 NÉGOCIATIONS DE M. DE LOMÉNIE . . . envoyé par le roy vers la royne d'Angleterre, l'an 1595. By [G. H.] Gaillard.
In *Notices et extraits des manuscrits de la bibliothèque du roi* pub. by *L'académie royale des inscriptions et belles-lettres*, ii (1789), pp. 103–13.

822 NÉGOCIATIONS, LETTRES ET PIÈCES DIVERSES relatives au règne de François II. By Louis Paris. Paris, 1841
Valuable for Anglo-French relations, 1559–60.

823   NEVERS, DUC DE. Mémoires . . . enrichis de plusieurs pièces du temps. By de Gomberville. 2 vols. Paris, 1665.
Contains many original papers bearing upon the marriage negotiations between Elizabeth and the two Valois princes, Henri and François. But cf. Hauser (23), iii, 107.

824   NOAILLES, Messieurs de. Ambassades en Angleterre. By R. A. de Vertot and C. Villaret. 5 vols. Leyden, 1763.
Three brothers, Antoine, François, and Gilles de Noailles, were ambassadors in England, successively, from 1553 to 1557, and in 1559. Originals in *Archives du Ministère des Affaires Étrangères*. Cf., the admirable statement on these papers in Harbison (590), 342–51.

825   ODET DE SELVE. Correspondance politique, 1546–9. By Germain Lefèvre-Pontalis. Paris, 1888.

826   ORIGINAL RECORD of . . . entry of King Henry VIII into Tournay . . . in 1513. By G. F. Beltz. *Arch.* xxvii (1838), 257–61.
From Tournay archives.

827   POULET, AMIAS. Copy-book of letters written during his embassy to France (A.D. 1577). By O. Ogle. *Roxburghe Club*, 1866.
Cover the period from May 1577 to Jan. 1578. Printed from a MS. in the Bodleian library. The originals of most of these letters are in the P.R.O. and have been calendared in the *Foreign Calendars, Elizabeth* (87). Valuable.

828   [STUBBES, JOHN.] The discoverie of a gaping gulf whereinto England is like to be swallowed by another French mariage, if the Lord forbid not the banns. . . . [Lond.], 1579.
This is the famous pamphlet against Elizabeth's marriage with the duc d'Alençon, for writing which Stubbes lost his right hand. Sir Philip Sidney's famous letter opposing the same marriage is printed in 630, iii, 51–60. An unpublished defence of the match by Henry Howard is in B.M., *Harl. MSS.* 180.

829   TREATY AGAINST THE TURKS, between Henry VIII and Francis I, concluded at Calais, 1532. By Joseph Burtt. *Arch. Jour.* x (1853), 338–41.

830   UNTON, HENRY. Correspondence. Ambassador from Queen Elizabeth to Henry IV, king of France, in the years MDXCI and MDXCII. By Joseph Stevenson. *Roxburghe Club*, 1847.
Invaluable for Anglo-French relations, 1591–2.

831   VERLOVING VAN ANJOU EN ELISABETH. *Kronijk von het Historisch Genootschaap*, xvii (1861), 192–5.
Two letters, dated in Nov. 1581, about the Alençon courtship.

832   WINWOOD, RALPH. Memorials of affairs of state in the reigns of Queen Elizabeth and King James I. By Edmund Sawyer. 3 vols. Lond. 1725.
Vol. i covers the period 1597–1603. Consists chiefly of correspondence of Winwood and Sir Henry Neville from France. A few papers on Spanish and Dutch affairs. Invaluable for Anglo-French relations between 1599–1603. The originals of most of Winwood's papers printed here, and many more besides are in the private collection of the duke of Buccleuch, at Montagu House (110).

(b) *Later Works*

For the French background, Lavisse, *Hist. de France*, v, vi, is the best general account. Note the references there cited. Harbison (590) is indispensable for

Mary's reign. Ascoli (323) is useful. Kervyn de Lettenhove (938) treats rather briefly of Elizabeth's relations to the Huguenots.

833   ATKINSON, E. G.   The cardinal of Chatillon in England, 1568–71. *Hug. Soc. proc.* iii (1888–91), 172–85.
Prints many documents.

834   BLACK, J. B.   Elizabeth and Henry IV. Oxf. 1914.
Brief.

835   BOURRILLY, V. L.   Le règne de François Ier, état des travaux et questions à traiter. *Revue d'histoire moderne et contemporaine*, iv (1902–3), 513–31, 585–603.
A masterly survey of the subject, indirectly valuable for contemporary Tudor England.

836   BOURRILLY, V. L.   François Ier et Henry VIII, l'intervention de la France dans l'affaire du divorce à propos de travaux récents. *Revue d'histoire moderne et contemporaine*, i (1899), 271–84.
Valuable bibliographically.

837   BOURRILLY, V. L.   Guillaume du Bellay, Seigneur de Langay. Paris, 1905.

838   BUISSON, ALBERT.   Le chancelier Antoine Duprat. Paris, 1935.

839   DECRUE, FRANÇOIS.   Anne de Montmorency. 2 vols. Paris, 1885–9.
Useful for Anglo-French relations from 1526 to 1541, and from 1547 to 1559.

840   DELABORDE, J. L.   Gaspard de Coligny, amiral de France. 3 vols. Paris, 1882.
Contains most of his correspondence.

841   DESCLOZEAUX, A.   L'ambassade de Sully en Angleterre en 1610 et les économies royales. *Revue historique*, xliv (1890), 68–71.
Argues to prove that Sully did not go to England in 1601.

842   DREUX, ANDRÉ.   Le premier divorce de Henry VIII et les relations entre la France et l'Angleterre de 1527 à 1534. *Positions des thèses soutenues . . . à l'école nationale des chartes.* Chalon-sur-Saône, 1900, pp. 43–62.

843   DUPUY, ANTOINE.   Histoire de la réunion de la Bretagne à la France. 2 vols. Paris, 1880.
Valuable for the early phases of Henry VII's foreign policy.

844   FERRIÈRE-PERCY, HECTOR DE LA.   La paix de Troyes avec l'Angleterre, 1563–4. *Revue des quest. hist.* xxxiii (1883), 36–75.

845   FERRIÈRE-PERCY, HECTOR DE LA.   Le xvie siècle et les Valois, d'après les documents inédits du British Museum et du Record Office. Paris, 1879.
A discussion of Anglo-French relations, with illustrative documents, practically confined to the period 1558–74. Valuable for Elizabeth's intrigues with the Huguenots, particularly after St. Bartholomew's Eve.

846   GOODACRE, E. B., Henry, earl of Derby's suite on his embassy to Paris in 1584–5. *Trans. Hist. Soc. Lancs. and Ches.* xcii (1941), 51–56.

847   GRINGORE, PIERRE.   Pierre Gringore's pageants for the entry of Mary Tudor into Paris. An unpublished manuscript. By C. R. Baskervill. Chicago, 1934.

848 HAMY, A. Entrevue de François Ier avec Henry VIII à Boulogne-sur-mer en 1532. Paris, 1898.
Contains a useful collection of documents.

849 HARBISON, E. H. French intrigue at the court of Queen Mary. *A.H.R.* xlv (1940), 533–51.

850 HUBAULT, G[USTAVE]. Ambassade de Michel de Castelnau en Angleterre, 1575–85. Saint-Cloud, [1856–7].
Makes use of unpublished material in the French archives and the valuable collection of contemporary copies of Castelnau's correspondence in the archives of the family of d'Esneval. Reveals an imperfect acquaintance with the English archives.

851 JACQUETON, GILBERT. La politique extérieure de Louise de Savoie. Paris, 1892.
Valuable for the diplomatic relations of England and France in 1525–6. Excellent critical bibliography.

852 KOSZUL, ANDRÉ. Les relations entre l'Alsace et l'Angleterre au xvie siècle. *Revue de littérature comparée*, ix (1929), 5–24.
Cultural relations.

853 LAFFLEUR DE KERMAINGANT, P. L'ambassade de France en Angleterre, sous Henri IV. 4 vols. Paris, 1886–95.
Covers the embassy of Jean de Thumery (sieur de Boissise), 1598–1602, and of Christophe de Harlay (comte de Beaumont), 1602–5. Vols. ii and iv contain *pièces justificatives*, chiefly letters of Henri IV not printed in 811. Invaluable for Anglo-French relations at the close of Elizabeth's reign.

854 MARCHAND, CHARLES. Le traité des Huguenots avec les Anglais en 1562. . . . *Revue des quest. hist.* lxxvii (1905), 191–200.
Cf. also other monographs on this subject cited by Hauser (23), iii, 192.

855 MATTINGLY, GARRETT. An early non-aggression pact. *Jour. Mod. Hist.* x (1938), 1–30.
The treaty of London, 1518.

856 MIGNET, F. A. M. La rivalité de François I et de Charles Quint. 2 vols. Paris, 1875.
The best general account of continental policies from 1515 to 1530. Especially valuable for the period of the Divorce.

857 NOUAILLAC, J. Le règne de Henri IV (1589–1610): sources, travaux et questions à traiter. *Revue d'histoire moderne et contemporaine*, ix (1907–8), 104–23, 348–63.
A masterly survey of the subject indirectly valuable for contemporary England.

858 PAULI, REINHOLD. Diplomatie im Jahre 1516. *Hist. Zeitschrift*, xiv (1865), 269–94.

859 PRÉVOST-PARADOL, [L. A.]. Élisabeth et Henri IV, 1595–1598. Paris, 1855; 1863.
Devoted chiefly to a study of the embassy of Hurault de Maisse in England, Nov. 1597 to Jan. 1598, and based upon his journal (817). Makes no use of unpublished English sources. Printed originally in Latin as a Ph.D dissertation (1855).

860 READ, CONYERS. The fame of Sir Edward Stafford. *A.H.R.* xx (1915), 292–313.
Attacks integrity of English ambassador to France, 1583–9. Cf. Pollard in *E.H.R.* xvi (1901), 572–7, and J. E. Neale in *E.H.R.* xliv (1929), 203–20, for a defence of his character, with Read's reply in *A.H.R.* xxxv (1930), 560–6.

861 ROBINSON, A. M. F. Queen Elizabeth and the Valois princes. *E.H.R.* ii (1887), 40–77.

862 RUBLE, J. E. A. DE. Le traité de Cateau-Cambrésis. Paris, 1889.
The standard work on the subject.

863 SALLES, GEORGES. La guerre et les négociations entre François Ier et Henry VIII du traité de Crépy au traité d'Ardres (septembre 1544–juin 1546). *Positions des thèses soutenues . . . à l'école nationale des chartes.* Mâcon, 1893.
Cf. also H. Courteault, *Blaise de Monluc, historien*, p. xviii.

864 THOMPSON, J. W. The wars of religion in France, 1559–76. Chicago, 1909.
Useful for Anglo-French affairs. Prints many English and French state papers in appendixes.

865 VAISSIÈRE, PIERRE DE. Charles de Marillac, ambassadeur et homme politique, sous François Ier, Henri II et François II (1510–60). Paris, 1896.
Marillac was French ambassador in England from March 1539 to March 1543. Cf. 804.

866 WEBER, B. C. The council of Fontainebleau (1560). *Archiv für Reformationsgesch.* xlv (1954), 43–62.

3. Spain

(a) *Sources*

For standard bibliographies on Spanish history see 26, 878, and 892. For the reign of Charles V the section on the empire should be consulted (*infra*, pp. 80–81); for Spain in the Low Countries, the section on the Low Countries (*infra*, pp. 75–80). Most of the material on the Elizabethan naval war with Spain is given in the section on the navy (*infra*, pp. 295ff.). Material relevant to Spanish relations with Scotland is printed in Teulet (4929). The *Cal. S.P., Spanish* (867–8) contains in trans. most of the material on Anglo-Spanish relations from Spanish and imperial sources, but they need to be supplemented and checked where possible by the *Documentos inéditos* (870).

867 CALENDAR OF STATE PAPERS, SPANISH. Vols. i, ii and supplementary vol., 1485–1525, by G. A. Bergenroth; vols. iii–vii, 1525–55, by Pascual de Gayangos; and the supplementary vol., 1513–42, by Garrett Mattingly; vol. viii, 1545–6 by M. A. S. Hume; vol. ix, 1547–9, by M. A. S. Hume and Royall Tyler; vols. x–xiii, 1550–8 by Royall Tyler. 13 vols. and 2 supplements. Lond. 1862–1954.
Vols. i–viii not always accurately edited or thorough in coverage. Calendar includes material from Brussels and elsewhere, as well as from Simancas.

868 CALENDAR OF STATE PAPERS, SPANISH, ELIZABETH. By M. A. S. Hume. 4 vols. Lond. 1892–9.
Very incomplete and too often careless. Should be supplemented by 870, 4929, and 923.

869 CLIFFORD, HENRY. The life of Jane Dormer, duchess of Feria. . . .
By J. Stevenson. Lond. 1887.
Jane Dormer, wife of Spanish ambassador to England under Mary. Clifford was Jane
Dormer's servant. Cf. her life in *D.N.B.* (9).

870 COLECCIÓN DE DOCUMENTOS INÉDITOS para la historia de
España. By M. F. Navarrete, Miguel Salvá, Pedro Sainz de Baranda, el
Marqués de la Fuensanta del Valle, *et al.* 112 vols. Madrid, 1842–95.
A collection of letters, and other original sources on Spanish history, taken from various
Spanish archives (principally Simancas). They deal chiefly with the sixteenth century,
and are preponderantly concerned with foreign affairs. There is much of incidental
value for English history to be found in vols. i, iii, xiv, lxxix, and lxxxi; and vols. lxxxvii,
lxxxix, xc, xci, and xcii are exclusively devoted to the correspondence between Philip II
and his ambassadors in England from 1558 to 1584, and contain the original text of
many letters, not invariably complete, in vols. i–iii of the *Spanish Calendar* (868).
   Index vols. published separately in 1885 and 1892 have been supplanted by *Catálogo
de la colección de documentos inéditos . . .* by Julian Paz, 2 vols., Madrid, 1930–1.
   A new edition of the *Documentos inéditos*, published by the duke of Alba and others (10
vols., Madrid, 1936–55) includes 2 vols. (vii and viii) devoted to treaties which contains
much on England, mostly printed in Rymer (88), Gairdner (396, 398), and elsewhere.
   The first 5 vols. of the *Nueva colección de documentos inéditos para la historia de España*
(6 vols., Madrid, 1892–6, by Francisco de Zabálburu and José Sancho de Rayon) contain the correspondence of Luíc de Requesens and Juan de Zúñiga with Philip II and
Granvelle between 1 Jan. and 7 Oct. 1574, and shed much light on English affairs.

871 COLLECTION DES VOYAGES DES SOUVERAINS DES PAY-BAS.
By L. P. Gachard and Charles Piot. 4 vols. Brussels, 1874–82.
Documents on Spanish marriage negotiations (1553–4) in vol. iv, app., pp. 83–453.

872 A DECLARATION OF THE CAUSES moving the Quenes Majestie . . .
to send a navy to the seas for the defense of the realmes against the king of
Spaines forces. Lond. 1596; repr. in *Somers Tracts* (296), i, 464–5.
The official explanation of the expedition under Essex and Howard against Spain.
Versions of this statement in Dutch, German, and Italian appeared also in 1596, and
a French version in 1597.

873 FOURQUEVAUX, M. DE. Dépêches. Ambassadeur du roi Charles IX
en Espagne, 1565–72. By l'Abbé Douais. 2 vols. Douai, 1896–1900.
Useful for Anglo-Spanish relations.

874 GONZÁLES, TOMÁS. Apuntamientos para la historia de Felipe II . . .
y la reina d'Inglaterra. *Memorias de la real academia de la historia,* vii (1832).
An English trans. was edited with an introduction and notes by Spencer Hall (Lond.
1865) under the title of *Documents from Simancas relating to the reign of Elizabeth* (1558–
68). It contains notes and transcripts of dispatches now lost.

875 MACHADO, ROGER. Journals. By James Gairdner. Lond. 1858.
In *Memorials of King Henry the Seventh* (398). French text and English trans. Relates
to an embassy to Spain in 1489, and to two embassies to Britanny in 1490.

876 A MEMORIAL OF LORD BURGHLEY on peace with Spain, 1588.
By W. F. Tilton. *A.H.R.* i (1895), 490–2.
An unpublished document from the B.M., *Cotton MS.*, dated 11 June 1588.

877 MUÑOZ, ANDRÉS. Viaje de Felipe II en Inglaterra. Saragossa, 1554; by
Pascual de Gayangos. *Sociedad de bibliófilos españoles,* no. 15. Madrid, 1877.
Muñoz was an inmate of the royal household, who accompanied Philip II to Corunna,
and got the rest of his story from letters and reports sent back to him.

(b) *Later Works*

The books dealing with English foreign policy in general cited above should be consulted. Several of the works cited in the section on Anglo-French relations contain pertinent material on Anglo-Spanish relations, notably 856, 858, 860, 862. For the reign of Charles V reference should be made to pp. 80 ff. *infra*; for Spanish affairs in Italy and in the Low Countries to pp. 75 ff., 83 ff. *infra*. The introductions to the various vols. of the *Cal. S.P., Spanish* (867–8) are useful though of very unequal value.

878   ALTAMIRA Y CREVEA, RAFAEL. Felipe, hombre de estado. Mexico, 1950.
A judicious essay with elaborate bibliographical apparatus.

879   BALLESTEROS Y BERETTA, ANTONIO. Historia de España. Barcelona, 1922–6.
The standard general history of Spain; extensive critical bibliographies. Vol. iii to 1516; vol. iv to 1700.

880   BINCHY, D. A. An Irish ambassador at the Spanish court, 1569–74. *Studies*, x (1921), 353–74, 573–84; xi (1922), 199–214; xii (1923), 83–105, 461–80; xiii (1924), 115–28; xiv (1925), 102–19.
Deals with Fitzgibbon, Stukely, and other Irishmen in Spain.

881   DEVOS, J. La Poste au service des diplomates espagnols accrédités auprès des cours d'Angleterre et de France, 1555–1598. *Bull. comm. roy. hist.* (Acad. Roy. de Belgique), ciii (1938), 205–67.

881a   DOUSSINAGUE, J. M. La política internacional de Fernando el Católico. Madrid, 1944.

882   FORNERON, HENRI. Histoire de Philippe II. 4 vols. Paris, 1881–2.
The standard life of Philip II, but inaccurate in details.

883   FERNANDEZ ALVAREZ, MANUEL. Felipe II, Isabel de Inglaterra y Marruécos. Madrid, 1951.

884   FERNANDEZ ALVAREZ, MANUEL. Origenes de la rivalidad naval hispano-inglesa en el siglo xvi. *Revista de las Índias*, viii (1947), 311–69.

885   FERNANDEZ ALVAREZ, MANUEL. Tres embajadores de Felipe II en Inglaterra. Madrid, 1951.
A reappraisal of Philip's policy towards England, 1558–68.

886   GIRARD, ALBERT. Note sur les consuls étrangers en Espagne avant le traité des Pyrénées. *Rev. hist. moderne*, n.s., ix (1934), 120–38.
Includes English consuls, 1532–1659.

887   LINNHOFF, LIESELOTTE. Spanische Protestanten und England. Emsdetten, 1934.
Contacts between Spanish and English reformers.

888   MATTINGLY, GARRETT. The reputation of Doctor De Puebla. *E.H.R.* lv (1940), 27–46.
De Puebla was the first resident ambassador in England.

889   HUME, M. A. S. The visit of Philip II. *E.H.R.* vii (1892), 253–80.

890   HUME, M. A. S. Philip II of Spain. Lond. 1897.

891   LAUGHTON, J. K. The Elizabethan naval war with Spain. *Cambr. Mod. Hist.* (20), iii, 294–327.

892   MERRIMAN, R. B. The rise of the Spanish empire. 4 vols. Lond. 1918–34.
Covers the period to 1598. The most scholarly account in English. Good bibliographies. Vol. iv uses unpublished archival material.

893   MOREL-FATIO, A. D. Bernardino de Mendoza. *Bull. hispan.* viii, Bordeaux, 1906.

894   PEARS, EDWIN. The Spanish armada and the Ottoman porte. *E.H.R.* viii (1893), 439–66.
Valuable. Cf. also *Cal. S.P., Venetian* (992), 1581–91, introduction, and *Trans. R.H. Soc.,* 4th ser., v (1922), 1–28. Additional documents are printed in Read (759), iii, 326–32.

895   PRESTAGE, EDGAR. The Anglo-Portuguese alliance. *Trans. R.H. Soc.,* 4th ser., xvii (1934), 69–100.

896   ZURITA, JERÓNIMO. Anales de la corona de Aragón. 6 vols. Saragossa, 1610–11.
The 5th and 6th vols. of this work have the special title, *Historia del Rey Don Hernando el Católico,* and contain the most valuable and detailed account of his foreign policy Zurita was made official chronicler of Aragón in 1548.

4. LOW COUNTRIES

(a) *Sources*

The most important sources are the *Letters and Papers, Henry VIII* (91), and the *Foreign Calendars, Edward VI–Elizabeth* (87), and the *Spanish Calendar* (868–9). For the period 1555–79, Kervyn de Lettenhove (923) is invaluable. For Leicester's expedition, cf. 274, 902, 907, and 909. There is a good deal of pertinent material in 905.
     Cf. *Ancaster MSS.* (97) for Willoughby's services in the Low Countries.

897   ACTES DES ÉTATS GÉNÉRAUX, 1576–85. By L. P. Gachard. 2 vols. Brussels, 1861–6.

898   ALBE, DUC D'. La correspondance sur l'invasion du Comte Louis de Nassau en Frise, en 1568, et les batailles de Heyligerlie et de Gemmingen. By L. P. Gachard. Brussels, 1850.

899   BOOM, G. DE. Documents concernant les relations d'Antoine de Ligne avec Philippe de Beau, Marguerite d'Autriche, Charles-Quint et Henri VIII, roi d'Angleterre. *Bull. comm. roy. hist.* (Acad. Roy. de Belgique), cxv (1950), 383–425.

900 BOR, PIETER. Oorspronck, begin en vervolgh der Nederlandsche oorlogen. 6 parts. Amsterdam, 1595–1601; revised ed. 4 parts, Amsterdam, 1679–84.
Prints many dispatches from Dutch envoys in England.

901 CORRESPONDANCE INÉDITE DE ROBERT DUDLEY, comte de Leycester, et de François et Jean Hotman. By P. J. Blok. Haarlem, 1911.
Valuable for Anglo-Dutch relations, 1582–1613, particularly for Leicester's intrigues with Dutch factions.

902 CORRESPONDENTIE VAN ROBERT DUDLEY, graaf van Leycester, en endere documenten betreffende zijn gouvernement-generaal in de neder-lander, 1585–8. By H. Brugmans. 3 vols. *Werken van het hist. Genootschap*, 3rd ser., lvi–lviii (1931).
Particularly valuable for material from Dutch archives. Cf. also P. T. Harmse van Haren, *Over enige niet-gedateerde brieven in de correspondentie van Leicester. Bijdragen voor de gesch. der Neder.* ii (1948), 78–83.

903 A DECLARATION OF THE CAUSES moving the queene of England to give aid to the defence of . . . the Lowe Countries. Lond. 1585.
The official statement of Elizabeth's reasons for assisting the Dutch in 1585. Repr. in *Somers Tracts* (296), i, 410–18. Versions of this statement in Latin, French, Dutch, German, and Italian also appeared in 1585.

904 DOCUMENTS INÉDITS relatifs à l'histoire du xvie siècle. By J. M. B. C. Baron Kervyn de Lettenhove. Brussels, 1883.
Chiefly on relations between Dutch rebels, England and France, 1568–84. Useful, though most of the documents included are in print elsewhere.

905 DOCUMENTS CONCERNANT LES RELATIONS entre le duc d'Anjou et les Pays-Bas. By P. L. Muller and A. Diegerick. 5 vols. *Werken van het hist. Genootschap*, n.s., li, lv, lvii, lx, lxi (1889–99).
Valuable for Elizabeth's relations with the duc d'Alençon and the Low Countries, 1576–84.

906 DORP, JONKHEER AREND VAN. Brieven en onuitgegeven stukken. By J. B. J. N. Ridder de van der Schueren. 2 vols. *Werken van het hist. Genootschap*, n.s., xliv, l (1887–8).
Correspondence and memoranda of a supporter of William the Silent, largely about military and diplomatic affairs, 1572–85.

907 DUDLEY, ROBERT, earl of Leicester. Correspondence during his government of the Low Countries in the years 1585 and 1586. By John Bruce. *Camden Soc.* xxvii (1844).
A valuable collection of documents upon Leicester's first visit to the Low Countries. Reprints the contents of a vol. of transcripts (*Ouvry MSS.*) and numerous state papers from the *Cotton MSS.* and the *Harleian MSS.* in the B.M. Aims to present 'a complete view of the correspondence between the earl and the English government', but has omitted several letters preserved in the P.R.O.
A number of documents pertinent to Leicester's government in the Low Countries are printed in *Kronijk van het hist. Genootschap*, xxii (1866), 279 ff.

908 FARNÈSE, ALEXANDRE, prince de Parme. Correspondance avec Philippe II, dans les années 1578, 1579, 1580 et 1581. By L. P. Gachard. Brussels, 1853.
Pt. i. No more published. Some of Parma's later correspondence is printed in 909.

909 GRANVELLE, CARDINAL. Correspondance (1565–1586). By E. Poullet and Charles Piot. 12 vols. Brussels, 1878–96.
Contains the cardinal's later correspondence. Valuable appendices containing some of the correspondence of prince of Parma with Philip II and documents (vol. xii) relative to secret negotiations for peace between Parma and Elizabeth, 1586–8. Cf. 910 for earlier correspondence.

910 GRANVELLE, CARDINAL. Papiers d'état. By Charles Weiss. 9 vols. Paris, 1841–52. In *Collection de documents inédits sur l'histoire de France.*
For Granvelle's later correspondence, cf. 909.

911 GUILLAUME LE TACITURNE. Correspondance. By L. P. Gachard. 6 vols. Brussels, 1847–57.
Correspondentie van Willem den Eerste, prins van Orange, 1551–1561, by N. Japikse, The Hague, 1934.

912 HOTMAN, JEAN. Brieven over het Leycestersche tijdvak uit die papieren van J. H. By R. Broersma and G. Busken Huet. *Bijdragen en Mededeelingen van het hist. Genootschap,* xxxiv (1913).
A valuable collection.

913 MARGUERITE D'AUTRICHE, duchesse de Parme. Correspondance avec Philippe II. By L. P. Gachard. 3 vols. Brussels, 1867–81.
One of a ser. entitled *Correspondances françaises des gouverneurs généraux des Pay-Bas avec Philippe II.* Continued in *Correspondance française de Marguerite d'Autriche, duchesse de Parma, avec Philippe II,* by J. S. Thiessen, vol. i, 1565–7; ii, Supplement, 1565–6, by H. A. E. van Gilden; iii, Supplement, 1566–8, *Werken van het hist. Genootschap,* 3rd ser., xlvii, lxxiv, lxxv (1925–42). Cf. also *Correspondance de Marguerite d'Autriche et ses ambassadeurs à la cour de France concernant l'exécution du traité de Cambrai, 1529–30,* by G. de Boom, *Comm. roy. d'histoire,* Brussels, 1935.

914 METEREN, E. VAN. Historie der nederlandsche ende haerder naburen oorlogen en geschiedenissen. Delft, 1599; rev. 1609; best ed. 1611; 1614.
The ed. of 1611 incorporated the last revisions of the author; the ed. of 1614 was revised under government supervision and is less trustworthy. Van Meteren was consul in London. Interesting details on commercial and diplomatic relations with England.

915 METEREN, E. VAN EN BOR, PIETER, Brieven van. By Z. W. Sneller. *Bijdragen en Mededeelingen van het hist. Genootschap,* lvi (1935), 261–81.
Notes and letters from London and elsewhere, 1592–9.

916 MONDOUCET, CLAUDE DE, résident de France aux Pays-Bas, 1571–4. Lettres et négociations. By L. Didier. 2 vols. *Trans. Acad. Reims,* lxxxvi, xc (1891–2).

917 OLDENBARNEVELDT, JOHAN VAN. Gedenkstukken. By M. L. van Deventer. 3 vols. The Hague, 1862.
Prints letters of Caron, agent of the Dutch estates in England.

918 OLDENBARNEVELDT, JOHAN VAN. Bescheiden betreffende zijn Staatkundigheid en zijn familie. By S. P. Haak. *Rijks Geschiedkundige Publicatiën,* lxxx. The Hague, 1934.

919 ORANGE-NASSAU, MAISON D'. Archives ou correspondance inédite. By G. Groen van Prinsterer. Première série, 10 vols. Leiden, 1835–47; deuxième série, 6 vols. Utrecht, 1857–62.
Valuable for Anglo-Dutch relations, 1560–1603. The 1st ser. and vols. i and ii of the 2nd ser. deal with the Elizabethan period.

920 PHILIPPE II. Correspondance sur les affaires des Pays-Bas. By L. P. Gachard. 5 vols. Brussels, 1848–79. 2nd. part. By Joseph Lefèvre. 3 vols. (in progress). Brussels, 1940–56.
The first part goes as far as 1577, the second part, 1577–91.

921 RAPPORT VAN DE NEDERLANDSCHE GEZANTEN, in 1585 naar Engeland gezonden om hulp te bekomen het ontzet van Antwerpen en een braktaat voor te dragen. *Kronijk van het hist. Genootschap*, xxii (1866), 215–77.
Report of a Dutch embassy sent to England in 1585 to secure relief for beleaguered Antwerp.

922 RELATIONS INÉDITES D'AMBASSADEURS VÉNITIENS dans les Pays-Bas sous Philippe II et Albert et Isabelle. By Gustave Hagemans. Brussels, 1865.
Extract from *Annales de l'Académie d'Archéologie de Belgique.*

923 RELATIONS POLITIQUES DES PAYS-BAS et de l'Angleterre sous le règne de Philippe II. By J. M. B. C. Baron Kervyn de Lettenhove and L. Gilliodts van Severen. 11 vols. Brussels, 1882–1900. In *Collection de chroniques belges inédites.*
A collection of unpublished documents from English, Spanish, Flemish, and other archives dealing with the diplomatic relations between England and the Low Countries. Unfinished. Covers period 1555–79. By far the most valuable collection of sources upon relations between England and the Low Countries for the period covered.

924 RESOLUTIËN DER STATEN GENERAAL van 1575 to 1609. By N. Japikse. *Rijkgeschiedkundige Publicatiën*, xxvi, xxxiii, xli, xliii, xlvii, li, lv, lvii, lxii, lxxi (1915–30), xcii (1950). Completed through 1603.

925 STUKKEN VOOR DE GESCHIEDENIS DER JAREN 1588–1595. *Kronijk van het hist. Genootschap*, xvi–xxi (1860–5), passim.

926 VERBAAL VAN DE LEGATIE VAN LEONINUS, van Loozen, Valcke en Frankena naar Engeland, in 1596. *Kronijk van het hist. Genootschap*, xxii (1866), 317–83.
The report of a Dutch embassy sent to England in 1596.

927 WILLIAMS, ROGER. The actions of the Lowe Countries. Lond. 1618; repr. in *Somers Tracts* (296), i, 329–82.
Treats of the Dutch wars from 1568 to 1576. Valuable as written by an English officer present in the Low Countries, particularly for the action of the English volunteers under Morgan. A seventeenth-century Dutch translation was published by J. T. B. Nyenhaus in 1864 under the title *Memoriën van Roger Williams*, in *Werken . . . hist. Genootschap*, n.s., iii (1864).

(b) *Later Works*

The relations of England with the Low Countries before 1555 form part of her relations with the Empire. H. Pirenne, *Histoire de Belgique* (4 vols., Brussels, 1902–11); A. Henne, *Règne de Charles Quint en Belgique* (10 vols., Brussels, 1858–60); and 933 are most useful for background. On Anglo-Dutch relations, 1555–1603, in addition to the books cited below, Pollard (363) and Froude (340) and Black (671) give good accounts. Read (759–60) is serviceable for the period 1558–98; Cheyney (690) for the period 1588–1603. Markham (3370) is useful. Motley's account (941) is very full for the period 1585–1603, but to be used with care in the light of Geyl (936). For the intrigues of Leicester in the Low Countries, cf. 1606. On trade relations, cf. pp. 254 ff. *infra.*

928 ALGEMEINE GESCHICHTE DER NEDERLANDEN. Deel V, De Tachtig jahrige Oorlog, 1567–1609. Utrecht, 1952.

929 ANTHEUNIS, LOUIS. Engelsche spionnen op het vasteland onder Elisabeth: Richard Baynes en John Nicholls. Bijd. *Gesch.* xxviii (1937), 219–36.

930 BEIJERMAN, HUGO. Oldenbarneveldt, de Staten van Holland en Leycester in 1585 en 1586. Deventer, 1847.

931 BLACK, J. B. Queen Elizabeth, the Sea Beggars and the capture of Brille, 1572. *E.H.R.* xlvi (1931), 30–47.

932 BLOK, P. J. De Watergeuzen in Engeland (1568–1572). *Bijdragen voor vaderlandsche Geschiedenis,* &c. 3rd ser., ix (The Hague, 1896), 226–63.
Cf. also J. H. Round, *Queen Elizabeth and the beggars of the sea,* in the *Athenæum,* no. 3545 (1895), 455–6.

933 BLOK, P. J. Geschiedenis van het nederlandsche volk. 8 vols. Groningen, 1892–1908; Eng. trans. by O. A. Bierstadt and Ruth Putnam. 5 vols. New York, 1898–1912.
The political narrative is somewhat abridged in the translation.

934 BROERSMA, R. Het tussenbestuur in het Leycestersche tijdvak. Goes, 1899.
Inadequate.

935 BRUGMANS, H. Engeland en de Nederlanden, 1558–76. Groningen, 1892.

936 GEYL, PIETER. Revolt of the Netherlands. Lond. 1932, 1958.

937 KERNKAMP, J. H. De handel van de Republiek in betrekking tot de diplomatie der groote Mogendheden in het jaar 1596. Bijd. *Vaderlandsche Gesch.,* reihe 7, iv (1934), 175–84.
The commerce of the Republic in relation to the diplomacy of the great powers in 1596

938 KERVYN DE LETTENHOVE, J. M. B. C. BARON. Les Huguenots et les gueux. . . . (1560–1585). 6 vols. Bruges, 1883–5.
Useful for relations of Elizabeth with French Huguenots and Dutch rebels, but very inaccurate in details.

939 LEMAN, AUGUSTE. Henry VIII et la neutralité des Pays-Bas en 1513. *Bull. Comm. Flamand,* 1938 (1939), 151–61.

940 MOTLEY, J. L. The rise of the Dutch republic. 3 vols. Lond. 1855.
Many later eds. Covers period to 1584.

941 MOTLEY, J. L. History of the United Netherlands from the death of William the Silent to the synod of Dort. 4 vols. Lond. 1860–7.
Many later eds. Contains fullest account of Anglo-Dutch relations, 1584–1609.

942 NEALE, J. E. Elizabeth and the Netherlands, 1586–7. *E.H.R.* xlv (1930), 373–96.
Deals with the financing of Leicester's expedition. Scholarly.

943 RACHFAHL, F. Wilhelm von Oranien und der niederländische Aufstand. 2 vols. Halle, 1906–8.
The standard life of Orange to 1569.

943a READ, CONYERS. Queen Elizabeth's seizure of the Duke of Alva's pay-ships. *Journ. of Mod. Hist.* v (1933), 443–64.

944 RENSON, G. De diplomatieke zending in Engeland van Frederik Perrenot, heer van Champagney (Jan, 1575–31 Maart, 1576). *Rev. Belge Philol. Hist.* xxvii (1949), 85–106.

945 RICHARDSON, W. C. Stephen Vaughan, financial agent of Henry VIII: a study of financial relations with the Low Countries. *Louis. State Univ. Stud.* iii, Baton Rouge, 1953.

946 ROGERS, E. F. Sir John Hackett, Henry VIII's ambassador in Malines *Med. et Hum.* vi (1950), 89–100.

947 STIRLING-MAXWELL, WILLIAM. Don John of Austria. 2 vols Lond. 1883.
Useful for English relations with the Low Countries, 1577–8. Cf. 948.

948 TÖRNE, P. O. DE. Don Juan d'Autriche et les projets de conquête de l'Angleterre . . . 1568–78. 2 vols. Helsingfors, 1915–28.
Scholarly.

948a WERNHAM, R. B. Mission of Thos. Wilkes to the United Provinces in 1590. *Studies presented to Sir Hilary Jenkinson*, Oxf. 1957, pp. 423–55.

5. THE HOLY ROMAN EMPIRE
(a) *Sources*

In general, cf. Dahlmann-Waitz (21). For Charles V, cf. Merriman (892), iii. *The Letters and Papers, Henry VIII* (91) and the *Cal. S.P., Foreign, Edward VI–Elizabeth* (87), are the most valuable sources on Anglo-German relations. Some material of importance is in Weiss (910). On trade relations, cf. pp. 254 ff. *infra*.

948b ASCHAM, ROGER. A report of the affairs and state of Germany. Lond. 1570; in *English Works of Roger Ascham*. Lond. 1904.
Written in 1558.

949 BRETT, JOHN A narration of the pursuit of English refugees in Germany under Queen Mary. By I. S. Leadam. *Trans. R.H. Soc.*, 2nd ser., xi (1897), 113–31.
A contemporary account, by a royal messenger, of a mission in the Empire in the years 1556–7.

950 BRIEFE UND AKTENSTÜCKE ZUR GESCHICHTE MAXIMILIAN I. By J. Chmel, Stuttgart, 1845.

951 BRIEFE DES PFALZGRAFEN JOHANN CASIMIR, mit verwandten Schriftstücken. By Friedrich von Bezold. 2 vols. Munich, 1882–4.
Covers the years 1576–86. Valuable for Elizabeth's dealings with Casimir in behalf of Dutch and French Protestants.

952 BRIEFE FRIEDRICH DES FROMMEN, Kurfürsten von der Pfalz, mit verwandten Schriftstücken. By August Kluckhohn. 2 vols. in 3 parts. Brunswick, 1868–72.
Covers the years 1559–76. Valuable for Elizabeth's dealings with the Palatinate in behalf of the French Huguenots.

953 BRIEFWECHSEL LANDGRAF PHILIPPS DES GROSSMÜTHI-
GEN von Hessen mit Bucer. By Max Lenz. 3 vols. Leipzig, 1880–91.
Publicationen aus den königlichen preußischen Staatsarchiven, Nr. 358. Important for
Anglo-Lutheran negotiations in the time of Henry VIII.

954 HUBATSCH, WALTHER. Europäische Briefe im Reformationszeitalter.
200 Briefe an Markgraf Albrecht von Brandenburg-Ansbach, Herzog in
Preußen. Kitzingen, 1949.

956 NUNTIATURBERICHTE AUS DEUTSCHLAND. Erste Abtheilung,
1533–59. By W. Friedensburg (vols. i–iv, viii–xi), L. Cordauns (vols. v–vii),
and G. Kupke (vol. xii). 12 vols. Gotha, 1892–1910. Zweite Abtheilung,
1560–72. By S. Steinherz and I. P. Dengel. 5 vols. Vienna, 1897–1926.
Dritte Abtheilung, 1572–85. By Joseph Hansen and K. Schnellhass. 5 vols.
Berlin, 1894–1909.

957 NUNTIATURBERICHTE AUS DEUTSCHLAND, 1585–90. By S.
Ehses, A. Meister, R. Reichenberger and J. Schweizer. 2 vols. in 5 parts.
Paderborn, 1895–1919.
These series of reports from papal agents in Germany contain scattered information
on Anglo-German relations.

959 QUEEN ELIZABETH AND SOME FOREIGNERS. By Victor von
Klarwill. Trans. T. N. Nash. Lond. 1928.
Prints 69 letters from Vienna archives, bearing chiefly upon marriage negotiations
between Elizabeth and the Archduke Charles. Carelessly edited.

960 SLEIDANUS or PHILIPPSON, JOANNES. Commentariorum de
statu religionis, reipublicae, carolo quinto Caesare, libri xxvi. Straßburg,
1555; by T. G. Boehme. 3 vols. Frankfort, 1785–6.
Valuable for Anglo-Lutheran negotiations temp. Henry VIII and Edward VI. An
English trans. with a continuation to 1563 was published by E. Bohun in London in
1689.

961 VENETIANISCHE DEPESCHEN VOM KAISERHOF. By I. Stich,
G. Turba, and A. F. Pribram. 3 vols. Vienna, 1889–95.
Covers the period 1538–76, with some seventeenth-century material. Contains many
papers of importance upon English relations with Germany not noticed in *Cal. S.P.,
Venetian* (992).

(b) *Later Works*

The best general histories of the empire are Egelhaaf (969) and Ritter (978).
On trade relations, cf. pp. 260 ff. *infra.* On special topics, cf. 709, 856, 858.

962 ARMSTRONG, EDWARD. The emperor Charles V. 2 vols. Lond.
1902; 1913.
Useful for English foreign affairs, particularly during the period of the Divorce, and
again for Edward VI, Lady Jane Grey, and the first year of Mary.

963 BASKERVILL, C. R. William Lily's verse for the entry of Charles V into
London [1522]. *Hunt. Lib. Bull.* no. ix (1936), 1–14.

964   BEHRENS, BETTY. The office of the English resident ambassador: its evolution as illustrated by the career of Sir Thomas Spinelly, 1509–22. *Trans. R.H. Soc.*, 4th ser., xvi (1933), 161–95.

965   BIHL, JOSEP. Württemberg und England im Zeitalter der Königin Elisabeth (1588–1603). *Württemberg. Viertelj. Landesgesch.* xlii (1936), 107–58.

966   BRANDI, KARL. Kaiser Karl V. 2 vols. Munich, 1937. Eng. trans., Lond. 1939.
Vol. ii contains documentation of great value, omitted from the Eng. trans

967   BUSCH, WILHELM. Cardinal Wolsey und die kaiserlich-englische Allianz, 1522–1525. Bonn, 1886.

968   BUSCH, WILHELM. Drei Jahre englischer Vermittlungspolitik: 1518–1521. Bonn, 1884.
Valuable.

969   EGELHAAF, G. Deutsche Geschichte im XVI Jahrhundert bis zum 1555. 2 vols. Stuttgart, 1889–92.
The most useful general account of the period.

970   HEIDRICH, PAUL. Der geldrische Erbfolgstreit. Kassel, 1896.
A brief monograph: important for the negotiations for the marriage of Henry VIII and Anne of Cleves.

971   HEPPE, H. L. J. Geschichte des deutschen Protestantismus in den Jahren 1555–1581. 4 vols. Marburg, 1852–9.
Useful for Elizabeth's relations with German protestant princes and for her various attempts to form a league with them.

972   KENNEDY, W. P. M. The imperial embassy of 1553–4 and Wyatt's rebellion. *E.H.R.* xxxviii (1923), 251–8.

973   MATTINGLY, GARRETT. A Humanist ambassador. *Jour. Mod. Hist.* iv (1932), 175–85.
Eustache Chapuys, ambassador of Charles V to England 1529–45.

974   MEYER, A. O. Die englische Diplomatie in Deutschland zur Zeit Eduards VI und Mariens. Breslau, 1900.

975   MÜLLER, ALBERT. Die Beziehungen Heinrichs VIII zu Anna von Cleve. Calw, 1907.

976   NIRRNHEIM, HANS. Hamburgs Gesandtschaft an König Heinrich VIII von England im Jahre 1534. *Z. d. Ver. f. Hamb. Gesch.* xl (1949), 26–62.

977   PRUESER, F. England und die Schmalkaldener, 1535–40. Leipzig, 1929.
A detailed study of the negotiations between Henry VIII and the German protestant princes.

978   RITTER, M. Deutsche Geschichte im Zeitalter der Gegenreformation und des dreißigjährigen Krieges (1555–1648). 3 vols. in 4 parts. Stuttgart, 1889–1908.
The best general account of the period.

979   SCHLOSSBERGER, A. Verhandlungen über die beabsichtigte Vermählung des Erzherzogs Karl von Österreich mit der Königin Elizabeth von England. *Forschungen zur deutschen Geschichte*, v, pt. i. Göttingen, 1865.

980 SCHNEEWIND, W. Die diplomatischen Beziehungen England mit der alten Eidgenossenschaft zur Zeit Elisabeth, Jakobs I., und Karl I., 1558–1649. *Basler Beitr. zur Geschichtswiss.* Fasc. 36 (1950).

981 SINGER, F. P. Die Beziehungen des Schmalkaldischen Bundes zu England im Jahre 1539. Greifswald, 1901.

982 STERN, ALFRED. Heinrich VIII und der Schmalkaldische Bund 1540. *Forschungen zur deutschen Geschichte*, x, 491–507. Göttingen, 1870.

983 ULMANN, HEINRICH. Englische Vermittlung im Jahre 1521. *Hist. Zeitschrift*, xxv (1871), 272–302.

984 ULMANN, HEINRICH. Kaiser Maximilian I. 2 vols. Stuttgart, 1891.
The standard life of Maximilian. Valuable for the foreign policy of Henry VII and early Henry VIII.

985 UNDREINER, G. J. Robert Wingfield. Erster ständiger englischer Gesandter am deutschen Hofe, 1464–1539. Fribourg, 1932.

986 WAITZ, GEORG. Lübeck unter Jürgen Wullenwever. 3 vols. Berlin, 1855.
Useful for Anglo-German relations in the early 1530's.

987 WERTHEIMER, EDUARD. Heiratsverhandlungen zwischen Elizabeth von England und Erzherzog Karl von Österreich, 1559–61. *Hist. Zeitschrift*, xl (1878), 385–432.

988 WURM, C. F. Die politischen Beziehungen Heinrichs VIII zu Marcus Meyer und Jürgen Wullenwever. Hamburg, 1852.

6. ITALY

English relations with Italy in the sixteenth century were of no great political importance. They were chiefly (1) commercial, principally with Venice, and to some extent with Florence; (2) religious, with the Papacy at Rome; (3) cultural. In these aspects Anglo-Italian relations are dealt with in chs. vi, vii, and x, *infra*.

(a) *Sources*

In addition to the *Letters and Papers, Henry VIII* (91) and the *Cal. S.P., Foreign, Edward VI–Elizabeth* (87) by far the most important source is the *Cal. S.P., Venetian* (992). Cf. also 4154, 4159.

989 ALBÈRI, EUGENIO. Relazioni degli ambasciatori veneti al senato durante il secolo decimo sesto. 15 vols. Florence, 1839–63.
Vols. i–vi of this great collection contain the reports which refer wholly or in part to England, and were separately issued in an *édition de luxe* in 1852.

990 CALENDAR OF STATE PAPERS, MILAN (1385–1618). By A. B. Hinds. Lond. 1912
Materials principally from state archives and Ambrosian library. Archive material chiefly for Sforza period, 1450–1535. Some material on English Roman Catholics temp. Elizabeth.

991   CALENDAR OF STATE PAPERS, ROME. Vol. i, Elizabeth, 1558–71; vol. ii, 1572–8. By J. M. Rigg. Lond. 1916–26.

Vol. i material scant because of strained relations between English and Roman governments. Fuller on relations between Mary, queen of Scots and Rome. (Cf. 5195.) Vol. ii contains much detailed information on relations of England with Spain and the Papacy. For a mission to Rome under Mary, cf. *Hardwicke papers* (280), i, 62–102.

992   CALENDAR OF STATE PAPERS, VENETIAN. Vols. i–ix, 1202–1603. By Rawdon Brown, Cavendish Bentinck, and Horatio Brown. Lond. 1864–98.

Especially valuable for the early part of the reign of Henry VIII and for Edward VI and Mary. Generally of slight value for Elizabeth's reign, but contains important material on Anglo-Turkish relations, 1583 ff. The introductions to the various volumes are excellent.

Dispatches from Venetian ambassadors at other European courts often contain English material. For those from France, cf. Hauser (23); for those from Germany, cf. 961; for those from the Low Countries, Pirenne (25).

993   CANESTRINI, G., and DESJARDINS, A. Négociations diplomatiques de la France avec la Toscane. 5 vols. Paris, 1865–75. In *Documents inédits sur l'histoire de France*.

Contains scattered material on Anglo-Tuscan and Anglo-French relations.

994   MICHELI (MICHIEL), GIOVANNI. Les dépêches de G. Michiel, ambassadeur de Venise en Angleterre pendant les années de 1554 à 1557, déchiffrées et publiées d'après les documents conservés aux archives nationales de Venise. By Paul Friedmann. Venice, 1869.

Valuable preface. L. Pasini published 36 pages of *Rettificazione ed aggiunte*, Venice, 1896.

(b) *Later Works*

England's direct political contacts with Italy during the sixteenth century were not close, but in the reign of Henry VII the relations were mainly commercial. They are well covered in Busch (406). For the reign of Henry VIII, Anglo-Italian relations are involved in the relations with the Empire and with France. For Italian influence on English political thinking associated chiefly with Machiavelli, cf. ch. iv *infra*, notably nos. 1468, 1477; 3576.

English relations with the Papacy are covered in ch. vi *infra*. Reference should also be made to the literature dealing with Henry VIII's first divorce (ch. ii *supra*). In addition to the general histories of the Papacy by Pastor and Ranke, Hübner's *Sixte Quint*, 3 vols., Leipzig, 1870; Brosch, *Geschichte des Kirchenstaates*, 2 vols., Gotha, 1880–2; P. Herre, *Papsttum und Papstwahl im Zeitalter Philipps II*, Leipzig, 1907, are useful for background.

Venetian relations are best covered in the introductions to the *Cal. S.P., Venetian* (992).

995   BALZANI, UGO. Un' ambasciata inglese a Roma; Enrico VII ad Innocenzo VIII: anno 1487. Rome, 1879.

Cf. *Edin. Rev.*, clix (1884), 256–63.

996   BASCHET, ARMAND. La diplomatie vénétienne. Les princes de l'Europe au xvi⁰ siècle . . . d'après les rapports des ambassadeurs vénétiens. . . . Paris, 1862.

Some facts about Elizabeth.

997 BEHRENS, BETTY. Origins of the office of English resident ambassador in Rome. *E.H.R.* xlix (1934), 640–56.

998 BONDIOLI, P. La battaglia di Marignano in una relazione a Enrico VIII d'Inghilterra, *Scritti storici e giuridici in memoria di Alessandro Visconti*. Milan, 1955, pp. 169–85.

999 GARRETT, C. H., and TOYNBEE, M. R. Tudor and Stuart relations with Savoy. *Times Lit. Supp.*, 16 Sept. 1939, 544.

1000 ROTH, C. England and the last Florentine republic 1527–30. *E.H.R.* xl (1925), 174–95.

7. OTHER COUNTRIES

1001 ANDERSSON, INGVAR. Erik XIV: s engelska underhandlingar. Studier i svensk diplomati och handelspolitik. *Skrifter utg. av Vetenskaps-Societeten i Lund.* xvii, Lund, 1935.
The English negotiations of Erik XIV of Sweden.

1002 BABINGER, FRANZ. Sherliana. 1. Sir Anthony Sherley's persische Botschaftsreise (1599–1601), 2. Sir Anthony Sherley's marokkanische Sendung (1605–6). Berlin, 1932.

1003 BURIAN, ORHAN. Interest of the English in Turkey as reflected in English literature of the Renaissance. *Oriens*, v (1952), 209–29.

1004 BURIAN, ORHAN. The report of Lello, third English ambassador to the Sublime Porte. *Ankara Univ., Dil. Tar. Cogr, Fak, Yayinl.* lxxxiii; *Ing. Dil. Edeb. Enstit.* iii, Ankara, 1952.

1005 FISHER, S. N. The foreign relations of Turkey, 1481–1512. *Illinois Studies in the Soc. Sc.* xxx, no. i (1948).

1006 JASNOWSKI, JOZEF. England and Poland in the sixteenth and seventeenth centuries. *Polish Science and Learning*, vii, Lond. 1948.

1007 KIRCHNER, WALTHER. England and Denmark, 1558–1588. *Jour. Mod. Hist.* xvii (1945), 1–15.

1008 MEWS, SIEGFRIED. Ein englischer Gesandtschaftsbericht über den polnischen Staat zu Ende des 16. Jahrhunderts. *Deutsch. und der Osten, Quellen und Forschungen zur Geschichte ihrer Beziehungen*, bd. 3. Leipzig, 1936.
An account of Poland by Sir George Carew in 1598.

1009 ODLOŽILIK, OTAKAR. Karel of Žerotín and the English court, 1564–1636. *Slavonic Rev.* xv (1937), 413–25.
A page at the English court c. 1585.

1010 SZUMSKA, URSZULA. Anglia a Polska w epoce humanizmu i reformacji. *Prace historyczno-kulturalne pod redakcija Stanislawa Lempickiego*, v. Lwów, 1938.
Cultural contacts of England and Poland.

1011 VAUGHAN, DOROTHY. Europe and the Turk, 1350–1700. Liverpool, 1954.

III

CONSTITUTIONAL HISTORY, 1485–1603

1. GENERAL WORKS

(a) *Sources*

The great mass of the sources on constitutional history fall under special classifications given below. The *Statutes* (1016) and the *Proclamations* (1017) contain important material upon virtually every phase of English life. Smith (1015) is the only contemporary account of the English government, but there is much in Coke (1532). Tanner (1018) is the best selected collection of documents. Pollard (400) prints much constitutional material for the reign of Henry VII.

1012 A BOOKE CONTAINING ALL SUCH PROCLAMATIONS as were published during the raigne of the late Queen Elizabeth. By Humphrey Dyson. Lond. 1618.

An extensive, though not quite complete, collection of Elizabeth's proclamations. The 3 extant copies of this book are in the Bodleian library, the Lambeth palace library, and the Grenville library at the B.M. The 3rd is the most complete. Cf. Jackson, W. A., *Humphrey Dyson and his collections of Elizabethan proclamations, Harvard Lib. Bull.* i (1947), 76–89.

1013 A COLLECTION OF CURIOUS DISCOURSES written by eminent antiquaries upon several heads on our English antiquities. By Thomas Hearne. Lond. 1720; with additions, 2 vols., Lond. 1775.

Contains many treatises of the late sixteenth and early seventeenth centuries upon law and the administration of justice, legal officials, the inns of courts, the court of Star Chamber, English money, divisions of land, &c.

1014 SELECT STATUTES AND OTHER DOCUMENTS illustrative of the reigns of Elizabeth and James I. By G. W. Prothero. Oxf. 1894; 1898.

The introduction contains a survey, now somewhat antiquated, of the Elizabethan and early Jacobean constitution.

1015 SMITH, THOMAS. De republica Anglorum, or a discourse on the commonwealth of England. Lond. 1583; best ed. by L. Alston, Cambr. 1906.

Four eds. appeared before 1600 and seven more by 1640. Smith borrowed from Harrison (615) as Harrison borrowed from Smith. The only contemporary account of the English government. Of some importance also in the history of English political theory.

1016 STATUTES OF THE REALM. By A. Luders, T. E. Tomlins, J. Raithby *et al.* 11 vols. Lond. 1810–28.

The most nearly complete collection of the statutes to 1713 and the only ed. to be consulted for historical purposes. For earlier eds. cf. vol. i, introduction, and app. A; for sixteenth-century eds. cf. Beale (1480), ch. i.

1017 TUDOR AND STUART PROCLAMATIONS, 1485–1714. By Robert Steele. 2 vols. Oxf. 1910.

Published under the direction of the earl of Crawford and originally as part of the *Bibliotheca Lindesiana*. Lists virtually every extant proclamation in chronological order with a brief summary of its contents. Vol. i, England and Wales; vol. ii, Scotland and

Ireland. Contains a series of reproductions of the royal arms. The introduction is useful and contains the text *in extenso* of the Irish *Modus tenendi parliamentum*.

The Society of Antiquaries possesses a valuable collection of proclamations, noticed from time to time in its *Proceedings*. Some of these for the reigns of Henry VII–Mary were published by the Society in facsimile, Oxf. 1897.

1018   TUDOR CONSTITUTIONAL DOCUMENTS, 1485–1603. By J. R Tanner. Cambr. 1922.
Well selected. The sectional introductions are scholarly.

(b) *Later Works*

The most important of the general constitutional histories are given in Gross (1), 121–4. Tanner's (1018) introductions are valuable for the whole period. Perhaps the best general account is in Holdsworth (1544), vol. iv. Cheyney (690) contains the best account of the Elizabethan constitution. Keir (1028) is useful.

1019   ANSON, W. R. Law and custom of the constitution. 2 vols. Oxf. 1886–92; 1907–9.
Deals with the modern English constitution, but gives some serviceable historical background.

1020   ADAIR, E. R. The statute of proclamations. *E.H.R.* xxxii (1917), 34–46.

1021   CAM, H. M. The decline and fall of English feudalism. *History,* xxv (1940), 216–33.

1022   DUNHAM, W. H. Lord Hastings' Indentured Retainers 1461–83. *Trans. Connect. Acad. A. and S.* xxxix (1955), 1–175.

1023   ELTON, G. R. The Tudor Revolution in government. Cambr. 1953.
Important and controversial interpretation of Thomas Cromwell's administrative reforms.

1024   GNEIST, H. R. Englische Verfassungsgeschichte. Berlin, 1882. English trans. by P. A. Ashworth. 2 vols. Lond. 1885; enl. ed., 2 vols., Lond. 1889.

1025   GROSS, CHARLES. Early history of the ballot in England. *A.H.R.* iii (1897), 456–63.
A few paragraphs on the sixteenth century.

1026   HALLAM, HENRY. Constitutional history of England, from the accession of Henry VII to the death of George II. 2 vols. Lond. 1827; 1846.
The numerous subsequent eds. are reprs. of the 1846 ed., the last to be revised by the author. Still of value, though subject to correction on many points.

1027   HURSTFIELD, J. The revival of feudalism in early Tudor England. *History,* xxxvii (1952), 131–45.

1028   KEIR, D. L. The Constitutional history of modern Britain, 1485–1937. Lond. 1938.
Useful. Cf. also Holdsworth (1544), iv.

1029   KOEBNER, RICHARD. 'The Imperial crown of this realm'; Henry VIII, Constantine the Great, and Polydore Vergil. *Bull. Inst. Hist. Research,* xxvi (1953), 29–52.

1030   MAITLAND, F. W. Collected papers. By H. A. L. Fisher. 3 vols. Cambr. 1911.
Essays, chiefly on legal history, most of them repr. from legal and historical jours. *Elizabethan gleanings* (iii, 157–209) are extremely valuable, particularly the paper on Elizabeth's acts of supremacy and uniformity.

1031   MAITLAND, F. W. The constitutional history of England. Lond. 1908.
Printed after the author's death from unrevised lecture notes. Contains an excellent brief section on the Tudor period.

1032   McILWAIN, C. H. Constitutionalism, ancient and modern. Ithaca, 1940; revised ed. 1947.

1033   MOSSE, G. L. Change and continuity in the Tudor constitution. *Speculum*, xxii (1947), 18–28.

1034   PICKTHORN, K. W. M. Early Tudor government. 2 vols. Cambr. 1934. Vol. i, Henry VII; ii, Henry VIII.
Useful, especially vol. i.

1035   THOMAS, J. H. Town government in the sixteenth century. Lond. 1933.
Slight. Cf. also, K. B. Smellie, *A history of local government*, Lond. 1946.

1036   THORNLEY, I. D. The treason legislation of Henry VIII (1531–1534). *Trans. R.H. Soc.*, 3rd ser., xi (1917), 87–124.

2. PARLIAMENT

A. GENERAL

(a) *Sources*

The *Statutes* (1016) and the *Journals* (1037, 1082, 1101) are the most valuable sources. Some of Elizabeth's speeches in Parliament or to delegations from Parliament are printed in *Nugae Antiquae* (289). The full authoritative texts of Elizabeth's speeches in her parliaments are given in Neale (1067). Cf. also 5214.

1037   D'EWES, SIMONDS. The journals of all the parliaments during the reign of Queen Elizabeth, both of the House of Lords and House of Commons, collected by Sir S. D'Ewes, revised and published by P. Bowes. Lond. 1682; 1693.
The most valuable source on the parliaments of Elizabeth; cf. also 1045, 1082, 1101, 1168, 1917.

1038   THE LORD KEEPER'S SPEECH to the parliament of 1592–3. By J. E. Neale. *E.H.R.* xxxi (1916), 128–37.

1039   [PARRY, C. H.] The parliaments and councils of England, chronologically arranged, from the reign of William I to the revolution of 1688. Lond. 1839.
A useful compilation, summarizing *Dugdale's writs*, the *Old parliamentary history*, and the journals of both houses, year by year.

1040   PRYNNE, WILLIAM. Brief register, kalendar and survey of the several kinds of all parliamentary writs. 4 vols. in 3. Lond. 1659.

1041 RETURN OF THE NAME OF EVERY MEMBER of the lower house
of the parliaments of England, Scotland and Ireland . . . 1213–1874. 3 vols.
Parl. papers, 1878, lxii, pts. i–iii.

The fullest list extant, but compiled solely from the extant writs and returns at the
P.R.O. and the Crown office lists, and incomplete. Pt. iii, the index, published in 1888,
contains valuable corrections and additions. A 4th vol., covering later returns published
in *Parl. papers*, lxii, contains further corrections. Cf. also W. W. Bean, *The parliamentary
returns of members of the House of Commons*, Lond. 1883, and *Interim report of the committee on House of Commons personnel and politics* (Cmd. 4130), Lond. 1931–2. A MS.
list of later corrections and additions is in the P.R.O.

1042 ROTULI PARLIAMENTORUM; ut et petitiones et placita in parlia-
mento (1278–1504). 6 vols. s.l., s.a. Index by J. Strachey, J. Pridden, and
E. Upham. Lond. 1832.

Other extracts from the Rolls were printed to supply the deficiencies in the Lords
Journals as late as Mary's first parliament. The MS. rolls, however, continue (in the
P.R.O.) to 49 Victoria—being confined after 1628 to the text of the statutes. Cf. Gross
(1), no. 2010.

1043 THOMAS CROMWELL'S PARLIAMENTARY LISTS. By A. F.
Pollard. *Bull. Inst. Hist. Research*, ix (1931), 31–43.

1044 SHOWER, BARTHOLOMEW. Cases in parliament resolved . . . upon
petitions and writs of error. Lond. 1698; by R. L. Loveland, 1876.

1045 TOWNSHEND, HAYWARD or HEYWOOD. Historical Collections,
an exact account of the last four parliaments of Elizabeth. Lond. 1680.

Townshend entered parliament in 1597; his work covers the period from 4 Feb. 1598 to
19 Dec. 1601. Cf. J. E. Neale, *The authorship of Townshend's 'Historical collections'*,
E.H.R. xxxvi (1921), 96–99; and Pollard's articles on the subject (1104–6).

1046 TWO LISTS SHOWING THE ALTERATIONS that have been made
in the House of Commons [1509–1625]. [By J. Roberts.] Lond. 1719; repr.
in *Somers Tracts* (296), xiii, 742–54.

1047 WILLIS, BROWNE. Notitia parliamentaria, or an history of the
counties, cities and boroughs in England and Wales . . . to which are sub-
joined lists of all the knights, citizens and burgesses. 3 vols. Lond. 1715–50;
vol. i, 1730.

An important authority on parliamentary elections, but full of inaccuracies. The 2nd
ed. of vol. i contains important additions.

(b) *Later Works*

There is no adequate history of parliament in the sixteenth century before 1558.
Pollard (1071) is the best general account. Stubbs (1081) is helpful for Henry
VIII. Neale's studies (1067, 1127) are definitive for Elizabeth. Cheyney (690)
gives some account of parliament during the last fifteen years of Elizabeth's
reign. Holdsworth (1544), iv, 166–90, should be consulted.

1048 ADAIR, E. R., and EVANS, F. M. Writs of assistance from 1558–1700.
E.H.R. xxxvi (1921), 356–72.

Concerns summons to parliament.

1049 AMOS, ANDREW. Observations on the statutes of the reformation
parliament. Lond. 1859.

Useful.

1050　BINDOFF, S. T. Parliamentary history, 1529–1688. In *V.C.H. Wilts.* v (1957), 111–69.
Excellent study of factions and elections in Wiltshire.

1051　CLIFFORD, FREDERICK. A history of private-bill legislation. 2 vols. Lond. 1885–7.

1052　COBBETT, WILLIAM. Parliamentary history of England from the Norman conquest in 1066 to the year 1803. 36 vols. Lond. 1806–20.
A still useful compilation, based upon the older printed sources. Frequently bound as the 1st ser. of *Hansard's debates*.

1053　COTTONI POSTHUMA. By James Howell. Lond. 1657; 1672; 1679.
Contains several studies by Sir Robert Cotton (1571–1631) on the relations of the crown to parliament, notably unique extracts (pp. 53–54) from lost journals of the House of Lords for 12 Henry VII.

1054　ELSYNGE, HENRY. The ancient method and manner of holding parliaments in England. Lond. 1660; 1663; 1675; by Thomas Tyrwhitt, 1768.
Elsynge was clerk of the House of Commons, 1632–48. A learned and able work.

1055　ELSYNGE, HENRY. Expedicio billarum antiquitus: an unpublished chapter of the second book of the manner of holding parliaments in England. By Catherine Strateman Sims. *Studies . . . Hist. of Repres. and Parl. Institutions*, xvi, Louvain, 1951.
Cf. also an article on the same subject by the same editor in *A.H.R.* xlii (1937), 225–43.

1056　ELTON, G. R. Parliamentary drafts, 1529–1540. *Bull. Inst. Hist. Research*, xxv (1952), 117–32.

1057　ELTON, G. R. A further note on parliamentary drafts in the reign of Henry VIII. *Bull. Inst. Hist. Research* xxvii (1954), 198–200.

1058　ELTON, G. R. The evolution of a Reformation statute. *E.H.R.* lxiv (1949), 174–97.

1059　EVANS, E. Of the antiquity of parliaments in England: some Elizabethan and early Stuart opinions. *History*, xxiii (1938), 206–21.

1060　GNEIST, H. R. Das englische Parlament in tausendjährigen Wandelungen. Berlin, 1886. Trans. R. J. Shea, *The English parliament in its transformations through a thousand years*, Lond. 1886; 4th ed. 1895; also trans. A. H. Keane, *The students' history of the English parliament*, Lond. 1887; 4th ed. 1895.
Brief on Tudor period and now rather antiquated.

1061　GREENING LAMBORN, E. A. A parliament roll of 1512. *Notes and Queries*, clxxxviii (1945), 248–50, 275–8; clxxxix (1946), 7–9.

1062　HAKEWEL, WILLIAM. Modus tenendi parliamentum, or the manner of holding parliaments in England. Lond. 1641; 1659; 1671.
The ed. of 1659 was much enlarged and improved, that of 1671 is a repr. Hakewel was a legal antiquary of the seventeenth century. Cf. note by E. Jeffries Davis on ed. of this work used by D'Ewes, in *E.H.R.* xxxiv (1919), 223–5. A hitherto unpublished chapter of Hakewel's book, on the Speaker of the House of Commons, is set forth in C. S. Sims, *The Speaker of the House of Commons, A.H.R.* xlv (1939), 90–95.

1063 McILWAIN, C. H. The high court of parliament and its supremacy. New Haven, 1910.
Emphasizes the judicial functions of parliament in the medieval period, but has valuable sections on the Tudor period.

1064 MAY, T. E. Treatise on the law, privileges, proceedings and usage of parliament. Lond. 1844; 10th ed. enlarged, 1893.

1065 NEALE, J. E. Queen Elizabeth's quashing of bills in 1597–8. *E.H.R.* xxxiv (1919), 586–8; xxxvi (1921), 480.

1066 NEALE, J. E. Parliament and the succession question in 1563 and 1566. *E.H.R.* xxxvi (1921), 497–520.
Prints documents illustrative of Elizabeth's tactics with parliament.

1067 NEALE, J. E. Elizabeth I and her Parliaments, 1559–1581. Lond. 1953; 1584–1603. Lond. 1957.
Indispensable both for politics and for puritanism. Cf. also 5214.

1068 PARLIAMENTARY OR CONSTITUTIONAL HISTORY of England. . . . (1066–1660). 24 vols. Lond. 1751–61; 1761–3.
Fuller than Cobbett (1052) for this period though supplemented by him. Commonly known as the *Old parliamentary history*.

1069 PETYT, WILLIAM. Jus parliamentorum or the ancient power, jurisdiction, rights and liberties of the high court of parliament. 2 pts. Lond. 1739.
Petyt was keeper of records in the Tower of London. He had a great knowledge of parliamentary precedents and legal antiquities. A defence of parliament against the views of courtiers of Restoration period.

1070 PETYT, WILLIAM. Miscellanea parliamentaria. Lond. 1680.
Contains precedents of freedom of arrest and censure of members, and an app. of instances where kings have consulted parliament in marriages, peace and war, and leagues.

1071 POLLARD, A. F. The evolution of Parliament. Lond. 1920; amended 1926.
The comments on the Tudor period are useful but need modification.

1072 POLLARD, A. F. The clerical organization of parliament. *E.H.R.* lvii (1942), 31–58.

1073 POLLARD, A. F. Receivers of petitions and clerks of parliament. *E.H.R.* lvii (1942), 202–26.

1074 PROTHERO, G. W. On two petitions presented by parliament to Queen Elizabeth. . . . *E.H.R.* ii (1887), 741–6.
Corrects a blunder in D'Ewes (1037). Cf. *E.H.R.* xxxvi (1921), 502, n. 2.

1075 [SELDEN, JOHN.] A brief discourse concerning the power of the peers and commons of parliament in point of judicature. Lond. 1640.
This is attributed to Selden but does not appear in the collected ed. of his works in 3 vols. which appeared in 1726.

1076 SELDEN, JOHN. Of the judicature in parliaments, a posthumous treatise wherein the controversies and precedents belonging to that title are methodically handled. Lond. s.a.; by David Wilkins, in *Collected works* (iii, 1587–1660), Lond. 1726.

1077   SIMS, C. S. 'The modern forme of the Parliaments of England.' *A.H.R.* liii (1948), 288–305.

1078   SMITH, G. B. History of the English parliament, together with an account of the parliaments of Scotland and Ireland. 2 vols. Lond. 1892.

1079   SMITH, GOLDWIN. Elizabeth and the apprenticeship of Parliament. *Univ. of Toronto Quar.* viii (1939), 431–9.

1080   SPELMAN, HENRY. Of parliaments. In *Reliquiae Spelmanniae*. By E. Gibson. Lond. 1698.
Also printed in *English works of Spelman*, Lond. 1723.

1081   STUBBS, WILLIAM. Parliament under Henry VIII.
Cf. 378

B. House of Lords

(a) *Sources*

In addition to those cited below reference should be made to 1037, 1038, 1042, 1045, 1067, 1071.

1082   JOURNALS OF THE HOUSE OF LORDS, 1509 ff. s.l., s.a. Index (vols. i–x). Lond. 1846.
These begin in 1510 and vols. i, ii cover the period to 1614. They should be used in connexion with *Calendars of the MSS. of the House of Lords* (152). For description of the journals, cf. A. F. Pollard, *The authenticity of the lords' journals in the sixteenth century*, Trans. R.H. Soc., 3rd ser., viii (1914), 17–40.

1083   JOURNAL OF THE HOUSE OF LORDS for April and May, 1559. By E. J. Davis. *E.H.R.* xxviii (1913), 531–42.

1084   DUGDALE, WILLIAM. A perfect copy of all summons of the nobility to the great councils and parliaments of this realm from xlix of King Henry the III, until these present times. Lond. 1685; repr. [1794].
Valuable. The repr. of 1794 bears date 1685 on title-page. Cf. 369 (pp. 330–66).

(b) *Later Works*

The best general account is 1093, the best peerage for historical purposes, 332. On the judicial functions of the House of Lords, cf. Holdsworth (1544), i, ch. iv. Reference should also be made to Coke (1532), pt. 4.

1085   BEVEN, T. The appellate jurisdiction of the House of Lords. *Law Quar. Rev.* xvii (1901), 155–70, 357–71.
Cf. also J. F. Macqueen, *Practical treatise on the appellate jurisdiction of the House of Lords*, &c., Lond. 1842, and J. W. Gordon, *The appellate jurisdiction of the House of Lords*, Lond. 1905.

1086   COLLIER, J. P. On Sir Nicholas Bacon, lord keeper, with extracts from some of his unprinted papers and speeches. *Arch.* xxxvi (1865), 339–48.

1087   CRUISE, W. The origin and nature of dignities or titles of honour. Lond. 1810; 1823.

1088 HALE, MATTHEW. The jurisdiction of the lords' house, or parliament considered according to ancient records. By Francis Hargrave. Lond. 1796.
Takes issue with Prynne (1095) *et al.* against their excessive claims regarding the original and appellate jurisdiction of the House of Lords.

1089 HARCOURT, L. W. V. His grace the steward and trial of peers. Lond. 1907.
Almost exclusively on medieval period.

1090 HUNT, T. An argument for the bishop's right in judging in capital causes in parliament. Lond. 1682.

1091 NICOLAS, N. H. Report of proceedings on claims to the barony of L'Isle. Lond. 1829.
Prints some material on House of Lords under Henry VIII.

1092 PALMER, F. B. Peerage law in England. Lond. 1907.
Deals with history of origin of peerage and of conflicting claims. Contains an app. of charters and patents, trans. into English.

1093 PIKE, L. O. The constitutional history of the House of Lords. Lond. 1894.
The standard authority on the subject. Contains something on the Tudor period, though largely concerned with earlier history.

1095 PRYNNE, W. A plea for the lords and house of peers. Lond. 1658.

1096 REPORTS FROM THE LORDS' COMMITTEES touching the dignity of a peer of the realm. 5 vols. Lond. 1820–9.
Based on a search of rolls, jours., and other documents and records. Admittedly imperfect and faulty, but contains much valuable information. Cf. Gross (1) no. 2944 for details of contents. Sometimes referred to as *Lord Redesdale's report.*

1097 WILKINSON, KOSMO. Personal story of the upper house. Lond. 1905.
Contains a chapter on *Personalities among the Tudor peers.*

C. House of Commons

(a) *Sources*

The Commons journals (1101) begin in 1547   There is no continuous record of their proceedings before that date.
   For the reign of Elizabeth, the most valuable sources are 1037 and 1045.

1099 HALL, ARTHUR. A letter sent by F. A. touching the proceedings in a private quarell and unkindnesse between Arthur Hall and Melchisidech Mallorie. Lond. 1579; in *Miscellanea antiqua anglicana* (pub. Robert Triphook), 1815.
The author was expelled from parliament for writing this; cf. Neale (1067), Wright (1137).

1100 HOOKER (*alias* VOWELL), JOHN. Journal for the session of 1571. *Trans. Devon Assoc.* xi (1879), 442–92.

1101 JOURNALS OF THE HOUSE OF COMMONS, 1547 ff. s.l., s.a.; repr. Lond. 1803 ff.; index (vols. i–xvii) by T. Vardon and T. E. May, Lond. 1852.
These journals begin in 1547. They do not contain debates, but are a record of proceedings and include many petitions. Vol. i goes to 1628. To be supplemented for Elizabeth's reign by D'Ewes (1037), and Townshend (1045). On these jours., cf. J. E. Neale, *Commons journals of the Tudor period* in *Trans. R.H. Soc.*, 4th ser., iii (1920), 136–70.

1102 [LAMBARDE, WILLIAM (?).] The orders, proceedings, punishments, and privileges of the commons house of parliament in England by W. L. Lond. 1641; repr. in *Harl. Misc.* (281), v, 258–67.
On the authorship of this tract, cf. *E.H.R.* xxxix (1924), 50, n. 3.

1103 POLLARD, A. F. An early Parliamentary election petition. *Bull. Inst. Hist. Research*, viii (1931), 156–66.
For Newcastle-under-Lyme, *c.* 1536.

1104 POLLARD, A. F., and BLATCHER, MARJORIE. Hayward Townshend's Journals. *Bull. Inst. Hist. Research*, xii (1934), 1–31.
Note and text of journal describing parliament of 1597–8.

1105 POLLARD, A. F. Hayward Townshend's Journals. *Bull. Inst. Hist. Research*, xiii (1935), 9–34.

1106 POLLARD, A. F. Hayward Townshend's Journals. *Bull. Inst. Hist. Research*, xiv (1937), 149–65; xv (1937), 1–18.

1107 SIMS, C. S. 'Policies in Parliaments' an early seventeenth century tractate on House of Commons procedure. *Hunt. Lib. Bull.* xv (1951), 45–58.
Author unknown, probably sat in Parliament of 1604.

1108 THE RED PAPER BOOK OF COLCHESTER. By W. G. Benham. Colchester, 1902.
Contains brief member's jour. of 1485 parliament.

(b) *Later Works*

In addition to the references cited below, 1071 is useful. Neale's contributions are all significant.

1109 ANDERTON, H. I. Robert Langton, M.P. for Newton in Makerfield, 1584–5, 1586–7, 1588–9 and 1593. *Notes and Queries*, clxix (1935), 186–8.

1110 BAYNE, C. G. The first House of Commons of Queen Elizabeth. *E.H.R.* xxiii (1908), 455–76, 643–82.
Supports the view that there was little or no attempt on the part of the government to pack this parliament.

1111 BENHAM, W. G. A parliamentary election in Colchester in 1571. *Essex Rev.* xlix (1940), 185–90.

1112 BLAIR, C. H. H. Members of Parliament for Newcastle upon Tyne (June 1377–January 1558); for Berwick upon Tweed (1529–1558) and Morpeth (1553–1558); *Arch. Aeliana*, 4th ser., xiv (1937), 22–66; Members of Parliament for Berwick upon Tweed and Morpeth 1558–1831. Ibid. xxiv (1946), 71–112.

1113 BLAIR, C. H. H. Members of Parliament for Northumberland (6th October 1399–20th January 1588). *Arch. Aeliana*, 4th ser., xii (1935), 82–132.

1114 BROWN, L. F. Ideas of representation from Elizabeth to Charles II. *Jour. Mod. Hist.* xi (1939), 23–40.

1115 BROWNE, A. L. Richard Pates [1516–88], M.P. for Gloucester. *Bristol and Glos. Arch. Soc. Trans. for 1934*, lvi (1935), 201–25.

1116 DASENT, A. I. The speakers of the House of Commons from the earliest times to the present day. Lond. 1911.
The standard work on the subject by a senior clerk of the House of Commons. It contains much on the topography of Westminster and on constitutional changes. Cf. also J. A. Manning, *The lives of the speakers of the House of Commons*, Lond. 1851.

1117 ELTON, G. R. The Commons' Supplication of 1532: Parliamentary manœuvres in the reign of Henry VIII. *E.H.R.* lxvi (1951), 507–34.
Cf. J. P. Cooper, The supplication against the ordinaries reconsidered. *E.H.R.* lxxii (1957), 616–41.

1118 GOODER, A. The parliamentary representation of the county of York, 1258–1832. Vol. i, *Yorks. Arch. Soc.*, rec. ser., xci for 1935 (1935), vol. ii, xcvi, 1937 (1938).

1119 GRAY, H. L. The influence of the Commons on early legislation. *Harvard Hist. Studies*, xxiv. Cambr., Mass., 1932.
Mainly fifteenth century, but important for parliamentary procedure at beginning of Tudor period.

1120 HATSELL, JOHN. Precedents of proceedings in the House of Commons. . . . 4 vols. Lond. 1781; best ed. by C. Abbott, Lord Colchester, Lond. 1818.
Written by the clerk of the House of Commons. A recognized authority. An earlier ed. of vol. i was published in 1776 under the title, *A collection of cases of privilege of parliament from the earliest records to 1628*.

1121 HORNYOLD-STRICKLAND, H. Biographical sketches of the members of parliament of Lancashire, 1290–1550. *Chetham Soc.*, n.s., xciii (1935).

1122 MAGEE, BRIAN. The first Parliament of Queen Elizabeth. *Dublin Rev.* cc (1937), 60–78.
Pro-Roman Catholic.

1123 NEALE, J. E. The commons' privilege of free speech in parliament. In *Tudor Studies* (379).
Scholarly.

1124 NEALE, J. E. Peter Wentworth. *E.H.R.* xxxix (1924), 36–54, 175–205.
Valuable.

1125 NEALE, J. E. Three Elizabethan elections. *E.H.R.* xlvi (1931), 209–39.
A valuable account of three contested county elections in Wales based on Star Chamber records.

1126 NEALE, J. E. More Elizabethan elections. *E.H.R.* lxi (1946), 18–44.

1127 NEALE, J. E. The Elizabethan House of Commons. Lond. 1949.
The only adequate treatise on the subject. Invaluable for elections and structure of the Commons and its procedure. Cf. also 1067.

1128 NOTESTEIN, WALLACE. The winning of the initiative by the House of Commons. *Proc. British Academy*, xi (1926), 125–76.
Chiefly concerned with seventeenth century, but excellent, as far as it goes, for sixteenth.

1129 POLLARD, A. F. A changeling member of parliament. *Bull. Inst. Hist. Research*, x (1932), 20–27.
M.P. for Weymouth.

1130 POLLARD, A. F. Queen Elizabeth's under-clerks and their Commons' Journals. *Bull. Inst. Hist. Research*, xvii (1939), 1–12.

1131 POLLARD, A. F. The under-clerks and the Commons' Journals. *Bull. Inst. Hist. Research*, xvi (1939), 144–67.

1132 POLLARD, A. F. A Protean clerk of the Commons. *Bull. Inst. Hist. Research*, xviii (1940), 49–51.

1133 PORRITT, EDWARD. The unreformed House of Commons. 2 vols. Cambr. 1903; 1909.
Contains a useful bibliography. Vol. i deals with England; vol. ii with Scotland and Ireland.

1134 REDLICH, J. Recht und Technik des englischen Parlamentarismus. Leipzig, 1905. Eng. trans. A. E. Steinthal, *Procedure of the House of Commons, a study of its history and present form*, 3 vols., Lond. 1908.
Contains historical notes on the Tudor period.

1135 USHER, R. G. The institutional history of the House of Commons, 1547–1641. *Washington Univ. Studies*, xi (1924), *Humanistic ser.* no. 2, 187–254.
Based on statistical tables compiled from the *Journals*.

1136 WEDGEWOOD, J. C., and HOLT, A. D. Biographies of the members of the House of Commons, 1439–1509. 2 vols. Lond. 1936; 1938.
Inaugural volumes of an abortive series. Detailed, but not always reliable, biographies.

1137 WRIGHT, HERBERT. Life and works of Arthur Hall of Grantham. Manchester, 1919.
Illustrative of privileges of House of Commons.

3. THE ADMINISTRATION

A. THE CROWN

(a) *Sources*

The functions of the crown on its administrative side were exercised by the council and privy council. Sources under that heading should be consulted, as well as the *Proclamations* (1017). Staunford (1518) is the one important treatise on the prerogative. For the theoretical position of the king, cf. ch. iv *infra*.

(b) *Later Works*

Holdsworth (1544), iv, 190–217, gives a good brief summary of the 'new' position of the crown in the sixteenth century, cf. also Figgis (1447).

1138 ALLEN, JOHN. Inquiry into the rise and growth of the royal prerogative in England. Lond. 1830; 1849.
Strongly Whig.

1139 BEAVAN, A. H. Crowning the king. Lond. 1902.
A good book, but marred by many inaccuracies.

1140 CHITTY, JOSEPH. A treatise on the law of the prerogatives of the crown; and the relative duties and rights of the subject. Lond. 1820.

1141 CHURCHILL, E. F. Dispensations under the Tudors and Stuarts. *E.H.R.* xxxiv (1919), 409–15.
Gives tariff for dispensations.

1142 CHURCHILL, E. F. The dispensing power and the defence of the realm *Law Quar. Rev.* xxxvii (1921), 412–41.

1143 CHURCHILL, E. F. The dispensing power of the crown in ecclesiastical affairs. *Law Quar. Rev.* xxxviii (1922), 297–316, 420–34.

1144 JOHNSON, M. F. The coronation of a king: the ceremonies, pageants and chronicles of coronations of all ages. Lond. 1902.
A valuable, accurate account.

1145 LEGG, L. G. W. English coronation records. Lond. 1883; Westminster, 1901.
Contains good brief accounts of English and Scottish coronation ceremonies, with documents. For further references to coronation ceremonies, regalia, &c., cf. Gross (1), nos. 922, 923, 925, 935.

1146 LEGG, L. G. W. The sacring of the English kings. *Arch. Jour.* li (1894), 28–43.

1147 MAITLAND, F. W. The crown as corporation.
Cf. 1030, iii, 244–70.

1148 POLLARD, A. F. The clerk of the crown. *E.H.R.* lvii (1942), 312–33.

1149 RICHARDSON, W. C. The surveyor of the King's prerogative. *E.H.R.* lvi (1941), 52–75.

1150 SCHRAMM, P. E. A History of the English coronation. Trans. by L. G. Wickham Legg. New York, 1937.

1151 TAYLOR, ARTHUR. The glory of regality: a treatise on the anointing and crowning of the kings and queens of England. Lond. 1820.
The best book on the subject.

B. Council and Privy Council

(a) *Sources*

An admirable guide to the MSS. and printed material on the council is E. R. Adair, *The sources for the history of the council in the sixteenth and seventeenth centuries. Helps for students of history*, no. 51 (1924).

The activities of the privy council must be sought for in every sort of public document. The *Acts* (1152) and the *Proceedings* (1153) are very brief and imperfect memoranda. The *Proclamations* (1017), the *Letters and Papers* (91), and the *Cal. S.P., Foreign* (87) and *Domestic* (86) are the most valuable sources.

1152 ACTS OF THE PRIVY COUNCIL of England. By J. R. Dasent. 32 vols. Lond. 1890–1907.
A continuation of 1153, covering the period from 1542 to 1604. A brief journal of the privy council meetings, not containing all the business transacted by the privy council. Gaps in the record, July 1543–May 1545; May 1559–70 (partly filled by rough notes, 1562–7); June 1582–Feb. 1586; Aug. 1593–Oct. 1595; Apr. 1599–Jan. 1600. A seventeenth-century compilation of extracts from the registers, 1550–1610 (B.M. Add. MS. 11402) contains a little from missing registers. Cf. E. R. Adair, *The privy council registers, E.H.R.* xxx (1915), 698–704, and *The rough copies of the privy council register,* ibid. xxxviii (1923), 410–22.

1153 PROCEEDINGS AND ORDINANCES of the privy council of England, 1386–1542. By N. H. Nicolas. 7 vols. Lond. 1834–7.
Vols. i–vi deal with period before 1485. Vol. vii covers the period from 10 Aug. 1540 to 8 Apr. 1542. Prefaced by an excellent dissertation on the functions and composition of the privy council. A brief memorandum of the council for 1528 is printed in *Bull. Inst. Hist. Research,* v (1927), 23–27.

(b) *Later Works*

There is a good account of the privy council under the Protector Somerset, in Pollard (567), and under Elizabeth, in Cheyney (690), i, ch. v. Cf. also Holdsworth (1544), iv, 56 ff.; and for Henry VIII, Dunham (1158–61).

1154 ADAIR, E. R. The first clerk of the privy council. *Law Quar. Rev.* xxxix (1923), 240–4.

1155 ADAIR, E. R. William Thomas: a forgotten clerk of the privy council. In *Tudor Studies* (379).

1156 BALDWIN, J. F. The king's council in England during the Middle Ages. Oxf. 1913.
A standard work, but barely reaches the Tudor period.

1157 DICEY, A. V. The privy council. Oxf. 1860; 1887.
A very good brief account of the subject.

1158 DUNHAM, W. H. The Ellesmere Extracts from the 'Acta Consilii' of King Henry VIII. *E.H.R.* lviii (1943), 301–18.

1159 DUNHAM, W. H. Henry VIII's whole council and its parts. *Hunt. Lib. Quar.* vii (1943), 7–46.

1160 DUNHAM, W. H. Wolsey's rule of the King's whole council. *A.H.R.* xlix (1944), 644–62.

1161 DUNHAM, W. H. The members of Henry VIII's Whole Council, 1509–27. *E.H.R.* lix (1944), 187–210.

1162 GLADISH, DOROTHY. The Tudor privy council. Retford, 1915.
Useful but very carelessly printed.

1163 HORNEMANN, KARL. Das Privy Council von England zur Zeit der Königin Elisabeth. Hanover, 1912.
A useful study, though not altogether reliable.

1164 LABAREE, L. W., and MOODY, R. E. The seal of the privy council. *E.H.R.* xliii (1928), 190–202.
The only adequate discussion of the subject.

1165 PALGRAVE, FRANCIS. An essay upon the original authority of the king's council. Lond. 1834.
A valuable contribution.

1166 PERCY, EUSTACE. The privy council under the Tudors. Oxf. 1907.
A brief sketch.

1167 POLLARD, A. F. Council, star chamber and privy council under the Tudors. *E.H.R.* xxxvii (1922), 337–60, 516–39; xxxviii (1923), 42–60.
Valuable, particularly for first half of sixteenth century.

1168 POLLARD, A. F. Lords' Journals. *E.H.R.* xxx (1915), 304.
Notes the presence among the Lords' Journals of a page from privy council register. Cf. E. R. Adair, *The privy council registers*, ibid., xxx (1915), 698–704, on same subject.

1169 READ, CONYERS. Walsingham and Burghley in Queen Elizabeth's privy council. *E.H.R.* xxviii (1913), 34–58.
Deals with factions in privy council, 1570–90.

1170 REID, R. R. The king's council of the north. Lond. 1921.
An exhaustive treatment of the subject. Contains a valuable bibliography. Cf. *Tudor Studies* (379), pp. 208–30, Brooks (1332–3), and Lapsley (1342).

1171 SKEEL, C. A. J. The council of the west. *Trans. R.H. Soc.*, 4th ser., iv (1921), 62–80.

1172 SOMERVILLE, R. Henry VII's 'Council learned in the law'. *E.H.R.* liv (1939), 427–42.

1173 TURNER, E. R. Privy council of England in the seventeenth and eighteenth centuries, 1603–1784. 2 vols. Baltimore, 1927–8.
Vol. i, chs. ii and iii, deal inadequately with the Tudor period.

C. CHANCERY—ADMINISTRATIVE SIDE

(a) *Sources*

The chancellor was originally the secretary of state for all departments and the custodian of the royal records. As keeper of the great seal all important public documents passed through his hands and were recorded in his office. Letters patent, letters close, treaties and statutes, &c., were all enrolled under his supervision. He therefore played an important part in the administrative business of the crown. By the sixteenth century his administrative duties had become relatively less important and his judicial duties more important. He continued, however, to exercise important administrative functions.

For the administrative records of his office, cf. Giuseppi (74), i, 9–46. For his judicial functions, cf. *infra*, pp. 145–7.

1174 INDEX OF ANCIENT PETITIONS of the chancery and the exchequer preserved in the P.R.O. *P.R.O. lists and indexes*, no. 1. Lond. 1892.
Index to names mentioned in petitions, addressed to king, council, parliament, and officers of state, Edward I–Henry VII. Cf. also *Index to the petitions to the king in council: Deputy keeper's report*, xxxiv (1873), 1–162.

1175 INVENTORY OF THE ROLLS, enrollments, and records of the chancery in the rolls chapel. *Deputy keeper's report*, iii (1842), app. ii, 135–55.

1176 LIST OF ANCIENT CORRESPONDENCE of the chancery and exchequer preserved in the P.R.O. *P.R.O. lists and indexes*, no. 15 (1902).
Royal letters, &c., Richard I–Henry VII. Cf. review by C. V. Langlois in *Jour. des savants*, n.s., ii (1904), 380–93, 446–53.

1177 LIST OF CHANCERY ROLLS, preserved in the P.R.O. 1 John ff. *P.R.O. lists and indexes*, no. 27 (1908).

(b) *Later Works*

Cf. in general, Holdsworth (1544), i, ch. v.

1178 BALDWIN, F. E. Proceedings in Chancery under Wolsey. *Bull. Inst. Hist. Research*, viii (1930), 17–20.

1179 CAMPBELL, JOHN. The lives of the lord chancellors and keepers of the great seal of England . . . till the reign of George IV. 7 vols. Lond. 1845–7; 10 vols., 1856–7.
Useful, but inaccurate. On Wolsey and the great seal, cf. 532.

1180 MAXWELL-LYTE, H. C. Historical notes on the use of the great seal of England. Lond. 1926.
Very valuable, though mainly devoted to the Middle Ages.

D. ADMINISTRATIVE OFFICERS

(a) *Sources*

There are a few contemporary or nearly contemporary tracts dealing with administrative officers in 1013, 1521, and 1522.

1181 BEALE, ROBERT. A treatise of the office of a councellor and principall secretarie, 1592. Printed in Read (759), i, app.

1182 CECIL, ROBERT. The state and dignity of a secretary of state's place. *Harl. Misc.* (281), v, 166–8.

1183 NICHOLAS FAUNT'S DISCOURSE touching the office of principal secretary of estate, &c., 1592. By Charles Hughes. *E.H.R.* xx (1905), 499–508.
'This Mr. Fante sometimes served Sir Fraunces Walsingham.'

1184 HERBERT, JOHN. Duties of a secretary. In Prothero, *Select documents* (1014), 166–8.

(b) *Later Works*

On this subject in general, cf. Cheyney (690), i, chs. ii and iii; Read (759–60) and Elton (1023).

1185 EVANS, F. M. G. The principal secretary of state: a survey of the office from 1558 to 1680. Manchester, 1923.
A helpful contribution to a vast and complicated subject.

1186 NICOLAS, N. H. Observations on the office of secretary of state. Printed in *Proceedings* (1153), vol. vi, intro.

1187 OTWAY-RUTHVEN, J. The King's secretary and the signet office in the 15th century. Cambr. 1939.
Useful background material.

E. PUBLIC FINANCE

1. *Exchequer*

(a) *Sources*

Most of the material for the study of national finance is in MS. The *P.R.O. lists and indexes* and the *Reports of the deputy keeper of public records* furnish guides to most of it. Giuseppi (74) should be consulted.

On the levy of the direct taxes, to wit, the tenth and fifteenth and the subsidy, the point of departure is the statute authorizing the tax in the *Statutes of the realm*. For the actual levy the most useful sources are the *Subsidy rolls* in the P.R.O. (Giuseppi, i, 111). There are, however, a great many local assessment lists preserved. Many of the assessments for particular dates and places have been printed. For those printed prior to 1912 reference should be made to Moore (2584), nos. 46, 121, 178, 179, 187, 207, 215, 252, 323, 383, 425, 442, 457, 465, 479, 518, 520, 545, 568, 576, 578, 622, 644, 661, 670, 683, 689. Cf. also Hall (2534), nos. 972, 973, 1020, 1021, 1032, 1041. For Northamptonshire, cf. Wake (1274); for Cambridge (4248); for Wilts., Ramsay (1211); for Bucks. (1207); for Wales (6327); for an assessment of the lawyers, cf. Inderwick (1619). Others are given in ch. xi *infra*. Surviving assessments for the tenth and fifteenth in the sixteenth century are rare, but there are a few in MS. in the B.M. The customs and the indirect taxes are considered under a separate section below. There is a great deal of scattered material on government finance in the *Cal. S.P., Domestic* and in the *Lansdowne* and *Cotton MSS.* in the B.M. Figures printed in Scott (3009) and Dietz (1216–19) need correction. For the reign of Edward VI the king's own writings should be consulted (555). On government borrowings abroad, cf. pp. 246–9 *infra*. Some source material on taxation is printed by Tawney and Power (2539), ii, 204–46. Cf. also 4154.

1188 THE ANCIENT KALENDARS AND INVENTORIES of the treasury of his majesty's exchequer, with other documents illustrating the history of that repository. By F. Palgrave. *Record Com.* 3 vols. Lond. 1836.

1189 CALENDAR OF DECREES of the court of general surveyors, 34–38 Henry VIII. *Deputy keeper's report*, xxx (1869), app., 166–96.

1190 CALENDAR OF TREASURY PAPERS, vol. i, 1557–1696. By J. Redington. Lond. 1868.
Only 3 pages before James I (petitions, accounts, instructions).

1191 CATALOGUE OF THE DOCUMENTS AND RECORDS now in the custody of the comptroller of the exchequer. *Deputy keeper's report*, ii (1841), app. ii, 190–248.
Auditors' privy seal books, Henry VII–Henry VIII. Auditors' receipt books, 1570 ff. Auditors' patent books, 1509–96. Under-treasurer's declarations of the state of the treasury, 1508–52. Tellers' views of accounts, 1558–1612. Tellers' views of payments and issues. Payments by royal warrant, 1559–86. Cf. also 1197.

1192 DEVON, F. Issues of the exchequer. Lond. 1837.
App. contains extracts from exchequer issue rolls, Edward IV–Elizabeth, translated.

1193 A DOCUMENT RELATING to the collection in Yorkshire of a subsidy under the act of 1601. By C. T. Clay. *Yorks. Arch. Jour.* xxxiii (1937), 309–13.

1194 ENROLMENTS OF CROWN LEASES, Henry VIII–James I.
Deputy keeper's report, xlix (1888), 209–360.
Index nominorum.

1195 EXCHEQUER RECORDS, catalogue of special commissions, 1 Elizabeth to 10 Victoria. Calendar of depositions taken by commission 1 Elizabeth to end of James I. *Deputy keeper's report,* xxxviii (1877).

1196 FANSHAWE, THOMAS. The practice of the exchequer court with its severall officers. Lond. 1658.
Originally written in Oct. 1572 for Lord Burghley (B.M., *Lansdowne MSS.* 171, f. 431) and later adapted to his successor as lord treasurer. The published version is from this adaptation.

1197 INVENTORIES OF THE BOOKS of the Pell office of the late receipt of the exchequer, 1559 ff. *Deputy keeper's reports,* iii (1842), app. ii, 156–86; iv (1843), app. ii, no. 6; vi (1845), app. ii, 221–43; vii (1846), app. ii, 213 ff.

1198 INVENTORIES OF THE RECORDS, &c. of the exchequer of pleas.
Deputy keeper's reports, ii (1841), app. ii, 93–135.

1199 INVENTORY OF ROLLS, accounts, assessments, inquisitions, petitions, certificates, or other documents, relating to the assessing and collection of the tallages, carucages, scutages, aids, subsidies, loans . . . &c. . . . among the records of the Queen's remembrancer in the exchequer. *Deputy keeper's reports,* iii (1842), app. ii, 3–104; iv (1843), app. ii, 2–29; v (1844), app. ii, 2–32.

1200 JONES, EDWARD. Index to records called the originalia (Henry III–George II). 2 vols. Lond. 1793–5.
Rolls containing notes of exchequer business and for the making up of accounts.

1200a LAY SUBSIDY ROLLS FOR . . . SUSSEX, 1524–5. By Julian Cornwall. *Sussex Record Soc. Pub.* lvi (1956).

1201 LIST AND INDEX OF DECLARED ACCOUNTS from the pipe office and the audit office (*c.* 1558–1830), preserved in the P.R.O. *P.R.O. lists and indexes,* no. 2 (1893).
An important series. Cf. 1221.

1202 LIST OF ORIGINAL MINISTERS' ACCOUNTS (to 1547) preserved in the P.R.O. *P.R.O. lists and indexes,* nos. 5, 8, 34 (1894–1910).
No. 34, Henry VII and Henry VIII, lists the original accounts of bailiffs, reeves, farmers, receivers, and other officers, collecting the issues of manors and lands—gives lands, county, date, officer. Includes accounts for Lancaster which are also listed in *Deputy keeper's report,* xlv, accounts formerly in Queen's remembrancer's office and other smaller collections described in part in *Deputy keeper's reports,* xx and xxi.

1203   LIST OF RENTALS AND SURVEYS and other analogous documents preserved in the P.R.O. *P.R.O. lists and indexes,* no. 25 (1908).
Chiefly records of the augmentation office of the exchequer, containing rentals, extents, surveys, valors, &c., Edward I–Charles II.

1204   LIST OF SPECIAL COMMISSIONS and returns in the exchequer, preserved in the P.R.O. *P.R.O. lists and indexes,* no. 37 (1912).
Descriptive list of special commissions of inquiry relating to concealed lands, possessions of persons attainted and of debtors to the crown; encroachments and intrusions, tithes, woods, ports, &c., Elizabeth ff.

1205   LIST OF VARIOUS ACCOUNTS formerly preserved in the exchequer, Henry II–George III. *P.R.O. lists and indexes,* no. 35 (1912).
Cf. Giuseppi (74), i, 78 ff.

1206   NOTICES OF TYTHE-SUITS enrolled in the exchequer of pleas. Edward IV–George III. *Deputy keeper's reports,* ii (1841), app. ii, 249–72.
Selected and abridged.

1207   SUBSIDY ROLL for the county of Buckingham, Anno 1524. By A. C. Chibnall and A. V. Woodman. *Bucks. Rec. Soc.* viii (1950).

1208   SURVEYS AND TOKENS. By H. E. Salter. *Oxf. Hist. Soc.* lxxv (1923).
Contains subsidy assessments for 1543, 1544.

1209   SUFFOLK IN 1524 AND 1568, being returns for subsidies granted in 1523 and 1566. By S. H. A. Harvey. 2 vols. *The Suffolk Green Books,* x, xii (1909).

1210   TAXATION IN SALFORD HUNDRED, 1524–1802. By James Tait. *Chetham Soc.,* n.s., xviii (1924).
Valuable introduction.

1211   TWO sixteenth century taxation lists 1545 and 1576. By G. D. Ramsay. *Wilts. Arch. and Nat. Hist. Soc.,* Rec. Branch, x (1954).
Valuable introduction.

1212   VALOR ECCLESIASTICUS. By John Caley and Jos. Hunter. 6 vols. Lond. 1810–34.
Survey of all ecclesiastical benefices in England and Wales, 26 Henry VIII, in order to carry out statute giving first-fruits and tenths to the king. Incomplete for several dioceses. Cf. A. C. Ewald, *Paper and parchment,* Lond. 1890, pp. 71–86.

(b) *Later Works*

The studies of Dietz (1216–19) are the only modern treatises based on an extensive study of the sources. Newton (1251) and Richardson (1226) are valuable on the reorganization of financial administration under the early Tudors. Scott (3009), iii, 485 ff., gives a useful but not always trustworthy account of national finances under Elizabeth with illustrative tables from the sources. On the financing of the Dutch wars, 1586–7, cf. 942.

On the levy and collection of the subsidy, Peyton (2664) and Ramsay (1211) are illuminating. Cf. also Tait's introduction to 1210.

1213   BEST, HENRY. The manner or forme of a distringas or levy. By C. B. Robinson. In *Rural economy in Yorkshire in 1641, Surtees Soc.* xxxiii (1857). Contains *The form or manner of collecting a subsidy* and *The manner of ratinge, assessinge, and levyinge of polle money.* Though written in the seventeenth century this tract throws much light on the detail of Tudor local practice.

1214   BONNER, G. A. The office of the king's remembrancer, showing the connexion with the old exchequer and the modern treasury. Lond. 1931.

1215   CANNAN, EDWIN. The history of local rates in England. By. W. A. S. Hewins. Lond. 1896.

1216   DIETZ, F. C. English government finance, 1485–1558. *Univ. of Illinois Studies in the Social Sciences,* ix (1920), no. 3. Contains a valuable note of MS. material available for financial history, pp. 233–7.

1217   DIETZ, F. C. English Public Finance, 1558–1641. New York, 1932.

1218   DIETZ, F. C. Finances of Edward VI and Mary. *Smith College Studies in History,* iii (1918), no. 2. A valuable study, with statistical app.

1219   DIETZ, F. C. The exchequer in Elizabeth's reign. *Smith College Studies in History,* viii (1923), no. 2. Mainly statistical. Attempts a complete yearly statement of receipts and expenditures of the exchequer, with comments.

1220   DOWELL, STEPHEN. A history of taxation and taxes in England from the earliest times to the present day. 4 vols. Lond. 1884; 1888. Inadequate.

1221   GEORGE, M. D. Notes on the origin of the declared account. *E.H.R.* xxxi (1916), 41–58. Contains references to MS. treatises on the organization and conduct of the exchequer.

1222   GILBERT, GEOFFREY. A treatise on the court of exchequer. Lond. 1758. App. contains an account of the origin and nature of the customs and of the method of charging and collecting the excise.

1223   JENKINSON, HILARY. Exchequer tallies. *Arch.* lxii (1911), 367–80. Mostly thirteenth century, but with some later material.

1224   LEWIS, A. H. A study of Elizabethan ship-money, 1588–1603. Philadelphia, 1928.

1225   MILLER, HELEN. Subsidy assessments of the peerage in the sixteenth century. *Bull. Inst. Hist. Research,* xxviii (1955), 15–34.

1226   RICHARDSON, W. C. Tudor Chamber administration, 1485–1547. Baton Rouge, 1952. Valuable. Contains, in an app., a useful biographical note on Sir R. Bray, Henry VII's minister.

1227   RICHARDSON, W. C. Some financial expedients of Henry VIII. *Econ. Hist. Rev.,* 2nd ser., vii (1954), 33–48.

1228   [STEVENS, JOHN.] The royal treasury of England, or an historical account of all taxes. Lond. 1725; 1733.

1229 THOMAS, F. S. The ancient exchequer of England. Lond. 1848.
One of the first attempts to discuss Tudor changes in exchequer organization.

1230 WARE, S. L. The Elizabethan parish in its ecclesiastical and financial aspects. Baltimore, 1908.

2. *Customs*

(a) *Sources*

Practically all of the sources are preserved in the P.R.O. and have not been printed. Cf. Giuseppi (74), ii, index, Customs.

1231 RATES OF THE CUSTOME HOUSE both inwarde and outwarde, the dyfference of measures and weyghte, &c. Lond. 1545.
This appears to be the first extant printed book of rates. One for the year 1507, preserved in MS., is printed by Gras (1235), pp. 694 ff. For other sixteenth-century eds. of books of rates, cf. *S.T.C.* (35), nos. 7688–90.

1232 RICHARD CARMARDEN'S A CAVEAT FOR THE QUENE (1570). By J. U. Nef. *Jour. Pol. Econ.* xli (1933), 33–57.
Carmarden was a customs official. The MS. here printed is in a private library in New York. It deals with corruption in collection of customs.

(b) *Later Works*

There is a good bibliography in Gras (1235).

1233 ATTON, HENRY, and HOLLAND, H. H. The king's customs, an account of maritime revenue and contraband traffic in England, Scotland and Ireland from the earliest times to the year 1800. 2 vols. Lond. 1908–10.
A popular history containing a good deal of miscellaneous material.

1234 DIETZ, F. C. Elizabethan customs administration. *E.H.R.* xlv (1930), 35–58.
Cf. 1239.

1235 GRAS, N. S. B. The early English customs system. *Harvard Econ. Studies,* xviii (1918).
Contains a valuable collection of documents, some in the sixteenth century. Useful bibliography.

1236 GRAS, N. S. B. Tudor 'Books of Rates', a chapter in the history of the English customs. *Quar. Jour. Econ.* xxvi (1912), 766–75.

1237 HALL, G. D. G. Impositions and the courts. *Law Quar. Rev.* lxix (1953), 200–18.

1238 HALL, HUBERT. A history of the custom-revenue in England, from the earliest times to the year 1827. 2 vols. Lond. 1885.
Valuable documents in appendixes.

1239 NEWTON, A. P. The establishment of the great farm of the English customs. *Trans. R.H. Soc.*, 4th ser., i (1918), 129–56.
Mainly Elizabethan. On the farming of the customs of the 'out ports' by Sir Francis Walsingham, 1585–90, cf. Read (759), iii, 383–91.

3. *Household and Purveyance*

(a) *Sources*

For the abundant material on the household in the P.R.O., cf. Giuseppi (74). Newton (1250) should be consulted on published and unpublished household ordinances. For a list of MS. account books of the treasurer of the chamber, temp. Henry VII, cf. Conway (5151), xvii ff.

1240   A COLLECTION OF ORDINANCES and regulations for the government of the royal household . . . Edward III to . . . William and Mary. By Sort, Gough, Topham, and Brand. *Soc. of Antiq.*, 1790.

1241   COLLIER, J. P. On a state manuscript of the reign of Henry VIII, the property of Sir Walter Calverley Trevelyan, bart. *Arch.* xxxvi (1855), 14–22. The MS. in question is the accounts of Sir Bryan Tuke, treas. of the Chamber. Cf. 91, v. 303–26.

1242   EXTRACTS FROM THE PRIVY PURSE EXPENSES of King Henry VII, 1491–1505. By S. Bentley. In *Excerpta historica*, Lond. 1831, pp. 85–133.

1243   HOUSEHOLD EXPENSES of the Princess Elizabeth during her residence at Hatfield, Oct. 1, 1551 to Sept. 30, 1552. By P. C. S. Smythe, Viscount Strangford. *Camden Misc.* ii (1853).

1244   A LIST OF RECORDS OF THE GREENCLOTH extant in 1610. By A. P. Newton. *E.H.R.* xxxiv (1919), 237–41.

1245   PRIVY PURSE EXPENSES of Elizabeth of York, with a memoir of Elizabeth of York and notes. By N. H. Nicolas. Lond. 1830.

1246   PRIVY PURSE EXPENSES of King Henry the Eighth, from November 1529 to December 1532. By N. H. Nicolas. Lond. 1827.

1247   PRIVY PURSE EXPENSES of the Princess Mary, daughter of King Henry the Eighth, afterwards Queen Mary. By F. Madden. Lond. 1831. With an introductory memoir and notes.

1248   SIR JOHN DAUNCE'S ACCOUNTS of money received from the treasurer of the king's chamber temp. Henry VIII. By C. T. Martin. *Arch.* xlvii (1883), 295–336.

(b) *Later Works*

Newton's essay (1250) and Woodworth (1253) are valuable.

1249   BRAY, WILLIAM. An account of the obsolete office of purveyor to the king's household. *Arch.* viii (1787), 329–62.

1250   NEWTON, A. P. Tudor reforms in the royal household. In *Tudor Studies* (379).

1251   NEWTON, A. P. The king's chamber under the early Tudors. *E.H.R.* xxxii (1917), 348–72.

1252   SEARS, L. M. Purveyance in England under Elizabeth. *Jour. Pol. Econ.* xxiv (1916), 755–74. Slight.

1253 WOODWORTH, ALLEGRA. Purveyance for the royal household in the reign of Queen Elizabeth. *Trans. Amer. Philos. Soc.*, n.s., vol. xxxv, pt. i, Philadelphia 1945.
Scholarly.

4. *Coinage and Currency*

(a) *Sources*

The various steps in the manipulation of the coinage by the Tudors may be traced in the *Proclamations* (1017). Part of the official records of the recoinage of 1560 are preserved in the *Declared Accounts*, P.R.O., and in *Lansdowne MSS.*, no. 4. There are a number of MS. treatises on the coinage preserved in the *Cal. S.P., Domestic*, P.R.O., and in the *Lansdowne* and *Cotton MSS.*, B.M. Tawney and Power (2539), ii, 176–203, print a number of pertinent documents. For the social and economic consequences of the coinage manipulation, cf. Scott (3009).

1254 GRUEBER, H. A. Handbook of the coins of Great Britain and Ireland in the British Museum. . . . Lond. 1899.

1255 MILNES, NORA. Mint records of Henry VIII. *E.H.R.* xxxii (1917), 270–3.
Valuable statement of the total coinage during first fifteen years of the reign of Henry VIII.

1256 PRYSE, JOHN. A manuscript treatise on the coinage, 1553. By W. A. J. Archibald. *E.H.R.* xiii (1898), 709–10.
Prints extracts.

1257 THE SUMMARIE OF CERTAINE REASONS which have moued the Quens Maiestie to procede in reformation of her base and course monies. . . . Lond. [1560]; *Harl. Misc.* (281), viii, 68–71.
Cf. Routledge (p. 10 *supra*) for tracts on the coinage preserved in the Bodleian library.

(b) *Later Works*

For general treatises, cf. Gross (1), nos. 372–81. The standard work is 1265.

1258 BROOKE, G. C. English Coins from the seventh century to the present. Lond. 1932; 1943; 1950; 1955.
pp. 162–201 on Tudors.

1259 CRAIG, JOHN. The Mint; a history of the London mint from A.D. 287 to 1948. Cambr. 1953.
Good on institutional, weak on economic side.

1260 FEAVEAYEAR, A. E. The Pound Sterling. A history of English money. Oxf. 1931.
Very useful.

1261 MILLIGAN, BURTON. Counterfeiters and coin clippers in the sixteenth and seventeenth centuries. *Notes and Queries*, clxxxii (1942), 100–5.

1262 OMAN, C. W. C. The Tudors and the currency, 1526–60. *Trans. R.H. Soc.*, 2nd ser., ix (1895), 167–88.
A study of the debasement and restoration of the coinage. Cf. Burgon, *Life of Gresham* (2933).

1263 OMAN, C. W. C. The coinage of England. Lond. 1931.

1264 READ, CONYERS. Profits on the recoinage of 1560–1. *Econ. Hist. Rev.* vi (1936), 186–93.
Corrects figures given in Froude (340) and Feaveayear (1260).

1265 RUDING, ROGERS. Annals of the coinage of Great Britain and its dependencies. 3 vols. Lond. 1817–19; best ed. Lond. 1840.
The most comprehensive work on the subject. Supersedes all earlier works. For list of these, see introduction, vol. i, pp. vii–ix. The 3rd vol. contains engraved plates of all the coins.

F. THE POST OFFICE

(a) *Sources*

1266 ORDERS SET DOWN . . . FOR THE POSTS, and articles set down . . . to be kept by the posts. Lond. 1584; by Edward Arber, Lond. 1897.
Two proclamations concerning the Post Office. Repr. in Arber, *Story of the Pilgrim fathers*, pp. 73–78, with other matter concerning the posts, pp. 78–86. Cf. Steele (1017), i, nos. 492, 773, 774, 833, 881.

1267 MARSHALL, C. F. Warrant for the payment for the carriage of government letters, April 1597. *Sussex Notes and Queries*, vi (1937), 154–5.

(b) *Later Works*

1268 HEMMEON, J. C. The history of the British Post Office. *Harvard Econ. Studies*, vii (1912).
For the earlier works on the subject by Joyce and Hyde, cf. Davies (8), no. 267.

1269 HOUSDEN, J. A. J. Early posts in England. *E.H.R.* xviii (1903), 713–18.
With a list of post towns in 1575.

1270 HOUSDEN, J. A. J. The merchant strangers' post in the sixteenth century. *E.H.R.* xxi (1906), 739–42.

1271 KAY, F. G. Royal Mail: the story of the posts in England from the time of Edward IV to the present day. Lond. 1951.

1272 OGILVIE, A. M. The rise of the English Post Office. *Econ. Jour.* iii (1893), 443–57.

1273 ROBINSON, HOWARD. The British Post Office: a history. Oxf. 1948; Lond. 1953.

4. LOCAL GOVERNMENT

A. THE LORD LIEUTENANT

(a) *Sources*

There is a good discussion of the sources in Scott Thomson (1278), pp. vii–x, and a useful bibliography in Wake (1274), pp. cxxxii–cxxxiii. Scott Thomson prints some documents in appendixes. The *Acts of Privy Council* (1152) should be consulted. There is a good deal of material in local collections, notably *Stiffkey papers* (1287), *Losely MSS.* (288), *Salisbury MSS.* (185), *Rutland MSS.* (181), and *Coke MSS.* (123).

1274 A COPY OF PAPERS RELATING TO MUSTERS, beacons, sub-sidies, &c. in . . . Northampton, A.D. 1586–1623. By J. Wake. *Northampton Rec. Soc.* iii (1926).
Papers of the deputy lieutenant of Northants. Contains a valuable introduction by J. E. Morris on the militia system.

1275 LANCASHIRE LIEUTENANCY UNDER THE TUDORS and Stuarts, the civil and military government of the county, as illustrated by a series of royal and other letters, orders of the privy council, the lord lieutenant, and other authorities. By J. Harland. 2 vols. *Chetham Soc.* xlix, l (1859).
Valuable.

1276 THE TWYSDEN LIEUTENANCY PAPERS 1583–1668. By G. S. Thomson. *Kent Arch. Soc.*, Records branch, x (1926).

(b) *Later Works*

1277 JACKSON, E. F. Office and actions of the lord lieutenant in Tudor England. Philadelphia, 1923.
Slight.

1278 THOMSON, G. SCOTT. Lords lieutenants in the sixteenth century: a study in Tudor local administration. Lond. 1923.
Valuable.

1279 THOMSON, G. SCOTT. The origin and growth of the office of deputy-lieutenant. *Trans. R.H. Soc.*, 4th ser., v (1922), 150–67.

B. JUSTICES OF THE PEACE

(a) *Sources*

The best bibliography of sixteenth-century treatises on the justices of the peace is in Beale (1480), 125–74. Putnam's discussion (1291) of some of these early treatises is admirable. Cf. also Holdsworth (1544), iv, 115–20. For an account of a MS. treatise by John Goldwell, a copy of which is in the Harvard Law Library, cf. *E.H.R.* xli (1926), 268–70.

1280 THE BOKE OF JUSTYCES OF PEAS. . . . Lond. 1506.
At least 32 eds. or issues in the sixteenth century, including several printed under the title of *The aucthoritie of al justices of peace*. Cf. Putnam (1291).

1281 FITZHERBERT, ANTHONY. L'office et auctoryte des justyces de peas. Lond. 1538 (French). English trans., *The newe boke of justices of the peas*. Lond. 1538.
At least 11 eds. before Crompton's enlargement of the French ed. in 1583 (1282).

1282 CROMPTON, RICHARD. L'office et aucthoritie de justices de peace. . . . Lond. 1583.

1283 FLEETWOOD, WILLIAM. The office of a justice of peace. Lond. 1658.
Written in 1565, a trans. in shortened form of Marowe's *De pace* of 1503. Cf. 1285 and *E.H.R.* xli (1926), 267–8.

1284 LAMBARD, WILLIAM. Eirenarcha: or the office of the justices of peace. Lond. 1581.
Long the standard authority; at least 13 eds. or issues between 1582 and 1620.
For an account of the original MS. and of the date of the 1st ed. as 1582 instead of 1581, cf. *E.H.R.* xli (1926), 260–70. With the later eds. were often bound up 1310.

1284a WILLIAM LAMBARD'S 'EPHEMERIS', 1580–8. By Conyers Read. *Hunt. Lib. Quar.* xv (1952), 123–58.
Lambard's diary as J.P. in Kent.

1285 MAROWE, THOMAS. De pace terre & ecclesie & conservacione eiusdem.
Written in 1503. First printed in Putnam (1291).

1286 PULTON, FERDINANDO. An abstract of all penall statutes which be generall. . . . Moreover the aucthoritie and duetie of all justices of peace, sherifes, coroners, eschetors. . . . Lond. 1577.
At least 8 eds. appeared before 1603.

1287 THE STIFFKEY PAPERS, the official papers of Sir Nathaniel Bacon of Stiffkey, Norfolk, a justice of the peace, 1580–1620. By H. W. Saunders. *Camden Soc.*, 3rd ser., xxvi (1915).
A selection from the Bacon papers in the Townshend collection (202). For omissions, cf. pp. xvii and xix.

1288 SUPPLEMENTARY STIFFKEY PAPERS. By F. W. Brooks. *Camden Misc.* xvi, 3rd ser., iii. *R.H.S.*, 1936.

1289 THE STATUTES whiche the iustices of peace, mayres . . . were of late commaunded . . . to put in execution. . . Lond. 1538.
Cf. Putnam (1291), pp. 27–28, and Beale (1480), nos. T 314–16.

(b) *Later Works*

The voluminous guide-books for justices of the peace which appeared during the seventeenth, eighteenth, and nineteenth centuries are not listed. For those of the seventeenth century, cf. Davies (8), pp. 45 ff. A partial list is printed in S. and B. Webb, *English local govt.* (3 vols. Lond. 1906–8), i, 295 n. The best modern account of the office in the sixteenth century is in Cheyney (690), ii, 313–42. Cf. also Holdsworth (1544), iv, 108 ff.

1290 BEARD, C. A. The office of justice of the peace in England, in its origin and development. New York, 1904.
Useful, but inadequate, being based almost entirely upon printed sources.

1291 PUTNAM, B. H. Early treatises on the practice of the justices of the peace in the fifteenth and sixteenth centuries. *Oxf. Studies in Social and Legal Hist.* vii (1926).
A very careful bibliography of known copies of all eds. of 1280, 1282, and 1284. Prints 1285. For eds. of 1280 discovered since 1924, cf. *Notes and Queries*, cxlviii (1925), no. 6.

1292 PUTNAM, B. H. Justices of the peace for 1558–1688. *Bull. Inst. Hist. Research,* iv (1926–7), 144–56.
Bibliographical.

1293 PUTNAM, B. H. Sixteenth century treatises for justices of the peace. *Univ. of Toronto Law Jour.* vii (1947), 137–61.

1294 GLEASON, J. H. The personnel of the Commissions of the peace, 1554–64. *Hunt. Lib. Quar.* xviii (1955), 169–77.

1296 SOMERVILLE, R. Lancashire justices of the peace in the fifteenth and sixteenth centuries. *Trans. Hist. Soc. Lancs. and Ches.* cii (1952), 183–8.
Cf. also R. S. France, *Lancashire justices of the peace in 1583, Trans. Hist. Soc. Lancs. and Ches.* xcv (1944), 131–3.

C. Quarter Sessions

(a) *Sources*

Only those printed quarter sessions records which cover some part of the Tudor period are included. For those of the next century, cf. Davies (8), ch. xi, sect. 3, *passim.*

1297 COX, J. C. Three centuries of Derbyshire annals, as illustrated by the records of the quarter sessions of the county of Derby, from Queen Elizabeth to Queen Victoria. 2 vols. Lond. 1890.

1298 QUARTER Sessions records with other records of the Justices of the peace for the county Palatine of Chester, 1559–1760, together with a few earlier miscellaneous records. By J. H. E. Bennett and J. C. Dewhurst. *Rec. Soc. Lancs. and Ches.* xciv (1940).

1299 GUIDE to archives and other collections of documents relating to Surrey Quarter Session records with other records of the Justice of the Peace for the county of Surrey. By Dorothy L. Powell. *Surrey Rec. Soc.* xxxii (1931).

1300 HERTFORD COUNTY RECORDS, 1581–1894. By W. J. Hardy. 3 vols. Hertford, 1905–10.
Vol. i contains chiefly notes and extracts from the *Sessions rolls,* 1581–1698.

1301 LANCASHIRE QUARTER SESSIONS RECORDS (1590–1606). By James Tait. *Chetham Soc.* lxxvii (1917).
Valuable introduction.

1302 MIDDLESEX COUNTY RECORDS. By J. C. Jeaffreson and W. J. Hardy. 6 vols. *Middlesex County Record Society* continued by *Middlesex County Council.* Lond. 1886 ff.
Vol. i covers the period from 1550 to 1603.

1303 THE STAFFORDSHIRE Quarter Session Rolls. By S. A. H. Burne. *Wm. Salt Arch. Soc.* i, 1581–9, 1929 (1931); ii, 1590–3, 1930 (1932); iii, 1594–7, 1932 (1933); *Stafford. Rec. Soc.* iv, 1598–1602, 1935 (1936).

1304 WEST RIDING SESSIONS ROLLS (1598–1602). By J. Lister. *Yorks. Arch. Soc.,* Rec. Ser., iii (1888).

1305 WILTSHIRE County Records: Minutes of Proceedings in sessions 1563 and 1574–92. By H. C. Johnson. *Wilts. Arch. and Nat. Hist. Soc.*, Rec. Branch, iv, Devizes, 1949.
Valuable introduction. Cf. 208.

1306 WORCESTERSHIRE COUNTY RECORDS. CALENDAR of the quarter sessions papers (1591–1643). By J. W. W. Bund. *Worcester Hist. Soc.*, 1900.

(b) *Later Works*

Cf. Cheyney (690), ii, ch. xxxvii *passim*, and Holdsworth (1544), iv, 142 ff. The introductions to Tait (1301), Bund (1306), and Johnson (1305) are serviceable.

1307 HAMILTON, A. H. A. Quarter sessions from Queen Elizabeth to Queen Anne, illustrative of local government and history, drawn from original records. Lond. 1878.
Selections from sessions rolls and depositions. The records relate chiefly to the county of Devon.

1308 HURSTFIELD, JOEL. County government, *c.* 1530–*c.* 1660. *V.C.H. Wilts.* v (1957), 80–110.

D. Sheriffs, Constables, Coroners, *and* Minor Officers

(a) *Sources*

Lambard (1310) gives the most serviceable contemporary account of these officials. For the rather extensive seventeenth-century handbooks on the subject, cf. Davies (8), pp. 45 ff., notably nos. 472 and 473. Holdsworth (1544), vi, 692–3, gives a list of pertinent publications between 1668 and 1700. For coroners' inquests in Middlesex, Edward VI to Elizabeth, cf. 1302.

1309 [FITZHERBERT, ANTHONY.] In this booke is contayned ye offices of sheryffes, bailliffes of liberties, escheatours, constables and coroners. Lond. [1538].
At least 17 eds. had appeared by 1573. Included in all editions of 1281. Cf. 1291, pp. 10–13.

1310 LAMBARD, WILLIAM. The duties of constables, borsholders, tything-men, and such other lowe ministers of the peace. Lond. [1582].
Eight eds. in the sixteenth century and 10 eds. in the seventeenth century. Frequently bound with 1284.
   To the ed. of 1602 is added, *Whereunto be adioyned, the seuerall offices of church-ministers and churchwardens, and ouerseers for the poore, surueighours of the highwayes, and distributors of the prouision against noysome fowle and vermin.*

1311 LIST OF SHERIFFS FOR ENGLAND AND WALES, from the earliest time to 1831. *P.R.O. lists and indexes*, no. 9 (1898).
For local lists, cf. Gross (1), nos. 1032 (Norfolk), 1086a (Staffordshire).

(b) *Later Works*

The best modern account of these officials in the later sixteenth century is in Cheyney (690), ii, chs. xxxviii–xli. For an historical account of the coroner's office, cf. Gross (1), no. 2047.

1312 FRASURE, L. D Shakespeare's constables. *Anglia*, lviii (1934), 384–91.

1313 LEE, W. L. M. A history of police in England. Lond. 1901; repr. 1905.

1314 MAITLAND, F. W. Justice and police. Lond. 1885.

1315 SIMPSON, H. B. The office of constable. *E.H.R.* x (1895), 625–41.

1315a REITH, C. A new study of police history. Edin. 1956.

1316 WEBB, SIDNEY and BEATRICE The story of the king's highway. Lond. 1913.

1317 WELLINGTON, R. H. The king's coroner, being a complete collection of the statutes relating to the office, together with a short history of the same. Lond. 1905–6.
Vol. i, *Statutes*; vol. ii, *Summary of procedure and cases from reporters.*

1318 WILSON, J. S. Sheriff's rolls of the sixteenth and seventeenth centuries. *E.H.R.* xlvii (1932), 31–45.

E. Courts Leet, Baron, Manorial Courts

(a) *Bibliography*

Gross (1), pp. 511–12, has a useful note on the subject. For contemporary legal treatises, cf. Beale (1480), 131–3. There is a good deal of bibliographical material in Hall (2534), M. F. Moore (2584), Lipson (2556), Hearnshaw (2580), and Hone (2582). For lists of manorial records in the P.R.O., the B.M., and in private hands, cf. Gross (1), p. 512. For borough courts, cf. ch. xi, *infra* (pp. 352 ff.). There is pertinent material also in ch. vii. 2 *infra* (pp. 217 ff.).

(b) *Sources*

No attempt is made to list here the records of particular courts many of which are printed in the publications of local historical societies. For those printed before 1912, cf. M. F. Moore (2584).

1319 CALTHROPE, CHARLES. The relation betweene the lord of a mannor and the coppyholder his tenant. . . . Lond. 1635.
Repr. in E. Coke, *Compleate copyholder*, Lond. 1650, and in *Manorial Soc. Pub.* x (1917). A reading delivered by Calthrope, who died in 1616.

1320 MODUS TENEND[I] CUR[IAM] BARON[UM] cum visu franc[i] plegii. Lond. [1506].
At least 23 separate eds. by 1552, and 4 in the seventeenth century; also bound up with at least 11 eds. of the *Boke* (1280). English trans., *Manorial Soc.*, Lond. 1916. Cf. also F. W. Maitland, *The court baron, Selden Soc.* iv (1891).

1321 MODUS TENENDI UNUM HUNDREDU[M] siue curiam de recordo. Lond. 1516 or 1521.
At least 14 separate eds. by 1547; also bound up with at least 11 eds. of the *Boke* (1280). Cf. also (1322). Beale (1480) gives 1521 for the date of the first ed.; *S.T.C.* (35) gives 1516.

1322   KITCHIN, JOHN. Le court leete, et court baron. Lond. 1579.

At least 7 separate eds. in the sixteenth century, and 3 in the seventeenth; also bound up with *The aucthoritie of al justices of peace* (1280).

English trans., *Jurisdictions: or, the lawful authority of courts leet, courts baron, court of marshalsea, court of pye-powder, and ancient demesne*, Lond. 1656.

A facsimile of the 1650 ed. was published by the *Manorial Soc.*, 1914.

(c) *Later Works*

There are none dealing specifically with the sixteenth century. Many of the seventeenth- and early-eighteenth-century treatises are illuminating. (Cf. Davies (8), pp. 45–57 *passim.*) Perhaps the best account is in S. and B. Webb, *English local govt. . . . the manor and borough*, 2 vols., Lond. 1908, though it is concerned primarily with the period following 1689. Holdsworth (1544), i, 132–51, 176–87, gives a brief account. Cf. also Hone (2582), Hearnshaw (2580) and Thomas (1035). Maitland's *Select pleas in manorial courts* (Gross (1), no. 2408) has a valuable introduction, though directly relevant to a much earlier period.

1323   BLOUNT, THOMAS. Fragmenta antiquitatis, antient tenures of land and jocular customs of some mannors. Lond. 1679; 1784; by I. Beckwitt, 1815; by W. C. Hazlitt, 1874.

The later eds. are entitled *Tenures of land and customs of manors*. Hazlitt's ed. is 'rearranged, corrected and enlarged'.

5. SPECIAL JURISDICTIONS

(a) *Sources*

Reference should be made to the list of *Court rolls* (1647) and the list of *Plea rolls* (1648) in the P.R.O. For printed collection of sources on Chester, Lancaster, and Durham, cf. Gross (1), nos. 2162, 2167, 2292, 2294–6, 2336, 2338–40, 2448–9, 2451–2, 2456–9, 2460.

The official records of the palatinates of Chester, Durham, and Lancaster, the duchy of Lancaster and the honour of Peveril are now in the P.R.O. Cf. Giuseppi (74), i, 296–336. For a discussion of the records of the palatinate of Durham, cf. Lapsley (1343), app. iii.

1323a   THE EARLDOM AND COUNTY PALATINE OF CHESTER. By Geoffrey Barraclough. Oxf. 1953. Reprinted from *Trans. Hist. Soc. Lancs. and Ches.* ciii.

1324   INVENTORY OF THE RECORDS relating to the royal forests in the Wakefield Tower (formerly). *Deputy keeper's report*, v (1844), 46–59. Cf. also *Report*, xx (1859), 126–7.

1325   THE LAWES AND STATUTES of the stannarie of Devon. Lond. 1600.

For the stannaries in general, cf. nos. (2806–7) *infra*.

1326   LIST OF RECORDS OF THE DUCHY OF LANCASTER (1066 ff.), preserved in the P.R.O. *P.R.O. lists and indexes*, no. 14 (1901).

A complete inventory of all types of records.

1327 LIST OF RECORDS OF THE PALATINATES of Chester, Durham and Lancaster, the honour of Peveril and the principality of Wales, preserved in the P.R.O. *P.R.O. lists and indexes,* no. 40 (1914).

1328 MANWOOD, JOHN. A brefe collection of the lawes of the forest. [Lond. 1592.]

1329 MANWOOD, JOHN. A treatise and discourse of the lawes of the forest. Lond. 1598.

1330 PLEADINGS AND DEPOSITIONS in the duchy court of Lancashire. By Henry Fishwick. 3 vols. *Rec. Soc. for Lancs. and Ches.* (1896–9).

1331 THE RIGHTS AND JURISDICTION of the county palatine of Chester. By J. B. Yates. 2 vols. *Chetham Misc.* ii, no. 1 (1854).

(b) *Later Works*

For works on the royal forests, cf. Gross (1), pp. 130–1. There is a good bibliography on Durham in Lapsley (1343). The *Victoria County Histories* (4203) of Chester, Durham, and Lancashire should be consulted. The introduction to 1330 is useful. On the special jurisdiction in the Stannaries, the Forest of Dean, and other mining districts, cf. nos. 2776–2815 *infra.*

1332 BROOKS, F. W. The Council in the North. *Hist. Assoc. Pamphlet.* Lond. 1953.

1333 BROOKS, F. W. York and the Council of the North. *St. Anthony's Hall Pub.* v (1954).

1335 DE LA ROGERIE, BOURDE. Occupation de Serk par les Français en 1549. *Soc. Guernsiaise Rept. and Trans. for 1938,* xiii (1939), 178–85.

1336 DICKIN, E. P. A history of Brightlingsea, a member of the Cinque Ports. Brightlingsea, 1939.

1337 EAGLESTON, A. J. The Channel Islands under Tudor government, 1485–1642. Cambr. 1949.

1338 EAGLESTON, A. J. The quarrel between the ministers and the civil power, 1581–5. *Soc. Guernsiaise Rept. and Trans. for 1936,* xii (1937), 481–90.
Presbyterianism in the Channel Islands.

1339 EAGLESTON, A. J. The dismissal of the seven jurats in 1565. *Soc. Guernsiaise Rept. and Trans. for 1936,* xii (1937), 508–16.

1340 EAGLESTON, A. J. Guernsey under Sir Thomas Leighton, 1570–1610. *Soc. Guernsiaise Rept. and Trans. for 1937,* xiii, (1938), 72–108.

1341 KEMPTHORNE, G. A. An Elizabethan swainmote court roll of Finchampstead bailiwick. *Berks. Arch. Jour.,* n.s., xxxvi (1932), 106–20.

1342 LAPSLEY, G. T. The problem of the north. *A.H.R.* v (1900), 440–66.
Cf. also 1170.

1343   LAPSLEY, G. T. The county palatine of Durham, a study in constitutional history. *Harvard Hist. Studies*, viii (1900).
Scholarly. Chiefly valuable for the medieval period.

1344   LEWIS, G. R. The stannaries.
Cf. 2806. The standard work on the subject. Cf. also *Laws and customs of the stannaries in Cornwall and Devon*, by Thomas Pearce, Lond. 1725.

1345   MURRAY, K. M. E. The Constitutional history of the Cinque Ports. *Univ. of Manchester Pub.* ccxxxv. Manchester, 1935.
Chiefly medieval but helpful for sixteenth century.

1346   MURRAY, K. M. E. Faversham and the Cinque Ports. *Trans. R.H. Soc.*, 4th ser., xviii (1935), 53–84.

1347   NISBET, JOHN. The history of the Forest of Dean. *E.H.R.* xxi (1906), 445–59.
Cf. also 2796.

1348   SAUNDERS, A. C. Jersey in the 15th and 16th centuries. Jersey, 1934.

1349   SOMERVILLE, ROBERT. History of the Duchy of Lancaster, vol. i, 1265–1603. Lond. 1953.
Important as a study and a quarry.

1350   TURNER, G. J. The justices of the forest south of the Trent. *E.H.R.* xviii (1902), 112–16.

1351   TURTON, R. B. The Honor and Forest of Pickering. 4 vols. *North Riding Rec. Soc.*, n.s., i–iv (1894).

6. MARCHES AND BORDERS

(a) *Sources*

For a general discussion of the sources and a bibliography of secondary works, cf. Tough (1361), pp. xi–xxv.

In addition to the works cited below a good deal of material relative to the Scottish border is to be found in *Cal. S.P., Foreign*, 1558–77 (87), *Cal. S.P., Domestic, Addenda* (86), *Cal. S.P., Scotland* (4924), *Acts of privy council* (1152), *Register of the privy council of Scotland* (4930), and *Accounts of lord high treasurer, Scotland* (4925); the following collections in the *Hist. MSS. Comm. Reports*: *Salisbury MSS.* (185), *Laing MSS.* (240), *Home of Wedderburn MSS.* (236), *Mar and Kellie MSS.* (243), *Athole and Home MS.* (219), and *Rutland MSS.* (181), and in the following: *Hamilton papers* (4926), *Sadler papers* (4958), *Bowes correspondence* (5303), *Melville's memoirs* (4989), and *Carey's memoirs* (603). The Border ballads should not be neglected.

On the Welsh borders, cf. 6262, 6296, 6297, 6300.

1352   THE BORDER PAPERS, calendar of letters and papers relating to the affairs of the borders of England and Scotland preserved in her Majesty's Public Record Office (1560–1603). By Joseph Bain. 2 vols. Edin. 1894–6.
Principally reports of border wardens. Material incomplete because of papers taken from collection to include in other series, especially *Domestic, Addenda* (86). Calendared fully.

1353 LEGES MARCHIARUM OR BORDER LAW; containing several original articles and treaties made and agreed upon by the commissioners of the respective kings of England and Scotland, &c. By William Nicholson. Lond. 1705.
Contains an app. of charters and records relating to treaties.

1354 EXTRACTS FROM THE COPY-BOOK OF LETTERS received by Sir Henry Witherington, knt. marshal of Berwick, between Nov. 1581 and Nov. 1592, preserved in the Ordnance office in the Tower of London. *Arch.* xxx (1844), 160–73.

1355 PUGH, T. B. 'The indenture for the Marches' between Henry VII and Edward Stafford (1477–1521), duke of Buckingham. *E.H.R.* lxxi (1956), 436–41.

(b) *Later Works*

Reference should be made to the general histories of the period of England, of Scotland, and of Wales, to the local histories of the English, Scottish, and Welsh border counties, to the histories of Berwick, Carlisle, and Newcastle, to Skeel (6300) and Reid (1170), and Thomas (6302), and to 6292, 6296–7.

1356 COULOMB, C. A. The administration of the English borders during the reign of Elizabeth. Philadelphia, 1912.
Slight.

1357 HODGKIN, THOMAS. The wardens of the northern marches. Lond. 1908.
Brief, but excellent.

1358 MACKENZIE, W. M. The debateable land. *Scot. Hist. Rev.* xxx (1951), 109–25.

1359 PEASE, HOWARD. The lord wardens of the marches of England and Scotland. Lond. 1913.
Based on printed sources. Superficial.

1361 TOUGH, D. L. W. The last years of a frontier. Oxf. 1928.
A history of the Scottish border under Elizabeth. Rather weak on institutional questions.

1362 WALLACE, H. M. Berwick in the reign of Queen Elizabeth. *E.H.R.* xlvi (1931), 79–88.
Deals with Berwick as a border fortress.

1363 WARDENS and Deputy Wardens of the Marches of England towards Scotland, in Northumberland and the English wardens of Berwick upon Tweed. *Arch. Aeliana,* xxviii (1950), 18–95.

IV

HISTORY OF POLITICAL THEORY

A. SOURCES

Titles in this section are arranged in the order of their publication.

There is a useful list of the more important contemporary works dealing with political theory in the sixteenth century in Allen (1432), pp. 517 ff.

Political theory in England in the sixteenth century dealt in large measure with the relations of church and state. A great deal of pertinent material is therefore to be found scattered through the works of ecclesiastical writers, given more fully in ch. vi *infra*; notably for the reign of Henry VIII, Cranmer (1718), Tyndale (1991), Gardiner (2103) and Sir Thomas More (450); for Edward VI, Latimer (1732), Lever (2105), and Hooper (1731); for Mary, Cardinal Pole (1739); for Elizabeth, the Anglicans Hooker (2170), Bancroft (2156, 2221, 2393–4), Whitgift (2181, 2417), Bridges (2445), and Bilson (2160), the Puritans Cartwright (2397–9, 2403) and Travers (1404), the Separatists Ainsworth (2454), Browne (2455–7), Barrow (2463), and Udall (2416), the Catholics Allen (2234–9) and Parsons (2269–73). There is something also in writers dealing primarily with social conditions such as Fish (1974) and Brinkelow (2098).

1364 DUDLEY, EDMUND. The tree of the commonwealth. Manchester, 1859; new ed. by D. M. Brodie, Cambr. 1948.
Written 1509. A definition of the royal position and duties by a sycophant. Cf. also C. M. Webster, *Notes and Queries*, clxvii (1934), 222–3.

1365 [MORE, THOMAS.] Libellus . . de optimo reip. statu, de qua nova insula Utopia . . . (commonly known as Utopia). Louvain, 1516; 1st Eng. trans. by Raphe Robynson, Lond. 1551; best Eng. ed. by J. R. Lumby, Lond. 1879.
A vast number of eds. and translations have appeared. Cf. J. H. Hexter, *More's Utopia: the biography of an idea*, Lond. 1952; Russell Ames, *Citizen Thomas More and his Utopia*, Lond. 1949; and G. B. Parks, *More's Utopia and geography*, *Jour. Eng. and German Philol.* xxxvii (1938), 224–36.

1366 TYNDALE, WILLIAM. The obedience of a Christian man and how Christian rulers ought to govern. Marlborow (but more probably Antwerp), 1528; by Richard Lovett, *Christian Classic Series*, Lond. 1885.
Also printed in Day's folio (1990) and in *Parker Soc.* ed. of Tyndale's *Works* (1991). Argues against the immunity of the clergy.

1367 [SAINT GERMAN, CHRISTOPHER.] Dialogus de fundamentis legum Anglie et de conscientia. Lond. 1528. Eng. trans. *Hereafter foloweth a dyaloge in Englysshe betwyxt a doctoure of dyuynyte and a student in the lawes of England*, Lond. [1530]; 1531; Cincinnati, 1874.
The ed. of 1531 contained 'newe addycyons' which were also separately published, Lond. 1531, under the title, *The new addicions, treating most specially of the power of the parlyament concerynge the spiritualitie and the spiritual jurisdiction*.
The Latin version includes disquisitions upon the canon law omitted in the Eng. trans. Cf. F. L. Baumer, *Christopher St. German: the political philosophy of a Tudor lawyer*, *A.H.R.* xlii (1937), 631–51; and Pearl Hogrefe, *The life of Christopher Saint German*, *Rev. Eng. Studies*, xiii (1937), 398–404.

1368 [SAINT GERMAN, CHRISTOPHER.] The secunde dyaloge in Englysshe bytwene a doctour of dyuynytye and a student. Lond. 1530; 1531; [Lond.], 1721; 15th ed., *Doctor and student; or, dialogues between a doctor of divinity and a student in the laws of England.* . . . Lond. 1751; Cincinnati, 1874.
To 15th ed. are added *thirteen chapters on the power and jurisdiction of the parliament*, &c. . . . omitted in all eds. between 1531 and 1751.

1369 MORE, THOMAS. A dyaloge of Syr Thomas More . . . wherein he treatyd dyuers matters, as of the veneration and worshyp of ymagys . . . wyth many othere thyngys touchyng the pestylant sect of Luther and Tyndale. . . . Lond. 1529; repr. in *English Works* (450).
Generally known as *A dialogue concerning heresies.*

1370 TYNDALE, WILLIAM. An answere unto Sir T. More's dialogue. [Antwerp? 1530]; repr. in Day (1990) and *Works* (1991).
A reply to 1369.

1371 ELYOT, THOMAS. The boke named the governour. Lond. 1531; by H. H. S. Croft, Lond. 1883; *Everyman Series*, Lond. 1907.
Seven other eds. appeared in the sixteenth century. Sets forth the ideal education of a ruler of the ideal commonwealth.

1372 MACCHIAVELLI, NICCOLÒ. I discorsi . . . . Florence, 1531. 1st Eng. trans. by E. Dacres, Lond. 1636; best Eng. ed. by L. J. Walker, 2 vols., Lond. 1950.
Written between 1513 and 1519. Cf. Felix Gilbert, *The composition and structure of Machiavelli's Discorsi, Jour. Hist. Ideas*, xiv (1953), 136-56.

1373 MACCHIAVELLI, NICCOLÒ. Il Principe. Florence, 1532. 1st Eng. trans. by E. Dacres. Lond. 1639.
Written in 1513. Cf. Felix Gilbert, *The humanist concept of the Prince and 'The Prince' of Machiavelli, Jour. Mod. Hist.* xi (1939), 449-83. Cf. Napoleone Orsini, *Elizabethan MS. Translations of Machiavelli's Prince, Jour. Warburg Inst.* i (1937), 166-9.

1374 [SAINT GERMAN, CHRISTOPHER.] A treatise concernynge the diuision betwene the spiryttualtie and temporaltie. Lond. [1532?].
One of the most important of early English books defining secular and ecclesiastical jurisdiction; called forth Sir Thomas More's *Apology* (1375).

1375 MORE, THOMAS. The apologye of Syr Thomas More. Lond. 1533; repr. in 450; by A. I. Taft, *E.E.T.S.* clxxx (1930).
An answer to 1374.

1376 [SAINT GERMAN, CHRISTOPHER.] Salem and Bizance (a dialogue betwixte two Englyshe men, whereof one was called Salem and the other Bizance). Lond. 1533.
An answer to 1375; answered in 1377.

1377 MORE, THOMAS. The debellacyon of Salem and Bizance. Lond. 1533; repr. in 450.
An answer to 1376.

1378 SAMPSON, RICHARD. Oratio quae docet hortatur admonet omnes potissimum Anglos regiae dignitati cum primis ut obediant, &c. Lond. 1533.
Attacks papal jurisdiction. Answered by Cardinal Pole (1382).

1379 BARNES, ROBERT. The supplication of Doctour Barnes unto the most gracyous Kynge Henrye the eyght, with the declaration of his articles condened by the byshops. Lond. [1532 or 4?]; repr. in Day (1990).

1380 [FOX, EDWARD.] Opus eximium de vera differentia regiae potestatis et ecclesiasticae. . . . Lond. 1534; repr. in Goldast (1428), iii, 23 ff.
An English trans. by Lord Henry Stafford was published in Lond. 1548. Attacks immunity of clergy.

1381 GARDINER, STEPHEN. De vera obedientia oratio. Lond. 1535; ed. with preface by E. Bonner, Hamburg, 1536; Eng. trans. [by John Bale?], Lond. 1553; later Eng. ed. by B. A. Heywood, Lond. 1870.
For the various eds. in Latin and Eng. with a discussion of Bonner's preface, cf. Muller (358), pp. 309–11. An Eng. trans. of this tract, with two other tracts of Gardiner never before printed, and ed. by Pierre Janelle has been published under the title *Obedience in church and state*, Cambr. 1930.

1382 POLE, REGINALD. Pro ecclesiasticae unitatis defensione. [Rome, 1536]; Ingolstadt, 1587.
A reply to 1378.

1383 STARKEY, THOMAS. An exhortation to the people instructynge theym to vnitie and obedience. Lond. [1540?].

1384 STARKEY, THOMAS. Dialogue between Pole and Lupset. By J. W. Cowper. *E.E.T.S.*, extra ser., xii (1871); new ed. by K. M. Burton, Lond. 1948.
An attempt to define a true commonwealth. Valuable also for discussion of social evils. Written before 1539 but not printed before 1871. Cf. F. L. Baumer, *Thomas Starkey and Marsilius of Padua*, *Politica*, ii (1936), 188–205.

1385 A NECESSARY DOCTRINE AND ERUDITION for any Christen man. Lond. 1543; repr. in 1903 *infra*; by T. A. Lacey, Lond. 1932.
Commonly known as *King Henry's book*.

1386 A SUPPLICATION OF THE POORE COMMONS. [Lond. 1546]; repr. in *A supplicacyon* (1974).

1387 BEKINSAU, JOHN. De supremo et absoluto regis imperio. Lond. 1546; repr. in Goldast (1428), i, 733–55.

1388 AN EXHORTATION CONCERNING GOOD ORDER and obedience. Printed in *Certayne sermons or homilies appoynted by the kynges maiestie*, &c., Lond. 1547; repr. in *Homilies appointed to be read in churches*, by J. Griffiths, Oxf. 1859.

1389 THOMAS, WILLIAM. The historie of Italie. . . . Lond. 1549.
Cf. also his *Discourses* printed in Strype (1849), ii, 365–93, and, more accurately, in A. d'Aubant's ed. of Thomas's *Works*, Lond. 1774. Reveals a strong Italianate influence. Cf. 463.

1390 CHEKE, JOHN. The hurt of sedicion howe grevous it is to a communewelth. Lond. 1549.
Sometimes known as *The true subject to the rebel*; 1st ed. published anonymously. Repr. in Holinshed (314), ed. 1587, iii, 1042–55.

1391 PONET (or POYNET), JOHN. A shorte treatise of politike power. . . . [Strasburg?], 1556; [Lond.], 1639; 1642.
One of the earliest systematic English books limiting the duty of obedience to the king.

1392   GOODMAN, CHRISTOPHER. How superior powers oght to be obeyd
. . . Geneva, 1558; repr. *Facsimile Text Society*, New York, 1932.
Strongly anti-Spanish, emphasizing limits of the obedience of subjects.

1393   GILBY, ANTHONY. An admonition to England and Scotland to call
them to repentance. Geneva, 1558; repr. in *Knox's Works* (1394), iv, 553–71.
Attacks Marian régime.

1394   KNOX, JOHN. Works of. By David Laing. 6 vols. Edin. 1846–64.
From the point of view of political theory the most important works of Knox are *The
Appellation, A letter addressed to the commonality of Scotland* and *The first blast of the
trumpet against the monstrous regiment of women*, all first published in Geneva in 1558.
John Aylmer replied to *The first blast* in *An harborowe for faithfull and trewe subjects*,
Strassburg, 1559. There is also a treatise in MS. by Henry Howard entitled *A dutifull
defense of the lawfull regiment of woman* preserved in *Lansdowne MSS.* 813 and *Harleian
MSS.* 7021, no. 11.

1395   JEWEL, JOHN. Apologia ecclesiae Anglicanae. Lond. 1562; trans. by
Ann Bacon, Lond. 1562; repr. by John Ayre, in *Works*, 4 vols., *Parker Society*,
1845–50.
The first methodical statement of the position of the Church of England. A work of
learning which exercised great influence. A Latin life of Jewel by L. Humphrey was
published in Lond. 1573.

1396   HALES, JOHN. A declaration of the succession of the crowne imperiale
of England. Lond. 1563; repr. in G. Harbin, *Hereditary right of the crown of
England asserted*, app. vii, p. 20, Lond. 1713.
Supports the claims of the Suffolk line.

1397   THE RIGHT OF SUCCESSION TO THE CROWN of England in
the family of the Stuarts . . . asserted and defended by Sir N. Bacon against
Sir A. Browne. By Nathaniel Booth. Lond. 1723.
The tract attributed here to Browne was by John Hales (cf. 1396), the one attributed to
Bacon is the second book of John Leslie's defence of Mary Q. of Scots (cf. 5180). An-
other tract supporting the Stuarts, written by Robert Waldegrave, was edited by J. P. R.
Lyell in the *E.H.R.* li (1936), 289–301.

1398   A LETTER ON THE ELIZABETHAN SUCCESSION QUESTION,
1566. By Mortimer Levine. *Hunt. Lib. Quar.* xix (1955), 13–38.
From a MS. in the Bodleian library.

1399   STAPLETON, THOMAS. A counterblast to M. Hornes vayne blaste
against J. Fekenham. . . . Louvain, 1567; repr. in *Opera* (2286).
The most elaborate and important of the works against the oath of supremacy, based
upon Feckenham's book of 1565 and Robert Horne's reply published in 1566 (*S.T.C.*
(35), no. 13818).
The substance of the *Counterblast* was probably written by Feckenham but revised
by Stapleton and published under his name.

1400   AN HOMILIE AGAYNST DISOBEDIENCE and wylful rebellion.
Lond. [1571?]; repr. in *Homilies* . . ., by J. Griffiths, Oxf. 1859.

1401   BULLINGER, HEINRICH. Bullae papisticae . . . contra . . . reginam
Elizabetham . . . promulgatae refutatio. Lond. 1571; Eng. trans. by A.
Golding, Lond. 1572.

1402　FIRST AND SECOND ADMONITION TO PARLIAMENT. s.l. 1572.
Cf. 2391–2.

1403　BRIDGES, JOHN. The supremacie of christian princes over all persons throughout these dominions . . . against the counterblast of T. Stapleton . . . and also against N. Sanders his *Visible monarchie*, &c. Lond. 1573.
Cf. also 2445.

1404　[TRAVERS, WALTER?] Ecclesiasticae disciplinae et Anglicanae ecclesiae . . . explicatio. [La Rochelle?], 1574.
An Eng. trans. (usually ascribed to Thomas Cartwright) was published [Zürich?] 1574 under the title, *A full and plain declaration of ecclesiastical discipline*.
For the authorship of this book and its publication, cf. 2437, pp. 135 ff. Often erroneously called *The book of discipline*, and so confused with the puritan book of discipline *par excellence*.
A statement of the Presbyterian position regarding church government.

1405　BLACKWOOD, ADAM. De vinculo: sive conjunctione religionis et imperii. Paris, 1575 (first 2 books); 1612 (3rd book).

1406　GENTILLET, INNOCENT. Discours sur les moyens de bien gouverner et en bonne paix un royaume, contre N. M. le Florentin. Lausanne, 1576; Eng. trans., Lond. 1602; later Eng. ed., Lond. 1608.
Commonly known as the *Anti Machiavel*. The basis for much English popular misconception of Machiavelli's theories.

1407　BODIN, JEAN. Les six livres de la république. Lyon, 1576; Latin trans. 1586; Eng. trans. (by R. Knolles), Lond. 1606; abridged ed. trans. by M. J. Tooley, Oxf. s.a.
The Latin trans. was made by Bodin himself with some augmentation of the French version. Eight French, 3 Latin, 1 Italian, 1 Spanish, and 1 German version appeared before 1594. Its influence on political thought in all western Europe was profound. Cf. G. L. Mosse, *The influence of Jean Bodin's Republique on English political thought*, *Med. et hum.* v (1948), 73–83.

1408　[BRUTUS, S. J.?] Vindiciae contra tyrannos. [Basel, 1579]; first French trans. s.l., 1581; first Eng. trans. [Amsterdam], 1581; by H. Laski, Lond. 1924.
Authorship in dispute—attributed to Duplessis-Mornay and to H. Languet, but cf. Allen (1432), p. 319, n. 2. Laski's ed. is a repr. of the bad Eng. trans. of 1689, with an excellent introduction. Exercised considerable influence on English political thinking in the seventeenth century.

1409　BUCHANAN, GEORGE. De jure regni apud Scotos dialogus. Edin. 1579; reissues in 1579 and 1580; later eds. Edin. 1580; 1581.
Usually repr. in eds. of *Buchanan's history* (4972). Subordinates the king to the will of the people. Influential upon seventeenth-century English political thinking. A new trans. by C. F. Arrowood was published in Austin, U.S.A., 1949. Cf. also J. H. Burns, *Three Scots Catholic critics of George Buchanan*, *Innes Rev.* i (1950), 92–109; and Camilla Hay, *George Buchanan et Adam Blackwood*, *Hum. et Renaissance*, viii (1946), 156–71.

1410　BLACKWOOD, ADAM. Apologia pro regibus adversus Georgii Buchanani dialogum de jure regni apud Scotos. Poitiers [1581]; Paris, 1588; by G. Naudé, in *Collected works*. Paris, 1644.
An able defence of the institution of monarchy.

1411   MERBURY, CHARLES. A briefe discourse of royall monarchie ... &c.
Lond. 1581.

1412   SMITH, THOMAS. De republica anglorum. . . . Lond. 1583.
Cf. 1015.

1413   BILSON, THOMAS. The true difference between christian subjection
and unchristian rebellion. Oxf. 1585; Lond. 1586.
Written at the request of Elizabeth in view of her aid to the Dutch against king of
Spain. Specifically a reply to Allen (2234).

1414   CROMPTON, RICHARD. A short declaration of the ende of traytors
and false conspirators against the state, and the duetie of subjects to their
souereigne governour. Lond. 1587.
Dedicated to Whitgift; a lawyer's view of obedience.

1415   [ROSSAEUS, G.?] De justa reipublicae christianae in reges impios et
haereticos auctoritate. Antwerp, 1592.
Ascribed to Rose, bishop of Senlis; by others to William Reynolds. The work of a
Catholic monarchomach. On Reynolds as author, cf. C. H. McIlwain, *Who was 'Ros-
saeus'?*, *Politica*, ii (1936), 156–9.

1416   COSIN, RICHARD. An apologie: of and for sundrie proceedings by
jurisdiction ecclesiasticall. Lond. 1591.
Chiefly in defence of the *ex-officio* oath. Cf. 2405.

1417   DOLEMAN, R. [Parsons, Robert]. A conference about the next suc-
cession to the crowne of England. . . . [Antwerp?], 1594.
Supports the right of subjects to alter the succession and favours the right of the
Infanta of Spain to succeed Elizabeth. Parsons was probably the author (cf.
Tierney's *Dodd* (1781), iii, 31, but cf. Code (2315), p. 54). Answered in 1420, 1423,
1428. Cf. McIlwain (1425), introduction, app. D.

1418   HOOKER, RICHARD. Of the lawes of ecclesiasticall politie. Books i–iv,
Lond. 1594; book v, 1597; books vi and vii, 1648; book vii, 1662; by J. Keble,
Oxf. 1836; best ed., 7th ed. of J. Keble revised by W. Church and F. Paget,
Oxf. 1888.
The 6th, 7th, and 8th books in their original form are said to have been destroyed by a
puritan. As we have them, the 6th book, though possibly by Hooker, does not, except
for the first two chapters, belong to his plan; the 7th and 8th books were evidently con-
structed from his rough notes. Cf. on them the introduction to ed. of 1888.
   Designed to show that puritan criticism of the Elizabethan church was unsound.
Easily the most important contribution to English political thought in the sixteenth
century. Cf. C. Looten, *Un avocat de l'église anglicane: Richard Hooker (1554–1600),
Of the laws of ecclesiastical polity (1592–3 et 1597)*, *Rev. Hist. Ecclés.* xxxiii (1937),
485–534.

1419   FLORENTINE HISTORIE written in the Italian tongue by Niccolò
Macchiavelli . . . and translated into English by Thomas Bedingfield. Lond.
1595.
Bedingfield's introduction reflects the influence of Italian thought on English political
philosophy.

1420   WENTWORTH, PETER. A pithie exhortation to her majestie for
establishing her successor to the crowne, whereunto is added a discourse

containing the author's opinion of the true and lawfull successor to her majestie. [Edin.], 1598.
Written in 1587 while Wentworth was in the Tower, to support James VI's claims to the succession. An answer to 1417.

1421   BARCLAY, WILLIAM. De regno et regali potestate adversus Buchananum, Brutum, Boucherium et reliquos monarchomachos. Paris, 1600.
Defends the royal power against Buchanan (1409), Brutus (1408), and Boucher, *De justa Henrici iii abdicatione*, Paris, 1589.

1422   HARINGTON, JOHN. A tract on the succession to the crown, A.D. 1602. . . . By C. R. Markham. *Roxburghe Club*, 1880.
Written to support claims of James of Scotland, but never printed before 1880. Contains many interesting sidelights on Elizabeth.

1423   [HAYWARD, JOHN]. An answer to the first part of a certaine conference concerning succession published not long since under the name of R. Doleman. Lond. 1603.
Supports succession of James and the divine right of kings. Cf. S. L. Goldberg, *Sir John Hayward, 'Politic' historian, Rev. Eng. Studies*, n.s., vi (1955), 233–44. Cf. 1417.

1424   CRAIG, THOMAS. Concerning the right of succession to the kingdom of England. By James Gatherer. 2 books. Lond. 1703.
Written in Latin 1603, but not published. Valuable preface by editor. One of the ablest expositions of the theory of the divine right of kings.

1425   JAMES I, The workes of the most high and mightie prince James . . . king of Great Britaine, France and Ireland. . . . By James, bishop of Winton. Lond. 1616; by C. H. McIlwain (*Political Works*), Cambr., U.S.A., 1918.
Contains the *Basilicon Doron* first published in 1599 and the *Trew law of free monarchies* published 1598. McIlwain's ed. contains an excellent introduction on Tudor political theory with a useful bibliography. A new ed. of the *Basilicon Doron* by James Craigie was published by the *Scot. Text. Soc.*, 3rd ser., xvi 1942 (1944); 3rd ser., xviii 1944 (1950).

1426   BARCLAY, WILLIAM. De potestate papae: an et quatenus in reges et principes seculares jus et imperium habeat. [Lond.] 1608; Pont-à-Mousson, 1608; Eng. trans., Lond. 1611; repr. in Goldast (1428), iii, 621 ff.
A famous posthumous denial of all temporal power to the pope. Answered in 1427.

1427   BELLARMINE, ROBERT. De potestate summi pontificis in rebus temporalibus adversus Gulielmum Barclaium. Rome, 1610.
The ablest contemporary exposition of the temporal claims of the papacy. Cf. 1426. For the life of Bellarmine, cf. J. Brodrick, *Robert Bellarmine, 1542–1621*, 2 vols., Lond. 1950.

1428   GOLDAST, MELCHIOR. Monarchia S. Romani imperii: sive tractatus de jurisdictione imperiali seu regia et pontificia seu sacerdotali deq. potestate imperatoris ac papae. 2 vols. [Frankfort?], 1611–14; 3 vols., 1668.
A valuable collection of sixteenth-century treatises defending monarchy chiefly against attacks of papal writers. References are to ed. of 1668.

1429   CAMDEN, WILLIAM. Discourse concerning the prerogative of the crown. By F. S. Fussner. *Proc. Amer. Philos. Soc.* ci, no. 2 (1957), 204–15.
From a MS. in Camden's hand (B.M., Stowe MS. 277), written in 1615.

1430 ROCABERTI, J. T. de. Bibliotheca maxima pontificia: in qua auctores melioris notae, qui hactenus pro sancta romana sede tum theologice tum canonice scripserunt, fere omnes continentur. 21 vols. Rome, 1898–9.
A great collection of writings on the papal side.

B. LATER WORKS

The best general account is Allen's (1432), particularly pt. ii. Also valuable are Baumer (1437) and Morris (1464). The works of Figgis, particularly (1447–8) are valuable. Some account of the political writings of the Marian refugees in Geneva is given in Martin (2149).

1431 ACTON, LORD. The history of freedom and other essays. By J. N. Figgis. Lond. 1909.
Contains, *inter alia*, *Political thoughts on the church* (repr. from *The Rambler*, 1858), *The protestant theory of persecution* (repr. from *The Rambler*, 1862).

1432 ALLEN, J. W. A history of political thought in the sixteenth century. Lond. 1928.
A brilliant account. Pt. ii deals with English thought.

1433 ARMSTRONG, E. The political theory of the Huguenots. *E.H.R.* iv (1889), 13–40.

1434 BAILEY, ALFRED. The succession to the English crown. . . . Lond. 1879.

1435 BAINTON, R. H. Changing ideas and ideals in the sixteenth century. *Jour. Mod. Hist.* viii (1936), 417–43.

1436 BASKERVILL, C. R. Sir Richard Morison as the author of two anonymous tracts on sedition. *Library*, 4th ser., xvii (1936), 83–87.
Morison (*d.* 1556), English ambassador to Charles V, published a defence of Henry VIII against Cochlaeus.

1437 BAUMER, F. L. The early Tudor theory of kingship. New Haven, 1940.

1438 BLAKEY, ROBERT. The history of political literature from the earliest times. Lond. 1855.
Of little value.

1439 BRADY, ROBERT. A true and exact history of the succession of the crown of England. 2nd ed. Lond. 1684.
Printed in *Introduction to old English history*, pp. 327 ff.

1440 BROWN, IVOR, English political theory. Lond. 1920.
Slight.

1441 CAMPBELL, L. B. Mirror for Magistrates. Oxf. 1938.

1442 DAVIES, E. T. The political ideas of Richard Hooker. Lond. 1946.

1443 D'ENTRÈVES, A. P. Richard Hooker in *The medieval contribution to political thought*. Oxf. 1939, 117–42.

1444 DOUARCHE, ARISTIDES. De tyrannicidio apud scriptores decimi sexti seculi. Paris, 1888.
A history of the theory of tyrannicide, with a valuable bibliography.

1445 DUNNING, W. A. A history of political theories, vol. ii, Luther to Montesquieu. New York, 1905.
Very brief on English contributions.

1446 FERGUSON, A. B. Renaissance realism in the 'Commonwealth' literature of early Tudor England. *Jour. Hist. Ideas*, xvi (1955), 287–305.

1447 FIGGIS, J. N. The theory of the divine right of kings. Cambr. 1896; enlarged, 1914.
A good historical account. The 2nd ed. includes an essay on Erastus and Erastianism.

1448 FIGGIS, J. N. From Gerson to Grotius, 1414–1625. Cambr. 1907; enlarged, 1916.
Valuable in general, but slight on England.

1449 FIGGIS, J. N. Political thought in the sixteenth century. In *Cambr. Mod. Hist.* (20), iii, ch. xxii.
An excellent summary, with bibliography.

1450 FIGGIS, J. N. Respublica Christiana. *Trans. R.H. Soc.*, 3rd ser., v (1911), 63–88; repr. in his *Churches in the modern state*, Lond. 1913.

1451 FIGGIS, J. N. On some political theories of the early Jesuits. *Trans. R.H. Soc.*, 2nd ser., xi (1897), 89–112.

1452 FOSTER, H. D. Political theories of the Calvinists before the Puritan exodus to America. *A.H.R.* xxi (1919), 481–503.
Valuable.

1453 FREUND, MICHAEL. Zur Deutung der Utopia des Thomas Morus. Ein Beitrag zur Geschichte der Staatsräson in England. *Hist. Zeit.* cxlii (1930), 254–78.

1454 GIERKE, OTTO. Johannes Althusius und die Entwickelung der naturrechtlichen Staatstheorien. Breslau, 1880; enlarged, 1902.

1455 GOOCH, G. P. The history of English democratic ideas in the seventeenth century. Cambr. 1898; by H. Laski, Lond. 1927.
Introduction pertinent to sixteenth century.

1456 HANCKE, E. B. Eine Studie über den Begriff der Souveränitat. By O. Gierke. *Untersuchungen zur deutschen Staats- und Rechtsgeschichte*. Breslau, 1894.

1456a HICKS, LEO. Father Robert Persons, S.J. and the book of Succession. *Recusant History*, iv (1957), 104–37.

1457 HUDSON, W. S. John Ponet (1516?–1556), advocate of limited monarchy. Chicago, 1942.

1458 JANET, PAUL. Histoire de la science politique dans ses rapports avec la morale. 3rd (rev.) ed. 2 vols. Paris, 1887.
The 1st ed. appeared in Paris, 1859, under the title *Histoire de la philosophie morale et politique*.
Slight on England.

1459   KEARNEY, H. F.   Richard Hooker: A reconstruction. *Cambr. Jour.* v (1952), 300–11.

1460   KREBS, RICHARD.   Die politische Publizistik der Jesuiten und ihrer Gegner in den letzten Jahrzehnten vor Ausbruch des dreißigjährigen Krieges. Halle, 1890.
Valuable.

1461   LAGARDE, GEORGES DE.   Recherches sur l'esprit politique de la réforme. Paris, 1926.
Contains a useful bibliographical note on the continental reformers and a list of recent books on their political theory.
   Valuable, but slight on England.

1462   LOSSEN, MAX.   Die Lehre vom Tyrannenmord in der christlichen Zeit. Munich, 1894.

1463   MICHAELIS, GOTTFRIED.   Richard Hooker als politischer Denker. *Historische Studien,* ccxxv, Berlin, 1933.

1464   MORRIS, CHRISTOPHER.   Political thought in England: Tyndale to Hooker. Oxf. 1954.
A good general account.

1465   MURRAY, R. H.   Political consequences of the reformation. Boston, 1926.
Interesting, but occasionally inaccurate.

1466   OSGOOD, H. L.   The political ideas of the Puritans. *Pol. Sci. Quar.* vi (1891), 1–28.

1467   PEARSON, A. F. S.   Church and state. Political aspects of sixteenth-century puritanism. Cambr. 1928.
Deals mainly with Thomas Cartwright's political ideas.

1468   PRAZ, MARIO.   Machiavelli and the Elizabethans. *Proc. Brit. Acad.* xiii (1928).
Cf. also E. Meyer, *Machiavelli and the Elizabethan drama,* in *Literarhistorische Forschungen,* i, Weimar, 1897; E. A. Greenlaw, *The influence of Machiavelli on Spenser,* in *Mod. Philol.* vii (1909–10), 187–202. Cf. also Napoleone Orsini, *Nuove ricerche sul machiavellismo nel rinascimento inglese, Rinascita,* i, no. 4 (1938), 92–101; no. 6 (1939), 299–304.

1469   SHIRLEY, F. J.   Richard Hooker and contemporary political ideas. Lond. 1949.

1470   SISSON, C. J.   The judicious marriage of Mr. Hooker and the birth of the laws of ecclesiastical polity. Cambr. 1940.

1471   THE SOCIAL AND POLITICAL IDEAS of some great thinkers of the renaissance and reformation. By F. J. C. Hearnshaw. Lond. 1925.
Contains essays on Sir Thomas More (by A. W. Read), Erasmus (by J. A. K. Thomson), Luther (by J. W. Allen), and Calvin (by W. R. Matthews).

1472   THE SOCIAL AND POLITICAL IDEAS of some great thinkers of the sixteenth and seventeenth centuries. By F. J. C. Hearnshaw. Lond. 1926.
Contains essays on Richard Hooker (by N. Sykes), King James I (by H. H. Chew), Bodin (by J. W. Allen), and Suarez (by A. L. Lilly).

1473   SOUTHGATE, W. M.   Erasmus: Christian humanism and political theory. *History*, xl (1955), 240-54.

1474   TAYLOR, H. O.   Thought and expression in the sixteenth century. 2 vols. New York, 1920.
Vol. ii, book iv, discusses England.

1475   TREUMANN, RUDOLF.   Die Monarchomachen, eine Darstellung der revolutionären Staatslehren des XVI Jahrhunderts, 1573-1599. Leipzig, 1895.

1476   ULLMAN, WALTER.   The development of the medieval idea of sovereignty. *E.H.R.* lxiv (1949), 1-33.

1477   WEISSBERGER, L. A.   Machiavelli and Tudor England. *Pol. Sci. Quar.* xlii (1927), 589-607.
Cf. also W. A. Phillips, *The influence of Machiavelli on the reformation in England, Nineteenth Century*, xl (1896), 907-18.

1478   WHITNEY, E. A.   Erastianism and divine right. *Hunt. Lib. Quar.* ii (1939), 373-98.

1479   WORMUTH, F. D.   The royal prerogative. New York, 1939.

V

HISTORY OF LAW

1. BIBLIOGRAPHY

In addition to the following bibliographical guides, the student should consult the catalogues of the libraries of the Inns of Court (cf. Gross (1), nos. 501, 521, 523–4); of the University library, Cambridge; and of the Harvard law school. The bibliographies in Holdsworth's new ed. of *Hist. Eng. law* (1544) are most valuable; see especially iv, 308–13; v, 355–78, *et al.*

1480 BEALE, J. H. A bibliography of early English law books. Cambr., U.S.A., 1926; supplement by J. A. Anderson, 1943.
The standard work for publications between 1480–1600. Very valuable. Cf. *A.H.R.* xxxii (1927), 640–1.

1481 BRIDGMAN, R. W. A short view of legal bibliography: containing some critical observations on the authority of the reporters and other law writers. . . . Lond. 1807.

1482 COWLEY, J. D. A bibliography of abridgments, digests, dictionaries, and indexes of English law to . . . 1800. *Selden Society*, 1932.

1483 HOLDSWORTH, W. S. Sources and literature of English law. Lond. 1925.
A description of types of legal material.

1484 INDEX TO LEGAL PERIODICALS and law library journals. New York, 1908 ff.
Publishes quarterly indexes of 71 English and American law journals.

1485 JONES, L. A., and F. E. CHAPMAN. An index to legal periodical literature. 5 vols. Boston, 1888–1928.
Lists 158 journals, earliest times to 1928.

1486 MAXWELL, W. H. A bibliography of English law. . . . Lond. 1925; Supplements, i–iv (1939–49).
Constitutes vol. i of Sweet and Maxwell's *Complete law book catalogue.* Based on old catalogues, it perpetuates ancient errors.

1487 MAXWELL, W. H. A complete list of British and colonial law reports and legal periodicals. Lond. 1913.

1488 MAXWELL, W. H. A legal bibliography of the British commonwealth of Nations. Lond. 1955.

1489 WINFIELD, P. H. The chief sources of English legal history. Cambr., U.S.A., 1925.
Valuable, but occasionally inaccurate in giving titles and eds.

1490 WORRALL, JOHN. Bibliotheca legum or compleat list of the law books of this realm. . . . Lond. 1732; 1800; 1806; 1808; (1810); 1819; &c.
The ed. of 1800 was compiled by E. Brooke and J. Rider; the ed. of 1806 and 1808, by John Clarke; the ed. of (1810) and 1819 by T. H. Hearne. Usually known as *Clarke's catalogue.*

2. GENERAL WORKS

A. Sources

The law books of the sixteenth century fall into the following groups:
  1. Collections of statutes.
  2. Decisions: year books, abridgements, and reports.
  3. Textbooks, books of practice (including collections of writs), and general treatises.
  4. Readings in the Inns of Court.

1. *Statutes*

For the statutes, cf. 1016, with the references there cited. Cf. also Winfield's discussion (1489); Beale's article in the *Harvard Law Rev.* xxxv (1921-2), 519-38, and Holdsworth (1544), iv, 307-13. V. B. Heltzel, *Ferdinando Pulton, Hunt. Lib. Quar.* xi (1947), 77-79, contains two letters from Pulton to Egerton concerning a project to reform the statutes.

2. *Decisions*

(a) *Year books*

A bibliography of printed eds. of the year books with notes of the libraries where they may be found is given in C. C. Soule, *Year Book Bibliography, Harvard Law Rev.* xiv (1901), 556-87. Beale (1480), ch. ii, gives perhaps the most accurate list. Cf. also *S.T.C.* (35), 213-18. Reference should also be made to W. H. Holdworth, *The year books, Law Quar. Rev.* xxii (1906), 360-82; W. C. Bolland, *The year books,* Cambr. 1921; J. Lambert, *Les year books de langue française,* Paris, 1928; J. Nicholson, *A register of manuscripts and printed year books extant,* Selden Soc., Lond. 1956; and Holdsworth (1544), ii, 525-56.

1491 LES REPORTS DE CASES (Edward II-27 Henry VIII). By John Maynard. 11 parts. Lond. 1678-80.
> This is the most nearly complete ed. of the year books but is badly edited and badly printed. The *Selden Soc.* is publishing scholarly eds. of the *Year books* but has not yet published any vols. for the Tudor period.

(b) *Abridgements*

Cf. Winfield (1489), ch. viii; Holdsworth (1544), ii, 543, is not so good but useful. The earliest printed abridgement is the one commonly ascribed to Nicholas Statham, which has no title-page but probably appeared about the year 1490 (Beale (1480), no. R 455). It does not go beyond 38 Henry VI. An English trans. by M. C. Klingel Smith, 2 vols., 1915, is very inaccurate. Cf. C. C. Williams, *A note on Statham's abridgement, W. Virginia Law Quar.* xlvi (1940), 233-45.

1492 BROOKE (or BROKE), ROBERT. La graunde abridgement. Lond. 1573; 1576; 1586.
> This abridgement adds to the material contained in Fitzherbert (1493) and is more systematically arranged.

1493 FITZHERBERT, ANTHONY. La graunde abridgement. Lond. 1516; 1565; 1577.

The most notable of sixteenth-century abridgements of the cases in the *Year books*. Cf. S. E. Thorne, *Fitzherbert's abridgement, Law Lib. Jour.* xxix (1936), 59–63; R. V. Rogers, *A source for Fitzherbert's La Graunde Abridgement, E.H.R.* lvi (1941), 605.

1494 [GREGORY, ARTHUR.] L'abridgement des cases concernant les titles plus materiall pur les estudients & practiciones des leyes du royalme. Lond. 1599.

Trans. and enl. by William Hughes under title, *Moot-book; a survey of the general titles . . . with cases,* Lond. 1663.

1495 TABULA LIBRI ASSISARUM. [Lond. 1517?]; Lond. 1555.

First published by Pynson. On the date cf. Holdsworth (1128), ii, 544, and Beale (1065), no. R 47 and p. 188. The ed. of 1555, by Rastell, bears the title *The abridgement of the booke of Assises.*

Summaries of selected cases. Not to be confused with *Tabula libri assisarum* [Lond. 1514–16?] which is confined to cases of Edward III's reign. Cf. Holdsworth (1544), ii, 537, 544.

(c) *Reports*

A table of the reports of the sixteenth and seventeenth centuries will be found in Holdsworth (1544), v, 358–63. Those for the sixteenth century are listed in Beale (1480), pp. 107–10. The characteristics of the several reporters are discussed in J. W. Wallace, *The reporters arranged and characterized . . .,* 4th ed., by F. F. Heard, Boston, 1882, and in V. V. Veeder, *The English reports, 1292–1865,* in *Harvard Law Rev.* xv (1901), 1–21, 109–57, repr. in part in *Select essays* (1144), ii, 123–54. Reference should also be made to Holdsworth's discussion of the reporters (1544), v, 355 ff. Cf. also Winfield (1489), pp. 183–99. The most important reporters for the Tudor period are Sir James Dyer (1512–82), Edmund Plowden (1518–85), and Sir Edward Coke (1552–1634). Cf. T. F. T. Plucknett, *The genesis of Coke's reports, Cornell Law Quar.* xxvii (1942), 190–213. Numerous abridgements and selections from sixteenth-century reports were printed in the seventeenth and eighteenth centuries. These also are listed in Holdsworth (1544), v, 358–63.

3. *Textbooks and Books of Practice*

For a general discussion of this type of legal literature, cf. Holdsworth (1544), v, 378 ff. These books may be classified as follows, though very often books of different classes were bound together and sold as a kind of convenient handbook:

  (a) Registers of writs and returns of writs.
  (b) Books of pleadings and precedents.
  (c) General treatises.
  (d) Law dictionaries.
  (e) Readings.

(a) *Registers of Writs and Returns of Writs*

1496 REGISTRUM OMNIUM BREVIUM tam originalium quam judicialium. Lond. 1531; 1553; 1595.

Cf. Maitland, *Collected papers* (1030), ii, 110–73, and Holdsworth (1540), ii, 513 ff.

1497 NATURA BREVIUM. Lond. [1496].
There were at least 17 French and 11 English eds. in the sixteenth century.
Sometimes called the *Old natura brevium* to distinguish it from Fitzherbert (1498).
For a table of contents, cf. Holdsworth (1544), ii, 640.

1498 FITZHERBERT, ANTHONY. La novel natura brevium. Lond. 1534.
At least 8 sixteenth-century eds. An Eng. trans. was published in 1682, edited by
Wadham Windham with a commentary by Sir Matthew Hale.

1499 RETURNA BREVIUM. Lond. 1516.
Beale (1480), pp. 135, 157-8, lists 17 eds. in the sixteenth century, besides 4 revised eds.
by John Kitchin.

(b) *Books of Pleadings and Precedents*

(1) General

1500 NOVAE NARRATIONES. Lond., s.a., 1561.
Beale (1480), p. 292, dates the 1st ed. conjecturally at 1496, and gives 3 eds. before 1600
Consists of precedents of pleading upon a number of writs commonly used.

1501 ARTICULI AD NARRATIONES NOVAS. . . . Lond. [1525?].
Beale (1480), p. 124, gives 8 sixteenth-century eds. On the character of this book, cf.
Holdsworth (1544), ii, 523.

1502 INTRATIONUM EXCELLENTISSIMUS LIBER. . . . Lond. 1510.
A book of precedents for pleading. The forerunner of many later books of entry of
which the most important are the so-called old *Book of entries*, Lond. 1545, Wm.
Rastell, *A colleccion of entries*, Lond. 1566; E. Coke, *A book of entries*, Lond. 1614.

**1503 DIUERSITE DE COURTZ ET LOUR JURISDICTIONS. . . . Lond.
1526.**
For other sixteenth-century eds. cf. Beale (1480), nos. T 1, 2, 110, 120-9. A brief discussion of the various courts of England. Cf. Holdsworth (1544), ii, 524.

**1504 PHAER or PHAYER, THOMAS. A newe boke of presidentes in maner
of a register. . . . Lond. 1543.**
At least 18 eds. appeared before 1600. A comprehensive collection of all kinds of legal
documents, besides a calendar of court sessions. Cf. Holdsworth (1544), v, 388.

**1505 WEST, WILLIAM. Symbolaeographia, which may be termed the art,
description or image of instruments, covenants, contracts of the notary or
scrivener. Lond. 1590.**
For later sixteenth-century eds. cf. *S.T.C.* (35), nos. 25267-79. The first part is a collection of precedents; in the 2nd ed. (1592) it was practically rewritten. The second part,
first published in 1594, contains *inter alia* a short treatise on equitable jurisdiction. Cf.
Holdsworth (1544), v, 389-90.

(2) Land laws

1506 THE OLD TENURES. Lond. [1496?].
The first dated ed. is 1525, but there were at least 4 earlier eds. Beale (1480), pp. 118-19,
gives 11 eds. in the sixteenth century. Repr. in T. E. Tomlin's ed. of *Littleton's tenures*,
Lond. 1841. Contains brief descriptions of the various kinds of tenures. Cf. Holdsworth (1544), ii, 575.

**1507 LITTLETON'S TENURES. Lond. [1480?]; best ed. by E. Wambaugh
[Washington, 1903].**
The earliest printed ed. is undated. Beale (1480), p. 299, conjectures 1480; Wambaugh,
1481 or 1482. The first English version appeared about 1532. Beale (1480), pp. 111-18,

gives 35 eds. in French and 23 in English before 1600. For an elaborate bibliography of eds., cf. Wambaugh's ed., pp. lxvii–lxxxiv. For Coke's famous commentary, cf. Davies (8), no. 477.

The first great book upon English law not written in Latin. Inspired by *Old tenures* and based upon the *Year books* but is much more than a summary of decisions. Contains a lucid account of the various tenures and estates in England. Cf. Holdsworth (1544), ii, 571–5.

1508   CARTA FEODI. Lond. [1506?].

The first known ed. is undated but conjectured by Beale (1480), p. 289, as 1506. Beale gives 25 eds. before 1600.

A small selection of forms of conveyances accompanied sometimes with short notes as to their proper use.

(3) Pleas of the Crown

1509   STAUNFORD, WILLIAM. Les plees del coron. Lond. 1557.

Beale gives 6 eds. before 1600. Founded almost entirely upon Bracton and the *Year books*.

(c) *General Treatises*

In addition to the works cited below reference should be made to Saint German's *Dialogue* (1367), which was widely used as a legal manual.

1510   CONSTABLE, ROBERT. Tertia lectura [at Lincoln's Inn] on Prerogativa Regis. By S. E. Thorne. New Haven, U.S.A., 1949.

1511   COWELL, JOHN. Institutiones juris Anglicani ad methodum institutionum Justiniani compositae et digestae. Cambr. 1605; Frankfort, 1630; Oxf. 1664; Eng. trans. by W. G. (?), Lond. 1651.

The only attempt between the Middle Ages and the nineteenth century to digest the common law according to the principles of the civil law. Cf. Holdsworth (1544), v, 21.

1512   EGERTON, THOMAS. A discourse upon the exposition and understanding of the statutes. By S. E. Thorne. San Marino, U.S.A., 1942.

From a MS. among the *Ellsmere MSS.* at the Huntington library. For the authorship cf. T. F. T. Plucknett, *Ellsmere on statutes*, *Law Quar. Rev.* lx (1944), 242 ff.

1513   [FULBECKE, WILLIAM.] A direction or preparative to the study of the lawe. Lond. 1600; 1620; repr. by T. H. Stirling, 1829.

Cf. Holdsworth (1544), v, 23.

1514   FULBECKE, W. A parallele or conference of the civil law, the canon law, and the common law, of this realme of England, &c. Lond. 1601–2; later ed., pt. i, Lond. 1618.

A series of dialogues pointing out the differences between the three systems of jurisprudence on various points. Cf. Holdsworth (1544), v, 22.

1515   LAMBARDE, WILLIAM. Archeion: or a commentary upon the high courts of justice in England. By Thomas Lambarde. Lond. 1635; by C. H. McIlwain and P. L. Ward, Cambr. U.S.A., 1957.

Completed, but not published, in 1591. Two eds. appeared in 1635, of which Thomas Lambarde's is the authoritative one. The 1957 ed. is based upon a collation of numerous manuscript copies of the text which are discussed in an appendix.

1516 PERKINS (or PARKINS), JOHN. A profitable booke treating of the lawes of England. Lond. 1528 (law French); 1555 (trans.).

The ed. of 1528 has the title-page *Incipit perutilis tractatus magistri Johnis Perkins sive explanatio quorundam capitulorum,* &c.; 4 other eds. appeared in law French before the Eng. trans. of 1555 and 9 subsequent Eng. eds. are known before the death of Elizabeth. Chiefly concerned with the land laws. Cf. Holdsworth (1544), v, 388.

1517 ROBINSON, RICHARD. A briefe collection of the Queene Majesties most high and most honourable courtes of recordes. By R. L. Rickard. *Camden Misc.* xx (1953).

A short treatise on the several royal courts written in the last decade of Elizabeth's reign, by a member of the Leathersellers Co. and based upon Alexander Fisher's MS. *Description of the courte of justice in England (S.P., Domestic, Eliz.* cx, no. 19). On Robinson's prolific literary output cf. *D.N.B.* (9).

1518 STAUNFORD [or Stanford or Stamford or Staundeford], WILLIAM. An exposition of the kinges prerogative, collected out of the great abridgement of justice Fitzherbert, and other olde writers of the lawes of England, &c. Lond. 1567.

Frequently made use of by later legal writers. Staunford was a member of parliament, a sergeant-at-law, and later, a judge of the court of common pleas. At least 6 eds. appeared before 1610.

1519 SWINBURNE, HENRY. Briefe treatise of testaments and last willes. Lond. 1590; by J. F. Powell, Lond. 1611; by James Wake, 3 vols., Lond. 1803.

Contains statutes, notes, and annotations.

(d) *Law Dictionaries*

1520 COWELL, JOHN. The interpreter, a book containing the signification of words; wherein is set forth the meaning of all . . . such words and terms as are mentioned in the laws written on statutes . . . requiring any exposition. Cambr. 1607; by Thomas Manley, Lond. 1637; augmented, 1672.

The best law dictionary of its day and still valuable. For its history, cf. McIlwain's ed. of *Works of James I* (1425), pp. lxxxvii–ix. For other dictionaries, cf. Cowley (1482).

(e) *Readings*

Lectures of Readers in the Inns of Court. Cf. in general Holdsworth (1544), ii, 506 ff.; 393 ff.; C. H. Williams, *Early law readings,* in *Bull. Inst. Hist. Research,* iii (1925–6), 96–101; and Putnam, *Early treatises* (1291), chs. v and vi, *passim.* Reference should also be made to pp. 142 ff. *infra,* on legal education. Holdsworth (1544), v, 497–9., gives a list of readings in print or in MS., taken from E. Brooke, *Bibliotheca legum Angliae* (1788), pt. ii, 191–6. Marow's *Readings,* delivered in 1503, are printed in Putnam (1291). Frowike's *Reading on the prerogative,* delivered in 1495, is printed in part in Smith's *Law Journal,* 1804–7, pp. 238–50, and in part in Constable (1510), where Constable's reading on the same subject, given in the same year, is printed in full. For a group of readings, all prior to 1489, cf. (1624). Bacon's *Reading on uses* is printed in Bacon's *Works* (by Spedding) (600), vii, 389–450. *Readings* by Sir James Dyer and Sir John Brograve were printed in Lond. 1648, and a *Reading* by Thomas Williams on trial by jury, in Lond. 1680. A complete list of sixteenth-century readings in print is a desideratum.

4. *Miscellaneous Collections of Legal Sources* (cf. 1013)

1521   COLLECTANEA JURIDICA. By Francis Hargrave. 2 vols. Lond. 1791–2.

1522   COLLECTION OF TRACTS relative to the law of England. By Francis Hargrave. Dublin, 1787.

B. LATER WORKS

Holdsworth (1544) is easily the most important general account. The studies by Maitland (1030) are valuable.

1523   ALLEN, C. K. Law in the making. Lond. 1927; 5th ed., 1951.

1524   AMES, J. B. Lectures on legal history and miscellaneous essays. Cambr., U.S.A., 1913.
Many of these have been reprinted from essays in 1562 and from legal periodicals; two especially notable are on the origin of trusts and the origin of uses.

1525   BLACKSTONE, WILLIAM. Commentaries on the laws of England. 4 vols. Lond. 1765–9.
8 eds. were published during the author's lifetime. No new ed. has appeared in England since the 21st in 1844. The last and best American eds. are Sharswood's in 1878 and Cooley's in 1884. There have been numerous adaptations, abridgements, and vols. of selections of which the best is Stephen's *New commentaries on the laws of England,* 1848–9, which reached a 9th ed. in 1883.

1527   CAMPBELL, J. The lives of the chief justices of England . . . till the death of Lord Mansfield. 3 vols. Lond. 1849–57; 4 vols. 1874.
Useful, but inaccurate.

1528   CECIL, EVELYN. Primogeniture, a short history of its development in various countries and its practical effects. Lond. 1895.

1529   CHALLIS, H. W. Law of real property in relation to conveyancing. Lond. 1885; 1892.

1530   CLARKSON, P. S., and WARREN, C. T. The law of property in Shakespeare and the Elizabethan drama. Baltimore, 1942.

1531   COOTE, CHARLES. Sketches of the lives and characters of eminent English civilians, with an historical introduction relative to the College of Advocates. Lond. 1804.

1532   COKE, EDWARD. Institutes of the laws of England. 4 pts. Lond. 1628–44; later ed. (pt. i only) by F. Hargrave and C. Butler, Lond. 1788.
Of the 4 pts. the 1st and most famous is a repr. of Littleton's *Tenures* with trans. and commentary; the 2nd is the text of a number of statutes from Magna Carta to James I; the 3rd deals with criminal law; the 4th with the jurisdiction of the various courts of law. A pioneer work of great historical interest. The ed. of 1788 (the 13th) is the basis of all later eds. of pt. i, commonly known as *Coke on Littleton.* The last 3 pts. published separately, 1642, 1644, 1644, have been published together in various eds. There have been several abridgements of pt. i. Cf. Holdsworth (1544), v, 456–93; also his article *The Elizabethan age in legal history, Iowa Law Rev.* xii (1927), 321–5, and his essay on Coke (1537) and S. E. Thorne, *Sir Edward Coke,* 1552–1952 (*Selden Soc. lect.* 1952), Lond. 1957. For Coke's personal library, cf. W. O. Hassall, *A catalogue of the library of Sir Edward Coke,* New Haven, 1950. Cf. 673.

1533 DIGBY, K. E. An introduction to the history of the law of real property, with original authorities. Oxf. 1866; 1876; 1884; by W. M. Harrison, Oxf. 1897.
A standard brief work on the subject for the use of students. In app. to pt. i, in tables i, ii, iii, there is a systematic arrangement of the main branches of the law at the beginning of the reign of Henry VIII.

1534 DUGDALE, WILLIAM. Origines juridiciales, or historical memorials of the English laws, courts of justice, &c. Lond. 1666; best ed., Lond. 1680.
Contains a chronology of the lords chancellors and other holders of judicial offices. The information given concerning the inns of court and chancery is particularly copious and curious. Abridgements appeared in 1685 and 1737.

1535 DUNCAN, J. L. The end and aim of law: ii, legal theories in England in the sixteenth and seventeenth centuries. *Juridical Rev.* i (1938), 257–81.

1536 ELTON, G. R. Informing for profit: a sidelight on Tudor methods of law enforcement. *Cambr. Law Jour.* xi (1954), 149–67.

1537 ESSAYS IN LEGAL HISTORY. By Paul Vinogradoff. Oxf. 1914.
Contains, *inter alia*: Holdsworth, *The influence of Coke on the development of English law*, pp. 297–311; W. B. Odgers, *A sketch of the history of the four Inns of Court*, pp. 233–60.

1538 FEARNE, CHARLES. Essay on the learning of contingent remainders and executory devices. Lond. 1772; 1791–5; by J. W. Smith, 2 vols., Lond. 1844.
A standard treatise.

1539 FIFOOT, C. H. S. English Law and its background. Lond. 1932.

1540 FIFOOT, C. H. S. History and sources of the common law; tort and contract. Lond. 1949.

1541 FOSS, EDWARD. Judges of England, with sketches of their lives and notices connected with the courts at Westminster, 1066–1864. 9 vols. Lond. 1848–64.
An indispensable work on the subject, but must be used with caution. Abridged under the title *Biographia juridica*, Lond. 1870.

1542 FOSS, EDWARD. Tabulae curiales: or tables of the superior courts of Westminster Hall, showing the judges who sat in them from 1066 to 1864; with the attorney- and solicitor-generals of each reign, an alphabetical list. Lond. 1865.

1543 HERBERT, T. A. History of the law of prescription in England. Lond. 1891.
Yorke prize essay for 1890.

1544 HOLDSWORTH, W. S. A history of English law. 3 vols. Lond. 1903–9; 13 vols., 1922–52; vol. i, 7th ed. rev. 1956.
The 1st ed. is chiefly confined to the period before 1485. The later ed. is the most comprehensive history of the subject. Vols. iv and v deal with the sixteenth and seventeenth centuries, but the other vols. contain much relevant material. This work is not only the most important history of English law in the Tudor period, but contains much on constitutional history. Valuable bibliographical notes. References herein are to the 2nd ed.

1545 JARDINE, DAVID. A reading on the use of torture in the criminal law of England previously to the commonwealth. Lond. 1837.
A learned discussion, with a good introduction describing the practice of reading. Extracts from original records in app.

1546 JENKS, EDWARD. A short history of English law. Lond. 1912.
From the earliest times to the end of 1911. Useful work within its brief compass, but not always accurate.

1547 JENKS, EDWARD. The story of the habeas corpus. *Law Quar. Rev.* xviii (1902), 64–77; repr. in *Select Essays* (1144), ii, 531–49.
The best account of the origin of habeas corpus.

1548 KENNY, C. S. History of the law of primogeniture in England and its effect upon landed property. Lond. 1878.
In *Two essays on the law of primogeniture* written with P. M. Lawrence.

1549 LATHAM, R. E. Curia Tremure. *E.H.R.* lxxi (1956), 428–33.
A local court held three times a year. May represent a survival of a primitive institution.

1550 LEAKE, S. M. Digest of the law of uses and profits of land. Lond. 1888.
Forms pt. iii of his digest of the law of property in land, perhaps the most useful treatise on uses.

1551 MAGUIRE, M. H. Attack of the common lawyers on the oath *ex officio*. *Essays in honor of C. H. McIlwain.* Cambr., U.S.A., 1936, pp. 199–229.

1552 MAITLAND, F. W. English law and the renaissance. Cambr. 1901; repr. in *Select Essays* (1144).
Deals with the threatened Romanization of English jurisprudence in the sixteenth century. Valuable.

1553 MAITLAND, F. W. Equity, also the forms of action at common law. Cambr. 1909; repr. 1936.
Throws much light on a difficult and obscure subject. Contains also a valuable history of the forms of action.

1554 PIKE, L. O. A history of crime in England. 2 vols. Lond. 1873–6.
The standard work.

1555 POTTER, HAROLD. An historical introduction to English law and its institutions. 3rd ed. Lond. 1948.

1556 PLUCKNETT, T. F. T. A concise history of the common law. 5th ed. Lond. 1956.

1558 REEVES, JOHN. A history of English law. 2 vols. (to 1509), Lond. 1783–4; 4 vols. (to 1558), 1787; vol. 5 (Elizabeth), 1829; by W. F. Finlason, 3 vols. 1869.
Displaced by Holdsworth (1544), but still of some value.

1559 REZNECK, SAMUEL. The trial of treason in Tudor England. *Essays in honor of C. H. McIlwain,* Cambr., U.S.A., 1936, pp. 258–88.

1560 SCRUTTON, T. E. The influence of Roman law in the law of England. Cambr. 1885.
Brief, but a good digest of existing materials.

1561 SCRUTTON, T. E. Land in fetters, or the history and policy of the laws restraining the alienation and settlement of land in England. Cambr. 1886.

1562 SELECT ESSAYS IN ANGLO-AMERICAN LEGAL HISTORY. 3 vols. Boston, 1907–9. Vol. i, Maitland, *English law and the renaissance*; Scrutton, *Roman law influence in chancery, church courts, admiralty, and law merchant*; Stubbs, *History of the canon law in England*; Holdsworth, *The development of the law merchant*; Bryce, *A comparison of the history of legal development at Rome and in England*; Zane, *The five ages of the bench and bar of England*. Vols. ii and iii, history of particular topics—many touch on sixteenth century.

1563 STEPHEN, J. F. A history of the criminal law of England. 3 vols. Lond. 1883.
Valuable, but uneven in treatment.

1564 THOMPSON, FAITH. Magna Carta. Minneapolis, 1948.

1565 USHER, R. G. The significance and early interpretation of the statute of uses. *Wash. Univ. (St. Louis) Studies*, i, pt. ii, no. 1 (1913).

1566 WINFIELD, P. H. The history of conspiracy and abuses of legal procedure. Cambr. 1921.

1567 [WYNNE, EDWARD]. A miscellany containing several law tracts. Lond. 1765.
Wynne usually wrote under the name Eunomus. This miscellany contains a tract entitled, *Observations touching the antiquity and dignity of serjeant-at-law*.

3. SPECIAL FIELDS OF LAW

A. ADMIRALTY

(a) *Sources*

For a brief account of the court and its records, cf. C. M. Andrews, *Guide to materials for American history in the Public Records Office*, Washington, 1914, vol. ii. For the early writers on the subject see Senior, *Early writers on maritime law*, Law Quar. Rev. xxxvii (1921), 323–36.

The Records of the Admiralty Court preserved in the P.R.O. are described in Giuseppi (74), i, 283 ff. Of these the most important for the Tudor period are:

(1) *Oyer and terminer records*, 1535–1834, being proceedings in trials for piracy and other crimes committed on the high seas.
(2) *Acts*, 1524–1786, which record the daily business of the court.
(3) *Examinations*, &c., 1536–1826, being depositions of witnesses, &c.
(4) *Libels*, 1519–1814. Original files of the court and chief source of information for Tudor period. Extracts from these are printed by Marsden (1570).
(5) *The black book* of the admiralty, by Travers Twiss, 4 vols., Lond. 1871–6, containing many of the fundamental laws governing admiralty cases. Cf. Gross (1), no. 2145.

1568 HIGH COURT of Admiralty examinations, 1637–8. By Dorothy Shilton and Richard Holworthy. *Anglo-Amer. Rec. Foundation* ii (1932).
Valuable for its introduction.

1569 MARSDEN, R. G. Reports, court of admiralty and upon appeal . . .
1758–74 . . . with extracts from the books and records of the high court of
admiralty and the court of the judges delegates 1584–1839, &c. Lond. 1885.

1570 SELECT PLEAS IN THE COURT OF ADMIRALTY. By R. G.
Marsden. 2 vols. *Selden Soc.* vi, xi (1892–7).
Contains, *inter alia*, pleas covering the period 1527–1602.

(b) *Later Works*

The best secondary account of the court and its work in the sixteenth century
is in 1570, introduction. Cf. also Holdsworth (1544), v, 123 ff., and Senior (2529).

1571 CLERKE, FRANCIS. Praxis supremae curiae admiralitatis. 5th ed.
Lond. 1798.

1572 MARSDEN, R. G. A digest of the cases relating to shipping, admiralty
and insurance law, from the reign of Elizabeth to the end of 1897. Lond. 1899.

1573 MARSDEN, R. G. Early prize jurisdiction and prize law in England.
E.H.R. xxiv (1909), 675–97; xxv (1910), 243–63; xxvi (1911), 34–56.

1574 MARSDEN, R. G. The high court of admiralty in relation to national
history, commerce and the colonization of America, A.D. 1550–1650. *Trans.
R.H. Soc.*, 2nd ser., xvi (1902), 69–96.

1575 ROSCOE, E. S. Early history of the English prize court. *Edin. Rev.*
ccxxxvii (1923) 133–40.

1576 RUDDOCK, A. A. The earliest records of the High Court of Admiralty,
1515–58. *Bull. Inst. Hist. Research*, xxii (1949), 139–51.

1577 SENIOR, WILLIAM. Judges of the high court of admiralty. *Mariner's
Mirror*, xiii (1927).

B. International Law

(a) *Sources*

For sixteenth-century English translations of continental works, cf. Holdsworth
(1544), v, 9.

1578 DE LEGATO ET ABSOLUTO PRINCIPE perduellionis reo. Oxf.
1587.
Deals with the case of ambassadors and princes conspiring against the life of another
prince in his territory. Possibly by one of Gentili's students. Applicable to the case of
Mary Stuart.

1579 DE LEGATIS ET LEGATIONIBUS, TRACTATII VARII. By V. E
Hrabar. Doepat, 1906.

1580 FULBECKE, WILLIAM. The pandects of the law of nations. Lond.
1602.
Cf. Holdsworth (1544), v, 9, n. 5.

1581   GENTILI, ALBERICO. De jure belli. Hanau, 1598; by T. E. Holland, Oxf. 1877; Eng. trans., 2 vols., *Classics of International Law*, xvi (1933).
Based upon lectures delivered at Oxford, 1588–9, and printed in London, 1588–9, under the title, *De jure belli commentatio prima, secunda et tertia.*
The most important of Gentili's works. For a good summary, cf. Nys (1602), 48–69.

1582   GENTILI, ALBERICO. De legationibus. Libri iii. Lond. 1585; Hanau, 1594; 1607; 2 vols., Oxf. 1924.
The ed. of 1924 in the series of *Classics of international law*, by J. B. Scott (*Carnegie Endowment for International Peace*) contains, in vol. i, a photographic reproduction of the ed. of 1594; in vol. ii, an Eng. trans. and an introduction by E. Nys. For a good summary, cf. Nys (1602), pp. 69–74.

1583   HOTMAN, JEAN. De la charge et dignité de l'ambassadeur. Paris, 1603; Eng. trans. Lond. 1603.

1584   SELDEN, JOHN. Mare clausum seu de dominio maris, libri duo. Lond. 1635; Eng. trans. Lond. 1652.

1585   SUTCLIFFE, M. The practice, proceedings and lawes of armes. Lond. 1593.
Deals with the justifiable causes of war and the way it must be waged.

(b) *Later Works*

The best general work is Nys (1604). His accounts of the early writers in 1602 are excellent. Holland's studies (1593–4) and Walker's (1607) are valuable.

1586   ADAIR, E. R. The exterritoriality of ambassadors in the sixteenth and seventeenth centuries. New York, 1929.

1587   BEHRENS, BETTY. Treatises on the ambassador written in the fifteenth and early sixteenth centuries. *E.H.R.* li (1936), 616–27.

1588   CHEYNEY, E. P. International law under Queen Elizabeth. *E.H.R.* xx (1905), 659–72.

1589   FENN, P. T. Origin of the right of fishing in territorial waters. Cambr., U.S.A., 1926.

1590   FRANCISCI, PIETRO DE, VECCHIO, GIORGIO DEL and others. Scritti e discorsi . . . Alberico Gentili. Rome, 1936.

1591   LES FONDATEURS DU DROIT INTERNATIONAL. By Antoine Tillet. Paris, 1904.
By various authors. Excellent.

1592   FULTON, T. W. The sovereignty of the sea. Edin. 1911.
Deals mainly with the Stuarts but has an admirable chapter on the Tudors.

1593   HOLLAND, T. E. An inaugural lecture on Albericus Gentilis. Lond. 1874; repr. in 1168.

1594   HOLLAND, T. E. Studies in international law. Oxf. 1898.

1595   JUSSERAND, J. A. A. J. The school for ambassadors and other essays. Lond. 1924.

1596 KALTENBORN, KARL VON. Die Vorläufer des Hugo Grotius auf dem Gebiete des Jus naturae et gentium, so wie der Politik in Reformationszeitalter. Leipzig, 1848.

1597 MATTINGLY, GARRETT. Renaissance diplomacy. Lond. 1954.

1598 MAULDE LA CLAVIÈRE, M.A., R. DE. La diplomatie au temps de Machiavel. 3 vols. Paris, 1892–3.

1599 NYS, ERNEST. Le droit de la nature et le droit des gens au xvii siècle. *Revue de droit internat.* xvi (1914), 245–86.

1600 NYS, ERNEST. Le droit de la guerre et les précurseurs de Grotius. Brussels, 1882.

1601 NYS, ERNEST. Études de droit international et de droit politique. 2 vols. Brussels, 1896–1901.

1602 NYS, ERNEST. Les initiateurs du droit publique moderne. Brussels, 1890.

1603 NYS, ERNEST. Notes pour servir à l'histoire littéraire et dogmatique du droit international en Angleterre. Brussels, 1888.

1604 NYS, ERNEST. Les origines du droit international. Brussels and Paris, 1894.
The best general work on the subject.

1605 RANDALL, H. J. History of contraband of war. *Law Quar. Rev.* xxiv (1908), 316–27.

1606 SMITH, D. B. Jean de Villiers Hotman. *Scot. Hist. Rev.* xiv (1916), 147–66.

1607 WALKER, T. A. A history of the law of nations. 2 vols. Cambr. 1899.

1608 WICQUEFORT, ABRAHAM DE. L'ambassadeur et ses fonctions. 2 vols. The Hague, 1681; best ed., 2 vols., Amsterdam, 1724; Eng. trans. Lond. (1716).
Uses a good deal of sixteenth-century illustrative material.

1609 ZELLER, G. Histoire des relations internationales: les temps modernes. I. De Christophe Columb à Cromwell. Paris, 1953.

C. LAW MERCHANT

(a) *Sources*

There is pertinent material on this subject in ch. vii, sect. 5, *infra* (pp. 246 ff.), and in sect. A, *supra* (p. 138).

1610 CALENDAR OF PLEA AND MEMORANDA ROLLS of the city of London. By A. H. Thomas. 5 vols. Cambr. 1926–54.

1611 MALYNES, GERARD DE. Consuetudo, vel lex mercatoria, or the ancient law-merchant. Lond. 1622.
A valuable contemporary statement on banking, exchange, &c.

1612 SELECT CASES IN THE LAW MERCHANT, 1270–1638. By Charles Gross and Hubert Hall. 3 vols. *Selden Soc.* xxiii, xlvi, xlix (1908–32).
Comprises cases tried in the central courts and in the fair, staple and tolsey courts, with a learned introduction on the development and decline of fair courts.

(b) *Later Works*

The only adequate account is in Holdsworth (1544), viii, ch. iv.

1613 CARTER, A. T. Early history of the law merchant in England. *Law Quar. Rev.* xvii (1901), 232–51.

1614 FLETCHER, E. G. M. The carrier's liability. Lond. 1932.

1615 PATON, G. W. Bailment in the common law. Lond. 1952.

1616 HUVELIN, P. Essai historique sur le droit des marchés et des foires. Paris, 1897.

1617 MITCHELL, WILLIAM. Essay on the early history of the law merchant. Cambr. 1904.

1618 SANBORN, F. R. Origins of the early English maritime and commercial law. New York, 1930.

4. LEGAL EDUCATION

(a) *Sources*

For a bibliography of registers of the inns of court, cf. 3755.

1619 A CALENDAR OF THE INNER TEMPLE RECORDS. By F. A. Inderwick. 5 vols. Lond. 1896–1937.
App. prints a roll of a subsidy levied upon members of the inns of court and chancery and officers of the courts of law, 1523.

1620 A CALENDAR OF MIDDLE TEMPLE RECORDS. By C. H. Hopwood. Lond. 1902.

1621 MIDDLE TEMPLE RECORDS: minutes of parliament, 1501–1703. By C. T. Martin. 4 vols. Lond. 1904–5.
Cf. J. R. V. Marchant, *Middle temple records, Law Quar. Rev.* xxi (1905), 346–56.

1622 THE MIDDLE TEMPLE BENCH BOOKS, being a register of benchers of the middle temple from the earliest records to the present time, with historical introduction. By A. R. Ingpen. Lond. 1912.
Chiefly valuable for the introduction on the history of the Temple, making use of some recently discovered MSS. of Sir Robert Brerewood, reader in 1638.

1623 THE PENSION BOOK OF GRAY'S INN (records of the Honorable Society), 1569–1800. By R. J. Fletcher. 2 vols. Lond. 1901–10.

1624 READINGS AND MOOTS AT THE INNS OF COURT. By S. E. Thorne. Vol. i, *Selden Soc.* lxxi (1955).

1625 THE RECORDS OF THE HONORABLE SOCIETY of Lincoln's inn: admissions, 1420–1893, and chapel registers. 2 vols. Lond. 1896.

1626 THE RECORDS OF THE HONORABLE SOCIETY of Lincoln's inn: the black books, 1422–1845. By J. D. Walker and W. P. Baildon. 4 vols. Lond. 1897–1902.

1627 REGISTER OF ADMISSIONS TO THE HONOURABLE SOCIETY OF THE MIDDLE TEMPLE, from the fifteenth century to . . . 1944. By H. A. C. Sturgess. 3 vols. Lond. 1949.

1628 WATERHOUSE, E. Fortescutus illustratus. Lond. 1663.
A commentary on Sir John Fortescue, containing (pp. 543–9) a report on the inns of court made to Henry VIII by N. Bacon *et al.*

(b) *Later Works*

Holdsworth (1544), ii, 484–512, gives the best modern account. For Dugdale's notable contributions, cf. 1534.

1629 BEDWELL, C. E. A. A brief history of the middle temple. Lond. 1909.
A repr. of articles in *Quar. Rev.* and other periodicals. A good brief account.

1630 BELLOT, H. L. L. The inner and middle temple. Lond. 1902.
A good popular account with an extensive bibliography.

1631 BUC or BUCK, GEORGE. The third university of England or a treatise of the foundations of all the colleges, within and about London. Lond. 1615.
Published at the end of Stow's *Annales* (317) ed. 1615, 958–88. The first attempt at a history of Gray's Inn.

1632 COWPER, FRANCIS. A prospect of Gray's Inn. Lond. 1951.

1633 CUNNINGHAM, TIMOTHY. History and antiquity of the four inns of court and of the nine inns of chancery, also of Serjeants inn and Scroops inn. Lond. 1780.
Extracted from Dugdale (1534).

1634 DOUTHWAITE, W. R. Gray's inn, its history and associations. Lond. 1886.

1635 HERBERT, WILLIAM. Antiquities of the inns of court and chancery, with a history of the English law. Lond. 1804.
By a painstaking antiquary.

1636 HOLDSWORTH, W. S. The disappearance of the educational system of the inns of court. *Univ. of Penna. Law Rev.* lxix (1920–1), 201–22.

1637 HURST, GERALD. A short history of Lincoln's Inn. Lond. 1946.

1638 MACKINNON, F. R. Inner Temple papers. Lond. 1948.

1639 MANNING, JAMES. Serviens ad legem. Lond. 1840.
A report on proceedings for the suppression of privileges of the serjeants-at-law. A useful account of the serjeants-at-law.

1640 MASTER WORSLEY'S BOOK on the history and constitution of the honorable society of the middle temple. By A. R. Ingpen. Lond. 1910.
Written 1733. Professes to describe the ancient 'constitution, customs, and usage' of the Temple. Not always accurate and not exhaustive. Ingpen's introduction is valuable on origin of inns of court and government and system of studies in the period following the Reformation.

1641 PEARCE, ROBERT. A history of the inns of court and chancery, including an account of the eminent men of the four learned and honorable societies. Lond. 1848; 1855.
1855 ed. is called *A guide to the inns of court and chancery*.

1642 PULLING, ALEXANDER. The order of the coif. Lond. 1884.
Badly arranged, but the only complete treatise on serjeants-at-law.

1643 WILLIAMSON, J. B. A history of the temple. Lond. 1924.

1644 WOOLRYCH, H. W. Lives of eminent serjeants-at-law on the English bar. 2 vols. Lond. 1869.

5. COURTS OF LAW

A. COMMON LAW

(a) *Sources*

For the High Court of Parliament, cf. ch. iii, sect. 2, *supra* (pp. 88 ff.).

The records of the central courts of common law fall roughly into three groups:

(a) The records of the court of king's bench.

(b) The records of the justices on circuit; to wit, the justices of assize, the justices of oyer and terminer, and of gaol delivery.

(c) The records of the court of common pleas.

For a general statement of the surviving records of these courts at the P.R.O., cf. Giuseppi (74), i, 219–57. Cf. also Gross (1), pp. 448–51.

(d) The records of the court of exchequer. The financial side of the exchequer is considered in ch. iii *supra* (pp. 101 ff.), and the sources in print relating both to its financial side and its judicial side (the exchequer of pleas) are listed there. For the records of the exchequer of pleas in the P.R.O., cf. Giuseppi (74), i, 173–7.

(e) The court of exchequer chamber—a court of appeal from errors in the court of exchequer and of king's bench. Two statutes pertinent to it are printed in Tanner (1018), pp. 343–6.

A good deal of material relevant to the common law courts will be found in sect. 2, *supra* (pp. 130 ff.). Reference should be made particularly to the *Year books, Abridgements, Reports, Books of practice,* and *Readings*.

1645 A COMPLETE COLLECTION OF STATE TRIALS and proceedings for high treason.... By William Cobbett, T. B. Howell, *et al.* 42 vols. Lond. 1816–98.
The standard ed. of state trials superseding earlier eds. by Hargreave, Emlyn, and others. The accounts, however, are not always official. Vol. i covers the period to 1603. J. W. Willis-Bund edited a selection of cases from this collection, 2 vols. Cambr. 1879–82.

1646 INVENTORY AND CALENDAR of the contents of the *Baga de secretis. Deputy keeper's reports*, iii, app. ii, no. 6; iv, app. ii, no. 7 (1842–3).
Brief summaries of indictments for high treason, &c. Cf. Giuseppi (74), i, 222–3.

1647 INVENTORIES OF THE RECORDS of the court of common pleas. *Deputy keeper's reports*, iii, app. ii, no. 2 (1842).

1648   LIST OF PLEA ROLLS OF VARIOUS COURTS, preserved in the
       Public Record Office. *P.R.O. lists and indexes*, no. 4. Lond. 1894; rev. 1910.
       Lists the rolls of the following courts: king's bench, common pleas, exchequer, eyres,
       Marshalsea, exchequer of the Jews, palatinates of Durham, Lancaster, Chester,
       Wales, &c.

1649   SELECT CASES IN THE EXCHEQUER CHAMBER. By M. Hem-
       mant. 2 vols. *Selden Soc.* li, lxiv (1933–48).
       Vol. 2 covers period 1461–1509.

1650   WALMYSLEY, THOMAS. Expenses of the judges of assize riding the
       Western and Oxford circuits, 1596–1601. By W. D. Cooper. *Camden Misc.*
       iv (1858).

(b) *Later Works*

Holdsworth (1544), i, 194–264; v, 339 ff., gives the best general account.

1651   BOOTE, RICHARD. Historical treatise of an action or suit at law and
       of the proceedings used in the king's bench and common pleas. Lond. 1766;
       1781; 1805.

1652   COOKE, GEORGE. Rules, orders and notices in the court of common
       pleas, from the 35th of Henry VI to Hilary term the 15th of George II. . . .
       Lond. 1742; 1747.
       2nd ed. to Trin. term 21 George II, 1747, inclusive, contains also the rules of king's
       bench sanctioned by parliament in 1604.

1653   HASTINGS, MARGARET. The court of common pleas in fifteenth
       century England. Ithaca, 1947.

1654   SMITH, L. B. English treason trials and confessions in the sixteenth
       century. *Jour. Hist. Ideas*, xv (1954), 471–98.

1655   THE RULES AND ORDERS OF THE COMMON PLEAS. Lond.
       1743.
       Extends from 1457 to 1743. An earlier coll. from 1457 to 1741 is annexed to 1652.

B. Chancery

(a) *Sources*

The chancery on its administrative side is dealt with in ch. iii, *supra* (pp. 101 ff.).
On its judicial side one must distinguish between its common law jurisdiction
and its equitable jurisdiction. For its records as a court of common law, cf.
Giuseppi (74), i, 46–47; as a court of equity, ibid. i, 47–56. There is a good discussion of the chancery records and of early treatises on the court of chancery
in Holdsworth (1544), v, 261 ff. Saint German (1367) is important. Cf. also
M. Dowling, *The equity side of chancery*, *Rev. Eng. Studies* viii (1932), 185–200.

1656   ACTA CANCELLARIA, or selections from the records of the court of
       chancery (1558–1624). By Cecil Monro. Lond. 1847.
       Valuable.

1657 BACON, NICHOLAS. Arguments exhibited in parliament whereby it
is proved that the persons of noblemen were attachable by law for contempts
in the high court of chancery. Lond. [1641?].
Repr. from MS. after Bacon's death.

1658 A CALENDAR OF PROCEEDINGS IN CHANCERY in the reign of
Queen Elizabeth; to which are prefixed examples of the earlier proceedings
in that court. . . . By J. Bayley. 3 vols. *Record Comm.*, Lond. 1827–32.
Based on P.R.O., *Early chancery proceedings*, bundles i and ii. Contains a number of
chancery bills and answers, with examples of proceedings, from the time of Richard II.

1659 CARY (CAREW), GEORGE. Reports on causes in chancery, collected
. . . out of the labours of Mr. William Lambert (Lambarde). Lond. 1650;
1668; 1820.
Short notes of points decided between 1537 and 1604.

1660 EARLY CHANCERY PROCEEDINGS, Staffordshire, Richard II–
Henry VII. *Wm. Salt Arch. Soc.*, n.s., vii (1904), 237 ff.

1661 CHANCERY PROCEEDINGS (Staffordshire) temp. Elizabeth, 1560–
70. *Wm. Salt Arch. Soc.*, n.s., ix (1906), 1–241; xxviii (1926), 59–150; series ii,
1558–79, 1931 (1933), 123–231; 1938 (1938), 1–201.

1662 INDEX OF CHANCERY PROCEEDINGS, preserved in the P.R.O.
Ser. ii, 1558–1660, 3 vols. Lond. 1896–1909. Vols. i and ii cover the period
1558–1621. *P.R.O. lists and indexes*, nos. 7, 24.
Lists second series of bills and answers in chancery not calendared in 1658 or indexed
in old MS. indexes in P.R.O. Adds materials previously misplaced in P.R.O.

1663 LISTS OF EARLY CHANCERY PROCEEDINGS preserved in the
P.R.O., 1386–1558. *P.R.O. lists and indexes*, nos. 12, 16, 20, 29, 38, 48, 50, 51,
54, 55 (1901–36).
Vols. 3–10 cover the period 1485–1558. Bills of complaint, answers, depositions, &c.,
calendared. Cf. also *Calendar of early chancery proceedings*, Richard II–Elizabeth,
Deputy keeper's report, xlix (1888), 201–8.

1664 ORDERS OF THE HIGH COURT OF CHANCERY, and statutes of
the realm relating to chancery, from the earliest period to the present time. By
G. W. Sanders. Lond. 1845.
Contains the general orders made by chancellors for regulation of chancery procedure.
They extend from 1388, but are not complete.

1665 REPORTS OF CASES decided by Francis Bacon in the high court of
chancery. By J. Ritchie. Lond. 1932.
Cf. W. S. Holdsworth, *Francis Bacon's decisions*, *Law Quar. Rev.* xlix (1933), 61 ff.

1666 SELECT CASES IN CHANCERY, 1364–1471. By W. P. Baildon.
Selden Soc. x (1896).

(b) *Later Works*

The best account of the court in the sixteenth and seventeenth centuries is in
Holdsworth (1544), v, 215–338.

1667 CAMPBELL, LORD. Consolidated general orders of the high court of
chancery, 1556–1895. Lond. 1860.
Issued by Lord Campbell with the concurrence of the other judges in chancery.

1668 [EGERTON, THOMAS?]. Certain observations concerning the office
of lord chancellor. Lond. 1657.
Attributed, probably mistakenly, to Egerton.

1669 HAKE, EDWARD. A dialogue on equity in three parts. By D. E. C.
Yale. New Haven, U.S.A., 1953.

1670 HOLMES, O. W. Early equity. *Law Quar. Rev.* i (1885), 162–74; repr.
in *Select essays* (1562), ii, 705–21.

1671 KERLY, D. MacK. A historical sketch of the equitable jurisdiction of
the court of chancery. Cambr. 1890.
Brief.

1672 ROBINSON, C. History of the high court of chancery. Richmond, 1882.

1673 SELDEN, JOHN. A brief discourse touching the office of lord chancellor
of England. Lond. 1672; by F. Hargrave, Lond. 1677; 1811.
The ed. of 1672 was transcribed by Dugdale from a copy. He added a catalogue of the
lord chancellors and lord keepers from the Norman conquest to 1671.

1674 SPENCE, GEORGE. The equitable jurisdiction of the court of chancery.
2 vols. Lond. 1846.
Really a history of the law of property. Much material about the courts of common law
and the common law itself. Especially valuable for the history of the court of chancery
and its equity jurisdiction. Many extracts from unprinted registers, especially in pt. ii,
books 1 and 2.

1675 TOTHILL, WILLIAM. Transactions of the high court of chancery
(England 1559–1646) by practice and precedent, with fees and special orders.
Lond. 1649; 1671; 1820.

1676 VINOGRADOFF, PAUL. Reason and conscience in sixteenth century
jurisprudence. *Law Quar. Rev.* xxiv (1908), 373–84.
Cf. Sir Frederick Pollock, *The transformation of equity*, in *Essays in legal history*, by
P. Vinogradoff, Oxf. 1913.

1677 WARD, P. L. William Lambard's collections on chancery. *Harvard
Lib. Bull.* vii (1953), 271–98.

C. The Prerogative Courts

The Court of Requests, of Star Chamber, and of Wards and Liveries are considered in detail below. The privy council in its judicial aspects and the special
conciliar courts of the north, of the west, and of Wales are dealt with in ch. iii
supra. W. C. Richardson, *A history of the Court of Augmentations*, is in press.
The other important prerogative courts, more fiscal than judicial in character,
to wit, the Court of First-Fruits and Tenths and of Surveyors still await adequate
treatment. Richardson (1226) and Elton (1023) give the best accounts in print.
The records of Augmentations for Wales and Monmouthshire have been published (6267). For the unpublished records of these courts cf. Giuseppi (74) i,
138–67. Illustrative documents are printed in Tanner (1015), 336–42. For the
Court of High Commission and the ecclesiastical courts in general, cf. ch. vi
infra.
On a proposal by Thomas Cromwell of an administrative court, cf. W. C.

Richardson, *The Court of Commonweal, Papers of the Michigan Acad. of Sc. Arts and Letters*, xix (1933), 459–76, and T. F. T. Plucknett, *Some proposed legislation of Henry VIII, Trans. R.H. Soc.*, 4th ser., xix (1936), 119–44.

1. *Court of Requests*

(a) *Sources*

1678   CAESAR, JULIUS. The ancient state, authority and proceedings of the court of requests. Lond. 1597.
This work, now very rare, is a treatise on the origin and functions of the court with a collection of records illustrative of its proceedings from the ninth year of the reign of Henry VII to the twenty-seventh year of Elizabeth.

1679   LIST OF PROCEEDINGS IN THE COURT OF REQUESTS preserved in the P.R.O. *P.R.O. lists and indexes*, no. 21 (1906).
Covers the period to the end of 1558, with a few later cases.

1680   SELECT CASES IN THE COURT OF REQUESTS, 1497–1569. By I. S. Leadam. *Selden Soc.* xii (1898).
The introduction, not always accurate, contains the best account of the court of requests.

(b) *Later Works*

The only adequate account is in Leadam (1680), intro. Cf. also 1544, i, 412–16.

1681   KEANE, D. D. Courts of requests, their jurisdiction and power. Lond. 1845.

1682   WINDER, W. H. D. The Courts of Requests. *Law Quar. Rev.* lii (1936), 369–94.

2. *The Court of Star Chamber*

(a) *Sources*

Many of the records of the Court of Star Chamber had already been lost by the time that Hudson wrote his treatise (1698), in the reign of James I. For a bibliography of extant records, MS. and in print, cf. 1700, pp. 4–22. An incomplete MS. catalogue of star chamber records by John Bruce is in B.M. Add. MS. 28201A, fol. 116. On proceedings relating to Wales, cf. 6263.

1683   ABSTRACTS OF STAR CHAMBER PROCEEDINGS relating to the county of Sussex, Henry VII to Philip and Mary (incl.). By P. D. Mundy. *Sussex Rec. Soc.* xvi (1913).

1684   CALENDAR OF STAR CHAMBER PROCEEDINGS. *Deputy keeper's report*, xlix (1888), app., 376–594.
This calendar has been superseded (to 1558) by 1687.

1685   CROMPTON, RICHARD. Star chamber cases, showing what causes properly belong to that court. Lond. 1630; 1641.
Selected from Crompton's *L'authoritié et jurisdiction des courts*, Lond. 1594.

1686   HAWARDE, JOHN. Les reportes del cases in camera stellata, 1593–1609. By W. P. Baildon. Lond. 1894.
Valuable.

1687   LIST OF PROCEEDINGS in the court of star chamber, 1485–1588, preserved in the P.R.O. *P.R.O. lists and indexes*, no. 13 (1901).

1688   PROCEEDINGS IN THE COURT OF THE STAR CHAMBER in the reigns of Henry VII and Henry VIII. By Gladys Bradford. *Somerset Rec. Soc.* xxvii (1911).
Valuable introduction.

1689   PROCEEDINGS IN THE COURT OF STAR CHAMBER, Stonor v. Dormer and others, 1491. By C. L. Kingsford. *E.H.R.* xxxv (1920), 421–32.

1690   SELECTED CASES BEFORE THE KING'S COUNCIL in star chamber (1477–1544). By I. S. Leadam. 2 vols. *Selden Soc.* xvi, xxv (1903–11). Valuable introduction. Cf. J. Gairdner's review in *E.H.R.* xix (1904), 774; xxvi (1911), 580.

1691   [TATE, FRANCIS?] Camera stellata: or an explanation of the most famous court of star chamber, with an account of the offences there punishable; the fees payable, and the orders for proceedings therein.
Published in vol. ii of the eds. of 1771 and 1775 of Hearne's *Curious discourses* (1013). Attributed there to Francis Tate, though Lambarde may have been the author.

1692   YORKSHIRE STAR CHAMBER PROCEEDINGS. By William Brown, H. B. McCall, J. Lister. *Yorks. Arch. Soc.*, rec. ser., xli, xlv, li, lxx (1909–27).
Temp. Henry VII and Henry VIII. Cf. *Yorks. Arch. Jour.* xii (1892–3), 489, and xiii (1894–5), 313, for appeals in the Star Chamber of bishop of Worcester against More. Cf. also *Yorks. Star Chamber proc.*, reign of Henry VIII, by W. P. Baildon, *Yorks. Arch. Jour.* xv (1898–9), 85–91.

(b) *Later Works*

In addition to the works cited below, Holdsworth (1544), i, 485 ff., and Leadam's introduction to 1690 should be consulted. Scofield (1700) is the standard account. Pollard's articles (1167) are important. Hudson's treatise (1698) is by far the best of the seventeenth-century studies and utilizes sources not now extant.

1693   BRAYLEY, E. W., and BRITTON, JOHN. History of the ancient palace and the late house of parliament at Westminster. Lond. 1836.
Contains various references to the Court of Star Chamber.

1694   BRUCE, JOHN. An outline of the history of the court of star chamber, in a letter from John Bruce. A second letter on the court of star chamber. *Arch.* xxv (1834), 342–93.
These letters, written in May and Dec. 1833, contain a brief outline based on the sources, together with 9 pages of extracts.

1695   BURNS, J. S. The star chamber, notices of the court and its proceedings, with a few additional notes of the high commission. Lond. 1870.

1696   CARTER, A. T. Council and star chamber. *Law Quar. Rev.* xviii (1902), 247–54.

1697   CHEYNEY, E. P. The court of star chamber. *A.H.R.* xviii (1912), 727–50.

1698 HUDSON, WILLIAM. A treatise on the court of star chamber. In *Collectanea juridica* (1521), vol. ii.
This treatise, which is a clear and able exposition of the subject, apparently written towards the close of the reign of James I, is corrected in some points by the articles of Bruce (1694).

1699 SCOFIELD, C. L. Accounts of star chamber dinners, 1593–4. *A.H.R.* iv (1899), 83–94.

1700 SCOFIELD, C. L. A study of the court of star chamber. Chicago, 1900.
A careful and scholarly account, with a bibliography of material in print and in MS.

1701 WILLIAMS, C. H. The so-called Star Chamber Act. *History*, xv (1930), 129–35.

3. *Court of Wards and Liveries*

(a) *Sources*

The unpublished records are mostly in the P.R.O., cf. Giuseppi (74), i, 274–8. There is scattered material in *Salisbury MSS.* (185). There is relevant material in Staunford (1518) and in Constable (1510).

(b) *Later Works*

1702 BELL, H. E. An introduction to the history and records of the Court of Wards and Liveries. *Cambr. Studies in English legal history.* Cambr. 1953.

1703 HURSTFIELD, JOEL. The Greenwich tenures of the reign of Edward VI. *Law Quar. Rev.* lxv (1949), 72–81.
Cf. also 1027.

1704 HURSTFIELD, JOEL. Lord Burghley as master of the Court of Wards. *Trans. R.H. Soc.*, 4th ser., xxxi (1949), 95–114.

1705 HURSTFIELD, JOEL. Wardship and marriage under Elizabeth I. *History Today*, iv (1954), 605–12.

1706 HURSTFIELD, JOEL. The profits of fiscal feudalism, 1541–1602. *Econ. Hist. Rev.*, 2nd ser., viii (1955), 53–61.

1706a HURSTFIELD, JOEL. The queen's wards: wardship and marriage under Elizabeth I. Lond. 1958.

VI

ECCLESIASTICAL HISTORY, 1485–1603

Bibliographies are printed in Gairdner (1785), Frere (2188b), Makower (2524), *Camb. Mod. Hist.* (20), ii and iii; Usher (2221), Pierce (2452), Pearson (2457), Dexter (2480), Whitley (p. 208 *infra*), and Pollen (1740).

For the voluminous controversial literature of the period, only part of which is given below, the lives of the controversialists in the *D.N.B.* (9) should be consulted, and the contemporary eds. of their writings checked from *S.T.C.* (35).

A useful work of reference is *Dictionnaire d'histoire et de géographie ecclésiastique*, by A. Baudrillant, A. de Meyer, and E. Van Cauwenbergh, Paris, 1936.

1. GENERAL WORKS

(a) *Sources*

Parliamentary enactments on religious affairs are set forth in the *Statutes of the realm* (1016); proclamations on the subject are calendared in (1017). Advertisements, articles, injunctions, and visitation articles of the official church, published before 1640 and still extant are listed in *S.T.C.* (35), pp. 220–5.

Much material for ecclesiastical history is to be found in the large general collections, such as *Letters and Papers Henry VIII* (91), *Cal. S.P., Domestic* (86); the *Spanish and Venetian calendars* (867–8), (992); the *Cal. S.P., Milan* (990); and, particularly, *Rome* (991); the *Acts of privy council* (1152), the *Salisbury MSS.* (185), and many of the private collections calendared by the Hist. MSS. Comm. Documents are printed in (1767), (1778), (1781), (1803), (1823); those printed in Strype's various works (570), (571), (1850), (2214–8), are very important, though not always accurately transcribed.

One of the most important collections of ecclesiastical sources is the publications of the *Parker Society* (54 vols., Cambr. 1842–55), comprising works of most of the Anglican reformers such as Coverdale, Tyndale, Cranmer, Hooper, Jewel, Latimer, Ridley, Grindal, Sandys, Pilkington, Whitgift, &c. (For individual titles, see under appropriate heading.)

1707 A COLLECTION OF ARTICLES, INJUNCTIONS, canons, orders, ordinances, and constitutions ecclesiastical, with other public records of the church of England. By Anthony Sparrow. Lond. 1661; 1684.
Useful, but largely superseded by Cardwell (1722).

1708 BALE, JOHN. Select Works. By Henry Christmas. *Parker Soc.*, 1849.
Contains examinations of Anne Askewe.

1709 BECCATELLI, LUDOVICO. The life of cardinal Reginald Pole. Trans. by B. Pye. Lond. 1776.
Italian life by Pole's secretary. The original Italian version and a contemporary Latin trans. by Andrew Dudith is printed in 1739.

1710 BECON, THOMAS. Works. 3 vols. Lond. 1560–4; by John Ayre. 3 vols. *Parker Soc.*, 1843–4.
A complete list of Becon's writings is given in *Athenae Cantabrigienses,* i, 247–9. Chiefly valuable for light on social conditions.

1711 BULLINGER, HEINRICH. Decades. 1st Eng. trans. by H. I. (?) Lond. 1577; by Thomas Harding, 4 vols. *Parker Soc.*, 1849–52.

1712 CODEX JURIS ECCLESIASTICI ANGLICANI. By Edmund Gibson. Lond. 1713; best ed., 2 vols., Oxf. 1761.
Indispensable. Commentary and introduction. For further information, cf. N. Sykes, *Edmund Gibson,* Lond. 1926, pp. 65–70.

1713 CONCILIA MAGNAE BRITANNIAE ET HIBERNIAE. . . . 446–1718. By David Wilkins. 4 vols. Lond. 1737.
Records of convocation so far as they were not destroyed by the fire of 1666. Invaluable, but transcriptions not always complete or accurate. For an epitome of this work, cf. Gross (1), no. 618.

1714 COVERDALE, MYLES. Writings and translations. Remains. By George Pearson. 2 vols. *Parker Soc.*, 1844–6.

1715 COX, J. C. Churchwardens' accounts. Lond. 1913.
A valuable general survey. Cf. also Elsbeth Phelipps, *List of printed churchwardens' accounts* in *E.H.R.* xv (1900), 335–41. Others have been printed since.

1716 COX, J. C. The parish registers of England. Lond. 1910.
App. ii contains a list of parish registers beginning in 1538 when they were made obligatory; app. iii a list of those beginning in 1539. App. iv lists those registers in print in 1909—some 600 all told. Various societies, some national and many local, are devoted to the publication of parish registers; cf. on this subject pp. 256–7. For the printed and unprinted registers of nonconformist and of foreign congregations in England, cf. pp. 257–9. Further reference on this subject should be made to A. M. Burke, *Key to the ancient parish registers of England and Wales,* Lond. 1908, and to B. L. Hutchins, *Parish and other accounts, Notes and Queries,* 9th ser., iv (1899), 301–2, 414–15, 452–3; v (1900), 63–64. Cf. W. E. Tate, *The parish chest: a study of the records of the parochial administration in England,* Cambr. 1946.

1717 CRANMER, THOMAS. Recantacyons. By Lord Houghton (R. M. Milnes) and James Gairdner. *Philobiblion Soc.*, 1885.
From a MS. written probably between 1556 and 1558.

1718 CRANMER, THOMAS. Works. By J. E. Cox. 2 vols. *Parker Society,* 1844–6.
This is the latest ed. of Cranmer's works, but an earlier ed., by H. Jenkyns, 4 vols., Oxf. 1833, is hardly, if at all, inferior.

1719 CROWLEY, ROBERT. Select works. By J. M. Cowper. *E.E.T.S.*, extra ser., xv (1872).
Prints five of Crowley's works, of which the most important, *The way to wealth* and *One and thyrtye epigrammes,* both first published, Lond. 1550, are valuable for social conditions. A complete list of his works is given in *D.N.B.* (9), art. Crowley.

1720 DAVIES, W. T. A bibliography of John Bale. *Oxf. Bibliog. Soc. Proc. and Papers,* v (1940), 203–79.

1721 DICKENS, A. G. Archbishop Holgate's apology. *E.H.R.* lvi (1941), 450–9.

1722 DOCUMENTARY ANNALS OF THE REFORMED CHURCH of England: being a collection of injunctions, declarations, orders, articles of inquiry, &c., from the year 1546 to the year 1716, with notes historical and explanatory. By E. Cardwell. 2 vols. Oxf. 1839; 1844.
A serviceable collection.

1723 DOCUMENTS ILLUSTRATIVE OF ENGLISH CHURCH HISTORY, compiled from original sources. By Henry Gee and W. J. Hardy. Lond. 1896.
Brief collection.

1724 DOCUMENTS ILLUSTRATING THE HISTORY of Saint Paul's Cathedral. By W. S. Simpson. *Camden Soc.*, 2nd ser., xxvi (1880).
Includes account of burning, 1561, and letter from bishop Aylmer to lord mayor, 1581.

1725 EVIDENCES ILLUSTRATIVE OF THE HISTORY of religion in Newcastle and Gateshead between the reformation and the revolution. By W. H. D. Longstaffe. *Surtees Soc.* l (1867), app. 259–482.
Miscellaneous, about 40 pages on the sixteenth century.

1726 FOXE, JOHN. Actes and monuments. Popularly known as *The book of martyrs*. Lond. 1563; by S. R. Cattley and George Townsend, 8 vols., Lond. 1837–41; by Josiah Pratt, 8 vols., Lond. 1870.
This work first appeared in Latin at Basel in 1559, under the title, *Rerum in ecclesia gestarum . . . narratio*. For further information on the value and various eds. and abridgements of this work, cf. *D.N.B.* (9), art. Foxe. S. R. Maitland demonstrated the inaccuracy of Cattley's ed. in *Six letters on Foxe's acts and monuments* (repr. from the *British Magazine*), 1837; and in *Notes on the contributions of the Revd. George Townsend . . . to the new edition of Foxe's martyrology*, Lond. 1841–2.
    A work of great industry, but strongly partisan and to be used with care. For a Roman Catholic estimate, cf. J. M. Stone, *John Foxe's book of errors, The Month*, xcv (1900), 352–69. Cf. also Mozley's defence of Foxe (1826).

1727 ORIGINAL LETTERS RELATIVE TO THE ENGLISH REFORMATION, 1531–58, chiefly from the archives of Zürich. By Hastings Robinson. 2 vols. *Parker Soc.*, 1846–7.
The Latin originals of these letters were printed under the title *Epistolae Tigurinae*, Cambr. 1848. The Simler collection of MSS. in Zürich contains much unprinted material on the same subject, cf. 2136, pp. vii–viii. Later letters are printed in 2182 *infra*.

1728 FOWLER, R. C. Episcopal registers of England and Wales. *Helps for students of history*, no. 1 (1918).
Useful small guide to episcopal archives, especially before the reformation.

1729 GORHAM, G. C. Gleanings of a few scattered ears during the period of the reformation in England. Lond. 1857.
Letters, 1533–88.

1730 HENNESSY, GEORGE. Novum repertorium ecclesiasticum parochiale londinense. Lond. 1898.
Supplements Newcourt (1736).

1731 HOOPER, JOHN. Early writings. By Samuel Carr. 2 vols. *Parker Soc.*, 1843. Later writings. By Charles Nevinson. 2 vols. *Parker Soc.*, 1852.

1732 LATIMER, HUGH. Works. By G. E. Corrie. 2 vols. *Parker Soc.*, 1844–5.
Cf. a sixteenth-century manuscript trans. of *Latimer's first sermon before Edward*, *P.M.L.A.* lx (1945), 959–1002.

1733 LE NEVE, JOHN. Fasti ecclesiae Anglicanae, or a calendar of the principal ecclesiastical dignitaries of England and Wales to 1715. Lond. 1716; by T. D. Hardy, 3 vols., Oxf. 1854.
A standard work of reference.

1734 THE LETTERS OF THE MARTYRS. By Myles Coverdale. Lond. 1564; by Edward Bickersteth, Lond. 1837.
Contains letters of Cranmer, Ridley, Hooper, Taylor, Saunders, Philpot, &c.

1735 NARRATIVES OF THE DAYS OF THE REFORMATION, chiefly from the MSS. of John Foxe the martyrologist, with two contemporary biographies of archbishop Cranmer. By J. G. Nichols. *Camden Soc.* lxxvii (1859).
Material not used by either Foxe or Strype.

1736 NEWCOURT, RICHARD. Repertorium ecclesiasticum parochiale londinense. 2 vols. Lond. 1708–10.
Institutions to benefices in dioceses of London, ordination of vicarages, &c. Cf. 1730.

1737 PARKER, MATTHEW. Correspondence, 1535–1575. By John Bruce and T. T. Perrowne. *Parker Soc.*, 1853.
Valuable.

1738 ROBERT PARKYN'S NARRATIVE OF THE REFORMATION. By A. G. Dickens. *E.H.R.* lxii (1947), 58–83.
Cf. *Robert Parkyn, A reformation chronicle*, by Justin McCann, *Ampleforth Jour.* xxxix (1934), 85–105. Cf. also on Robert's brother John, A. G. Dickens, *John Parkyn, fellow of Trinity College, Cambridge, Pro. Cambr. Antiq. Soc.* xliii (1950), 21–29.

1739 POLE, REGINALD. Epistolae Reginaldi Poli . . . et aliorum ad se. By A. M. (Giralamo) Quirini. 5 vols. Brescia, 1744–57.
The most important source of information on Pole's career. 349 letters of Pole are calendared in *Cal. S.P., Venetian*, v, (992), omitted in Quirini.

1740 POLLEN, J. H. Sources for the history of Roman Catholics in England, Ireland, and Scotland from the reformation period to that of emancipation, 1533 to 1795. *Helps for students of history*, no. 39 (1921).
Very brief, but useful.

1741 RECORDS OF THE NORTHERN CONVOCATION (1279–1714). By G. W. Kitchin. *Surtees Soc.* cxiii (1906).

1742 THE REGISTER OF RICHARD FOX, Lord Bishop of Durham, 1494–1501. By M. P. Howden. *Surtees Soc.* cxlvii (1932).

1743 THE REGISTERS OF OLIVER KING, Bishop of Bath and Wells, 1496–1503, and Hadrian de Castello, Bishop of Bath and Wells, 1503–1518. By H. C. Maxwell-Lyte. *Somerset Rec. Soc.* liv (1937).

1744 THE REGISTERS OF ROBERT STILLINGTON, Bishop of Bath and Wells, 1466–1491, and Richard Fox, Bishop of Bath and Wells, 1492–1496. By H. C. Maxwell-Lyte. *Somerset Rec. Soc.* lii (1937).

1745 THE REGISTERS OF CUTHBERT TUNSTALL, Bishop of Durham, 1530–59, and James Pilkington, Bishop of Durham, 1561–76. By Gladys Hinde. *Surtees Soc.* clxi (1952).

1746 THE REGISTERS OF THOMAS WOLSEY, Bishop of Bath and Wells, 1518–1523, John Clarke, Bishop of Bath and Wells, 1523–1541, William Knyght, Bishop of Bath and Wells, 1541–1547, and Gilbert Bourne, Bishop of Bath and Wells, 1554–1559. By H. C. Maxwell-Lyte. *Somerset Rec. Soc.* lv (1940).

1747 RIDLEY, NICHOLAS. Works. By Henry Christmas. *Parker Soc.*, 1841.

1748 SANDERS, NICHOLAS. De origine ac progressu schismatis Anglicani liber. Cologne, 1585.
The work of a contemporary Catholic controversialist. It was continued by E. Rishton from the accession of Elizabeth to 1585. The whole was trans. into English and ed., with an introduction and notes by D. Lewis, Lond. 1877. On Sanders see J. H. Pollen in *E.H.R.* vi (1891), 36–47. On variations in content of Latin, French, and English versions, cf. Constant (2003, Eng. tran.), i, 132 n., 207 n., 443.

1749 STUBBS, WILLIAM. Registrum sacrum Anglicanum; an attempt to exhibit the course of episcopal succession in England. Oxf. 1858; best ed. Oxf. 1897.
Useful for reference; contains lists of bishops.

1750 SYNODALIA. A collection of articles of religion, canons and proceedings of convocations in the province of Canterbury from the year 1547 to the year 1717. By Edward Cardwell. 2 vols. Oxf. 1842.
Most of the documents are to be found in Wilkins (1713). Notes and historical comments not always accurate.

1751 THOMPSON, A. H. Parish history and records. *Helps for students of history*, no. 15 (1919).
Useful brief discussion of types of material and guide to principal printed sources.

1752 THORNLEY, I. D. Sanctuary register of Beverley. *E.H.R.* xxxiv (1919), 393–7.

1753 VISITATION ARTICLES AND INJUNCTIONS of the period of the reformation. By W. H. Frere and W. M. Kennedy. 3 vols. *Alcuin Club collections*, xiv–xvi (1910).
Valuable. Goes to 1575. Continued in no. 2168, *infra.*

(b) *Later Works*

This section includes secondary works covering the whole period or a large portion of it. Works dealing with particular reigns are classified under the appropriate sections below. The best general view of the ecclesiastical history of the period is to be got from Gairdner (1785), 1485–1558, and Frere (2188b), 1558–1625.

The older histories like Burnet and Collier, save for documents of value which they may contain, are chiefly of worth as revealing the state of knowledge in the periods in which they were written and the differing conceptions of the reformation held by various parties in the two centuries that succeeded.

Much material for ecclesiastical history is to be found in the general histories of the period, such as Froude (340), *Cambr. Mod. Hist.* (20), ii–iii; Fisher (339), Pollard (363), Mackie (354) and Black (671). Cf. also 4649.

1754 AINSLIE, J. L. The doctrines of ministerial order in the reformed churches of the sixteenth and seventeenth centuries. Edin. 1940.

1755 BAILEY, D. S. Thomas Becon and the reformation in England. Edin. 1952.

1756 BAILEY, SHERWIN. Robert Wisdom under persecution, 1541–43. *Jour. Eccles. Hist.* ii (1951), 180–9.

1757 BARNAUD, J. Les causes économiques de la réforme en Angleterre. *Études Theol. et relig.* vii (1932), 27–49.

1758 BASKERVILLE, GEOFFREY. A sister of Archbishop Cranmer. *E.H.R.* li (1936), 287–9.

1759 BERTRAND, PIERRE. Genève et la Grande-Bretagne, de John Knox à Oliver Cromwell. Geneva, 1948.

1760 BLENCH, J. W. John Longland and Roger Edgeworth. Two forgotten preachers of the early sixteenth century. *Rev. Eng. Studies*, n.s., v (1954), 123–43.

1761 BIRON, R., and BARENNES, J. Reginald Pole. Paris, 1923.
Catholic biography from printed sources. Good. Cf. also 1868.

1762 BLUNT, J. H. The reformation of the church of England, its history, principles and results. Lond. 1869; 2 vols. 1878–82.
High Anglican point of view; vol. i, 1514–47; vol. ii, 1547–62. 1st ed. includes vol. i only.

1763 BONNAR, ALPHONSUS. The Greenwich Franciscans in the sixteenth century. *Cath. Rec. Soc.*, 35th Report (1940).

1764 BOONE, H. L'infructueuse ambassade du Cardinal Pole. *Mém. de la soc. d'émulation de Cambrai*, lxxxv (1937), 213–49.

1765 BROMILEY, G. W. Thomas Cranmer: Archbishop and Martyr. Lond. 1955.
Cf. idem. *Thomas Cranmer: theologian*, Lond. 1956.

1765a BROMILEY, G. W. Nicholas Ridley, 1500–1555, scholar, bishop, theologian, martyr. Lond. 1953.

1766 BROOKS, F. W. The social position of the parson in the sixteenth century. *Brit. Arch. Assoc. Jour.*, 3rd ser., x (1948), 23–37.

1767 BURNET, GILBERT. History of the reformation of the church of England. 3 vols. Lond. 1679–1715; best ed. by Nicholas Pocock, 7 vols., Oxf. 1865.
An answer to Sanders, *De origine* (1748). A work of great learning and value. Contains many documents.

1768   CARLYLE, R. M., and CARLYLE, A. J. Hugh Latimer. Boston, 1899.

1769   CHESTER, A. G. Hugh Latimer: Apostle to the English. Philadelphia,
1954.
Scholarly.

1770   CHILD, G. W. Church and state under the Tudors. Lond. 1890.
App. of documents.

1771   COLLIER, JEREMY. An ecclesiastical history of Great Britain, chiefly
of England, from the first planting of Christianity to the end of the reign of
king Charles the Second, with a brief account of the affairs of religion in
Ireland. 2 vols. Lond. 1708–14; by Thomas Lathbury, 9 vols., Lond. 1852.
High Anglican position.

1772   CREHAN, J. H. The return to obedience. New judgement on Cardinal
Pole. *The Month*, n.s., xiv (1955), 221–9.

1773   CREHAN, J. H. St. Ignatius and Cardinal Pole. *Arch. Hist. Soc. Iesu*,
xxv (1956), 72–98.

1774   CREMEANS, C. D. The reception of Calvinistic thought in England.
Ill. Studies in Soc. Sc. xxxi. Urbana, 1949.

1775   CROSSE, G. A short history of the English reformation. Lond. 1950.

1776   DALTON, HERMANN. Johannes à Lasco, Beitrag zur Reformationsgeschichte Polens, Deutschlands, und Englands. Gotha 1881. Trans. (part)
H. J. Evans. *John à Lasco: his earlier life and labours*. Lond. 1886.

1777   DEMAUS, ROBERT. Hugh Latimer. *Religious Tract Soc.* Lond.
1869; 1882; 1886; rev. by A. R. B., 1903; abridged by Newman Watts, 1935.

1778   DEMAUS, ROBERT. William Tyndale. Lond. 1871; by Richard
Lovett, *Religious Tract Soc.*, Lond. 1886.
App. of documents.

1779   DICKENS, A. G. Aspects of intellectual transition among the English
parish clergy of the Reformation period. A regional example (South Yorkshire). *Archiv für Reformationsges.* xliii (1952), 51–69.

1780   DIXON, R. W. History of the church of England from the abolition of
the Roman jurisdiction. 6 vols. Oxf. 1878–1902.
Extends from 1529 to 1570. High Anglican view. Vols. v and vi ed. Henry Gee. See
review by A. F. Pollard, in *E.H.R.* xvii (1902), 577, and an unsigned review in *Church
Quar. Rev.* liv (1902), 339.

1781   DODD, CHARLES (*pseud.* for Tootel, Hugh). The church history of
England from 1500 to the year 1688, chiefly with regard to Catholicks. 3 vols.
Brussels (probably Lond.), 1737–42; best ed. by M. A. Tierney, 5 vols.,
Lond. 1839–43.
Roman Catholic. Valuable documents and notes appended by Tierney. Tierney's ed.
ends at 1675.

1782   DU BOULAY, F. R. H. Archbishop Cranmer and the Canterbury
temporalities. *E.H.R.* lxvii (1952), 19–36.

1783   FREEMAN, E. A. Cardinal Pole. *Historical Essays*, 4th ser., Lond.
1892.

1784 FULLER, THOMAS. Church history of Britain from the birth of Jesus
Christ until the year 1648. Lond. 1655; best ed. by J. S. Brewer, 6 vols., Oxf.
1845.
Anglican viewpoint. Valuable.

1785 GAIRDNER, JAMES. The English church in the sixteenth century,
from the accession of Henry VIII to the death of Mary. Lond. 1902.
Good brief bibliographies at the end of each ch. Vol. iv of *A history of the English
church*, by Stephens and Hunt.

1786 GAIRDNER, JAMES. Lollardy and the reformation in England. 4 vols.
Lond. 1908–13.
Covers the period from the fourteenth century to 1555. The last vol. ed. and partly
written by William Hunt after Gairdner's death.
Reveals, particularly in the earlier vols., a strong bias against 'heresy' in all forms.

1787 GARRETT, C. H. The legatine register of Cardinal Pole, 1554–57.
Jour. Mod. Hist. xiii (1941), 189–94.

1788 GEE, J. A. Tyndale and the 1533 English *Enchiridion* of Erasmus.
P.M.L.A. xlix (1934), 460–71.

1789 GILLOW, JOSEPH. A literary and biographical history, or bibliographical dictionary, of the English Catholics from the breach with Rome to
the present time. 5 vols. Lond. 1885–1903.
Primarily biographical, from Roman Catholic viewpoint. Valuable.

1790 GRAY, C. M. Hugh Latimer and the sixteenth century: an essay in
interpretation. Cambr., U.S.A., 1950.

1791 GWATKIN, H. M. Church and state in England to the death of queen
Anne. By E. W. Watson. Lond. 1917.
Inaccurate. Strong sympathy with Protestant and Puritan movements.

1792 HAILE, MARTIN. Life of Reginald Pole. Lond. 1910.

1793 HARDWICK, CHARLES. A history of the Christian church during
the reformation. Cambr. 1856; by William Stubbs, Lond. 1877.
A brief sketch still of value.

1794 HENDRICKS, LAWRENCE. The London charterhouse, its monks
and its martyrs. Lond. 1889.

1795 HERIOT, D. B. Anabaptism in England during the 16th and 17th centuries. *Congregational Hist. Soc. Trans.* xii (1935), 256–71; xii (1936), 312–20.

1796 HEYLYN, PETER. Ecclesia restaurata or the history of the reformation
of the church of England. Lond. 1661; 1670; 1674; by J. C. Robertson,
Eccles. Hist. Soc., Cambr. 1849.
The last ed. contains a life of Heylyn by J. Barnard. High church Anglican viewpoint.

1798 HOOK, W. F. The lives of the archbishops of Canterbury. 12 vols.
Lond. 1860–76.
Valuable, but to be used with care.

1799 HUGHES, PHILIP. The eve of the reformation. *Dublin Rev.* cciv
(1939), 147–59.

1800 HUGHES, PHILIP. Rome and the counter-reformation in England. Lond. 1942.

1801 HUGHES, PHILIP. The reformation in England. Vol. i: The King's proceedings. Lond. 1950; Vol. ii: Religio Depopulata. Lond. 1953; Vol. iii: 'True religion now established.' Lond. 1954.

1802 HUGHES, PHILIP. A popular history of the reformation. Lond. 1957.
A good, Roman Catholic account of the reformation on the continent and in England.

1803 HYLAND, St. G. K. A century of persecution under Tudor and Stuart sovereigns, from contemporary records (at Loseley). Lond. 1920.
Many documents printed in full. For the *Loseley MSS.* cf. 288.

1804 INGRAM, T. D. England and Rome; a history of the relations between the papacy and the English state and church, from the Norman conquest to 1688. Lond. 1892.
Maintains that Tudor supremacy was the same as that of medieval English kings.

1805 JACOBS, H. E. A study in comparative symbolics; the Lutheran movement in England during the reigns of Henry VIII and Edward VI, and its literary monuments. Philadelphia, 1890; 1908.
Trustworthy.

1806 JACQUOT, JEAN. Sébastien Castellion et l'Angleterre: quelques aspects de son influence. *Hum. et Ren.* xv (1953), 15–44.

1807 JANELLE, PIERRE. L'Angleterre était-elle vouée au protestantisme? *Bull. Hist. et scientif. de l'Auvergne*, lxiv (1944), 155–98.

1808 JORDAN, W. K. The development of religious toleration in England from the beginning of the English reformation to the death of Queen Elizabeth. Cambr., U.S.A., 1932.
3 subsequent volumes, covering the seventeenth century, were published in 1934, 1938, 1940.

1809 LAW, T. G. A calendar of the English martyrs of the sixteenth and seventeenth centuries; with an introduction. Lond. 1876.
Useful.

1810 LEE, F. G. Reginald Pole, cardinal archbishop of Canterbury. Lond. 1898.
Uncritically laudatory.

1811 LINDSAY, T. M. A history of the reformation. 2 vols. Edin. 1906.
Vol. ii pertinent. This refers to the reformation on the continent as well as in England.

1812 LIVES OF THE ENGLISH MARTYRS. By Bede Camm. 2 vols. Lond. 1904–5.
Vol. i, 1535–45, deals with those who were declared blessed by Leo XIII in 1886 and 1895; vol. ii, 1570–83. Roman Catholic viewpoint.

1813 LIVES OF THE ENGLISH MARTYRS. By J. H. Pollen and E. H. Burton. Lond. 1914.
2nd ser. Cf. (1812) above. Deals with the martyrs (1583–1603) declared venerable. Biographical notes and documentary extracts.

1814 MACKINNON, J. The origins of the reformation. Lond. 1939.

1815   MAITLAND, S. R. Essays on subjects connected with the reformation in England. Lond. 1849; by A. W. Hutton, Lond. 1898.
Critical of the reformers.

1816   MALDEN, H. E. Notes on the local progress of protestantism in England in the sixteenth and seventeenth centuries. *Trans. R.H. Soc.*, 2nd ser., ii (1885), 61–76.

1817   MASON, A. J. Thomas Cranmer. Lond. 1898.
Brief.

1818   MERLE D'AUBIGNÉ, J. H. Histoire de la réformation du seizième siècle. 5 vols. Paris, 1849–53; trans. by H. White, Edin. 1853.
Vol. v, *Réformation d'Angleterre.* Valuable.

1819   MESSENGER, E. C. The reformation, the mass and the priesthood. A documented history with special reference to the question of Anglican orders. 2 vols. Lond. 1936, 1937.
Cf. Gustave Constant, *The reformation, the mass and the priesthood, Downside Rev.* liv (1936), 522–7; and E. C. Messenger, *The reformation, the mass and the priesthood. A reply,* ibid. lv (1937), 56–63.

1820   MOORE, A. L. Lectures and papers on the history of the reformation in England and on the continent. Lond. 1890.
Fragmentary, but suggestive. High Anglican.

1821   MOORMAN, J. R. H. History of the Church. Lond. 2nd ed. 1954.

1822   MOREAU, E. DE, JANELLE, P., and JOURDA, P. La crise religieuse du XVIᵉ siècle. *Histoire de l'église depuis les origines jusqu'à nos jours.* By A. Fliche and Eug. Jarry, T. xvi. Paris, 1950.

1823   MORRIS, JOHN. The troubles of our Catholic forefathers, related by themselves. 3 vols. Lond. 1872–7.
Illustrated. Ill-digested, but with important documents.

1824   MORTIMER, C. G., and BARBER, S. C. The English bishops and the reformation, 1530–1560, with a table of descent. Lond. 1936.

1825   MOZLEY, J. F. William Tyndale. Lond. 1937.

1826   MOZLEY, J. F. John Foxe and his book. Lond. 1940.

1827   MULLER, J. A. Stephen Gardiner. Cf. 358.

1827a   MUMFORD, A. A. Hugh Oldham, 1452–1519. Bishop of Exeter. Lond. 1936.

1828   PARKER, T. M. The English reformation to 1558. Lond. 1950.

1829   PASTOR, LUDWIG, FREIHERR VON. Geschichte der Päpste seit dem Ausgang des Mittelalters. Vols. i–xiii (to 1644, in progress). Freiburg, 1891–1929. Eng. trans., 23 vols. (to 1605, in progress), by F. I. Antrobus, R. F. Kerr. Lond. 1891–1933.
Roman Catholic viewpoint.

1830   PAYNE, E. A. The Anabaptists of the 16th century and their influence in the modern world. Lond. 1949.

1831   PENNINGTON, E. L. The episcopal succession during the English reformation. Lond. 1952.

1832   PERRY, G. G. A history of the English church from the accession of Henry VIII to the silencing of convocation in the eighteenth century. Lond. 1878.
Good brief sketch.

1833   POLLARD, A. F. Thomas Cranmer and the English reformation, 1489–1556. Lond. 1904; 1926.
Weak theologically.

1833a   PORTER, H. C. Reformation and reaction in Tudor Cambridge. Cambr. 1958.

1834   RANKE, LEOPOLD VON. Die römischen Päpste. In *Sämmtliche Werke*, vols. xxxvii–xxxviii. Leipzig, 1874 ff. Eng. trans. by E. Foster, 3 vols., Lond. 1902–3.

1835   RATCLIFF, E. C. The liturgical work of Archbishop Cranmer. *Jour. Eccles. Hist.* vii (1956), 189–203.

1836   RIDLEY, J. G. Nicholas Ridley: a biography. Lond. 1957.

1838   RUPP, E. G. Studies in the making of the English protestant tradition, mainly in the reign of Henry VIII. Lond. 1947.

1839   SCHENK, W. Reginald Pole, cardinal of England. Lond. 1950.

1840   SCHENK, W. Cardinal Pole. *Church Quar. Rev.* cxlvii (1949), 174–84.

1841   SCHENK, W. The student days of Cardinal Pole. *History*, xxxiii (1948), 211–25.

1842   SCHÖFFLER, HERBERT. Die Anfänge des Puritanismus: Versuch einer Deutung der englischen Reformation. *Kölner anglistische Arbeiten*, xiv, Leipzig, 1932.

1843   SIMONS, P. Die Anfänge der englischen Reformation. *Tijdschrift voor geschiedenis*, Groningen, xxxiii (1941), 31–41, 135–47.

1844   SLOOTMANS, C. J. F. Engelsche Lutheranen op te jaarmarkten te Bergen op Zoom, 1526–35. *Taxandria*, xlix (1942), 52–56, 63–72.

1845   SMITH, H. M. Pre-reformation England. New York, 1938.

1846   SMITH, H. M. A commentary on Trevisan. *Church Quar. Rev.* cxxi (1935), 71–96.

1847   SMITH, L. B. Tudor prelates and politics. *Princeton studies in history*, viii. Lond. 1953.

1848   SOAMES, HENRY. The history of the reformation of the church of England. 4 vols. Lond. 1826–8.
Anglican point of view. Henry VIII to 1563. An abridgement published in Lond. 1828.

1849   STRYPE, JOHN. Ecclesiastical memorials, relating chiefly to religion, and the reformation of it, and the emergencies of the church of England under King Henry VIII, King Edward VI, and Queen Mary I, with large appendices, containing original papers, records, &c. Lond. 1721; best ed. 3 vols. In *Works*, Oxf. 1820–40.
Valuable for its documents.

1850 STRYPE, JOHN. Memorials of the most reverend father in God, Thomas Cranmer, sometime lord archibshop of Canterbury. Lond. 1694; 2 vols., Oxf. 1840; 2 vols., Lond. 1853; 3 vols., Oxf. 1848–54.
Documentary material, sometimes carelessly given. In the last 2 eds. the documents have been re-ed.

1851 STURGE, CHARLES. Cuthbert Tunstal: churchman, scholar, statesman, administrator. Lond. 1938.

1852 SYKES, NORMAN. Crisis of the reformation. Lond. 1938.

1853 SYKES, NORMAN. The Church of England and non-episcopal churches in the sixteenth and seventeenth centuries. Lond. 1948.

1854 THOMPSON, E. M. The Carthusian order in England. Lond. 1930.

1855 THORNLEY, I. D. The destruction of sanctuary. In *Tudor Studies* (379), 182–207.

1856 A TRACTARIAN BRITISH CRITIC [Townsend, George]. The life and defence of . . . Edmund Bonner, bishop of London. Lond. 1842.

1857 TYPICAL ENGLISH CHURCHMEN. By W. E. Collins. 2 vols. *Church Hist. Soc.*, Lond. 1902.
Ser. i, from Parker to Maurice, contains chapters on Matthew Parker by H. Gee and on Richard Hooker by A. J. Mason; ser. ii, from Wyclif to Gardiner, chapters on Cuthbert Tunstall by G. H. Ross-Lewin and on Stephen Gardiner by J. Gairdner.

1858 WAKE, WILLIAM. The state of the church and clergy of England. Lond. 1703.
Valuable.

1859 WHARHIRST, G. W. The reformation in the diocese of Lincoln as illustrated by the life and work of Bishop Longland, 1521–47. *Lincs. Archit. and Arch. Soc. Reports and Papers* (1939), 137–76.

1860 WHARTON, HENRY (*pseud.* Anthony Harmer). A specimen of some errors. Lond. 1693.
Attack on Burnet (1767).

1861 WHITAKER, W. B. Sunday in Tudor and Stuart times. Lond. 1933.

1862 WHITE, H. C. The Tudor books of private devotion. Madison, 1951.

1864 WILBY, N. M. St. Thomas More and the refugees in Flanders. *Dublin Rev.* cxcix (1936), 315–29.

1865 WINTERS, WILLIAM. John Foxe, the martyrologist and his family. *Trans. R.H. Soc.* v (1877), 28–82.

1866 WORDSWORTH, CHRISTOPHER. Ecclesiastical biography, or lives of eminent men connected with the history of religion in England from the commencement of the reformation to the revolution. 6 vols. Lond. 1810; 1839; 1853.
The ed. of 1839 has a new introduction and additional lives.

1867 WRIGHT, L. B. The significance of religious writings in the English renaissance. *Jour. Hist. Ideas*, i (1940), 59–68.

1868 ZIMMERMAN, ATHANASIUS. Kardinal Pole, sein Leben und seine Schriften, ein Beitrag zur Kirchengeschichte des 16 Jahrhunderts. Regensburg, 1893.
The best life of Pole, by a Jesuit.

(c) *Protestant Refugees in England*

The best general account is in 1875 which, however, approaches the subject from an economic point of view; for which cf. also ch. vii, *infra* (p. 249). The publications of the *Huguenot Society of London* deal with the history of many of the French and Walloon churches in England.

1869 LES ACTES DES COLLOQUES des églises françaises et des synodes des églises étrangères réfugiées en Angleterre, 1581–1651. By A. C. Chamier. *Hug. Soc. Pub.* ii (1890). Index issued separately.

1870 BEEMAN, G. B. The early history of the Strangers' Church, 1550 to 1561. *Hug. Soc. Proc.* xv (1935), 261–82.

1871 BEVIS MARKS RECORDS, being contributions to the history of the Spanish and Portuguese congregation of Lond. By L. D. Barnett. Pt. i. The early history of the congregation from the beginning until 1800. Oxf. 1940.
Deals with a Jewish synagogue.

1872 BURN, J. S. The history of the French, Walloon, Dutch, and other foreign protestant refugees settled in England, from the reign of Henry VIII to the revocation of the edict of Nantes: with notices of their trade and commerce. Lond. 1846.

1873 COWELL, H. J. Valérand Poullain: a precursor of congregationalism? *Congregational Hist. Soc. Trans.* xii (1934), 112–18.

1874 CROSS, F. W. History of the Walloon and Huguenot church at Canterbury. *Hug. Soc. Pub.* xv (1898).
Contains a number of documents concerning the life and industries of the Huguenots in the sixteenth and seventeenth centuries.

1875 CUNNINGHAM, WILLIAM. Alien immigrants to England. Lond. 1897.
General, but including a valuable ch. on the Tudor period.

1876 ÉGLISE FRANÇAISE DE THREADNEEDLE STREET. Actes du consistoire de l'église française de Threadneedle Street, Londres. Vol. i. 1560–5. By Elsie Johnson. *Hug. Soc. Pub.* xxxviii (1937).

1877 FLOWER, R. E. W. The Dutch and Walloon 'strangers' in Norwich. *Brit. Mus. Quar.* x (1935), 32–34.

1878 KERKERAADS-PROTOCOLLEN der nederduitsche Vluchtelingenkerk te London, 1560–3. By A. A. Van Schelven. *Werken d. historisch Genootschap*, 3rd ser., xliii (1921).

1879 LETTERS OF DENIZATION and acts of naturalization for aliens in England, 1509–1603. By William Page. *Hug. Soc. Pub.* viii (1893).
For a list of lists of strangers in England cf. *Hug. Soc. Proc.* i (1885–6), 21–24.

1880 LINDEBOOM, J. Austin friars: history of the Dutch reform church in London, 1550–1950. Trans. D. de Iongh. The Hague, 1950.

1881 A LIST OF STRANGERS IN LONDON in 1567 and 1568. By A. W. C. Hallen. *Genealogical Mag.* i (1897), 45–48; 109–12.
This is a printing of B.M., *Lansdowne MS.* x. 62.

1882 MOENS, W. J. C. The Walloons and their church at Norwich, 1565–1832. *Hug. Soc. Pub.* i (1888).

1883 MOENS, W. J. C. Walloon settlements and the French church at Southampton. *Hug. Soc. Proc.* iii (1892), 53–76.
For other short papers on foreign congregations in England, cf. ibid. ii, iii, v, viii.

1884 MORANT, VALERIE. The settlement of protestant refugees in Maidstone during the sixteenth century. *Econ. Hist. Rev.*, 2nd ser., iv (1951), 210–14.

1885 NORWOOD, F. A. The London Dutch refugees in search of a home, 1553–4. *A.H.R.* lviii (1952), 64–72.

1886 RAHLENBECK, CHARLES. Les refugiés belges du seizième siècle en Angleterre. *Revue trimestrielle*, 2nd ser., viii (1856), 1–48.
Contains little that is original. Cf. also *Quelques notes sur les réformés flamands et Wallons du seizième siècle refugiés en Angleterre. Hug. Soc. Proc.* iv (1894), 22–44.

1887 RETURNS OF ALIENS dwelling in the city and suburbs of London from the reign of Henry VIII to that of James I. 4 vols. By R. E. G. Kirk and E. F. Kirk. *Hug. Soc. Pub.* x (1900–8), parts 1–4.

1888 SHAW, W. A. The English government and the relief of protestant refugees. *Hug. Soc. Proc.* v. (1898), 343–423.

1889 SCHICKLER, LE BARON F. DE. Les églises du refuge en Angleterre. 3 vols. Paris, 1892.

1890 SMILES, SAMUEL. The Huguenots, their settlements, churches, and industries in England and Ireland. Lond. 1867.

1891 STRIDE, E. E. A bibliography of some works relating to the Huguenot refugees, whence they came and where they settled. *Hug. Soc. Proc.* i (1885–6), 130–50.

1892 VAN SCHELVEN, A. A. Nederduitsche Vluchtelingen-kerken der 16 eeuw in Engeland en Deutschland. The Hague, 1909.
Chs. 3 and 5 deal with refugees in England, 1544–53, 1559–76. Prints in app. many letters from the archives of the reformed church of Emden.

1893 VERHEYDEN, A. L. E. Une correspondance inédite adressée par des familles protestantes des Pays-Bas à leurs coreligionnaires d'Angleterre (11 novembre 1569–25 fevrier 1570). *Bull. comm. roy. hist.* (Académie royale de Belgique), cxx (1955), 95–257.

1894 WORMAN, E. On MSS. in the University library, Cambridge, relating to Huguenots and other refugees. *Hug. Soc. Proc.* vii (1905), 230–52.

1895 WYATT, THOMAS. Aliens in England before the Huguenots. *Hug. Soc. Proc.* xix (1953), 74–94.

2. ARTICLES OF RELIGION AND THE PRAYER BOOK

(a) *Sources*

Arranged in order of dates of publication. For contemporary eds. of ecclesiastical advertisements, articles, canons, and visitation articles, cf. *S.T.C.* (35), pp. 220–5; cf. also 5451.

1896 HENRY VIII. Assertio septem sacramentorum. Lond. and Rome, 1521; best. ed. by Louis O'Donovan, New York, 1908.
Ed. 1908 contains Latin original and Eng. trans. with illustrative documents and a bibliography.
Against Luther. Won for Henry the title *defensor fidei*.

1897 ARTICLES DEVISED BY THE KINGES HIGNES MAJESTIE to stablyshe Christen quietnes and unitie amonge us and to avoyde contentious opinions. Lond. 1536.
The *Ten articles*. Repr. in no. 1903 *infra*.

1898 THE INSTITUTION OF A CHRISTIAN MAN. Lond. 1537.
The *Bishop's book*. Repr. in no. 1903 *infra*.

1899 A NECESSARY DOCTRINE AND ERUDITION for any Christen man, set furthe by the kynges maiestie of Englande, &c. Cf. 1385.
The *King's book*.

1900 CERTAYNE SERMONS OR HOMILIES appoynted by the kynges maiestie to be declared and redde in churches (the *First book of homilies*). The second tome of homilies, of such matters as were promised and instituted in the former part of homilies, set out by the authorities of the queenes maiestie (the *Second book of homilies*). Lond. 1547–63; by John Griffiths, Oxf. 1859.
The ed. of 1859 has the title: *The two books of homilies appointed to be read in churches*.

1901 THE BOOKE OF THE COMMON PRAIER and administracion of the saramentes, and other rites and ceremonies of the churche, after the use of the church of England (the *First book* of Edward VI). Lond. 1549; 1844; by Vernon Staley, *Library of liturgiology and ecclesiology for English readers*, ii. Lond. 1903.

1902 THE BOKE OF COMMON PRAYER, and administration of the sacramentes, and other rites and ceremonies in the churche of Englande (the *Second book* of Edward VI). Lond. 1552; 1883.

1903 FORMULARIES OF FAITH put forth by authority during the reign of Henry VIII. By Charles Lloyd. Oxf. 1825.
Repr. of the *Ten articles* (1897), the *Bishop's book* (1898), and the *King's book* (1899).

1904 THE TWO BOOKS OF COMMON PRAYER, set forth by authority of parliament in the reign of King Edward the sixth, compared. By Edward Cardwell. Oxf. 1838; 1841.

1905 CARDWELL, EDWARD. A history of conferences and other proceedings connected with the book of common prayer from the year 1558 to the year 1690. Oxf. 1840; 1849.
Sequel to 1904. The two are intended to give a complete documentary history of the English liturgy from the reformation on. The documents are extemely useful, the historical comments of less value.

1906 THE TWO LITURGIES, A.D. 1549, and A.D. 1552, with other documents set forth by authority in the reign of King Edward VI. By Joseph Ketley. *Parker Soc.*, 1844.

1907 LITURGIES AND OCCASIONAL FORMS OF PRAYER set forth in the reign of Queen Elizabeth. By W. K. Clay. *Parker Soc.*, 1847.

1908 THE BOOK OF COMMON PRAYER, with notes, legal and historical. By A. J. Stephens. 3 vols. *Eccles. Hist. Soc.*, 1849–54.

1909 TROUBLES CONNECTED WITH THE PRAYER BOOK of 1549. Cf. 557.

1910 THE CANONS OF 1571, in English and Latin, with notes. By W. E. Collins. *Church Hist. Soc.* xl (1889).

1911 CRANMER'S LITURGICAL PROJECTS. By J. W. Legg. *Henry Bradshaw Soc.* i (1915).
Two draft attempts at producing an English breviary from a MS. once belonging to Cranmer. Introduction, notes, app. Scholarly.

(b) *Later Works*

The standard history of the English prayer book is 1930.

1912 BIRCHENOUGH, EDWYN. The Prymer in English. *Library*, 4th ser., xviii (1937), 177–94.

1913 BIRCHENOUGH, EDWYN. An unknown edition of Henry VIII's prymer. *Bodleian Quar. Rec.* viii (1935), 16.

1914 BRIGHTMAN, F. E. The litany under Henry VIII. *E.H.R.* xxiv (1909), 101–4.

1915 BURNET, GILBERT. An exposition of the thirty-nine articles of the church of England. Lond. 1699; Oxf. 1814.

1916 BUTTERWORTH, C. C. The English primers, 1529–45: their publication and connection with the English bible and the reformation in England. Philadelphia, 1953.

1918 COBB, C. S. The rationale of ceremonial, 1540–3, with notes and appendices and an essay on the regulation of ceremonial during the reign of King Henry VIII. *Alcuin Club*, 1910.
Documents and plates. Careful ed. of *Lambeth MS. book of ceremonies.*

1919 COLLIGAN, J. H. The Genevan service book of 1555. Manchester, 1932.

1920 GAIRDNER, JAMES. Henry VIII's English litanies. *E.H.R.* xxiii (1908), 530–3.

1921 GASQUET, F. A., and BISHOP, EDMUND. Edward VI and the book of common prayer. An examination into its origin and early history, with an appendix of unpublished documents. Lond. 1890.
Valuable. See *The true history of the Edwardine ordinal, Church Quar. Rev.* xliv (1897), 123–47.

1921a GEE, HENRY. The Elizabethan prayer book and ornaments, with an app. of documents. Lond. 1902.

1922 GIBSON, E. C. S. The thirty-nine articles. Lond. 1898.

1923 HARDWICK, CHARLES. A history of the articles of religion. Cambr. 1851; Lond. 1904.
The standard account. App. of documents, 1536–1615.

1924 HARRINGTON, E. C. Pope Pius IV and the book of common prayer. Lond. 1856.

1925 MESSENGER, E. C. The Lutheran origin of the Anglican ordinal. Lond. 1934.

1926 PARKER, JAMES. The first prayer-book of Edward VI compared with the successive revisions of the book of common prayer. Oxf. 1877.

1927 PARKER, JAMES. Did Queen Elizabeth take 'other order' in the 'advertisements' of 1566? Oxf. 1878.

1928 PARKER, JAMES. The ornaments rubric; its history and meaning. Oxf. 1881.

1929 POLLEN, J. H. The alleged papal sanction of the Anglican liturgy. *The Month*, c (1902), 274–80.

1930 PROCTER, FRANCIS, and FRERE, W. H. A new history of the book of common prayer, with a rationale of its offices. On the basis of the former work by Francis Procter, revised and rewritten by W. H. Frere. Lond. 1901; 1914.
The standard history of the English prayer book.

1931 PULLAN, LEIGHTON. The history of the book of common prayer. Lond. 1909.

1932 RATCLIFF, E. C. The Book of common prayer of the Church of England: its origins and revisions, 1549–1661. Lond. 1949.

1933   SCHAFF, PHILIP. The creeds of Christendom. 3 vols. New York, 1877.
Historical discussion, i, 592–701; text of English and Scottish formularies, iii, 437–525; considerable bibliographical material.

1934   SYMONDS, H. E. The council of Trent and Anglican formularies. Oxf. 1933.

1935   TIMMS, G. B. Dixit Cranmer. *Church Quar. Rev.* cxliii (1947), 217–34; cxliv (1947), 33–51.
Cf. Gregory Dix, *Dixit Cranmer et non timuit. A supplement to Mr. Timms, Church Quar. Rev.* cxlv (1948), 146–76; cxlvi (1948), 44–60.

1936   TOMLINSON, J. T. The prayer book, articles and homilies. Lond. 1897.
Of value if used with caution.

3. THE ENGLISH BIBLE

This section does not pretend to be exhaustive. For early eds. of the bible and parts of the bible in English both on the continent and in England, cf. *S.T.C.* (35), pp. 47–64.

(a) *Sources*

1937   COTTON, HENRY. Editions of the bible and parts thereof in English. Lond. 1821; Oxf. 1852.

1938   THE ENGLISH HEXAPLA. Lond. 1841.
Contains Tyndale's new testament, ed. of 1534; Coverdale's, 1539; the Genevan, 1557; and the Rhemish, 1582.

1939   FACSIMILE TEXTS. The first printed English new testament, translated by William Tyndale. By Edward Arber. Lond. 1871.
Extensive introduction by the editor. Cf. *The New Testament translated by William Tyndale, 1534. A reprint of the edition of 1534 with the translator's prefaces and notes and the variants of the edition of 1523.* By N. H. Wallis, for the *Roy. Soc. of Lit.,* Cambr. 1938.

1940   FRY, FRANCIS. The bible by Coverdale, MDXXXV. Lond. 1867.
Facsimiles.

1941   FRY, FRANCIS. A bibliographical description of the editions of the new testament; Tyndale's versions in English, &c. Lond. 1878.
Facsimiles.

1942   FRY, FRANCIS. A description of the great bible, 1539, and the six editions of Cranmer's bible, &c. Lond. 1865.
Facsimiles.

1943   MOMBERT, J. I. English versions of the bible. Lond. 1883.
Handbook with collated texts and comparative tables. Includes Tyndale's, Coverdale's, Matthew's and Taverner's versions; the Great Bible, Genevan, Rheims, and Douay bibles.

1944 POLLARD, A. W. Records of the English bible, the documents relating to the translation and publication of the bible in English, 1525–1611. Oxf. 1911.
Valuable documentary collection.

1945 TYNDALE, WILLIAM. Doctrinal treatises and introductions to different portions of the holy scriptures. By Henry Walter. *Parker Soc.*, 1848.

1946 TYNDALE, WILLIAM. Exposition and notes on sundry portions of the holy scriptures. By Henry Walter. *Parker Soc.*, 1849.
Exposition of St. Matthew, chs. v–vii and 1 epistle of St. John, and marginal notes on Matt. chs. i–xxi. Includes repr. of *Practyse of prelates*. For the original eds. of Tyndale's commentaries, cf. *S.T.C.* (35), pp. 569–70.

(b) *Later Works*

Westcott (1960) is the standard history.

1947 ANDERSON, CHRISTOPHER. The annals of the English bible. 2 vols. Lond. 1845–55.

1948 BROWN, JOHN. The history of the English bible. Cambr. 1911.
Good, brief, popular sketch.

1949 CARLETON, J. G. The part of Rheims in the making of the English bible. Oxf. 1902.

1950 CHESTER, J. L. John Rogers. Lond. 1861.
Discusses his part in the early English versions of the bible.

1951 EADIE, JOHN. The English bible. 2 vols. Lond. 1876.
Traces history of English bible from Anglo-Saxon times to 1611.

1952 EASON, CHARLES. The Geneva bible. Notes on its production and distribution. Dublin, 1937.

1953 GUPPY, HENRY. Miles Coverdale and the English bible, 1488–1568. *John Rylands Lib. Bull.* xix (1935), 300–28.

1954 GUPPY, HENRY. The royal 'injunctions' of 1538 and the 'Great Bible', 1539–1541. *John Rylands Lib. Bull.* xxii (1938), 31–71.

1955 HUTTON, H. H., and WILLOUGHBY, H. R. The ignored Taverner bible of 1539. *The Crozier Quar.* (1939), 161–76.

1956 ISAACS, J. The Sixteenth century English version. In *The Bible in its ancient and English versions*. By H. W. Robinson. Oxf. 1950; repr. with apps. 1954.

1957 LUPTON, J. H. Versions (English). In *Dict. of the bible*. By James Hastings. Extra vol. Edin. 1904.

1958 MOULTON, W. F. The history of the English bible. Lond. 1878–82.
Facsimiles.

1959 MOZLEY, J. F. Coverdale and his bibles. Lond. 1953.

1960 WESTCOTT, B. F. A general view of the history of the English bible. Lond. and Cambr. 1868; Lond. 1872; best ed. by W. A. Wright, Lond. 1905.
Valuable.

1961 WHITLEY, W. T. Thomas Matthew of Colchester and Matthew's Bible of 1537. A study of editing and publishing. *Essex Rev.*, xliii (1934), 1–6, 82–87, 155–62, 227–34; xliv (1935), 40–44; lvi (1947), 73–74.

1962 WHITLEY, W. T. Thomas Matthew's bible [1537]. *Church Quar. Rev.* cxxxv (1937), 48–69.

1963 WHITLEY, W. T. The English bible under the Tudor sovereigns. Lond. 1937.

1964 WILLOUGHBY, H. R. The Coverdale psalter and the quatrocentenary of the printed English bible. Chicago, 1935.

1965 WILLOUGHBY, H. R. Current errors concerning the Coverdale bible. *Jour. Bibliog. Literature*, lv (1936), 1–13.

1966 WILLOUGHBY, H. R. The first authorized English bible and the Cranmer preface. Chicago, 1942.

4. HENRY VII AND HENRY VIII, 1485–1547

A. General

(a) *Sources*

Practically all the official correspondence relative to Henry VIII's relations to the church are printed in *Letters and Papers Henry VIII* (91), but virtually all the important collections of sources upon the history of his reign contain material on religious history. The bibliographies at the chapter-endings in Gairdner (1785) are particularly useful for source material. The works of Cranmer (1718) and Latimer (1732), Pole's letters (1739), More's works (450), Merriman's ed. of Cromwell's letters (520), Nichols's *Narratives of the reformation* (1735), Strype's *Ecclesiastical memorials* (1849), Foxe's *Acts and monuments* (1726), and Pocock's ed. of Burnet (1767) are of first-rate importance for this period.

Many of the books written in this period which are listed in the chapter on Political Theory (ch. iv *supra*) are pertinent to this section.

1967 CHAPTER ACTS OF THE CATHEDRAL CHURCH of St. Mary of Lincoln, A.D. 1536–47. By R. E. G. Cole. 3 vols. *Lincoln Rec. Soc.* xii (1915), xiii (1917), xv (1923).

1968 DAVIS, E. J. The authorities for the case of Richard Hunne, 1514–15. *E.H.R.* xxx (1915), 477–88.

1969 DICKENS, A. G. A new prayer of Sir Thomas More. *Church Quar. Rev.* cxxiv (1937), 224–37.

1970 ERASMUS, DESIDERIUS. Opera. By Le Clerc. 10 vols. Leyden, 1703–6.
Erasmus's works and correspondence throw a great deal of light upon conditions in the church in England before the breach with Rome. For his correspondence, cf. 1979.

1971 AN UNPRINTED LETTER OF JOHN COLET. *A.H.R.* xxxix (1934), 696–9, by W. K. Ferguson.

1972 VIE DU BIENHEUREUX MARTYR JEAN FISHER, CARDINAL (1535). Text anglais et traduction latine du xvie siècle. By Fr. van Ortroy, Bollandiste. From *Analecta Bollandiana*, x (1891), xii (1893). Brussels, 1893.
This was the original text upon which Thomas Bayly's pirated 'Life' (Lond. 1655) was based. Cf. *Saint John Fisher. The earliest English Life*, by Philip Hughes, Lond. 1935. Cf. also edition by Ronald Bayne, *E.E.T.S.*, extra ser., cxvii (1921).

1973 LINCOLN DIOCESE DOCUMENTS. By Andrew Clark. *E.E.T.S.* cxlix (1914).
76 documents, 1450–1544. Includes 37 wills, proceedings in archidiaconal courts, proceedings against heretics, steps taken by bp. Longland for acceptance of the royal supremacy.

1974 [FISH, SIMON.] A supplicacyon for the beggers. Lond. [1529?]; by J. Meadows Cowper, *E.E.T.S.*, extra ser., xiii (1871); by Edward Arber, *English Scholar's Library*, no. 4, Lond. 1878.
Ed. of 1871 also contains *A supplycacyon to our moste soueraigne lorde kynge Henry the eyght (1544)*, and *A supplication of the poore commons (1546)*, both of which are attributed by the editor to Henry Brinkelow. All three deal with the ignorance and worldliness of the clergy.
Answered by Sir Thomas More in his *Supplycacyon of soulys*, Lond. [1529?].

1975 FISHER, JOHN. English works. By J. E. B. Mayor. *E.E.T.S.*, extra ser., xxvii (1876).

1976 GOODALE, JOHN. The lyberties of the cleargy, collected out of the lawes of the realme, both necessary for vycars and curates. Lond. [1540?].

1977 HOPE, W. H. ST. J. On an inventory of the goods of the collegiate church of the Holy Trinity, Arundel, taken 1st Oct. 9 Henry VIII (1517). *Arch.* lxi (1908), 61–96.

1978 LETTERS OF RICHARD FOX, 1486–1527. By P. S. and H. M. Allen. Oxf. 1928.

1979 OPUS EPISTOLARUM DES. ERASMI ROTERDAMI. By P. S. Allen, H. M. Allen, and H. W. Garrod. 12 vols. Oxf. 1906–58. Vol. xii, the index volume, was edited by P. S. Allen, Barbara Flower, and Elizabeth Rosenbaum.
For an Eng. trans. of most of these letters, cf. *The epistles of D. Erasmus*, by F. M. Nichols, 3 vols., Lond. 1901–18.

1980 PETERBOROUGH LOCAL ADMINISTRATION. The foundation of Peterborough cathedral, A.D. 1541. Pt. ii of Tudor documents. By W. T. Mellows. *Northamp. Rec. Soc.* xiii (1941).

1981 RECORDS OF THE REFORMATION: the divorce, 1527–33. By Nicholas Pocock. 2 vols. Oxf. 1870.
Documents.

1982 THE REGISTER OF CHARLES BOTHE, bishop of Hereford (1516–35). By A. T. Bannister. 2 vols. *Cantilupe Soc.* Hereford, 1921.

1983 THE REGISTER OF RICHARD FOX, while bishop of Bath and Wells, 1492–4. By E. C. Batten. Lond. 1889.
With valuable life of bishop Fox.

1984   REGISTRUM THOME WOLSEY CARDINALIS ecclesie Wintoniensis administratoris. By Herbert Chitty. *Canterbury and York Soc.* xxxii (1926).
Register of church and bishopric of Winchester, 1529–30.

1985   REGISTRA STEPHANI GARDINER et Johannis Poynet, episcoporum Wintoniensium (1531–47, 1551–2). By Herbert Chitty. *Canterbury and York Soc.* xxxvii (1930).
Chiefly on Gardiner's episcopate.

1986   THE SERMON AGAINST THE HOLY MAID OF KENT, delivered at Paul's Cross, 23 November, 1533 and at Canterbury, Dec. 7. By L. E. Whatmore. *E.H.R.* lviii (1943), 463–75.

1987   SIMPSON, W. S. On a newly-discovered MS. containing statutes compiled by Dean Colet for the government of the chantry priests and other clergy in St. Paul's Cathedral. *Arch.* lii (1890), 145–74.

1988   A SUBSIDY COLLECTED IN THE DIOCESE OF LINCOLN in 1526. By H. E. Salter. Oxf. 1909.

1989   A TREATYSE CONCERNINGE DIVERS OF THE CONSTITUCYONS prouynciall and legatines. Lond. [1535?].
Sometimes attributed to Saint German.

1990   TYNDALL, J. FRITH, and DOCT. BARNES, The whole workes of W. 2 vols. Lond. 1572–3.
Commonly known as Day's ed. from the publisher's name.

1991   TYNDALE, WILLIAM. Works. By Henry Walter. 3 vols. *Parker Soc.*, 1848–50.
There is an earlier ed. of the works of Tyndale and Frith, by Thomas Russell, 3 vols. Lond. 1828–31. Cf. also 1366, 1370, and 1990.

1992   VISITATIONS OF THE DIOCESE OF NORWICH, 1492–1532. By Augustus Jessopp. *Camden Soc.*, new ser., xliii (1888).
Documents.

1993   VISITATIONS AND MEMORIALS OF SOUTHWELL MINSTER. By A. F. Leach. *Camden Soc.*, new ser., xlviii (1891).
Good picture of manner of life and working of a collegiate church, 1469–1547.

1994   THE VISITATIONS AND INJUNCTIONS of Cardinal Wolsey and Archbishop Cranmer to the priory of Worcester in 1526 and [1534?]. By J. M. Wilson. Worcester, 1924.
Cf. *E.H.R.* xl (1925), 87–92.

1995a   VISITATIONS IN THE DIOCESE OF LINCOLN, 1517–31. By A. H. Thompson. *Lincoln Rec. Soc.* xxxiii (1940), xxxv (1944), xxxvii (1947).

(b) *Later Works*

The best summary of the facts is in Gairdner (1785). Fisher (339), Mackie (354), Pollard's *Henry VIII* (531), are valuable, as is also Froude's account (340) despite his bias. Gasquet's studies on various phases of the subject (2017, 2073–4) are a more scholarly presentation of the Roman Catholic view than is Lingard's (353). On Cardinal Morton, cf. Jenkins in 379, *supra*, on Sir Thos. More, cf. Bridgett (474).

1996   ALLEN, P. S. Dean Colet and Archbishop Warham. *E.H.R.* xvii (1902) 303–6.

1997   ABBADESSA, GIUSEPPE. Il P. Angelo da Sciacca e la sua relazione dello scisma anglicano. *Arch. Stor. Siciliano*, n.s., liv (1934), 76–88.

1998   ANTHEUNIS, LOUIS. Note sur John Harris, secretaire privé de chancelier Thomas Morus (1510?–79). *Rev. Hist. Eccles.* xxxiii (1937), 535–40.

1999   ARROWSMITH, R. S. The prelude to the reformation. Lond. 1923.
A useful study of church life from Wycliffe to the breach with Rome.

2000   BRIDGETT, T. E. The life of the blessed John Fisher. . . . Lond. 1888.

2001   CAMPBELL, W. E. Erasmus in England. *Dublin Rev.* ccxi (1942), 36–49.

2002   CHESTER, A. G. Robert Barnes and the burning of the books. *Hunt. Lib. Quar.* xiv (1951), 211–21.

2003   CONSTANT, GUSTAVE. La réforme en Angleterre, le schisme anglican, Henry VIII. Paris, 1930. Eng. trans. by R. E. Scantlebury, Lond. 1934. Alterations in the trans. approved by the author.
Impartial and scholarly.

2004   CONSTANT, GUSTAVE. Les évêques Henriciens sous Henry VIII. *Revue des quest. hist.* xci (1912), 384–425.

2005   CONSTANT, GUSTAVE. Politique et dogme dans les confessions de foi de Henri VIII, roi d'Angleterre. *Revue historique*, clv (1927), 1–38.

2006   CONSTANT, GUSTAVE. Clément VII et le divorce d'Henri VIII, 1527–33. *Mélanges* (1932), 145–62.

2007   CONSTANT, GUSTAVE. The schism of Henry VIII: some question of evidence. *Clergy Rev.* x (1935), 429–37.

2008   CONSTANT, GUSTAVE. Formularies of faith during the reign of Henry VIII. *Downside Rev.* liv (1936), 155–64.

2009   COWELL, H. J. Erasmus's personal and literary associations with England. *Huguenot Soc. Proc.* xv (1936), 428–55.

2010   DAWLEY, P. M. Henry VIII and the church: an essay on some aspects of the reformation in England. *Hist. Mag. of the Episcopal Church*, xvi (1947), 246–59.

2011   DICKENS, A. G. Robert Holgate: Archbishop of York and president of the King's council in the north. Lond. 1955.

2012   DICKENS, A. G. The marriage and character of Archbishop Holgate. *E.H.R.* lii (1937), 428–42.

2013   DICKENS, A. G. The northern convocation and Henry VIII. *Church Hist. Rev.* cxxvii (1938), 84–102.

2014   DU BOYS, ALBERT. Catherine d'Aragon et les origines du schisme Anglican. *Société générale de librairie catholique*. Paris, 1880; trans. by C. M. Yonge, 2 vols., Lond. 1881.

2015   FRÉDÉRICQ, PAUL. La fin de William Tyndale brûlé à Vilvorde en 1536. *Mélanges d'histoire offerts à M. Charles Bémont* (Paris, 1913), pp. 473–80.

2016 GANSS, H. G. Sir Thomas More and the persecution of heretics. *Amer. Cath. Quar.* xxv (1900), 531–48.

2017 GASQUET, F. A. The eve of the reformation. Lond. 1900.
Moderate Roman Catholic viewpoint.

2018 HENRY VIII AND THE ENGLISH REFORMATION. *Edin. Rev.* ccvi (1907), 306–25.

2019 HUGHES, PHILIP. Some aspects of the papacy as Henry VIII knew it. *Clergy Rev.* v (1933), 89–103.

2020 HUTTON, W. H. The religious writings of Sir Thomas More. *E.H.R.* iv (1889), 667–83.

2021 HYMA, A. Erasmus and the Oxford Reformers, 1493–1503. *Ned. Archief voor kerkgesch.*, n.s., xxv (1932), 69–93, 97–134; xxxviii (1951), 65–85.
The second article covers the period 1503–19.

2022 JANELLE, PIERRE. La controverse entre Étienne Gardiner et Martin Bucer sur la discipline ecclésiastique, 1541–8. *Revue des sciences religieuses,* vii (1927), 452–66.

2023 JANELLE, PIERRE. L'Angleterre catholique à la veille du schisme Paris, 1935.
Valuable. Relates chiefly to S. Gardiner.

2024 JANELLE, PIERRE. Humanisme et unité chrétienne: John Fisher et Thomas More. *Études.* ccxxiii (1935), 442–60.

2025 LEWIS, JOHN. The life of Dr. John Fisher. 2 vols. Lond. 1855.

2026 LUMSDEN, C. B. The dawn of modern England, being a history of the reformation in England, 1509–25. Lond. 1910.

2027 LUPTON, J. H. The influence of Dean Colet upon the reformation of the English church. Lond. 1893.

2028 LUPTON, J. H. A life of John Colet. Lond. 1887.
Contains the best text of Colet's sermon to convocation. Cf. 3745.

2029 REYNOLDS, E. E. St. John Fisher. Lond. 1955.

2030 SEEBOHM, FREDERIC. The Oxford reformers (of 1498) being a history of the fellow work of John Colet, Erasmus, and Thomas More. Lond. 1867; rev. and enl. 1869; 1887.

2031 THURSTON, HERBERT. The canon law of the divorce. *E.H.R.* xix (1904), 632–45.

B. The Dissolution of the Monasteries

(a) *Sources*

The *Letters and Papers* (91) are of first-rate importance. Cf. also 1212.

2032 ABSTRACT OF THE BAILIFF ACCOUNTS of monastic and other estates in the county of Warwick . . . for the year . . . 1547. By W. B. Bickley and W. F. Carter. *Dugdale Soc. Pub.* ii (1923).

2033 ARCHBISHOP WARHAM'S VISITATION OF MONASTERIES, 1511. By Mary Bateson. *E.H.R.* vi (1891), 18–35.

2034 A SELECTION OF MONASTIC RECORDS AND DISSOLUTION PAPERS. By J. S. Purvis. *Yorks. Arch. Soc.*, rec. ser., lxxx (1931). *Miscellanea*, iii, 1–148.

2035 CALENDAR OF ENROLMENTS OF CROWN LEASES by the surveyors-general 34–38 Henry VIII. *Deputy keeper's reports*, xxv (1864), 1–22.
Disposition of monastic lands.

2036 CATALOGUES OF THE DEEDS OF SURRENDER of certain abbeys, priories, &c. . . . (Henry VIII and Edward VI) . . . known as 'the surrenders' . . . in the custody of . . . the master of the rolls. *Deputy keeper's reports*, viii (1847), app. 2, pp. 1–51.

2037 CHANCAEUS, MAURITIUS, or CHAUNCY, MAURICE. Historia aliquot . . . martyrum, maxime octodecim Cartusianorum. Mainz, 1550; Bruges, 1583; by V. M. Doreau, Lond. 1888.
The last part of this work was reprinted at Ghent in 1608, under the title *Commentariolus de vitae ratione et martyrio octodecim Cartusianorum, qui in Anglia, sub rege Henrico VIII trucidati sunt*. An Eng. trans. of the whole entitled *The History of the sufferings of eighteen Carthusians in England* was published in Lond. 1890. Another trans. (from a unique MS.) entitled *The passion and martyrdom of the holy Carthusian fathers*, by G. W. S. Curtis, Lond. 1935.

2038 CLARK-MAXWELL, W. G. The report of the commissioners in the survey of 1536 of the Abbey of Buildwas at its dissolution. *Shropshire Arch. and Nat. Hist. Soc.* xlvi (1933).

2039 COLLECTANEA ANGLO-PREMONSTRATENSIA. By F. A. Gasquet. 3 vols. *Camden Soc.*, 3rd ser., vi, x, xii (1904–6).
Bishop Redman's visitations of the Premonstratensian houses in England.

2040 THE NORFOLK MONASTERIES at the time of the suppression by Henry VIII. By A. Jessopp. *Norfolk Antiq. Misc.* ii (1883) 434–63.
Cf. also 1992.

2041 THE DURHAM HOUSEHOLD BOOK, or the accounts of the bursar of the monastery of Durham, 1530–4. By James Raine. *Surtees Soc.* xviii (1844).
In extenso, classified by subject of expenditure.

2042 INSTRUCTIONS OF KING HENRY VIII for the general visitation of the monasteries and nunneries, 1538–9. In *Ten Scarce Books in English Literature* (298).

2043 INVENTORIES AND VALUATIONS of religious houses at the time of the dissolution, from the public record office. By M. E. C. Walcott. *Arch.* xliii (1871), 201–49.

2044 INVENTORY OF THE ORIGINAL ACKNOWLEDGEMENTS of the royal supremacy, made by the religious houses . . . temp. Henry VIII . . . and deposited in the treasury of receipt of the exchequer. *Deputy keeper's reports*, vii (1846), app. 2, pp. 279–307.

2045 INVENTORY OF PARTICULARS FOR GRANTS, preserved among the records of the late augmentation office (Henry VIII–1 Elizabeth). *Deputy keeper's reports*, ix (1848), app. 2, pp. 148–232; report x (1849), app. 2, pp. 223–309.
Material for disposition of abbey lands, arranged alphabetically by grantees.

2046 REGISTER OR CHRONICLE OF BUTLEY PRIORY, SUFFOLK, 1510–35. By A. G. Dickens. Winchester, 1951.

2047 THE LAST DAYS OF PETERBOROUGH MONASTERY. By W. T. Mellows. Pt. i: Tudor documents, *Northamp. Rec. Soc.* xii (1948).

2048 THREE CHAPTERS OF LETTERS relating to the suppression of monasteries. By Thomas Wright. *Camden Soc.* xxvi (1843).
142 letters, chiefly from Cotton MSS. originally probably in Cromwell papers. Some from Scudamore papers, B.M. Some of letters printed by Bishop Burnet (1767).

2049 THE VISITATION OF THE MONASTERY OF THAME, 1526. By G. G. Perry. *E.H.R.* iii (1888), 704–22.

2050 WILLIAMS, JOHN. Account of the monastic treasures confiscated at the dissolution of the various houses in England. By W. B. Turnbull. *Abbotsford Club*, 1836.
Williams was master and treasurer of the jewels of King Henry VIII.

2051 YORKSHIRE MONASTERIES, SUPPRESSION PAPERS. By J. W. Clay. *Yorks. Arch. Soc.*, rec. ser., xlviii (1912).

(b) *Later Works*

Gasquet (2073) is the standard Roman Catholic account. Savine (2091) and Liljegren (2082) are good on the economic aspects of the subject. On the situation in Wales, cf. 6395, 6449, 6459, 6464–6, 6468; on Ireland, 6050, 6055, 6056.

2052 ANDREWS, F. B. Pershore on the eve of the suppression, A.D. 1534–9. *Birm. Arch. Soc. Trans. and Proc.* lvi (1934), 77–101.

2053 ARCHBOLD, W. A. J. The Somerset religious houses. Cambr. 1892.
Contains much information about landed property, prices, wage, and charities.

2054 BARNARD, E. A. B. John Stonywell, abbot of Pershore, 1527–39. *Worcs. Arch. Soc. Trans. for 1937*, n.s., xiv (1938), 30–44.

2055 BASKERVILLE, GEOFFREY. The dispossessed religious after the suppression of the monasteries. In *Essays in history presented to R. L. Poole*. By H. W. C. Davis, Oxf. 1927.
Cf. also *Trans. Bristol and Gloucester Arch. Soc.* xlix (1928), 63–122.

2056 BASKERVILLE, GEOFFREY. An attempt to divorce an ex-nun, 1541. *E.H.R.* li (1935), 504–6.

2057 BASKERVILLE, GEOFFREY. English monks and the suppression of the monasteries. Lond. 1937.
Cf. Walter Gumbley, *Mr. Baskerville and the monks*, *Blackfriars*, xviii (1937), 340–51.

2058 BASKERVILLE, GEOFFREY. The depossessed religious in Surrey. *Surrey Arch. Coll.* xlvii (1941), 12–28

2059 BATES, J. G. The dissolution of Axholme Priory. *Lincs. Mag.* iii (1937), 225–7.

2060 CAMM, BEDE. Nine martyr monks. The lives of the English Benedictine martyrs beatified in 1929. Lond. 1931.

2061 CARAMAN, P. P. G. An English monastic reformer of the xvith century. *Clergy Rev.* xxviii (1947), 1–16.

2062 COLVIN, H. M. The dissolution of Dale Abbey. *Jour. of Derbys. and Nat. Hist. Soc.*, n.s., xvii, lxiv (1943), 1–25.

2063 COULTON, G. G. The last generations of mediaeval monachism. *Speculum*, xviii (1943), 437–57.

2064 COULTON, G. G. Five centuries of religion, iv: the last days of mediaeval monachism. Cambr. 1950.

2065 COUNCER, C. R. The dissolution of the Kentish monasteries. *Arch. Cant.* xlvii (1936), 126–43.

2066 DAVIS, E. J. The beginning of the dissolution: Christ church, Aldgate, 1532. *Trans. R.H. Soc.*, 4th ser., viii (1925), 127–50.
Account of first monastery dissolved by king without papal sanction.

2067 DICKENS, A. G. An Elizabethan defender of the monasteries. *Church Quar. Rev.* cxxx (1940), 236–62.

2068 DUGDALE, W. Monasticon anglicanum. 3 vols. Lond. 1665–73; best ed. (augmented) by J. Caley, H. Ellis, and B. Bandinel, 8 vols. Lond. 1817–30; repr., 6 vols. Lond. 1846.
Collection of documents on English and Welsh monastic houses, with a history of each house.

2069 DOREAU, VICTOR-MARIE. Henry VIII et les martyrs de la Chartreuse de Londres. Paris, 1890.
Facsimiles of old prints.

2070 ELTON, G. R. The Quondam of Rievaulx. *Jour. Eccles. Hist.* vii (1956), 45–60.

2071 EVANS, ALLAN. Battle Abbey at the dissolution: income: *Hunt. Lib. Quar.* iv (1941), 393–442; expenses, vi (1942), 53–101; *Actors in the account rolls of Battle Abbey*, vi (1942), 103–5.

2072 FLOWER, R. E. W. The last pre-dissolution survey of Glastonbury lands [*c.* 1515–19]. *Brit. Mus. Quar.* x (1936), 69–72.

2073 GASQUET, F. A. Henry VIII and the English monasteries. 2 vols. Lond. 1888–9; 1906.
Roman Catholic view-point. Cf. G. G. Coulton, *Medieval Studies* (Lond. 1930), pp. 84–107. Cf. also M. D. Knowles, *Cardinal Gasquet as a historian, Creighton lecture, 1956*, Lond. 1957.

2074 GASQUET, F. A. The last abbot of Glastonbury and his companions. Lond. 1885; 1934.

2076 GREENSLADE, S. L. The last monks of Durham cathedral priory. *Durham Univ. Jour.*, n.s. x (1949), 107–13.

2076a HABAKKUK, H. J. The market for monastic property, 1539–1603. *Ec. Hist. R.*, 2nd ser. x (1958), 362–80.

2077 HAY, DENYS. The dissolution of the monasteries in the diocese of Durham. *Arch. Aeliana*, 4th ser., xv (1938), 69–114.

2078 HENDRIKS, LAWRENCE. The London charter house, its monks and martyrs, with a short account of the English Carthusians after the dissolution. Lond. 1889.

2079 HODGETT, G. A. J. The dissolution of the religious houses in Lincolnshire and the changing structures of society. *Lincs. Archit. and Arch. Soc. Rep. and Papers*, iv (1951), 83–99.

2080 KNOWLES, DAVID. The case of St. Albans Abbey in 1490. *Jour. Eccles. Hist.* iii (1952), 144–58.

2081 LÉOTAUD, ALBAN. The journal of Prior William More of Worcester. *Dublin Rev.* cciii (1938), 302–15.

2082 LILJEGREN, S. B. The fall of the monasteries and the social changes in England leading up to the great revolution. *Lunds Universitets Årsskrift*, N.F., Avd i, Bd. 19, Nr. 10 (1924).
Useful.

2083 LILLIE, H. W. R. The English martyrs and English criminal law *Clergy Rev.* xii (1936), 294–309. *Ibid.* xiii (1937), 281–90.

2084 MATHEW, DAVID and GERVASE. The reformation and the contemplative life. A study of the conflict between the Carthusians and the state. Lond. 1934.

2085 MOORMAN, J. H. R. The grey friars in Cambridge, 1225–1538. Cambr. 1952.

2086 MORRIS, JOHN. The relics of St. Thomas of Canterbury. Canterbury, 1888.
Discusses the spoliation of Becket's shrine.
  Cf. also on this subject J. H. Pollen, in *The Month*, cxxxvii (1921), 119, 324.

2087 PANTIN, W. A. English monks before the suppression of the monasteries. *Dublin Rev.* cci (1937), 250–70.

2088 PRESTON, A. E. The demolition of Reading Abbey. *Berks. Arch. Jour.* xxxix (1935), 107–44.

2089 ROOKE, G. R. Dom William Ingram and his account book, 1504–33. *Jour. Eccles. Hist.* vii (1956), 30–44.

2090 SALZMAN, L. F. The last prior of Lewes. *Sussex Arch. Coll.* lxxvi (1935), 178–82.

2091   SAVINE, A. English monasteries on the eve of the dissolution. *Oxford studies in social and legal history*, i (1909).
Based largely on *Valor ecclesiasticus* (1212). Valuable chiefly for economic aspects of the monasteries.
   Cf. also Snape, R. H., *English monastic finances in the later middle ages*, Cambr. 1926.

2092   THOMSON, G. SCOTT. The dissolution of Woburn Abbey. *Trans. R.H. Soc.*, 4th ser., xvi (1933), 129–60.

2093   SPARROW, A. C. Blessed Thomas Beche. *Downside Rev.* xli (1943), 1–10, 88–97.
Beche [*alias* Mandell] was the last abbot of Colchester.

2094   TANNER, THOMAS. Notitia monastica: an account of all abbeys, &c., in England and Wales. . . . Lond. 1744; later ed. (with additions by J. Nasmith), Cambr. 1787.
Valuable.

2095   TURNER, J. B. Abbot Edward Kirkby, thirty-fifth abbot of Rievaulx, 1528?–33. *Ampleforth Jour.* xliii (1938), 203–9.

2096   WHATMORE, L. E. George Lazenby, monk of Jervaux: a forgotten martyr [1535]. *Downside Rev.* lx (1942), 325–8.

2097   WILSON, G. B. Beitrag zur Vorgeschichte der Auflösung der Klöster in England und Wales, speciell unter der Regierung Heinrichs VIII. Halle, 1900.

2098   YOUINGS, J. A. The terms of disposal of the Devon monastic lands, 1536–58. *E.H.R.* lxix (1954), 18–38.

5. EDWARD VI AND MARY

A. GENERAL

(a) *Sources*

Most of the important sources on the religious history of Edward VI and Mary are given in sect. 1, *supra* (pp. 151 ff.). Strype's *Ecclesiastical memorials* (1849) and his *Life of Cranmer* (1850) are useful for both reigns, as are the works of Latimer (1732), Ridley (1747), Hooper (1731), and Cranmer (1718). The writings of Stephen Gardiner, the most prominent of the Roman Catholic leaders, are given in the bibliography in Muller (358); Gardiner's letters are in 286. Foxe's *Acts and monuments* (1726) is still, despite its bias, the most valuable source on the Marian persecutions. Cardinal Pole's correspondence (1739) is important for Mary's reign.

2098a   BRINKELOW, HENRY. Complaynt of Roderyck Mors, somtyme a gray fryre, unto the parliament howse of England his natural cuntry, for the redresse of certen wicked lawes, evel customs, and cruel decreys (Lond. 1548); by J. M. Cowper, *E.E.T.S.*, extra ser., xxii (1874).
Ed. 1874 contains also Roderigo Mors (Brinkelow), *The lamentacyon of a Christen agaynst the cytye of London*. Complains of conditions brought about by reformation. Valuable on enclosures, rack renting and other economic problems. Cf. also 1974.

2099 BUCER, M. Scripta Anglicana. Basel, 1577.

2100 CHANTRY CERTIFICATES. Surveys of the chantries, &c., in accordance with the terms of the act for the dissolution of the chantries, 1547.
On the reports of the commissioners to survey the chantries, cf. in general Giuseppi (74), i, 140–1. The reports from several counties have been printed, to wit: *Somerset*, by E. Green, *Somerset Rec. Soc.* ii (1888); *Gloucester*, by Sir J. Maclean, *Trans. Bristol and Gloucester Arch. Soc.* viii (1883–4), 229–308; *York*, by William Page, 2 vols., *Surtees Soc.* xci, xcii (1894–5); *Shropshire*, by A. H. Hamilton, *Shropshire Arch. and Nat. Hist. Soc. Trans.*, 3rd ser., x (1910), 269–392; *Sussex*, by J. R. Ray, *Sussex Rec. Soc.* xxxvi (1930); *Kent*, by Arthur Hussey, *Kent Arch.* Soc., Rec. Branch, xii (1935); *Duchy of Lancaster in Norfolk*, by B. Cozens-Hardy, *Norfolk Arch.* xxix (1946), 201–10; *Canterbury and neighborhood*, supplementary to Kent chantries, by Charles Cotton, *Kent Rec.* xii, supplement; *Cornwall*, by L. S. Snell, *Documents towards a history of the Reformation in Cornwall*, Exeter, 1953; 1955; *Bingley* (Yorks.), by E. E. Dodd, *Brad. Antiq.*, n.s., viii (1954), 91–99; *Teesdale*, *Teesdale Rec. Soc. Pub.*, no. 2, Barnard Castle, 1937. Cf. for Wales, 6452.

2101 THE EDWARDIAN INVENTORIES FOR EXETER. *Alcuin Club*, 1916.

2102 FIOREBELLI, ANTONIO (Bishop of Lavello). Ad Philippum et Mariam reges de restituta in Anglia reglione, oratio. Louvain, 1555.

2103 GARDINER, STEPHEN. An explication and assertion of the true Catholique fayth, touchyng the moost blessed sacrament of the aulter, with confutaction of a booke written against the same. (Rouen, 1551).
Reply to Cranmer. Repr. in Cranmer's *Works* (1718).

2104 A DIOCESAN VISITATION OF 1553. By W. D. Peckham. *Sussex Arch. Coll.* lxxvii (1936), 93–105.

2105 LEVER, THOMAS. Sermons. Lond. 1550; *Arber Reprints*, Lond. 1871.

2106 TUNSTALL, CUTHBERT. De veritate corporis et sanguinis Domini Nostri Jesu Christi in eucharistia. Paris, 1554.
One of the ablest works of the Roman Catholic reaction.

2107 BISHOP WAKEMAN'S VISITATION ARTICLES for the diocese of Gloucester, 1548. By W. T. M. Kennedy. *E.H.R.* xxxix (1924), 252–6.

2108 WATSON, THOMAS. Holsome and Catholyke doctryne concerninge the seven sacramentes of Chryste's church. Lond. 1558; by T. E. Bridgett, Lond. 1876.
A vigorous Roman Catholic treatise. 1876 ed. includes biographical notice of the author.

2109 WENDEL, FRANÇOIS. Un document inédit sur le séjourn de Bucer en Angleterre. *Rev. d'hist. et de philso. religieuses*, xxxiv (1954), 223–34.

(b) *Later Works*

Gairdner (1785), Mackie (354), Pollard (567), Constant (2097), Read (760), and Hughes (1801), should be consulted.

2110 BAILEY, ALFRED. A legal view of Cranmer's execution. *E.H.R.* vii (1892), 466–70.

2111 BASKERVILLE, GEOFFREY. Elections to convocation in the diocese of Gloucester under Bishop Hooper. *E.H.R.* xliv (1929), 1–32.
An important contribution on the effect of the religious changes in the sixteenth century upon the clergy in a part of one diocese.

2112 BASKERVILLE, GEOFFREY. Married clergy and pensioned religious in Norwich diocese, 1555. *E.H.R.* xlviii (1933), 43–64, 199–228.

2113 BORNKAMM, HEINRICH. Martin Bucers Bedeutung für die europäische Reformationsgeschichte. *Schriften des Vereins für Reformationsges.* clxix (1952).

2114 BRETTON, R. Bishop Robert Ferrar. *Halifax Antiq. Soc. Trans. for 1934* (1935), 193–266.

2115 BROWN, W. J. Rowland Taylor, the protestant martyr, 1509–55. *Trans. Worcs. Arch. Soc.*, n.s., xxx (1954), 72–77.

2116 CONSTANT, GUSTAVE. La chute de Somerset et l'élévation de Warwick. Leurs conséquences pour la réforme en Angleterre (Octobre 1549–Juillet 1553). *Rev. Hist.* clxxii (1933), 422–54.

2117 CONSTANT, GUSTAVE. La réforme en Angleterre, ii . . . Edouard VI (1547–53). Paris, 1939. Eng. trans. by E. I. Watkin, Lond. 1942.

2118 DARLINGTON, IDA. The Reformation in Southwark. *Hug. Soc. Proc.* xix (1955), 65–81.

2119 DAVENPORT, J. Notes on the bishopric of Worcester, 1547–59. Worcester, 1916.

2120 DICKENS, A. G. Some popular reactions to the Edwardian reformation in Yorkshire. *Yorks. Arch. Jour.* xxxiv (1939), 151–69.

2121 EELLS, HASTINGS. Martin Bucer. New Haven, U.S.A., 1931.

2122 FRERE, W. H. The Marian reaction in its relation to the English clergy. *Church Hist. Soc.* xviii (1896).
Study of episcopal registers.

2123 GAIRDNER, JAMES. Bishop Hooper's visitation of Gloucester, 1551. *E.H.R.* xix (1904), 98–121.

2124 HARVEY, A. E. Martin Bucer in England. Marburg, 1906.
Doctor's thesis. App. contains original letters of Bucer. Useful bibliography.

2125 HOPF, CONSTANTIN. Martin Bucer and the English reformation. Oxf. 1946.
Corrects a serious blunder in 2136.

2126 HUGHES, PHILIP. A hierarchy that fought, 1554–9. *Clergy Rev.* xviii (1940), 25–39.

2127 LANG, AUGUST. Martin Bucer in England. *Archiv für Reformationges.* xxxviii (1941), 230–9.

2128 LEE, F. G. King Edward the sixth, supreme head. Lond. 1886–9.
Work of a Romanizing Anglican extremist.

2129 THE MARIAN PERSECUTION. *Church Quar. Rev.* xxxii (1891), 188–204.

2130 MESSENGER, E. C. Bishop Bonner and Anglican orders. *Dublin Rev.* cxcviii (1936), 100–10.

2131 POCOCK, NICHOLAS. The condition of morals and religious beliefs in the reign of Edward VI. *E.H.R.* x (1895), 417–44.

2132 POPE, HUGH. The Oxford and Cambridge deputations on the Holy Eucharist, 1549. *Irish Eccles. Rec.*, 5th ser., lix (1942), 403–24, lx (1942), 41–53.

2133 POLLARD, A. F. The reformation under Edward VI. *Cambr. Mod. Hist.* (20) ii, 474–511.

2134 PRICE, F. D. Gloucester diocese under Bishop Hooper, 1551–3. *Bristol and Gloucs. Arch. Soc. Trans. for 1938*, lx (1939), 51–151.

2135 QUINN, EDWARD. Bishop Tunstall's treatise on the Holy Eucharist. *Downside Rev.* li (1933), 674–89.

2136 SMYTH, C. H. Cranmer and the reformation under Edward VI. Cambr. 1926.
Controversial, but based on scholarly research. Contains a good bibliography of continental reformers whose work influenced the Edwardian reformation. Cf. 2125.

2137 WHITEBROOK, J. C. Thomas Thirlby: his forbears and relatives. *Notes and Queries*, clxxxvi (1944), 172–5; 198–201.

B. English Protestant Refugees, 1553–8

Cf. Foxe (1726), Strype (1849), Bertie (670), Read (759), Goff (793), Knox (1394).

2138 BAXTER, J. H. Alesius and other reformed refugees in Germany. *Scot. Church Hist. Soc. Rec.* v (1934), 93–102.

2139 COWELL, H. J. English protestant refugees in Strasbourg, 1553–8. *Hug. Soc. Proc.* xv (1934), 69–120.

2140 COWELL, H. J. The sixteenth century English speaking refugee churches at Strasbourg, Basle, Zurich, Aarau, Wesel and Emden. *Hug. Soc. Proc.* xv (1937), 612–65.

2141 COWELL, H. J. The sixteenth century English speaking refugee churches at Geneva and Frankfurt. *Hug. Soc. Proc.* xvi (1939), 209–30.

2142 GARRETT, C. H. The Marian Exiles. A study in the origins of Elizabethan puritanism. Cambr. 1938.
Valuable, but to be used with caution.

2143 GARRETT, C. H. John Ponet and the confession of the banished ministers. *Church Quar. Rev.* cxxxvii (1943), 47–74; (1944), 181–204.

2144 HINDS, A. B. The making of the England of Elizabeth. Lond. 1895.
An account of English protestant refugees on the continent of Europe during the reign of Mary.

2145 JUNG, RUDOLF. Die englische Flüchtlingsgemeinde in Frankfurt am Main, 1554–9. Frankfort, 1910.
Archival material.

2146 KNOX, JOHN. A narrative of the proceedings and troubles of the English congregation at Frankfort on the Main, 1554–5. In *Works* (1394), iv, 41–49.
Printed from a MS. with illustrative documents.

2147 LEADAM, I. S. Narrative of the pursuit of the English refugees in Germany under Queen Mary. *Trans. R.H. Soc.*, 2nd ser., xi (1897) 113–31.

2148 LIST OF ENGLISH REFUGEES at Frankfort-on-Main, 1557. *Hug. Soc. Proc.* iv (1894), 86–89.

2149 MARTIN, CHARLES. Les protestants anglais refugiés à Genève au temps de Calvin, 1555–60. Geneva, 1915.
Contains a good bibliography of the publications of this group at Geneva.

2150 MILLATT, T. B. Three Marian exiles. *Essex Rev.* lii (1943), 190–4.

2151 MULLINS, E. L. C. Note on an unsigned letter to John Abell at Strasbourg. *E.H.R.* lxii (1947), 213–17.

2152 PECK, G. T. John Hales and the Puritans during the Marian exile. *Church Hist.* x (1941), 159–77.

2153 SOUTHGATE, W. M. The Marian exiles and the influence of John Calvin. *Hist.* xxvii (1942), 148–52.

2154 NARRATIVE OF MRS. ROSE THROCKMORTON . . . written in her 85th year, 1610. In Adam Stark. *The history and antiquities of Gainsburgh.* 2nd ed. Lond. 1843.
MS. is in B.M., Add. MS. 43827 A and B. Cf. E. G. Millar. *Narrative of Mrs. Rose Throckmorton, Brit. Mus. Quar.* ix (1935), 74–76.

2155 WHITTINGHAM, WILLIAM. A brieff discours off the troubles begonne at Franckford in Germany Anno Domini 1554, abowte the booke off common prayer and ceremonies. [Zurich?], 1575; Lond. 1846.
Important for puritan beginnings. Repr. in Knox's *Works* (1394), iv, pp. 1–40.

6. ELIZABETH

A. Anglicanism

(a) *Sources*

Only the outstanding works of the Anglican divines are given below. Adequate bibliographies will be found under their biographies in the *D.N.B.* (5). Anglican works dealing with nonconformity and with Roman Catholicism will be found in the appropriate sections following. A great deal of source material dealing with Anglicanism is printed in the appendixes to Strype's *Annals of the reformation* (2214), and his lives of eminent Anglican divines (2215–18). *Cal. S.P., Domestic* (86), *Acts of privy council* (1152), *Proclamations* (1017), and the *Salisbury MSS.* (185) are of primary importance.

Works dealing with ecclesiastical law and institutions are given in sect. 7 *infra* (pp. 210 ff.). For the correspondence of Wm. Chaderton, Bishop of Chester, see Peck (277), book iii, 2–52.

2156 BANCROFT, RICHARD. A sermon preached at Paules Crosse the 9 of Februarie, being the first Sunday in the parliament, anno 1588. Lond. 1588; 1637; 1709.
Significant for its implication of the necessity of apostolic succession.

2157 TRACTS ASCRIBED TO RICHARD BANCROFT. By Albert Peel. Cambr. 1953.

2158 BISHOP BARLOW'S CONSECRATION AND ARCHBISHOP PARKER'S REGISTER: with some new documents. By Claude Jenkins. *Church Hist. Soc. Pub.* xvii (1935).

2159 BAYNE, C. G. Visitation of the province of Canterbury, 1559. *E.H.R.* xxviii (1913), 636–77.
Proceedings of the commissioners who carried out the royal visitation of 1559.

2160 BILSON, THOMAS. The perpetual government of Christe's church. Lond. 1593; by Robert Eden, Oxf. 1842.
Thorough-going defence of the Anglican theory. Cf. also 1413.

2161 COLLECTION OF ORIGINAL LETTERS from the bishops to the privy council, 1564, with returns of the justices of the peace and others classified according to their religious convictions. By Mary Bateson. *Camden Soc. Misc.* ix (1893).
Cf. *Salisbury MSS.* (185), pt. i, p. 306.

2162 THE CORRESPONDENCE OF DR. MATTHEW HUTTON, archbishop of York, with a selection from the letters, &c., of Sir Timothy Hutton, his son, and Matthew Hutton, his grandson. By James Raine. *Surtees Soc.* xvii (1843).
Much valuable correspondence between the court and Hutton, bishop of Durham and later archbishop of York, concerning affairs of state in the county and on the border and concerning matters of religion, 1565–1605.

2163 COSIN, RICHARD.
Cf. no. 1416 *supra.*

2164 DIOCESIS CANTUARIENSIS: registrum Matthei Parker, 1559–75. By W. H. Frere. Parts 1–8. *Canterbury and York Soc.*, pts. ix, x, xi, xx, xxx, xl, lii, lxxii, lxxviii, lxxxiii, xciii, xciv, 1907–35.
Omits documents published by *Parker Soc.* (1737). Valuable.

2165 DIOCESE OF NORWICH. Bishop Redman's visitation, 1597. By J. F. Williams. *Norfolk Rec. Soc.* xviii (1946).

2166 DAVIS, E. J. Archbishop Parker's register. *E.H.R.* xxxiv (1919), 257–60.

2167 THE DECLARACYON OF THE PROCEDYNGE of a conference begon at Westminster the laste of Marche, 1559 . . . Lond. [1560?]; repr. in Holinshed (314), ed. 1587, iii, 1182.

2168 ELIZABETHAN EPISCOPAL ADMINISTRATION. By W. P. M. KENNEDY. 3 vols. *Alcuin Club*, 1925.
Contains visitation articles and injunctions, 1579–1603. A continuation of 1753. Cf. Kennedy, *Visitation articles and injunctions, 1576–1603*, in *E.H.R.* xxxii (1917), 273–6.

2169 GRINDAL, EDMUND. Remains. By William Nicholson. *Parker Soc.*, 1843.

2170 HOOKER, RICHARD. Of the lawes of ecclesiasticall politie.
Cf. no. 1418 *supra*.

2171 THE INJUNCTIONS AND OTHER ECCLESIASTICAL PROCEEDINGS of Richard Barnes, bishop of Durham (1577–87). By James Raine. *Surtees Soc.* xxii (1850).

2172 JEWEL, JOHN. An apologie, or answere, in defence of the church of England.
Cf. no. 1395 *supra*.

2173 THE LIFE AND DEATH OF MR. WILLIAM WHITTINGHAM, deane of Durham, who departed this life Anno Domini 1579, June 10. By M. A. E. Green. *Camden Soc. Misc.* vi (1870).
Written perhaps in 1603. Pertinent documents from the P.R.O. printed in an app.

2174 LINCOLN EPISCOPAL RECORDS in the time of Thomas Cooper, bishop of Lincoln A.D. 1571 to A.D. 1584. By C. W. Foster. *Canterbury and York Soc.* xi (1913).
A full description of a bishop's activity, including an act-book, 3 register books, 2 returns of the clergy of diocese, &c. Valuable. Cf. Kathleen Major, *The Lincoln diocesan records*, *Trans. R.H. Soc.*, 4th ser., xxii (1940), 39–66; and idem, *Handlist of the records of the bishop of Lincoln and the archdeacons of Lincoln and Stow*, Oxf. 1953. Cf. also E. S. De Beer, *Resignation deeds of the diocese of Lincoln*, *Bull. Inst. Hist. Research*, xix (1942), 57–66.

2175 NOWELL, ALEXANDER. Cathechismus, sive prima institutio disciplinaque pietatis Christianae. Lond. 1570; by G. E. Corrie. *Parker Soc.*, 1853.
Influential Anglican defence. For Nowell's other writings, with a careful discussion of the eds. of his three catechisms, cf. *D.N.B.* (9), art. A. Nowell.

2176 PAULE, GEORGE. The life of the most revered prelate J. Whitgift. Lond. 1612; repr. in Wordsworth, *Ecclesiastical biography* (1866); iv.
Favourable to Whitgift.

2177 PILKINGTON, JAMES, bishop of Durham. Works. By J. Scholefield. *Parker Soc.*, 1842.

2178 SARAVIA, HADRIAN À. De diversis ministrorvm Evangelii gradibus, sicvt a Domino fuerunt instituti, & traditi ab Apostolis ... liber. Lond. 1590; Eng. trans. by A. W. Street, Oxf. 1840.
A treatise on the different degrees of the Christian priesthood. A defense of episcopacy by a learned Fleming, which called forth a reply from Beza. Cf. *D.N.B.* (9) art. Saravia.

2179 THE STATE OF THE CHURCH in the reigns of Elizabeth and James I. By C. W. Foster. vol. i. *Lincoln Rec. Soc.* xxiii (1926).
Documents relate to diocese of Lincoln. Valuable introduction.

2181 WHITGIFT, JOHN. Works. By John Ayre. 3 vols. *Parker Soc.*, 1851–3.

2182 THE ZÜRICH LETTERS, comprising the correspondence of several English bishops and others with some of the Helvetian reformers during the reign of Queen Elizabeth. By Hastings Robinson. 2 vols. *Parker Soc.*, 1842–5.
Vol. i, 1558–79; vol. ii (2nd ser.), 1558–1602. Earlier letters from the Zürich archives are given in 1727.
For the correspondence of Michel de l'Hôpital with Sir Thos. Smith on the Anglican church, cf. Hauser (23), ii, no. 1277.

(b) *Later Works*

The best general account is in Frere (2188b). Cf. also Strype (2215–18), Pollard (368), Froude (340), Black (671), Read (759–60), Neale (743).

2183 BIRT, H. N. The deprivation of clergy in Elizabeth's reign. *Dublin Rev.* cxxvi (1900), 25–45, 313–42.

2184 BIRT, H. N. The Elizabethan religious settlement, a study of contemporary documents. Lond. 1907.
Roman Catholic viewpoint. Critical of Gee (2188c).

2185 BROOK, V. J. K. Whitgift and the English church. Lond. 1957.

2186 CARTER, C. S. The real Matthew Parker. *Church Quar. Rev.* cxxxvi (1943), 205–20.

2187 CHADWICK, OWEN. Richard Bancroft's submission. *Jour. Eccles. Hist.* iii (1952), 58–73.

2188 DAWLEY, P. M. John Whitgift and the reformation. Lond. 1955.

2188a FREEMAN, E. A. Archbishop Parker. *Historical Essays*, 4th ser. Lond. 1892.

2188b FRERE, W. H. The English church in the reigns of Elizabeth and James I. Lond. 1904.
Vol. v of *A history of the English church*, by Stephens and Hunt. Excellent. Good brief bibliographies at the chapter ends.

2188c GEE, HENRY. The Elizabethan clergy, and the settlement of religion, 1558–64. Oxf. 1898.
Documents. A careful attempt to investigate the treatment of the clergy at the beginning of Elizabeth's reign. Cf. 2184, and on the same subject 2356 and 2366.

2189 HEMBRY, P. M. The death of Thomas Godwin, Bishop of Bath and Wells (1584–90). *Proc. Somerset Arch. and Nat. Hist. Soc.* xcvi (1952), 78–107.

2190 HERR, A. F. The Elizabethan sermon, a survey and bibliography. Philadelphia, 1940.

2191 HICKS, LEO. The ecclesiastical supremacy of Queen Elizabeth. *The Month*, clxxxiii (1947), 170–7.

2192 HICKS, LEO. Elizabethan royal supremacy and contemporary writers. *The Month*, clxxxiv (1948), 216–28.

2193 HILL, CHRISTOPHER. Economic problems of the church. From Archbishop Whitgift to the Long Parliament. Oxf. 1956.

2194 KENNEDY, W. P. M. Archbishop Parker. Lond. 1908.
Cf. W. W. Gregg, *Books and bookmen in the correspondence of Archbishop Parker. Library*, 4th ser., xvi (1935), 243–79.

2195 KENNEDY, W. P. M. The 'Interpretations' of the bishops and their influence on Elizabethan episcopal policy. *Alcuin Club Tracts*, Lond. 1908.

2196 KENNEDY, W. P. M. Parish life under Queen Elizabeth. Lond. 1914.

2197 KLEIN, A. J. Intolerance in the reign of Elizabeth, queen of England. Boston, 1917.
Lacks penetration. Careful bibliography.

2198 LEE, F. G. The church under Queen Elizabeth. 2 vols. Lond. 1880; rev., 1892.
Romanizing Anglican. Hostile to reformation and its leaders.

2199 MACCOLL, MALCOLM. The reformation settlement. Lond., 1899; rev., 1901.
Important controversial work. High Anglican point of view. 1901 ed. contains reply to Maitland (2200). Cf. *E.H.R.* xvi (1901), 376–9.

2200 MAITLAND, F. W. Canon MacColl's new convocation. *Fortnightly Rev.* lxxii (1899), 926–35.
Criticism of 2199. Repr. in *Collected papers* (1030), iii, 119 ff.

2201 MAITLAND, F. W. Elizabethan gleanings. 1900–3. i. *Defender of the faith and so forth. E.H.R.* xv (1900), 120–4. ii. *Queen Elizabeth and Paul IV*, ibid. xv, 424–30. iii. *Pius IV and the English church service*, ibid. xv, 530–2. iv. *Thomas Sackville's message from Rome*, ibid. xv, 757–60. v. *Supremacy and uniformity—observations on the acts of supremacy and uniformity, based upon an examination of the actual parchment rolls*, ibid. xviii (1903), 517–32.
Repr. in 1030, iii, 157–209. For a dissent by Hubert Hall from Maitland on the *et cetera* clause in Elizabeth's title, cf. *The Athanæum*, 2 May, 1908, p. 543.

2202 McGINN, D. J. The admonition controversy. New Brunswick, U.S.A., 1949.
Defends Whitgift's position.

2203 NEALE, J. E. The Elizabethan acts of supremacy and uniformity. *E.H.R.* lxv (1950), 304–32.
Of great significance.

2204 NEALE, J. E. Parliament and the Articles of Religion, 1571. *E.H.R.* lxvii (1952), 510–21.

2205 PRESSEY, W. J. State of the church in Essex, in 1563. *Essex Rev.* xlvi (1937), 144–57.

2206 PRICE, F. D. The abuses of excommunication and the decline of ecclesiastical discipline under Queen Elizabeth. *E.H.R.* lvii (1942), 106–15.

2207 PRICE, F. D. An Elizabethan church official—Thomas Powell, chancellor of Gloucester diocese. *Church Hist. Rev.* cxxviii (1939), 94–112.

2208 PRICE, F. D. The commission for ecclesiastical causes for the dioceses of Bristol and Gloucester, 1574. *Trans. Bristol and Glos. Soc.* lix (1938), 61–184.

2209 QUYNN, D. M. The early career of John Gordon, dean of Salisbury. *Hum. et Ren.* vii (1945), 118–38.

2210 RYAN, L. V. The Haddon-Osorio controversy (1563–1583). *Church Hist.* xxii (1953), 142–54.

2211 SHIRLEY, F. J. Elizabeth's first Archbishop. Lond. 1948.

2212 SISSON, R. A. William Perkins, apologist for the Elizabethan church of England. *Mod. Lang. Rev.* xlvii (1952), 495–502.

2213 SOAMES, HENRY. Elizabethan religious history. Lond. 1839; 1856.
Moderate Anglican.

2214 STRYPE, JOHN. Annals of the reformation and establishment of religion, and other various occurrences in the church of England (during Queen Elizabeth's happy reign), together with an appendix of original papers of state, records and letters. 4 vols. Lond. 1709–31; Oxf. 1820–40.
Contains most valuable documentary material, sometimes inaccurately or carelessly given.

2215 STRYPE, JOHN. Historical collections of the life and acts of the right reverend father in God, John Aylmer, lord bishop of London. . . . Lond. 1701; Oxf. 1821.
Valuable documentary material, sometimes carelessly given.

2216 STRYPE, JOHN. The history of the life and acts of the most reverend father in God, Edmund Grindal. . . . Lond. 1710; Oxf. 1821.
Documents.

2217 STRYPE, JOHN. The life and acts of Matthew Parker, the first archbishop of Canterbury in the reign of Queen Elizabeth. . . . Lond. 1711; 3 vols. Oxf. 1821.
Valuable documents, to be used with care.

2218 STRYPE, JOHN. The life and acts of John Whitgift, D.D., the third and last lord archbishop of Canterbury, in the reign of Queen Elizabeth. . . . Lond. 1718; 3 vols. Oxf. 1822.
Important documents, to be used with care.

2219 THOMPSON, B. M. H. The consecration of Archbishop Parker. Lond. 1934.

2220 THOMPSON, J. V. P. Supreme governor: a study of Elizabethan ecclesiastical policy and circumstance. Lond. 1940.

2221 USHER, R. G. The reconstruction of the English church. 2 vols. New York, 1910.
Largely devoted to Richard Bancroft, but valuable for Elizabethan conditions in general.

2222 WALL, JAMES. William Whittingham of Chester (? 1524–79). *Church Quar. Rev.* cxxii (1936), 74–87.

2223 WALTON, ISAAK. Life of Richard Hooker. Lond. 1665; repr. in
Walton's *Lives*, 1670. Many eds. since.
    Keble's introduction to his ed. of Hooker's *Works* with the corrections of Church and
    Paget (1418) is valuable. Cf. on the same subject, the bibliography in *D.N.B.* (9), art.
    Hooker; also V. Staley, *Richard Hooker*, Lond. 1907; R. H. Murray, *Richard Hooker
    and his teaching*, Lond. 1934; L. S. Thornton, *Richard Hooker*, Lond. 1924; Morris
    (1464); Sisson (1470).

2224 WHITE, F. O. Lives of the Elizabethan bishops of the Anglican church.
Lond. 1898.

2225 WHITEBROOK, J. C. The consecration of Matthew Parker, archbishop
of Canterbury. Lond. 1945.
    Main thesis not accepted, but useful material on Kitchen of Llandaff.

2226 WHITEBROOK, J. C. The consecration of Matthew Parker. *Notes and
Queries*, cxc (1946), 5–9, 178–80, 203–6.
    Reviewed in *Notes and Queries*, lxxxix (1946), 219–20, and reviewers reply to White-
    brook's reply ibid. cxc (1946), 69–71. See also L. G. H. Horton-Smith, *George Acworth
    (c. 1534–c. 1592) public orator of Cambridge*, ibid. cxci (1946), 90–92, 114–16, cxcii
    (1947), 58–59, cxcv (1950), 136–7.

2227 WILLIAMS, J. F. An episcopal visitation in 1593. *Norfolk Arch.* xxviii,
1943 (1945), 29–82.

2228 WOODHOUSE, H. F. The doctrine of the church in Anglican theology,
1547–1603. Lond. 1954.

2229 WRIGHT, L. B. William Perkins: Elizabethan apostle of practical
divinity. *Hunt. Lib. Quar.* iii (1940), 171–96.

2230 YOUNG, J. A. C. A bibliographical sketch of John Young, bishop of
Rochester, with emphasis on his relations with Edmund Spenser. *Indiana
Univ. Studies*, xxi, Study no. ciii. Bloomington, 1935.

B. ROMAN CATHOLICISM

(a) *Sources*

The *Acts of privy council* (1152), the *Cal. S.P., Domestic* (86), the *Statutes of the
realm* (1016), and the *Proclamations* (1017) are particularly valuable sources as
are the *Cal. S.P., Spanish* (868), *Rome* (991), *Milan* (990), and the correspondence of French ambassadors in England (*supra*, pp. 66 ff.). The *Cal. S.P.,
Foreign* (87), should be consulted on the subject of Roman Catholic refugees on
the Continent. Much important source material has been printed by the *Catholic
Record Soc.* Cf. also 634.

   The Roman Catholic controversial writers have not been listed fully.
   In addition to those given below reference should be made to the bibliography
in Code (2315). Cf. also *A catalogue of Catholic books in English, printed abroad
or secretly in England, 1558–1640*, by A. F. Allison and D. M. Rogers, in *Biog.
Studies* (1956), vol. iii, pts. 3 and 4; pt. 5, 341–68. Cf. also Chap. iv *supra*.

   A valuable annotated bibliography of the contemporary literature on the controversy between the Jesuits and Seculars is printed in *Law* (2347), pp. cxxviii–
cliii.

2231 LETTER FROM GEORGE ACWORTH TO LORD BURGHLEY, 15 October, 1573. By L. G. H. Horton-Smith. *Notes and Queries*, cxcv (1950), 337–8.

2232 LETTER FROM GEORGE ACWORTH TO CARDINAL POLE. . . . 1558. By L. G. H. Horton-Smith. *Notes and Queries*, cxcv (1950), 178–80, 233–6.

2233 LETTER FROM GEORGE ACWORTH TO QUEEN ELIZABETH, written from Venice on 13th December, 1558. By L. H. G. Horton-Smith. *Notes and Queries*, cxcv (1950), 266–9.
Cf. idem, *George Ackworth*, s.l. (privately printed), 1953.

2234 [ALLEN, WILLIAM.] A true, sincere, and modest defense of the English Catholiques . . . against a . . . libel entituled, 'The execution of justice in England'. Ingolstadt, 1584; *The Catholic Library*, no. 2. 2 vols. Lond. 1914.
Allen's response to Burghley's tract (2244). A Latin version appeared the same year at Douai.

2235 ALLEN, WILLIAM. An apologie and true declaration of the institution of the two English colleges. [Rheims], 1581.
Defending the Roman Catholic colleges at Rome and Rheims.

2236 ALLEN, WILLIAM. An admonition to the nobility and people of England and Ireland, concerning the present warres. . . . (Antwerp), 1588; by Eupater (I. Mendham). Lond. 1842.
A vicious attack upon the character of Queen Elizabeth, put forth just before the sailing of the Armada, in which Allen urged all good Englishmen to abandon her. An abridgement of the *Admonition* entitled, *A declaration of the sentence of deposition of Elizabeth . . . pretensed queene of England*, was published in 1588.

2237 ALLEN, WILLIAM. The copie of a letter written by M. Doctor Allen: concerning the yielding up of . . . Dauentrie . . . by Sir William Stanley. Antwerp, 1587; by Thomas Heywood, *Chetham Soc.* xxv (1851).
Defends Stanley's surrender of Deventer to the Spanish and urges other English commanders, 'upon pain of damnation, to do the like'. Latin, Italian, and French translations appeared in 1587 and 1588.

2238 ALLEN, WILLIAM. Letters and memorials of. By T. F. Knox. *Records of the English Catholics under the penal laws*, ii (Lond. 1882).

2239 ALLEN, WILLIAM. Some correspondence of 1579–85, from the Jesuit archives. By Patrick Ryan. *Cath. Rec. Soc. Misc.* vii (1911), 12–105.

2240 THE ARCHPRIEST CONTROVERSY. Documents relating to the dissensions of the Roman Catholic clergy, 1597–1602. By T. G. Law. 2 vols. *Camden Soc.*, n.s., lvi (1896), lviii (1898).
From the *Petyt MSS.* (175) with a valuable introduction.

2241 BRIDGEWATER, JOHN. (Aquipontanus, Joannes). Concertatio ecclesiae Catholicae in Anglia. 2 vols. Treves, 1583; enlarged, 1584.
Contemporary martyrology.

2242 BRISTOW, RICHARD. A brief treatise of diverse plaine and sure wayes to find out the truthe in this time of heresy. Antwerp, 1594.

2243 LORD BURGHLEY'S MAP OF LANCASHIRE, 1590. By Joseph Gillow. *Cath. Rec. Soc. Misc.* iv (1907), 162–216.
Burghley's notes on recusancy in Lancashire in 1590.

2244 [BURGHLEY, LORD.] The execution of justice in England. . . . Lond. 1583; by F. L. Baumer, New York, 1939.
A defence of Elizabeth's treatment of the Roman Catholics. Printed in *Somers Tracts* (296), i, 189–208, in *Harl. Misc.* (281), i, 489–513, and in Holinshed (314), ed. 1587, iii, 1358 ff. Latin, Dutch, and Italian versions appeared in 1584.

2245 [BURGHLEY, LORD?] A declaration of the favourable dealing of her majesty's commissioners, appointed for the examination of certain traitors. . . . Lond. 1583.
A defence of the use of torture in examining Catholics. Printed in *Somers Tracts* (296), i, 209–12, and in *Harl. Misc.* (281), i, 514–17. Ascribed, on doubtful evidence, to Burghley.

2246 CIRCIGNANI, NICCOLÒ. Ecclesiae anglicanae trophaea. Rome, 1584.
Martyrology.

2247 A COPIE OF A LETTER, lately sent by a gentleman . . . to a friend of his . . . concerning D. Storie. (Lond.), 1571.
Published by authority. A justification of the execution of Dr. Story. Printed in *Harl. Misc.* (281), i, 398–405.

2248 COPLEY, THOMAS. Letters of . . . to Queen Elizabeth and her ministers. By R. C. Christie. *Roxburghe Club*, 1897.
Copley was one of the most prominent of English Roman Catholic refugees in France. Letters date from 1572 to 1584.

2249 CRESSWELL, JOSEPH. Historia de la vida y martyrio que padeció en Inglaterra, . . . 1595, el P. Henrique Valpolo, . . . con el martyrio de otros quatro sacerdotes. . . . Madrid, 1596.
A French trans. of the life of Walpole appeared at Arras, 1597. For a slightly inaccurate list of Cresswell's writings. cf. *D.N.B.* (9), art. Joseph Cresswell.

2250 PHILOPATRIS, JOHN (Cresswell, Joseph). An advertisement written to a secretarie of my lord treasurers of Ingland. [Lond. 1592].
This is directed against the queen's proclamation against the Catholics of 1591 and follows closely Parson's later pamphlet on the same subject (2270).

2251 PERNE, JOHN (Cresswell, Joseph). Exemplar litterarum missarum a Germania ad D. Guilielmum Cecilium consiliarium regium. [Lond.?] 1592.
Against Elizabeth's proclamation of 29 Nov. 1591. Cf. Parsons (2270).

2252 A DECLARATION OF THE LIFE AND DEATH OF JOHN STORY. Lond. 1571.
Printed by authority. Justifies the execution of Story. Repr. in *Harl. Misc.* (281), i, 408–19.

2253 DIOCESAN RETURNS OF RECUSANTS for England and Wales, 1577. By Patrick Ryan. *Cath. Rec. Soc. Misc.* xii (1921), 1–114.

2254 THE FIRST AND SECOND DIARIES of the English College, Douai, and an app. of unpublished documents. By T. F. Knox. *Records of the English Catholics under the penal laws*, i (Lond. 1878).

2255 THE DOUAY COLLEGE DIARIES, third, fourth, and fifth, 1598–1654. By E. H. Burton and T. L. Williams. 2 vols. *Cath. Rec. Soc.* x, xi (1911).
Contains also the Rheims report, 1579–80.

2256 AN ELIZABETHAN RECUSANT HOUSE, comprising the life of the Lady Magdelen, Viscountess Montague (1538–1608). Trans. from Latin of Dr. Richard Smith by Cuthbert Fursdon. By A. C. Sothern. Lond. 1954.

2257 THE ENGLISH BENEDICTINE NUNS of Brussels and Winchester, 1598–1856. By Joseph Hansom. *Cath. Rec. Soc. Misc.* ix (1914), 174–203.

2258 THE ESTATE OF THE ENGLISH FUGITIVES under the king of Spaine and his ministers. Lond. 1595.
A curious, contemporary pamphlet on English Roman Catholic fugitives on the continent under Elizabeth.

2259 THE EXCOMMUNICATION OF QUEEN ELIZABETH. By M. Petriburg [Mandell Creighton]. *E.H.R.* vii (1892), 81–88.
Two documents illustrating the attitude of Roman Catholics upon this subject.

2260 JOHN GERARD, THE AUTOBIOGRAPHY OF AN ELIZABETHAN. By Philip Caraman. Lond. 1951.

2261 HARDING, THOMAS. A confutation of a book (by Bishop Jewel) entitled, 'An apologie of the church of England'. Antwerp, 1565.
Harding represented the Roman Catholic position in a controversy with Jewel. For a complete list of Harding's writings, cf. *D.N.B.* (9), art. T. Harding.

2262 IMPORTANT CONSIDERATIONS, which ought to move all . . . Catholics . . . to acknowledge . . . that the proceedings of her Majesty . . . have been both mild and merciful. Lond. 1601; by J. Mendham, Lond. 1831.
The most complete statement on the anti-Jesuit side. Preface contains *The Epistle*, by W. Watson.

2263 LETTER FROM THE VEN. CHRISTOPHER ROBINSON to the Rev. Richard Dudley, describing the martyrdom of the Ven. John Boste, 1594. By Lord Herries. *Cath. Rec. Soc. Misc.* i (1905), 85–99.

2264 TWO LETTERS OR REPORTS ON RECUSANCY by Bishop Barnes, 1570 and 1585. By J. H. Pollen. *Cath. Rec. Soc. Misc.* xii (1921), 115–19.

2265 LIBER RUBER VENERABILIS COLLEGII ANGLORUM DE URBE. By Wilfred Kelly. I. Annales collegi. Pars prima, nomina alumnorum. A.D. 1579–1630. *Cath. Rec. Soc.* xxxvii (1940).

2266 MUNDAY, ANTHONIE. The English Romayne life. Lond. 1582; repr. Lond. 1925.
An account of the English college at Rome by a notable English spy.

2267 OFFICIAL LISTS OF PRISONERS for religion from 1562–1602. By J. H. Pollen. *Cath. Rec. Soc. Misc.* i (1905), 47–71; ii (1905), 219–88.

2268 PARSONS, ROBERT. Annals of the English college at Seville, with accounts of other foundations at Valladolid, St. Lucar, Lisbon, and St. Omers. By J. H. Pollen. *Cath. Rec. Soc. Misc.* ix (1914), 1–24.
Cf. also 2279.

2269 [PARSONS, ROBERT.] A brief discours, contayning certayne reasons
why Catholiques refuse to goe to church. Douay, 1580.
Answered by John Field in *A caveat for Parsons Howlet, 1581;* by Perceval Wiburn,
Checke or reproofe of M. Howlet's untimely schreeching in her majestie's eares, 1581; and
by William Fulke, *Briefe confutation of a popish discourse, lately set forth, 1581.*

2270 PHILOPATER, ANDREAS (Parsons, Robert). Elizabethae Angliae
reginae haeresim Calvinianam propugnantis saevissimum in Catholicos sui
regni edictum . . . promulgatum Londoni 29 Novembris 1591. Lyons, 1592.
A French trans. was published in Lyons, 1593. Cf. Meyer (2356), English trans.,
p. 351, n. For a list of the published works of Parsons, cf. his life in *D.N.B.* (9).

2271 PARSONS, ROBERT. An epistle of the persecutions of Catholickes in
Englande. Douay [1582?].
A Latin version, *De persecutione Anglicana libellus* was printed in Rome, 1582.

2272 [PARSONS, ROBERT.] A treatise of three conversions of England from
Paganism to Christian religion. 3 vols. (St. Omer), 1603–4.
Answered by Matthew Sutcliffe, *The subversion of R. Parsons his worke, entituled,
A treatise of three conversions of England, 1606.*

2273 THE MEMOIRS OF FATHER ROBERT PARSONS. By J. H.
Pollen. *Cath. Rec. Soc. Misc.* ii (1905), 12–218; iv (1907), 1–161.
Valuable on dissensions among the Roman Catholics.

2267 LETTERS AND MEMORIALS OF FATHER ROBERT PERSONS,
S.J., Vol. i, 1578–88. By Leo Hicks. *Cath. Rec. Soc.* xxxix (1942).

2275 PRISONERS IN THE FLEET, 1577–80. By J. H. Pollen. *Cath. Rec.
Soc. Misc.* xii (1921), 130–1.

2276 REBORA, P. L'opera d'uno scrittore Toscano sullo scisma d'Inghilterra
ed una lettera della regina Elisabetta. *Archiv. Stor. Ital.* xciii (1935), 233–54.

2277 RECUSANTS AND PRIESTS. March, 1588. By J. H. Pollen. *Cath.
Rec. Soc. Misc.* xii (1921), 120–9.

2278 RECUSANT ROLLS, 1592–3. By M. M. C. Calthrop. *Cath. Rec. Soc.*
xviii (1916).

2279 REGISTERS OF THE ENGLISH COLLEGE AT VALLADOLID,
1589–1862. By Edwin Henson. *Cath. Rec. Soc.* xxx (1930).
Pages 1–80 on Tudors.

2280 [ROWLANDS, RICHARD *alias* VERSTEGEN, RICHARD.] Thea-
trum crudelitatum haereticorum nostri temporis. Antwerp, 1587; French
trans. Antwerp, 1588.
A Roman Catholic narrative of Elizabeth's treatment of the Roman Catholics.

2281 SANDERS, NICHOLAS. Report to Cardinal Moroni on the change of
religion in 1558–9. By J. H. Pollen. *Cath. Rec. Soc. Misc.* i (1905), 1–46.
From Vatican archives.

2282 SOME HOSTILE 'TRUE REPORTS' OF THE MARTYRS. By
A. C. Newdigate. *Cath. Rec. Soc. Misc.* xv (1932), 389–436.

2283 SOME LETTERS AND PAPERS OF NICHOLAS SANDER, 1562–80. By J. B. Wainewright. *Cath. Rec. Soc. Misc.* xiii (1926), 1–57.

2284 SOUTHWELL, ROBERT. An epistle of comfort to the reverend priestes, and to the honorable worshipful, and other of the lay sorte restrayned in durance for the Catholike faith. [Paris? 1593?]; [Douay?], 1605.
Written 1591.

2285 SOUTHWELL, ROBERT. A humble supplication to her maiestie, printed anno 1595. (By Henry Garnett and George Blackwell.) [Douay, 1600?]; by R. C. Bald, New York, 1953.
Written in 1591, probably first issued 1600 at Douay or St. Omer and not in 1595 as the title indicates. A MS. copy in the Huntington library (*Ellesmere MS*. 2089) is dated 31 Dec. 1592. For a complete bibliography of Southwell's writings, cf. *D.N.B.* (9), art. R. Southwell.

2286 STAPLETON, THOMAS. Opera omnia. 4 vols. Paris, 1620.
Stapleton was probably the ablest of the Roman Catholic controversialists in the disputes between Catholic and Anglican under Elizabeth. For complete bibliography of his writings, cf. *D.N.B.* (9), art. T. Stapleton.

2287 TOWER BILLS, 1575–89, 1595–1681. By J. H. Pollen. *Cath. Rec. Soc. Misc.* iii (1906), 4–29; iv (1907), 217–46.
Printed with these are the Gatehouse certificates, 1592–1603. Roman Catholics imprisoned in two London prisons, the Tower and the Gatehouse.

2288 UNPUBLISHED DOCUMENTS relating to the English martyrs, 1584–1603 By J. H. Pollen. 2 vols. *Cath. Rec. Soc.* v, xxi (1908, 1914).

2289 WATSON, WILLIAM. A decacordon of ten quodlibeticall questions concerning religion and state. [Douay?] 1602.
By an anti-Jesuit Catholic.

2290 WEBSTER, R. 'The copie of a double letter.' *Downside Rev.* liv (1936), 165–87.
Note and text of a Roman Catholic account of a Protestant martyrdom at Rome, 1581.

2291 WESTON, WILLIAM. The autobiography of an Elizabethan. Trans. from Latin by Philip Caraman. New York, 1955.
Printed earlier in Morris (1823), ser. ii.

2292 CONCLUSION OF THE AUTOBIOGRAPHY of Fr. Wm. Weston, S.J., 1589–1603. By J. H. Pollen. *Cath. Rec. Soc. Misc.* i (1905), 72–85.

2293 YEPES, DIEGO DE. Historia particular de la persecución de Inglaterra. Madrid, 1599.
Contemporary martyrology.

(b) *Later Works*

The best account from the Anglican viewpoint is in Frere (2188b). Among Roman Catholic historians Pollen's work (2366) is notable for its honest scholarship. Meyer (2356) is the best general account. *The Month* (a Roman Catholic magazine, Lond. 1874 ff.) contains many scholarly articles. On the episcopal succession in the English Roman Catholic Church, cf. Brady (6005). Cf. also Read (759, 760), *passim.*

2294 ALLISON, A. F. Franciscan books in English, 1559–1640. *Biog. Stud.* iii (1955), 16–65.

2295 ALLISON, A. F. The writings of Fr. Henry Garnet, S.J. (1555–1606). *Biog. Stud.* i (1951), 7–21.

2296 ANSTRUTHER, GODFREY. Vaux of Harrowden, a recusant family. Newport, 1953.

2297 ANTHEUNIS, LOUIS. Élisabeth Ière d'Angleterre et les catholiques. *Rev. Hist. Eccles.* xlix (1954), 491–8.

2298 ANTHEUNIS, LOUIS. Un réfugié catholique aux Pays-Bas: Sir Roger Ashton (*d.* 1592). *Rev. Hist. Eccles.* xxvii (1931), 589–91.

2299 ANTHEUNIS, LOUIS. Un réfugié anglais, traducteur de Louis de Grenade: Richard Hopkins, 1546–94. *Rev. Hist. Eccles.* xxxv (1939), 70–77.

2300 ANTHEUNIS, LOUIS. Een Engelsche uitgewekene in de Spaansche Nederlanden. John Bolt, priester en musicus, 1563–1640. *Bijd. Gesch.* xxviii (1937), 1–10.

2301 ANTHEUNIS, LOUIS. Un Jésuite anglais aux Pays-Bas espagnols: Sir Edward Stanley (1564–1639). *Rev. Hist. Eccles.* xxxii (1936), 360–5.

2302 ANTHEUNIS, LOUIS. Dr. John Ramridge, balling en professor aan de Louvense Universiteit (149?–1568). *Bull. comm. roy. hist.* (Académie royale de Belgique), cxvi (1951), 153–200.

2303 BAYNE, C. G. Anglo-Roman relations, 1558–65. *Oxf. Hist. and Lit. Studies,* ii (1913).
App. of 68 selected documents from the archives of England, Spain, France, Austria, and Belgium. Valuable.

2304 BELLESHEIM, A. Wilhelm, Cardinal Allen . . . und die englischen Seminare auf dem Festlande. Mainz, 1885.

2305 BOWLER, HUGH. Exchequer Dossiers: I. The recusancy of Venerable John Talbot, gentleman. *Biog. Stud.* ii (1953), 4–22.

2306 BOWLER, HUGH. Exchequer Dossiers: II. The recusancy of Venerable Bretton: gentleman and of Frances, his wife. *Biog. Stud.* ii (1953), 111–34.

2307 BOYAN, PEARL, and LAMB, G. A. Francis Tregian, Cornish recusant. Lond. 1955.

2308 BRIDGETT, T. E., and KNOX, T. F. The true story of the Catholic hierarchy deposed by Queen Elizabeth. Lond. 1889.
Roman Catholic viewpoint.

2309 BURTON, F. H. Handlist of secular clergy, 1559–1800. *Biog. Stud.* ii (1933), 71–80.

2310 BUTLER, CHARLES. Historical memoirs of the English, Irish, and Scottish catholics since the reformation. 2 vols. Lond. 1819; 3rd (augmented) ed., 4 vols. Lond. 1822.
Apps. of original documents.

2311　BUTLER, DOM., and POLLEN, J. H.　Doctor Gifford in 1586. *The Month*, ciii (1904), 243–58, 348–67.
Throws light upon factions among the English Roman Catholic refugees in France.

2312　CAMM, BEDE.　The adventures of some church students in Elizabethan days. *The Month*, xci (1898), 375–85.

2313　CHALLONER, RICHARD.　Memoirs of missionary priests and other Catholics of both sexes that have suffered death in England on religious accounts from the year 1577 to the year 1684. 2 vols. Lond. 1741–2; Edin. 1878; by J. H. Pollen, Lond. 1923.
Uncritical. Illustrated. 1878 ed. bears title *Martyrs to the Catholic faith*.

2314　CHAMBRUN, C. L. DE.　Shakespeare and the Elizabethan statutes. *Dublin Rev.* cxcvii (1936), 84–98.
On Shakespeare's possible connexion with recusancy.

2315　CODE, J. B.　Queen Elizabeth and the English catholic historians. *Recueil de travaux publiés par les membres des conférences d'histoire et de philologie*, 2nd sér., 33e fasc. Louvain, 1935.

2316　CONSTANT, GUSTAVE.　La nonciature de Perpaglia auprès d'Elisabeth (1560). In *Mélânges d'histoire offerts à M. Charles Bémont* (Paris, 1913), 509–20.
App. of documents from the archives at Simancas.

2317　CORBOY, JAMES.　Father James Archer, 1550–1625 (?), Fr. Henry Fitzsimon, 1566–1643, Father Christopher Holywood, 1559–1626. *Studies*, xxxiii (1944), 99–107; xxxii (1943), 260–6; xxxiii (1944), 243–9.

2318　D'ELBOUX, R. H.　The venerable Thomas Pylcher. *Biog. Stud.* iii (1955), 334–7.

2319　DEVLIN, CHRISTOPHER.　Southwell and the Marprelates. *The Month*, clxxxv (1948), 88–95.

2320　DEVLIN, CHRISTOPHER.　Richard Topcliffe. *The Month*, n.s., v (1951), 151–63.

2321　DEVLIN, CHRISTOPHER.　The patriotism of Robert Southwell. *The Month*, n.s., x (1953), 345–54.

2322　DEVLIN, CHRISTOPHER.　The failure of the English Inquisition. *The Month*, n.s., xiii (1955), 101–9.

2323　DEVLIN, CHRISTOPHER.　The life of Robert Southwell, poet and martyr. Lond. 1956.

2324　DICKENS, A. G.　The first stages of Romanist recusancy in Yorkshire. 1560–90. *Yorks. Arch. Jour.* xxxv (1941), 157–81.

2325　DODDS, M. H. (and others).　The daughters of Thomas Percy, seventh earl of Northumberland [executed 1572]. *Notes and Queries* (1935), 165–6, 231, 246–7.

2326　THE ENGLISH MARTYRS.　*Papers from the summer school of Catholic studies at Cambridge, 1928.* By Bede Camm. Cambr. 1929.

2327　FABRE, F.　The English college at Eu, 1582–1592. *Cath. Hist. Rev.* xxxvii (1951), 257–80.

2328 FOLEY, HENRY. Records of the English province of the Society of Jesus. 7 vols. Lond. 1877–84.
Portraits. Documents. Unskilfully done, but with material of value.

2329 FORSTER, A. M. C. The venerable George Errington. *Biog. Stud.* iii (1956), 322–33.

2330 GASQUET, F. A. Hampshire recusants in the time of Elizabeth. In *The old English Bible and other essays* (Lond. 1897), 319–82.
Roman Catholic viewpoint. Many documents.

2331 GERARD, JOHN. Father Garnet and his accusers. *The Month*, xcii (1898), 144–52.

2332 GERSON, A. J. English recusants and the Spanish Armada. *A.H.R.* xxii (1917), 589–94.

2333 GUILDAY, PETER. The English Catholic refugees on the continent, 1558–1795. Vol. i, *The English colleges and convents in the Catholic low countries, 1558–1795*. Lond. 1914.
Strong Roman Catholic point of view. Domestic history of various religious communities. Little general bearing on English or continental history. On Welsh Catholic refugees, cf. 6483. On English and Scottish Cath. colleges in Paris, cf. 6004.

2334 HAILE, MARTIN. Cardinal Allen. Lond. 1913.
Somewhat partial. Haile is a pseud. for Marie Hallé.

2335 HICKS, LEO. Cardinal Allen and the society [of Jesus]. *The Month*, clx (1932), 342–53; 434–43; 528–36.

2336 HICKS, LEO. The English College, Rome and vocations to the Society of Jesus, March, 1579–July, 1595. *Arch. Hist. Soc. Iesu.* iii (1934), 1–36.

2337 HICKS, LEO. Allen and Deventer (1587). *The Month*, clxiii (1934), 507–17.

2338 HICKS, LEO. The Catholic exiles and the Elizabethan religious settlement. *Cath. Hist. Rev.* xxii (1936), 129–48.

2339 HICKS, LEO. An Elizabethan propagandist: the career of Solomon Aldred. *The Month*, clxxxi (1945), 181–91.

2340 HICKS, LEO. Cardinal Allen's admonition. *The Month*, clxxxv (1948), 232–42; clxxxvi (1949), 30–39.

2341 HICKS, LEO. The foundation of the college of St. Omers. *Arch. Hist. Soc. Iesu*, xix (1950), 146–80.

2342 HICKS, LEO. Sir Robert Cecil, Father Persons and the succession 1600–1. *Arch. Hist. Soc. Iesu*, xxiv (1955), 95–139.

2343 JANELLE, PIERRE. Robert Southwell, the writer. A study in religious inspiration. Lond. 1935.

2344 JESSOPP, AUGUSTUS. One generation of a Norfolk house: a contribution to Elizabethan history. Norwich, 1879; Lond. 1913.
Roman Catholic sufferers under the penal laws.

2345 LANGSTON, J. N. Robert Alfield, schoolmaster of Gloucester, and his sons [Thomas, executed 1585, and Robert]. *Trans. Bristol and Glos. Arch. Soc.* lvi (1935), 141–63.

2346 LAW, T. G. Cuthbert Mayne and the bull of Pius V. *E.H.R.* i (1886), 141–4.

2347 LAW, T. G. A historical sketch of the conflicts between Jesuits and seculars in the reign of Queen Elizabeth, with a reprint of Christopher Bagshaw's 'True relation of the faction begun at Wisbich', and illustrative documents. Lond. 1889.
Valuable, with an annotated bibliography of importance.

2348 LEA, K. M. Sir Anthony Standen and some Anglo-Italian letters. *E.H.R.* xlvii (1932), 461–77.
On Standen, cf. Read (759), iii, 277 ff.

2349 LEATHERBARROW, J. S. The Lancashire Elizabethan recusants. *Chetham Soc.*, n.s., cx (1947).

2350 LECHAT, ROBERT. Les refugiés anglais dans les pays-bas espagnols durant le règne d'Elisabeth. Louvain, 1914.
Excludes Scottish and Irish refugees and deals with the English only while they remain in the Netherlands. Very fair. Valuable.

2351 MATTINGLY, GARRETT. William Allen and Catholic propaganda in England. *Travaux d'Humanisme et Renaissance*, xxviii (1957), 325–39.
Relates to a MS., s.a., in the Folger library, here ascribed to Allen, *c.* 1584, previously printed in *De Conquesto Angliae per Hispanos tempore Elizabethae reginae*, 1869.

2352 McDONNELL, MICHAEL. Edmund Campion, S.J., and St. Paul's School. *Notes and Queries*, cxciv (1949), 46–49, 67–70, 90–92.

2353 MAGEE, BRIAN. The English recusants. A study of the post-reformation Catholic survival and the operation of the recusancy laws. Lond. 1938.

2354 MERRICK, M. M. James Duckett: a study of his life and times. Lond. 1947.

2355 MERRIMAN, R. B. Some notes on the treatment of English Catholics in the reign of Queen Elizabeth. *A.H.R.* xiii (1908), 480–500.
Deals mainly with an early project to establish a Roman Catholic colony in America.

2356 MEYER, A. O. England und die katholische Kirche unter Elisabeth und den Stuarts. *Bibliothek des kgl. preußischen historischen Instituts in Rom.* vi (Rome, 1911).
Of first importance. Indications of place and nature of unpublished sources. Dispassionate. An English trans. by J. R. McKee, London, 1916, was revised by the author and carries the *imprimatur* of the Roman church.

2357 MORUS, H. Historia provinciae Anglicanae Societatis Jesu. St. Omer. 1660.
For disputes in the English college at Rome.

2358 MORRIS, JOHN. The kalendar and rite used by the Catholics since the time of Elizabeth. *Arch.* lii (1890), 113–28.

2359 MOTT, AGNES. A Dominican martyr in Hampshire. *Blackfriars*, xvi (1935), 766–73.

2360 NEWDIGATE, C. A. Quelques notes sur les catalogues des martyrs anglais dits de Chalcedoine et de Paris. *Anal. Boll.* lvi (1938), 308–33.

2361 NOTES ON THOS. NORTON, M.P., and state proceedings in matters of religion, 1581–2. *Arch.* xxxvi (1855), 97–119.

2362 O'CONNELL, J. R. Richard Topcliffe, priest-hunter and torturer. *Dublin Rev.* cxcv (1934), 240–55.

2363 PHILIPPEN, L. J. M. De avonturen van Robertus Ellyatus, 1577–1609. *Bijd. Gesch.* xxviii (1937), 279–89.

2364 PHILLIPS, G. E. The extinction of the ancient hierarchy. Lond. 1905

2365 PLUNKETT, FRANCIS. The life of Francis Tregian. By P. A. Boyan. *Cath. Rec. Soc.* xxxii (1932), 1–44.
Plunkett was a seventeenth-century Cistercian.

2366 POLLEN, J. H. The English Catholics in the reign of Queen Elizabeth: a study of their politics, civil life, and government, 1558–80, from the fall of the old church to the advent of the counter-reformation. Lond. 1920.
Moderate Roman Catholic viewpoint. Scholarly and valuable.

2367 POLLEN, J. H. The politics of English Catholics during the reign of Queen Elizabeth. *The Month*, xcix (1902), 43–60, 131–48, 290–305, 394–411, 600–18; c (1902), 71–87, 176–88.
Particularly valuable for the Parry Plot.

2368 POLLEN, J. H. Religious terrorism under Queen Elizabeth. *The Month*, cv (1905) 271–89.

2369 POLLEN, J. H. Spurious records of Tudor martyrs. *The Month*, lxxxiv (1895), 217–28.

2370 POLLEN, J. H. The institution of the Arch-priest Blackwell, 1595–1602. Lond. 1916.

2371 REA, W. F. The authorship of 'News from Spagne and Holland' and the bearing on the genuineness of the confessions of the Blessed Henry Walpole, S.J.' *Biog. Stud.* i (1951), 220–30.

2372 REEL, CASSIAN. Father Constantine, O.F.M. Cap. 15? –1616. *Biog. Stud.* ii (1953), 23–36.

2373 ROGERS, D. M. Venerable Robert Sutton of Stafford, a note on his family and early life. *Biog. Stud.* ii (1953), 150–66.

2374 ROGERS, D. M. A bibliography of the published works of Thomas Wright, 1561–1623. *Biog. Stud.* i (1952), 262–80.

2375 ROWSE, A. L. Nicholas Roscarrock and his lives of the saints. *Studies in social history. A tribute to G. M. Trevelyan.* By J. H. Plumb. Lond. 1955, pp. 1–31.

2376 SIMPSON, RICHARD. Edmund Campion, a biography. Lond. 1867; 1896.
Valuable, but partisan Roman Catholic.

2377 STROUD, THEODORE. Father Thomas Wright: a test case for toleration. *Biog. Stud.* i (1951), 189–219.

2378 SOUTHERN, A. C. Elizabethan recusant prose, 1559–82: a historical and critical account of the books of Catholic refugees printed and published abroad and at secret presses in England, together with an annotated bibliography of the same. Lond. 1950.

2379 SOUTHERN, A. C. Recusancy in the North Riding of Yorkshire (c. 1590). *Biog. Stud.* ii (1953), 135–49.

2380 STONOR, R. J. Stonor: a Catholic sanctuary in the Chilterns. Newport, Mon., 1951.

2381 SUNDERLAND, F. H. J. John Finglow, martyr, 1555–8 August 1586 (York). *Downside Rev.* liv (1936), 424–8.

2382 TAUNTON, E. L. The history of the Jesuits in England, 1580–1773. Philadelphia, 1901.
App. contains résumé of principal writings of Robert Parsons. Deals with the political activity of the Jesuits.

2383 THOMPSON, B. H. Anthony Munday's journey to Rome, 1578–9. *Durham Univ. Jour.* xxxiv (1941), 1–14.

2384 THURSTON, HERBERT. Catholic writers and Elizabethan readers. *The Month,* lxxxii (1894), 457–76; lxxxiii (1895), 231–45, 383–99.

2385 VEECH, T. M. Dr. Nicholas Sanders and the English reformation 1530–81. *Recueil de travaux . . . conferences d'histoire et de philol.,* 2nd ser., 32e fasc. Louvain, 1935.

2386 WAUGH, EVELYN. Edmund Campion. Lond. 1935.

2387 WEBSTER, RAYMUND. 'Conference' at Wisbech. A glimpse of Bishop Watson and Abbot Feckenham in 1580. *Downside Rev.* liv (1936), 323–45.

2388 WEBSTER, RAYMUND. Richard Broughton, 'a priest in persecution'. *Downside Rev.* liv (1936), 495–514.

2389 WICKES, GEORGES. Henry Constable, poet and courtier, 1562–1613 *Biog. Stud.* ii (1954), 272–300.

C. PURITANISM

1. *General*

(a) *Sources*

The most important printed collections of sources on the activity of the Puritans are *A part of a register* (2406); *The second parte of a register* (2407); *Puritan manifestoes* (2410); and Usher's *Presbyterian movement* (2409). Strype's *Annals* (2214), and his *Whitgift* (2218), contain much pertinent material. Cf. also sect. D *infra* (pp. 206 ff.).

There are useful bibliographies in 2221 and 2480.

No attempt is made to give an exhaustive list of the writings of the Elizabethan

Puritans. For those of lesser importance reference should be made to their lives
in the *D.N.B.* (9). Cf. the arts. there on Robert Beale, Edward Dering, John
Field, John Fox, Antony Gilbey, John Knewstub, Thomas Sampson, Laurence
Tomson, Thomas Wilcox, and others.

For the political theories of the Puritans, cf. ch. iv, *supra*.

2390 AN ABSTRACT OF CERTAIN ACTS OF PARLIAMENT; of
certaine her maiesties injunctions; of certain canons, constitutions and
synodalles prouincall; established and in force for the peaceable gouernment
of the church. Lond. 1584.
A lawyer's attempt to prove the laws favourable to Puritan claims. Replied to by
Richard Cosin (2402).

2391 AN ADMONITION TO THE PARLIAMENT. s.l. 1572.
Two different eds. were printed the same year (1572). Repr. in *Puritan manifestoes*
(2410). Of prime importance for puritanism.

2392 A SECOND ADMONITION TO THE PARLIAMENT. s.l. 1572;
repr. in *Puritan manifestoes* (2410).
Significant.
Generally ascribed to but probably not by Thomas Cartwright.

2393 BANCROFT, RICHARD. Daungerovs positions and proceedings,
published and practised within this iland of Brytaine, vnder pretence of
reformation and for the presbiteriall discipline. Lond. 1593; 1640.
Information of value as to puritan movements. Repr. in condensed form in 2409.

2394 BANCROFT, RICHARD. A survay of the pretended holy discipline,
contayning the beginninges, successe, parts, proceedings, authority, and
doctrine of it. Lond. 1593.
Highly important Anglican criticism of Puritanism.

2395 BOWND, NICHOLAS. The doctrine of the sabbath plainely layde
forth, and soundly proved by testimonies both of holy Scripture, and also of
olde and new ecclesiasticall writers. Lond. 1595; enl. 1606.
The first influential exposition of the Puritan conception of Sunday. 1606 ed. enlarged
as *Sabbathum veteris et novi testamenti*, or, *the true doctrine of the Sabbath*.

2396 BRADSHAW, WILLIAM. English Puritanism, containeing the maine
opinions of the rigidest sort of those that are called Puritanes in the realme of
England. [Amsterdam?], 1605.
Written by a moderate Puritan divine. For a list of Bradshaw's known works, cf.
D.N.B. (9), art. W. Bradshaw.

2397 CARTWRIGHT, THOMAS. A replye to an answere made of M. Dr.
Whitgifte agaynste the admonition to the parliament by T. C., s.l. 1574.
For a list of Cartwright's known works, cf. his life in *D.N.B.* (9). Many of his letters and
other papers are printed in apps. to Pearson (2437). A treatise on the *ex officio* oath,
probably by Cartwright, is printed in 146, ii, 432–6.

2398 CARTWRIGHT, THOMAS. The second replie of T[homas] C[art-
wright] against Maister Doctor Whitgiftes second answer, touching the
churche discipline. [Zürich?], 1575.

2399 CARTWRIGHT, THOMAS. The rest of the second replie of T[homas]
Cartwright: agaynst Master Doctor Whitgifts second answer, touching the
church discipline. s.l. 1577.

2400 CARTWRIGHTIANA. By Albert Peel and Leland H. Carlson. *Elizabethan non-conformist texts*, vol. i, Lond. 1951.

2401 COSIN, RICHARD. Conspiracie for pretended reformation, viz. presbyteriall discipline; a treatise discovering the late designments and courses held for advancement thereof by W. Hackett, E. Coppinger, and H. Arthington. Lond. 1592; repr. 1699.
Official account of the Hacket plot.

2402 COSIN, RICHARD. An answer to the two first and principall treatises of a certeine factious libell, put foorth latelie without name of author or printer, and without approbation of authoritie vnder the title of 'An Abstract'. Lond. 1584.
Important Anglican reply to 2390. For Cosin's work on the *ex officio* oath, cf. 1416.

2403 A DIRECTORY OF CHURCH GOVERNMENT anciently contended for and, as far as the times would suffer, practicid by the first non-conformists in the days of Queen Elizabeth. Found in the study of . . . T. Cartwright, after his decease, &c. Lond. 1644; by Peter Lorimer, Lond. 1872.
This is an English trans. of the book of discipline compiled by English Presbyterians in the 1580's. The Latin original, in two parts, has been printed from MS. copies as an app. to Paget's introduction to Hooker's *Works* (1418), and by A. F. S. Pearson in *Der älteste englische Presbyterianismus*. Not to be confused, as it often is, with Travers's work (1404). Cf. on this subject Pearson's *Cartwright* (2437), 256–7.

2404 FENNER, DUDLEY. A counter-poyson, modestly written for the time, to make answer to the obiections and reproaches, wherewith the annswerer to the abstract would disgrace the holy discipline of Christ. [Lond.?], 1584.
A Puritan reply to 2402. For other writings of Fenner, cf. his life in *D.N.B.* (9).

2405 [MORICE, JAMES.] A briefe treatise of oathes exacted by ordinaries and ecclesiasticall judges, to answere generallie to all such articles or interrogatories, as pleaseth them to propound. [Lond. 1600?].
Printed anonymously. Reply by a Puritan and a common lawyer to Cosin's *Apologie* (1416). Another ed. was printed in Middelburg (*c.* 1600?).

2406 A PART OF A REGISTER, contayninge sundrie memorable matters, written by diuers godly and learned in our time, which stande for and desire the reformation of our church according to the pure worde of God, and the lawe of our lande. By Robert Waldegrave. [Middelburg, 1593].
A repr. of 33 Puritan tracts of much value. It might well be reprinted. For table of contents, cf. Peel (2407), i, 30–33.

2407 THE SECOND PARTE OF A REGISTER. By Albert Peel. 2 vols. Cambr. 1915.
Calendar of MSS. under that title intended for publication by the Puritans about 1593, now in Dr. Williams's library, London. Valuable.

2408 A PETITION DIRECTED TO HER MOST EXCELLENT MAIESTIE. [1590?].
An important defence of the Puritan reformers by a learned lawyer.

2409 THE PRESBYTERIAN MOVEMENT in the reign of Queen Elizabeth, as illustrated by the minute book of the Dedham classis, 1582–9. By R. G. Usher. *Camden Soc.*, 3rd ser., viii (1905).
Original material of value, carefully discussed.

2410 PURITAN MANIFESTOES: a study of the origin of the puritan revolt. By W. H. Frere and C. E. Douglas. *Church Hist. Soc.* lxxii (1907). By Norman Sykes. Lond. 1954.
Indispensable. The 1954 ed. has a valuable new preface.

2411 A REMONSTRANCE: or plain detection of some of the favlts and hideous sores of svch sillie syllogismes and impertinent allegations, as ovt of sundrie factious pamphlets and rhapsodies, are cobled vp together in a booke entituled *A demonstration of discipline*. Lond. 1590.
Anglican reply to John Udall (2416).

2412 ROGERS, RICHARD, and WARD, SAMUEL. Two Elizabethan Puritan diaries. By M. M. Knappen. Chicago, 1933.

2413 SUTCLIFFE, MATTHEW. A treatise of ecclesiasticall discipline. . . . Lond. 1590; rev. 1591.
Anglican rejection of Puritan positions. For a list of Sutcliffe's known controversial works both with the Puritans and the Romanists, cf. his life in *D.N.B.* (9).

2414 TRAVERS, WALTER.
Cf. 1404 above. For Travers's controversial writings, cf. his life in *D.N.B.* (9).

2415 UDALL, JOHN. The state of the church of Englande laide open in a conference between Diotrephes a byshop, Tertullus a papist, Demetrius a vsurer, Pandocheus an inne-keeper and Paule a preacher of the words of God. s.l. 1588; by Edward Arber, Lond. 1880.
Extreme Puritan. 1880 ed. in *English Scholar's Library* bears title *Diotrephes*.

2416 UDALL, JOHN. A demonstration of the trueth of that discipline which Christe hath prescribed in his worde for the gouernment of his church, . . s.l. 1588; by Edward Arber, Lond. 1880.
Extreme Puritan. For the Anglican reply, cf. 2411.

2417 WHITGIFT, JOHN. The defense of the aunswere to the admonition, against the replie of T. C., Lond. 1574; repr. in *Works* (2181).
Important Anglican reply to the Puritan positions of Thomas Cartwright.

2418 WHITGIFT, JOHN. An answere to a certen libel entituled an admonition to the parliament. Lond. 1572; enl. 1573; repr. in *Works* (2181).
An answer to 2391.

(b) *Later Works*

Of the older books, Brook's *Lives* (2421) and Neal (2436) are still useful. Frere (2188b) gives a good summary; Pierce (2452) is useful though partisan; Usher's *Reconstruction* (2221) presents the best case for the Anglican position. Pearson (2437) is sound and scholarly. Knappen (2433) is the best general account. For the political aspects of puritanism cf. Froude (340), Pollard (363), Black (671), Read (759, 760); on their parliamentary activities Neale (1067, 1124).

2419 BENHAM, W. G. Twelve Colchester persons indicted for heresy in 1566. *Essex Rev.* i (1941), 157–62.

2420 BORGEAUD, CHARLES. Cartwright and Melville at the university of Geneva, 1569–74. *A.H.R.* v (1899), 284–90.

2421 BROOK, BENJAMIN. The lives of the Puritans, . . . from the reformation under Queen Elizabeth to the Act of Uniformity in 1662. 3 vols. Lond. 1813.
Partisan and to be used carefully. Contains a good deal of value.

2422 BROOK, BENJAMIN. Memoir of the life and writings of Thomas Cartwright, B.D. Lond. 1845.

2423 CLARK, H. W. History of English nonconformity from Wiclif to the close of the nineteenth century. 2 vols. Lond. 1911–13.
Vol. i pertinent. Good.

2424 COLLIGAN, J. H. The Honourable William Whittingham of Chester (? 1524–79). Chester, 1934.

2425 CRAIG, HARDIN. The Geneva Bible as a political document. *Pacific Hist. Rev.* vii (1938), 40–49.

2426 DRYSDALE, A. H. History of the Presbyterians in England. Lond. 1889.
Inaccurate.

2427 GOLDING, L. T. An Elizabethan Puritan, Arthur Golding, the translator of Ovid's *Metamorphoses* and also of John Calvin's *Sermons*. New York, 1937.

2428 GREENSLADE, S. L. William Whittingham, dean of Durham, 1524–78. *Durham Univ. Jour.* viii (1946), 28–36.

2429 HALLER, WILLIAM. The rise of Puritanism, or the way to the New Jerusalem as set forth in pulpit and press from Thomas Cartwright to John Lilburne and John Milton, 1570–1643. New York, 1938.

2430 HEYLYN, PETER. Aërius redivivus: or, the history of the presbyterians from the year 1536 to . . . 1647. Oxf. 1670.
Violently anti-Puritan.

2431 HOLDEN, W. P. Anti-Puritan satire, 1572–1642. *Yale Studies in Eng.* cxxvi. New Haven, 1954.

2432 HOPKINS, SAMUEL. The Puritans during the reigns of Edward VI and Queen Elizabeth. 3 vols. Boston, 1859–61.
Strongly puritan.

2433 KNAPPEN, M. M. Tudor Puritanism: a chapter in the history of idealism. Chicago, 1939.

2434 MARSDEN, J. B. History of the early Puritans, from the reformation to . . . 1642. Lond. 1853.
This work does not advance much beyond Neal (2436).

2435 MUSS-ARNOLT, W. Puritan efforts and struggles, 1550–1603; a bio-bibliographical study. *Amer. Jour. Theology*, xxiii (1919), 345–66, 471–99.
Useful.

2436 NEAL, DANIEL. The history of the Puritans, or protestant non-conformists; from the reformation in 1517, to the death of Queen Elizabeth.

4 vols. Lond. 1732–8; by Joshua Toulmin, 5 vols., Bath, 1793–7; by J. O. Choules, 2 vols., New York, 1844.

Widely influential, but prejudiced and often inaccurate. 1793 ed. the best.

2437　PEARSON, A. F. S. Thomas Cartwright and Elizabethan Puritanism, 1535–1603. Cambr. 1925.

App. of pertinent documents. Bibliography. Valuable.

2438　SHAW, W. A. Elizabethan Presbyterianism. *E.H.R.* iii (1888), 655–67.

2439　SMITH, H. M. The case of Robert Wright. *Church Quar. Rev.* cxii (1931), 98–107.

2440　SMITHEN, F. J. Presbyterianism in England in the reign of Queen Elizabeth. *Presbyter. Hist. Soc. Eng.*, extra pubs., i (1937).

On Presbyterianism in the Channel Islands, cf. 1338.

2441　VETTER, THEODOR. Literarische Beziehungen zwischen England und der Schweiz im Reformationszeitalter. Zürich, 1901.

Throws light upon relationship between English puritanism and Switzerland.

2442　WHITLEY, W. T. Thomas Helwys. *Baptist Quar.*, n.s., vii (1934), 241–54.

2443　WILSON, J. D. Richard Schilders and the English Puritans. *Trans. Bibliog. Soc. Lond.* xi (1909–11), 65–114.

2. *The Martin Marprelate Controversy*

The principal works included in this controversy are set forth by Arber (2448), 197–200. The authorship of the Marprelate tracts themselves has never been definitely established. Field, Udall, Penry, Job Throgmorton, Barrow, and others have been suspected. Some of the tracts were reprinted by Petheram (2453), others by Arber in the *English Scholar's Library*; the six important ones by Pierce (2450). For the attitude of the Puritan leaders, notably Cartwright, towards Martin and his work, cf. Pearson (2437), 277 ff. Much of the source material on the controversy is printed in Arber (2448).

2444　BONNARD, G. La controverse de Martin Marprelate 1588–90. Geneva, 1916.

No discussion of authorship.

2445　BRIDGES, JOHN. A defence of the government established in the chvrch of Englande for ecclesiasticall matters. Lond. 1587.

Started the Marprelate controversy.

2446　C[OOPER], T[HOMAS]. An admonition to the people of England; wherein are answered, not onely the slaunderous untruethes, reprochfully uttered by Martin the libeller, but also many other crimes by some of his broode, &c. Lond. 1589; by E. Arber, *English Scholar's Library*, no. 15 (1895).

The official reply to Martin Marprelate's epistle. Called forth his tract, *Hay any worke for Cooper, &c.*

2447　[FULKE, WILLIAM.] A briefe and plaine declaration, concerning the desires of all those faithfull ministers that haue and do seeke for the discipline and reformation of the church of Englande. Lond. 1584.

Written by Fulke though ascribed on the title-page to Dudley Fenner. Answered by Bridges (2445), whose work in turn brought on the Marprelate controversy. For other writings by Fulke and his controversies with the Romanists, cf. his life in *D.N.B.* (9).

2448 AN INTRODUCTORY SKETCH to the Martin Marprelate controversy. By Edward Arber. Lond. 1879; *English Scholar's Library*, 1895.
Prints many documents pertinent to the controversy.

2449 McGINN, D. J. The real Martin Marprelate [John Penry]. *P.M.L.A.* lviii (1943), 84–107.
Neale (1067), ii, 105, 194–220, argues in favour of Job Throckmorton.

2450 THE MARPRELATE TRACTS, 1588, 1589. By William Pierce. Lond. 1911.
Repr. of *The epistle, The epitome, Mineralls, Hay any worke, Theses Martinianae, The just censure, The protestatyon.* Spelling and punctuation modernized, with notes historical and explanatory. For the original eds. cf. *S.T.C.* (35), p. 394.

2451 MASKELL, WILLIAM. A history of the Martin Marprelate controversy in the reign of Queen Elizabeth. Lond. 1845.
Anglo-Catholic viewpoint. Prejudiced against Puritans.

2452 PIERCE, WILLIAM. An historical introduction to the Marprelate tracts. A chapter in the evolution of religious and civil liberty in England. Lond. 1909.
Indispensable, though partisan. Bibliography.

2453 PURITAN DISCIPLINE TRACTS. By John Petheram. 6 vols. Lond. 1843–7.
Reprs. of some of the more important Marprelate tracts.

D. SEPARATISM

(a) *Sources*

The line between Puritanism and separatism is not easy to draw with accuracy. Only the more important works of the recognized separatists are here given. For the later development of separatism and its connexion with the New England Pilgrims reference should be made to Dexter (2480) and to Davies (8).

2454 [AINSWORTH, HENRY.] A trve confession of the faith and hvmble acknovvledgment of the alegeance vvhich vve hir maiesties subjects, falsely called Brovvnists doe hould. . . . [Amsterdam?], 1596; repr. in Walker (2473), pp. 49–74.
A creed, theory of the church, and programme for action. Ainsworth was leader of the separatist congregation at Amsterdam. For his other writings, cf. his life in *D.N.B.* (9).

2455 BROWNE, ROBERT. A booke which sheweth the life and manners of all true Christians and howe vnlike they are vnto Turkes and Papistes and heathen folke. Middelburg, 1582.
Extracts repr. in Walker (2473). Fundamental for separatism.

2456 BROWNE, ROBERT. A treatise of reformation without tarrying for anie, and of the wickedness of those preachers which will not reforme till the magistrate commaunde or compell them. Middelburg, 1582; by T. G. Crippen, *Trans. Congregational Hist. Soc.*, no. 2 (1901).
Important not merely for the separatist position but for the separatist criticism of puritanism.

2457 BROWNE, ROBERT. A true and short declaration, both of the gather-
ing . . . together of certaine persons and also of the lamentable breach . . .
which fell amongst them. s.l. [1584?]; repr. in *The Congregationalist.* Lond.
1888.
Autobiographical. Extracts from it occur in Bancroft's *Sermon at Paul's Cross,* 1588
(2156).

2458 BROWNE, ROBERT. The retraction of Robert Browne. . . . By C.
Burrage. Oxf. 1907.
Written in 1588.

2459 THE BROWNISTS IN NORWICH AND NORFOLK about 1580;
some new facts, together with 'A treatise of the church and the kingdome of
Christ', by R. H. [Robert Harrison?]. By Albert Peel. Cambr. 1920.
From MS. in Dr. Williams's library, London. Cf. 2407.

2460 BURRAGE, CHAMPLIN. The early English dissenters in the light of
recent research (1550–1641). 2 vols. Cambr. 1912.
Documents. Indispensable.

2461 A COLLECTION OF CERTAINE SCLAUNDEROUS ARTICLES
gyven out by the bisshops against such faithfull Christians as they now
vniustly deteyne in their prisons, togeather with the answeare of the said
prisoners therunto. Also the some of certain conferences had in the fleete,
according to the bisshops bloudie mandate with two prisoners there (Barrow
and Greenwood?) [Dort? 1590?].
A separatist publication. Presents the arguments in favour of separatism. Probably
written by Barrow, Greenwood, and Penry while in prison.

2462 [BARROWE, HENRY, and GREENWOOD, JOHN.] A trve descrip-
tion, ovt of the word of God, of the visible church. [Dort?], 1589; repr. in
Walker (2473), pp. 33–40.
Separatist picture of a true church, its officers and administration.

2463 BARROWE, HENRY. A brief discovery of the false church. [Dort?],
1590.
Extreme separatist criticism of the church of England.

2464 [BARROWE, HENRY, and GREENWOOD, JOHN.] A plaine refuta-
tion of M. Giffarde's booke, intituled, 'a short treatise against the Donatistes
of England'. [Dort?], 1591; [Lond. 1605?].
A defence of the separatist position. Cf. 2465.

2465 GIFFORD, GEORGE. A short treatise against the Donatists of England,
whome we call Brownists. Lond. 1590.
A Puritan criticism of separatism. Cf. 2464.

2466 GIFFORD, GEORGE. A plaine declaration that our Brownists be full
Donatists. Lond. 1590.
A Puritan criticism of separatism. A reply to 2467.

2467 GREENWOOD, JOHN. An annswer to George Gifford's pretended
defence of read prayers and devised leitourgies, with the vngodly cavils and
vvicked sclanders comprised in the first part of his book entituled, 'A short
treatise against the Donatists of England'. [Dort?], 1590.
A reply to 2465.

2468   THE WRITINGS OF ROBERT HARRISON AND ROBERT BROWNE. By Albert Peel and L. H. Carlson. *Elizabethan Nonconformist Texts*, vol. ii. Lond. 1953.

2469   KNEWSTUB, JOHN. A confutation of monstrous and horrible heresies taught by H. N. (Henrick Niclaes) and embraced of a number who call themselves the familie of love. Lond. 1579.

2470   PENRY, JOHN. The appellation of John Penri vnto the highe court of parliament from the bad and injurious dealing of the archb. of Canterb. and other his colleagues of the high commission. [Lond.], 1589.
The Welsh dissenter. Reputed author of the Marprelate tracts. For a list of his writings, cf. *S.T.C.* (35), p. 449.

2470a   THE NOTEBOOK OF JOHN PENRY, 1593. By Albert Peel. *Camden Soc.*, 3rd ser., lxvii (1944).

2471   ROGERS, JOHN. The displaying of an horrible secte of gross and wicked heretiques, naming themselves the familie of love, with the lives of their authours (i.e. D. Joris and H. Niclas). Lond. 1578.

2472   ROGERS, JOHN. An answere unto a wicked and infamous libel, made by Christopher Vitel, one of the chief English elders of the pretended family of love. Lond. 1579.

2473   WALKER, WILLISTON. The creeds and platforms of Congregationalism. New York, 1893.

(b) *Later Works*

The most complete bibliography is in 2480; cf. also W. T. Whitley, *A Baptist bibliography*, i, 1526–1776. Lond. 1916.

The works of Burrage (2476–7), of Dale (2479), of Dexter (2480), of Peel (2485), and of Powicke (2487–8) are most noteworthy.

2474   BRAGHT, T. J. VAN. A martyrology of the churches of Christ commonly called Baptists, during the era of the reformation. By E. B. Underhill. 2 vols. *Hanserd Knollys Soc.* viii (1850–3).
Trans. from the Dutch.

2475   BROWNE, JOHN. History of Congregationalism and memorials of the churches in Norfolk and Suffolk. Lond. 1877.

2476   BURRAGE, CHAMPLIN. John Penry, the so-called martyr of Congregationalism, as revealed in the original record of his trial and in documents relating thereto. Lond. 1913.

2477   BURRAGE, CHAMPLIN. The true story of Robert Browne (1550?–1633), father of Congregationalism, including various points hitherto unknown or misunderstood, with some account of the development of his religious views, and an extended and improved list of his writings. Lond. 1906.
Indispensable.

2478   CROSBY, THOMAS. The history of the English Baptists from the reformation to the beginning of the reign of King George I. 4 vols. Lond. 1738–40.

2479   DALE, R. W., and DALE, A. W. W. History of English Congregationalism. Lond. 1907.
The best general account.

2480   DEXTER, H. M. The Congregationalism of the last three hundred
years, as seen in its literature: with special reference to certain recondite,
neglected or disputed passages. New York, 1880.
Valuable discussions and a remarkable bibliography.

2481   DEXTER, H. M., and DEXTER, MORTON. The England and
Holland of the Pilgrims. Boston, 1905.
A careful piece of work.

2482   EVANS, B. The early English baptists. 2 vols. Lond. 1862–4.

2483   HALLEY, R. Lancashire: its Puritanism and non-conformity. 2 vols.
Manchester, 1869.

2484   HANBURY, BENJAMIN. Historical memorials relating to the inde-
pendents, or Congregationalists; from their rise to the restoration of the
monarchy, A.D. MDCLX. 3 vols. Lond. 1839–44.
Ill-digested, but of value.

2485   PEEL, ALBERT. The first Congregational churches: new light on
separatist congregations in London, 1567–81. Cambr. 1920.

2486   PIERCE, WILLIAM. John Penry, his life, times and writings. Lond.
1923.
Bibliography. Valuable on the religious condition of Wales.

2487   POWICKE, F. J. Henry Barrow, separatist (1550?–93), and the exiled
church of Amsterdam. London. 1900.
Careful and painstaking.

2488   POWICKE, F. J. Robert Browne, pioneer of modern congregationalism.
Lond. 1910.

2489   UNDERWOOD, A. C. A history of the English Baptists. Lond. 1947.

2490   SMITH, D. C. Robert Browne, Independent. *Church Hist.* vi (1937),
289–349.

2491   USHER, R. G. The pilgrims and their history. New York, 1918.
Holds that the pilgrims were not subject to active persecution in England from church
or state. Bibliographical notes.

2492   WADDINGTON, JOHN. Congregational history, 1567–1700, in relation to contemporaneous events, and the conflict for freedom, purity and
independence. Lond. 1874; 1880.
Partisan, and not always careful.

2493   WADDINGTON, JOHN. John Penry, the pilgrim martyr 1559–93.
Lond. 1854.
Brief, uncritical, but contains valuable excerpts from contemporary documents.

7. THE CONSTITUTIONAL HISTORY OF THE CHURCH OF ENGLAND

Cf. on this subject Gross (1), pp. 141–9. For parish registers, cf. 1716; for church wardens' accounts, 1715, for bishops' registers, 1742–6, 1787, 2166; for episcopal visitations, 1992–4, 2104, 2107, 2164, 2165, 2168, 2180, 2227. For the Elizabethan controversy between Anglican and Puritans over the *ex-officio* oath, cf. sect. 6, *supra* (pp. 200 ff.). Reference should also be made to ch. iv, *supra* (pp. 118 ff.), particularly for the relations between Church and State.

(a) *Sources*

2494 ABSTRACT OF THE ACT BOOK OF THE ARCHDEACON OF HUNTINGDON'S COURT. By F. G. Emmison. *Trans. East Herts. Arch. Soc.* viii, 1930–1 (1933), 187–94.

2495 THE ARCHDEACON'S COURT: liber actorum, 1584. Vol. i trans. E. R. Brinkworth. *Oxf. Rec. Soc.* xxiii (1942); pt. ii, xxix (1946).

2496 ARCHDEACON HARPSFIELD'S VISITATION, 1557, together with visitations of 1556 and 1558. By L. E. Whatmore and W. Sharp. *Cath. Rec. Soc.* xlv–xlvi (1950–1).

2497 AN ARCHIDIACONAL VISITATION OF 1502. By C. E. Woodruff. *Arch. Cant.* xlvii (1935), 13–54.

2498 BRINKWORTH, E. R. The study and use of archdeacon's court records, illustrated from Oxford Records, 1566–1759. *Trans. R.H. Soc.*, 4th ser., xxv (1943), 93–119.

2499 CALENDAR OF ADMINISTRATIONS in the consistory court of Lincoln, 1540–1659. By C. W. Foster. *Index Library*, lii (1921).

2500 DEPOSITIONS AND OTHER ECCLESIASTICAL PROCEEDINGS from the courts of Durham . . . from 1311 to the reign of Elizabeth. *Surtees Soc.* xxi (1846).
Particularly valuable for depositions relating to the rebellion of 1569.

2501 LYNDWOOD, WILLIAM. Provinciale seu constitutiones Anglie. Oxf. [1481?]; Lond. 1525; Oxf. 1679.
Beale (1480) dates the first ed. 1481; *S.T.C.* (35), 1483. Beale gives fifteen Latin and one Eng. trans. in the sixteenth century.
This *digest in five bookes of the synodal constitutions of the province of Canterbury* deals with a period earlier than the Tudors but is fundamental for English canon law.

2502 NORWICH CONSISTORY COURT DEPOSITORIES, 1499–1512, 1518–30. Calendared by E. D. Stone; revised and arranged by B. Cozens-Hardy, *Norfolk Rec. Soc. Bull.* x (1938).

2503 PALMER, W. M. The archdeaconry of Cambridge and Ely, 1599. *Trans. Cambr. and Hunt. Arch. Soc.* vi (1938), 1–28.

2505 PRICE, F. D. Elizabethan apparitors in the diocese of Gloucester. *Church Quar. Rev.* cxxxiv (1942), 37–55.

2506   REFORMATIO LEGUM ECCLESIASTICARUM. Lond. 1571; by Edward Cardwell. Oxf. 1850.
1850 ed. published under title, *The reformation of the ecclesiastical laws as attempted in the reigns of King Henry VIII, King Edward VI and Queen Elizabeth.*

2507   RIDLEY, THOMAS. A view of the civile and ecclesiastical law, and wherein the practice of them is streitned and may be relieved within this land. Lond. 1607; by J. Gregory, Oxf. 1675.
Seeks to show the scope of jurisdiction of ecclesiastical courts and to defend bishops in controversy over prohibitions.

2508   SELECT XVI CENTURY CASES IN TITHE from the York diocesan registry. By J. S. Purvis. *Yorks. Arch. Soc.*, rec. ser., cxiv (1949).

2509   A SERIES OF PRECEDENTS AND PROCEEDINGS in criminal causes, 1475–1640, extracted from the act books of ecclesiastical courts in the diocese of London. By W. H. Hale. Lond. 1847.
Introductory essay on the English ecclesiastical law and the jurisdiction of the ecclesiastical courts. Valuable.

2510   STUBBS, WILLIAM. Report of the commissioners appointed to inquire into the constitution and working of the ecclesiastical courts (Historical appendix to vol. i). *Parliamentary papers*, 1883, xxiv.
Collection of acts and cases, with comments of high value. For the controversy provoked by this publication, cf. Gross (1), nos. 767, 768a, 769.

(b) *Later Works*

2511   BURN, RICHARD. Ecclesiastical law. 2 vols. Lond. 1760; by R. Phillimore, 4 vols., Lond. 1842.
Consists largely of extracts of the laws very judiciously selected and arranged alphabetically. By additions of subsequent editors its original value has been greatly enhanced.

2512   BURN, J. S. The high commission, notices of the court and its proceedings. Lond. 1865.

2513   THE CANON LAW OF THE CHURCH OF ENGLAND. Being the report of the archbishops' commission on Canon Law together with proposals for a revised body of Canons. Lond. 1947.

2514   DIBDIN, L. T. Church courts, an historical inquiry into the status of the ecclesiastical courts. 2nd ed. Lond. 1882.

2514a   DIBDIN, L. T., and CHADWICK–HEALEY, C. E. English church law and divorce. Lond. 1912.
Valuable.

2515   FINCHAM, W. X. Notes from the ecclesiastical court records at Somerset house. *Trans. R.H. Soc.*, 4th ser., iv (1921), 103–39.
Extracts printed mostly from sixteenth century.

2516   FOSTER, G. J. Doctors' commons; its courts and registries with a treatise on probate court business. Lond. 1868.

2517 GIBSON, EDMUND. Synodus Anglicana: or the constitution and proceedings of an English convocation shown from the acts and registers thereof to be agreeable to the principles of an episcopal church. Lond. 1702; by Edward Cardwell. Oxf. 1854.
Deals mainly with sixteenth and seventeenth centuries.

2518 HODY, HUMPHREY. A history of English councils and convocations and of the clergy's sitting in parliament. Lond. 1701.
Useful. Cf. on the same subject, Gross (1), nos. 764–6.

2519 HOOPER, WILFRED. The court of faculties. *E.H.R.* xxv (1910), 670–86.

2520 JOYCE, J. W. England's sacred synods: a constitutional history of the convocations of the clergy. Lond. 1855.

2521 LATHBURY, T. History of the convocation of the church of England. Lond. 1842; 1853.

2522 LAW, J. T. Forms of ecclesiastical law or the mode of conducting suits in the consistory courts. Lond. 1851.
Contains some historical matter and notes on seventeenth and eighteenth-century books of practice in the ecclesiastical courts.

2523 MAITLAND, F. W. Roman canon law in the church of England. Lond. 1898.
Asserts that the Roman canon law was valid in England before the reformation. For the controversial literature on this subject, cf. Gross (1), nos. 767 and 769.

2524 MAKOWER, FELIX. Die Verfassung der Kirche von England. Berlin, 1884; Eng. trans. Lond. 1895.
Important. Bibliography.

2525 PHILLIMORE, ROBERT. Ecclesiastical law of the church of England. 2 vols. Lond. 1873; by C. F. Jemmett and W. G. F. Phillimore, Lond. 1895.
Considerable historical matter is included.

2526 PRESSEY, W. J. The surplice in Essex during Elizabethan and Stuart times. *Essex Rev.* xlv (1937), 36–45.

2527 RICHIE, C. I. A. The ecclesiastical courts of York. Lond. 1956.

2528 SELDEN, JOHN. The historie of tithes, that is, the practice of payment of them, the positive laws made for them, the opinions touching the right of them. [Lond.], 1618.
Still the best authority on the history of tithes. Suppressed by court of high commission for questioning that tithes are payable by divine right.

2529 SENIOR, WILLIAM. Doctors' commons and the old court of admiralty: a short history of the civilians in England. Lond. 1922.

2530 SPELMAN, HENRY. History and fate of sacrilege. Lond. 1698; 1853; by F. C. S. Warren, Lond. 1895.
Written about 1633 by the celebrated ecclesiastical lawyer and antiquary.

2532 USHER, R. G. The rise and fall of the high commission. Oxf. 1913.

2533 WOODCOCK, B. L. Medieval ecclesiastical courts in the diocese of Canterbury. Lond. 1952.

VII

ECONOMIC HISTORY

1. GENERAL

(a) *Bibliography*

There is no adequate bibliography on the subject as a whole. Bibliographies on special topics are listed below under the appropriate sections. Gross (1), sects. 25, 72, and pp. 609–10, gives the important general works printed before 1910. Palgrave (2565) contains bibliographical notices of the authorities on the topics with which it deals. Cunningham (2546), ii, pt. 2, gives a selected list of contemporary works printed and unprinted, arranged chronologically. This is incomplete, but useful, particularly for unprinted material. He also gives a long list of secondary authorities. Scott's (3009) list of authorities, i, p. xxvii, will also be found useful, particularly for unpublished MSS. and contemporary pamphlets. Shorter bibliographies are in Lipson (2556), Unwin (2693), Bland, Brown, and Tawney (2536), and Westerfield (2694), but none of these is either critical or exhaustive. A convenient annual list of new contributions to English economic history, beginning 1925, is printed in the *Econ. Hist. Rev.*, 1927 ff. For works in Russian on English economic history, cf. ibid. i (1927–8), 208–34. For Scottish and Irish economic history, cf. chs. xii, xiii, *infra*.

The following periodicals will be found serviceable both for their articles and for their book reviews:

Agricultural History Review. Lond. 1953 ff.
Annales d'histoire économique et sociale. Paris, 1929 ff.
Economica. Lond. 1921 ff.
The Economic History Review. Lond. 1927 ff.
The Economic Journal. Lond. 1891 ff.
Journal of Economic and Business History. Cambr., U.S.A., 1928–32.
Journal of Political Economy. Chicago, 1893 ff.
Quarterly Journal of Economics. Boston, 1887 ff.
Vierteljahrschrift für Sozial- und Wirtschaftsgeschichte. Leipzig, 1903 ff.

2534 A SELECT BIBLIOGRAPHY of the study, sources, and literature of English medieval economic history. By Hubert Hall. Lond. 1914.
Contains much of value for sixteenth century. Cf. also E. Lipson, *The sources available for the study of medieval economic history* in *Trans. R.H. Soc.*, 3rd ser., x (1916), 115–58.

2535 TAWNEY, R. H. Studies in bibliography: modern capitalism. *Econ. Hist. Rev.* iv (1933), 336–56.

(b) *Sources*

Most of the sources on economic history relate to some particular aspect of the subject and will be noticed in the appropriate sections below. There is a great deal of miscellaneous unprinted material in the P.R.O. The fiscal and the judicial records of the crown are particularly rich in information upon almost every phase of economic life. Scattered through the domestic state papers are numerous contemporary discourses on economic subjects, particularly from 1558 onwards. Notices of these in the printed calendars are very inadequate. There is much material of the same sort in the B.M., notably in the *Cotton, Lansdowne,* and *Harleian MSS.* Among private collections the *Salisbury MSS.* (185) deserve particular attention.

The official attitude towards matters economic is often revealed in the *Acts of the Privy Council* (1152), the *Royal Proclamations* (1017), and the *Statutes of the Realm* (1016). The preambles of statutes concerning economic matters often present the official diagnosis of the economic ills they are designed to correct. The *Journals of the House of Commons* (1101) and *D'Ewes Journal* (1037) are also valuable, as are town and quarter-sessions records.

Tawney and Power (2539) is easily the best of the general collections of source material. Many contemporary writers deal with the economic ills of the time. Perhaps the most important is Hales (2537). Dudley's *Tree of the Commonwealth* (1364), More's *Utopia* (1365), and Starkey's *Dialogue between Pole and Lupset* (1384) are also of first-rate importance. Harrison's *Description* (615) should be consulted.

The works of some of the divines also deserve attention, e.g. Bucer, *De regno Christi* (2099), Latimer's *Sermons* (1732), Crowley, *Epigrams* and *One way to wealth* (1719), Becon, *The jewel of joy* (1710), Lever, *Sermons* (2105). Interesting sidelights on English economic conditions are thrown by the reports of the Venetian ambassadors in Albèri (989) and in the Venetian calendars (992).

2536   ENGLISH ECONOMIC HISTORY, SELECT DOCUMENTS. By A. E. Bland, P. A. Brown, R. H. Tawney. Lond. 1914.
The collection extends from the earliest times to 1846 and the documents in pt. ii, 1485–1660, with their introductions, are of much value.

2537   [HALES, JOHN?] A discourse of the common weal of this realm of England. By Elizabeth Lamond. Cambr. 1893; repr. 1929.
This is the definitive ed. of *A compendious or briefe examination of certayne ordinary complaints, of divers of our countrymen in these our dayes . . .*, by W. S. Gentleman, Lond. 1581. The original ed. and the repr. by F. J. Furnivall in the *New Shakespeare Soc.*, ser. vi, no 3 (1876), bear the additional titles *A briefe conceipte touching the common weal of this realme of Englande* and *A briefe conceipte of English policy.* The work was attributed to William Stafford until shown by Miss Lamond, *E.H.R.* vi (1891), 284–305, to be derived from a MS. by John Hales written in 1549. An important source. Cf. Cunningham (2546), 3rd ed., iii, 552. Cf. also A. C. Terson, *John Hales, économiste anglais du milieu du XVIe siècle: sa doctrine et son temps,* Avallon, 1907; and Nasse, in *Zeit. für die gesamte Staatswissenschaft,* xix (1863), 5 ff., 369 ff. Some scholars maintain that Sir Thomas Smith was the author. Cf. E. Hughes, *The authorship of the discourse of the common weal,* Bull. *John Ryland's Lib.* xxi (1937), 167–75; Jean-Yves le Branchu, *Écrits notables sur la monnaie,* i (Paris, 1934), pp. lvii–xciv.

2538   PAULI, R. Drei volkswirthschaftliche Denkschriften aus der Zeit Heinrichs VIII. von England. *Abhandlungen der königlichen Gesellschaft der Wissenschaften zu Göttingen.* Göttingen, 1878.
Contains (1) *A treatise concerning the staple and the commodities of this realm* (probably by Clement Armstrong); (2) *How the comen people may be set to work, an order of a comenwelth*; (3) *How to reform the realme in settyng them to worke and to restore tillage.*

2539 TUDOR ECONOMIC DOCUMENTS. By R. H. Tawney and Eileen
Power. 3 vols. *Univ. of London Hist. Ser.*, no. 14. Lond. 1924.
An extensive and admirably chosen mass of material, much of it not elsewhere in print,
illustrative of all phases of economic history.

(c) *Later Works*

Lipson (2556) is the best general account. Cunningham (2546) is valuable.
Ashley (2541) though old is still useful.

In addition to the works cited below, the chapters dealing with economic life
in the various vols. of the *Victoria County History* (4203) should be consulted.

2540 ASHLEY, W. J. The economic organization of England. Lond. 1914.
Brief, but suggestive.

2541 ASHLEY, W. J. An introduction to English economic history and
theory. 2 vols. Lond. 1888–92.
Pt. ii has valuable chapters on the Tudor period.

2542 BINDOFF, S. T. Clement Armstrong and his treatises of the commonweal. *Econ. Hist. Rev.* xiv (1944), 64–73.

2543 BRENTANO, LUJO. Eine Geschichte der wirtschaftlichen Entwicklung
Englands. 3 vols. Jena, 1927–8.
Vol. ii covers the sixteenth century.

2544 CHALK, A. F. Natural law and the rise of economic individualism in
England. *Jour. Pol. Econ.* lix (1951), 332–47.

2545 CLARK, G. N. The wealth of England from 1496–1760. Lond. 1946.

2546 CUNNINGHAM, WILLIAM. The growth of English industry and
commerce. 2 vols. in 3 pts. Cambr. 1882; rev. 1890–2; rev. 1903–5; rev.
1907–10.
Covers the whole period of English history and treats with learning and insight all
phases of economic life and theory. Provided with valuable appendixes and a bibliography. The last ed. is the best. Cf. also William Cunningham, *Western civilization in
its economic aspects*, Cambr. 1900, vol. ii, for a general treatment.

2547 DARBY, H. C. The draining of the Fens. Lond. 1940; 1956.

2548 DOBB, MAURICE. Studies in the development of capitalism. Lond.
1946.
Socialist viewpoint.

2549 FISHER, F. J. The development of London as a centre of conspicuous
consumption in the sixteenth and seventeenth centuries. *Trans. R.H. Soc.*,
4th ser., xxx (1948), 37–50.

2550 FISHER, F. J. The development of the London food market, 1540–1640.
Econ. Hist. Rev. v (1935), 46–64.

2551 HAWEIS, J. O. W. Sketches of the reformation and Elizabethan age
taken from the contemporary pulpit. Lond. 1844.
Illustrative material from sermons on the parochial clergy, state of public morals,
superstitions, usury, state of poor, &c.

2552 HAMILTON, E. J. American treasure and the rise of capitalism (1500–
1700). *Economica*, ix (1929), 338–57.

2553 HUGHES, EDWARD. Studies in administration and finance, 1558–1825, with special reference to the history of salt taxation in England. Manchester, 1934.

2554 JACKMAN, W. T. The development of transportation in modern England. 2 vols. Cambr. 1916.

2555 KERRIDGE, ERIC. The movement of rent, 1540–1640. *Econ. Hist. Rev.*, 2nd ser., vi (1953), 16–34.

2556 LIPSON, EPHRAIM. The economic history of England. Vol. i, Lond. 1915; 5th ed. 1929; 7th ed. 1937; vols. ii and iii, 1931; 5th ed. 1948; 1956.
The best general account to the middle of the eighteenth century.

2558 NEF, J. U. Prices and industrial capitalism in France and England, 1540–1640. *Econ. Hist. Rev.* vii (1937), 155–85.

2559 NEF, J. U. English and French industrial history after 1540 in relation to the constitution. In *The constitution reconsidered*. By Conyers Read. New York, 1938, pp. 79–103.

2560 NEF, J. U. Industry and government in France and England, 1540–1640. *Amer. Philol. Soc.* xv (1940).

2561 NEF, J. U. Industrial Europe at the time of the reformation (*c.* 1515–*c.* 1540). *Jour. Pol. Ec.* xlix (1941), 1–40, 183–224.

2562 NEF, J. U. War and economic progress, 1540–1640. *Econ. Hist. Rev.*, xii (1942), 13–38.
Cf. also ibid., *War and human progress*, Cambr., U.S.A., 1950.

2563 NEF, J. U. The genesis of industrialism and of modern science. In *Essays in honor of Conyers Read*, Chicago, 1953, pp. 200–69.

2564 OCHENKOWSKI, W. VON. Englands wirtschaftliche Entwicklung im Ausgange des Mittelalters. Jena, 1879.
Important chapters on landholding, the gilds, the staple and foreign trade.

2565 PALGRAVE, R. H. I. Dictionary of political economy. 3 vols. Lond. 1894–9; by Henry Higgs, Lond. 1923–6.

2566 O'BRIEN, S. An essay on the economic effects of the reformation. Lond. 1923.
Arrives at many of the conclusions reached by Tawney (2576), but is a much less scholarly work.

2567 ROBERTSON, H. M. Sir Belvis Bulmer, a large-scale speculator of Elizabethan and Jacobean times. *Jour. Econ. and Bus. Hist.* iv (1931), 99–120.

2568 ROBERTSON, H. M. Aspects of the rise of economic individualism. Cambr. 1933.
Cf. J. Brodrick, *The economic morals of the Jesuits*, Lond. 1934, for an attack on Robertson's views.

2569 ROGERS, J. E. T. Six centuries of work and wages. Oxf. 1884.
Theories not generally accepted.

2570 ROGERS, J. E. T. A history of agriculture and prices in England. 7 vols. Oxf. 1866–1900.
Supplementary prices on corn (wheat) are printed in Gras (2982). Cf. also 2855, 2865.

2571 ROOVER, RAYMOND DE. Scholastic economics: survival and lasting influence from the sixteenth century to Adam Smith. *Quar. Jour. Econ.* lxix (1955), 161–90.

2572 SÉE, HENRI. L'évolution du capitalisme moderne. Paris, 1926.
A good short introduction to modern economic history. Cf. also idem, *L'Évolution du capitalisme en Angleterre du XVIᵉ siècle au commencement du XIXᵉ, Revue de synthèse historique*, xl (1926), 31–49.

2573 SHAKESPEARE'S ENGLAND. 2 vols. By C. T. Onions. Oxf. 1917.
Vol. i, chs. 11 and 12, deal with economic topics, with bibliographical notes appended, and many useful illustrations. Ch. 11 is reprinted in Unwin (2575), 302–36.

2574 SOCIAL ENGLAND. 6 vols. By H. D. Traill. Lond. 1897; by J. S. Mann, 1901–4.
A co-operative work. The last part of vol. ii and vol. iii have a mass of information on all phases of the economic and social life of the period, with bibliographies. The 2nd ed. contains excellent illustrations.

2575 STUDIES IN ECONOMIC HISTORY: The collected papers of George Unwin. By R. H. Tawney. Lond. 1927.
Contains several essays and book reviews pertinent to the sixteenth century.

2576 TAWNEY, R. H. Religion and the rise of capitalism. Lond. 1926; 1938.
A brilliant study. Chiefly concerned with England to 1700. For a criticism of earlier writers on the subject, cf. p. 319, n. 32. Cf. also Tawney's earlier articles on this subject in *Jour. Pol. Econ.* xxxi (1923), 461–93; 637–74; 804–25.

2577 TAYLOR, E. G. R. The surveyor. *Econ. Hist. Rev.* xvii (1947), 121–33.

2578 WALKER, P. C. G. Capitalism and the reformation. *Econ. Hist. Rev.* viii (1937), 1–19.

2. RURAL CONDITIONS: LANDHOLDING, VILLEINAGE, ENCLOSURES, ETC.

(a) *Bibliography*

For a more complete list of the bibliographies printed before 1910, cf. Moore (2584), 78–80. Gross (1), pp. 511–12, has a very useful note on the subject.

2579 DAVENPORT, F. G. A classified list of printed original materials for English manorial and agrarian history during the middle ages. *Radcliffe College Monographs*, no. 6. Boston, 1894.
Includes much material for the sixteenth and seventeenth centuries. Valuable, but out of date. The introduction contains a useful discussion of the general character of the sources of manorial history.

2580 HEARNSHAW, F. J. C. Leet jurisdiction in England, especially as illustrated by the records of Southampton. *Southamp. Rec. Soc.*, 1908.
Bibliography, pp. 386–95. Prints also (pp. 156–60) a list of court rolls printed before 1908.

2581 HALL, HUBERT. A classified list of agrarian surveys in the P.R.O. *Economica*, ii (1922), 28–50.

2582   HONE, N. J. The manor and manorial records. Lond. 1906.
In the series *Antiquary's Books*. App. i contains lists of manor court rolls in (a) the custody of the ecclesiastical commissioners and of the land revenue office, in P.R.O., (b) the B.M., (c) Lambeth Palace library, (d) Bodleian library. Also contains, pp. 312–22, a bibliography of manorial literature. Useful for scattered material in publications of local societies. For other manorial records in the P.R.O., cf. *Lists and Indexes*, nos. 6 (1896) and 25 (1908). For lists of manor court rolls in private hands, cf. *Manorial Soc. Monographs*, nos. 1, 2, 4, by A. L. Hardy, Lond. 1907–10.

2583   MACDONALD, D. Agricultural writers from Sir Walter Henley to Arthur Young (1200–1800). Lond. 1908.
Bibliography, pp. 199–224.

2584   MOORE, M. F. Two select bibliographies of mediaeval historical study. Lond. 1912.
A classified list of work relating to English manorial and agrarian history from the earliest times to the year 1660. Valuable. The app. contains a useful list of periodical publications dealing with manorial history.

2585   THIRSK, JOAN. The content and sources of English agrarian history after 1500. *Agric. Hist. Rev.* iii (1955), 66–79.

(b) *Sources*

There are good general discussions of the sources in Davenport (2579), in Moore (2584), and in Thirsk (2585). MacDonald (2583) lists the contemporary agricultural writers. Manor court rolls, surveys, rentals, extents, terriers, &c., are very numerous, and many of them have been printed in English local archaeological and historical periodicals. Those printed before 1910 are listed in Moore (2584), who also gives convenient lists of local publications which print manorial material. The *Manorial Soc. Monographs*, Lond. 1907, &c., are particularly noteworthy. For unpublished material in general, cf. Hone (2582). Some manorial surveys are printed in county histories. Cf. particularly *C.H. Northumberland* (4660), i, 350 ff.

Contemporary comment on rural conditions, particularly on the enclosure movement, is far scattered. Cf. More's *Utopia* (1365); Hales's *Discourse* (2537); Harrison's *Description* (615); the sermons of Latimer (1732) and Lever (2105); the works of Cranmer (1718), Tyndale (1991), and James Pilkington (2177); Nowell's *Catechism* (2175); Brinkelow's *Complaint* (2098a); Bacon's *Catechism* (1710); Robt. Crowley's *Select works* (1719); Starkey's *Dialogue* (1384); William Forrest, *Pleasant poesie of princelie practice* (in Starkey, *England in the reign of Henry VIII*, E.E.T.S., extra ser., xxxii (1878), app.); Stubbes's *Anatomy of abuses*, Lond. 1583.

Pauli (2538) prints two contemporary tracts on enclosures. Tawney and Power (2539), i, 1–90; iii, 12–81, give much illustrative material from contemporary sources, some of it not elsewhere in print. Some pertinent material is included in ch. iii *supra* (pp. 108 ff.), on local government.

2586   ABSTRACT OF THE BAILIFFS' ACCOUNTS of monastic and other estates in the county of Warwick, 1546–7. . . . By W. B. Buckley. *Dugdale Soc.* ii (1923).

2587 BENESE, RYCHARDE. This boke sheweth the maner of measurynge of all maner of lande, as well of woodlande as of lande in the felde. Southwark [1537?].
4 eds. appeared before 1570. Contains a few pages of valuable general statements concerning contemporary land customs.

2588 BEST, HENRY. Rural economy in Yorkshire n 1641. . . . By C. B. Robinson. *Surtees Soc.* xxxiii (1857).
Though later, is valuable for the details of farming practice.

2589 THE BOOK OF JOHN ROWE, steward of the manors of lord Bergavenny, 1597–1622. By W. H. Godfrey. *Sussex Rec. Soc.* xxxiv (1928).

2590 THE BUCKHURST TERRIER, 1587–8. By Ernest Straker. *Sussex Rec. Soc.* xxxix (1933).

2591 THE LORDSHIP OF CAUSE, 1540–1. *Trans. Shrop. Arch. Soc.* liv (1951–8), 45–68, 327–37.

2592 CERTAYNE CAUSES GATHERED TOGETHER, wherein is shewed the decaye of England only by the great multitude of shepe. . . . By J. M. Cowper. *E.E.T.S.*, extra ser., xiii (1871).
Written about 1550–3.

2593 CHEYNEY, E. P. Social changes in England in the sixteenth century, as reflected in contemporary literature, part i, Rural changes. . . . *University of Pennsylvania Series in Philology, Literature, and Archaeology*, iv, 2 (1895).
No further parts published.

2594 CLARK, ANDREW. Copyhold tenure at Felsted, Essex. *E.H.R.* xxvii (1912), 517–22.
Interesting excerpts from a 1576 MS. survey.

2595 A COLLECTION OF RECORDS AND DOCUMENTS relating to the hundred and manor of Crondal in the county of Southampton. . . . By F. J. Baigent. *Hampshire Rec. Soc.* iii (1891).

2596 THE DOMESDAY OF INCLOSURES, 1517–18. Extant returns to chancery for Berks, Bucks, Cheshire, Essex, Leicestershire, Lincolnshire, Northants, Oxon, Warwickshire, by the commissioners of inclosures in 1517; Bedfordshire, 1518, with Dugdale's MS. notes of Warwickshire inquisitions 1517, 1518, 1549. . . . By I. S. Leadam. 2 vols. *R.H.S.*, 1897.
Cf. for Nottingham, no. 4674 *infra*.

2597 EXTENTS AND SURVEYS OF MANORS in the S.W. of England. By Humberton. *Topographer and Genealogist*, i (2834).
Temp. Philip and Mary.

2598 EXTRACTS FROM THE COURT ROLLS of the manor of Wimbledon. I Edward IV to 1864. . . . By the Common Committee. Wimbledon. Lond. 1866.
In two parts. A general work containing valuable excerpts from manor court records.

2599 FITZHERBERT, [ANTHONY?]. The boke of husbandry. Lond.
1523; by W. W. Skeat. *Eng. Dialect Soc.* xiii (1881).
No less than 10 eds. appeared before 1600. Repr. 1767 (by Vansittart) in *Certain
ancient tracts concerning the management of landed property.* For a discussion of the
authorship, cf. *E.H.R.* xii (1897), 225; *D.N.B.* (9), art. Sir Anthony Fitzherbert, and
Quar. Jour. Econ. xviii (1903–4), 588–93. A practical manual for the husbandman.

2600 FITZHERBERT, [ANTHONY?]. Boke of surveying. Lond. 1523.
No less than 10 eds. appeared before 1600. Repr. by Vansittart (cf. 2599). For authorship, cf. references cited under 2599 *supra*.

2601 HERESBACH, CONRAD. Foure bookes of husbandry . . . conteyning
the whole arte and trade of husbandry, with the antiquitie, and commendation
thereof. Newely Englished and increased. . . . By Barnabe Googe, Lond. 1577.
Translated from the German and enlarged. At least 6 eds. of this trans. appeared before
1615.

2602 HOARE, C. M. The history of an East Anglian soke. . . . Bedf. 1918.
A history of the soke of Gimingham in Norfolk.

2603 LEIGH, VALENTINE. Most profitable and commendable science of
surveying of landes, tenements, &c. Lond. 1577.
4 other eds. appeared before 1600. Commended by Norden.

2604 MASCALL, LEONARD. The first booke of cattell. Lond. 1587.

2607 PLATT, HUGH. The jewell house of art and nature. Conteining divers
rare and profitable inventions, together with sundry new experimentes in the
art of husbandry, distillation and moulding. Lond. 1594.

2609 SCOT, REGINALD. A perfite platforme of a hoppe garden, and necessarie instructions for the making and mayntenaunce thereof. . . . Lond. 1574;
1576; 1578.

2610 A SIXTEENTH-CENTURY survey and year's account of the estate
of Hornby Castle, Lancashire. By W. H. Chippindall. *Chetham Soc.*, n.s.,
cii (1939).

2611 SURVEY OF THE LANDS OF WILLIAM, first earl of Pembroke.
By C. R. Straton. 2 vols. *Roxburghe Club*, 1909.
A valuable series of extents and surveys between 1545 and 1573.

2612 SURVEYS OF THE MANORS of Robertsbridge, Sussex and Michelmarsh, Hampshire, and of the demesne lands of Walden in Rolvenden, Kent,
1567–70. By R. H. D'Elboux. *Sussex Rec. Soc.* xlvii (1944).

2613 TUSSER, THOMAS. A hundreth good points of husbandrie. . . . Lond.
1557; 1573; by W. F. Manor, Lond. 1812; by Dorothy Hartley, Lond. 1931;
by E. V. Lucas, Lond. 1931.
Ed. of 1573 and subsequent eds. are entitled *Five hundreth points of good husbandrie . . .
with huswiferie.* . . . An amusing collection of maxims concerning farming and rural
life given in doggerel verse. Very popular. At least 20 eds. appeared before 1640.
Hartley's ed. contains other writings of Tusser.

(c) *Later Works*

The general works of Ashley (2541), Cunningham (2546), and Lipson (2556)
have valuable chapters on the subject. Cf. also 4529, 4552.

For the enclosure movement, Gonner (2647) gives the best account of the economic factors prompting enclosure; Tawney (2676) of its social consequences. For a detailed study of local conditions reference should be made to the chapters on agriculture in the different vols. of the *Victoria County History* (4203). The conditions on monastic lands and the economic consequences of the dissolution of the monasteries are discussed in Savine (2091), Liljegren (2082), and Habakkuk (2076).

2614   ALLISON, K. J. The sheep-corn husbandry of Norfolk in the sixteenth and seventeenth centuries. *Agric. Hist. Rev.* v (1957), 12–30.

2615   ASHLEY, W. J. The character of villein tenure. *E.H.R.* viii (1893), 294–7.
See Leadam (2656).

2616   BERESFORD, M. W. Lot acres. *Econ. Hist. Rev.* xiii (1943), 74–79.

2617   BERESFORD, M. W. Lost villages of Yorkshire. *Yorks. Arch. Jour.* xxxvii (1948–51), 474–91; xxxviii (1952–5), 44–70, 215–40, 280–309.

2618   BERESFORD, M. W. Glebe terriers and open-field Leicestershire. *Trans. Leics. Arch. Soc.* xxiv (1949), 77–126.

2619   BERESFORD, M. W. The deserted villages of Warwickshire. *Trans. Birm. Arch. Soc.* lxvi (1950), 46–106.

2620   BERESFORD, M. W. The poll tax and census of sheep, 1549. *Agric. Hist. Rev.* i (1953), 9–15; ii (1954), 15–29.

2621   BERESFORD, M. W. The lost villages of England. Lond. 1954.
Cf. J. D. Gould, *Mr. Beresford and the lost villages, Agric. Hist. Rev.* iii (1955), 107–13.

2622   BRADLEY, HARRIET. The enclosures in England. New York, 1918.
Suggestive, but conclusions open to question. Cf. R. Lennard, *The alleged exhaustion of the soil in medieval England, Econ. Jour.,* xxxii (1922), 12–27.

2623   CHEYNEY, E. P. The disappearance of English serfdom. *E.H.R.* xv (1900), 20–37.

2624   CORBETT, W. J. Elizabethan village surveys. *Trans. R.H. Soc.,* 2nd ser., xi (1897), 67–89.

2625   CORNWALL, JULIAN. Farming in Sussex, 1560–1640. *Sussex Arch. Coll.* xcii (1954), 48–92.

2626   CURTLER, W. H. R. The enclosure and redistribution of our land. Oxf. 1920.

2627   DAVENPORT, F. G. The economic development of a Norfolk manor, 1086–1565. Cambr. 1906.
An excellent study of the two manors of Forncett as typical rural communities, with valuable appendixes, most of which, however, refer to medieval conditions.

2628   FABER, RICHARD. Die Entstehung des Agrarschutzes in England. By G. F. Knapp and L. Brentano. *Abhandlungen aus dem staatswissenschaftlichen Seminar zu Straßburg,* v (1888).

2629   FUSSELL, G. E. Four centuries of Cheshire farming systems, 1500–1900. *Trans. Hist. Soc. Lancs. and Ches.* cvi (1955), 52–77.

2630　FUSSELL, G. E. Four centuries of farming systems in Devonshire: 1500–1900. *Trans. Devon. Assoc.* xxxiii (1951).

2631　FUSSELL, G. E. Four centuries of farming systems in Derbyshire: 1500–1900. *Jour. Derbys. Arch. Nat. Hist. Soc.* lxxi (n.s. xxiv) (1952), 1–37.

2632　FUSSELL, G. E. Four centuries of farming systems in Sussex: 1500–1900. *Sussex Arch. Coll.* xc (1952), 60–101.

2633　FUSSELL, G. E. Four centuries of farming systems in Shropshire: 1500–1900. *Trans. Shrop. Arch. Soc.* liv (1951–2), 1–29.

2634　FUSSELL, G. E. Missing Tudor books on farming. *Times Lit. Supp.*, no. 1864 (1937), 788.

2635　FUSSELL, G. E. Rowland Vaughan. An Elizabethan agriculturist. *Estate Mag.* xxxvi (1936), 738–41.

2636　FUSSELL, G. E. Early English books on fruit trees. *Estate Mag.* xxxvii (1937), 94–95.

2637　FUSSELL, G. E. The old English farming books from Fitzherbert to Tull, 1523–1730. Lond. 1947.

2638　FUSSELL, G. E. Crop nutrition in Tudor and early Stuart England. *Agr. Hist. Rev.* iii (1955), 95–106.

2639　FUSSELL, G. E. Four centuries of Leicestershire farming. *Studies in Leics. agrarian history, Trans. Leics. Arch. Soc.* xxiv (1949), 159–76.

2640　FUSSELL, G. E. Farming systems from Elizabethan to Victorian days in the north and east Ridings of Yorkshire. York, 1944.

2641　GARNIER, R. M. History of the English landed interest. 2 vols. Lond. 1892.
This and the succeeding work, although semi-popular and not entirely critical, are made invaluable by the author's familiarity with the actual rural life of which he writes.

2642　GARNIER, R. M. Annals of the British peasantry. Lond. 1895.

2643　GAY, E. F. Inclosures in England in the sixteenth century. *Quar. Jour. Econ.* xvii (1903), 576–97.
A pioneer work. Figures now open to question.

2644　GAY, E. F. The inquisitions of depopulation in 1517 and the domesday of inclosures. *Trans. R.H. Soc.*, 2nd ser., xiv (1900), 101, 231–67, and 286–303.
Largely critical of Leadam (2596 and 2654).

2645　GAY, E. F. Zur Geschichte der Einhegungen in England. Berlin, 1902.
Berlin Ph.D. thesis. A valuable study.

2646　GAY, E. F. The midland revolt and the inquisitions of depopulation of 1607. *Trans. R.H. Soc.*, 2nd ser., xviii (1904), 195–237.
About one-third of this article refers to the sixteenth century.

2647　GONNER, E. C. K. Common land and inclosure. Lond. 1912.
Valuable for the economic factors prompting enclosure.

2648　GRAY, H. L. English field systems. *Harvard Hist. Studies*, xxii (1915).
The standard book on the subject.

2649 HOSKINS, W. G. The reclamation of the waste in Devon, 1550–1800. *Econ. Hist. Rev.* xiii (1943), 80–92.

2650 HOSKINS, W. G. The Leicestershire farmer in the sixteenth century. In *Essays in Leicestershire history.* Liverpool, 1950.

2651 HOSKINS, W. G. The deserted villages of Leicestershire. In *Essays in Leicestershire history.* Liverpool, 1950.

2652 HOSKINS, W. G. The rebuilding of rural England, 1570–1640. *Past and Present,* iv (1953), 44–56.

2653 JOHNSON, A. H. The disappearance of the small landowner. Oxf. 1909.
Ford lectures, 1909. Lecture iii is a valuable survey of enclosures from the fifteenth to the seventeenth centuries.

2654 LEADAM, I. S. The inquisition of 1517. Inclosures and evictions. *Trans. R.H. Soc.,* 2nd ser., vi (1892), 167–314; vii (1893), 127–292; viii (1894), 251–331; xiv (1900), 267–86.
Printed from *Lansdowne MSS.* i, 153, with introduction, notes, and appendixes. Cf. Gay's criticisms (2644).

2655 LEADAM, I. S. The last days of bondage in England. *Law Quar. Rev.* ix (1893), 348–65.

2656 LEADAM, I. S. The security of copyholders in the fifteenth and sixteenth centuries. *E.H.R.* viii (1893), 684–96.
Answering Ashley's criticism (2615).

2657 LENNARD, REGINALD. Custom and change in sixteenth century England. *E.H.R.* xxviii (1913), 745–8.
A short but significant contribution to the problem of fixity of tenure.

2658 MALDEN, H. E. Bondmen in Surrey under the Tudors. *Trans. R.H. Soc.,* 2nd ser., xix (1905), 305–7.

2659 NASSE, ERWIN, Über die mittelalterliche Feldgemeinschaft und die Einhegungen des sechzehnten Jahrhunderts in England. Bonn, 1869.
This was the earliest of the modern studies on the enclosure movement. An English trans. (by H. A. Ouvry) was published, Lond. 1871, by the *Cobden Club.*

2660 ORWIN, C. S. and C. S. The open fields. Oxf. 1938; 1954.

2661 PALMER, W. M. Enclosures at Ely, Downham, and Littleport, A.D. 1548. *Trans. Cambs. and Hunts. Arch. Soc.* v (1936), 369–84.

2662 PARKER, L. A. The agrarian revolution at Cotesbach, 1501–1612. *Trans. Leics. Arch. Soc.* xxiv (1949), 41–76.

2663 PURVIS, J. S. A note on XVI century farming in Yorkshire. *Yorks. Arch. Jour.* xxxvi (1944–7), 435–54.

2664 PEYTON, S. A. The village population in the Tudor lay subsidy rolls. *E.H.R.* xxx (1915), 234–50.
Indicates that fixity of population was less than generally supposed. Much valuable information on the assessment of the subsidy.

2665 PROTHERO, R. W. (LORD ERNLE). English farming past and present. Lond. 1912; 1919.
Supersedes his earlier work, *The pioneers and progress of English farming* (1888). Valuable, especially by reason of the familiarity of the author with rural conditions. App. contains a useful list of early writers on agriculture.

2666 RODGERS, H. B. Land use in Tudor Lancashire; the evidence of the final concords, 1450–1558. *Inst. of British Geographers, Trans. and Papers,* 1955.

2667 SALAMAN, R. N. The history and social influence of the potato. Cambr. 1949.

2668 SAVINE, ALEXANDER. English customary tenure in the Tudor period. *Quar. Jour. Econ.* xix (1904–5), 33–80.
This is a summary in English of the author's Russian work on the English village of the Tudor period.

2669 SAVINE, ALEXANDER. Bondmen under the Tudors. *Trans. R.H. Soc.,* 2nd ser., xvii (1903), 235–89.
A valuable article with statistics. Cf. 2658.

2670 SAVINE, ALEXANDER. Copyhold cases in the early chancery proceedings. *E.H.R.* xvii (1902), 296–303.
Fifteenth-century origins of sixteenth-century conditions.

2671 SCRIVEN, JOHN. A practical treatise on copyhold tenure and court keeping. 2 vols. Lond. 1816–23.
A useful statement of the legal side of landholding. Title of 2nd vol. differs somewhat from 1st.

2672 SEMEONOV, V. P. Enclosures and peasant revolts in England in the sixteenth century. Moscow, 1949.
In Russian. Cf. *Econ. Hist. Rev.,* 2nd ser., iii (1950), 138–9.

2673 STEFFEN, G. F. Studien zur Geschichte der englischen Lohnarbeiter, 1401–1662. 3 vols. Stuttgart (1903–6).
This is a German trans. (by Margarite Langfeldt) from a Swedish original. Largely based on Rogers (2570). Contains (i, 365–8) price tables, 1541–1662.

2674 STRATTON, C. R. An English manor in the time of Elizabeth. *Wilts. Arch. and Nat. Hist. Mag.* xxxii (1902), 288–310.

2675 TATE, W. E. Enclosure acts and awards relating to Warwickshire. *Trans. Birm. Arch. Soc.* lxv (1949), 45–104.

2676 TAWNEY, R. H. The agrarian problem in the sixteenth century. Lond. 1912.
A valuable work, particularly on the social aspects of the problem.

2677 TROW-SMITH, R. English husbandry. Lond. 1951.

2678 TROW-SMITH, R. A history of British livestock husbandry to 1700. Lond. 1957.

2679 THIRSK, JOAN. Farming in Kesteven, 1540–1640. *Linc. Archit. and Arch. Soc. Reports and Papers,* n.s., vi (1955–6), 37–53.

2680 THIRSK, JOAN. Fenland farming in the sixteenth century. *Dept. of Local Hist. Occ. Papers,* no. 3. Univ. Coll. of Leicester, 1953.

3. INDUSTRY AND INDUSTRIAL ORGANIZATION

A. GENERAL

(a) *Bibliography*

The general bibliographies in Cunningham (2546), Lipson (2556), Scott (3009), and Westerfield (2694) should be consulted; also Unwin (2693) and Ashley (2541), bibliographical note, ii, ch. 2.

Industrial organization in the sixteenth century was almost entirely local in character. Reference should therefore be made to bibliographies cited under local history.

(b) *Sources*

Selected documents are printed in (2539), i, 90–140; and in (2536), 279–302. The printed records of many towns contain important material, cf. Gross (1), nos. 2716a (Beverley), 2477 (Preston), 2487 (Leicester), 2684a (Stratford), 2685 (Knowle), 2744, 2750a (York), 2546a (Norwich), 2681a (Coventry), 864 (Chester), 2276 (Reading). Cf. ch. xi *infra*.

The attitude of the national government towards industry is set forth in the *Statutes* (1016), the *Proclamations* (1017), and the *Acts of Privy Council* (1152), cf. also sect. 4 *infra* (pp. 239 ff.). Scattered material is to be found in *Letters and Papers Henry VIII* (91), *Cal. S.P., Domestic, Edward VI–Elizabeth* (86), and in the vols. of the *Hist. MSS. Comm.*, pp. 10 ff. *supra*. The records of the Court of Star Chamber (1683–92) disclose a good deal of industrial litigation.

For contemporary comments on industrial questions, cf. Hales (2537), Harrison (615), Pauli (2538), Crowley's works (1719), Lever's sermons (2105), and Deloney's works (2682).

2681 CHOLMELEY, WILLIAM. The request and suite of a true-hearted Englishman. By W. J. Thomas. *Camden Soc. Misc.* ii (1853).
Written in the year 1553. An interesting essay on the industrial and commercial condition of England.

2682 DELONEY, THOMAS. The pleasant history of John Winchcomb . . . called Jack of Newberry, the famous . . . clothier. Lond. 1597; by J. O. Halliwell, Lond. 1859; best ed. F. O. Mann, Oxf. 1912.
The 10th ed. appeared in 1637. Contains a metrical account of a sixteenth-century cloth factory. Cf. also A. Chevalley, *Thomas Deloney: le roman des métiers au temps de Shakespeare*, Paris, 1926; and Kuehn, G. W. *The novels of Thomas Deloney as source for climate of opinion in sixteenth-century economic history*, *Jour. Pol. Econ.* xlviii (1940), 865–75.

2683 ENGLISH GILDS. By J. T. Smith and L. J. Smith. *E.E.T.S.* xl (1870).
With an introduction by Lujo Brentano on the history and development of English gilds, also printed separately (Lond. 1870). The documents printed are almost all of them earlier than 1485. Brentano's brilliant essay is unreliable.

(c) *Later Works*

Unwin (2693) is the standard account. Cf. also Lipson (2556), i, Cunningham (2546), and Ashley (2541), and Unwin's chapter in *Shakespeare's England* (2573), i, ch. xi. On the effect of the Chantries Act of 1547 upon gild organization Ashley (2541), ii, ch. ii, controverts the position of Rogers (2569), Brentano (2683), and the original position of Cunningham, later modified (e.g. ed. 1905, i, 522). Cf. also on this subject Kramer (2689) and *Chantries certificates* (2100).

2684　CAMP, C. W. The artisan in English literature. New York. 1924.

2685　CUNNINGHAM, WILLIAM. The formation and decay of crafts gilds. *Trans. R.H. Soc.*, 2nd ser., iii (1886), 371–92.

2686　DUNLOP, O. J. English apprenticeship and child labour. Lond. 1912.

2687　GAY, M. R. Aspects of Elizabethan apprenticeship. In *Facts and factors in economic history*. Cambr., U.S.A., 1932.

2688　GROSS, CHARLES. The gild merchant. 2 vols. Oxf. 1890.
The standard work. Vol. ii contains documents.

2689　KRAMER, STELLA. The English craft gilds: studies in their progress and decline. New York, 1927.

2689a　KRAMER, STELLA. The English craft gilds and the government. New York, 1905.

2690　NEF, J. U. A comparison of industrial growth in France and England from 1540 to 1640. *Jour. Pol. Econ.* xliv (1936), 289–317, 505–33, 643–66.

2691　NEF, J. U. The progress of technology and the growth of large scale industry in Great Britain, 1540–1640. *Econ. Hist. Rev.* v (1934), 3–24.

2692　MARSHALL, T. H. Capitalism and the decline of the English gilds. *Cambr. Hist. Jour.* iii (1929), 23–33.

2693　UNWIN, GEORGE. Industrial organization in the sixteenth and seventeenth centuries. Oxf. 1904.
A valuable detailed study of the crafts and companies in the latter part of the sixteenth and early part of the seventeenth centuries; with bibliography. Written of western Europe in general, but referring more specifically to England.

2694　WESTERFIELD, R. B. Middlemen in English business. . . . *Trans. Connect. Acad. of Arts and Sciences*, xix (1915), 111–445.
Though dealing specifically with the period 1660–1760 contains much of value for earlier period.

B. Local Industries

1. *The London Companies*

(a) *Bibliography*

2695　WELCH, CHARLES. The bibliography of the livery companies of the city of London. Lond. 1890.

(b) *General Works*

2696　CHEESEWRIGHT, R. J. An historical essay on the livery companies of London with a short history of the worshipful company of cutlers of London. [Croydon], 1881.
Of slight value.

2697 COOTE, H. C. Ordinances of some secular gilds. *Trans. Lond. and Middx. Arch. Soc.* iv (1871).
Includes ordinances of glovers, blacksmiths, shearmen, and water-bearers.

2698 CITY OF LONDON LIVERY COMPANIES COMMISSION. *Parliamentary papers*, 1884, xxxix, 5 parts.

2699 HAZLITT, W. C. The livery companies of the city of London. Lond. 1892.
A work containing much material rather uncritically used.

2700 HERBERT, WILLIAM. The history of the twelve great livery companies of London; principally compiled from their grants and records. 2 vols. Lond. 1837.
Prints many documents. Often inaccurate but indispensable.

2701 UNWIN, GEORGE. The gilds and companies of London. Lond. 1908; 3rd ed. 1938.
In the series *Antiquary's Books*. Valuable.

(c) *Histories of the separate companies*

Books on the separate London companies are arranged below alphabetically by trades. Nearly all of them contain both source material and comment. They vary greatly in scholarly attributes. The best are 2707, 2713, 2715, 2733.

(1) Barber Surgeons

2702 YOUNG, SIDNEY. The annals of the barber surgeons of London. Lond. 1890.
With many documents. Cf. also 4048.

(2) Bakers

2703 THRUPP, SYLVIA. A short history of the worshipful company of bakers of London. Lond. 1933.

(3) Basket Makers

2704 BOBART, H. H. Records of the basket makers' company. Lond. 1911.
Prints many documents.

(4) Blacksmiths

2705 ADAMS, A. The history of the worshipful company of blacksmiths from early times until the year 1785. Lond. 1951.

(5) Carmen

2706 BENNETT, E. The worshipful company of carmen of London: a short history. Lond. 1952.

(6) Carpenters

2707 RECORDS OF THE WORSHIPFUL COMPANY OF CARPENTERS. By Bower Marsh. 4 vols. Oxf. 1913–16; vol. v, Warden's account book, 1571–91, by John Ainsworth, Phillimore, 1937; vol. vi, Court book, 1573–94, Lond. 1939.

2708 JUPP, E. B. An historical account of the worshipful company of carpenters of the city of London. Lond. 1848; by W. W. Pocock, Lond. 1887.
Prints many documents.

(7) Cloth Workers

2709 THE ORDINANCES OF THE CLOTH WORKERS' COMPANY. Lond. 1881.
Documents; cf. also *The charters . . . granted to . . . the cloth workers co.* Lond. 1881.

(8) Coopers

2710 COOPERS' COMPANY: HISTORICAL MEMORANDA, Charters, Documents, &c. By J. F. Firth. Lond. 1848.

2711 FOSTER, WILLIAM. A short history of the worshipful company of coopers of London. Cambr. 1944.

(9) Cordwainers

2712 MANDER, C. H. W. A descriptive and historical account of the . . . cordwainers of . . . London. Lond. 1932.

(10) Cutlers

Cf. also Cheesewright (2696).

2713 WELCH, CHARLES. History of the cutlers' company of London and of the minor cutlery crafts, with biographical notices of early London cutlers. 2 vols. Lond. 1916–23.
Vol. ii completed by Herbert Welch. Valuable. Prints many documents.

(11) Drapers

2714 CONNELL-SMITH, G. The ledger of Thomas Howell. *Econ. Hist. Rev.*, 2nd ser., iii (1951), 363–70.
Howell was a draper.

2715 JOHNSON, A. H. The history of the worshipful company of drapers 5 vols. Oxf. 1914–22.
Vols. i and ii cover period to 1603. Scholarly.

(12) Dyers

2716 ROBINS, E. C. Some account of the history and antiquities of the worshipful company of dyers. *Trans. of Lond. and Middx. Arch. Soc.* v (1881), 441–76.

(13) Founders

2717 WILLIAMS, W. M. Annals of the . . . founders . . . of London. [Lond.] 1867.
Prints documents, but slight before 1600.

(14) Girdlers

2718 SMYTHE, W. D. An historical account of the . . . girdlers of . . . London. Lond. 1905.
Slight.

(15) Goldsmiths

2719 HEAL, AMBROSE. The London goldsmiths, 1200–1800. Cambr. 1935.

2720 PRIDEAUX, W. S. Memorials of the goldsmiths' company, being gleanings from their records between the years 1335 and 1815. 2 vols. Lond. 1896.
Chiefly on the seventeenth century.

(16) Grocers

2721 HEATH, J. B. Some account of the worshipful company of grocers of the city of London. Lond. 1829; enl. 1854; 1869.
Scholarly. Prints many documents, but slight on sixteenth century. Cf. also *List of the wardens of the grocers company from 1345 to 1907*, by W. W. Grantham, Lond. 1907

2722 REES, J. A. The worshipful company of grocers, an historical retrospect, 1345–1923. Lond. 1923.
Slight.

(17) Horners

2723 COMPTON, C. H. The history of the worshipful company of horners of London. *Jour. Brit. Arch. Assoc.* xxxv (1882), 372–9.
Cf. also H. G. Rosedale, *Some notes on the old book of the . . . horners*, [Lond.] 1911.

(18) Ironmongers

2724 NICHOLL, JOHN. Some account of the worshipful company of ironmongers. Lond. 1851; enl. 1866.
Prints documents.

2725 NOBLE, T. C. A brief history of the . . . ironmongers, London, A.D. 1351–1889. Lond. 1889.
Contains an app. on the blacksmiths' company. Cf. also 2697.

(19) Joiners

2726 ANNALS OF THE . . . JOINERS OF . . . LONDON. By H. L. Phillips. Lond. 1915.
Documents, but very slight on sixteenth century.

(20) Leathersellers

2727 BLACK, W. H. History and antiquities of the worshipful company of leathersellers of the city of London. Lond. 1871.

(21) Masons

2728 CONDER, JR., EDWARD. Records of the hole crafte and fellowship of masons. Lond. 1894.
Prints some source material, but slight on sixteenth century.

(22) Mercers

2729 ACTS OF COURT OF THE MERCERS' COMPANY, 1453–1527. By Laetitia Lyell and F. D. Watney. Cambr. 1936.

2730 CHARTERS, ORDINANCES AND BYE-LAWS of the mercers' company (1393–1808). Lond. 1881.

2731 WATNEY, J. History of the mercers' company. . . . Lond. 1914.
Very slight.

(23) Merchant Taylors

2732 THE CHARTERS OF THE MERCHANT TAYLORS' COMPANY. By F. M. Fry and R. T. D. Sayle. s.l. 1937.

2733 CLODE, C. M. Memorials of the guild of merchant taylors of the fraternity of St. John the Baptist in the city of London. Lond. 1875.
Prints many documents. Valuable.

2734 CLODE, C. M. The early history of the guild of merchant taylors. 2 vols. Lond. 1888.

2735 FACSIMILE OF ANCIENT DEEDS of the merchant taylors, 1331–1531. Lond. 1889.

(24) Painter-stainers

2736 ENGLEFIELD, W. A. D. History of the painter-stainers. . . . Lond. 1923.
Slight.

(25) Paviors

2737 WELCH, CHARLES. History of the worshipful company of paviors of the city of London. [Lond.] 1909.
Slight, but prints documents.

(26) Pewterers

2738 WELCH, CHARLES. History of the worshipful company of pewterers of the city of London. 2 vols. Lond. 1902.

(27) Plumbers

2739 WALDO, F. J. Short history of the worshipful company of plumbers. 2nd ed. Lond. 1923.
Slight.

(28) Poulters

2740 JONES, P. E. The worshipful company of poulters of the city of London. Lond. 1939.

(29) Saddlers

2741 SHERWELL, J. W. Descriptive and historical account of the guild of saddlers. . . . [Lond.], 1889.
Slight on sixteenth century.

(30) Shipwrights

2742 RECORDS OF THE WORSHIPFUL COMPANY OF SHIP-WRIGHTS. Vol. i, 1428–1780. By C. H. Ridge. Lond. 1940; vol. ii, 1728–1858, Lond. 1946.

2743 SHARPE, R. R. A short account of the worshipful company of ship-wrights. Lond. 1876.

(31) Skinners

2744 RECORDS OF THE SKINNERS OF LONDON, Edward I to James I. By J. J. Lambert. Lond. 1934.

2745 WADMORE, J. F. History and antiquities of the company of skinners. Lond. 1902.
Scholarly; prints documents.

(32) Stationers

2746 RIVINGTON, C. R. The records of the worshipful company of stationers. 2nd ed. Edin. 1883.
Cf. also idem, *A short account of the . . . Stationers.* Lond. 1903.

2747 HODGSON, SIDNEY. The worshipful company of stationers and newspaper makers. Lond. 1953.
Cf. also 36, 3678.

(33) Tallow-chandlers

2748 MONIER-WILLIAMS, M. F. Records of the . . . tallow-chandlers. Vol. i (no more published). Lond. 1897.

(34) Turners

2749 STANLEY-STONE, A. C. The . . . turners of London. Lond. 1925.
Slight, but prints documents.

(35) Tylers

2750 BELL, W. G. A short history of the worshipful company of tylers and bricklayers of the city of London. Lond. 1939.

(36) Vintners

Cf. also (3012).

2751 MILBOURN, THOMAS. The vintners' company. Lond. 1888.
Slight, but prints documents.

(37) Watermen

2752 HUMPHERUS, H. History of the . . . company of watermen and lightermen of the river Thames. 3 vols. Lond. [1887–9?].

(38) Weavers

2753 CONSITT, FRANCES. The London weavers' company. Oxf. 1933.

2. *Local Industries outside London*

(a) *Sources*

2754 ACTS AND ORDINANCES OF THE COMPANY OF MERCHANT TAYLORS IN THE CITY OF YORK. By B. Johnson. York, 1949.

2755 CALENDAR OF THE BRISTOL APPRENTICE BOOK, 1532–65. Pt. i: 1532–42. By D. Hollis. *Bristol Rec. Soc.* xiv (1949).

2756 MINNS, E. H. A Cambridge vintner's accounts, *c.* 1511. *Proc. Cambr. Antiq. Soc.* xxxiv (1934), 50–58.

2757 THE EARLIEST BOOK OF THE DRAPERS' COMPANY of Shrewsbury. By I. M. Rope and C. H. Drinkwater. *Shrop. Arch. and Nat. Hist. Soc. Trans.*, 4th ser., iii (1913), 135–262; iv (1914), 195–247; ix (1923–4), pt. ii, 258–77; x (1925–6), 193–208; xi (1927–8), 141–82.

2758 PROCEEDINGS, MINUTES and ENROLMENTS of the company of Soapmakers [Bristol], 1562–1642. By H. E. Matthews. *Bristol Rec. Soc. Pub.* x (1940).

(b) *Later Works*

2759 FOWLER, J. T. Account book of William Wray, draper at Ripon, 1581–1602. *Antiquary*, xxxii (1896), 54–375 *passim*.

2760 GROOMBRIDGE, M. J. The city gilds of Chester. *Jour. Chester and N. Wales Archit., Arch., and Hist. Soc.* xxxix (1952), 93–108.

2761 FRETTON, W. G. Memorials of the fullers' gild at Coventry. Coventry, 1878.

2762 HIBBERT, F. A. The influence and development of English gilds as illustrated by the history of the craft gilds of Shrewsbury. Cambr. 1891.

2763 JONES, L. The antiente company of smiths and others commonly called hammermen. *Shrop. Arch. and Nat. Hist. Soc. Trans.,* 1st ser., xi (1888), 291–324.

2764 LAMBERT, J. M. Two thousand years of gild life ... with a full account of the gilds and trading companies of Kingston-upon-Hull. Hull, 1891.
The principal value of this work is in the documents it contains respecting the companies of Hull, principally in the sixteenth century.

2765 LEIGHTON, W. A. The gilds of Shrewsbury. *Shrop. Arch. and Nat. Hist. Soc. Trans.,* 1st ser., iv (1881), 193–292; v (1882), 265–97; vii (1884), 408–30; viii (1885), 269–412.

2766 MENDENHALL, T. C. The Shrewsbury drapers and the Welsh wool trade in the XVI and XVII centuries. Lond. 1953.
On records of shearmen, discovered since, cf. *Jour. Nat. Lib. Wales,* viii (1953–4), 110.

2767 MENDENHALL, T. C. The social status of the more prominent Shrewsbury drapers, 1560–1660. *Trans. Shrop. Arch. Soc.* liv (1953), 163–70.

C. The History of Particular Industries

1. General

Much pertinent material on particular industries will be found in sects. A and B *supra.* The arts as distinguished from the crafts are dealt with in ch. x *infra,* cf. particularly pp. 326 ff.

2768b SALZMAN, L. F. English industries of the middle ages. Lond. 1913; Oxf. 1923.
One of the best accounts of mining and industrial technique. 2nd ed. reproduces many valuable contemporary illustrations.

2. Textiles

The manufacture of textiles, notably woollen cloths, was easily the most important of English industries in the sixteenth century. It was a matter of great concern to the state, as appears in the *Acts of Privy Council* (1152), the *Royal proclamations* (1017), and the *Statutes* (1016). Its importance in foreign trade and through foreign trade upon foreign policy was profound. Reference should therefore be made to section 7 *infra* (pp. 249 ff.), on trade, and to ch. ii *supra* on foreign policy.

2768c BOWDEN, P. J. Wool supply and the woollen industry. *Econ. Hist. Rev.,* 2nd ser., ix (1956), 44–58.

2768d DALE, M. K. The London silkwomen of the fifteenth century. *Econ. Hist. Rev.* iv (1933), 324–45.

2768e DANIELS, G. W. The early history of the English cotton industry. Manchester, 1920.
A small but significant work with only slight reference to the use of cotton in the sixteenth century.

2768f HEATON, HERBERT. The Yorkshire woollen and worsted industries. *Oxf. Hist. and Lit. Studies*, x (1920).
Cf. also K. G. Ponting, *A history of the west of England cloth industry*. Lond. 1957.

2768g HEWART, BEATRICE. The cloth trade in the north of England in the sixteenth and seventeenth centuries. *Econ. Jour.* x (1900), 20–31.

2768h JAMES, JOHN. History of the worsted manufacture in England. Lond 1857.
Chiefly on the period since 1600.

2768i LIPSON, EPHRAIM. English woollen and worsted industries. Lond. 1921; rev. ed. 1953.

2770 McCLENAGHAN, BEATRICE. The Springs of Lavenham and the Suffolk cloth trade in the fifteenth and sixteenth centuries. Ipswich, 1924.

2771 PERRY, R. The Gloucestershire woollen industry 1100–1690. *Trans. Bristol and Glos. Arch. Soc.* lxvi (1947), 49–137.

2771a POSTHUMUS, N. W. De neringen in de Republiek. *K. Nederlandsche Akad. Wetenschappen Meded., Afd. Letterkunde,* lxxxiv, ser. B (1937), 1–83.
Includes regulations for bays and says in Norwich, 1581, 1583.

2772 RAMSAY, G. D. The Wiltshire woollen industry in the sixteenth and seventeenth centuries. *Oxf. Hist. Stud.*, Lond. 1943.

2773 RAMSAY, G. D. The distribution of the cloth industry in 1561–2. *E.H.R.* lvii (1942), 361–9.

2774 SMITH, JOHN. Chronicon rusticum commerciale, or memoirs of wool. 2 vols. Lond. 1747; 1756–7.
The best work on this subject.

2775 WILLIAMS, N. J. Two documents concerning the new draperies. *Econ. Hist. Rev.*, 2nd ser., iv (1952), 353–8.

3. *The Extractive Industries*

(a) *Bibliography*

For early treatises on mining and metallurgy, cf. Agricola (2777), Hoover's trans., app. ii. Cf. also Lewis (2806), 281–8.

2776 FERGUSON, JOHN. Bibliotheca chemica. 2 vols. Glasgow, 1906.
Contains many titles on mining and metallurgy.

(b) *General*

Salzman (2768b) contains a good brief account of the technique of mining. The articles on the extractive industries in the vols. of the *Victoria County Histories* (4203) are of first-rate importance. Scott (3009), ii, 383 ff., deals with early mining companies. On the status of free miners, cf. *V.C.H. Glos.* ii, 214 ff. On early mining law, cf. Lewis (2806), 65–85. Tawney and Power (2539), i, 229–92, print many documents, most of them not elsewhere in print. The work of Sir John Pettus, *Fodinae Regales* (Lond. 1670) and *Fleta Minor* (Lond. 1683), dealing with mining and mineral law in the seventeenth century, are useful. Cf. also *A collection of scarce and valuable treatises upon metals, mines, and minerals* (Lond. 1740).

2777   AGRICOLA (BAUER), GEORG. De re metallica. Basel, 1556.
The most important book on mining and metallurgy between 1500 and 1700. Describes minutely various methods of mining, smelting, &c. Contains many valuable illustrative woodcuts. An English trans. by Herbert and Lou H. Hoover, published in Lond. 1912, 1950, contains a sketch of author, a bibliography of his writings, and elaborate footnotes on the text by a mining engineer. The original illustrations are reproduced. App. ii of trans. contains a useful survey of the literature of mining and metallurgy to 1556. Cf. also *Lazarus Erekar's Treatise on Ores and Assaying.* Trans. from German ed. of 1580. By A. G. Sisco and C. S. Smith. Chicago, 1951.

2778   BEKKER, ERNST. Deutsche Bergleute, Münzverfeinerer und Lands-knechte in England. *Giessener Studien aus dem Gebiet der Geschichte, Beiträge zur englischen Geschichte im Zeitalter Elisabeths,* i (1899), 1–17.
An interesting account of a company formed to develop English mines.

2779   DONALD, M. B. Burchard Kranich (*c.* 1515–78), miner and Queen's physician, Cornish mining stamps, antimony and Frobisher's gold. *Annals of Science,* vi (1950), 308–22.

(c) *Coal*

(1) Sources

A great deal of MS. material bearing on the subject is to be found in the P.R.O. and in the Corporation records of Newcastle. The *MSS. of Lord Middleton* (163) are valuable as are the *Extracts from the Records of the . . . hostmen, New-castle-on-Tyne* (by F. W. Dendy, *Surtees Soc.* cv (1901)). Owen's *Description of Pembrokeshire* (6335) contains something on Welsh coal-mining. Platt's pamphlet (2780) is almost the only contemporary treatise dealing with the use of coal. Cf. Agricola (2777) for illustrations of mining technique. R. Greene (4166) has something to say about the dishonesty of coal dealers. Cf. also Tawney and Power (2539), i. 267–89.

2780   PLATT, HUGH. A new, cheap and delicate fire of cole-balles, wherein sea cole is by mixture of other combustible bodies both sweetened and multi-plied. Lond. 1603.
Cf. C. F. Mullett, *Hugh Plat: Elizabethan virtuoso, Studies in honor of A. H. R. Fair-child, Univ. of Missouri Studies,* xxi (1946), i, 91–118.

(2) Later Works

Nef (2787) is much the best history. The chapters on coal mining in the *Victoria County Histories* (4203) and in the *C.H. of Northumberland* (4660) are generally good, cf. also 4663.

2781   BAILEY, F. A. Early coal mining in Prescot, Lancashire. *Trans. Hist. Soc. Lancs. and Ches.* xcix (1947), 1–20.

2782   BANKES, J. H. M. Records of mining in Winstanley and Orrell, near Wigan. *Trans. Lancs. and Ches. Antiq. Soc.* liv (1939), 31–64.

2783   DALE, H. B. The fellowship of woodmongers. Lond. 1924.
Unscholarly, but useful for the early London coal trade.

2784   CROFTON, R. C. Lancashire and Cheshire coal mining records. *Trans. Lancs. and Ches. Antiq. Soc.* vii (1889), 26–73.
A collection of extracts from documents in print. Useful.

2785   GALLOWAY, R. L. A history of coal mining in Great Britain. 2 vols. Lond. 1882.
This work and the one following are still valuable. The *Annals* contains more material, but the *History* alone includes Scotland.

2786   GALLOWAY, R. L. Annals of coal mining and the coal trade. Lond. 1898–1904.

2787   NEF, J. U. The rise of the British coal industry. 2 vols. Lond. 1932.
The standard work.

2788   STONE, LAWRENCE. An Elizabethan coal mine. *Econ. Hist. Rev.*, 2nd ser., iii (1950), 97–106.

2789   SWEEZY, P. M. Monopoly and competition in the English coal trade, 1550–1850. *Harvard Econ. Stud.* lxiii. Cambr., U.S.A., 1938.

2790   TAYLOR, T. J. The archaeology of the coal trade. *Arch. Inst. of Gt. Brit. and Ireland Proc. at Newcastle 1852* (Lond. 1858), i, 150–223.
Cf. also J. B. Simpson, *Coal mining by the monks*, Newcastle, 1910.

(d) *Iron*

(1) Sources

There is very little in print. Accounts of iron works in Sussex and in Wales, 1541–68, are printed in part in *De Lisle and Dudley MSS.* (124), 305–21, and there is scattered material in other private collections, notably in *Lord Middleton's MSS.* (163) and in *Salisbury MSS.* (185). The P.R.O. contains much material, some of it calendared in *Letters and Papers, Henry VIII* (91), some of it briefly indexed in *Cal. S.P., Domestic* (86), much of it in *Exchequer K.R.* accounts, and elsewhere, still unprinted.

(2) Later Works

2791   BECK, LUDWIG. Die Geschichte des Eisens. 5 vols. Brunswick, 1884–1903.
The standard work.

2792   JENKINS, RHYS. The beginnings of iron-founding in England. In *Collected Papers*. Cambr. 1936.

2793   LOWER, M. A. Iron works of the county of Sussex. *Sussex Arch. Coll.* ii (1849), 169–220; iii (1850), 240–8; xviii (1866), 10–16.

2794   LLEWELLIN, W. Sussex iron masters in Glamorganshire. *Arch. Cambr.*, 3rd ser., ix (1863), 81–119.
Prints documents, chiefly sixteenth century.

2795 LLEWELLIN, W. Some account of the iron and wire works of Tintern. *Arch. Cambr.*, 3rd ser., ix (1863), 291–318.
Prints documents, chiefly sixteenth century.

2796 NICHOLLS, H. G. Iron making in the olden times as instanced in the ancient mines, forges and furnaces of the forest of Dean, &c. Lond. 1866.
Cf. also on the forest of Dean mines, *Brit. Arch. Jour.* xvii; Rudder, *Gloucestershire* (4398) and *V.C.H. Glos.* (4203). Cf. also *Reports of the Dean forest commissioners, Parl. papers*, 1835, vol. xxxvi, and *Report from the select committees on Dean forest, Parl. papers*, 1874, vol. ii. Cf. also 1347; *The commoners of Dean Forest*, by C. E. Hart, Gloucester, 1951; and *The verderers and Speech-Court of the Forest of Dean*, idem, Gloucester, 1950.

2797 STRAKER, ERNEST. Wealden iron . . . a history of the industry from the earliest times. . . . Lond. 1931.
A history of iron works in Sussex, Surrey, and Kent.

2798 PELHAM, R. A. The establishment of the Willoughby ironworks in north Warwickshire in the sixteenth century. *Univ. of Birm. Hist. Jour.* iv (1953), 18–29.

2799 PELHAM, R. A. The migration of the iron industry towards Birmingham during the sixteenth century. *Trans. Birm. Arch. Soc.* lxvi (1950).

2800 MATHEW, DAVID and GERVAISE. Iron furnaces in South-eastern England and English ports and landing-places, 1578. *E.H.R.* xlviii (1933), 91–99.

2801 NEF, J. U. Note on the progress of iron production in England, 1540–1640. *Jour. Pol. Econ.* xliv (1936), 398–403.

2802 SCHUBERT, H. R. The first cast-iron cannon made in England. *Jour. Iron and Steel Inst.* cxlvi (1942), 131–40.

2803 SCHUBERT, H. R. History of the British iron and steel industry from *c.* 450 B.C. to A.D. 1775. Lond. 1957.

2804 SCHUBERT, H. R. Shrewsbury letters. A contribution to the history of ironmaking. *Jour. Iron and Steel Inst.* clv (1947), 521–5.

2805 SCHUBERT, H. R. The economic aspect of Sir Henry Sidney's steel works at Robertsbridge, in Sussex and Boxhurst, in Kent. *Jour. Iron and Steel Inst.* clxiv (1950), 278–80.

(e) *Tin*

There is a useful bibliography in Lewis (2806), 281–8.

2806 LEWIS, G. R. The stanneries: a study of the English tin mines. *Harvard Econ. Ser.* iii (1908).
The standard work. Cf. also Lewis's article on tin-mining in Cornwall in *V.C.H. Cornwall* (4203).

2807 JENKIN, A. K. H. The Cornish miner. Lond. 1927.
Deals chiefly with economic and social position of the tin-miner. Chs. iii and iv cover the period 1500–1800.

(f) Gold, Silver, Lead, Copper, and other Minerals

Cf. in general Salzman (2768b). The incorporated companies organized or encouraged by the crown to exploit these precious and semi-precious metals are dealt with in Scott (3009), ii, 383 ff.

On lead and silver mining in England there is no good general account. The three chief lead-mining districts are Alston Moor (Cumberland), Derbyshire, and the Mendips (Somerset). Cf. *V.C.H. Cumberland, Derby, and Somerset* (4203). Gold was never found in paying quantities in England.

2808 ABRAHAMS, ISRAEL. Joachim Gaunse: a mining incident in the reign of Queen Elizabeth. *Trans. Jew. Hist. Soc.* iv (1899–1901), 82–103.
Copper-mining—with an app. of documents.

2809 COLLINGWOOD, W. G. The Keswick and Coniston mines in 1600 and later. *Trans. Cumb. and Westmor. Antiq. and Arch. Soc.*, n.s., xxviii (1928), 1–32.

2810 DAVIES, D. S. The records of the mines royal and the mineral and battery works. *Econ. Hist. Rev.* vi (1936), 209–13.

2811 DONALD, M. B. Elizabethan copper. The history of the company of mines royal, 1568–1605. Lond. 1955.

2812 ELIZABETHAN KESWICK, extracts from the original account books, 1564–77, of the German miners, in the archives of Augsburg. By W. G. Collingwood. *Cumb. and Westmor. Antiq. and Arch. Soc.*, Tract. ser., viii (1912).
Important source material.

2813 GOUGH, J. W. The mines of Mendip. Oxf. 1930.
Scholarly.

2814 HAMILTON, H. The English brass and copper industries to 1800. Lond. 1926.

2815 JENKINS, RHYS. The alum trade in the fifteenth and sixteenth centuries and the beginnings of the alum industry in England. In *Collected Papers*. Cambr. 1936.

2816 MONKHOUSE, F. J. Some features of the historical geography of the German mining enterprises in Elizabethan lakeland. *Geography*, xxviii (1943), 107–13.

2817 PELHAM, R. A. The Birmingham plateau in the sixteenth century. In *Birmingham and its regional setting. Brit. Assoc. Handbook, 1950*, 144–52.

2818 SINGER, CHARLES. The earliest chemical revolution. An essay in the historical relations of economics and technology, illustrated from the alum trade. Lond. 1948.

4. The Fisheries

There is an excellent short bibliography in Jenkins (2821). The international aspects of the question and the attitude of the English government towards the fisheries are ably discussed in Fulton (1592), ch. iii. On Burghley's attitude towards the fisheries, cf. Read (760). The only important contemporary writers on the subject are Hitchcock (2820) and Dee (2819). Harrison (615) has a short chapter on 'fish usually taken upon our coasts'.

2819 DEE, JOHN. General and rare memorials pertayning to the perfecte arte of nauigation. Lond. 1577; in *Eng. Garner* (279) ii, 61–70.
The running title is *The British monarchy*. Claims the fisheries adjacent to the British coast for England. Fulton (1592), 100 ff., gives a summary of Dee's views. Cf. also Dee's unpublished letter to Sir E. Dyer on the subject in *Harl. MSS.* 249, f. 95.

2820 HITCHCOCK, ROBERT. A pollitique platt for the honour of the prince, the greate profite of the publique state, relief of the poore, etc. Lond. 1580; in *Eng. Garner*, ii (279), 133–68.
An interesting plan for a system of state-founded fisheries. For a discussion of Hitchcock's project, cf. Fulton (1592), 95 ff.

2821 JENKINS, J. T. The herring and the herring fisheries. Lond. 1927.
Brief but scholarly. Contains a good bibliography.

2822 KEYMER, JOHN. Observations made upon the Dutch fishing about the year 1601. Demonstrating that there is more wealth raised out of herrings and other fish. . . . Lond. 1664.
Probably submitted to James I in 1605 or 1606, but not printed until 1664. Cf. Fulton (1592), 126 ff.

2823 ROWSE, A. L. The Plymouth pilchard fishery, 1584–91. *Econ. Jour.*, hist. supp., 1932, 461–72.

2824 SAMUEL, A. M. The herring: its effect on the history of Britain. Lond. 1918.

5. *Miscellaneous Industries*

Many of these are dealt with in ch. x *infra*.

2825 CHAFFERS, WILLIAM. Gilda aurifabrorum: a history of English goldsmiths and plate workers. Lond. 1883.

2826 FLEMING, A. P. M., and BROCKLEHURST, H. J. A history of engineering. Lond. 1925.

2827 HURRY, J. B. The woad plant and its dye. Oxf. 1930.
In the main a history of the woad industry.

2828 JENKINS, RHYS. Paper-making in England, 1459–1788. In *Collected Papers*. Cambr. 1936.

2829 KNOOP, DOUGLAS, and JONES, G. P. The medieval mason: an economic history of English stone building in the later Middle Ages and early modern times. Manchester, 1933.

2830 KNOOP, DOUGLAS, and JONES, G. P. The sixteenth century mason. Lond. 1937.

2831 NOTES UPON THE EARLIER HISTORY of the manufacture of paper in England. *Hug. Soc. Proc.* viii (1905–7), 177–220.
Cf. also Edw. Heawood, *Sources of early English paper supply*, *Library*, 4th ser. (1930), 282–307, 427–54, D. C. Coleman. The British paper industry, 1495–1860. Oxf. 1958.

2832 STAHLSCHMIDT, J. C. L. Surrey bells and London bell-founders. Lond. 1884.
A contribution to the comparative study of bell inscriptions. Cf. also, by the same author, *The church bells of Hertfordshire* (Lond. 1886) and *The church bells of Kent: their inscriptions, founders, uses, and traditions* (Lond. 1887). Cf. also H. B. Walters, *The church bells of England*, Lond. 1912, and the bibliography there given.

4. GOVERNMENT REGULATION OF ECONOMIC LIFE

A. GENERAL

(a) *Sources*

The most valuable sources are the *Statutes* (1016), the *Royal Proclamations* (1017), and the *Acts of Privy Council* (1152). A great deal of material is scattered through the *Letters and Papers, Henry VIII* (91), the *Cal. S.P., Domestic* (86), and the *Hist. MSS. Comm. reports* (pp. 10 ff. *supra*). Burghley's papers at Hatfield (185) and particularly in the *Lansdowne MSS.* reveal his constant interest and intervention in economic problems. The accounts of the collectors of the ulnage, Edward III to James I, are in P.R.O. Exchequer K.R. accounts, bundles 339–47.
Pertinent documents are printed in Bland (2536), 317 ff., and in Tawney and Power (2539), ii *passim*.

2833 THE ASSYSE OF BREAD AND ALE and other things. Lond. (not before 1534); by E. W. Ashbee, Lond. 1869.
With interesting pictures of the different forms of loaves. For various extant eds. of the assize of bread and ale in the sixteenth century, cf. *S.T.C.* (35), 20–21.

2834 THE ASSIZE OF BREAD BOOK 1477–1517. By R. C. Anderson. *Southampton Rec. Soc.*, 1923.
Deals with assize of bread in Southampton, also with wool sales and entrance fees to trades there.

(b) *Later Works*

On the mercantile system in general, Cunningham (2546), ii, 13–171, is useful, though misleading on Burghley's economic policy; cf. Read (760). Tawney (2676), 313–400, discusses admirably the policy of the government towards agrarian problems. Heaton (2768f) contains a useful chapter (iv) on the state regulation of the cloth industry. Ashley (2541) and Lipson (2556) should also be consulted. For the official attitude towards money lending, cf. 2955; towards the gilds, 2689; towards the corn trade, 2982 and 3000.

2835 BALDWIN, F. E. Sumptuary legislation and personal regulation in England. Baltimore, 1926.

2836 DAVIES, M. R. GAY. The enforcement of English apprenticeship; a study in applied mercantilism, 1563–1642. Cambr., U.S.A., 1956.
Valuable. Based largely on court records.

2837 GRAMPP, W. D. The liberal elements in English mercantilism. *Quar. Jour. Econ.* lxvi (1952), 456–501.

2838 HARPER, L. A. The English navigation laws. New York, 1939.

2839 HEATON, HERBERT. Heckscher on mercantilism. *Jour. Pol. Econ.* xlv (1937), 370–93.

2840 HECKSCHER, E. F. Mercantilism. Trans. Mendel Shapiro. 2 vols. Lond. 1935.
The standard work.

2841 HECKSCHER, E. F. Revisions in economic history. V. Mercantilism. *Econ. Hist. Rev.* vii (1936), 44–54.

2842 HOOPER, WILFRID. The Tudor sumptuary laws. E.H.R. xxx (1915), 433–49.

2843 JOHNSON, E. A. J. Predecessors of Adam Smith. Lond. 1937.

2844 KERRIDGE, ERIC. The returns of the inquisition of depopulation. *E.H.R.* lxx (1955), 212–28.

2845 LOHMANN, F. Die staatliche Regelung der englischen Wollindustrie vom XV. bis zum XVIII. Jahrhundert. *Schmoller's Forschungen,* lxxvii (1900), 1–100.

2846 MORGAN, F. C. The regulations of the city of Hereford, including the assize of bread and ale, 1557. Oxf. 1945.

2847 NICHOLAS, F. J. The assize of bread in London during the sixteenth century. *Econ. Jour.,* hist. supp., 1932, pp. 323–48.

2848 PEARCE, BRIAN. Elizabethan food policy and the armed forces. *Econ. Hist. Rev.* xii (1942), 39–46.

2849 PINCHBECK, IVY. The state and the child in sixteenth-century England. *Brit. Jour. of Sociology,* vii (1956), 273–85; viii (1957), 59–74.

2850 READ, CONYERS. Mercantilism: the old English pattern of a controlled economy. In *The Constitution reconsidered.* New York, 1938.

2851 READ, CONYERS. Tudor economic policy. In *Making of English History.* By R. L. Schuyler. New York, 1952, pp. 195–201.

2852 REES, J. F. Mercantilism. *History,* n.s., xxiv (1939), 129–35.

2853 STONE, LAWRENCE. State control in sixteenth century England. *Econ. Hist. Rev.* xvii (1947), 103–20.

2854 WEBB, S. and B. The history of liquor licensing in England. Lond. 1903.

B. PRICES

Sir William Beveridge's great work, of which vol. i has been published (2855) supplants Rogers (2570), whose references are obscure and his sources limited. Some useful figures on corn prices are in Gras (2982). Abundant unprinted material exists in the P.R.O. and in private collections, but it is far scattered.

Any consideration of current prices must be based upon a knowledge of the conditions governing buying and selling, which varied widely in different localities and were often artificially controlled by local and national regulations. Price variations are often to be explained also by variations in standards of weights and measures. Very little information on this subject is available, but reference may be made to *Select tracts and table books relating to English weights and measures, 1100–1742*, by H. Hall and F. J. Nicholas; *Camden Misc.* xv (1929); W. H. Prior in *Bull. Ducange*, i (1924–5), 77–79, 141–79; H. R. Snape, *Monastic finances* (2091), app. C; W. A. Donisthorpe, *A system of measures*, Lond. 1895, pp. 204–21; W. Hallock and H. T. Wade, *Evolution of weights and measures*, Lond. 1911; E. W. Robertson, *Historical essays*, Lond. 1876, pp. 65 ff.; A. Robinson, *A record of old weights and measures in Norfolk*, *Norfolk Arch.* xxv, 1934 (1935), 207–19; and to the bibliography in *Camden Misc.* xv (1929), 55–58.

The rise of prices in the sixteenth century was a matter of considerable contemporary concern. On this subject, cf. particularly Hales's *Discourse* (2537), Latimer's *Sermons* (1732), and *Policies to reduce this realm of Englande unto a prosperous wealthe and estate*, 1549 (printed in Tawney and Power (2539), iii, 311–45). For the effect of the debasement of the coinage upon prices, cf. Oman (1262).

2855 BEVERIDGE, WILLIAM. Prices and wages in England from the twelfth to the nineteenth century. Vol. i: Price tables: mercantile era. Lond. 1939.

2856 BOWDEN, P. J. Movements in wool prices, 1490–1610. *Yorks. Bull. Econ. and Soc. Research*, iv (1952), 109–24.
Cf. J. F. Wright, *A note on Mr. Bowden's index of wool prices*, ibid. vii (1955), 156–8; S. Pollard, *A second note on Mr. Bowden's 'wool prices'*, ibid. vii (1955), 159–61.

2857 COWPER, J. M. Tudor prices in Kent, chiefly in 1577. *Trans. R.H. Soc.*, ser. i (1875), 169–86.

2858 GREEN, EMANUEL. On the poor and some attempts to lower the price of corn in Somerset, 1548–1638. *Proc. Bath Nat. Hist. and Antiq. Field Club*, iv (1881), 1–49.

2859 HARING, C. H. American gold and silver production in the first half of the sixteenth century. *Quar. Jour. Econ.* xxix (1915), 433–74.
Cf. 2552.

2860 JACOB, W. An historical enquiry into the production and consumption of the precious metals. Philadelphia, 1832.

2861 LUTZ, H. L. Inaccuracies in Rogers' History of Prices. *Quar. Jour. Econ.* xxiii (1908–9), 350–8.

2862 McARTHUR, E. A. Prices at Woodstock in 1604. *E.H.R.* xiii (1898), 711–16.

2863 PEELE, JAMES. The pathwaye to perfectnes in th' accomptes of debitour and creditour; in manner of a dialogue very pleasante and profitable for merchantes. Lond. 1553; 1569.
For a good short essay on sixteenth-century treatises on accounting, cf. R. D. Richards, *Early history of the term capital*, *Quar. Jour. Econ.* xl (1926), 329–38, 547–8. Cf. also Cosmo Gordon in *Trans. Bibliog. Soc.* xiii (1916), 145; M. L. Hartsough in *Jour. Econ. and Bus. Hist.* iv (1932), 539, n. 1; P. De Waal, *De engelsche Vertaling van Jan Ympyn's nieuwe Instructie*, *Econ. Hist. Jaarboek.* xviii (1934), 1–58; and *Studies in the history of accounting*, by A. C. Littleton and B. S. Yamey, Lond. 1956.

2864 SOETBEER, ADOLF. Edelmetall Produktion und Werthverhältniß zwischen Gold und Silber seit der Entdeckung Amerikas bis zur Gegenwart. Gotha, 1879.

2865 USHER, A. P. Prices of wheat and commodity price indexes for England, 1259–1930. *Harvard Rev. of Econ. Statistics*, xiii (1931), 103–13.

2866 WIEBE, GEORG. Zur Geschichte der Preisrevolution des 16. und 17. Jahrhunderts. *Staats- und socialwissenschaftliche Beiträge*, ii, pt. ii. Leipzig, 1895.
A general work, but containing much about England.

C. WAGE ASSESSMENTS

(a) *Sources*

In addition to the wage assessments in print which are given below, a few others are preserved in proclamations, namely, for Canterbury, 1576, Higham Ferrers, 1595, and New Sarum, 1595 (cf. Steele, *Proclamations* (1017), i, nos. 703, 877, and 878). A considerable number for London (1565, 1573, 1576, 1578, 1580, 1584, 1585, 1587, 1588, and 1589) are preserved in the MS. Guildhall journals. There is one for Exeter, 1563, in the corporation records, one for Colchester, 1583, in the *Essex Session Books* (Gross (1), no. 2358) and two for Hertfordshire, 1589 and 1594, in the *Hertford Session Rolls* (1300). For a Welsh wage assessment cf. 6512.
The following assessments are in print:

2867 *1560—Northants.*
B. H. Putnam: *Northamptonshire wage assessments of 1560 and 1667. Econ. Hist. Rev.* i (1927), 124–34.

2868 *1561—Bucks.*
W. A. S. Hewins: *Regulation of wages by the justices of the peace. Econ. Jour.* viii (1898), 340–6.

2869 *1563—Kent*
B. H. Putnam: *The earliest form of Lambarde's Eirenarcha and a Kent wage assessment of 1563. E.H.R.* xli (1926), 260–73.

2870 *1563—Lincoln*
V.C.H. Lincs. ii, 330.

2871 *1563—London*
Carpenters' wages assessed by court of carpenters' company, in Jupp (2708).

2872 *1563—Maidstone*
C. E. Woodruff: *Wages paid at Maidstone. Arch. Cantiana*, xxii (1897), 316–19.

2873 *1563—Rutland*
In Rogers (2570), iv, 120.

2874 *1563—York*
A. Raine, *York Civic Records*, vi, 58–60 (4878).

2875 *1564—Exeter*
Records of Exeter, Hist. MSS. Comm., (1916), 50–51.

2876 *1570—Chester*
Morris (4268), 367.

2877 *1570—Kingston-upon-Hull*
Dyson (1012), f. 77.

2878 *1576—Chester*
Morris (4268), 409.

2879 *1577—Doncaster*
W. J. Hardy: *Calendar to the records of the borough of Doncaster* (Doncaster, 1899–1903), iii, 210.

2880 *1586—London*
Tawney and Power (2539), i, 364.

2881 *1592—Hertfordshire*
W. J. Hardy (1300), i, 8.

2882 *1592—Liverpool*
J. A. Picton: *Selections from the municipal archives* (Liverpool, 1883), i, 114.

2883 *1593—Chester*
Morris (4268), 376–8.

2884 *1593—East Riding, Yorks.*
Eden (2918), iii, app.; Steele (1017), i, no. 862.

2885 *1594—Canterbury*
Civis: *Minutes Coll. from ancient records . . . of . . . Canterbury* (Canterbury, 1800–1).

2886 *1594—Devonshire*
A. H. A. Hamilton (1307), 12–13.

2887 *1594—Liverpool*
J. A. Picton (2882), i, 114.

2888 *1595—Cardigan*
Dyson (1012), f. 331b.

2889 *1595—Lancashire*
Rogers (2570), vi, 689.

2890 *1596—Chester*
Eden (2918), iii, app. 3.

2891 *1597—Chester*
Morris (4268), 367.

2892 *1602—Wiltshire*
Wiltshire Q. S. Records (1305), 162–7.

(b) *Later Works*

2893 BEVERIDGE, WILLIAM. Westminster wages in the manorial era. *Econ. Hist. Rev.*, 2nd ser., viii (1955), 18–35.

2894 BROWN, E. H. P., and HOPKINS, S. V. Seven centuries of building wages. *Economica*, n.s., xxii (1955), 195–206.

2895 HEATON, H. Wages in Yorkshire in the seventeenth and eighteenth centuries. *Econ. Jour.* xxiv (1914), 218–35.

2896 HEWINS, W. A. S. The regulation of wages by the justices of the peace. *Econ. Jour.* viii (1898), 340–6.

2897 HUTCHINS, B. L. The regulation of wages by gilds and town authorities. *Econ. Jour.* x (1900), 404–11.

2898 KELSALL, R. K. Wage regulation under the statute of artificers. Lond. 1938.

2899 KNOOP, DOUGLAS, and JONES, G. P. Overtime in the age of Henry VIII. *Econ. Jour.*, hist. supp., (1938), 13–20.

2900 McARTHUR, E. A. 'The boke longyng to a justice of the peace' and the assessment of wages. *E.H.R.* ix (1894), 305–14, 554; xiii (1898), 297.

2901 McARTHUR, E. A. The regulation of wages in the sixteenth century. *E.H.R.* xv (1900), 445–55.

2902 TAWNEY, R. H. The assessment of wages in England by the justices of the peace. *Vierteljahrschrift für Sozial- und Wirtschaftsgeschichte*, xi (1913), 307–37, 533–64.
A scholarly account of the application of the wage assessment clause in the *Statute of Artificers* (5 Eliz. c. 4).

D. Patents and Monopolies

There is a useful bibliography in Price (2907). The best general discussion is in Cheyney (690), ii, ch. 36. Scott (3009) contains a good deal of scattered material. Unwin (2693),164 ff., discusses one important phase of the subject. A vigorous attack upon monopolies written about 1587 is printed from a MS. by Tawney and Power (2539), iii, 265. For other pertinent material, including the debates in parliament in 1601, cf. ibid. ii, 246–95. On English patent law, cf. J. W. Gordon, *Monopolies by patents*, Lond. 1897.

2903 DAVIES, D. S. The early history of the patent specification. *Law Quar. Rev.* l (1934), 86–109, 260–274.

2904 DAVIES, D. S. Acontius, champion of toleration, and the patent system. *Econ. Hist. Rev.* vii (1936), 63–66.

2905 HUGHES, EDWARD. The English monopoly of salt in the years 1563–71. *E.H.R.* xl (1925), 334–50.

2906 HULME, E. W. The history of the patent system under the prerogative and at common law. *Law Quar. Rev.* xii (1896), 141–54; xvi (1900), 44–56.
Descriptions of many sixteenth-century grants of monopoly.

2907 PRICE, W. H. The English patents of monopoly. *Harvard Econ. Studies*, i (1906).
Covers the period from 1558 to 1640; a valuable work, containing many documents in appendixes.

2908   TURTON, R. B. The alum farm: together with a history of the origin, development and eventual decline of the alum trade in north-east Yorkshire. Whitby, 1938.

2909   WAGNER, D. O. The common law and free enterprise: an early case of monopoly. *Econ. Hist. Rev.* vii (1937), 217–20.

E. Poor Relief

(a) *Sources*

The footnotes to chs. i and ii of Webb (2928) contain a great mass of pertinent bibliographical material. Tawney and Power (2539), ii, 296–368, and iii, 405–58, print many documents. The official policy can be traced in the *Proclamations* (1017) and the *Statutes* (1016). Cf. also Harrison (615), bk. ii, ch. 10, and Hitchcock (2820).

The extensive literature on rogues and vagabonds is dealt with on p. 351 *infra*.

2910   ARTH, HENRY. Provision for the poore now in penurie; out of the storehouse of God's plentie. Lond. 1597.
A discussion of the problem of relieving the poor. Extracts are printed in Tawney and Power (2539), iii, 444 ff.

2911   BOWEN, THOMAS. Extracts from the records and court books of Bridewell hospital. Lond. 1798.
Cf. also Thomas Bowen, *Remarks upon the report of a select committee on Bridewell hospital*, Lond. 1799.

2912   THE HOUSES OF CORRECTION at Maidstone and Westminster. By S. A. Peyton. *E.H.R.* xlii (1927), 251–61.

2913   HOWES, JOHN. Contemporaneous account . . . of the formation and early history of Christ's hospital. Lond. 1889.
Contains two dialogues, one dealing with the beginning of Christ's hospital, Bridewell, and the hospital of St. Thomas the apostle, the other with abuses committed in the government of the poor in London. Both of these are printed virtually in full in Tawney and Power (2539), iii, 415–43.

2914   LIST OF PROCEEDINGS OF COMMISSIONERS for charitable uses. *P.R.O. lists and indexes*, no. 10 (1899).
Lists, inquisitions, and decrees of commissioners appointed to administer the sections of the poor laws of 1597 and 1601 which applied to the abuse of charitable bequests, &c.

2915   SALTER, F. R. Some early tracts on poor relief. Lond. 1926.
Prints five early sixteenth-century tracts dealing with the relief of the poor on the continent.

2916   VIVES, J. L. De subventione pauperum sive de humanis necessitatibus. Bruges, 1526.
The earliest treatise exclusively devoted to poor law policy. Written in England. Salter (2915) prints an Eng. trans. with annotations; cf. also Webb (2928), 36 ff.

(b) *Later Works*

The best account is in Leonard (2923). Ashley (2541), ii, 305–76, and Cheyney (690), ii, chs. 35 and 41 should be consulted. For local administration of poor relief, cf. Ware (1230).

2917 DARIVAS, BASILE. Étude sur la crise économique de 1593–7 en Angleterre et la loi des pauvres. *Rev. d'hist. econ. et soc.* xxx (1952), 382–98.

2918 EDEN, F. M. The state of the poor; or a history of the labouring classes in England from the conquest to the present period. . . . 3 vols. Lond. 1797; abridged by A. G. L. Rogers, Lond. 1928.
Chiefly valuable for eighteenth century, but contains much material for the sixteenth century.

2919 ELTON, G. R. An early Tudor poor law. *Econ. Hist. Rev.*, 2nd ser., vi (1953), 55–67.

2920 EMMISON, F. G. Poor relief accounts of two rural parishes in Bedfordshire, 1563–1598. *Econ. Hist. Rev.* iii (1931), 102–16.

2921 EMMISON, F. G. The care of the poor in Elizabethan Essex. Recently discovered records. *Essex Rev.* lxii (1953), 7–28.

2922 GRAY, B. K. A history of English philanthropy from the dissolution of the monasteries to the taking of the first census. Lond. 1905.

2923 LEONARD, E. M. The early history of English poor relief. Cambr. 1900.
A thorough and valuable study covering the period 1514–1644. Cf. *The relief of the poor by the state regulation of wages*, E.H.R. xiii (1898), 91–93.

2924 MEMORANDA, REFERENCES AND DOCUMENTS relating to the royal hospitals. Lond. 1836.

2925 NICHOLLS, GEORGE. A history of the English poor law. 2 vols. Lond. 1854; by H. G. Willink and T. Mackay. 3 vols. Lond. 1898–9.

2926 RIBTON-TURNER, C. J. A history of vagrants and vagrancy and beggars and begging. Lond. 1887.
Deals mainly with England, but contains chapters on Scotland and Ireland.

2927 STEINBICKER, C. R. Poor relief in the sixteenth century. *Studia Facultas Theologica*, xlviii. Washington, 1937.

2928 WEBB, SIDNEY and BEATRICE. English local government; English poor law history. Part i, the old poor law. Lond. 1927.
Chs. 1 and 2 refer to the sixteenth century. Scholarly. Valuable bibliography in footnotes.

5. MONEY AND BANKING, USURY

A. The Money Market

The best contemporary account of the Antwerp money market is in Guicciardini (2929). Valuable material is printed by Tawney and Power (2539), iii, sect. 3, and by Schanz (3010), ii, 611–43. A number of contemporary treatises in MSS. are preserved among the *Cotton MSS.* in the B.M., notably in *Otho* E x, most of them more or less damaged by fire. There is an excellent bibliography on the early history of English banking in Richards (2940).

For treatises on sixteenth-century accounting, cf. 2863. For public finance and the coinage, cf. ch. iii *supra* (pp. 101–8).

(a) *Sources*

2929 GUICCIARDINI, L. Descrittione di tutti i paesi bassi. Antwerp, 1567; French trans. by F. De Belle-Forest, Antwerp, 1582.
The best contemporary description of the Antwerp money market. Extracts from the French trans. are printed in Tawney and Power (2539), iii, 149–73.

2930 MALYNES, GERARD DE. England's view, in the unmasking of two paradoxes: with a replication unto the answer of Maister John Bodine. Lond. 1603.
An essay on prices, exchange, and money, based on two economic 'paradoxes' presented by Malestroit to the French king, answered by John Bodin, and this answer now discussed by Malynes.
Cf. also 1611.

2931 MALYNES, GERARD DE. A treatise of the canker of England's commonwealth. Lond. 1601.
Concerning the balance of trade, money, and exchange: with an app. giving prices from purchase and sale of East Indian goods.
Cf. also 1611.

(b) *Later Works*

The best modern treatise on the sixteenth-century money market is Ehrenberg (2935). Goris (2936) is also excellent. Tawney's introduction to Wilson (2955) is the best thing on usury in English. Holdsworth's (1544) chapter on the law merchant (viii, 99–245) should be consulted.

2932 BUCKLEY, H. Sir Thomas Gresham and the foreign exchanges. *Econ. Jour.* xxxiv (1924), 589–601.

2933 BURGON, J. W. The life and times of Sir Thomas Gresham. 2 vols. Lond. 1839.
Particularly valuable on English borrowings abroad. Documents. Gresham's official accountings of his borrowings in the continental money market, Edward VI to Elizabeth, are preserved in P.R.O., K.R. Declared Accounts.

2934 CUNNINGHAM, WILLIAM. The progress of capitalism in England. Cambr. 1916.
A small but suggestive work.

2935 EHRENBERG, RICHARD. Das Zeitalter der Fugger: Geld-kapital und Creditverkehr in 16. Jahrhundert. 2 vols. Jena, 1896; repr. 1922.
The best general work on the sixteenth-century money market. An Eng. trans. (by H. M. Lucas) under the title *Capital and finance in the age of the renaissance* (Lond. 1928). The trans. omits vol. i, chs. 4 and 5; vol. ii, sect. iii.

2936 GORIS, J. A. Étude sur les colonies marchandes méridionales à Anvers de 1488 à 1567. Louvain, 1925.
Contains much valuable material on the sixteenth-century money market.

2937 HOLDEN, J. M. The history of negotiable instruments in English law. Lond. 1955.

2938 MARTIN, J. B. The grasshopper in Lombard street. Lond. 1892.
The grasshopper was the sign over Gresham's house. Prints documents on early history of banking, chiefly seventeenth century but some sixteenth century.

2939　PRICE, F. G. H. A handbook of London bankers, 1667–1876. Lond. 1876.
Prints one Elizabethan document.

2940　RICHARDS, R. D. The early history of banking in England. Lond. 1929.
Scholarly. Contains a valuable bibliography.

2941　ROOVER, RAYMOND DE. Early accounting problems of foreign exchange. *The Accounting Rev.* xix (1944), 381–407.

2942　ROOVER, RAYMOND DE. What is dry exchange? A contribution to the study of English mercantilism. *Jour. Pol. Econ.* lii (1944), 250–66.

2943　ROOVER, RAYMOND DE. Le contrat de change depuis la fin du treizième siècle jusqu'au début du dix-septième. *Rev. belge de philologie et d'histoire,* xxv (1946–7), 111–128.

2944　ROOVER, RAYMOND DE. Gresham on foreign exchange: an essay on early English mercantilism with the text of Sir Thomas Gresham's memorandum for the understanding of the exchange. Cambr., U.S.A., 1949.
Gresham's authorship open to question.

B. Usury

(a) *Sources*

For the attitude of the sixteenth-century clergy towards usury, cf. Haweis (2551), ch. xii.

2945　F. F. W. A list of anti-usury books. *Notes and Queries,* ser. 5, vol. x (1878), 281, 341, 422; vol. xi (1879), 63, 163, 262, 361.
Cf. also ser. 4, vol. xii (1873), 335, and ser. 9, vol. iv (1899), 235.

2946　A[CHELEY] T[HOMAS]. The massacre of money. Lond. 1602.
An essay against usury in verse.

2947　BACON, FRANCIS. Of usury. Lond. 1625.
First printed in the 1625 ed. of Bacon's essays.

2948　[CAESAR, PHILIP, and HEMINGIUS, NICHOLAS]. A general discourse against the damnable sect of usurers, grounded upon the worde of God . . . wherunto is annexed another godlie treatise concernying the lawfull use of ritches. Lond. 1578.
A trans. by Thomas Rogers of two Latin treatises, published in Germany, the first by Philip Caesar in 1569, the second from the works of Nicholas Hemingius.

2949　THE DEATH OF USURY, or the disgrace of usurers. Cambr. 1594.

2950　LODGE, THOMAS. Alarum against usurers. Lond. 1584. By E. W. Gosse, *Complete works of Thomas Lodge, Hunterian Club,* i (1883).

2951　MALYNES, GERARD DE. Saint George for England, allegorically described. Lond. 1601.
A little essay against usury.

2952　MOSSE, MILES. The arraignment and conviction of usurie; that is the iniquitie and unlawfulness of usurie displayed in six sermons preached at Saint Edmunds Burie in Suffolk upon Proverbs, xxviii, 8. Lond. 1595.

2953   SANDERS, NICHOLAS. A briefe treatise of usurie. Louvain, 1568.

2954   S[MITH], H[ENRY]. The examination of usury, in two sermons. Lond. 1591.
   A condemnation of usury and explanations of its moral evil, notwithstanding its legality, by an eloquent puritan divine.

2955   WILSON, THOMAS. A discourse uppon usurye by waye of dialogue and oracions, for the better varietye and more delite of all those that shall reade thys treatise. Lond. 1572; 1584; by R. H. Tawney, Lond. 1925.
   Written in 1569. Ed. of 1925 contains very valuable introduction covering sixteenth-century monetary theory and practice.

(b) *Later Works*

Tawney's introduction to Wilson (2955) is the best account. Cf. also Ashley (2541), i, ch. vi, and Tawney (2576).

2956   CUNNINGHAM, WILLIAM. Christian opinion on usury with special reference to England. Edin. 1884.

6. ALIEN IMMIGRANTS

The records of foreign congregations in England (p. 163 *supra*) are important for economic activities. Selected documents are printed in Tawney and Power (2539), i, 240–324. A great deal of documentary material has been published by the Huguenot Society of London. Cf. also F. A. Norwood, *The reformation as an economic force, Studies in Church Hist.* v, Chicago, 1942.

The *Victoria County Histories* (4203) of the south-eastern counties, notably of Norfolk, Suffolk, Essex, and Kent, contain accounts of the economic activities of foreign communities as do the town histories of Norwich, Colchester, Canterbury, and other towns of the south-east.

For the activities of aliens in new industries, cf. 2906, 2907; for their activities in mining, pp. 233 ff. *supra*.

2957   O'NEIL, B. H. ST. J. Stepan von Haschenberg, an engineer to King Henry VIII and his work. *Arch.* xci (1945), 137–55.

2958   REDSTONE, V. B. Alien settlers in Ipswich in 1485. *East Anglian Misc.* 16, 17, 19 (1937).

2959   RÖSLER, MARGARETE. Die Lebensweise der Ausländer in England im späteren Mittelalter und in der Renaissance. *Eng. Studien,* lxviii, no. 1 (1933), 17–56.

2960   TAUBE, EDWARD. German craftsmen in England during the Tudor period. *Econ. Jour.,* hist. supp., (1939), 167–78.

7. COMMERCE

A. GENERAL

(a) *Sources*

The state regulation of commerce can be traced in the *Statutes* (1016), the *Proclamations* (1017), and the *Acts of Privy Council* (1152). Reference should also be made to the section on customs duties (p. 105 *supra*). Treaties are printed in Rymer (88), though the French treaty of 1572, missing there, is given in Dumont (808). The *Letters and Papers, Henry VIII* (91), *Cal. S.P., Foreign* (87), *Spanish* (867–8), and *Venetian* (992), all contain important material, as does the correspondence of French ambassadors in England (pp. 66–69 *supra*). Kervyn de Lettenhove (923) is valuable on Anglo-Dutch trade 1555–79. Tawney and Power (2539), ii, 1–133, print significant documents on commerce, colonization, and shipping. Pollard (400), ii, 265 ff., reprints commercial documents for Henry VII. Schanz (3010), ii, prints many documents not elsewhere in print. Hakluyt (3137) is invaluable on the newer fields of trade. On Anglo-Spanish trade cf. 2714. Cf. also 4426.

The most important sources not in print are the *Port books* (Giuseppi (74), i, 109, 158) and the *Admiralty Records* (ibid. i, 283 ff.) in the P.R.O. A considerable number of contemporary discourses on commercial questions in MS. are preserved in the B.M., notably among the *Lansdowne MSS.* and in the *Cal. S.P., Domestic, Elizabeth*, at the P.R.O.

For the art of navigation and shipbuilding, cf. pp. 279–82 *infra*. For the navy, cf. pp. 295–305 *infra*.

2961 I. B. [John Browne]. The merchants aviso. Lond. 1589. By Patrick McGrath. Cambr., U.S.A., 1957.
An important manual of instructions.

2962 EARLY ENGLISH TRACTS ON COMMERCE. By J. R. McCulloch. Lond. 1859; *Econ. Hist. Soc.*, Lond. 1952.

2963 ENGLISH FOREIGN TRADE UNDER ELIZABETH. By Conyers Read. *E.H.R.* xxix (1914), 515–24.
A list undated (*c.* 1580) of commodities of trade between England and her foreign trade connexions. Repr. in Gras (2982), 429–39, and in Tawney and Power (2539), iii, 199–210. Cf. *The libell of English policy* (Gross (1), no. 2800) for a rhymed summary of the principal commodities of English trade, written 1436.

2964 A PAPER CONCERNING A FREE MART in England and a discourse about the reformation of many abuses.
Two documents printed in *Remains of Edward VI* (555) and in Burnet (1767), ed. 1848, iv, 239–42 and 244–6.

2965 A PRINTED LETTER OF THE LONDON HANSA OF MERCHANTS (3 March 1526). By M. E. Kronenberg. *Oxf. Bibliog. Soc. Pub.*, n.s., i (1949), 25–32.

2966 SELECT CHARTERS OF TRADING COMPANIES A.D. 1530–1707. By C. T. Carr. *Selden Soc.* xxviii (1913).

(b) *Later Works*

Cunningham (2546) and Lipson (2556) furnish the most important general accounts. Busch (406) has valuable chapters on trade under Henry VII, and Cheyney (640) on trade under Elizabeth. There are no detailed accounts of Anglo-French or Anglo-Spanish trade except 2976. On French trade, besides Boissonade (2970) and Simon (3012), the histories of Bordeaux (2997) and of Rouen (2980) should be consulted. The Spanish trading charter of 1530 is printed in Carr (2966), the charter of 1577 in Shillington and Chapman (3011), 313–26. Scott (3009) is invaluable on the joint stock trading companies.

On fairs and markets, the general works are given in Gross (1), nos. 856, 1218, 1221, 1225, 1261. Lipson (2556), i, ch. vi, is excellent.

2967 ANDERSON, ADAM. An historical and chronological deduction of the origin of commerce . . . containing an history of the great commercial interests of the British Empire. 2 vols. Lond. 1764.
A vast body of facts, uncritically collected and often inaccurate.

2968 BASSINGHAM, W. J. London markets: their origins and history. Lond. 1935.

2969 BOISSONADE, P. Le mouvement commercial entre la France et les Iles Britanniques au XVIᵉ siècle. *Revue historique*, cxxxiv, cxxxv (1920), 1–27, 193–228.
Stresses the importance of the French export trade to England.

2970 BOISSONNADE, P. Le socialisme d'État. L'industrie et les classes industrielles en France. . . . (1458–1661). Paris, 1927.
Contains some useful references to French commercial relations with England.

2971 BOURNE, H. R. F. English merchants. Memoirs in illustration of the progress of British commerce. 2 vols. Lond. 1866; 1898.
An uncritical résumé of one phase of English commerce. Cf. also idem, *English seamen under the Tudors*, 2 vols., Lond. 1868.

2972 BRAUDEL, FERNAND. La Mediterranée et le monde méditerranéen à l'époque de Philippe II. Paris, 1949.

2973 BRIDBURY, A. R. England and the salt trade in the later Middle Ages. Oxf. 1955.

2974 BURWASH, DOROTHY. English merchant shipping, 1460–1540. Toronto, 1947.

2975 CAWSTON, GEORGE, and KEANE, A. H. The early chartered companies, A.D. 1296–1858. Lond. 1896.
An outline sketch of the history of the staplers, the merchants adventurers, the Russia, Eastland, Levant, East India, and Hudson Bay companies, with some valuable appendixes.

2976 CONNELL-SMITH, GORDON. Forerunners of Drake. A study of English trade with Spain in the early Tudor period. Lond. 1954.

2977 DICKIN, E. P. Notes on the coast shipping and sea borne trade of Essex, 1565–77. *Essex Arch. Soc. Trans.*, n.s., xvii (1926), 153–64.

2978 DURHAM, H. F. Relation of the crown to trade under James I. *Trans. R.H. Soc.*, 2nd ser., xiii (1899), 199–247.
Valuable introductory statements on the status of trade under Elizabeth.

2979 FISHER, F. J. Commercial trends and policy in sixteenth century England. *Econ. Hist. Rev.* x (1940), 95–117.

2980 DE FRÉVILLE DE LORME, C. E. Mémoire sur le commerce maritime de Rouen. Rouen, 1857.

2981   FRIIS, ASTRID. Alderman Cockayne's project and the cloth trade. Copenhagen and Lond. 1927.
Valuable material on the sixteenth century.

2982   GRAS, N. S. B. The evolution of the English corn market from the twelfth to the eighteenth century. *Harvard Econ. Studies*, xiii (1915).
Valuable appendixes of corn prices supplementing Rogers (2570).

2983   GOULD, J. D. The crisis in the export trade, 1586–1587. *E.H.R.* lxxi (1956), 212–22.

2984   GUTTREY, D. R. Stourbridge market in Tudor times. *Trans. Worcs. Arch. Soc.*, n.s., xxx (1954), 16–38.

2986   HEWINS, W. A. S. English trade and finance chiefly in the seventeenth century. Lond. 1892.
Brief.

2987   HOGDEN, M. T. Fairs of Elizabethan England. *Econ. Geog.*, xviii (1942), 389–400.

2988   JONES, J. R. Some aspects of London mercantile activity during the reign of Queen Elizabeth. In *Essays in honor of Conyers Read*. Chicago, 1953. pp. 186–99.
Based upon the port books.

2989   JURIEN DE LA GRAVIÈRE, J. P. E. Les marins du xvᵉ et xviᵉ siècle. 2 vols. Paris, 1879.
Covers a number of English voyages to Russia and the East.

2990   KINGSBURY, S. M. A comparison of the Virginia company with the other English trading companies of the sixteenth and seventeenth centuries. *Annual Report of the Am. Hist. Assoc.* 1906, i, 161–76.
Includes a bibliography of commercial companies.

2991   KNEISEL, ERNST. 'The evolution of the English corn market.' *Jour. Econ Hist.* xiv (1954), 46–52.

2992   LUCAS, C. P. The beginnings of English overseas enterprise. A prelude to the empire. Oxf. 1917.
Suggestive.

2993   MACPHERSON, DAVID. Annals of commerce, manufactures, fisheries, and navigation . . . of the British empire and other countries from the earliest accounts to . . . 1801. 4 vols. Lond. 1805.
The portion between 1492 and 1760 covering vol. ii and one-half of vol. iii is virtually a repr. of Anderson (2967).

2994   McCUTCHEON, K. L. Yorkshire fairs and markets to the end of the eighteenth century. *Thoresby Soc.* xxxix (1939).

2995   THE MARITIME TRADE OF THE PORT OF BLAKENEY which included Cley and Wiveton, 1587 to 1590. By B. Cozens-Hardy. *Norfolk Rec. Soc.* viii (1936), 15–37.

2996   MARTIN, FREDERICK. History of Lloyd's and of marine insurance in Great Britain. Lond. 1876.

2997   MICHEL, F. Histoire du commerce . . . à Bordeaux. Bordeaux, 1867.

2998 MILLER, L. R. New evidence on the shipping and imports of London. *Quar. Jour. Econ.* xli (1927), 740–60.
An analysis of London shipping based upon the Port Books.

2999 MORGAN, F. C. Trade in Hereford in the 16th century. *Woolhope Nat. F.C. Trans. for 1936–38* (1938), 1–20.

3000 NAUDÉ, W. Die Getreidehandelspolitik der europäischen Staaten. Berlin, 1896.

3001 RAMSAY, G. D. The smugglers' trade: a neglected aspect of English commercial development. *Trans. R.H. Soc.*, 5th ser., ii (1952), 131–57.

3002 RAMSAY, G. D. English overseas trade during the centuries of emergence. Lond. 1957.

3003 RAMSEY, PETER. Overseas trade in the reign of Henry VII: the evidence of customs accounts. *Econ. Hist. Rev.*, 2nd ser., vi (1953), 173–82.

3004 RAMSEY, PETER. Some Tudor merchants' accounts. In *Studies in the history of accounting*. By A. C. Littleton and B. S. Yamey. Lond. 1956.

3005 REYNOLDS, BEATRICE. Elizabethan traders in Normandy. *Jour. Mod. Hist.* ix (1937), 289–303.

3006 RUDDOCK, A. A. The Trinity house at Deptford in the sixteenth century. *E.H.R.* xlv (1950), 458–76.

3007 RUDDOCK, A. A. London capitalists and the decline of Southampton in the early Tudor period. *Econ. Hist. Rev.*, 2nd ser., ii (1949), 137–51.

3008 SCHÄFER, DIETRICH. Deutschland und England im Welthandel des 16ten Jahrhunderts. *Preußische Jahrbücher*, lxxxiii (1896), 268–81.

3009 SCOTT, W. R. The constitution and finance of English, Scottish, and Irish joint stock companies. 3 vols. Cambr. 1910–12.
The standard work. Of great importance. Contains much for the sixteenth but more for the seventeenth century. Includes a useful chapter on public finance under Elizabeth. Useful bibliography in vol. i.

3010 SCHANZ, GEORG. Englische Handelspolitik gegen Ende des Mittelalters . . . des Zeitalters . . . Heinrich VII. und Heinrich VIII. 2 vols. Leipzig, 1881.
The most valuable and detailed existing study of money, prices, and economic policy in England, her shipping and trade with the rest of Europe, and her part in early exploration between 1485 and 1547. Vol. ii is made up of contemporary documents.

3011 SHILLINGTON, V. M., and CHAPMAN, A. B. W. The commercial relations of England and Portugal. Lond. s.a.
Two essays, one on the medieval period, the second covering the period 1487–1807. Contains the charter of the merchants trading to Spain and Portugal and other documents. Contains a bibliography of printed and MS. sources. Cf. also A. B. W. Chapman, *The commercial relations of England and Portugal 1487–1807*, in *Trans. R.H. Soc.*, 3rd ser. (1907), 157–79.

3012 SIMON, A. L. The history of the wine trade in England. 3 vols. Lond. 1906–9.
Vol. ii on sixteenth century. Valuable Cf. also idem, *Bibliotheca Bacchica*, vols. i and ii, Lond. 1927–32.

3013 STONE, LAWRENCE. Elizabethan overseas trade. *Econ. Hist. Rev.*, 2nd ser., ii (1949), 30–58.
Important.

3014 THRUPP, S. L. The merchant class of mediaeval London (1300–1500). Chicago, 1948.

3015 TUPLING, G. H. Lancashire markets in the sixteenth and seventeenth centuries. *Trans. Lancs. and Ches. Antiq. Soc.* lviii (1945–6), 1–34; lix (1947), 10–34.
Cf. idem. *An alphabetical list of the fairs and markets of Lancashire, recorded before 1701*, ibid. li (1937), 86–110.

3016 USHER, A. P. The growth of English shipping, 1572–1922. *Quar. Jour. Econ.* xlii (1928), 465–78.
Gives a few figures on the English mercantile marine and its tonnage under Elizabeth.

3017 WILLIAMS, D. I. Trade relations between Jersey, Guernsey and Welsh ports in Elizabethan times. *Soc. Guernesiaise Bull.* (1934), 261–70.

3018 WILLIAMS, N. J. Francis Shaxton and the Elizabethan port books. *E.H.R.* lxvi (1951), 387–95.

3019 WILLIAMS, N. J. The London port books. *Trans. Lond. and Middx. Arch. Soc.* xviii, pt. i (1955), 1–14.

3020 WILLIAMSON, J. A. Maritime enterprise, 1485–1558. Oxf. 1913.
Valuable for a period upon which little has been written.

3021 WILLIAMSON, J. B. The foreign commerce of England under the Tudors. Oxf. 1883.
Brief. Chiefly devoted to early Tudors.

3022 WROTH, L. C. An Elizabethan merchant and man of letters. *Hunt. Lib. Quar.* xvii (1954), 299–314.

B. THE STAPLERS, MERCHANT ADVENTURERS, THE HANSA, AND TRADE WITH THE LOW COUNTRIES

(a) *Sources*

Cf. sect. A *supra*, particularly Schanz (3010); Pollard (400), K. de Lettenhove (923), and the *Cal. S.P., Foreign, Elizabeth* (87) and *Cal. S.P., Spanish* (867–8). Some important letters on Anglo-Dutch trade are printed in Burgon (2933). An excellent survey of literature on the Hanseatic league is in *Jour. Econ. and Bus. Hist.* ii (1930), 585–602. The records of the Staplers are now in the B.M., Add. MSS. 43847–52; Add. Ch. 70834.

3023 [ARMSTRONG, CLEMENT.] A treatise concerninge the staple and the commodities of this realme. In Pauli (2538).

3024 BRONNEN TOT DE GESCHIEDENIS VAN DEN HANDEL met Engeland, Schotland en Ierland. Tweede deel, 1485–1585, eerste stuk, 1485–1558; tweede stuk, 1558–85. By H. J. Smit. *Rijks Geschiedkundige Pub.* lxxxvi, xci. 'S-Gravenhage, 1942, 1950.

3025 THE CELY PAPERS. Selection from the correspondence and memoranda of the Cely family, merchants of the staple 1475–88. By H. E. Malden. *Camden Soc.*, 3rd ser., i (1900).
Letters, bills, memoranda. Nearly all before 1485.

3026 COLLINS, A. J. The records of the merchants of the staple of England. *Brit. Mus. Quar.* x (1936), 31–32.

3027 EXTRACTS FROM THE RECORDS of the merchant adventurers of Newcastle-upon-Tyne. By F. W. Dendy and J. R. Boyle. 2 vols. *Surtees Soc.* xciii and ci (1895, 1899).
A valuable collection of documents mostly of the sixteenth and seventeenth centuries.

3028 A GENERAL COURT OF THE MERCHANT ADVENTURERS in 1547. By W. P. M. Kennedy. *E.H.R.* xxxvii (1922), 105–7.

3029 HANSERECESSE VON 1477–1530 (3rd ser.). By Dietrich Schäfer and Friedrich Techen. 9 vols. *Verein für hansische Geschichte.* Leipzig, 1881–1913.

3030 INVENTARE HANSISCHER ARCHIVE des 16. Jahrhunderts. By K. Höhlbaum, H. Keussen, and P. Sunson. *Verein für hansische Geschichte.* 3 vols. Leipzig, 1896–1913.
Vols. i and ii include Kölner Inventare to 1591; vol. iii Danziger Inventare, 1531–91.

3031 LONDONER URKUNDEN ÜBER DEN STAHLHOF, 1549–1622. By K. Höhlbaum. *Hansische Geschichtsblätter*, viii (1895), 152–64.
A calendar of MSS. in London concerning the relations between England and the Hansa for the years 1549–1622.

3032 LYELL, LAETITIA. The problem of the records of the merchant adventurers. *Econ. Hist. Rev.* v (1935), 96–98.

3033 THE MERCHANT ADVENTURERS OF ENGLAND; their laws and ordinances with other documents. By W. E. Lingelbach. *Trans. and reprints . . . pub. by the Univ. of Penns.*, 2nd ser., ii (1902).
The *laws and ordinances* of 1608 preceded by a short history of the Merchant Adventurers Company and followed by a number of documents of the period 1407–1805.

3034 THE ORDINANCE BOOK OF THE MERCHANTS OF THE STAPLE. By E. E. Rich. *Cambr. Studies in Econ. Hist.* Cambr. 1937.

3035 THE STAPLE COURT BOOKS of Bristol. By E. E. Rich. *Bristol Rec. Soc.* v (1934).

3036 THE YORK MERCERS AND MERCHANT ADVENTURERS 1356–1917. By Maud Sellers. *Surtees Soc.* cxxix (1917).
Some two-thirds of this vol. refers to the Tudor period. Introduction valuable.

3037 WHEELER, JOHN. A treatise of commerce. . . . Middelburgh, 1601; Lond. 1601; by G. B. Hotchkiss. New York, 1931.
A defence of the monopoly of the merchant adventurers by the secretary of the Company. For a contemporary attack, cf. Tawney and Power (2539), iii, 265–76.

(b) *Later Works*

On the staplers, Jenckes (3049) is useful but brief. The introduction to *The Cely Papers* (3025) should be consulted, as well as Sandeman (372).

On the merchant adventurers Lingelbach (3033) though brief is serviceable. Unwin's views (3062) are significant. Hagedorn (3048) throws light on their trade with Emden.

On the Hansa and England, Schanz (3010) and Schulz (3060) though not always in agreement are both excellent for the period to 1547; Ehrenberg (3047) from 1547 to 1603.

There is no adequate account of Anglo-Dutch commercial relations in the sixteenth century. Busch (406) should be consulted for Henry VII. Fulton (1592) is suggestive.

3038 BENSE, J. F. Anglo-Dutch relations from the earliest time to the death of William III. Lond. 1925.
An historical introduction to a dictionary of the low Dutch element in the English vocabulary. Slight.

3039 BRAKEL, S. VAN. De hollandsche handelscompagnieen der zeventiende eeuw. The Hague, 1908.
Contains some matter of value for Tudor period.

3040 BRAKEL, S. VAN. Die Entwicklung und Organisation der Merchant Adventurers. *Vierteljahrschrift für Sozial- und Wirtschaftsgeschichte*, v (1907), 401–32.

3041 BRUGMANS, H. Engeland en de Nederlanden in de eerste jaren von Elizabeth's Regeering (1558–1567). Groningen, 1892.
Ph.D. thesis. Devoted largely to commercial relations.

3042 CARUS-WILSON, E. M. The origins and early development of the merchant adventurers' organization in London as shown in their own mediaeval records. *Econ. Hist. Rev.* iv (1932), 147–76.
Important.

3043 DE SMEDT, OSKAR. De engelse Natie te Antwerpen in de 16e Eeuw. (1496–1582). 2 vols. Antwerpen, 1950–4.

3044 CLEPHAN, R. C. The Hanseatic confederation with special reference to the . . . trading connections with Newcastle-upon-Tyne. Newcastle, 1893.
Repr. from *Arch. Aeliana*, n.s., xvi (1894), 211–48.

3045 COTTON, WILLIAM. An Elizabethan guild of the city of Exeter. An account of the proceedings of the society of merchant adventurers during the latter half of the sixteenth century. Exeter, 1873.

3046 EDLER, FLORENCE. Winchcombe kerseys in Antwerp (1538–44). *Econ. Hist. Rev.* vii (1936), 57–62.

3047 EHRENBERG, RICHARD. Hamburg und England im Zeitalter der Königin Elisabeth. Jena, 1896.
An important monograph on sixteenth-century trading relations.

3048 HAGEDORN, BERNHARD. Ostfrieslands Handel und Schiffahrt im 16. Jahrhundert. 2 vols. *Abhandlungen zur Verkehrs- und Seegeschichte*, iii, vi (1910–12).
Valuable for English trade relations with Emden.
   The 2nd vol. appeared under the title *Ostfrieslands Handel und Schiffahrt vom Ausgang des 16. Jahrhunderts bis zum Westfälischen Frieden* (1580–1648). Cf. Unwin's review of vol. i in *Studies* (2575), 379–82.

3049 JENCKES, A. L. The origin, the organization, and the location of the staple of England. Philadelphia, 1908.
Prints the charters of the merchants of the staple of 1561 and 1617.

3050 KASER, K. Handelspolitische Kämpfe zwischen England und die Niederländer, 1563–66. Stuttgart, 1892.

3051 KURZINNA, WERNER. Der Name Stahlhof. *Hansische Geschichtsblätter*, xviii (1912), 429–61.
Concerning the origin of the name of the London steelyard.

3052 LAPPENBERG, J. M. Urkundliche Geschichte des hansischen Stahlhofes zu London. 2 vols. Hamburg, 1851.
With many documents.

3053 LATIMER, J. History of the society of merchant adventurers of the city of Bristol. Bristol, 1903.

3054 LINGELBACH, W. E. The merchant adventurers at Hamburg. *A.H.R.* ix (1904), 265–87.
With especial reference to their dissolution in 1809.

3055 LINGELBACH, W. E. The internal organization of the merchant adventurers of England. *Trans. R.H. Soc.*, 2nd ser., xvi (1902), 19–67.

3056 PAULI, REINHOLD. Der hansische Stahlhof in London. Bremen, 1856.

3057 POLNITZ, GOTZ, FREIHERRN VON. Fugger und Hanse: Ein hundertjähriges Ringen um Ostsee und Nordsee. *Schwäbische Forschungsgemeinschaft bei der Kommission fur Függergeschichte*, xi. Tübingen, 1953.

3058 SARTORIUS, G. F. C. Geschichte des hanseatischen Bundes. 3 vols. Göttingen, 1802–8.
Book 17 in vol. iii, 307–428, includes much of value for English relations.

3059 SCHANZ, GEORG. Die Handelsbeziehungen zwischen England und den Niederlanden, 1485–1547. Wurzburg, 1879.

3060 SCHULZ, FRIEDRICH. Die Hanse und England von Edwards III. bis auf Heinrichs VIII. Zeit. *Abhandlungen zur Verkehrs- und Seegeschichte*, v (1911).
Valuable on the early Tudors. Makes some corrections of Schanz (3010).

3061 TE LINTUM, C. De merchant adventurers in de Nederlanden. Ein bijdragetot de geschiedenis von den engelschen handel met Nederland. The Hague, 1905.

3062 UNWIN, GEORGE. The merchant adventurers company in the reign of Elizabeth.
Lectures delivered in Oxford, 1913. Printed in part in *Econ. Hist. Rev.* i (1927), 35–64; in full in *Studies* (2575), 133–220. Suggestive.

3063 WALFORD, CORNELIUS. An outline history of the Hanseatic league, more particularly in its bearings upon English commerce. *Trans. R.H. Soc.* ix (1881), 82–136.

3064 WILLIAMS, E. Staple inn, customs house, wool court and inn of chancery. Lond. 1906.

3065 WINCHESTER, BARBARA. Tudor family portrait. Lond. 1955.
The family of John Johnson, merchant stapler, based on correspondence in P.R.O., S.P., Domestic, supplementary.

C. Russian and Baltic Trade

(a) *Sources*

On the Russian trade a good deal of important material is printed in Hakluyt (3137). The *Cal. S.P., Foreign, Elizabeth* (87) yield something. On the English sources in general, cf. Wretts-Smith (3086). For sources in Russian, printed and unprinted, cf. Lubimenko, *Correspondence of Queen Elizabeth with the Russian Czars, Trans. R.H. Soc.*, 3rd ser., ix (1915), 111–22.

English trade in the Baltic centres around the rivalry between the Hansa and the Eastland Co. The *Cal. S.P., Foreign, Elizabeth* (87), particularly after 1580, contains much material, as does the *Acts of Privy Council* (1152).

3066 THE ACTS AND ORDINANCES OF THE EASTLAND COMPANY. By Maud Sellers. *Camden Soc.*, 3rd ser., xi (1906).

3067 BANG, N. E. Tabeller over Skibsfart og Varetransport gjennem Oeresund, 1497–1660. 2 vols. Copenhagen, 1906, 1922.
Valuable statistics on English ships passing into the Baltic and paying the Danish sound dues.

3068 EARLY VOYAGES AND TRAVELS to Russia and Persia by Anthony Jenkinson and other Englishmen. By E. D. Morgan and C. H. Coote. 2 vols. *Hakluyt Soc.* lxxii, lxxiii (1886).
With a valuable introduction and a large number of documents not elsewhere accessible.

3069 TOLSTOY, GEORGE. The first forty years of intercourse between England and Russia. St. Petersburg, 1875.
A collection of documents given both in English and Russian, 1553–93. Valuable.

3070 RUSSIA AT THE CLOSE OF THE SIXTEENTH CENTURY. By E. A. Bond. *Hakluyt Soc.* xx (1856).
Contains Giles Fletcher, *Of the Russe commonwealth*, Lond. 1591, Jerome Horsey, *Travels*, and many documents.

(b) *Later Work*

Lubimenko's articles use Russian material. For the financial organization of the Russia Co., Scott (3009), ii, 36–52 has been superseded by Willan (3089).

On the Eastland Co., cf. (3072), (3085). Unwin (3062) throws light on the relations of the Eastland Co. to the Merchant Adventurers. Cheyney (690), i, ch. xv, has a good chapter on both the Russian and Baltic trades.

3071 CASIMIR, NICHOLAS, BARON DE BOGOUSHEVSKY. The English in Muscovy during the sixteenth century. *Trans. R.H. Soc.* vii (1878), 58–129.
Prints documents.

3072 DEARDORFF, N. R. English trade in the Baltic during the reign of Elizabeth. In *Studies in the history of English commerce in the Tudor period.* New York, 1912.

3073 HAMEL, J. Tradescant der ältere in Russland: der Handelsverkehr zwischen England und Rußland in seiner Entstehung. St. Petersburg and Leipzig, 1847.
A valuable paper presented to the Imperial Academy of Sciences in St. Petersburg and published separately in German. The so-called trans. by Leigh is so extensively rearranged and modified as to be practically a new work.

3074 ENGLAND AND RUSSIA: comprising the voyages of John Tradescant the Elder, Sir Hugh Willoughby, Richard Chancellor, Nelson, and others, to the White Sea, &c. By J. S. Leigh. Lond. 1854.
Based on 3073, but of independent value.

3075 HILL, C. E. Danish sound dues and the command of the Baltic. Durham, U.S.A., 1926.
A brief but scholarly history. Good bibliography.

3076 LUBIMENKO, INNA. The correspondence of Queen Elizabeth with the Russian Czars. *A.H.R.* xix (1914), 525–42.
Contains valuable references to the Russian sources.

3077 LUBIMENKO, INNA. Les marchands anglais en Russie au seizième siècle. *Revue historique*, cix (1912), 1–26.

3078 LUBIMENKO, INNA. Les projets d'alliance anglo-russe aux seizième et dix-septième siècles. *Revue d'histoire diplomatique*, xxxviii (1924), 61–74.

3079 LUBIMENKO, INNA. Trois lettres inédites d'Elizabeth d'Angleterre à la cour de Russie. In *Mélanges d'histoire offerts à M. Charles Bémont* (Paris, 1913), pp. 549–57.

3080 LUBIMENKO, INNA. Les relations commerciales et politiques de l'Angleterre avec la Russie avant Pierre le Grand. Paris, 1933.

3081 PULS, H. Die Beziehungen zwischen England und Rußland im xvi und xvii. Jht., unter Berücksichtigung des zeitgenössischen englischen Schrifttums über Rußland. Hambourg, 1941.

3082 RUFFMAN, K. H. Das Rußlandbild im England Shakespeares. Göttingen, 1952.

3083 VAUGHN, E. V. English trading expeditions into Asia under . . . the Muscovy Company (1557–81). In *Studies in the history of English commerce in the Tudor period*. New York, 1912.

3084 VILENSKAJA, E. S. K. Istorii russko-anglijskich otnošenij v xvi v.: Neizdannaja zapiska Dž. Flečera koroleve Elizavete. *Istoričeskie Zaviski*, xxix (1949), 123–34.
Russo-English relations. Sixteenth century. Unpublished note of Fletcher to Elizabeth.

3085 VOLCKMANN, E. Der Grundstein britischer Weltmacht. Würzburg, 1923.
Economic relations of England and Prussia to the reign of James I, chiefly the Eastland Co. Scholarly.

3086 WRETTS-SMITH, MILDRED. The English in Russia during the second half of the sixteenth century. *Trans. R.H. Soc.*, 4th ser., iii (1920), 72–102.
Scholarly. Useful discussion of sources.

3087 WILLAN, T. S. The Russia Company and Narva, 1558–81. *Slavonic Rev.* xxxi (1953), 405–19.

3088 WILLAN, T. S. The Muscovy merchants of 1555. Manchester, 1953.

3089 WILLAN, T. S. Early history of the Russia company, 1553–1603. Manchester, 1956.

3090 YAKOBSON, S. Early Anglo-Russian relations (1553–1613). *Slavonic Rev.* xiii (1935), 597–610.

D. The Mediterranean: North and West Africa: The East Indies

(a) Sources

The Mediterranean

The *Cal. S.P., Venetian* (992) is the most valuable source for trade relations with the Near East. There is some material in the *Cal. S.P., Foreign* (87). For the dispatches of the English agents at Constantinople, cf. 894 and 3129. Hakluyt (3137) and Purchas (3138) are generally useful. For sources on trade relations with Persia, cf. 3068.

The African Trade

In addition to the sources cited below the *Cal. S.P., Foreign* (87), the *Cal. S.P., Spanish* (868), the Hawkins voyages (3186), and Hakluyt (3137), should be consulted. Williamson prints a contemporary account of the third Hawkins voyage in his *Life of Hawkins* (3190), app.

The East Indies

The systematic development of the trade belongs to the seventeenth century and is adequately dealt with in Davies (8). For a general guide to the English official sources, cf. W. Foster, *A guide to the India office records 1600–1858*, Lond. 1919. *Cal. S.P., Colonial* (85), ii, deals with the far east.

3091 THOMAS FENNER AND THE GUINEA TRADE. By K. R. Andrews. *Mariner's Mirror*, xxxviii (1952), 312–14.
Reproduces Fenner's deposition in the Admiralty records.

3092 CHARTERS GRANTED TO THE EAST INDIA COMPANY from 1601; also the treaties and grants made with or obtained from the princes and powers in India from the year 1756 to 1772. s.l., s.a.
This large and valuable collection of charters and other documents was presumably issued by the East India company.

3093 THE DAWN OF BRITISH TRADE TO THE EAST INDIES as recorded in the court minutes of the East India company, 1599–1603. By Henry Stevens. Lond. 1886.
Printed from the MSS. preserved in the India office, London. A valuable record.

3094 EARLY TRAVELS IN INDIA, 1583–1619. By W. Foster. Oxf. 1921.

3095 EUROPEANS IN WEST AFRICA, 1450–1560. By J. W. Blake. 2 vols. *Hakluyt Soc.*, 2nd ser., lxxxvi–lxxxvii (1942).

3097	FEDERICI, CESARE. The voyage and travel of M. Caesar Frederick, merchant of Venice into the East Indies, the Indies and beyond the Indies. Trans. T[homas] H[ickock]. Lond. 1588.

3098	LETTERS RECEIVED BY THE EAST INDIA COMPANY from its servants in the East, transcribed from the original correspondence. By F. C. Danvers. Lond. 1896.
Only one letter in the Tudor period.

3099	LINSCHOTEN, J. H. VAN. J. H. van Linschoten—his discourse of voyages into the East and West Indies. Trans. W. Philip. Lond. 1598; by P. A. Fiele and A. C. Burnell, 2 vols., *Hakluyt Soc.* lxx and lxxi (1885).
A trans. of the first part of Linschoten's *Itinerario*, published in 1596. Of much influence.

3100	OF THE NEW LANDES AND OF YE PEOPLE founde by the messengers of the kynge of Portyngale named Emanuel. Antwerp [1511?]; by Edward Arber, cf. 3253.
A curious little book printed in English on the continent and probably giving the English the first real knowledge in published form in their own language of the recent discoveries of the Portuguese. *S.T.C.* (35), no. 7677, conjectures the date to be 1520, Arber, 1511.

3101	PARRY, WILLIAM. A new and large discourse of the travels of sir Anthony Sherley, knight, by sea and over land to the Persian empire. Lond. 1601; by J. P. Collier, *Collier's Reprints,* ii, Lond. 1864.

3102	R., H. News from the Levant Seas. Describing the many perrilous events of the most worthey deserving gentleman, Edward Glenham, Esq. Lond. 1594; repr. *Collier's Illustrations of old Eng. Lit.* i, Lond. 1866.
On this pamphlet and on another printed 3 years earlier, cf. Life of Ed. Glemham [*sic*] in *D.N.B.* (9) and *S.T.C.* (35), nos. 11921, 20572.

3103	THE REGISTER OF LETTERS, etc. of the governour and company of merchants of London trading into the East Indies, 1600–19. By George Birdwood and William Foster. Lond. 1893.
A repr. of a MS. vol. of miscellaneous documents of the East India company compiled probably by its secretary between 1606 and 1619.

3104	SANDERSON, JOHN. The travels of, in the Levant, 1584–1602. By William Foster. *Hakluyt Soc.,* 2nd ser., lxvii (1931).
Important documents in app.

3105	SHIRLEY, E. P. The Sherley brothers. An historical memoir of the lives of Sir Thomas Sherley, Sir Anthony Sherley, and Sir Robert Sherley. *Roxburghe Club,* 1848.
Prints *in extenso* many letters of these merchants and adventurers in Morocco, Persia, and the east, *c.* 1600 and after.

3106	LES SOURCES INÉDITES DE L'HISTOIRE DU MAROC. Première série. *Archives et bibliothèques d'Angleterre.* By Henry de Castries. Vols. i, ii. Paris, 1918–25.

3107	THE PILGRYMAGE OF SIR RICHARD GUYLFORDE to the Holy Land, A.D. 1506. Lond. 1511; by Henry Ellis. *Camden Soc.* li (1851).
Written by Guilford's chaplain.

3108   THE VOYAGES OF SIR JAMES LANCASTER to Brazil and the East Indies, 1591–1603. By William Foster. *Hakluyt Soc.*, 2nd ser., lxxxv (1940).

(b) *Later Works*

The Mediterranean

Busch (406) is good on Mediterranean trade under Henry VII. Pohlmann (3127) throws some light upon trade relations between England and Florence. Cheyney (690) has a good account of the Mediterranean trade under Elizabeth. The introductions to *Cal. S.P., Venetian* (992) are valuable. There is something in the histories of Turkey by Knollys, Zinkheisen, and Hammer-Purgstall (3118). Cf. also 894.

North and West Africa

The best account for the period before 1558 is in Williamson (3020). On the early slave trade to the Guinea coast Williamson's *Hawkins* (3190) is also serviceable. Bekker (3110) deals with a later phase of the subject.

The East Indies

This trade belongs chiefly to the Stuart period. On the origin and early organization of the East India company, Scott (3009) is valuable. Hunter (3121) is the standard history.

3109   DE ALBERTI, LEONORA, and CHAPMAN, A. B. W. English merchant traders and the Spanish inquisitions in the Canaries during the reign of Queen Elizabeth. *Trans. R.H. Soc.*, 3rd ser., iii (1909), 237–53; xxiii (1912).
Though primarily concerned with the Inquisition contains much about trade.

3110   BEKKER, ERNST. Der Afrikahandel der Königin Elisabeth von England und ihr Handelskrieg mit Portugal 1569–77. *Giessener Studien aus dem Gebiete der Geschichte: Beiträge zur englischen Geschichte im Zeitalter Elisabeths.* Giessen, 1899.

3111   BLAKE, J. W. European beginnings in West Africa, 1454–1578. *Roy. Emp. Soc. Imperial Studies,* xiv. Lond. 1937.

3112   BRUCE, J. Annals of the honourable East India company from 1600 to 1707–8. 3 vols. Lond. 1810.
Bruce was historiographer to the company and keeper of its records.

3113   BURIAN, ORHAN. Türk-İngiliz münasebetlerinin ilk yılları. *Ankara Üniv. Dil. Tar. Coğr. Fak. Derg.* ix (1951), 1–17.
First years of Anglo-Turk relations, 16th century.

3114   CAILLÉ, J. Le commerce anglais avec la Maroc pendant la seconde moitié du xvi siècle. *Rev. Africaine,* lxxxiv (1940), 186–219.

3115   CHEW, S. C. The Crescent and the Rose. Islam and England during the Renaissance. New York, 1937.

3116 EPSTEIN, MAX. The early history of the Levant company. Lond. 1908.
Contains the charter of the company of 1605, and several other documents in an app.

3117 FOSTER, WILLIAM. England's quest of eastern trade. Lond. 1933.

3118 HAMMER-PURGSTALL, BARON J. VON. Geschichte des osmanischen Reichs. 10 vols. Budapest, 1828.
Vol. iii is pertinent.
A French trans. revised by the author, edited by J. J. Hillert, was published, 18 vols., Paris, 1835–44.

3119 HORNIKER, A. L. William Harborne and the beginning of Anglo-Turkish diplomatic and commercial relations. *Jour. Mod. Hist.* xiv (1942), 289–316.
Cf. Read (759) iii, 225–8, 326–32.

3120 HORNIKER, A. L. Anglo-French rivalry in the Levant from 1583 to 1612. *Jour. Mod. Hist.* xviii (1946), 289–305.

3121 HUNTER, W. W. A history of British India. 2 vols. Lond. 1899–1900.
The standard history. For other histories, cf. Davies (8), no. 3789.

3122 JENKINSON, HILARY. The records of the English African companies. *Trans. R.H. Soc.*, 3rd ser., vi (1912), 185–220.
Valuable as guide to MS. material.

3123 KERNKAMP, J. H. De Handel op den Vijand, 1572–1609. 2 vols. Utrecht, 1934.
English and Dutch trade with the enemy (Spain).

3124 KRISHNA, BAL. Commercial relations between England and India, 1601–1757. Lond. 1924.

3125 KURAT, AKDES NIMET. Türk-İngiliz münasebetlerinin baslangici ve gelismesi (1553–1610). *Ankara Üniv. Dil. Tar. Coğr. Fak. Yayınl.* lxxxiv, *Tar. Enstit*, x. Ankara, 1953.
Anglo-Turkish relations, 1553–1610.

3126 MEYERSTEIN, E. H. W. Troubles of Devonshire mariners in Spanish ports, 1550. *Mariner's Mirror*, xxxv (1949), 146–50.

3127 POHLMANN, ROBERT. Die Wirthschaftspolitik der Florentiner Renaissance und das Princip der Verkehrsfreiheit. In *Preisschriften hrsg. von der fürstlichen Jablonowskischen Gesellschaft*, xxi (Leipzig, 1878).

3128 RAWLINSON, H. G. British beginnings in Western India, 1579–1657. Oxf. 1920.

3129 RAWLINSON, H. G. Embassy of William Harborne to Constantinople. 1583–8. *Trans. R.H. Soc.*, 4th ser., v (1922), 1–27.
Cf. Read (545), iii, 326–32, for correspondence of Harborne. Cf. B.M. *Lansdowne MS.* 57, no. 23, ff. 65–66, for a short summary of Harborne's services at Constantinople written by himself.

3130 ROWLAND, A. L. England and Turkey, the rise of diplomatic and commercial relations. In *Studies in English commerce and exploration in the reign of Elizabeth*. Philadelphia, 1925.

3131 RUDDOCK, A. A. Italian merchants and shipping in Southampton, 1270–1600. *Southampton Rec. Soc.*, n.s., i (1951).

3134 WILLAN, T. S. Some aspects of English trade with the Levant in the sixteenth century. *E.H.R.* lxx (1955), 399–410.

3135 WOOD, A. C. A history of the Levant Company. Lond. 1935.

VIII

DISCOVERY, EXPLORATION, AND COLONIZATION

A. GENERAL

(a) *Sources*

The *Cal. S.P.*, *Colonial Series* (85) are with Hakluyt (3137) and Purchas (3138) the most important sources. Much of the important source material has been published by the Hakluyt Soc. On the explorations of particular men, cf. pp. 268–76 *infra*; on America, cf. pp. 276–9 *infra*. The sections dealing with Russian trade, the Levant trade, and trade in the far East and with Africa should also be consulted (pp. 260–4 *supra*).

3136 DOCUMENTS CONCERNING ENGLISH VOYAGES TO THE SPANISH MAIN, 1569–1590. By I. A. Wright. *Hakluyt Soc.*, 2nd ser., lxxi (1932).

The Spanish documents were selected from the archives of the Indies at Seville. The volume also contains some English accounts of the voyages.

3137 HAKLUYT, RICHARD. The principall navigations, voiages and discoveries of the English nation, made by sea or over land. . . . Lond. 1589; 3 vols. 1599–1600; by R. H. Evans, 5 vols., Lond. 1809–12; by Walter Raleigh, 12 vols., Glasgow, 1903–5.

Ed. of 1599 includes everything contained in the 1st ed. except that all matter connected with Sir John Mandeville is omitted, different accounts of two or three voyages are substituted, and the matter is wholly rearranged. In some copies *The Voyage to Cadiz* is wanting, having been suppressed by order.

Ed. of 1903–5 is an exact repr. of ed. of 1599–1600 and is on the whole the best ed. It contains a good introductory essay by Prof. Walter Raleigh.

The convenient *Everyman's Library* ed., 8 vols., omits a few things from the 2nd ed.

The editorial portion contributed by Hakluyt, although small, is valuable. The industry with which the narratives were collected, and the extent to which they have disappeared except as they have been preserved in this collection make it absolutely invaluable.

References throughout are to the 1903–5 ed.

3137a HAKLUYT, RICHARD. THE ORIGINAL WRITINGS AND CORRESPONDENCE of the two Richard Hakluyts. By E. G. R. Taylor. 2 vols. *Hakluyt Soc.*, 2nd ser., lxxvi, lxxvii (1935).

3138 HAKLUYTUS POSTHUMUS OR PURCHAS HIS PILGRIMES contayning a history of the world, in sea voyages and lande-travells by Englishmen and others. By Samuel Purchas. Lond. 1625; 20 vols., Glasgow, 1905–7.

The narratives included are for the most part such as had been collected by Hakluyt but not printed by him. Many are, however, of a somewhat later period. Not to be confused with two other works by Purchas of a very similar title. Cf. *D.N.B.* (9), art. Purchas.

3139 THE HISTORY OF TRAVAYLE in the West and East Indies and other countreys lying eyther way towardes the fruitfull and ryche Moluccaes. By Richard Eden and Richarde Willes. Lond. 1577.
A rearrangement with omissions and additions of *Decades of the Newe World* (3258).

3140 MÜNSTER, SEBASTIAN. A treatyse of the newe India, with other new founde landes and ilandes, as well eastwarde as westwarde. Trans. Rycharde Eden. Lond. 1553; by Edward Arber, cf. 3253.
A trans. of part of Sebastian Münster's *Cosmographia* (Basel, 1544).

3141 NARRATIVES OF VOYAGES towards the north west, in search of a passage to Cathay and India, 1496 to 1631. By Thomas Rundall. *Hakluyt Soc.* v (1849).

3142 A NEW INTERLUDE AND A MERY of the nature of the iiii elements. Lond. [1539?]; by J. O. Halliwell-Phillipps, *Percy Soc.* xxii (1848); by E. Arber, cf. 3253.
In *Garrick Collection of Plays* in B.M. Probably written by John Rastell. Date of publication in dispute. *D.N.B.* (art. Rastell) favours 1519; *S.T.C.* (35), no. 20722, 1525; but cf. Steele, in *Library*, 4th ser., ix (1929) 90–91. Earliest known narrative of some of the earliest English voyages of discovery to the west.

3143 SOME SPANISH REACTIONS TO ELIZABETHAN colonial enterprises. By D. B. Quinn. *Trans. R.H. Soc.*, 5th ser., i (1951), 1–23.

(b) *Later Works*

In addition to the books cited below a careful account of discovery and exploration down to 1558 is given in Williamson (3020). Reference should be made also to sects. B and C *infra*. Cf. also (1574). On Welsh maritime enterprise, cf. 6272, 6509.

3144 ANDREWS, K. R. New light on Hakluyt. *Mariner's Mirror*, xxxvii (1951), 299–308.

3145 BARROW, JOHN. A chronological history of voyages into the Arctic regions undertaken chiefly for the purpose of discovering a north-east, north-west or polar passage between the Atlantic and Pacific. Lond. 1818.
A book of old-fashioned learning.

3146 BEAZLEY, C. R. Exploration under Elizabeth, 1558–1603. *Trans. R.H. Soc.*, 2nd ser., ix (1895), 119–65.

3147 BOURNE, H. R. F. English seamen under the Tudors. 2 vols. Lond. 1868.
The 1st vol. alone is concerned with exploration and trade; the 2nd is devoted to privateering and warlike expeditions.

3148 FRENCH, J. M. Raleigh, Frobisher and the great carack of Spain. *Notes and Queries*, clxxiv (1938), 327–30.

3149 FROUDE, J. A. English seamen in the sixteenth century. Lond. 1895.
Should be used with care in matters of detail.

3150 GIRTIN, TOM. Richard Hakluyt, scholar at Oxford. *Geog. Jour.* cxix (1953), 208–12.

3151 KNORR, K. E. British colonial theories, 1570–1850. Oxf. 1944.
An economic interpretation.

3152 LYNAM, EDWARD. Richard Hakluyt and his successors. *Hakluyt Soc.*, 2nd ser., xciii (1946).

3153 McCANN, F. T. English discovery of America in 1585. Lond. 1952.
Very useful book.

3154 McINTYRE, R. A. William Sanderson: Elizabethan financier of discovery. *William and Mary Quar.*, 3rd ser., xii (1956), 184–201.
Sanderson contributed to the exploits of John Davis, Raleigh, &c.

3155 MANHART, G. B. English search for a north-west passage in the time of Queen Elizabeth. Philadelphia, 1924.

3156 NEWTON, A. P. The European nations in the West Indies, 1493–1688. *The Pioneer Histories*. By V. T. Harlow and J. A. Williamson. Lond. 1933.

3157 OAKESHOTT, W. Founded upon the seas: A narrative of some English maritime overseas enterprises, 1550–1616. Cambr. 1942.

3158 PARKS, G. B. Richard Hakluyt and the English voyagers. *Amer. Geog. Soc. Pub.* New York, 1928.
Contains, in app. iv, a list of English books on geography and travel.

3159 PENROSE, BOIES. Travel and discovery in the Renaissance, 1420–1620. Cambr., U.S.A., 1952.
Particularly good on Portuguese and Spanish adventurers.

3160 RALEIGH, WALTER. The English voyages of the sixteenth century. Lond. 1906.
Repr. from Hakluyt (3137), vol. xii. A spirited and suggestive essay.

3161 TAYLOR, E. G. R. Early empire-building projects in the Pacific Ocean, 1565–1585. *Hispanic Amer. Hist. Rev.* xiv (1934), 296–306.
Projects found in the writings of John Rastell and others.

3162 TAYLOR, E. G. R. Richard Hakluyt. *Geog. Jour.* cix (1947), 165–74.

3163 TAYLOR, E. G. R. The early navigator. *Geog. Jour.* cxiii (1949), 58–61.

3164 TAYLOR, E. G. R. Master Hore's voyage of 1536. *Geog. Jour.* lxxvii (1931), 469–70.

3165 WALKER, GEORGE. Puritan salt. The story of Richard Madox, Elizabethan venturer. Lond. 1935.

3166 WILKINSON, CLENNEL. The English adventurers. Lond. 1931.

3167 WITTEK, PAUL. The Turkish documents in Hakluyt's 'Voyages'. *Bull. Inst. Hist. Research*, xix (1942), 121–39.

3168 WRIGHT, L. B. Religion and empire, the alliance between piety and commerce in English expansion, 1558–1625. Chapel Hill, 1943.

3169 WRIGHT, L. B. Elizabethan politics and colonial enterprise. *North Carol. Hist. Rev.* xxxii (1955), 254–69.

B. THE EARLY EXPLORERS

For Thomas Cavendish, the Circumnavigator, cf. his life in *D.N.B.* (9), for George, Earl of Cumberland, cf. 3501.

(1) THE CABOTS

(a) *Bibliography*

Winship's admirable bibliography (3170) obviates the necessity of any exhaustive list of the voluminous literature on this subject. The work of Williamson (3185) is most valuable; also Deane's essay on the Cabots in Winsor (3278b). Reference should also be made to the bibliographical note in Channing (3270), i, 55.

3170 WINSHIP, G. P. Cabot bibliography, with an introductory essay on the careers of the Cabots. New York, 1900.
An admirable guide to all sources of information on the subject.

(b) *Sources*

Harrisse (3179) prints nearly all the important evidence dealing with the Cabot voyages. Markham prints the documents relative to the 1497 voyage in his *Journal of Columbus* (Hakluyt Soc., Lond. 1893). *Cal. S.P., Spanish* (867), i, and *Cal. S.P., Venetian* (992), i, contain something of value.

3171 THE NORTHMEN, COLUMBUS AND CABOT, 985–1503. By J. E. Olson and E. G. Bourne. *Original Narratives of Early American History*. New York, 1906.
Includes letters from Italian diplomats in London, 1497–8.

3172 NOTICES CONCERNING JOHN CABOT and his son Sebastian . . . from original manuscripts in the Macrian library at Venice. By Rawdon Brown and Edward Cheney. *Philobiblon Soc., Bibliographical and Historical Miscellanies*. Lond. 1854–6.

3173 AN EARLY GRANT TO SEBASTIAN CABOT, 1504. By A. P. Newton. *E.H.R.* xxxvii (1922), 564–5.

(c) *Later Works*

The work of Williamson (3185) is the standard account. Also valuable are the works of Harrisse (3179–81), Beazley (3174), Dawson (3176), and Weare (3184) are all good.

3174 BEAZLEY, C. R. John and Sebastian Cabot; the discovery of North America. New York, 1898.

3175 [BIDDLE, RICHARD.] A memoir of Sebastian Cabot with a review of the history of maritime discovery. Philadelphia, 1831.
One of the earliest of modern contributions to the subject of discovery, giving occasion for a large number of critical articles, for which see Winship (3170).

3176 DAWSON, S. E. The voyages of the Cabots in 1497 and 1498; with an attempt to determine their land-fall and to identify their island of St. John. *Proc. and Trans. Roy. Soc. of Canada*, xii (1894), 51–112; 2nd ser., ii (1896), 3–28; 2nd ser., iii (1897), 139–268.

3177　ERRERA, CARLO. La spedizione di Sebastiano Caboto al Rio della Plata. *Archivio Storico Italiano*, 5th ser., xv (1895), 1–62.

3178　FERNANDEZ DURO, CESAREO. Los Cabotos. *Boletín de la Real Academia de la Historia*, xxii (1893), 257–82.

3179　HARRISSE, HENRY. Jean et Sébastien Cabot, leur origine et leurs voyages. Paris, 1882.
Gives text of all sources known at time of publication.

3180　HARRISSE, HENRY. John Cabot, the discoverer of North-America and Sebastian his son. Lond. 1896.
A careful study of all disputed questions concerning the Cabots, with many of the documents.

3181　HARRISSE, HENRY. The outcome of the Cabot quatercentenary. *A.H.R.* iv (1898–9), 38–61.
Valuable bibliographical notes.

3182　MEDINA, J. T. El Veneciano Sebastian Caboto al servicio de España. 2 vols. Santiago de Chile, 1908.
Although these vols are devoted to the career of Cabot in Spain, the short chapters concerning his early and late life are significant for his connexion with England.

3183　PASTOR, C. P. Sebastian Caboto en 1533 y 1548. *Boletín de la Real Academia de la Historia*, xxii (1893), 257–82.

3184　WEARE, G. E. Cabot's discovery of North America. Lond. 1897.
A good account with many documents.

3185　WILLIAMSON, J. A. The voyages of the Cabots and the English discovery of North America under Henry VII and Henry VIII. Lond. 1929.
Cf. also by the same author, *The voyages of John and Sebastian Cabot*, Hist. Assoc. Pamphlet, no. 106. Lond. 1937.

(2) SIR JOHN HAWKINS

(a) *Sources*

The best discussion of the sources on Hawkins is in Williamson (3190), *passim*. For his earlier career there is some material in R. H. Worth, *Calendar of Plymouth municipal records* (4329), and some of his personal papers are printed in 3526. Markham's ed. of *Hawkins's voyages* (3186) needs to be supplemented by another account of the third voyage printed in Williamson (3190). Hakluyt (3137) is of first-rate importance. For Hawkins's naval career reference should be made to pp. 295–304 *infra*, particularly to Corbett (3451) and Laughton (3518).

3186　THE HAWKINS' VOYAGES during the reigns of Henry VIII, queen Elizabeth and James I. By C. R. Markham. *Hakluyt Soc.* lvii (1878).
Narratives and works of four members of the Hawkins family, with valuable introductory matter, including a repr. of 3187. Includes also an account of the voyage of Edward Fenton, 1582.

3187　HAWKINS, RICHARD. Observations of Sir Richard Hawkins, knight, on his voyage into the South Sea, A.D. 1593. Lond. 1622; by C. R. D. Bethune, *Hakluyt Soc.* i (1847); repr. in 3186; new ed. by J. A. Williamson, Lond. 1933.

3188 RUMEU DE ARMAS, ANTONIO. Los viajes de John Hawkins a America, 1562–1595. *Univ. of Seville Pub. School of Hispano-Amer. Stud.* xxxv, 2nd ser., mono. no. 9. Seville, 1947.

3189 THE THIRD VOYAGE OF SIR JOHN HAWKINS, 1567–8. By Edward Arber. Westminster, 1895.

A collection of state papers and other MSS. and reprs. of original narratives relating to the affair of San Juan de Ulua. Cf. also Michael Lewis, *Fresh light on San Juan de Ulua*, *Mariner's Mirror*, xxii (1936), 324–45; xxiii (1937), 295–315, who reproduces some new documents on Hawkins's adventure.

Another contemporary account of this voyage is printed in Williamson (3190), 491–534. A narrative based on Spanish sources by C. S. Arizmendi is printed in *Boletín del Instituto de Estudios Americanistas* (Seville, 1913–14), 55.

For a discussion of the sources of this voyage in general, cf. Williamson (3190), 142–4.

(b) *Later Works*

The earlier unsatisfactory lives of Hawkins in Campbell (3466) and Southey (3497) are supplanted by Williamson (3190).

3190 WILLIAMSON, J. A. Sir John Hawkins, the times and the man. Oxf. 1927; rev. ed. 1949.

Scholarly. Valuable bibliography and app. 1st ed. is more complete.

(3) SIR FRANCIS DRAKE

(a) *Sources*

The best discussion of the sources for Drake's career is in Corbett (3212), appendixes to vols. i and ii. Cf. also Williamson (3220). Relevant material from Spanish archives is printed in Nuttall (3202), Wagner (3218), and Jameson (3204). The *Cal. S.P., Spanish, Elizabeth* (868) should also be consulted. Some material from French archives is printed in 3252. Hakluyt (3137) is of first-rate importance.

For Drake's naval exploits reference should be made to pp. 295–304 *infra*, particularly to Corbett (3451) and to Laughton (3518).

3191 BIGGES (*et al.*), CAPT. WALTER. A summarie and true discourse of Sir Francis Drake's Indian voyage (1585–6) begun by Capt. Walter Bigges, continued after his death by his lieutenant Master Crofts or some other . . . with geographical mappes . . . diligently made by Baptista Boazio. By Thomas Gates. Lond. 1589.

2 eds. appeared in 1589. Never reprinted though most of it is given in Hakluyt (3137) x, 97 ff. For an unpublished contemporary account of this voyage and for the Spanish sources, cf. Corbett (3212), ii, 411.

3192 DE LA RONCIÈRE, CHARLES. Un atlas inconnu de la dernière expédition de Drake (vues prises de son bord). Paris, 1909.

Reproduced (with commentary) from the original atlas in the Bib. Nat. Cf. the *Mariner's Mirror*, ii (1912), 135.

3193 DE VEGA CARPIO, LOPE F. Dragontea. 1602; by F. Cerda y Rica. Madrid, 1776–9.

A poem of the last expedition of Drake and Hawkins, 1595–6. Ed. of 1776–9 is included in Lope de Vega's *Obras Sueltas*, published in 21 vols.

3194 EPHEMERIS EXPEDITIONIS NORREYSII ET DRAKI in Lusi-
taniam. Lond. 1589; Frankfort, 1590.

3195 FLETCHER, FRANCIS. The world encompassed by Sir Francis
Drake . . . carefully collected out of the notes of Master Francis Fletcher.
By Francis Drake (nephew of the navigator). Lond. 1628; by W. S. W. Vaux,
Hakluyt Soc. xvi (1854).
Vaux's ed. gives in appendixes various other narratives and documents relating to the
voyage. See Corbett (3212), i, app. E.

3196 GREEPE, THOMAS. The true and perfecte newes of the exploytes
performed by Syr Francis Drake. Lond. 1587; reproduced with notes and
bibliography by D. W. Waters, Hartford, 1955.
A ballad giving particulars not found elsewhere.

3197 [HASLOP, H.] Newes out of the coast of Spaine. The true report of
the honourable service . . . performed by Sir Francis Drake . . . upon Cales.
Lond. 1587.

3198 JENNER, G. A Spanish account of Drake's voyages. *E.H.R.* xvi (1901),
46–66.
Extracts from Pedro Simon's *Noticias Historiales de las Conquistas de Tierra Firma,*
written c. 1623, bearing upon Drake's expeditions to South America in 1585–6.

3199 LENG, ROBERT. Sir Francis Drake's memorable service done against
the Spaniards in 1587. By Clarence Hopper. *Camden Misc.* v (1863).
The author was one of Drake's fellow-soldiers.

3200 MAYNARDE, THOMAS. Sir Francis Drake his voyage, 1595. By
W. D. Cooley. *Hakluyt Soc.* iv (1849).
The author was captain of a company of troops and a member of the council of war.
Includes also a Spanish account of Drake's attack upon Puerto Rico.

3201 NICHOLS, PHILIP. Sir Francis Drake reviv'd . . . By Sir Francis
Drake (the younger). Lond. 1626; by Edward Arber, Westminster, 1895.
See Corbett (3212), i, app. D.

3202 NUTTALL, ZELIA. New light on Drake, 1577–80. *Hakluyt Soc.,*
2nd ser., xxxiv (1914).
Documents from Spanish and Mexican archives pertinent to Drake's voyage of circumnavigation. Cf. also M. M. de Peralta, *Costa Rica, Nicaragua y Panama en el siglo XVI*
(Madrid, 1883), which contains several original letters from Spanish officials in America
at the time of Drake's attack upon their possessions in the South Seas.

3203 SAVILE, HENRY. A libell of Spanish lies . . . concerning some part
of the last voyage of Sir Francis Drake. Lond. 1596; repr. by Hakluyt (3127),
x, 246–65.

3204 SOME NEW SPANISH DOCUMENTS dealing with Drake. By A. K.
Jameson. *E.H.R.* xlix (1934), 14–31.

3205 A TRUE COPPIE OF A DISCOURSE written by a gentleman em-
ployed in the late voyage of Spaine and Portingale. Lond. 1589; *Collier's
Reprints,* Lond. 1870.
Repr. also in Hakluyt (3137), vi, 470–527, where it is doubtfully attributed to Col.
Antonie Wingfield.

(b) *Later Works*

The best lives of Drake are Corbett (3212) and Williamson (3220), both scholarly works which displace the earlier life by Barrow (3206). An excellent account of Drake's naval exploits is in Oppenheim's ed. of Monson (3448). Reference may also be made to the account of Drake in Campbell (3466), Southey (3497), Clowes (3467), and in 3526.

3206 BARROW, JOHN. Life, voyages and exploits of Sir Francis Drake. Lond. 1843.
Valuable mainly for the documents printed.

3207 BENSON, E. F. Sir Francis Drake. Lond. 1927.

3208 BISHOP, R. P. Drake's course in the north Pacific. *Brit. Colum. Hist. Quar.* iii (1939), 151–82.
This article contains extracts from the sources.

3209 ¶ CALLENDER, GEOFFREY. Drake and his detractors. *Mariner's Mirror,* vii (1921), 66–74, 98–105, 142–52.
Analyses the evidence against Drake in the Doughty affair.

3210 CALLENDER, GEOFFREY. Fresh light on Drake. *Mariner's Mirror,* ix (1923), 16–28.
A discussion of a rediscovered contemporary Spanish poem by Juan de Castellaños on Drake's descent upon Carthagena.

3211 CHRISTY, MILLER. The silver map of the world, a contemporary medallion commemorative of Drake's great voyage 1577–80. Lond. 1900.
A critical examination of the geographical results of Drake's circumnavigation.

3212 CORBETT, J. S. Drake and the Tudor navy. With a history of the rise of England as a maritime power. 2 vols. Lond. 1898; 1899.
A standard life. Scholarly. Valuable bibliographical notes in appendixes. The 2nd ed. corrects a few errors in the 1st.

3212a CORBETT, J. S. The successors of Drake. Lond. 1900; 1932.

3213 DRAKE'S PLATE OF BRASS. Evidence of his visit to California in 1579. *California Hist. Soc.,* spec. pub., xiii (1937), 1–57; xiv (1938), 1–26.
A collection of essays by various historians. Cf. also H. E. Bolton, ibid. xvi (1937), 1–16; J. A. Williamson, *Geog. Jour.* xci (1938), 543–5; R. B. Haselden, *California Hist. Soc. Quar.* xvi (1937), 271; and J. B. Brebner, *Canadian Hist. Assoc. Report for 1937* (1937), 72–75.

3214 DYER, F. E. Drake's voyage of circumnavigation. *Mariner's Mirror,* ix (1923), 194–201.
Reproduces sketches which accompany Fletcher's contemporary account of the voyage. Cf. also W. H. Kerr, *The treatment of Drake's circumnavigation in Hakluyt's 'Voyages', 1589,* Papers Bibliog. Soc. Amer. xxxiv (1940), 281–302.

3215 ELIOT-DRAKE, E. F. The family and heirs of Sir Francis Drake. 2 vols. Lond. 1911.
Contains, besides details of Sir F. Drake's life, valuable appendixes of documents relating to the voyage of circumnavigation.

3216 HARTE, W. J. Historical revisions: lxxvi. Some recent views of Drake's voyage around the world. *History,* xx (1936), 348–53.

3217 ROBINSON, GREGORY. The evidence about the Golden Hind.
Mariner's Mirror, xxxv (1949), 56–65.

3218 WAGNER, H. R. Sir Francis Drake's voyage around the world. San
Francisco, 1925.
Holds that Drake's purpose was primarily to reach the Moluccas and open up the spice
trade. Prints many documents from English and Spanish sources. Cf. *A.H.R.* xxxiv
(1928), 114–17.

3219 WILLIAMSON, J. A. Books on Drake. *History*, xii (1928), 310–21.
A review of recent books on Drake, notably Corbett (3212), Nuttall (3202), and Wagner
(3218), with a useful discussion of the sources for Drake's career.

3220 WILLIAMSON, J. A. The age of Drake. *Pioneer Histories*. Lond.
1938; 1946; 1952.
Excellent.

(4) SIR MARTIN FROBISHER

(a) *Sources*

The most important sources for Frobisher's explorations are printed in Hakluyt
(3137) and by Collinson (3227). Cf. also 3252. There is some unpublished
material utilized by Marsden (3230) and Eliot (3228) in the Admiralty records.
For Frobisher's naval exploits reference should be made to pp. 295–304 *infra*.

3221 BEST, GEORGE. A true discourse of the late voyages of discoverie . . .
under the conduct of Martin Frobisher, General. Lond. 1578; repr. in
Hakluyt (3137), vii, 250–83; new ed. by Vilhjalmur Stefansson and Eloise
McCaskill, 2 vols., Lond. 1938.
The 1938 ed. is from original text of Best, together with numerous other versions,
additions, &c. Cf. also E. G. R. Taylor, *Voyages of Martin Frobisher*, *Geog. Jour.* xci
(1938), 360–3. Cf. also 2779.

3222 DE MARTINI FORBISSERI Angli navigatione in regiones occidentis
et septentrionis narratio historica. Noriberga, 1580.
A Latin trans. by D. Joan from a French account of Frobisher's second voyage of 1577.

3223 ELLIS, THOMAS. A true reporte of the third and last voyage into
Meta Incognita, 1578. Lond. 1578; repr. in Hakluyt (3137), vii, 231–42.

3224 CHURCHYARDE, THOMAS. A prayse and reporte of Maister Mar-
tyne Forboisher's voyage to Meta Incognita. Lond. 1578.

3225 FROBISHER'S THIRD VOYAGE, 1578. By G. B. Parks. *Hunt. Lib.
Bull.* no. 7 (1935), 181–90.
Contains documents.

3226 SETTLE, DIONYSE. A true reporte of the laste voyage into the
West and Northwest regions . . . in 1577 . . . worthily atchieved by Captaine
Frobisher. Lond. 1577; repr. in Hakluyt (3137), vii, 211–30.
An account of Frobisher's second voyage. Cf. G. P. Parks and Roland Baughman,
The two versions of Settle's Frobisher narrative, *Hunt. Lib. Quar.* ii (1938), 59–68.

3227 THE THREE VOYAGES OF MARTIN FROBISHER in search of a
passage to Cathaia and India by the Northwest. By Richard Collinson.
Hakluyt Soc. xxxvii (1867).
The accounts reprinted from Hakluyt, with many illustrative documents. Valuable.

(b) *Later Works*

3228 ELIOT, K. M. The first voyages of Martin Frobisher. *E.H.R.* xxxii (1917), 89–92.

3229 JONES, FRANK. The life of Sir Martin Frobisher, knight, containing a narrative of the Spanish Armada. Lond. 1878.
A popular but meritorious work.

3230 MARSDEN, R. G. The early career of Martin Frobisher. *E.H.R.* xxi (1906), 538–44.

(5) SIR HUMPHREY GILBERT

(a) *Sources*

Hakluyt (3137), Slafter (3233) and Quinn (3234) print virtually all the pertinent material. Some foreign comments are to be found in the *Cal. S.P., Spanish* (868) and in the French dispatches (3252).

3231 GILBERT, HUMPHREY. A discourse of a discoverie for a new passage to Cataia. By George Gascoigne. Lond. 1576; repr. in Hakluyt (3137), vii, 158–90.

3232 PECKHAM, GEORGE. A true reporte, of the late discoveries and possession taken . . . of the new-found landes by . . . Sir Humfrey Gilbert. Lond. 1583; repr. in Hakluyt (3137), viii, 89–131.

3233 SIR HUMPHREY GILBERT AND HIS ENTERPRISE of colonization in America. By Carlos Slafter. *Prince Soc.*, 1903.
Prints pertinent narratives from Hakluyt (3137) and letters from S.P., Domestic, in the P.R.O.

3234 THE VOYAGES AND COLONIZING ENTERPRISES of Sir Humphrey Gilbert. By D. B. Quinn. 2 vols. *Hakluyt Soc.*, 2nd ser., lxxxiii–lxxxiv (1940).

(b) *Later Works*

In addition to Gosling (3235), Slafter (3233) furnishes a useful account in his introduction. Longfellow's well-known poem on Gilbert's death is inaccurate in details.

3235 GOSLING, W. G. The life of Sir Humphrey Gilbert, England's first empire builder. Lond. 1911.
With many documents: devoted especially to Gilbert's activities in colonization

(6) SIR WALTER RALEIGH

(a) *Bibliography*

Cf. Winsor (3278b), iii, 121–6; and T. N. Brushfield, *Bibliography of Sir Walter Raleigh*, 2nd ed., Exeter, 1908.

(b) *Sources*

Most of the materials pertinent to Raleigh's ventures in the new world are printed in Tarbox (3237). Much also is printed in Hakluyt (3137). Edwards (609) prints Raleigh's correspondence.

3236 RALEGH, WALTER. The discouerie of the large, rich and bewtiful empire of Guiana. . . . Lond. 1596; by R. H. Schomburgk, *Hakluyt Soc.* iii (1848).
Ed. of 1848 contains many valuable notes. Also repr. in Hakluyt (3137), x, 338–431.

3237 SIR WALTER RALEGH AND HIS COLONY in America. By I. N. Tarbox. *Prince Soc.*, 1884.
Reprints Ralegh's charter and various accounts of his Virginia venture, from Hakluyt (3137).

3238 RALEGH, WALTER. Works. By Thomas Birch. 2 vols. Lond. 1751; 8 vols., Oxf. 1829.

(c) *Later Works*

There are many popular lives of Raleigh, but (609) and (3245) give all the important facts. For his adventure in North America reference should be made to sect. C *infra*, and in South America to Williamson (3278a).

3239 GRIFFITHS, G. M. An account book of Raleigh's voyage, 1592. *Jour. Nat. Lib. Wales*, vii (1952), 347–53.

3240 HARLOW, V. Raleigh's last voyage. Lond. 1933.
Cf. also C. L'Estrange Ewen, *Notes and Queries*, clxxiv (1938), 254–6.

3241 QUINN, D. B. Raleigh and the British Empire. Lond. 1947.

3242 QUINN, D. B. The failure of Raleigh's American colonies. *Essays in British and Irish history in honour of James Eadie Todd*. Lond. 1949. pp. 61–85.

3243 SANDISON, H. E. Raleigh's orders once more. *Mariner's Mirror*, xx (1934), 323–30.

3244 SHIRLEY, J. W. Sir Walter Raleigh's Guiana finances. *Hunt. Lib. Quar.* xiii (1949), 55–69.

3245 STEBBING, W. Sir Walter Raleigh. Oxf. 1891; 1899.

3246 STRATHMANN, E. C. Sir Walter Raleigh: a study in Elizabethan skepticism. Lond. 1951.
Cf. also A. M. C. Latham, *A birth date for Sir Walter Raleigh*, *Études Angl.* ix (1956), 243–5; J. Denham, *La date du mariage de Sir Walter Raleigh*, ibid. 193–211; and C.F.T. Brooke, *Sir Walter Ralegh as poet and philosopher*, *Eng. Lit. Hist.* v (1938), 93–112.

3247 THOMPSON, EDWARD. Sir Walter Raleigh: the last of the Elizabethans. Lond. 1935.

(7) Sir John Davis

His works and much of his correspondence are given in Markham (3248).

3248 THE VOYAGES AND WORKS OF JOHN DAVIS, the navigator. By A. H. Markham. *Hakluyt Soc.* lix, pt. i (1880).
With a valuable introduction and bibliographical appendixes. Includes his treatises, *The worldes hydrographical description*, 1595, and *The seaman's secrets*, 1607.

3249   MARKHAM, C. R. A life of John Davis, the navigator, 1550–1605. . .
Lond. 1889.
The standard life.

C. AMERICA

Reference should be made to sect. B *supra* (pp. 268–76).

(a) *Bibliography*

Winsor (3278b), i, pp. xi–xviii, prints a useful though now rather antiquated
bibliography of American bibliographies; iii contains valuable bibliographical
essays on the Cabot voyages, on the Hawkins and Drake voyages, on exploration
to the north-west, on Raleigh, on Norumbega and its English explorers. Winsor,
iii, 199–206, prints also a useful list of the earliest English books on America.
A. B. Hart, *The American nation*, i, *The European background of American history*,
by E. P. Cheyney, and iv, *England in America*, by L. G. Tyler, contain useful
bibliographical chapters. A good selected bibliography is in the *Harvard guide
to American history*, by Oscar Handlin *et al.*, Cambr. 1954, which is a revision
of the *Guide to the study of American history*, by E. Channing, A. B. Hart, and
F. J. Turner, 3rd ed., Boston, 1912.

For MS. material relating to the early history of the English in America,
students should consult:

> *Guide to the items relating to American history in the reports of the English
> historical MSS. Comm.*, by J. F. Jameson, *Annual Report Am. Hist. Assoc.
> 1898*, Washington, 1899.
> *Guide to the MSS. material for the history of the United States to 1783 in the
> British Museum, in minor London archives and in the libraries of Oxford and
> Cambridge*, by C. M. Andrews and F. G. Davenport, Washington, 1918.
> *Guide to the material for American history to 1783 in the Public Record Office
> of Great Britain*, by C. M. Andrews, 2 vols., Washington, 1912–14.
> *List of books relating to America in the registers of the London Company of
> Stationers from 1562 to 1638*, by P. L. Phillips, *Annual Report Amer. Hist.
> Assoc. 1896*, i, 1249–61, Washington, 1897.

Further bibliographical references of a general nature are printed in Davies (8),
355–7, and Stanley Pargellis and D. J. Medley, *Bibliography of British history,
the eighteenth century, 1714–1789*, Oxf. 1951, pp. 452–3.

(b) *Sources*

The *Cal. S.P., Colonial*, i, and ix (85), are of first-rate importance. Hakluyt
(3137) prints practically all of the extant accounts of early English adventurers
in America. One or two are added by Purchas (3138).

3250   BRERETON, JOHN. A briefe and true relation of the discoverie of the
north part of Virginia. Lond. 1602; repr. in 3251; by Luthers Livingston,
New York, 1903.
An account of Gosnold's voyage of 1602 by one of his company.

3251   COLLECTIONS OF THE MASSACHUSETTS HISTORICAL
SOCIETY. 3rd ser., viii. Boston, 1843.
Prints sources relating to Gosnold's and Mace's voyage to America in 1602, chiefly
from Purchas (3138).

3252 DESPATCHES OF CASTELNAU de la Mauvissière (on Frobisher, Gilbert, de la Roche, Drake), 1577–81. By J. F. Jameson, *A.H.R.* xxxi (1926), 285–96.
Contemporary reports by the French ambassador in England.

3253 THE FIRST THREE ENGLISH BOOKS ON AMERICA, by E. Arber. Westminster, 1895.
Includes 3100, 3140, 3258.

3254 FURTHER ENGLISH VOYAGES TO SPANISH AMERICA, 1583–94. By I. A. Wright, *Hakluyt Soc.*, 2nd ser., xcix (1951).

3255 HAKLUYT, RICHARD. Divers voyages touching the discoverie of America and the ilands adjacent unto the same. Lond. 1582; by J. W. Jones, *Hakluyt Soc.* vii (1850).
Ed. of 1850 contains valuable introduction, notes, and appendixes.

3256 HAKLUYT, RICHARD. A particular discourse concerninge the greate necessitie and manifolde commodytics . . . by the Westerne discoveries lately attempted. By Charles Deane. In *Doc. history of the state of Maine* (8 vols., Portland, U.S.A., 1869–1909), ii.
Written in 1584. Very similar in content and arrangement to Captain Carlile's *Briefe and summary discourse*, written April 1583, in Hakluyt (3137), viii, 134–47. Generally known as Hakluyt's *Discourse on Western planting*.

3257 HARIOT, THOMAS. A briefe and true report of the new-found land of Virginia. Lond. 1588; Frankfort, 1590; repr. in Hakluyt (3137), viii, 348–86.
The 2nd ed. contains drawings by John White. It was repr. in facsimile by the *Holbein Soc.*, Lond. 1893. For the White drawings, cf. E. Hale in *Arch. Americana*, iv (1860), 21. For bibliographical data, cf. Winsor (3278b), iii, 123, n. 1.

3258 MARTYR ANGLERIUS, PETER. The decades of the newe worlde or west India, conteynyng the navigations and conquestes of the Spanyardes. Rycharde Eden, translator. Lond. 1555; by Edward Arber, cf. 3253.
This trans. marks an important step in the knowledge by the English people of exploration and discovery.

3259 THE ROANOKE VOYAGES, 1584–90. By D. B. Quinn. *Hakluyt Soc.*, 2nd ser., civ–cv (1955).

3260 SAILORS' NARRATIVES OF VOYAGES along the New England coast, 1524–1624. By G. P. Winship. Boston, 1905.
Contains portions of a number of the early narratives of discovery, some not included in Hakluyt.

3261 SPANISH DOCUMENTS concerning English voyages to the Caribbean, 1527–68. By I. A. Wright. *Hakluyt Soc.*, 2nd ser., lxii (1929).
Papers drawn from the archives of the Indies at Seville.

3262 THE VOYAGE OF ROBERT DUDLEY . . . to the West Indies, 1594–5. By G. F. Warner. *Hakluyt Soc.*, 2nd ser., iii (1899).
Three parallel accounts of this voyage with a valuable app.

3263 VOYAGE OF THE BARBARA TO BRAZIL, Anno 1540. By R. G. Marsden. *Naval Miscellany* (*Navy Rec. Soc.*), ii (1912), 3–66.
Drawn from Admiralty records. Cf. also R. G. Marsden on the same subject in *E.H.R.* xxiv (1909), 96–100.

3264 VOYAGES OF THE ELIZABETHAN SEAMEN to America. By E. J. Payne. 2 vols. Lond. 1880; 2 vols., Oxf. 1893–1900.
A selection of some of the most important narratives from Hakluyt (3137), with some introductory material.

3265 TRAVELS AND WORKS OF CAPT. JOHN SMITH. By Ed. Arber. Westminster, 1884; 2 vols. Edin. 1910.
First book, pt. 1, 304–41, contains Smith's abridgements of accounts of early voyages to America, chiefly from Hakluyt (3137).

(c) *Later Works*

Of the innumerable general histories of the English in America, the more important are given in Davies (8). Merriman (2355) discusses an early project to establish a Roman Catholic settlement in America. On the Raleigh settlements in North Carolina, cf. Hawks (3273). Williamson (3020) writes of an early colonial project in North America under Henry VII.

3266 BOURNE, E. G. The naming of America. *A.H.R.* x (1904–5), 41–51.

3267 BIGGAR, H. P. Precursors of Jacques Cartier. Ottawa, 1911.
Cf. also idem, *An expedition to America in 1527*, in *Mélanges* (3079), 459–72.

3268 BREBNER, J. B. The explorers of North America, 1492–1806. *Pioneer Histories*. Lond. 1933.

3269 BROWN, ALEXANDER. The genesis of the United States. 2 vols. Boston, 1891.
Contains remarkable lists and short biographies of all characters even remotely connected with early colonization.

3270 CHANNING, EDWARD. A history of the United States. 6 vols. New York, 1905–25.
Vol. i covers early English exploration and colonization. Useful bibliographical notes.

3271 CONNELL-SMITH, G. English merchants trading to the new world in the early sixteenth century. *Bull. Inst. Hist. Research*, xxiii (1950), 53–67.

3272 HARTE, W. J. Some evidence of trade between Exeter and Newfoundland up to 1600. *Trans. of the Devon Assoc.* lxiv (1932).

3273 HAWKS, F. L. History of North Carolina. 3 vols. Fayetteville, N.C., 1857–8.
Vol. i deals with the English settlement at Roanoke, 1584–91.

3274 KIRKPATRICK, F. A. The first recorded English voyage to the West Indies. *E.H.R.* xx (1905), 115–24.

3275 KOHL, J. G. A history of the discovery of the east coast of North America . . . from 990 to . . . 1578. *Documentary History of the State of Maine* (8 vols. Portland, U.S.A., 1869–1909), i.
A full account of voyages to the NE. coast of America by all nations, with many documents and maps. Scholarly. Especially valuable for the Cabot voyages and for early maps.

3276 LOWERY, WOODBURY. Jean Ribaut and Queen Elizabeth. *A.H.R.* ix (1903–4), 456–9.

3277 QUINN, D. B. Preparation for the 1585 Virginia voyage. *William and Mary Quar.*, 3rd ser., vi (1949), 208–36.

3278 SAUNDERS, A. C. Newfoundland and the Channel Islands. *Soc. Guernesiaise Report and Trans. for 1933*, xii (1934), 42–56.

3278a WILLIAMSON, J. A. The English colonies in Guiana and on the Amazon. Oxf. 1923.
Pp. 17–29 deal with the period before 1604.

3278b WINSOR, JUSTIN. A narrative and critical history of America. 8 vols. Boston, 1884–9.
Vol. iii deals with early English exploration and colonization. Particularly valuable for its bibliographical notes.

D. THE ART OF NAVIGATION

(a) *Sources*

In the latter half of the sixteenth century practical treatises on the art of navigation became numerous. A valuable bibliography of these is printed in Markham's ed. of *Works of John Davis* (3248), pp. 339–67, though the bibliographical details are not always scrupulously accurate. There is also a useful list in Winsor (3278b), iii, 207–8. The earlier works on navigation were chiefly continental. Three Spanish works in particular were well known in England and translated editions of them appeared (cf. 3281, 3284, 3286).

In addition to these there were the so-called *Rutters of the Sea*, being descriptions of coast-lines and sailing-courses often printed with old law codes governing maritime questions. The oldest of these was in French, printed early in the sixteenth century at Rouen under the title, *Le routier de la mer iusques au fleuve de Jourdain*. Numerous English translations appeared (3287).

There were finally several series of astronomical almanacs or *Ephemerides*, of which perhaps the best known in England were those of Johannes Stadius.

The first marine atlas was published by Lucas J. Wagenaar in 1584, and an English version appeared in 1588 (3289).

Besides the works mentioned below, books pertaining to the art of navigation were contributed by Thomas Digges, John Dee, John Blagrave, Robert Tanner, Thos. Blundeville, Simon Forman, Robert Hues, Thos. Harriot, William Barlow, Edward Wright, William Gilbert, and Robert Norman. On all of these cf. Markham (3248).

3279 BOURNE, WILLIAM. A booke called the treasure for traueilers . . . contayning very necessary matters for all sorts of traueilers, eyther by sea or by lande. Lond. 1578.
An ed. was published in 1641 under the title, *A mate for mariners*.
Bourne also wrote *Inventions and devices very necessary for all generalles and captaines or leaders of men, as well by sea as by land* (Lond. 1578) and several nautical almanacs.

3280 BOURNE, WILLIAM. A regiment for the sea. . . . Lond. [1573 or 1574?].
The dates of the 1st and 2nd eds. are uncertain. Markham (3248) gives 1573 and 1577, but cf. *S.T.C.* (35), nos. 3422–3. At least 10 eds. appeared before 1632. The ed. of 1592 was corrected and enlarged by Thos. Hood; that of 1596 contained also *An hydrographicall discourse to shew the passage unto Cattay five manner of waies, two of them knowen and the other three supposed* as well as Hood's *The mariners guide* (3285).

3281 CORTES, MARTIN. The arte of nauigation. Richard Eden, translator. Lond. 1561.
A very popular work trans. from the Spanish of Martin Cortes, *Breve compendio de la sphera de la arte de navegar,* &c., published at Seville in 1551. As many as 8 eds. of this trans. with some corrections and augmentations appeared before 1616.

3282 DAVIS, JOHN. The seaman's secrets. . . . etc., etc. 1594; by A. H. Markham, cf. 3248.
No copy of 1st ed. extant. At least 8 eds. appeared in the seventeenth century. The ed. of 1880 is a repr. of the ed. of 1607.

3283 DAVIS, JOHN. The worldes hydrographical discription, wherein is proved . . . that the worlde in all his zones . . . is habitable and in seas . . . navigable. Lond. 1595; by A. H. Markham, cf. 3248.

3284 GUEVARA, ANTONIO DE. A book of the inuention of the art of nauigation. Lond. 1578.
An Eng. trans. of *Libros de los inventores del arte de marear y de muchos trabajos que se passen en las galeras,* Antwerp, 1550, written by Guevara, bp. of Mondonedo.

3285 HOOD, THOMAS. The mariners guide. . . . . Lond. 1596.
On Hood, cf. Markham (3248), 360, on the date of publication, cf. *S.T.C.* (35), no. 13696

3286 MEDINA, PEDRO DE. The arte of nauigation. Trans. J. Frampton. Lond. 1581; 1595.
A trans. of *Arte de Navegar,* Valladolid, 1545. A very popular book on the continent, where it appeared in numerous French and Dutch eds.

3287 THE RUTTER OF THE SEA, with the laws of the yle of Auleron. By Robert Coplande. Lond. 1528.
This is an Eng. trans. of a French *Routier.* Of this 1st ed. no copy appears to be extant. Many subsequent eds. appeared in the sixteenth century. For an account of these, cf. Markham (3248), 355, where 6 eds. are cited, *S.T.C.* (35) gives only 4 (nos. 11551–4). Cf. also W. Senior in *Mariner's Mirror,* vi (1920), 243–6.
The earliest extant ed. is apparently that of 1536, of which there is a unique copy in Lincoln's Inn library.

3288 A SIXTEENTH CENTURY MS. navigating manual in the Society's library. By E. G. R. Taylor. *Geog. Jour.* lxxviii (1931), 346–52.

3289 WAGENAAR, L. J. The mariners mirrour, together with the rules and instruments of navigation, first made by Luke Wagenaar of Enchuisen. By Anthony Ashley. Lond. 1588.
An English version of Wagenaar's *Spieghel der Zeevaardt van de navigatrie de westersche Zee,* Antwerp, 1584, the first marine atlas, of which 4 Dutch eds. had appeared by 1596.

(b) *Later Works*

3290 BOSANQUET, E. F. Notes on further addenda to English printed almanacks and prognostications to 1600. *Library,* 4th ser., xviii (1937), 39–66.

3291 BOSANQUET, E. F. The Flye, 1569. *Library*, 4th ser., xviii (1937), 195–200.
Pictorial tide-table in Philip Moore's *Almanack*.

3292 CRASTER, EDMUND. Elizabethan globe at Oxford. *Geog. Jour.* cxvii (1951), 24–26.

3293 CRONE, G. R. 'The Mariners' Mirrour' 1558. *Geog. Jour.* cxix (1953), 455–8.

3294 GUNTHER, R. T. Quadrants, astrolabes, nocturnals, &c. *Oxf. Hist. Soc.* lxxviii (1923).
Cf. idem, *The great astrolabe and other scientific instruments of H. Cole, Arch.* lxxv; (1926), 273–317; *The mariner's astrolabe, Roy. Geog. Soc. Jour.* lxxii (1928), 342–5; and *The astrolabe of Queen Elizabeth, Arch.* lxxxvi (1937), 65–72. Cf. 3967.

3295 HEATHCOTE, N. H. DE V. Early nautical charts. *Annals of Science*, i (1936), 13–28.
Contains account of sixteenth-century writers on the subject.

3296 STEPHENS, A. E. 'The booke of the sea carte': a seaman's manual of the sixteenth century. *Imago Mundi*, ii (1937), 55–59, iii (1939), 71.

3297 WALLIS, H. M. Further light on the Molyneux globes. *Geog. Jour.* cxxi (1955), 304–11.

E. SHIPS AND SEAMEN

The best accounts of Elizabethan ships and shipping are in Corbett (3212), i, ch. 12, and Oppenheim (3557). Reference should also be made to *Shakespeare's England* (2573), i, ch. 5. Many short contributions to the subject appear in *Mariner's Mirror*, Lond. 1911 ff.

A useful bibliography of early books on shipbuilding and rigging is printed by R. C. Anderson in *Mariner's Mirror*, x (1924), 52–64, but no English book is cited before 1620.

3298 ABELL, WESTCOTT. The Shipwright's trade. Cambr. 1948.
Contains reproductions of Elizabethan architect's plans and Sir Anthony Deane's drawings.

3299 ADAIR, E. R. English galleys in the sixteenth century. *E.H.R.* xxxv (1920), 497–512.

3300 ANDERSON, R. C. The Grace de Dieu of 1446–86. *E.H.R.* xxxiv (1919), 584–6.

3301 ANDERSON, R. C. Henry VIII's great galley. *Mariner's Mirror*, vi (1920), 274–81.

3302 AYDELOTTE, FRANK. Elizabethan seamen in Mexico and ports of the Spanish Main. *A.H.R.* xlviii (1942), 1–19.

3303 BELL, DOUGLAS. Elizabethan seamen. Lond. 1936.

3304 BROOKS, F. W. A wage scale for seamen, 1546. *E.H.R.* lx (1945), 234–46.

3305 CHARNOCK, J. History of marine architecture. 3 vols. Lond. 1800–2.
Valuable, but not always trustworthy.

3306 CLOWES, G. S. L. Ships of the early explorers. *Roy. Geog. Soc. Jour.* lxix (1927), 216–35.

3307 DAMER, J. W. Lists of Bristol ships, 1571 and 1572. *Trans. Bristol and Glos. Arch. Soc.* lii (1930), 117–22.

3308 DYER, F. E. The Elizabethan sailorman. *Mariner's Mirror*, x (1924), 133–46.
Deals with the common sailor. Cf. also C. A. G. Bridge, *Did Elizabeth starve and rob her seamen? Nineteenth Century*, l (1901), 774–89.

3309 HAGEDORN, BERNHARD. Die Entwicklung der wichtigsten Schiffs-typen bis ins 19. Jahrhundert. Berlin, 1914.

3310 LAUGHTON, L. G. C. Old ship figure-heads and sterns. Lond. 1925.
Scholarly. Cf. also H. S. Vaughan, *Figureheads of ships, Henry VIII, Mariner's Mirror*, iv (1914), 37–43.

3311 LAUGHTON, L. G. C. The inventory of the Great Barque, 1531. *Mariner's Mirror*, v (1919), 21–22.

3312 LOVEGROVE, H. Shipping in a sixteenth century plan of Winchelsea and Rye. *Mariner's Mirror*, xxxiii (1947), 187–98.

3313 MANWARING, G. E. The dress of the British seamen from the earliest times to 1600. *Mariner's Mirror*, viii (1922), 324–33; ix (1923), 162–73.

3314 MAINWARING, HENRY. The seaman's dictionary. Lond. 1644; by G. E. Manwaring, *Navy Rec. Soc.* lvi (1923).
A book of definitions of nautical terms. For a bibliography of nautical dictionaries, cf. L. G. C. Laughton, *A bibliography of nautical dictionaries, Mariner's Mirror*, i (1911), 84–90.

3315 NANCE, R. M. Some ships of 1541–2. *Mariner's Mirror*, vii (1921), 368–73.
Cf. idem, *The ship of the Renaissance, Mariner's Mirror*, xli (1955), 180–98, 281–98.

3316 SMITH, JOHN. An accidence or the pathway to experience, necessary for all young seamen. Lond. 1626; repr. in *Works* (3265), ii, 785–804.
A practical guide for seamen.

3317 TINNISWOOD, J. T. Anchors and accessories, 1340–1640. *Mariner's Mirror*, xxxi (1945), 84–105.

3318 WHALL, W. B. Shakespeare's sea terms explained. Lond. 1910.

3319 WHALL, W. B. The Great Harry. *Mariner's Mirror*, iv (1914), 65–69.
Cf. J. A. Williamson, *The two ships named Great Harry, Blackwood's Mag.* cxcvi (1914), 205–15; and Gregory Robinson, *The Great Harry, Mariner's Mirror*, xx (1934), 85–92.

3320 WHALL, W. B. Ships of 1529. *Mariner's Mirror*, iv (1914), 174–8.

IX

MILITARY AND NAVAL HISTORY

A. MILITARY HISTORY

1. BIBLIOGRAPHY

There is a useful short bibliography in *Shakespeare's England* (2573), i, 126, 140; in Wake (1274), cxxii–cxxiii; and in Spaulding (3322).

3321 COCKLE, M. J. C. A bibliography of English military books up to 1642 and of contemporary foreign books. By H. D. Cockle. Lond. 1900.
Includes books on the art of war, but omits histories of battles and campaigns.

3322 SPAULDING, T. M. Elizabethan military books. *John Quincy Adams Memorial Studies.* Washington, 1948, pp. 495–507.

3323 SPAULDING, T. M. Early military books in the Folger library. *Amer. Military Hist. Foundation Jour.* i (1937), 91–100.
Chiefly sixteenth-century military books.

2. GENERAL

(a) *Sources*

3324 CHURCHYARD, THOMAS. A generall rehearsall of warres, wherein is five hundred severall services of land and sea. . . . Lond. [1579].
The running title is *Churchyard's choice.* Reviews the exploits of English soldiers and sailors from Henry VIII to early Elizabeth.

(b) *Later Works*

Cruickshank (3327) is the best book on the subject. Fortescue (3329) is still valuable.

3325 BELGION, MONTGOMERY. 'Disarmament' in the sixteenth century. *Dublin Rev.* cxciv (1934), 1–15.

3326 CRANFILL, T. M., and BRUCE, D. H. Barnaby Rich: a short biography. Austin, 1953.
Author and soldier, 1540?–1617. Cf. H. J. Webb, *Barnabe Rich—sixteenth century military critic, Jour. Eng. and German. Philol.* xlii (1943), 240–52.

3327 CRUICKSHANK, C. G. Elizabeth's army. Oxf. 1946.
The best book on the subject.

3328 DENISON, G. T. A history of cavalry from the earliest times. Lond. 1877.
Of little value.

3329 FORTESCUE, J. W. A history of the British army. 13 vols. Lond. 1899–1930.
The standard account. Vol. i, bk. ii, chs. 2–5, deals briefly with the Tudor period.

3330 FURSE, G. A. Military operations beyond the seas. 2 vols. Lond. 1897.
Of slight value. Vol. ii is historical.

3331 GROSE, FRANCIS. Military antiquities respecting a history of the English army from the conquest to the present time. 2 vols. Lond. 1786–8; 1801; 1812.
Valuable. The ed. of 1801 includes a repr. of F. Grose, *A treatise on ancient armour and weapons, illustrated . . .*, Lond. 1785.

3332 LLOYD, E. M. A review of the history of infantry. Lond. 1908.

3333 SCOTT, [J.] S. D. The British army: its origin, progress and equipment. 3 vols. Lond. 1868–80.
Narrative account of military events. Treatment also topical, especially in vol. ii.

3334 STRATHMANN, E. A. John Brende: soldier and translator. *Hunt. Lib. Quar.* i (1938), 421–37.

3335 WAGGONER, G. R. An Elizabethan attitude toward peace and war. *Philol. Quar.* xxxiii (1954), 20–33.

3336 WEBB, H. J. Military newsbooks during the age of Elizabeth. *Eng. Studies*, xxxiii (1952), 241–51.

3337 WEBB, H. J. Elizabethan soldiers: a study in the ideal and the real. *Western Humanities Rev.* iv (1950), 19–33, 141–54.

3338 WEBB, H. J. Classical histories and Elizabethan soldiers. *Notes and Queries*, cc (1955), 466–9.

3339 WEBB, H. J. Thomas Digges, an Elizabethan combat historian. *Military Affairs*, xiv (1950), 53–56.
Discusses Digges's anonymous publication in 1590 on Leicester's relief of Sluys in 1587. Cf. idem, *Two additions to the military bibliography of Thomas Digges*, Mod. Lang. Quar. xii (1951), 131–3.

3. HISTORY OF MILITARY OPERATIONS

(a) *Henry VII*

(1) *Sources*

Reference should be made to Campbell's (397) and Gairdner's (396) collections; to Polydore Vergil (320), Hall (312), Kingsford (304), and to Bacon's *Henry VII* (403).

(2) *Later Works*

Busch (406) and Fisher (339) are the best general accounts. Dupuy (843) is useful for the wars in Brittany, and Molinet (819) for the Flemish campaigns.

3340 BROOKE, RICHARD. Visits to fields of battle in England in the fifteenth century. Lond. 1857.
Includes eleven fields. Accounts mainly topographical. Useful for Bosworth and Stoke, particularly Stoke.

3341 HUTTON, WILLIAM. The battle of Bosworth field. Birmingham, 1788.
Cf. also 6308.

(b) *Henry VIII*

(1) *Sources*

By far the most valuable sources are the *Letters and Papers* (91), though there is some military material in the Spanish (867) and Venetian (992) calendars.

Among the chroniclers Hall (312) and Holinshed (314) are the most useful. Lord Herbert of Cherbury (510) should also be consulted.

On the Scottish wars reference should be made to 4926, 4929, 4958, 5125, 5130, 5135; on the Irish wars to 5733, 5736, 5739, 5745; on the French wars to 807, 826.

3342 LETTERS AND PAPERS relating to the war with France, 1512–13. By Alfred Spont. *Navy Rec. Soc.* x (1897).

3343 LA ROTTA DE FRANCCIOSI a Terroano novamente facta. La Rotta de Scocesi. *Roxburghe Club*, 1825.
    Two contemporary Italian poems—the first originally printed in Rome 1513. An app. contains notes and letters relating to Flodden. A trans. is printed in 3351.

(2) *Later Works*

The best accounts are in Fisher (339) and Froude (340) and Mackie (354); cf. on the Scottish wars, 4996, 4999, 5019, 5147, 5149, 5156, 5161, 5163, 5165, 5166; on the Irish wars, 5827, 5835, 5907, 5909, 5915, 5919; on the French wars, 856, 863.

3344 ANSCOMBE, ALFRED. Pregent de Bidoux's raid in Sussex in 1514. *Trans. R.H. Soc.*, 3rd ser., viii (1914), 103–11.

3345 BUSCH, WILHELM. Englands Kriege im Jahre 1513. Guingate und Flodden. *Hist. Vierteljahrsschr.* xiii (1910), 1–69.

3346 GAIRDNER, JAMES. On a contemporary drawing of the burning of Brighton in the time of Henry VIII. *Trans. R.H. Soc.*, 3rd ser., i (1907), 19–32.

3347 HOCQUET, A. Tournai et l'occupation anglaise, 1513–19. *Annales Soc. Hist. Tournai*, 1900.

3348 LAUGHTON, L. G. C. The burning of Brighton by the French. *Trans. R.H. Soc.*, 3rd ser., x (1916), 167–73.

3349 LOGAN-HOME, G. J. N. Battle of Ancrum Moor, 1545. *Berwick Nat. Club Hist. for 1933*, xxviii (1934), 159–65.

3350 MABON, W. W. The story of Cessford Castle. *Berwick Nat. Club Hist. for 1933*, xxviii (1934), 145–55.
    This article includes account of Surrey's assault, 1523.

3351 MACKENZIE, W. M. The secret of Flodden with 'the rout of the Scots'. Edin. 1931.
    Includes a trans. of 3343.

(c) *Edward VI and Mary*

(1) *Sources*

(i) General

Holinshed (314) and Grafton (306) are the most useful of the contemporary chronicles. There is some material in the Spanish (867) and Venetian (992) calendars.

(ii) The French Wars

Cal. S.P., Foreign (87) is the most important. It includes dispatches relating to Calais. *The chronicle of Calais* (318) has valuable appendixes. Cf. also 923. For contemporary French accounts of the siege of Boulogne, cf. Hauser (23), ii, no. 1326; of the battle of St. Quentin, ibid. ii, nos. 1253, 1259, 1387–9; of the loss of Calais, ibid. ii, nos. 1255, 1392–3.

(iii) The Scottish Wars

The Scottish calendar (4924) and *The Hamilton papers* (4926) are the most important. Cf. also 4929. For contemporary accounts of the battle of Pinkie Cleugh, cf. 5122, 5140.

3352 GREY OF WILTON, ARTHUR, LORD. A commentary of the services and charges of William, Lord Grey of Wilton, K.G. By P. de M. Grey Egerton. *Camden Soc.* xl (1847).
Gives an account of the siege of Guisnes, by an officer present there.

3353 THE WINNING OF CALAIS BY THE FRENCH, January, 1558. *English Garner* (279), iv, 173–214.
A collection of contemporary narratives.

(2) *Later Works*

The best general accounts are in Froude (340), Mackie (354), Pollard (363), and (567), and Tytler (554); on the Scottish wars, cf. (4996), (5007), (5155), (5168), (5171); on the French wars, (333), (334); *Lavisse, Hist. de France*, v, pt. ii, ch. iii, with the references cited on p. 124; H. Fornernon, *Les ducs de Guise et leur époque* (2 vols., Paris, 1877), i; Decrue (839), and Delaborde (840).

3354 McROBERTS, DAVID. The Fetternear Banner. *Innes Rev.* vii (1956), 69–86.
Made *c.* 1520, used in the Battle of Pinkie, 1547, and carried by Leslie.

3355 OMAN, C. W. C. The Battle of Pinkie, September 10, 1547. *Arch. Jour.* xc (1934), 1–25.
As represented in unpublished drawings in the Bodleian library. Article also includes a note by C. de W. Crookshank.

(d) *Elizabeth*

(1) *Sources*

(i) The Scottish Wars

The most important contemporary material is in 1352, 4924, and 4926. The *Salisbury MSS.* (185) contain much Scottish material. Of the chronicles Camden (302) and Holinshed (314) are the best. Knox (5449) is valuable.

3356 DRURY, WILLIAM. Proclamation on the entry of the English forces into Scotland. Edin. 1573; repr. in *English Garner* (279), v, 89.
  A single sheet.

(ii) The Irish Wars

The most important contemporary material is in 5733, 5736. The *Salisbury MSS.* (185) contain a good deal about Ireland. Cf. on Sidney's military enterprises, 629; on those of Essex, 289, 601, 608, 5792, 5794, 5810, 5824. Among the chroniclers Holinshed (314), Stanihurst (5823), and particularly Camden (302) are the most useful. Camden's *Britannia* (4190) contains an account of O'Neill's rebellion. Cf. also 5788, 5795, 5811, 5814, 5821.

3357 CHURCHYARD, THOMAS. Fortunate farewell to the earl of Essex. Lond. 1599.
  Cf. 3324. Includes Sidney's wars in Ireland.

(iii) The Low Countries

Cf. in general, pp. 75–78 *supra*. The most important contemporary material to 1579 is in 923; down to 1588 in 87. Leicester's correspondence (907) is useful for his campaigns, and there is scattered material in 185, 274, 629. The *Ancaster MSS.* (97) should be consulted for Willoughby's campaigns. On the military efforts of the duc d'Alençon, cf. 905.

On the Spanish side, cf. 870, 908, 909–10, 913, 920. Among the English chroniclers, Holinshed (314), Stow (317), and Camden (302) are of some value. Bor (900) and Meteren (914) are the best of the contemporary Dutch chronicles. Williams (927) is useful for the military actions of English volunteers in the Low Countries, 1568–76. For contemporary accounts of the campaigns of Norris and Leicester, cf. 3409, 3413.

3358 CHURCHYARD, THOMAS. A lamentable and pitiful description of the wofull warres in Flaunders. Lond. 1578.

3359 METEREN, EMANUEL VAN. A true discourse historicall of the succeeding governors in the Netherlands and the civil wars . . . with the memorable services of our . . . English . . . soldiers especially under Sir John Norice . . . from the yeere 1577 until the yeere 1589, and afterwards in Portugall, France, Britaine and Ireland until the yeere 1598. Trans. T. C[hurchyard] and R. Ro[binson]. Lond. 1602.
  Trans. from van Meteren's chronicle (914) with additions.

3360 VERE, FRANCIS. The commentaries of Sir Francis Vere, being diverse pieces of service, wherein he had command . . . published by William Dillingham. Cambr. 1657; repr. in *English Garner* (279), vii, 57–184.
  Vere's account of the wars breaks off suddenly in the account of the siege of Ostend, 1601. Dillingham completed the story of the siege and added two narratives of the battle of Ostend. Cf. also *S.T.C.* (35), no. 24652.

(iv) The French Wars

Cf. in general, pp. 66–69 *supra*. For English intervention in the first French civil war, cf. *Cal. S.P.*, *Foreign* (87), Cabala (274), Forbes (611), Kervyn de Lettenhove (923), and the French sources cited in Hauser (23), iii, nos. 1421,

1562, 1563, and p. 198. For English campaigns in France, 1589 ff., cf. Birch (799), Edmondes (810), Winwood (832), Unton (830), and *Ancaster MSS.* (97).

There is a journal of Lord Willoughby preserved in B.M. *Cotton MSS., Galba*, E vi. French sources are cited in Hauser (23), iv, 64 ff., 90–99, 155. Meteren (3359) is valuable for Norris's French campaigns. Cf. also *S.T.C.* (35), nos. 13156, 18654, and 18655.

3361 CONINGSBY, THOMAS. Journal of the siege of Rouen, 1591. By J. G. Nichols. *Camden Soc. Misc.* i (1847).
By an English officer who took part in the siege. A gap in his account, 5 Sept. to 3 Oct., is filled from another MS. by Rachel Poole in *E.H.R.* xvii (1902), 527–37. Cf. also R. B. Wernham, *Queen Elizabeth and the siege of Rouen, 1591, Trans. R.H. Soc.*, 4th ser., xv (1932), 163–79.

3362 NEWS FROM SIR ROGER WILLIAMS... Lond. 1591.
A report on progress of the French wars, 1589–90.

(2) *Later Works*

The best general account of military operations before 1588 is in Froude (340); after 1588, in Cheyney (690). Pollard (363) and Black (671) are briefer but useful. For the Scottish wars, Brown (4996), Lang (5007), and MacKenzie (5011) are the best accounts; cf. also (666), (5635), and (5268). For the Irish wars, the best accounts are by Falls (3366–7); cf. also (5827), (5842), (5862), (5864), (5877), (5887), and (5903). The Dutch wars are most amply treated in Motley (940–1); more accurately in Geyl (936). Bertie (670) should be consulted for Willoughby's actions. Neale (942) deals with the financing of Leicester's expedition. On the French wars, there is nothing better than Froude and Cheyney. Cf. also Mackie (354), Black (671), Neale (743), Read (760), and Matthew (355).

3363 BURNE, A. H. The siege of Ostend [1601]. *Roy. Artillery Jour.* lxv (1938), 238–53.

3364 CHRISTY, MILLER. Queen Elizabeth's visit to Tilbury, in 1588. *E.H.R.* xxiv (1919), 43–61.
Cf. A. J. Collins, *The progresses of Queen Elizabeth to the camp at Tilbury, 1588, Brit. Mus. Quar.* x (1936), 164–7, which is based upon a map in the B.M. Cf. also E. P. Pickin, *The army at Tilbury, 1588, Trans. Essex Arch. Soc.*, n.s., xxiii (1942), 49–53.

3365 DAVIS, H. H. The military career of Thomas North. *Hunt. Lib. Quar.* xii (1949), 315–21.

3366 FALLS, CYRIL. Elizabeth's Irish Wars. Lond. 1950.
The best account.

3367 FALLS, CYRIL. Mountjoy: Elizabethan general. Lond. 1955.
Charles Blount, Lord Mountjoy, earl of Devonshire, last viceroy in Ireland.

3368 FALLS, CYRIL. The Elizabethan soldier in Ireland. *History today*, i (1951), 40–45.

3369 HENRY, L. W. The earl of Essex as strategist and military organizer (1596–7). *E.H.R.* lxviii (1953), 363–93.
Reappraisal of Essex as a strategist.

3370 MARKHAM, C. R. The fighting Veres; lives of Sir Francis Vere . . . and of Sir Horace Vere. Lond. 1888.
Valuable for the military operations of the last decade of Elizabeth's reign.

3371 OWEN, L. V. D. Sir Roger Williams and the Spanish power in the Netherlands. *Army Quar.* xxxiv (1937), 53–66.

3372 WERNHAM, R. B. Queen Elizabeth and the Portugal expedition of 1589. *E.H.R.* xlvi (1951), 1–26, 194–218.
Valuable.

4. The Mustering of the Tudor Army and its Organization

(a) *Sources*

There is a good deal of unprinted material in the P.R.O. among the Domestic papers and scattered through the records of the Exchequer as well as in the *Harleian* and *Lansdowne MSS.* in the B.M.; at Lambeth and in the *Salisbury MSS.* (185). The *Acts of Privy Council* (1152), the *Proclamations* (1017), and the *Statutes* (1016) are important. A good deal of information about current abuses in the army can be gathered from instructions to commanders of expeditions to Ireland, France, and the Low Countries scattered through the *Cal. S.P., Ireland* (5736) and the *Cal. S.P., Foreign* (87). The *Foljambe Papers* (138) are valuable, and reference should also be made to 1274–6. Some material of a later date is illuminating, cf. Davies (8), nos. 2810 and 2836, and Rich (4074).

3373 CERTIFICATE OF MUSTERS in the county of Somerset, 1569. By Emanuel Green. *Somerset Rec. Soc.* xx (1904).
Very complete returns and valuable introduction.

3374 CLERICAL MUSTERS in St. Albans archdeaconry, 1590. By William Brigg. *Herts. Genealogist and Antiquary*, i (1895), 113–19.

3375 MUSTER LISTS FOR STAFFORDSHIRE, 1539. *Wm. Salt Soc.*, n.s., iv (1901), 213–57; v (1902), 233–324; vi (1903), 61–87.

3376 MUSTER LIST OF YORKSHIRE, 1535, 1539. By W. P. Baildon. *Thoresby Soc.* iv (1895), 245–60; ix (1899), 99–111, 299–310; xv (1909), 111–21.

3377 THE MUSTER RETURNS FOR DIVERSE HUNDREDS IN THE COUNTY OF NORFOLK, 1569, 1572, 1574, and 1577. Pt. i, by M. A. Farrow and H. L. Bradfer-Lawrence, *Norfolk Rec. Soc. Pub.* vi (1935); Pt. ii, by M. Farrow and Percy Millican, ibid. vii (1936), 119–225.

3378 MUSTER ROLL OF BABERGH HUNDRED, 1577, 1579. By V. B. Redstone. *East Anglia Miscellany* (1937), 43–44, 46–47, 50, 52–53, 59–61, 64, 66, 69.

3379 MUSTER ROLLS FOR THE HUNDRED OF NORTH GREEN-HOE, co. Norfolk (*c.* 1523). *Norfolk Rec. Soc.* i (1931), 41–68.

3380 NOTES ON A SIXTEENTH CENTURY KEIGHLEY MUSTER ROLL. By H. I. Judson. *Bradford Antiq.*, n.s., vi (1931), 389–97.

3381 PAPERS RELATING TO THE TRAINED SOLDIERS of Shropshire in the reign of Queen Elizabeth. By William Phillips. *Trans. Shrop. Arch. and Nat. Hist. Soc.*, 2nd ser., ii (1890), 215–94; iii (1891), 93–146.

3382 SHROPSHIRE MUSTER LISTS OF 1538. *Trans. Shrop. Arch. and Nat. Hist. Soc.* 3rd ser., viii (1908), 245–86.

3383 SURREY MUSTERS, 1544–1684. *Surrey Rec. Soc.* iii (1919).
A valuable collection; cf. also *Surrey musters*, 1588–1626, by A. R. Bax, *Surrey Arch. Soc. Coll.* xvi (1901), 137–67.

(b) *Later Works*

The best account is Cruickshank (3327). Wake (1274), Introduction and Thomson (1278), ch. 4 are also useful. There is a good deal of information about county levies in *V.C.H.* (4203). Fortescue (3329) is valuable. Cf. also Pearce (2848).

3384 BRUCE, JOHN. Report on the arrangements which were made for the internal defence of these kingdoms when Spain projected the invasion and conquest of England. . . . s.l. 1798.
Prepared for Pitt when he feared a French invasion. Prints many documents.

3385 CRUICKSHANK, C. G. Dead-pays in the Elizabethan army. *E.H.R.* liii (1938), 93–97.
Cf. idem, *Elizabethan pensioner reserve*, ibid. lvi (1941), 637–9.

3386 GREEN, EMANUEL. The preparations in Somerset against the Spanish Armada. A.D. 1558–88. Lond. 1888.
A valuable account incorporating much source material.

3387 HOGG, O. F. G. The 'gunner' and some other early masters of ordnance. *Roy. Artillery Jour.* lxii (1936), 463–73.
Sir Sampson Norton (d. 1517), Sir William Skeffington (d. 1535), and Sir Christopher Morris (1490?–1544).

3388 JORGENSEN, P. A. Moral guidance and religious encouragement for the Elizabethan soldier. *Hunt. Lib. Quar.* xiii (1950), 241–59.

3389 NOBLE, T. C. The names of those persons who subscribed towards the defence of this country at the time of the Spanish Armada, 1588. Lond. 1886.
This list originally published Lond. 1798, when a French invasion was threatened. Noble repr. it and undertook to prove that the list was substantially correct.

3390 NOBLE, W. M. Huntingdonshire and the Spanish Armada. Lond. 1896.

3391 WEBB, H. J. Elizabethan field artillery. *Military Affairs*, xix (1955), 197–202.
Discusses the organization, personnel, equipment, and tactics of the artillery.

3392 WEBB, H. J. The science of gunnery in Elizabethan England. *Isis*, xlv (1954), 10–21.

5. Arms and Armour

(a) *Sources*

There are notable collections of English arms and armour in the Tower of London, Windsor Castle, and the Wallace collection (London). Almost all the later works on the subject contain excellent illustrations; cf. particularly Grose (3331), Meyrick (3406), Gardner (3402), and Ffoulkes (3399). Contemporary treatises on the art of war (pp. 292–4 *infra*) are valuable, notably Smythe (3426), Barwick (3408), and Williams (3433). Harrison (615) gives a useful contemporary description of 'great' ordnance. Monumental effigies supply important information cf. Gross (1), 74. On Irish armour, cf. nos. 5865, 5866, 6080.

3393 ASCHAM, ROGER. Toxophilus, the scole of shootinge. . . . Lond. 1545; 1571; 1589; best ed. by W. A. Wright (in *English works of Roger Ascham*). Cambr. 1904.
The best known of all books on archery. A strong plea for the long bow, both in peace and war. Cf. also on this same subject Harrison (615) and Smythe (3426).

3394 A LETTER OF SIR HENRY LEE, 1590, on the trial of iron for armour. By H. A. Dillon. *Arch.* li (1888), 167–77.

(b) *Later Works*

The best of the earlier treatises is Grose (3331); Traill (2574), iii, and *Shakespeare's England* (2573), i, contain useful short accounts with brief bibliographies. Morris's introduction to Wake (1274) and Ffoulkes (3400) are the best accounts. Firth's *Cromwell's army*, Lond. 1921, though dealing with a later period, throws much valuable light upon sixteenth-century conditions. Corbett's *Drake* (3212), i, 3 ff. is good for naval ordnance. Reference should also be made to the catalogues of the Windsor and Tower armouries and of the Wallace collection.

3395 BOVILL, E. W. Queen Elizabeth's gunpowder. *Mariner's Mirror*, xxxiii (1947), 179–86.

3396 CLEPHAN, R. C. The military handgun of the 16th century. *Arch. Jour.* lxvii, n.s., xvii (1910), 109–50.

3397 DILLON, VISCOUNT. The Tudor battle flag. *Arch. Jour.* lxv, n.s., xv (1908), 282–6.
Cf. idem, *Tilting in Tudor times*, ibid. lv, n.s., v (1898), 296–321; *Barriers and foot combats*, ibid. lxi, n.s., xi (1904), 276–308; *The rack*, ibid. lxii, n.s., xii (1905), 37–47; *The gun called policy*, ibid. lxv, n.s., xv (1908), 265–9; and *Armour and arms in Shakespeare*, ibid. 270–81.

3398 FFOULKES, C. J. Armour and weapons. Oxf. 1909.
Well illustrated.

3399 FFOULKES, C. J. The armourer and his craft from the eleventh to the sixteenth century. Lond. 1912.
Well illustrated. Cf. also idem, *The armourers company of London* . . . *Arch.* lxxvi (1926), 41–58.

3400 FFOULKES, C. J., and HOPKINSON, E. C. Sword, lance and bayonet: a record of the arms of the British army and navy. Cambr. 1938.

3401 FFOULKES, C. J. Gun founders of England. Cambr. 1937.

3402 GARDNER, J. S. Armour in England from the earliest times to the seventeenth century. Lond. 1898.
Beautifully illustrated.

3403 HEWITT, J. Ancient armour and weapons in Europe. 3 vols. Oxf. 1855-60.

3404 LAKING, G. F. A record of European armour and arms through seven centuries. 5 vols. Lond. 1920-2.

3405 LUARD, JOHN. A history of the dress of the British soldier from the earliest period to the present time. Lond. 1852.

3406 MEYRICK, S. R. A critical inquiry into ancient armour. 3 vols. Lond. 1824; 1842.
Cf. also idem, *Engraved illustrations of ancient arms and armour*, 2 vols., Lond. 1830; 1854.

6. THE ART OF WAR

(a) *Sources*

There were several translations of classical authors on the art of war in Tudor times, notably of Vegetius and of Frontinus. These are given in Cockle (3321). Many English works on the subject are simply translations of continental authors.

3407 BARRET, ROBERT. The theorike and practise of moderne warres, discoursed in dialogue wise. Lond. 1598.
A compilation from foreign writers.

3408 BARWICK, HUMFREY. A briefe discourse, concerning the force and effect of all manuall weapons of fire, and the disability of the long bowe or archery. . . . Lond. [1594?].
Written to refute Smythe's arguments (3426) in favour of the long bow.

3409 BLANDY, WILLIAM. The castle, or picture of pollicy shewing forth the duety, quality, profession of a perfect and absolute souldiar, the martiall feates lately done by our English nation, under the conduct of John Noris general of the army of the states in Freisland. . . . Lond. 1581.

3410 BOURNE, WILLIAM. The arte of shooting in great ordnance. Lond. 1587; 1643.
First English work on gunnery.

3411 CATANEO, GIROLAMO. Most briefe tables to know howe many ranckes of footemen go to the making of a just battayle. Trans. by H[enry?] G[rantham?]. Lond. 1574.

3412 CLAYTON, GYLES. The approved order of martiall discipline, with every particular offycer his offyce and dutie . . . whereunto is adioyned a second booke, for the true ordering and imbattelling of any number soever. . . . Lond. 1591.
Cf. also idem, *A brief discourse of martial discipline*, Middelburgh, 1587.

3413 DIGGES, THOMAS. An arithmeticall militare treatise, named stratioticos: . . . together with the modern militare discipline, offices, lawes and dueties in every wel governed campe and armie to be observed. . . . Lond. 1579; 1590.
This book was apparently begun by Leonard Digges, father of Thomas. The 2nd ed. (1590) contains an account and a defence of Leicester's efforts to relieve Sluys in 1587.

3414 DUDLEY, ROBERT, EARL OF LEICESTER. Lawes and ordinances set down by Robert, earle of Leycester, in the Lowe Countires: fit to be observed by all such as shall serve her Maiestie under him. [Lond. 1586.]

3415 GARRARD, WILLIAM. The artc of warre. By [Robert] Hitchcock. Lond. 1591.
Consists almost entirely of extracts from some of the best-known military writers of the day. Hitchcock corrected and finished it and added *A generall proportion and order of provision for a yere* . . . *to victuall a garrison of one thousande souldiours*, which was repr. in *English Garner* (279), ii, 207–24.

3416 IVE, PAUL. The practise of fortification. . . . Lond. 1589; 1597.
Ive also published *Instructions for the warres . . . discoursing of the method of militarie discipline, from the French of . . . William de Bellay* . . ., Lond. 1589.

3417 KNYVETT, SIR HENRY. The defense of the realm. Lond. 1596; 1906.

3418 MACCHIAVELLI, NICCOLÒ. The arte of warre. . . . Trans. by Peter Whitehorne. Lond. 1562; 1573; 1588.

3419 PROCTOR, T[HOMAS]. Of the knowledge and conducte of warres. . . . Lond. 1578.
First technical military book written by an Englishman, otherwise of little importance, all the information being extracted from the ancients.

3420 RICH, BARNABY. Allarme to England, fore-shewing what perilles are procured where the people liue without regarde of martiall lawe. Lond. 1578; 1578.

3421 RICH, BARNABY. Farewell to Militarie profession. Lond. 1581.
Cf. also T. M. Cranfill, *Barnaby Rich: an Elizabethan reviser at work*, Studies in Philol. xlvi (1949), 411–18.

3422 RICH, BARNABY. A right exelent and pleasant dialogue betwene Mercury and an English souldier. [Lond. 1574.]
Exposes ill use of the English soldier. Defends archery.

3423 RICH, BARNABY. A pathway to military practise. Containinge offices, lawes, disciplines and orders to be observed in an army. . . . Lond. 1587.

3424 RICH, BARNABY. A souldiers wishe to Briton's welfare. Lond. 1604. Pt. ii. The fruites of long experience. Lond. 1604.
For a complete list of Rich's works, cf. *D.N.B.* (9), art. B. Rich.

3425 S., R. A briefe treatise, to prooue the necessitie and excellence of the vse of archerie. Lond. 1596.
By a disciple and admirer of Sir John Smythe (3426).

3426 SMYTHE, JOHN. Certain discourses . . . concerning the formes and effects of diuers sorts of weapons . . . also, of the great sufficiencie, excellencie, and wonderful effects of archers. . . . Lond. 1590.
Commonly called *The book on weapons*. A protest against the changes in the military art which had been gaining ground and were now being tested in the Low Countries. The book charged Leicester with incompetence and corruption and was suppressed.

3427 SMYTHE, JOHN. Instructions, obseruations, and orders mylitarie. Requisite for all chieftaines, captaines, and higher and lower men of charge. . . . Lond. 1595.
Written in 1591. Further arguments for use of long bow.

3428 SMITH, THOMAS. The arte of gunnerie. . . . Lond. 1600; 1628; 1643.
The 2nd ed. bore the title: *The complete souldier, containing the whole art of gunnery with certaine new and rare additions concerning fire-works* . . .; the ed. of 1643: *The art of gunnery*.

3429 STATUTES AND ORDINANCES of warre. Lond. [1493]; 1513; 1544.
These were ordinances for the government of the English army abroad. Cf. *S.T.C.* (35), nos. 9332–4.

3430 STYWARD, THOMAS. The pathwaie to martiall discipline. . . . Lond. 1581.
Compilation from many sources.

3431 TARTAGLIA, NICCOLO. Three bookes of colloquies concerning the arte of shooting in great and small peeces of artillerie. . . . Trans. by Cyprian Lucar. Lond. 1588.
Tartaglia dedicated his book to Henry VIII.

3432 VENN, THOS. Military and maritime discipline. Lond. 1672.
Sir Francis Vere's 'notes of direction how far every man's office in a regiment doth extend and the duty of every officer' is published in this, pp. 186–93.

3433 WILLIAMS, ROGER. A briefe discourse of warre. Lond. 1590; repr. in *English Garner* (279), v, 158.
Contains some personal reminiscences. Favours the musket and pike and condemns the long bow.

(b) *Later Works*

For modern treatises on the history of the art of war, cf. Gross (1), 133–5. Oman (3436), Fortescue (3329) and Wake (1274) are the best on the Tudor period. Lloyd (3332) contains a good sketch of infantry tactics. On Ireland cf. 5860 and 5893.

3434 JORGENSEN, P. A. Theoretical views of war in Elizabethan England. *Jour. Hist. Ideas*, xiii (1952), 469–81.

3435 KOHLER, G. Die Entwickelung des Kriegswesens von der Mitte des 11. Jahrhunderts. 3 vols. in 5. Greslau, 1886–9; index, 1890; supplement, 1893.
The standard work on the subject.

3436 OMAN, C. W. C. A history of the art of war in the sixteenth century.
  Lond. 1937.
  Book iv is entitled 'Military history of England under the Tudors'. Cf. C. T. Atkinson,
  Soc. Army Hist. Research Jour. xvi (1937), 152–7.

B. NAVAL HISTORY

A great deal of material pertinent to naval history is included in the sections
on commerce (pp. 249–64 *supra*) and on exploration and discovery (pp. 268–76
supra). On the admiralty court, cf. pp. 138–9 *supra*, on the art of navigation, pp. 279–81 *supra*.

I. BIBLIOGRAPHIES

There is a good deal of valuable bibliographical material in Corbett's works
on Drake (3212) and his successors (3468). Cf. also the bibliographies in 3219,
in 20, iii, 816 ff., in 2, iv, chs. 4 and 5, and in 2573, i, 168 ff. The best general
bibliography is 3437; the best guide to periodical literature is 3440.

3437 ADMIRALTY LIBRARY. Subject catalogue of printed books. Pt. i,
  Historical section. By W. G. Perrin. Lond. 1912.
  The best general bibliography for naval history.

3438 CALLENDER, G. S. Bibliography of naval history. Pt. i. *Historical
  Assoc. Leaflets*, no. 58 (1924).

3439 LAUGHTON, L. G. C. Bibliography of naval literature. *Lean's Royal
  N. List.* Jan. 1906; Jan. 1910.

3440 MANWARING, G. E. A bibliography of British naval history. Lond.
  1930.
  Covers MS. material and articles in periodicals, but omits books.

2. GENERAL

(a) *Sources*

For Henry VIII the most valuable source is the *Letters and Papers* (91), for the
rest of the century the *Cal. S.P., Domestic*, in the P.R.O., very inadequately
calendared in 86. The *Foreign Calendars* (87) are very important as far as they
go—and there is some material in the Spanish (867–8) and Venetian (992)
Calendars, and in the *Salisbury MSS.* (185), the *Foljambe Papers* (138), and the
Coke MSS. (123). The *Documentos Ineditos* (870) are valuable, and Duro (3478)
prints many other Spanish documents. The *Acts of Privy Council* (1152) often
furnish administrative details. Reference should also be made to contemporary
chroniclers, particularly to Hall (312), Holinshed (314), Camden (302), Stow
(317), and Speed (316). Hakluyt (3137) is very valuable for the sea war with
Spain under Elizabeth; Purchas (3138) less so. There is an account of Elizabeth's navy in Harrison (615). Reference should be made in general to the
sections on commerce (pp. 249–64 *supra*) and on discovery and exploration
(pp. 268–76 *supra*); and on military history, particularly 3342, 3360 and 3384.

3441 BYTHARNE, JEHAN. Book of war by sea and land, 1543. *Navy Rec. Soc.* xx (1902).

3442 DOCUMENTOS RELATIVOS a la toma y saco de Cadiz por los Ingleses . . . 1596. *Documentos ined.* (870), xxxvi.

3443 DOWNTON, NICHOLAS. The firing . . . of the carrack, Las Cinquo Llagas by . . . the earl of Cumberland, 1600. *Eng. Garner* (279), 2nd ed., i, pt. ii, pp. 145–50.

3444 DUDLEY, ROBERT. Voyage to the West Indies, 1594–5. *Hakluyt Soc.*, 2nd ser., iii (1879).
Dudley's account of his piratical expedition to the Spanish West Indies (also printed in 3137) together with another account by George Wyatt.

3445 ELLIS, HENRY. Naval expeditions, 1588–1603, with lists of the fleet *Arch.* xxxiv (1852), 296–349.

3446 ELLIS, HENRY. Account of an ancient drawing representing the attack of the French upon Brightlenstone in 1545. *Arch.* xxiv (1832), 292–8.
The naval operation of which this formed a part is related minutely by Du Bellay (807).

3447 MANSELL, ROBERT. A true report of the service done upon certaine gallies. Lond. 1602; repr. in C. A. Maunsell and E. P. Statham, *History of the family of Maunsell*, i (1917).
Mansell's account of his attack upon six Spanish galleys in 1602.

3448 MONSON, WILLIAM. Naval tracts in 6 books. By M. Oppenheim. *Navy Rec. Soc.* xxii, xxiii, xliii, xlv, xlvii (1902–14).
First printed in Churchill's *Voyages*, iii. An early version of bk. i was printed in 1682 under the title *Megalopsychy*. The MS. was completed in 1624. Bks. i and ii deal with naval actions under Elizabeth; bks. iii to vi deal with naval administration. Cf. W. C. Abbott, *A true Elizabethan: Sir William Monson, Conflicts with oblivion*, Cambr., U.S.A., 1935.

3449 MOTE, HUMPHREY. The Primrose of London, with her valiant adventure on the Spanish coast. Lond. 1585; by E. W. Ashbee, Lond. 1871.

3450 NAVAL SONGS AND BALLADS. By C. H. Firth. *Navy Rec. Soc.* xxxiii (1908).

3451 PAPERS RELATING TO THE NAVY during the Spanish war, 1585–7. By J. S. Corbett. *Navy Rec. Soc.* xi (1898).
Valuable.

3452 RALEIGH, WALTER. A report of the truth of the fight about the iles of Azores. Lond. 1591; repr. in *Somers Tracts* (296) i, 465–73; Hakluyt (3137), vii, 38–53, and elsewhere.
The last fight of the *Revenge*. Cf. Pierre LeFranc, *Un inédit de Ralegh sur la conduite de la guerre* (1596–7), *Études anglaises*, viii (1955), 193–211; and J. H. Stibbs, *Ralegh's account of Grenville's fight at the Azores in 1591*, North Carolina Hist. Rev. xxvii (1950), 20–31.

3453 RALEIGH, WALTER. A relation of the Cadiz action, 1596.
First printed in Cayley's *Raleigh* (Lond. 1805), and later in 3238, vol. viii.

3454 THE SEAMAN'S TRIUMPH, declaring the honourable actions . . . at the taking of the great carrick. . . . Lond. 1592; by E. W. Ashbee, Lond. 1872.

3455 SLINGSBY, WILLIAM. The voyage to Calis in Andalusia . . . by Sir W. Slyngisbie, employed in that service (1596). By J. S. Corbett. *Navy Rec. Soc.* xx (1902).

3456 THE TAKING OF THE MADRE DE DIOS, 1592. By C. L. Kingsford. *Navy Rec. Soc.* xl (1912).
Prints contemporary accounts by Francis Seall, Sir John Burgh, and others. Cf. W. R. Drake, *Notes upon the capture of the great carrack in 1592*, Arch. xxxiii (1849), 209–40. Cf. also 3454.

3457 THOMAS COBHAM and the capture of the St. Katherine. By R. G. Marsden. *E.H.R.* xxiv (1909), 290–1.

3458 THE VOYAGE TO CADIZ in the second edition of Hakluyt's *Voyages*. By C. E. Armstrong. *Papers Bibliog. Soc. Amer.* xlix (1955), 254–62.
Describes, in the light of Essex's fall from favour, the state of title-page to vol. i and the presence or absence of the leaves containing the Cadiz account in the 1598–1600 edition of the voyage.

(b) *Later Works*

On maritime enterprise under the early Tudors, cf. 3020. The best account of the Tudor navy under Elizabeth is in Corbett (3212). Oppenheim's introduction to Monson (3448) is valuable. The best naval history is Clowes (3467). Hume (350) gives an account of the Lisbon expedition of 1589 from Spanish sources. The lives of the great Elizabethan seafarers, particularly Hawkins, Drake and Frobisher, listed in ch. viii *supra* (pp. 269–74), are important. Also valuable is Rowse (3495). Of the general political histories Froude (340), Fisher (339), Black (671), Read (759), Pollard (363), and Cheyney (690) are the best for naval history. The maritime histories of the various English counties given in *V.C.H.* (4203) are often valuable.

3459 ALBREN, PEDRO DE. Historia del saqueo de Cadiz por los Ingleses en 1596. Cadiz, 1866.

3460 ANDREWS, K. R. Appraisements of Elizabethan privateermen. *Mariner's Mirror*, xxxvii (1951), 76–79.

3461 BARRINGTON, MICHAEL. The most high-spirited man on earth: Sir Richard Grenville's last fight, Sept. 1591, new evidence. *Mariner's Mirror*, xxxvi (1950), 350–3.

3462 BARROW, JOHN. Memoirs of the naval worthies of Queen Elizabeth's reign. . . . Lond. 1845.
A popular account of slight value. Prints a few documents.

3463 BRÉARD, C. and P. Documents relatifs à la marine normande . . . aux xvie et xviie siècles. *Soc. de l'histoire de Normandie.* Rouen, 1889.
Cf. also idem, *Le vieux Harfleur et ses marins*, Rouen, 1897. Both of these are of some value for Anglo-French naval relations.

3464 CALLENDER, G. S. The evolution of sea power under the first two Tudors. *History*, v (1920), 141–58.

3465 CALLENDER, G. S. The naval campaign of 1587. *History*, iii (1918), 82–91.

3466 CAMPBELL, JOHN. Lives of the British admirals, containing a naval history from the earliest periods. 4 vols. Lond. 1742–4; by H. R. Yorke. 8 vols. Lond. 1812–17.
Many subsequent eds. Antiquated but still useful.

3467 CLOWES, W. L., and others. A history of the royal navy from the earliest times to the death of Queen Victoria. 7 vols. Lond. 1897–1903.
A useful compilation, documented.

3468 CORBETT, J. S. The successors of Drake. Lond. 1900.
The best naval history for the period 1595–1603.

3469 COTTON, R. W. An Elizabethan adventurer (John Chudleigh). *Macmillan's Mag.* lxxi (1895), 190–4.
There is no account of Chudleigh in the *D.N.B.*

3470 DE LA RONCIÈRE, CHARLES. Histoire de la marine française. 5 vols. Paris, 1900–20.
The standard history of the French navy. Valuable for Anglo-French naval relations.

3471 DAVIES, G. S. The romance of a forgotten seaman. *Cornhill Mag.*, n.s., xlix (1920), 668–76.
There is a life of G. Fenner in *D.N.B.* (9).

3472 DERRICK, CHARLES. Memoirs of the rise and progress of the royal navy. Lond. 1806.
Chiefly valuable for early naval lists—notably for 1517, 1548, 1552, 1557, 1565, 1578, 1588, 1603. Cf. also J. Bree, *Cursory Sketch* (Lond. 1827), 212–22, and Ellis (290), 2nd ser., i, 218–22.

3473 DYER, F. E. Reprisals in the sixteenth century. *Mariner's Mirror*, xxi (1935), 187–97.
The Anglo-French incidents and negotiations resulting from the plundering of five French ships by Callis and Court in 1572.

3474 ENTICK, JOHN. A new naval history, or complete view of the British marine, the royal navy and merchant service, lives of admirals and navigators; laws and regulations of the navy and for trade and commerce. Lond. 1757.
Brief and antiquated, but of some value.

3475 EWEN, C. H. L'E. Captain John Ward, arch-pirate. Paignton, 1939.
Fl. 1607–15.

3476 EWEN, C. H. L'E. The golden chalice: a documented narrative of an Elizabethan pirate. Paignton, 1939.
John Callice or Challis of Tintern.

3477 EWEN, C. H. L'E. Organized piracy round England in the sixteenth century. *Mariner's Mirror*, xxxv (1949), 29–42.

3478 FERNANDEZ DURO, CESAREO. Armada Española, desde la union de los reinos de Castilla y de Aragon. 9 vols. Madrid, 1895–1930.
Valuable appendixes of documents, calendars, and bibliographies. Cf. also, by the same author, *Disquisiciones nauticas*, Madrid, 1877, and *La conquista de las Azores en 1583*, Madrid, 1886.

3479 GOLDINGHAM, C. S. The expedition to Portugal, 1589. *Roy. Unit. Serv. Inst. Jour.* lxiii (1918), 469–78.

3480 GOLDINGHAM, C. S. The navy under Henry VII. *E.H.R.* xxxiii (1918), 472–88.

3481 GOLDINGHAM, C. S. Warships of Henry VIII. *Unit. Serv. Mag.* (Lond.) clxxix (1919), 453–62.

3482 GUGLIELMIOTTI, ALBERTO. Storia della marina pontificia. 10 vols. Rome, 1886–93.

3483 HANNAY, DAVID. Short history of the British navy. 2 vols. Lond. 1898–1908.

3484 JURIEN DE LA GRAVIÈRE, J. P. E. Les chevaliers de Malte et la marine de Philippe II. 2 vols. Paris, 1887.

3485 LAUGHTON, J. K. From Howard to Nelson. Lond. 1899.
Brief naval biographies.

3486 LECKY, H. S. The king's ships; together with the most important historical episodes connected with the successive ships of the same name. . . . 3 vols. Lond. 1913–14.

3487 LEDIARD, THOMAS. Naval history of England, 1066–1714. 2 vols. Lond. 1735.
Supplanted by 3467.

3488 M'LELLAN, D. T. H. Murder and the Bodleian. *Blackwoods Mag.* ccxxxvii (1935), 513–25.
Essex, Antonio Perez, and the Cadiz expedition.

3489 MATHEW, DAVID. Cornish and Welsh pirates in the reign of Elizabeth. *E.H.R.* xxxix (1924), 337–48.

3490 OPPENHEIM, MICHAEL. Spanish treasure fleets in the sixteenth century. In Monson (3448), ii, 309–40.
Cf. also on this subject, C. H. Haring, *Trade and navigation between Spain and the Indies, Harvard Econ. Studies,* xix (1918).

3491 RICHMOND, HERBERT. Statesmen and sea power. Oxf. 1946.

3492 RICHMOND, HERBERT. The Navy as an instrument of policy, 1558–1727. By E. A. Hughes, Cambr. 1953.

3493 ROBINSON, GREGORY. The loss of H.M.S. Revenge, 1591. *Mariner's Mirror,* xxxviii (1952), 148–50.

3494 ROUND, J. H., and OPPENHEIM, M. The royal navy under Queen Elizabeth. *E.H.R.* ix (1894), 709–15.

3495 ROWSE, A. L. Sir Richard Grenville of the Revenge, an Elizabethan hero. Lond. 1937; 1949.
Excellent. Cf. also idem, Raleigh lecture, *Sir Richard Grenville's place in English history. Brit. Acad. Pro.* (1957), 79 ff.

3496 RUIDIAZ Y CARAVIA, E. Florida: su conquista y colonización. 2 vols. Madrid, 1893.
Valuable for the Spanish defence system in the West Indies and especially for the correspondence of Pero Menéndez de Avilés, Capt.-Gen. of the Indian trade.

3497 SOUTHEY, ROBERT. Lives of the British admirals. 5 vols. Lond. 1833–40.

3498 STANDING, P. C. Henry VIII's lord high admiral (Sir E. Howard). *Unit. Serv. Mag.* (Lond.) cxliv (1901), 448–56.

3499 WATERS, D. W. Limes, lemons and scurvy in Elizabethan and early Stuart times. *Mariner's Mirror*, xli (1955), 167–9.

3500 WEBB, J. G. William Sabyn of Ipswich: an early Tudor sea-officer and merchant. *Mariner's Mirror*, xli (1955), 209–21.

3501 WILLIAMSON, G. C. George, third earl of Cumberland, 1558–1605. Cambr. 1920.
Reproduces or epitomizes a good deal of valuable MS. material.

3502 WILLIAMSON, J. A. The ocean in English history. Oxf. 1941.

3. The Defeat of the Spanish Armada

(a) *Sources*

There is an excellent discussion of the sources for this campaign in Corbett (3212), ii, 412 ff. The Spanish sources, given in part in the *Cal. S.P., Spanish* (868), are best given in Fernandez Duro (3511). Most of the important English sources are printed in Laughton (3518). The *Salisbury MSS.* (185) are useful. On the military preparations to meet the Armada, cf. 3384–92.

3503 ARMSTRONG, EDWARD. Venetian despatches on the Armada and its results. *E.H.R.* xii (1897), 659–78.
An analysis of the Venetian dispatches relating to the Armada in the Venetian calendar (992).

3504 ANONYMOUS LETTER TO MR. JOHN STANHOPE . . . reporting the dispersion of the Spanish armada. *Arch.* xxxviii (1860), 246–51.
Printed with this is an English report on the strength of the Armada, dated 1 July 1588.

3505 CAPTAIN CUELLAR'S ADVENTURES in Connaught and Ulster, 1588. By H. Allingham. Lond. 1897.
Pt. ii gives a trans., by Robert Crawford, of Cuellar's narrative from the Spanish text in Fernandez Duro (3511). An earlier trans. appeared in *Spanish Armada tracts*, by H. D. Sedgwick, Lond. 1895, which is adversely criticized by Crawford in the introduction to his version.

3506 CERTAIN ADUERTISEMENTS OUT OF IRELAND, concerning the losses to the Spanish nauie. . . . Lond. 1588; repr. in *Harl. Misc.* (281), ii, 47–59.
Consists mainly of examinations of Spanish prisoners. A French version and three different Dutch versions were printed in 1588.

3507 DELONEY, THOMAS. Three ballads on the Armada fight. Lond. 1588; repr. in *Eng. Garner* (279), vii, 39–56.
These ballads were published, each one separately, in 1588. For their titles cf. *S.T.C.* (35), nos. 6557–8, 6565.

3508 DOCUMENTS ILLUSTRATING THE HISTORY OF THE SPANISH ARMADA. By G. P. B. Naish. *The Naval Misc.* iv (1952), *Navy Rec. Soc.* 1–84.

3509 DOCUMENTS RELATIVE TO THE SPANISH ARMADA and the defense of the Thames. By W. Jerdan. *British Arch. Assoc.* ix (1853), 330-6.

3510 ESTRADA, PEDRO. Account of the Armada voyage. By M. Oppenheim. *Navy Rec. Soc.* xxiii (1902), 299-308.
An undated letter from a Spanish soldier in the Armada to his brother, ed. from a trans. in the *Calthorpe MSS.* (113).

3511 FERNANDEZ DURO, CESAREO. La armada invincible. 2 vols. Madrid, 1884-5.
A collection of Spanish official papers and narratives with an introduction. One important Spanish document, omitted in this collection, Duro subsequently printed in 3478, iii, app.

3512 LORD BURGHLEY ON THE SPANISH INVASION. By W. F. Tilton. *A.H.R.* ii (1896), 93-98.
Prints a MS. dated 25 Feb. 1587-8. Cf. 646.

3513 MARTEN, ANTHONY. An exhortation to stirre up the mindes of all her maiesties faithfull subiects. . . . Lond. [1588]; repr. in *Harl. Misc.* (281), ii, 85-108.
Put forth immediately after the defeat of the Armada.

3514 ORDERS SET DOWNE BY THE DUKE OF MEDINA to be obserued in the voyage toward England. Lond. 1588; repr. in *Harl. Misc.* (281), ii, 42-47.
Trans. from the Spanish.

3515 A PACKE OF SPANISH LYES. Lond. 1588; repr. in *Somers Tr.* (296), i, 453-63, and *Harl. Misc.* (281), ii, 117-29.
Prints, in parallel columns, false Spanish reports of the Armada's success and refutations of them. A Dutch trans. appeared in 1589.

3516 PAZ SALAS, PEDRO DE. La felicissima armada que el rey Don Felipe . . . mando juntar en el puerto de la ciudad de Lisboa. . . . Lisbon, 1588.
A complete list of the Spanish ships with their commanders, tonnage, &c., published just before the Armada sailed. The copy of this book in the B.M. contains MS. notes by Lord Burghley. French, Dutch, German, Italian, and English translations were published in 1588.

3517 PIGAFETTA, FILIPE. Discorso supra l'ordinanza dell'armata Catholica. Rome, 1588.

3518 STATE PAPERS relating to the defeat of the Spanish Armada, anno 1588. By J. K. Laughton. *Navy Rec. Soc.* i and ii (1894).
The best collection of English sources.

3519 UBALDINO, PETRUCCIO. A discourse concerninge the Spanishe fleete invadinge Englande in the yeare 1588 . . . written in Italian by P. Ubaldino and trans. Trans. Robert Adams. Lond. 1590.
Ubaldino wrote two versions, in Italian, neither of them published and both preserved in MS. in B.M. Reg. 14, A x and xi. An English version of Ubaldino's first account, and probably the original which he used, is printed in Laughton (3518), i, pp. i ff. Ubaldino's second version was not completed. It was evidently written at Drake's instigation. Adams trans. the first Ubaldino version. On this whole subject, cf. Corbett (3212), ii, 412 ff.

(b) *Later Works*

The best account of the Armada campaign is in Corbett (3212). Froude (340) and Pollard (363) should be consulted, and the general naval histories, notably Clowes (3467). For the parts played by Hawkins, cf. Williamson (3190), for Frobisher (3229). The introduction to Fernandez Duro (3511) is excellent for the Spanish side of the story. Tilton (3538) is a careful review of the authorities. Cf. also Black (671) and Read (759).

3520 CLARKE, SAMUEL. England's remembrancer: containing a true and full narrative of . . . the Spanish invasion of 1588. Lond. 1657; Westminster, 1820.
An early account of the Armada. The 1820 ed. appeared in the series *Historical and biographical tracts*, i, no. 1.

3521 COLVILLE, ROBERT. The Armada and the post office. *Chambers Jour.*, 8th ser., viii (1939), 503–5.

3522 COZENS-HARDY, B. Norfolk coastal defences in 1588. *Norfolk Arch.* xxvi (1938), 310–14.

3523 DYER, F. E. Scotsmen and the Armada. *Chambers Jour.*, 8th ser., iii (1934), 865–8.

3524 FROUDE, J. A. The Spanish story of the Armada. Lond. 1882.
Many subsequent eds. Based upon Fernandez Duro (3511).

3525 GREEN, W. S. The wrecks of the Spanish Armada on the Irish coast. *Roy. Geog. Soc. Jour.* xxvii (1906), 429–48.

3526 HAWKINS, M. W. S. Plymouth Armada heroes. Plymouth, 1888.
Valuable for its use of local records.

3527 HISTORY OF THE SPANISH ARMADA . . . containing . . . lists . . . of its ships, land forces, mariners . . . and military stores . . . and also of the . . . forces raised . . . for the defense of this realm. Lond. 1759.

3528 HUME, M. A. S. The defeat of the Armada. *Fortnightly Rev.* lxviii (1897), 286–96.

3529 HUME, M. A. S. Some survivors of the Armada in Ireland. *Trans. R.H. Soc.*, 2nd ser., xi (1897), 41–66.

3530 KER, W. P. The Spanish story of the Armada. *Scot. H.R.* xvii (1920), 165–77.

3531 LEWIS, MICHAEL. Armada guns: a comparative study of English and Spanish armaments. *Mariner's Mirror*, xxviii (1942), 41–73, 104–47, 231–45, 259–90; xxix (1943), 3–39, 100–21, 163–78, 203–31.

3531a MATTINGLY, GARRETT. The Invincible Spanish Armada (in progress).

3532 PINE, JOHN. The tapestry hangings of the house of lords representing the several engagements between the English and Spanish fleets . . . 1588. Lond. 1739.
For the historical value of these, cf. Corbett (3212), ii, 420.

3533 ROSE, J. H. Was the failure of the Spanish Armada due to storms? *Proc. Brit. Acad. for 1936*, xxii (1937), 207–44.

3534 SALTILLO, MARQUÉS DE. El duque de Medina Sidonia y la jornada a Inglaterra en 1588. *Bol. Bibliog. Menendez Pelayo*, xvi (1934), 167-77.

3536 STÜBEL, BRUNO. Einige Relationen über die Armada, 1588. *Mittheilungen des Instituts für oesterreichische Geschichtsforschung*, xx (1899), 620-30.
An analysis of some obscure continental contemporary pamphlets descriptive of the Armada. Many of these in French, German, Latin, Italian, and Dutch are preserved in the B.M. and reveal a concerted effort to broadcast the news of the English victory.

3537 THOMSON, ALEXANDER, John Holles. *Jour. Mod. Hist.* viii (1936), 145-72.
Served against Armada, 1588 and in Azores expedition, 1597.

3538 TILTON, W. F. Die Katastrophe der spanischen Armada. . . Freiburg-im-B., 1894.
Valuable for its exhaustive documentation.

3539 WATERS, D. W. The Elizabethan navy and the Armada campaign. *Mariner's Mirror*, xxxv (1949), 90-138.

3540 WESTROPP, T. J. Notes on the Armada ships lost on the coast of Clare, 1588. *R.S.A.I.*, 4th ser., ix (1889), 131-3.

3541 WINDEATT, E. Fitting of two ships at Dartmouth, 1588. *Devon Assoc.* xii (1880), 312-21.

4. ORGANIZATION AND ADMINISTRATION OF THE NAVY

(a) *Sources*

Monson (3448), iii, contains a detailed account of the lord high admiral and the officers under him.

3542 BEATSON, R. Lists of the lord high admirals, 872-1806. In his *Political Index*, i, Lond. 1806.

3543 A COMPLETE LIST OF THE ROYAL NAVY OF ENGLAND in 1599. By W. Latham. *Arch.* xiii (1807), 27-34.

3544 EDWARD VI. Names of all his majesty's ships, etc. (undated). *Arch.* vi (1782), 218-20.

3545 ELIZABETH. Account of all the queen's ships of war, and the warlike stores aboard the navy, 1578. In *Royal Ordinances* (1240).

3546 FIGHTING INSTRUCTIONS, 1530-1816. By J. S. Corbett. *Navy Rec. Soc.* xxix (1905).

3547 HOWARD, CHAS., earl of Nottingham. Instructions and articles to be observed in the queen's ships. *Naval Chronicle*, viii (1802), 474-6.

3548 MONTGOMERIE, JOHN. Treatise concerning the mayntenance of the navie.
Several copies of this exist in MS. Notably in B.M. Add. MSS. 18035, written in 1570. Another copy (Add. MSS. 20042) contains additions made by the author in 1588. This last MS. is printed in large part in E. Bridges, *Censura literaria*, Lond. 1805, vol. v. Cf. also J. Mountgomery, *Thinges nedefull for this present state*, by E. M. Thompson, *Arch.* xlvii (1883), 209–41.

3549 NAVAL ACCOUNTS AND INVENTORIES of the reign of Henry VII, 1485–8, 1495–7. By Michael Oppenheim. *Navy Rec. Soc.* viii (1896).

3550 RALEIGH, WALTER. Judicious essays upon the first invention of shipping . . . the navy royal and sea services, etc. In *Works* (3238), viii.

(b) *Later Works*

On the reforms in the administration of the navy by Sir John Hawkins, cf. Williamson (3190). Oppenheim (3557) is much the best general account.

3551 BEER, E. S. DE. The lord admiral and the administration of the navy. *Mariner's Mirror*, xiii (1927), 45–50.

3552 COLLIER, J. P. On the charge . . . of the English navy in the middle of the reign of Queen Elizabeth, with a letter . . . from Sir John Hawkins. . . . *Arch.* xxxiii (1849), 191–4.

3553 GOLDINGHAM, C. S. The personnel of the Tudor navy and the internal economy of the ships. *Unit. Serv. Mag.* (Lond.) clxxvii (1918), 427–51.

3554 JOHNS, A. W. The principal officers of the navy. *Mariner's Mirror*, xiv (1928), 32–39.
Devoted mainly to the sixteenth century.

3555 LLOYD, CHRISTOPHER. The title of lord high admiral. *Mariner's Mirror*, xl (1954), 236–7.
First used by William, 1st Lord Howard of Effingham, 1555. Cf. D. W. Waters, *Lord Howard as seaman, 1578*, *Mariner's Mirror*, xli (1955), 336–7.

3556 MARSDEN, R. G. The vice-admirals of the coast. *E.H.R.* xxii (1907), 468–77; xxiii (1908), 736–57.

3557 OPPENHEIM, MICHAEL. History of the administration of the royal navy. Lond. 1896.
Covers the period to 1660. Valuable.

3558 OPPENHEIM, MICHAEL. The royal and merchant navy under Elizabeth. *E.H.R.* vi (1891), 465–94.

3559 SETON, BRUCE. The vice-admiral of Scotland and the quest of the golden penny. *Scot. H.R.* xx (1923), 122–8.

3560 SPARLING, H. H. Mariners of England before the Armada. *Eng. Illust. Mag.* viii (1891), 647–54.
Contains original documents and contemp. prints.

5. Naval Architecture

For Elizabethan tonnage measurements, cf. Corbett's *Drake* (3212), ii, 421–6. Cf. also ch. viii *supra* (pp. 281–2), and Corbett (3451), 337–41.

3561 CANO, T. Arte para fabricar, fortificar y aparejar naos de guerra y merchante. Seville, 1611.

3562 CLEVES, PHILIP, DUKE OF. Instruction de toutes manières de guerroyer tant par terre que par mer et des choses y servantes. Paris, 1558.

3563 CRESCENTIO, BARTHOLOMEO. Nautica mediterranea. Rome, 1601.
Written in 1595, deals with building of various classes of warships and their armament, navigation, &c.

3564 GARCIA DE PALACIO, DIEGO. Instruction nauthica. Mexico, 1587.

6. The Art of Naval Warfare

The best general account is in Corbett (3212), i, 1–60.

3565 GOLDINGHAM, C. S. Development of tactics in the Tudor navy. *Unit. Serv. Mag.* (Lond.) clxxviii (1918), 207–15.

3566 SAVORGNANO, MARIO, CONDE DE DELGRADO. Arte militare terrestre e maritima secondo la ragione e l'uso de piu valerosi capitani antichi et moderni. By Cesare Campana. Venice, 1599.
Written before 1591, probably about 1570.

7. Naval Armaments

Cf. Bourne (3410).

3567 ANDERSON, R. C. Armaments in 1540. *Mariner's Mirror*, vi (1920), 281.
Gives in detail guns in 10 ships of the R.N.

3568 CORBETT, J. S. Guns and gunnery in the Tudor navy. *Navy Rec. Soc.* xi (1898), app. A.

3569 LEWIS, MICHAEL. The guns of the *Jesus of Lübeck*. *Mariner's Mirror*, xxii (1936), 324–45.
The flagship of Sir John Hawkins.

3570 PERRIN, W. G. Early naval ordinance. *Mariner's Mirror*, vi (1920), 51–53.

X

CULTURAL AND SOCIAL HISTORY

In this chapter, no attempt at completeness is made. The titles here given are designed to serve simply as guides to special bibliographies of the several subjects and to standard works of reference or volumes most generally useful.

1. GENERAL CULTURE

This section might properly include every book written in or about the sixteenth century. It is confined to books of a general character not readily classifiable elsewhere. Perhaps the best contemporary survey of English culture in the sixteenth century is in Harrison (615). The publications of the *Early English Text Society*, the *Percy Society*, the *Spenser Society*, and the *New Shakespeare Society* are especially important. Reference should be made to 3597. The best modern survey is *Shakespeare's England* (2573) with its useful bibliographies and its excellent illustrations. Cf. 345.

3571 ABRAMS, ANNIE. English life and manners in the later middle ages. Lond. 1913.
Good general discussion, touching such subjects as housekeeping, education, amusement.

3572 BUCKLEY, G. T. Atheism in the English renaissance. Chicago, 1932.

3573 BUSH, DOUGLAS. The renaissance and English humanism. Toronto, 1939.

3574 BYRNE, M. ST. C. Elizabethan life in town and country. Lond. 1925; 1934; 1950; 7th ed. rev. 1954.

3575 DITCHFIELD, P. H. England of Shakespeare. Lond. 1917.

3576 EINSTEIN, LEWIS. The Italian renaissance in England. Lond. 1902; 1935.
Cf. also Praz (1468) and Weissberger (1477).

3577 EINSTEIN, LEWIS. Tudor ideals. Lond. 1921.

3578 AN ELIZABETHAN JOURNAL. By G. B. Harrison. 3 vols. Lond. 1928–39; 1955.
A haphazard, uncritical collection of news items for the period 1591–1603.

3579 ENGLAND IN SHAKESPEARE'S DAY. By G. B. Harrison. Lond. 1928.
A collection of passages from sixteenth-century literature illustrating life and literature of the period.

3580 THE ENGLISH HOME. By M. St. C. Byrne. Lond. 1930.
Translations of French dialogues by Claudius Holyband and Pierre Erondelle, Elizabethan writers of French lesson books. For the sources of these dialogues cf. *S.T.C.* (35), nos. 6738 ff., 10513 ff. Cf. also W. B. Austin, *Claudius Hollyband: an Elizabethan schoolmaster*, *Notes and Queries*, clxxvii (1939), 237–40.

3582 HALL, HUBERT. Society in the Elizabethan age. Lond. 1886; 3rd ed. 1888.
A scholarly book, based largely upon the records of the Darrell family, with an app. of documents.

3583 HARTLEY, D., and ELLIOT, M. Life and work of the people of England. 2 vols. Lond. 1925.
A collection of pictures from contemporary sources. Vol. ii illustrates the sixteenth century. Cf. also the illustrations in Harrison (346), and in Tenison (780).

3584 HYMA, ALBERT The continental origins of English humanism. *Hunt. Lib. Quar.* iv (1944), 1–25.

3585 JOHNSON, F. R. Thomas Hill: an Elizabethan Huxley. *Hunt. Lib. Quar.* vii (1952), 329–51.

3586 KOCHER, P. H. The Old Cosmos: a study of Elizabethan science and religion. *Hunt. Lib. Quar.* xv (1952), 101–21.

3588 LEE, SIDNEY. The French renaissance in England. Oxf. 1910.
Chiefly concerned with literary relations, but touches also on education, printing, and social customs.

3589 ORSINI, NAPOLEONE. Studii sul rinascimento italiano in Inghilterra, con alcuni testi inglese inediti. Florence, 1937.
Elizabethan translations of Machiavelli, Ghismonda and Guicciardini, Bruno, &c.

3590 QUENNELL, M. and C. H. B. A history of everyday things in England. 2 vols. Lond. 1918–19; 1930; rev. ed., vol. i, by Peter Quennell, Lond. 1957.

3591 REBORA, PIERO. Aspetti del'umanesimo in Inghilterra. *Rinascita*, ii (1939), 366–414.

3592 ROPE, H. E. G. The 'Italianate' Englishman. *The Month*, n.s., xi (1954), 93–103.
Roger Ascham.

3593 SALZMAN, L. F. England in Tudor times. Lond. 1926.
Good brief descriptions of social life and industries, fully illustrated.

3594 SCHRINNER, WALTER. Castiglione und die englische Renaissance. *Neue deutsche Forschungen*, 234, *Abteilung englische Philologie*, bd. 14. Berlin, 1939.

3595 STEPHENSON, H. T. Shakespeare's London. New York, 1906.
A lively account of social customs.

3596 STEPHENSON, H. T. The Elizabethan people. New York, 1910.
Refers especially to amusements.

3597 TILLYARD, E. M. W. The English renaissance: fact or fiction. Baltimore, 1952.

3598 WALKER, ALICE. The reading of an Elizabethan: some sources of the prose pamphlets of Thomas Lodge. *Rev. Eng. Studies*, viii (1932), 264–81.

3599 WASSERMAN, E. R. The scholarly origin of the Elizabethan revival. *Eng. Lit. Hist.* iv (1937), 213–43.

3600 WHITE, H. C. Social criticism in popular religious literature of the sixteenth century. New York, 1944.

2. LITERATURE

A. BIBLIOGRAPHY

No attempt is here made to give a bibliography of sixteenth-century English literature. The titles selected are merely guides or preliminary studies touching the various types of literature of the period. With the exception of Shakespeare and Spenser, no individual author is singled out for special mention. Notes on these are included because so much of the discussion of the literature centres around them. The best general bibliography to English literature in the sixteenth century is 5. Reference should also be made to the annual bibliography of English studies published in a supplement to *Publications of the Modern Language Association* and *Recent Literature of the Renaissance* published annually in the April issue of *Studies in Philology* (Univ. of N. Carolina). Also useful are *The Years Work in English Studies* (Oxford) and the *Annual Bibliography— English Language and Literature* (Modern Humanities Research Association).

B. GENERAL WORKS

The following publications are of great general value: *Publications of the Shakespeare Society*, Lond. 1841–53; of the *New Shakespeare Society*, Lond. 1874–86; of the *Spenser Society*, Manchester, 1867–94; *Tudor Facsimile Texts*, by J. S. Farmer, Lond. 1907 ff.; *Bodley Head Quartos*, by G. B. Harrison, 15 vols., Lond. 1923–6; *English Reprints*, by E. Arber, 7 vols., Lond. 1868–70. Cf. 5, 6.

On the subject of pamphleteering, consult the introduction to vol. i of *Works of Thomas Nashe*, by R. B. McKerrow, 5 vols., Lond. 1904–10.

3601 BALLADS FROM MANUSCRIPTS. By F. J. Furnivall and W. R. Morfill. 2 vols. *Ballad Soc.* Lond. 1868–73.
Covers the period 1502–1603. Valuable editorial notes.

3602 BERDAN, J. M. Early Tudor poetry, 1485–1547. New York, 1920.
Contains excellent essays on the social background of the period and a useful bibliography.

3603 BROOKE, C. F. TUCKER. The renaissance. Part II of *A Literary History of England*. By A. C. Baugh. New York, 1948.

3604 CRAIG, HARDIN. The Enchanted Glass. The Elizabethan mind in literature. Oxf. 1936.

3605 EDWARDS, H. L. R. Skelton, the life and times of an early Tudor poet. Lond. 1949.

3606 GAMZUE, B. B. Elizabeth and literary patronage. *P.M.L.A.* xlix (1934), 1041–9.

3607 GRIERSON, H. J. C. Cross currents in English literature of the seventeenth century. Lond. 1929.
Contains much on the sixteenth century.

3608 HELTZEL, V. B. Sir Thomas Egerton as patron. *Hunt. Lib. Quar.* xi (1948), 105–27.

3609 HERFORD, C. H. Studies in the literary relations of England and Germany in the sixteenth century. Cambr. 1886.

3610 HUDSON, HOYT. The epigram in the English renaissance. Princeton, 1947.

3611 JOHN, L. C. The Elizabethan sonnet sequences: studies in conventional conceits. *Columbia Univ. Studies in Eng. and Compar. Lit.*, no. 138. New York, 1938.

3612 JUSSERAND, J. A. A. J. Le roman au temps de Shakespeare. Paris, 1888; trans. Elizabeth Lee (*The English novel in the time of Shakespeare*), Lond. 1890.

3612a KINGSFORD, C. L. English historical literature of the fifteenth century. Oxf. 1913.
Invaluable.

3613 AN ANALYTICAL INDEX TO THE BALLAD-ENTRIES (1557–1709) in the Registers of the Company of Stationers of London. Chapel Hill, 1924.

3614 ROSENBERG, ELEANOR. Leicester: patron of letters. New York, 1955.
Corrects errors in 3616.

3615 SCHELLING, F. E. English literature during the lifetime of Shakespeare. New York, 1910.

3616 SHEAVYN, PHOEBE. The literary profession in the Elizabethan age. Manchester, 1909.
Discusses relations of writers with their patrons, publishers, censors, readers, and audiences. Cf. 3614, p. 12, n. 6.

3617 SIMPSON, PERCY. Literary piracy in the Elizabethan age. *Oxf. Bibliog. Soc. Pub.* (1947), n.s., i (1949), 1–23.

3618 STAUFFER, D. A. English biography before 1700. Cambr., U.S.A., 1930.
Contains a bibliography of biographies.

3619 UNDERHILL, J. G. Spanish literature in the England of the Tudors. New York, 1899.

3620 WILSON, F. P. The English jestbooks of the sixteenth and early seventeenth centuries. *Hunt. Lib. Quar.* ii (1939), 121–58.

3621 WRIGHT, L. B. The Elizabethan middle-class taste for history. *Jour. Mod. Hist.* iii (1931), 175–97.
A useful survey of historical writing and translating under Elizabeth.

3622 WRIGHT, L. B. Middle-class culture in Elizabethan England. Chapel Hill, 1935.
Cf. also W. M. Dodd, *Elizabethan middle-class culture*, Quar. Rev. cclxvi (1936), 272–84.

3623 ZOCCA, L. R. Elizabethan Narrative Poetry. New Brunswick, 1950.

C. Drama

Useful bibliographies are given in 5, 6, and in Chambers (3627). The former contains bibliographies of the works of the several dramatists, none of whom, with the exception of Shakespeare, is separately listed here.

The *Malone Society* reprints are authoritative editions of Elizabethan plays. The *Malone Society Collections*, 2 vols., Lond. 1907–13, and *The English drama and stage under the Tudor and Stuart princes, 1543–1664*, by W. C. Hazlitt, *Roxburghe Club*, Lond. 1869, both contain important documents for stage history. *Materialien zur Kunde des älteren englischen Dramas*, by von W. Bang, Louvain, 1902–14, continued as *Materials for the study of the old English drama*, by H. de Vocht, 1927 ff., reprints many Tudor plays and other materials.

The standard bibliography of the printed drama is Greg (3633). Cf. also F. G. Fleay, *A chronicle history of the London stage, 1559–1642*, Lond. 1890, and F. G. Fleay, *A biographical chronicle of the English drama, 1559–1642*, 2 vols., Lond. 1891.

3624 ADAMS, J. Q. Shakespearean playhouses. A history of English theatres from the beginnings to the restoration. Boston, 1917.
Still the best concise treatment.

3625 ALBRIGHT, E. M. Dramatic publication in England, 1580–1640. *Modern Language Assoc. Monographs*, no. 2. New York, 1927.

3626 BASKERVILL, C. R. The Elizabethan jig and related song drama. Chicago, 1929.

3627 CHAMBERS, E. K. The Elizabethan Stage. 4 vols. Oxf. 1923.
The most complete treatment of the subject. Contains an extensive bibliography of material for social as well as dramatic history. Other good discussions of the drama with valuable bibliographies are to be found in F. E. Schelling, *Elizabethan drama, 1558–1642*, 2 vols., Boston, 1908; W. J. Lawrence, *The Elizabethan playhouse and other studies*, Stratford-on-Avon, 1912; C. F. T. Brooke, *The Tudor drama*, Lond. 1912; cf. also E. K. Chambers, *The medieval stage*, 2 vols., Oxf. 1903; cf. Beatrice White, *An index to The Elizabethan stage*, Oxf. 1934.

3628 CLARK, E. G. Elizabethan fustian: a study in the social and political background of the drama, with particular reference to Christopher Marlowe. Vol. i. New York, 1937; vol. ii Raleigh and Marlowe, New York, 1941.

3629 COLSON, PERCY. Sixteenth and seventeenth century masques. *Connoisseur*, cii (1938), 241–46.

3630 CREIZENACH, WILHELM. The English drama in the age of Shakespeare. Trans. C. Hugon. Philadelphia, 1916.
A trans. of vol. iv of Wilhelm Creizenach, *Geschichte des neueren Dramas*, 6 vols., Halle, 1893–1916. Contains a valuable biliography.

3631 DOCUMENTS RELATING TO THE OFFICE OF THE REVELS. By A. Feuillerat. 2 vols. Louvain, 1908–14.
Cf. S. A. Tannenbaum, *Shakespeare forgeries in the revels accounts*, New York, 1928; A. E. Stamp, *The disputed revels accounts*, Oxf. 1931; Arnold Edinborough, *The early Tudor revels office*, Shakes. Quar. ii (1951), 19–25; and F. S. Boas, *Queen Elizabeth, the revels office and Edmund Tilney*, Annual E. Howland lecture, *1937*, Oxf. 1938.

3632 GILDERSLEEVE, V. C. Government regulation of the Elizabethan drama. New York, 1908.

3633 GREG, W. W. A Bibliography of the English printed drama to the restoration. 2 vols., Lond. 1939, 1951. *Illus. Monographs issued by the Bibliog. Soc.*, XXIV, i and ii. Vol. i: Stationers' records; Plays to 1616; vol. ii: Plays, 1617–89; Latin plays; Lost plays.

3634 GREG, W. W. Dramatic documents from the Elizabethan playhouses. Stage plots, Actors' parts, Prompt books. 2 vols. Oxf. 1931.
Vol. i: Commentary; vol. ii: Reproductions and transcriptions.

3635 GRIFFIN, W. J. Notes on early Tudor control of the stage. *Mod. Lang. Notes*, lvii (1942), 50–54.

3636 HARBAGE, ALFRED. Annals of English drama, 975–1700: an analytical record of all plays, extant or lost, chronologically arranged and indexed by authors, titles, dramatic companies, &c. Philadelphia, 1940.

3637 HARBAGE, ALFRED. Elizabethan acting. *P.M.L.A.* liv (1939), 685–708.

3638 HARRISON, G. B. Shakespeare's fellows. Lond. 1923.

3639 HENSLOWE'S DIARY. By W. W. Greg. 2 vols. Lond. 1904–8.
The best documentary source for the drama. Contains admirable editorial comment and a valuable list of plays and persons. For additional material, see *Henslowe papers*, by W. W. Greg, Lond. 1907; *The Alleyn papers*, by J. P. Collier, *Shakespeare Soc. Pub.* ii (1843).

3640 MURRAY, J. T. English dramatic companies, 1558–1642. 2 vols. Lond. 1910.
Contains much information on players outside London as well as in the city. Extensive documentary app. Cf. also 2573 for a discussion of playhouses.

3641 RINGLER, WILLIAM. The first phase of the Elizabethan attack on the stage, 1558–79. *Hunt. Lib. Quar.* v (1942), 391–418.

3642 SPENS, JANET. Elizabethan drama. Lond. 1922.
Treats the folk aspect of the Elizabethan drama.

D. SHAKESPEARE

It is impossible to furnish here a guide to the innumerable editions of Shakespeare's works and to the voluminous critical, biographical, and controversial literature about him. A full list (to the year 1910) will be found in William Jaggard, *Shakespeare bibliography . . .*, Stratford-on-Avon, 1911; for more recent works, W. Ebisch and L. L. Schücking, *Shakespeare bibliography*, Oxf. 1931; *Supplement for Years 1930–5*, Oxf. 1937, should be consulted. *Shakespeare Quarterly (Shakespeare Society of America)*, 1950 ff., prints an annual bibliography of Shakespeare studies.

The chapters on Shakespeare in the *Cambr. Hist.* (6), vol. v, and the accompanying bibliographies furnish a useful guide. Cf. also 5, *index* 'Shakespeare'. Chambers (3643) prints excellent selected bibliographies at the heads of his chapters on the separate plays and, at the end of vol. ii, a useful list of the most important books on the subject (published before 1929).

There is an extensive literature on political allusions in Shakespeare's plays. For the general studies on this subject, cf. Chambers (3643), i, 308. For the studies of particular plays from this point of view, cf. Chambers's separate bibliographies for the separate plays, particularly i, 409 (*Hamlet*); i, 459 (*Othello*); i, 471 (*Macbeth*); 8, 464 (*King Lear*); i, 350 (*Midsummer Night's Dream*); i, 350 (*Richard II*), and i, 332 (*Love's Labour 's Lost*).
On Shakespeare's Welsh characters, cf. 6510a.

3643 CHAMBERS, E. K. William Shakespeare. 2 vols. Oxf. 1930.
The standard comprehensive account. Contains extensive bibliographies covering the Shakespeare literature.

3644 CAMPBELL, L. B. Shakespeare's histories: mirrors of Elizabethan policy. San Marino, 1947.

3645 DRAPER, J. W. Political themes in Shakespeare's later plays. *Jour. Eng. German. Philol.* xxxv (1936), 61–93.

3646 TILLYARD, E. M. W. Shakespeare's history plays. Lond. 1944.

E. SPENSER

3647 CARPENTER, F. I. A reference guide to Edmund Spenser. Chicago, 1923.
A useful guide to eds. of Spenser's work and to critical and biographical literature. Continued by Alice Parrott, *A critical bibliography of Spenser from 1923 to 1928*, *Studies in Philology*, xxv (1928), 468–90. Consult also H. S. V. Jones, *Spenser handbook*, New York, 1930, and the bibliography in 6, iii, ch. xi. Cf. also D. F. Atkinson, *Edmund Spenser, a bibliographical supplement*, Baltimore, 1937.

3648 SPENSER, EDMUND. The works of Edmund Spenser. A variorum edition. By Edwin Greenlaw, C. G. Osgood, F. M. Padelford, *et al.* 9 vols. Baltimore, 1932–49.
Includes a biography of Spenser by A. C. Judson.

F. LITERARY CRITICISM

3649 ATKINS, J. W. H. English literary criticism: the Renaissance. Lond. 1947.
One of a series of volumes on criticism in England.

3650 ELIZABETHAN CRITICAL ESSAYS. By G. Gregory Smith. 2 vols. Oxf. 1904.
Contains all the more important texts and an admirable introduction. Additional texts are printed in the *Bodley Head Quartos*.

3651 RALLI, AUGUSTUS. A history of Shakespeare criticism. 2 vols. Oxf. 1932.

3652 SPINGARN, J. E. A history of literary criticism in the renaissance. New York, 1899; rev. 1908; 1925.
Largely continental, but contains illuminating chapters on English criticism and a useful bibliography.

3653 SWEETING, E. J. Early Tudor criticism, linguistic and literary. Oxf. 1940.

3654 WHITE, H. O. Plagiarism and imitation during the English renaissance: a study in critical distinctions. *Harvard Stud. in Eng*. xii. Cambr., U.S.A., 1935.

G. LANGUAGE

For the language of the sixteenth century, the most generally useful work of reference is the *Oxford English Dictionary*, by J. A. H. Murray, *et al*., 10 vols., Lond. 1888–1928.
A list of sixteenth-century dictionaries will be found in 6, iii, ch. xx.

3655 ABBOTT, E. A. A Shakespearean grammar. Lond. 1869; 1874.

3656 DAVIES, CONSTANCE. English pronunciation from the fifteenth to the eighteenth century: a handbook to the study of historical grammar Lond. 1934.

3657 DOBSON, E. J. English pronunciation. 2 vols. Oxf. 1957.
The standard work.

3658 ELLIS, A. J. On early English pronunciation; with especial reference to Shakespeare and Chaucer. 5 vols. *E.E.T.S*., extra ser., ii, vii, xiv, xxiii, lvi. Lond. 1869–89.
Vol. i deals with the fifteenth to seventeenth centuries.

3659 JOHN HART'S WORKS ON ENGLISH ORTHOGRAPHY AND PRONUNCIATION [1551, 1569, 1570]. By Bror Danielsson. Pt. i. Stockholm, 1955.
Prints Hart's works *verbatim* and *literatim* with his biography and bibliography. A model of careful scholarship.

3660 JONES, R. F. The triumph of the English language. A survey of opinions concerning the vernacular from the introduction of printing to the Restoration. Palo Alto, 1951.

3661 KÖKERITZ, HELGE. Shakespeare's pronunciation. New Haven, 1953.

3662 MATTHEWS, WILLIAM. The vulgar speech of London in the XV–XVIIth centuries. *Notes and Queries*, clxxii (1937), 2–5, 21–24, 40–42, 56–60, 77–79, 92–96, 112–15, 130–3, 149–51, 167–70, 186–8, 204–6, 218–21, 241–3.

3663 ORSINI, NAPOLEONE. 'Policy' or the language of Elizabethan machiavellianism. *Jour. Warburg Court. Inst*. ix (1946), 122–34.

3664 SCHMIDT, ALEXANDER. Shakespeare-lexicon. 2 vols. Berlin and Lond. 1874–5; 3rd ed. by G. Sarrazin, Berlin, 1902.

3665 SKEAT, W. W., and MAYHEW, A. L. A glossary of Tudor and Stuart words, especially from the dramatists. Oxf. 1913.

3666 STARNES, D. T. Renaissance dictionaries: English–Latin and Latin–English. Austin, Texas, 1954.

H. PRESS AND CENSORSHIP

3667 CLYDE, W. M. The struggle for the freedom of the press from Caxton to Cromwell. *St. Andrews Univ. Pub*. xxxvii. Lond. 1934.

3668　FOWELL, F., and PALMER, F.　The censorship in England, from the earliest times. Lond. 1913.
Cf. Albright (3625) and Gildersleeve (3632).

3669　SHAABER, M. A.　Some forerunners of the newspaper in England, 1476–1622. Philadelphia, 1929.

3670　SIEBERT, F. S.　Freedom of the press in England, 1476–1776: the rise and decline of government controls. Urbana, 1952.

3671　WILLIAMS, J. B.　A history of English journalism to the foundation of the Gazette, 1665. Lond. 1908.

I. PRINTING AND PUBLISHING

(a) *Books*

For the best general account, cf. *Cambr. Hist.* (6), iv.

The most complete list of books printed in England before 1640 will be found in *S.T.C.* (35). Cf. also A. W. Pollard, *Catalogue of books printed in the fifteenth century now in the British Museum*, 6 vols., Lond. 1908–30; cf. also Ames (27) and McKerrow (31).

3672　AN ANTHOLOGY OF ELIZABETHAN DEDICATIONS AND PREFACES. By Clara Gebert. Philadelphia, 1934.
Valuable on subject of patronage and its effect upon the creative artist.

3673　BENNETT, H. S.　English books and readers, 1475–1557. Cambr. 1952.
A history of the book trade. Excellent. Cf. also idem, *Printers, authors, and readers, 1475–1557, Library*, 5th ser., iv (1949), 155–65.

3674　BENNETT, H. S.　Notes on English retail book prices, 1480–1560. *Library*, 5th ser. v (1950), 172–8.
Cf. also article by F. R. Johnson on same subject, *1550–1640*, ibid. 83–112.

3675　GREG, W. W.　Books and bookmen in the correspondence of Archbishop Parker. *Library*, 4th ser., xvi (1935), 243–79.

3676　GREG, W. W.　Some aspects and problems of London publishing between 1550 and 1650. *Lyell lectures*, 1955. Oxf. 1956.

3677　POLLARD, A. W.　Shakespeare's fight with the pirates. . . . Lond. 1917; rev. 1920.
Discusses the regulation of the book trade.

3678　RECORDS OF THE COURT OF THE STATIONERS CO., 1576 to 1640. . . . Vol. i by W. W. Greg and E. Boswell; vol. ii by W. A. Jackson. *Bibliographical Soc.* Lond. 1931–57.
For the registers of the stationers, cf. 36. A good account of the company, of copyright, &c., is in H. R. Tedder, *The official record of current literature, Trans. Bibliog. Soc.* i (1893), 147–64. For the history of the company before 1557, cf. Graham Pollard, *Library*, 4th ser., xviii (1937), 1–38; for the company's constitution, cf. ibid. 235–60. Cf. also Cyprian Blagden, *The English stock of the stationers company, an account of its origins, Library*, 5th ser., x (1955), 163–85. On the records, cf. *Times Lit. Supp.*, 3 May 1957, p. 280.

(b) *Printers*

The transactions of the *Bibliographical Society of London*, the monographs published by the society, and their periodical, *The Library*, contain accounts of individual printers and of the book trade in special localities. Cf. also Ames (27), McKerrow (31).

3679 ANTHEUNIS, LOUIS. Engelsche drukkers in de Spaansche Neder-landen: John Fowler, Lawrence Kellam. *Bijd. Gesch.* xxvii (1937), 114–27, 147–57.

3680 BLADES, WILLIAM. The biography and typography of William Caxton. 2 vols. Lond. 1861–3; rev. 1882; 1897.
The standard life. For supplement, cf. S. De Ricci, *A census of Caxtons*, *Bibliog. Soc.*, Oxf. 1909. Cf. also E. G. Duff, *William Caxton, Caxton Club*, Chicago, 1905.

3681 BYROM, H. J. Some exchequer cases involving members of the book trade, 1534–58. *Library*, 4th ser., xvi (1936), 402–17.

3682 DAVENPORT, C. J. Thomas Berthelet, royal printer and bookbinder to Henry VIII. *Caxton Club*, Chicago, 1901.

3683 DAVIES, H. W. Devices of the early printers, 1457–1560. Lond. 1935.
Their early history and development.

3684 THE DAY BOOK OF JOHN DORNE. By F. Madan. *Oxford Historical Soc. Collectanea*, i (1885), 71–177.
The accounts of an Oxford bookseller.

3685 DUFF, E. G. A century of the English book trade . . . 1457 to . . . 1557. Lond. 1905.
Short notices of printers, bookbinders, &c. Cf. also W. W. Greg, *Richard Robinson and the Stationers' register*, Mod. Lang. Rev. l (1955), 407–13; and Bruce Dickins, *Stationers made free of the city in 1551/2 and 1552*, Trans. Cambr. Bibliog. Soc. i (1950), 194–5.

3686 GIBSON, S., and ROGERS, D. M. The earl of Leicester and printing at Oxford. *Bodleian Lib. Rec.* ii (1949), 240–5.

3687 HAND-LISTS OF ENGLISH PRINTERS, 1501–56. 3 parts. Lond. 1895–1905.
Cf. also 31.

3688 HOPPE, H. R. John Wolfe, printer and publisher, 1579–1601. *Library*, 4th ser., xiv (1933), 241–88.

3689 JENKINS, HAROLD. The life and work of Henry Chettle. Lond. 1934.
Elizabethan printer and dramatist.

3690 JOHNSON, JOHN, and GIBSON, STRICKLAND. Print and privilege at Oxford to the year 1700. Oxf. 1946.

3691 MADAN, FALCONER. The early Oxford press; a bibliography of printing and publishing at Oxford, '1468'–1640. Oxf. 1895.
Cf. also *Some account of the Oxford University press, 1468–1921*, Oxf. 1922.

3692 McKERROW, R. B. The Elizabethan printer and dramatic manuscripts. *Library*, 4th ser., xii (1931), 253–75.

3693 MORRISON, P. G. Index of printers, publishers and booksellers in . . . a short-title catalogue of books . . . 1475–1640. Charlottesville, 1950.

3694 PLOMER, H. R. Abstracts from the wills of English printers and stationers from 1492 to 1630. *Bibliographical Soc.* Lond. 1903.

3695 ROBERTS, S. C. A history of the Cambridge university press, 1521–1921. Cambr. 1921.

3695a ROSENBERG, ELEANOR. Giacopo Castelvetro, Italian publisher in Elizabethan London. *Hunt. Lib. Quar.* vi (1943), 119–48.

3696 SHAABER, M. A. The meaning of the imprint in early printed books. *Library*, n.s., xxiv (1944), 120–41.

3697 SIMPSON, PERCY. Proof-reading in the sixteenth and seventeenth centuries. Oxf. 1935.
Cf. W. A. Jackson in *Colophon*, n.s. (1935), 254–60, for a review of Simpson's book.

3698 WILLOUGHBY, E. E. A printer of Shakespeare: the books and times of William Jaggard. Lond. 1934.

3699 WORMAN, E. J. Alien members of the book trade during the Tudor period. *Bibliographical Soc.* Lond. 1906.
Compiled from lists of aliens published by the Huguenot Society of London.

(c) *Typography*

3700 CURTIS, G. B. A study in Elizabethan typography. *Baconiana*, 3rd ser., xxiv (1939), 6–21.

3701 DICKINS, BRUCE. The Irish broadside of 1571 and Queen Elizabeth's types. *Trans. Cambr. Bibliog. Soc.* i (1949), 48–68.

3702 DUFF, E. G. Early English printing. A series of facsimiles of all the types used in England during the fifteenth century. Lond. 1896.

3703 ISAAC, F. S. English and Scottish printing types [1501–58]. 2 vols., Lond. 1930–2.
Facsimiles showing all the types used during this period.

3704 ISAAC, F. S. English printers' types of the sixteenth century. Milford, 1936.

3705 JOHNSON, A. F. Sources of Roman and Italic types used by English printers in the sixteenth century. *Library*, 4th ser., xvii (1936), 70–82.

3706 McKERROW, R. B. Printers' and publishers' devices in England and Scotland, 1485–1640. *Bibliographical Soc. Monographs*, xvi. Lond. 1913.

3707 McKERROW, R. B., and FERGUSON, F. S. Title-page borders used in England and Scotland, 1485–1640. *Illust. Monographs Issued by the Bibliog. Soc.* xxi. Oxf. 1933.

(d) *Handwriting, Shorthand, Punctuation, Water-marks*

The standard book on handwriting is Jenkinson (80); on shorthand, cf. ibid., p. 93, n. 2.

3708 BENHAM, W. G. The charm of penmanship. Examples from Colchester court rolls of 1547-8. *Essex Rev.* xlviii (1939), 112-24.

3709 BRIQUET, C. M. Les filigranes. Paris, 1907.
The standard work on paper water-marks. Cf. also Le Clert, *Le papier*, 2 vols. Mâcon, 1926.

3710 DE BEAU CHESNE, JOHN, and BAILDON, JOHN. A booke containing divers sortes of hands, as well English as French secretarie. Lond. 1571
The first writing-master's book produced in England. At least 5 eds. appeared by 1615.

3711 HEAL, AMBROSE. The English writing-masters and their copy-books, 1570-1800. Cambr. 1931.
The introduction, by Stanley Morison, traces the development of English handwriting.

3712 JENKINSON, HILARY. Notes on the study of punctuation of the sixteenth century. *Rev. Eng. Studies*, ii (1926), 152-8.

3713 MATTHEWS, W. Peter Bales, Timothy Bright and William Shakespeare. *Jour. Eng. German. Philol.* xxxiv (1935), 483-510.
Shorthand writers.

3714 MORLEY, MORRIS. John Willis: Elizabethan stenographer. The art of stenographie, 1602. *Notes and Queries*, clxxxix (1945), 222-7. Cf. ibid. 112-14.

3715 TANNENBAUM, S. A. The handwriting of the renaissance. New York, 1930.
Cf. idem, *Problems in Shakespeare's penmanship*, New York, 1927.

(e) *Bookbinding*

3716 KER, N. R. Fragments of medieval manuscripts used as paste-downs in Oxford bindings with a survey of Oxford binding, *c.* 1515-1620. *Oxf. Bibliog. Soc. Pub.*, n.s., v (1954).

3717 MOSS, W. E. Bindings from the library of Robert Dudley, earl of Leicester, K.G. 1533-88; a new contribution to the history of English sixteenth century gold-tooled bookbindings. Crawley, 1939.

3718 POLLARD, GRAHAM. Changes in the style of bookbinding, 1550-1830. *Library*, 5th ser., xi (1956), 71-94.

3719 PRIDEAUX, S. T. An historical sketch of bookbinding. Lond. 1893.
Contains collection of documents and good bibliography. Material on the subject is also contained in the *Trans. Bibliog. Soc.* iv (1896), 144-8; vii (1902), 123-62; viii (1904), 25-38. Cf. also W. Y. Fletcher, *English bookbindings in the British Museum*, Lond. 1895; Strickland Gibson, *Early Oxford bindings*, Bibliog. Soc., Oxf. 1903.

3. LEARNING AND SCHOLARSHIP

A. GENERAL

Much of the learned writing of the time related to religious questions and to questions of political theory and is included in chs. iv and vi *supra*. For the controversy over the pronunciation of Greek, cf. 358, p. 121, together with the lives of Sir John Cheke and Sir Thomas Smith in *D.N.B.* (9). On popular short cuts to learning, cf. L. B. Wright, *Handbook learning of the renaissance middle class, Studies in Philol.* (Univ. of N. Carolina), xxviii (1931), 58–87.

3720　ADAMS, E. N. Old English scholarship in England, 1566–1800. *Yale Studies in English*, lv. New York, 1917.

3721　CONLEY, C. H. The first English translators of the classics. New Haven, 1927.

3722　DEAN, L. F. Tudor theories of history writing. *Univ. of Michigan contributions in Modern Philol.* i. Ann Arbor, 1947.

3723　DICK, H. G. Thomas Blundeville's *The true order and Methode of wryting and reading hystories (1574)*. *Hunt. Lib. Quar.* iii (1940), 149–70.

3724　ENGLISH HISTORICAL SCHOLARSHIP IN THE SIXTEENTH AND SEVENTEENTH CENTURIES. By Levi Fox. *Dugdale Soc.* Lond. 1956.

3725　FORDYCE, G. J. Louvain and Oxford in the sixteenth century. *Rev. belge de philol. et d'hist.* xii (1933), 645–52.

3726　HOWELL, W. S. Logic and rhetoric in England, 1500–1700. Princeton, 1956.

3727　LAMBLEY, K. The teaching and cultivation of the French language in England during Tudor and Stuart times. Manchester, 1920.

3728　MADAN, FALCONER. The Bodleian library. Lond. 1919.
Includes a description of sixteenth-century collections.

3730　PALMER, H. R. List of English editions of Greek and Latin classics printed before 1641. *Bibliographical Soc.* 1911.
Cf. H. B. Lathrop, *Translations from the classics into English from Caxton to Chapman, 1475–1620, Univ. of Wisconsin Studies in Lang. and Lit.*, no. 35 (1933).

3731　SANDYS, J. E. A history of classical scholarship. 3 vols. Cambr. 1903–8; 1921.

3732　SCOTT, M. A. Elizabethan translations from the Italian. Boston, 1916.

3733　SIMONINI, R. C. Italian scholarship in renaissance England. *Univ. of North Carolina Stud. in Compar. Lit.* iii. Durham, 1952.

3734　TILLEY, ARTHUR. Greek studies in England in the early sixteenth century. *E.H.R.* liii (1938), 221–9, 438–56.

3735　TRIMBLE, W. R. Early Tudor historiography, 1485–1548. *Jour. Hist. Ideas*, xi (1950), 30–41.

3736　TUDOR TRANSLATIONS. 1st ser. by W. E. Henley. Lond. 1892–1909; 2nd ser. by Charles Whibley, Lond. 1924 ff.
Cf. F. O. Matthiessen, *Translation, an Elizabethan Art.* Cambr., U.S.A., 1931.

B. Individual Scholars

The writings of individual scholars are generally well listed in their 'lives' in *D.N.B.* (9). On Colet, Erasmus, and More, cf. in general Seebohm (2030); for the writings of Erasmus, cf. 1970; of More 450. The best life of Colet is 2028; the best life of More 474. The biographies of Erasmus by E. Emerton (New York, 1899) and by Preserved Smith (New York, 1923) are useful popular accounts. Allen's notes on Erasmus's correspondence (1979) are valuable. A useful survey of literature on Erasmus by E. W. Nelson is in *Jour. Mod. Hist.* i (1929), 88–102. The best life of Thomas Elyot is in Croft (3783); the best life of William Grocyn, by Montagu Burrows, is in *Oxf. Hist. Soc. Collectanea*, ii (1890), 319–80. For Lupset, cf. J. A. Gee, *Life and works of T. Lupset*, New Haven, U.S.A., 1928; for Linacre, cf. 4033.

There is a good chapter on Antiquaries in *Cambr. Hist.* (6), iii, ch. 15.

3737 BYRNE, M. ST. C. The first Lady Burghley. *National Rev.* ciii (1934), 356–63.

3738 BYRNE, M. ST. C. The mother of Francis Bacon. *Blackwood's Mag.*, ccxxxvi (1934), 758–71.

3739 CAIUS, JOHN. The works of, with a memoir of his life, by John Venn. By E. S. Roberts. Cambr. 1912.

3740 FLOWER, ROBIN. Laurence Nowell and the discovery of England in Tudor times. *Brit. Acad. Proc. for 1935*, xxi (1937), 48–73.

3741 HARVEY, GABRIEL. Marginalia. By G. C. M. Smith. Stratford-on-Avon, 1913.
Contains his notes on his books.

3742 HUNT, E. W. Dean Colet and his theology. Lond. 1956.

3743 LIMENTANI, LODOVICO. Giordano Bruno a Oxford. *Civiltà moderna*, ix (1937), 254–80.

3744 LOOTEN, C. Giordano Bruno (1548–1600) à Londres. *Rev. Litt. Comparée*, xix (1939), 201–12.

3745 MARRIOTT, J. A. R. The life of John Colet. Lond. 1933.

3746 PELLEGRINI, A. M. Giordano Bruno and Oxford. *Hunt. Lib. Quar.* v (1942), 303–16.

3747 RICE, E. F. John Colet and the annihilation of the natural. *Harvard Theol. Rev.* xlv (1952), 141–63.

3748 RYAN, L. V. Walter Haddon: Elizabethan latinist. *Hunt. Lib. Quar.* xvii (1954), 99–124.

3749 VAN NORDEN, LINDA. Sir Henry Spelman on the chronology of the Elizabethan college of antiquaries. *Hunt. Lib. Quar.* xiii (1950), 131–60.

3750 WHEATLEY, WILLIAM. The history of Edward Latymer and his foundation, including the life of William Latymer. Lond. 1936.

3751 WHITING, M. B. The learned and virtuous Lady Bacon. *Hibbert Jour.* xxix (1931), 270–83.

3752 YATES, F. A. Giordano Bruno's conflict with Oxford. *Jour. Warburg Inst.* ii (1939), 227–42.
Cf. also Napoleone Orsini, *Appunti su G. Bruno in Inghilterra, l'avversario di Oxford*, *Gior. Critico Filosofia Ital.* xviii (1937), 41–43.

3753   WALTERS, H. B. The English antiquaries of the sixteenth, seventeenth and eighteenth centuries. Lond. 1934.

4. EDUCATION

A. General

3754   BEALES, A. C. F. Education under Mary Tudor. *The Month*, n.s., xiii (1955), 342–51.

3755   BIBLIOGRAPHY OF REGISTERS (printed) of the universities, inns of court, colleges and schools of Great Britain and Ireland. By Marjorie Johnson. *Bull. Inst. Hist. Research*, ix (1931), 19–30, 65–83, 154–70.

3756   CASPARI, FRITZ. Humanism and the social order in Tudor England. Chicago, 1954.
Essays on educational ideas of Erasmus, More, Eliot, Shakespeare, Sidney, and Spenser.

3757   A CYCLOPEDIA OF EDUCATION. By Paul Monroe. 5 vols. New York, 1914–15.
Contains good articles on the period.

3758   GRAVES, F. P. A history of education during the middle ages and the transition to modern times. Lond. 1910.

3759   HEXTER, J. H. The education of the aristocracy in the renaissance. *Jour. Mod. Hist.* xxii (1950), 1–20.

3760   WOODWARD, W. H. Studies in education during the age of the renaissance, 1400–1600. Cambr. 1906.
Cf. also Norman Wood, *The reformation and English education*. Lond. 1931.

3761   YATES, F. A. Italian teachers in Elizabethan England. *Jour. Warburg Inst.* i (1937), 103–16.

B. Universities

For the histories of the separate colleges at Cambridge and Oxford, cf. Davies (8), nos. 2268, 2274.

(a) *Cambridge*

3761a   ALUMNI CANTABRIGIENSIS. By John Venn and S. A. Venn. 4 vols. Cambs. 1922–7.

3762   CAMBRIDGE GRACE BOOKS, 1454–1659. By S. M. Leathes (Book *A*, 1454–88), M. Bateson (Book *B*, 1488–1544 in two parts), W. G. Searle (Book Γ, 1501–42), John Venn (Book Δ, 1542–89), J. and J. A. Venn (*The book of matriculations and degrees*, 1544–1659). Cambr. 1898–1913.
Contain lists of students matriculating and receiving degrees. Cf. also *Early honour lists of University of Cambridge, 1498–1747*, by C. M. Neale, Bury St. Edmunds, 1909.

3763   COOPER, C. H. and T. Athenae cantabrigienses. 2 vols. Cambr. 1858–61.
Biographies of Cambridge worthies. Cf. also Davies (8), no. 2262.

3764 PEACOCK, GEORGE. Observations on the statutes of the university of Cambridge. Lond. 1841.
Valuable on sixteenth-century Cambridge.

3765 MULLINGER, J. B. The university of Cambridge from the earliest times to the accession of Charles the first. 2 vols. Cambr. 1873–84.

(b) *Oxford*

3766 FOSTER, JOSEPH. Alumni oxonienses: the members of the university of Oxford, 1500–1714. 4 vols. Oxf. 1891–2.
The matriculation register of the university, alphabetically arranged, with notes.

3767 MALLET, C. E. A history of the university of Oxford. 3 vols. Lond. 1924–7.
Vol. ii covers the sixteenth and seventeenth centuries.

3768 PLUMMER, CHARLES. Elizabethan Oxford. *Oxf. Hist. Soc.* viii (1886).

3769 REGISTER OF THE UNIVERSITY OF OXFORD. By C. W. Boase and A. Clark. 5 vols. *Oxf. Hist. Soc.* i, x, xi, xii, xiv (1884–9).

3770 WOOD, ANTHONY À. Athenae oxonienses. 2 vols. Oxf. 1692; by Philip Bliss. 4 vols. 1813–20.
Biographies of Oxford worthies.

C. GRAMMAR SCHOOLS

The *Victoria County Histories* (4203) contain notices of schools and quotations from foundations and statutes. Most of these accounts have been prepared by A. H. Leach and are valuable. No attempt has been made to list the numerous histories of individual schools. Some of the more important ones are listed in 2573, i, 249. Cf. also *Cambr. Hist.* (6), viii, ch. xix with bibliog., and Gross (1), no. 2711. A useful list of histories of schools published 1946–56 is in Lancaster (i. b 1), nos. 4054–96.

3771 ALLEN, P. S. A sixteenth-century school. *E.H.R.* x (1895), 738–44.
Prints a contemporary MS. containing school rules and discusses conduct of schools.

3772 BALDWIN, T. W. William Shakespeare's Petty school. Oxf. 1943.

3773 BALDWIN, T. W. William Shakespeare's small Latine and lesse Greeke. 2 vols. Oxf. 1944.

3774 BROWN, J. H. Elizabethan schooldays: an account of the English grammar schools in the second half of the sixteenth century. Lond. 1933.

3775 LEACH, A. F. English schools at the reformation, 1546–8. Westminster, 1896.
Prints many documents illustrating the founding and history of the schools in existence in 1548.

3776 STOWE, A. R. M. English grammar schools in the reign of Queen Elizabeth. New York, 1908.

3777　WATSON, FOSTER. The English grammar schools to 1660; their curriculum and practice. Cambr. 1908.
Excellent bibliography and account of sixteenth-century educational literature. Much Tudor material has also been printed by the same author in *The curriculum and text-books of English schools in the first half of the seventeenth century*, Trans. Bibliog. Soc. vi (1900), 159–267. Cf. also A. W. Tuer, *History of the horn-book*, 2 vols., Lond. 1896.

D. PEDAGOGY

3778　ANDERS, A. The Elizabethan A B C with the catechism. *Library*, 4th ser., xvi (1935), 33–48.

3779　ASCHAM, ROGER. The scholemaster, or plaine and perfite way of teaching children to understand, write and speak in Latin tong, but specially purposed for the private brynging up of youth in Ientlemen and noble mens houses. . . . Lond. 1570; by W. A. Wright, in Ascham's *English Works*, Cambr. 1904.
Cf. also G. B. Parks, *The first draft of Ascham's 'Scholemaster'*, Hunt. Lib. Quar. i (1938), 313–27. Cf. 3592.

3780　BENNDORF, CORNELIA. Die englische Pädagogik im 16. Jahrhundert, wie sie dargestellt wird im Wirken und in den Werken von Elyot, Ascham und Mulcaster. Vienna, 1905.
Contains a bibliography of pedagogical treatises.

3781　BRINSLEY, JOHN. Ludus literarius; or the grammar school. Lond. 1612.

3782　CONYBEARE, JOHN. Letters and exercises of the Elizabethan schoolmaster, John Conybeare. . . . By F. C. Conybeare. Lond. 1905.

3783　ELYOT, THOMAS. The boke named the governour. Lond. 1531; best ed. by H. H. S. Croft, 2 vols., Lond. 1883; in *Everyman's Library*, Lond. 1907.
The first book on the subject of education written and printed in English. At least 8 eds. were published before 1581.

3784　MULCASTER, RICHARD. Positions wherein those circumstances be examined necessarie for the training up of children. Lond. 1581; abridged ed. by J. Oliphant, Glasgow, 1903.

3785　MULCASTER, RICHARD. The first part of the elementarie which entreateth of right writing of our English tung. . . . Lond. 1582.
Cf. Foster Watson, *Mulcaster and his 'elementarie'*, Lond. 1893.

3786　NELSON, WILLIAM. The teaching of English in Tudor grammar schools. *P.M.L.A.* xlix (1952), 119–43.

3787　PAFORT, ELOISE. A group of early Tudor school-books. *Library*, 4th ser., xxvi (1946), 227–61.

3788　PRICE, H. T. Grammar and composition in the sixteenth and seventeenth centuries. *Jour. of Eng. German Philol.* xxxviii (1939), 540–8.

3789　SCHULZ, H. C. The teaching of handwriting in Tudor and Stuart times. *Hunt. Lib. Quar.* vi (1943), 381–425.

3790 VIVES, JUAN LUIS. Linguae latinae exercitatio. Lond. 1539; trans. by Foster Watson (*Tudor school boy life*), Lond. 1908.
Especially valuable because the exercises consist of dialogues on all phases of school life. On Vives, cf. Foster Watson, *Vives el gran Valenciano, Hispanic Notes and Monographs*, iv, Lond. 1922. Cf. also Henry de Vocht, *Vives and his visits to England, Monumenta Humanistica Lovaniensia*, iv, Louvain, 1934.

3791 WALLACE, K. R. Rhetorical exercises in Tudor education. *Quar. Jour. Speech*, xxii (1936), 28–51.

5. MUSIC

A. GENERAL HISTORY

There is an excellent bibliography in Woodfill (3827). On Welsh music, cf. 6541.

3792 BONTOUX, GERMAINE. La chanson en Angleterre au temps d'Élisabeth. Oxf. 1936.

3793 BOYD, M. C. Elizabethan music and musical criticism. Philadelphia, 1940.

3794 BRENNECKE, ERNEST. John Milton the elder and his music. *Columbia Univ. Studies in Musicology*, ii. New York, 1938.

3795 BRENNECKE, ERNEST. A day at Christ Church, 1573. *Music and Letters*, xix (1938), 22–35.

3796 DICTIONARY OF MUSIC AND MUSICIANS. By George Grove. 4 vols. and index. Lond. 1879–90; by J. A. F. Maitland, 5 vols., Lond. 1904–9; by H. Colles, Lond. 1927–8.
The best authority for biographies of musicians.

3797 DOLMETSCH, MABEL. Dances of England and France from 1450 to 1600. Lond. 1949.

3798 FELLOWES, E. H. Orlando Gibbons and his family. Oxf. 1925; 1951.

3799 FELLOWES, E. H. William Byrd. Oxf. 3rd ed. 1936.

3800 FLOOD, A. H. G. Early Tudor composers. Oxf. 1925.
Oxford musical essays.

3801 FRASER, R. An amateur Elizabethan composer, John Hall. *Music and Letters*, xxxiii (1952), 328–32.

3802 FRASER, R. Early Elizabethan songs, John Hall's Court of Virtue, 1565. *Musica disciplina*, vii (1953), 199–203.

3803 GLYN, M. H. About Elizabethan virginal music and its composers. 2nd ed., Lond. 1934.

3804 HARRIS, D. G. T. Musical education in Tudor times (1485–1603). *Proc. of the Musical Assoc.* (1939), 109–39.

3805 HENRY, LEIGH. Dr. John Bull, 1562–1628. Lond. 1937.

3806 KNIGHTS, E. S. William Byrd and Stondon Massey. *Essex Rev.* xliii (1934), 31–35.

3807 LA MUSIQUE INSTRUMENTALE DE LA RENAISSANCE: études reunies et presentées. *Journées internationales d'études*. By Jean Jacquot. Paris, 1955.

3808 McQUAID, JOHN. Music and the administration after 1560. *Innes Rev.* iii (1952), 14–21.

3809 MILNER, R. H. The study of Elizabethan music. *Études anglaises*, vi (1953), 214–25.

3810 MORLEY, THOMAS. A plaine and easie introduction to practicall musicke. By E. H. Fellowes. *Shakespeare Assoc. Fac.* xiv (1937).

3811 MURRAY, GREGORY. William Byrd. *Downside Rev.* lv (1937), 64–72.

3812 NAGEL, WILIBALD. Geschichte der Musik in England. 2 vols. Strassburg, 1894–7.
Deals chiefly with the Tudor period and is a recognized authority.

3813 NEWTON, RICHARD. English lute music of the golden age. *Music Assoc. Proc. for 1938–9* (1939), 63–90.

3814 PATTISON, BRUCE. Notes on early music printing. *Library*, 5th ser., iv (1949), 1–13.

3815 PATTISON, BRUCE. Literature and music in the age of Shakespeare. *Musical Assoc. Proc.* lx (1934), 67–86.

3816 PATTISON, BRUCE. Music and poetry of the English renaissance. Lond. 1948.

3817 REESE, GUSTAVE. Music in the renaissance. New York, 1954.

3818 STEELE, ROBERT. The earliest English music printing; a description and bibliography of English printed music to the close of the sixteenth century. *Bibliographical Soc.* Lond. 1903.
For a guide to MSS. as well as early printed sources, see Henry Davey, *History of English music*, Lond., s.a.

3819 STERNFIELD, F. W. Music in the schools of the reformation. *Musica disciplina*, ii (1948), 99–122.

3820 STEVENS, J. E. Rounds and canons from an early Tudor song book. *Music and Letters*, xxxii (1951), 29–37.

3821 TAYLOR, S. DE B. Thomas Tompkins (1576–1656): a great Elizabethan composer. A short account of his life and works. s.l. 1935.

3822 UHLER, J. E. Thomas Morley and the first music for the English burial service. *Renaissance News*, ix (1956), 144–6.

3823 VAN DEN BORREN, CHARLES. Les origines de la musique de clavier en Angleterre. Brussels, 1912; Eng. trans. by J. E. Matthew. Lond. [1914].
Contains detailed account of sixteenth-century virginal and organ music.

3824 WALKER, ERNEST. A history of music in England. Oxf. 1907.
Contains the best account of sixteenth-century music. The *Oxford history of music*, by W. H. Hadow, 6 vols., Oxf. 1901–5, is weak on the sixteenth century, although it contains valuable examples of music.

3825 WESTRUP, J. A. William Byrd (1543–1623). *Music and Letters*, xxiv (1943), 125–30.

3826 WOODFILL, W. L. Education of professional musicians in Elizabethan England. *Med. et hum.* vi (1950), 101–8.

3827 WOODFILL, W. L. Musicians in English society from Elizabeth to Charles I. *Princeton Stud. in History*, ix. Princeton, 1953.
Scholarly. Excellent bibliography.

B. Ecclesiastical

3828 BUMPUS, J. S. A history of English cathedral music, 1549–1889. 2 vols. Lond. 1908.

3829 EARLY ENGLISH ORGAN MUSIC (16TH CENTURY). Trans. and ed. M. H. Glyn. Vol. i. *Plainsong and medieval Music Soc. Pub.* 1939.

3830 FELLOWES, E. H. English cathedral music from Edward VI to Edward VII. Lond. 1942.

3831 PFATTEICHER, C. F. John Redford, organist and almoner of St. Paul's Cathedral, in the reign of Henry VIII. Kassel, 1934.

3832 PULVER, JEFFREY. The organist's post. *Organ*, xvi (1937), 244–50; xvii (1937), 50–54.
The early history of church organs in England.

3833 SHAW, WATKINS. From Tallis to Tomkins: a survey of church music, c. 1550–c. 1650. *Church Music Soc. Occasional Paper*, xxii. Oxf. 1953.

3834 STEVENS, D. W. Tudor church music. New York, 1955.

3835 STEVENS, D. W. A unique Tudor organ mass. *Musica disciplina*, vi (1952), 167–75.

3836 TUDOR CHURCH MUSIC. By P. C. Buck *et al.* 10 vols. Lond. 1923–30.
Very valuable.

C. Popular

3837 CHAPPELL, WILLIAM. A collection of national English airs. 2 vols. Lond. 1838–40; by H. E. Wooldridge (*Old English popular music*). 2 vols. Lond. 1893.

D. Madrigal

3838 FELLOWES, E. H. The English madrigal composers. Oxf. 1921; 1948.
Contains complete list of all madrigals and works of each composer. Based largely on Edward F. Rimbault, *Bibliotheca madrigaliana*, Lond. 1847. For a complete description of the so-called 'Queen Elizabeth's virginal book', cf. E. W. Naylor, *An Elizabethan virginal book*, Lond. 1905.

3839 OBERTELLO, ALFREDO. Madrigali italiani in Inghilterra: storia, critica, testi. Milano, 1949.

E. Music on the Stage, and at the Court

3840 COOKE, GREVILLE. Queen Elizabeth and her court musicians. *Musical Times*, lxxix (1938), 419–21.

3841 COWLING, G. H. Music on the Shakespearean stage. Cambr. 1913.
For detailed discussion of the chief musical allusions in the plays of Shakespeare, see Louis C. Elson, *Shakespeare in music*, Boston, 1901.

3842 NAGEL, WILIBALD. Annalen der englischen Hofmusik . . . 1509–1649. *Monatshefte für Musikgeschichte*, xxvi, suppl. Leipzig, 1894.
Contains source extracts year by year.

3843 NAYLOR, E. W. Shakespeare and music. Lond. 1896.

F. Musical Instruments

3844 GALPIN, F. W. Old English instruments of music, their history and character. Chicago, 1911.
Good illustrated account of the various instruments and valuable bibliography.

3845 RIMBAULT, E. F. The early English organ builders and their works. Lond. 1864.
Cf. Stanley Mayes, *An Organ for the Sultan* [1599], Lond. 1956.

6. THE FINE ARTS

A. Architecture

(a) *General*

For church decoration, cf. Bond (3926) and the following by the same author: *Fonts and font covers*, Lond. 1908; *Screens and galleries*, Lond. 1908; *The chancel of English churches*, Lond. 1916. On church glass and church brasses, cf. Drake (3937) Macklin (3922), and Andrews (4457).

3846 BUILDINGS OF ENGLAND. By N. Pevsner. 11 vols. *Penguin Books*. Lond. 1951–4.

3847 BLOMFIELD, REGINALD. History of renaissance architecture in England, 1500–1800. 2 vols. Lond. 1897.
A standard work on the subject.

3848 CROSSLEY, F. H. Timber building in England from early times to the end of the xviith century. Lond. 1951.

3849 CUDWORTH, C. L. Dutch influence in East Anglian architecture. *Proc. Cambr. Antiq. Soc.* xxxvii (1937), 24–42.

3850 ENGLISH MEDIEVAL ARCHITECTS, a biographical dictionary down to 1550. . . . By John Harvey and Arthur Oswald. Lond. 1954.

3851 GOTCH, J. A. Early renaissance architecture in England. Lond. 1901.
Covers period 1500–1625 and contains a good bibliography.

3852 GOTCH, J. A., and BROWN, W. T. Architecture of the renaissance in England. 2 vols. Lond. 1891–4.
Profusely illustrated from buildings built between 1560 and 1635. Other illustrations will be found in C. J. Richardson, *Architectural remains of the reigns of Elizabeth and James I*, i, Lond. 1840. Wyatt Papworth, *The renaissance and Italian styles of architecture*

in Great Britain, Lond. 1883, contains a useful chronological list of buildings and artists. Many valuable architectural documents are to be found in the app. to Ernest Law, *The history of Hampton Court Palace in Tudor times*, 3 vols., Lond. 1855. Reference should also be made to 4195.

3853 HARVEY, JOHN. Tudor architecture. New York, 1952.

3854 KNOOP, DOUGLAS, and JONES, G. P. The decline of the mason architect in England. *Jour. Roy. Inst. Brit. Archit.*, 3rd ser., xliv (1937), 1004-7.

3855 LEES-MILNE, JAMES. Tudor Renaissance. Lond. 1951.
Deals with painting and architecture, chiefly architecture. Excellent illustrations.

3856 SALZMAN, L. F. Building in England down to 1540. Oxf. 1952.

3857 SHUTE, JOHN. The first and chief groundes of architecture used in all the auncient and famous monyments. Lond. 1563; 1584.
The principal Elizabethan treatise on architecture. Cf. also Sir Henry Wotton, *The elements of architecture*, Lond. 1624.

3858 WIFFEN, MARCUS. An introduction to Elizabethan and Jacobean architecture. Lond. 1952.

(b) *Domestic Architecture*

Descriptions of extant Tudor houses are in great abundance, from local guide books to the authoritative publications of the *Royal Commission on Historical Monuments* (4195) which is still incomplete. Excellent articles on famous country houses have been for forty years in course of publication in *Country Life*, admirably illustrated, most of these by H. A. Tipping, Christopher Hussey, and Arthur Oswald. Tipping (3864) is largely derived from these articles. Chamberlain (3859) and Summerson (3863) both deal with the subject. On famous Elizabethan houses, like Theobalds, no longer extant, Summerson is valuable.

3859 CHAMBERLAIN, S. Tudor homes of England. New York, 1929.
Describes extant houses. Good pictures and architects' drawings. Cf. also W. A. Seaby, *Wellington House: The Elizabethan mansion of Sir John Popham, knight, Trans. Somerset Arch. and Nat. Hist. Soc.* xcvii (1953), 153–62; Arthur Oswald, *Ladston Hall, Yorkshire, Country Life*, lxxxiv (1938), 556–61, 580–5; Arthur Oswald, *Ingatestone Hall, Essex, Country Life*, lxxxiii (1938), 64–69.

3860 GARNER, THOMAS, and STRATTON, ARTHUR. The domestic architecture of England during the Tudor period. 2 vols. Lond. 1911; rev. 1929.
This is the standard work. The following are also valuable: John Clayton, *A collection of the ancient timber edifices of England*, Lond. 1846; P. H. Ditchfield, *The manor houses of England*, Lond. 1910; J. A. Gotch, *The growth of the English house*, Lond. 1910 (brief); Joseph Nash, *The mansion of England in olden time*, 4 vols., Lond. 1839–49; by Charles Holme, Lond. 1905. Cf. also 4195. Cf. also Arthur Stratton, *Introductory handbook to the styles of English architecture*, pt. ii, *Tudor and Renaissance*, 2 vols. Lond.; 3rd ed. 1938.

3861 ROSENBERG, L. C. Cottages, farmhouses, and other minor buildings in England of the sixteenth, seventeenth and eighteenth centuries. New York, 1923.
Cf. also M. W. Barley, *Farmhouses and cottages, 1550–1725, Econ. Hist. Rev.*, 2nd ser., vii (1955), 291–306.

3862   STRATTON, A. J. The English interior. Lond. 1920.

3863   SUMMERSON, JOHN. Architecture in Britain, 1530–1830. Lond. 1953; rev. ed. 1955.
Standard work on domestic architecture. Cf. idem, *John Thorpe and the Thorpes of Kingscliffe*, *Archit. Rev.*, Nov. 1949, 291–300 and *Three Elizabethan architects*, *Bull. John Rylands Lib.* xl (1957), 202–28.

3864   TIPPING, H. A. English homes, period ii . . . early Tudor; period iii . . . late Tudor and early Stuart. Lond. 1922; 1924.
Beautifully illustrated. Cf. also H. A. Tipping, *English homes*, periods i and ii. Vol. ii, *Medieval and early Tudor, 1066–1558*, Lond. 1937.

(c) *Landscape Architecture and Gardens*

In this connexion Harrison's chapter on gardens (615) and Sir Francis Bacon's essay *Of gardens* should not be neglected. Cf. also *Shakespeare's England* (2573), i, ch. 12.

3865   AMHERST, ALICIA (Mrs. Evelyn Cecil). A history of gardening in England. Lond. 1895; 1910.

3866   ARBER, AGNES. Herbals, their origin and evolution: a chapter in the history of botany, 1470–1670. Cambr. 1912; enl. ed. 1938.
Contains a good bibliography and a descriptive list of herbals published in the Tudor period. Among the most important are: William Turner, *A new herball*, Lond. 1551, 1568; Didymus Mountain (pseud. for Thomas Hill), *A most briefe and pleasaunt treatise teachinge howe to dress a garden*, Lond. 1563; Rembert Dodoens, *A nievve herball; or historie of plantes*, trans. Henry Lyte, Lond. 1578; John Gerard, *The herball, or generall historie of plantes*, Lond. 1597; by Thomas Johnson, Lond. 1633; by Marcus Woodward, Lond. 1927.
   For facsimiles from herbals, of 1526, 1551, 1570–1, 1578, 1597, and 1629, see J. F. Payne, *English herbals*, *Trans. Bibliog. Soc.* xi (1909–11), 299–310.

3867   BLOMFIELD, REGINALD. The formal garden in England. 8 vols. Lond. 1901.
The best historical account. Chiefly Tudor.

3868   TAYLOR, G. C. The garden at Breccles Hall, Norfolk. *Country Life*, lxxxiii (1938), 194–9.

B. PAINTING, PORTRAITURE, SCULPTURE

As there was very little native sixteenth-century painting there is little literature on the subject. Reference should be made to such general works as Ernest Chesneau, *La peinture anglaise*, *Bibliothèque de l'enseignement des beaux-arts*, Paris, s.a., and Salomon Reinach, *Répertoire des peintures du moyen âge et de la renaissance, 1280–1580*, 3 vols., Paris, 1905–10.

   Such painting as was done in England was largely portraiture. On this subject Spielmann (3894) gives the best general account. For miniature painters in addition to Foster (3882) the lives of Nicholas Hilliard, Isaac Oliver, and Federigo Zuccaro in *D.N.B.* (9) should be referred to.

   The best gallery of English sixteenth-century portraits is the National Portrait Gallery in London, but there are many valuable private collections—notably those at Hatfield House, and at Penshurst.

For the first half of the century Holbein was the outstanding portrait-painter in England. His drawings of royal and famous personages, the originals of which are preserved at Windsor Castle, are well known and have been often reproduced (notably by Bartalozzi). Zuccaro's portraits are perhaps the best known for the reign of Elizabeth. Extant portraits of sixteenth-century notables are usually listed with their 'lives' in *D.N.B.* (9).

3869 ADAMS-ACTON, MURRAY. Structural ceilings of the early Tudor houses. *Connoisseur*, cxxiii (1949), 75–82.

3870 ANECDOTES OF PAINTING IN ENGLAND, with some account of the principal artists . . . collected by . . . Mr. George Vertue and published . . . by Mr. H. Walpole. 4 vols. Strawberry Hill, 1762–71; by R. N. Wornum. 3 vols. Lond. 1849.
Cf. Davies (8), no. 2547.

3871 AUERBACH, ERNA. Tudor artists. Lond. 1954.
Excellent. Includes biographical notes.

3872 BAKER, C. H. C., and CONSTABLE, W. G. English painting of the sixteenth and seventeenth centuries. New York, 1930.
The first scientific study of the period of English portraiture from the death of Holbein to the close of the seventeenth century, containing a large series of reproductions hitherto inaccessible to the general public.

3873 CHAMBERLAIN, A. B. Hans Holbein the younger. 2 vols. Lond. 1913.
Gives a good general view of painting of the period as well as a discussion of Holbein's work. Cf. J. G. Nichols, *Notices of the contemporaries and successors of Holbein, Arch.* xxxix (1863), 19–46; G. Scharf, *Additional observations,* ibid. 47–56.

3874 CHEW, S. C. The iconography of *A Book of Christian Prayers* (1578). *Hunt. Lib. Quar.* viii (1945), 293–305.

3875 CUST, L. H. Exhibition illustrative of early English portraiture. *Burlington Fine Arts Club*, Lond. 1909.
Valuable introduction.

3876 CUST, L. H. Historical and descriptive catalogue of the National Portrait Gallery (originally compiled by Sir George Scharf). 2 vols. Lond. 1901–2.

3877 CUST, L. H. Notes on foreign artists of the reformed religion working in England from about 1560 to 1660. *Hug. Soc. Proc.* vii (1903), 45–82.

3878 DORMER, E. W. Two historic Berkshire portraits at Burlington House. *Berks. Arch. Jour.*, n.s., xxxviii (1934), 33–36.
Sir Edward Hoby and Sir Henry Unton.

3879 EDEN, F. S. Heraldic Parliament rolls. *Connoisseur*, xciv (1934), 363–6.
Miniatures in the rolls of parliament marking the openings of parliament under Henry VIII.

3880 ESDAILE, K. A. English church monuments, 1510–1840. Lond. 1946.

3881 ESDAILE, K. A. The inter-action of English and Low-country sculpture in the sixteenth century. *Jour. of Warburg and Court. Inst.* vi (1943), 80–88.

3882 FOSTER, J. J. British miniature painters and their works. Lond. 1898.
Cf. the further references on this subject in Davies (8), no. 2557.

3883   GANZ, P. Holbein and Henry VIII. *Burl. Mag.* lxxxiii (1943), 269–73.

3884   HICKS, H. L., and BLAIR, C. H. H. Renaissance monuments in the cathedral church of St. Nicholas, Newcastle. *Arch. Aeliana*, 4th ser., xvi (1939), 1–30.

3885   HIGGINS, ALFRED. On the work of Florentine sculptors in England in the early part of the sixteenth century. *Arch. Jour.*, 2nd ser. vol. i (1894), 129–220.

3885a   ILLUSTRATED CATALOGUE of a loan collection of portraits of English historical personages who died before 1625. By C. F. Bell and Rachael Poole. Oxf. 1904.
Useful for many portraits in private collections not easily accessible. Cf. also Davies (8), nos. 2568, 2570.

3886   JONES, E. A. Some notes on Nicholas Hilliard, miniaturist and gold-smith, *c.* 1547–1617. *Connoisseur*, cxiii (1943), 3–6.

3887   MORGAN, F. C. Two Hereford sixteenth-century sculptors, John Gildon and Epiphanius Evesham. *Trans. Woolhope Nat. F. Club for 1933–5*, pt. iii (1938), 111–18.

3888   O'DONOGHUE, F. M. A descriptive and classified catalogue of portraits of Queen Elizabeth. Lond. 1894.

3889   THE PAINTINGS OF HANS HOLBEIN. By Paul Ganz. Lond. 1956.
Contains reproductions of all of Holbein's extant paintings—but not his drawings.

3890   POPE-HENNESSY, JOHN. Nicholas Hilliard and mannerist art theory. *England and the Mediterranean tradition studies in art, history and literature.* Oxf. 1945. pp. 69–80.

3891   READER, F. W. Tudor domestic wall-paintings. *Arch. Jour.* xcii (1936), 243–86; xciii (1937), 220–62.
Cf. also articles on wall-painting by idem in *London Naturalist for 1933* (1934), 45–48; *Rec. of Bucks.* xii (1933), 368–98; and *Trans. East Herts. Arch. Soc.* xi (1942), 142–53. Cf. articles by E. T. Leeds, *Oxoniensia*, i (1936), 144–50; and G. M. Benton, *Suffolk Inst. Arch. Proc.* xxii (1935), 108.

3892   REYNOLDS, GRAHAM. Nicholas Hilliard and Isaac Oliver. *Vict. and Albert Mus. Handbook.* Lond. 1947.
Contains brief biographies of Hilliard and Oliver and reproductions of many of their miniatures. Cf. Noel Blakiston, *Nicholas Hilliard at court*, *Burl. Mag.* xcvi (1954), 17–18.

3893   ROBERTSHAW, WILFRED. An early local portrait. *Bradford Antiq.*, n.s., vii (1950), 319–26.
Margaret Layton of Rawdon.

3894   SPIELMANN, M. H. British portrait painting to the opening of the nineteenth century. 2 vols. Berlin, 1910.

3895   THREE INVENTORIES OF THE YEARS 1542, 1547, and 1549–50 of pictures in the collections of Henry VIII and Edward VI. By W. A. Shaw. *Court. Inst. Texts for the Study of Art History*, i. Lond. 1937.

3896 VIVIAN-NEAL, A. W. The Tudor and Stuart plasterwork of west Somerset. *Proc. Somerset Arch. and Nat. Hist. Soc.* xcvi (1952), 143–51.

3897 WATERHOUSE, E. K. Painting in Britain, 1530–1790. *Penguin Books.* Lond. 1953.

3898 WOLTMANN, A. F. and G. A. Holbein und seine Zeit. 2 vols. Leipzig, 1866–8; trans. F. E. Bunnett, Lond. 1872.

3899 WOODWARD, JOHN. Tudor and Stuart drawings. Lond. 1952.

3900 WYATT, M. D. On the foreign artists employed in England during the sixteenth century. Lond. 1868.

C. Engraving

3901 CATALOGUE OF ENGRAVED BRITISH PORTRAITS . . . in the British Museum. With supplement and indexes. By F. M. O'Donoghue and H. M. Hake. 6 vols. Lond. 1908–25.

3902 CATALOGUE OF PRINTS AND DRAWINGS in the British Museum, Division I, Political and personal satires. 4 vols. Lond. 1870–83.

3903 COLVIN, SIDNEY. Early engraving and engravers in England, 1545–1695. Lond. 1905.

App. contains list of engravers' works. Much useful personal information about the engravers is to be found in M. C. Salaman, *The old engravers of England in their relation to contemporary life and art,* Lond. 1906; and in *The first century of English engraving,* by the same author in *The Studio,* 1908, special spring number.

3904 THE HEADS OF ILLUSTRIOUS PERSONS of Great Britain engraven by Houbraken and Vertue, with their lives and characters. By T. Birch. 2 vols. Lond. 1743.

Engraved reproductions of many sixteenth-century portraits, of which some of the originals have disappeared.

3905 HIND, A. M. Engraving in England in the sixteenth and seventeenth centuries. Pt. i, the Tudor period. Cambr. 1952; pt. ii, the reign of James I. Cambr. 1955.

The standard book. Copious illustrations. Many Elizabethan portraits in pt. ii.

3906 HODNETT, EDWARD. English woodcuts, 1480–1535. *Bibliog. Soc. Illus. Monographs,* xxii. Oxf. 1935.

3907 LEVIS, H. C. A descriptive bibliography of the most important books in the English language, relating to the art and history of engraving and the collecting of prints. Lond. 1912; Supplement and index, 1913.

Very useful. See also G. Bourcard, *Graveurs et gravures, France et étranger: essai de bibliographie, 1540–1910,* Paris, 1910.

3908 THORPE, W. A., and MAYNARD, JOSEPHINE. An Elizabethan connoisseur. *Trans. Lond. and Middx. Arch. Soc.,* n.s., viii (1938), 31–47.

Hugh Offley of Chester, worker in leather.

7. CRAFTS

A. GENERAL

Sixteenth-century English craftsmen were not conspicuous for either the quality or quantity of their work. The volumes listed below deal in some measure with work done in England by foreigners. The records of the English workers are to be found in the records of their gilds rather than their products. Cf. ch. vii *supra* (pp. 225–39).

The Victoria and Albert Museum contains the best collections of all varieties of British crafts, and its library, the National Art Library, is rich in literature dealing with the minor arts. Catalogues of the collections and lists of books in the library should be consulted. Note particularly catalogues of collections of pottery and porcelain (Lond. 1899), and English goldsmiths' work (Lond. 1920), and also the published lists of books on furniture (Lond. 1885), glass (Lond. 1887), and textiles, lace, and needlework (Lond. 1888).

3909 VALLANCE, AYMER. Art in England during the Elizabethan and Stuart periods. *The Studio*, special spring number. Lond. 1908.
A valuable sketch covering various aspects of the decorative arts.

B. METAL-WORK AND JEWELLERY

Cf. Hamilton (2814) and Chaffers (2825).

3910 CHAFFERS, WILLIAM. Hallmarks on gold and silver plate. . . . Lond. 1863; 1922.
Valuable for reference.

3911 CRIPPS, W. J. Old English plate, ecclesiastical, decorative and domestic. Lond. 1878; 1926.

3912 EVANS, JOAN. English jewellery from the fifth century to 1800. Lond. 1921.

3913 EVANS, JOAN. Magical jewels of the middle ages and the renaissance, especially in England. Oxf. 1922.

3914 EVANS, JOAN. History of jewellery, 1100–1870. Lond. 1953.

3915 GARDNER, J. S. Old silver work, chiefly English, from the fifteenth to the eighteenth centuries. Lond. 1903.

3916 GASK, NORMAN. Silver spoons in Tudor times seen in nine typical examples. *Connoisseur*, cv (1940), 242–5.

3917 HOW, G. E. P. and J. P. English and Scottish silver spoons: medieval to late Stuart and pre-Elizabethan hallmarks on English plate. 3 vols. Lond. 1953.

3918 JACKSON, C. J. English goldsmiths and their marks. Lond. 1905; 1922.

3919 JACKSON, C. J. Illustrated history of English plate. Lond. 1911.

3920 LISTER, R. Decorative wrought iron work in Great Britain. Lond. 1957.

3921 MASSÉ, H. J. L. J. Pewter plate; a historical and descriptive handbook. Lond. 1904; 1910.
For hall-marks on pewter, see C. A. Markham, *Pewter marks and old pewter ware*, Lond. 1909; and L. I. Wood, *Scottish pewter ware and pewterers*, Edin. 1904.

3922 MACKLIN, H. W. The brasses of England. Lond. 1907.
Mostly medieval, but contains three chapters on the Tudor period. See also E. R. Suffling, *English church brasses from the thirteenth to the seventeenth centuries*, Lond. 1910. Cf. 4457.

3923 MURPHY, B. S. English and Scottish wrought iron work. Lond. 1904.

3924 WEAVER, LAWRENCE. English leadwork; its art and history. Lond. 1909.
Contains bibliography.

C. Furniture and Woodcarving

3925 ADAMS-ACTON, MURRAY. Wall seats and settles of the sixteenth century. *Connoisseur*, cxxi (1948), 16–21.

3926 BOND, FRANCIS. Wood carving in English churches. 2 vols. Lond. 1910.
Much material on woodcarving will also be found in books on furniture and architecture.

3927 CESCINSKY, HERBERT. Two English oak cabinets of the early sixteenth century. *Burl. Mag.* lxxiv (1939), 187–93.

3928 JOURDAIN, M. English decoration and furniture during the Tudor, Elizabethan and early Stuart periods. Lond. 1922.

3929 MACQUOID, PERCY. A history of English furniture. 3 vols. Lond. 1904–8; 4 vols. 1919.
The standard work on English furniture. Vol. i covers the period 1500–1660.

3930 MACQUOID, P., and EDWARDS, R. Dictionary of English furniture from the middle ages to the late Georgian period. 3 vols. Lond. 1924–7.

3931 PURVIS, J. S. The use of continental woodcuts and prints by the 'Ripon School' of woodcarvers in the early sixteenth century. *Arch.* lxxxv (1936), 107–28.

3932 SYMONDS, R. W. The craft of furniture making in the sixteenth and seventeenth centuries. *Connoisseur*, xcix (1937), 130–6.

3933 SYMONDS, R. W. The domestic furnishings of the Elizabethans. *Burl. Mag.* lxxxviii (1946), 8–15.

3934 WENHAM, EDWARD. Oak motifs in English furniture: the Elizabethan and early Stuart periods. *Connoisseur*, xcvii (1936), 134–9.

D. Ceramics, Glass, and Glass Painting

3935 BUCKLEY, F. History of old English glass. Lond. 1925.

3936 CHAFFERS, WILLIAM. Marks and monograms on European and oriental pottery and porcelain. . . . Lond. 1863; 1912.
A standard work of reference.

3937   DRAKE, MAURICE. A history of English glass-painting. Lond. 1912.

3938   FRANCIS, G. R. Old English drinking glasses. Lond. 1926.

3939   HARTSHORNE, ALBERT. Old English glasses . . . to the end of the eighteenth century. Lond. 1897.

3940   HONEY, H. B. English pottery and porcelain. Lond. 1934.

3940a HULME, E. W. English glass-making in the sixteenth and seventeenth centuries. *Antiquary*, xxx (1894), 210–14, 259–63.
Cf. also J. A. Knowles, *Dispute between English and foreign glass-painters in the sixteenth century*, Antiq. Jour. v (1925), 148–57.

3941   KENYON, G. M. A Sussex yeoman family as glassmakers. *Sussex Notes and Queries*, vii (1939), 171–3.
The Strudwicks of Idehurst.

3942   RACKHAM, BERNARD. Early Tudor pottery. *Trans. Eng. Ceramic Circle*, ii (1939), 15–25.
Cf. also by the same author, *Farnham pottery of the sixteenth century*, Surrey Arch. Coll. lii (1952), 50–55.

3943   SOLON, L. M. E. Ceramic literature. . . . Lond. 1910.
A useful list is also contained in *List of works in the New York Public Library relating to ceramics and glass*, New York, 1908.

3944   THORPE, W. A. English glass. Lond. 1935.

3945   WILMER, D. Early English glass . . . of the sixteenth, seventeenth, and eighteenth centuries. Lond. 1909.

3946   WINBOLT, S. E. Wealden glass: the Surrey-Sussex glass industry, 1261–1615. Hove, 1934.

3947   WOODFORDE, CHRISTOPHER. Glass painters in England before the Reformation. *Proc. Suffolk Inst. Arch. and Nat. Hist.* xxii (1936), 231–43.
Cf. idem, *The painted glass in Withcote church*, Burl. Mag. lxxv (1939), 17–22; *The Norwich school of glass painting in the fifteenth century*, New York, 1950; *English stained and painted glass*, Oxf. 1954.

E. Weaving, Lace-making, Needlework

3948   AUDEN, J. E. White ladies. *Trans. Shrop. Arch. Soc.* clviii (1937), ii–iii.
Sixteenth-century embroidery.

3949   KENDRICK, A. F. English embroidery. Lond. 1905.
Cf. also further material by the same author in *A book of old embroidery*, The Studio, 1921; and *English decorative fabrics of the sixteenth to eighteenth centuries*, Lond. 1935.

3950   NEVINSON, J. L. Needlework in the home in the time of Queen Elizabeth and James I. *Embroidery*, iv (1936), 77–80.

3951   PALLISER, FANNY. History of lace. Lond. 1864; rev. by M. Jourdain and A. Dryden, 1902; New York, 1911.

3952 THOMSON, W. G. Tapestry weaving in England . . . to the end of the eighteenth century. Lond. 1914.

3953 GÖBEL, HEINRICH. Wandteppiche. 4 vols. Leipzig, 1923–8.

8. SCIENCE

A. GENERAL

For catalogues and guides, cf. Davies (8), nos. 2625–9; for metallurgy, cf. Agricola (2777).

3954 BUTTERFIELD, H. The origins of modern science, 300–1600. Lond. 1949.

3955 A COLLECTION OF LETTERS illustrative of the progress of science in England . . . Elizabeth to . . . Charles II. By J. O. Halliwell-Phillips. *Historical Soc. of Science.* Lond. 1841.

3956 DORAN, MADELEINE. On Elizabethan 'credulity' with some questions concerning the use of the marvellous in literature. *Jour. Hist. Ideas,* i (1940), 151–76.

3957 GUNTHER, R. T. Early science in Oxford. 4 vols. Oxf. 1921–5.

3958 JACQUOT, JEAN. Humanisme et science dans l'Angleterre élizabéthaine: l'œuvre de Thomas Blundeville. *Rev. d'hist. des sciences et de leurs applications,* iv (1953), 189–202.

3959 KOCHER, P. H. Science and religion in Elizabethan England. San Marino, 1953.

3960 McCOLLEY, GRANT. William Gilbert and the English reputation of Giordano Bruno. *Annals of Science,* ii (1937), 353–4.

3961 MASON, S. F. The scientific revolution and the Protestant reformation. *Annals of Science,* ix (1953), 64–87; 154–75.

3962 PARSONS, E. J. S., and MORRIS, W. F. Edward Wright and his work. *Imago Mundi,* iii (1939), 61–71.
Wright was an hydrographer, *c.* 1558–1615.

3963 SMITH, PRESERVED. A history of modern culture. Vol. i, The great renewal, 1543–1687. New York, 1930.
Considerable material on the history of science. Useful bibliographies.

3964 THORNDIKE, LYNN. A history of magic and experimental science. 6 vols. New York, 1934–41.
Vols. v and vi cover the sixteenth century.

3965 WOLF, ABRAHAM. A history of science, technology and philosophy in the 16th and 17th centuries. Lond. 1935.

B. ASTRONOMY AND ASTROLOGY

For a brief bibliography, cf. 2573, i, 460. Nautical-astronomical literature is covered in nos. 3279–97, *supra.*

3966 BRYANT, W. W. A history of astronomy. Lond. 1907.

3967   GABB, G. H. The astrological astrolabe of Queen Elizabeth. *Arch.* lxxxvi (1936), 101–3.

3968   HELLMAN, C. D. The comet of 1577: its place in the history of astronomy. *Stud. in Hist. Econ. and Pub. Law*, no. 510. New York, 1944.

3969   HOUZEAU, J. C., and LANCASTER, A. Bibliographie générale de l'astronomie. 2 vols. Brussels, 1882–7.

3970   JOHNSON, F. R. Astronomical thought in Renaissance England: a study of the English scientific writings from 1500 to 1645. Baltimore, 1937.

3971   JOHNSON, F. R. The influence of Thomas Digges on the progress of modern astronomy in sixteenth century England. *Osiris*, i (1936), 390–410.

3972   JOHNSON, F. R., and LARKEY, S. V. Thomas Digges, the Copernican system and the idea of the universe in 1575. *Hunt. Lib. Bull.* v (1934), 69–117.

3973   LARKEY, S. V. Astrology and politics in the years of Elizabeth's reign. *Bull. Inst. of Hist. Medicine*, iii (1935), 171–86.

3974   SMITH, C. F. John Dee, 1527–1608. Lond. 1909.
Cf. also J. O. Halliwell, *The private diary of John Dee, Camden Soc.* xix (1842), and M. R. James, *List of manuscripts formerly owned by Dr. John Dee, Trans. Bibliog. Soc.*, 1921, suppl. i; S. C. McCulloch, *John Dee: Elizabethan doctor of science and magic, South Atlantic Quar.* l (1951), 72–85; and Luigi Firpo, *John Dee, scienziato, negromante e avventuriero, Rinascimento*, anno iii (1952), 25–84. Cf. also 2819.

3975   WILSON, F. P. Some English mock-prognostications. *Trans. Bibliog. Soc.*, 2nd ser., xix (1938), 6–43.
Astrology in the sixteenth and seventeenth centuries.

C. CHEMISTRY AND ALCHEMY

Since alchemy was illegal in England to the end of the Stuarts, there are no English treatises on the subject in this period. Cf. bibliography in *Shakesp. Engl.* (2573), i, 474; and in Ferguson (2776). Cf. also 2818.

3976   BOLTON, H. C. A. Literature of alchemy. *Pharmaceutical Rev.* xix (1901), 150–5, 195–9.

3977   BOLTON, H. C. A. Select bibliography of chemistry, 1492–1892. *Smithsonian Misc. Collections*, vols. xxxvi, xxxix, xli, xlv. Washington, 1893; supplements, 1899; 1901; 1904.

3978   STILLMAN, J. M. The story of early chemistry. New York, 1924.

D. GEOGRAPHY

There is a good bibliography of early books on the subject in Parks (3158), app. iv. Cf. also ch. viii *supra* (pp. 265–7), and sect. 12 *infra* (pp. 348–51). For contemporary maps of England, cf. Camden (4190), and Norden (4201).

3979   BARLOW, ROGER. A briefe summe of geographie. By E. G. R. Taylor. *Hakluyt Soc.*, 2nd ser., lxix (1932).

3980   THE HISTORICAL GEOGRAPHY OF ENGLAND BEFORE 1800. By H. C. Darby. Cambr. 1936.

3981 SUGDEN, E. H. A topographical dictionary to the works of Shakespeare and his fellow dramatists. Manchester, 1925.

3982 TAYLOR, E. G. R. Instructions to a colonial surveyor in 1582. *Mariner's Mirror*, xxxvii (1951), 48–62.

3983 TAYLOR, E. G. R. Tudor geography, 1485–1583. Lond. 1930.
Contains a survey of English geographical literature with a catalogue of English geographical and kindred works printed and in MS. to 1583.

3984 TAYLOR, E. G. R. Later Tudor and early Stuart geography, 1583–1650. Lond. 1934.
A sequel to (3983). Continues the valuable bibliography also.

3985 TAYLOR, E. G. R. Leland's England and Camden's England. In 3980, pp. 330–86.

E. MATHEMATICS

Cf. *D.N.B.* (9), art. Thos. Harriot.

3986 BALL, W. W. R. A short account of the history of mathematics. Lond. 1888; 1915.

3987 CAJORI, FLORIAN. History of mathematics. Lond. 1894; 1919.

3988 DE MORGAN, A. Arithmetical books from the invention of printing to the present time. Lond. 1847.

3989 THE EARLIEST ARITHMETICS IN ENGLISH. By R. Steele. *E.E.T.S.*, extra ser., cxviii (1922).
Prints a number of sixteenth-century treatises.

3990 JOHNSON, F. R., and LARKEY, S. V. Robert Recorde's mathematical teaching and the anti-Aristotelian movement. *Hunt. Lib. Bull.*, no. vii (1935), 59–87.

3991 KLOYDA, Sister M. Linear and quadratic equations, 1550–1660. *Osiris*, iii (1937), 165–92.

3992 TAYLOR, E. G. R. The mathematical practitioners of Tudor and Stuart England. Cambr. 1954.

F. NATURAL HISTORY, BIOLOGY, ZOOLOGY, BOTANY

For botany, cf. Arber (3866). There are short bibliographies of botany and zoology in *Shakesp. Engl.* (2573), i, 498, 515. Reference should also be made to the books of Turberville on hunting and falconry; cf. *D.N.B.* (9), art. Geo. Turberville.

3993 BARTHOLOMAEUS, ANGLICUS. De proprietatibus rerum. Basel [*c.* 1470]; Eng. trans. J. Trevisa [Lond. 1495]; Lond. 1535; by Stephen Batman (Batman upon Bartholome his booke . . .), Lond. 1582.
A standard book on natural science in the sixteenth century. Written in the thirteenth century. Trevisa's trans. was made in 1390 but first printed in 1495.

3994 CHALLONER, J. The early progress of British geology. I. From Leland to Woodward, 1538–1728. *Annals of Science*, ix (1953), 124–53.

3995 GESNER, CONRAD. Historia animalium. 5 vols. Zurich, 1551–87.
The starting-point for modern zoology, popularized by Edward Topsell in *The historie of four-footed beastes* . . ., Lond. 1608.

3996 JACKSON, B. D. Guide to the literature of botany. Lond. 1881.

3997 LOCY, W. A. Growth of biology. New York, 1925.

3998 PHIPSON, EMMA. The animal-lore of Shakespeare's time. Lond. 1883.

3999 SEAGER, H. W. Natural history in Shakespeare's time. Lond. 1896.
A collection of extracts from contemporary sources.

4000 SHIPLEY, A. E. Zoology in the time of Shakespeare. *Edin. Rev.* ccxvi (1912), 117–38.

4001 TURNER, WILLIAM. Avium praecipuarum. . . . Lond. 1544; by A. H. Evans (Turner on Birds), Lond. 1903.
The first scientific English treatise on natural history. Cf. also G. E. Fussell, *William Turner, the father of English botany, Estate Mag.* xxxvii (1937), 367–70.

4002 WOTTON, EDWARD. De differentiis animalium libri decem. Paris, 1552.

G. Physics

4003 CAJORI, FLORIAN. History of physics in its elementary branches. Lond. 1899; rev. New York, 1929.

4004 GILBERT, WILLIAM. De magnete, magneticisque corporibus, et de magno magnete tellure. . . . Lond. 1600; trans. *Gilbert Club.* Lond. 1900.
The beginning of modern electrical science and the greatest contribution of the period to natural science. Cf. S. P. Thompson, *Gilbert of Colchester*, Lond. 1891.

9. MAGIC AND WITCHCRAFT

There is an excellent chapter on this subject in *Shakesp. Engl.* (2573), i, 546. Cf. also 3974 and 5539.

4005 CURTIS, S. C. Trials for witchcraft in Guernsey. *Soc. Guernesiaise Report and Trans.* xiii (1938), 109–43.

4006 LONGFORD, W. W. An accusation of witchcraft, 1582. *Trans. Hist. Soc. Lancs. and Ches.* xcii (1941), 203–6.
Against Ellen Wynstanley.

4007 MURRAY, M. A. Witchcraft in western Europe. Oxf. 1921.

4008 NOTESTEIN, WALLACE. A history of witchcraft in England from 1558 to 1718. Washington, 1911.

4009 SCOT, REGINALD. The discoverie of witchcraft. Lond. 1584; by Brinsley Nicholson, Lond. 1886; 1930.

10. MEDICINE AND DISEASE

For catalogues and guides, cf. Davies (8), nos. 2696–9; for contemporary literature, Pilcher (4044). On the craft of surgery, cf. Young (2702).

There were many English translations of the works of continental physicians and surgeons in circulation in sixteenth-century England, notably those of John Vigo (*S.T.C.* (35), nos. 24720–6), Girolamo Ruscelli, known as Alexis of Piedmont (ibid., nos. 293–312), and Nicholas Monardes (ibid., nos. 18005–7). The works of Ambroise Paré, the great French surgeon, though well known in sixteenth-century England, were not translated until 1634 (ibid., no. 19189).

The principal contemporary English writers, in addition to those listed below, were John Banister, Thomas Cogan, and Thomas Gale. For an account of their lives and writings, cf. their 'lives' in the *D.N.B.* (9).

The most popular of the books on household remedies were 4014, 4023, 4027.

4010 ALBION, GORDON. Caius of Cambridge. *Clergy Rev.*, n.s., xvi (1939), 115–24.

4011 BAYON, H. P. William Gilbert, 1544–1603, Robert Fludd, 1574–1637, and William Harvey, 1578–1657, as medical exponents of Baconian doctrines. *Royal Soc. of Medicine Proc. for 1938–9, Hist. of Med. Sect.* xxxii (1939), 31–42.

4012 BENHAM, W. G. Dr. William Gilbred of Tymperlys, Colchester. *Essex Rev.* xlviii (1939), 36–39.
Physician to Queen Elizabeth and James I, c. 1544–1603.

4013 BLOOM, J. H., and JAMES, R. R. Medical practitioners in the diocese of London, licensed under the Act of 3 Henry VIII, c. 11. An annotated list, 1529–1725. Cambr. 1935.

4014 BORDE or BOORDE, ANDREW. A compendyous regyment or a dyetary of helth. Lond. [1542?]; by F. J. Furnivall, *E.E.T.S.*, extra ser., x (1870).

4015 BRADFORD, C. A. Hugh Morgan, Queen Elizabeth's apothecary. Lond. 1939.

4016 BULLEIN, WILLIAMS. A dialogue bothe pleasaunt and pietifull . . . against the fever pestilence. Lond. 1564; by M. W. and A. H. Bullein, *E.E.T.S.*, extra ser., lii (1888).
For other treatises by Bullein, cf. *S.T.C.* (35), nos. 4033–42. Cf. also W. H. Welply, *An unanswered question—Bullein and Hilton, Notes and Queries*, ccii (1957), 3–6.

4017 CAIUS, JOHN. A boke or counseill against the disease called the sweate. . . . Lond. 1552.

4018 CLOWES, WILLIAM. Profitable and necessarie booke of observations: an Elizabethan book of surgery and medicine. By T. Starnes and C. D. Leake. New York, 1944.

4019 CLOWES, WILLIAM. Selected writings of William Clowes, 1544–1604. By F. N. L. Poynter. Lond. 1948.

4020 CREIGHTON, CHARLES. A history of epidemics in Britain from A.D. 664 to the extinction of the plague. 2 vols. Cambr. 1891.
Contains valuable information about social conditions especially in the sixteenth and seventeenth centuries.

4021 EDGAR, I. I. Elizabethan conceptions of the physiology of the circulation. *Annals Med. Hist.*, n.s., viii (1936), 359–70, 456–65.

4022 EDGAR, I. I. Medical practice and the physician in Elizabethan England and in Shakespeare's dramas. *Medical Life*, xli (1934), 331–50.

4023 ELYOT, THOMAS. The castel of helth. Lond. 1534.
The earliest extant ed. is 1539. 13 eds. appeared in the sixteenth century.

4024 FULTON, J. F. Early medical humanists: Leonicenus (1428–1524), Linacre (1460–1524), and Thomas Elyot (d. 1546). *New Eng. Jour. Med.* ccv (1934), 141–6.

4025 GARRISON, F. H. Introduction to the history of medicine. . . . Philadelphia, 1913; 4th ed. rev., Philadelphia, 1929.

4026 HALLIDAY, F. E. Queen Elizabeth and Dr. Burcot. *History Today*, v (1955), 542–4.
Said to have been the physician who cured Elizabeth of small-pox in 1562. Later employed to assay the ore from Frobisher's adventures. The full name was Burcot Raurych.

4027 HERE BEGYNNETH A NEW BOKE OF MEDECYNES, intytulyd the treasure of pore men. . . . Lond. 1526.
Probably a trans. of the popular medieval treatise of Petrus Hispanus (Pope John XXI) entitled *Thesaurus pauperum*. It is a book of household remedies. At least 10 eds. appeared in the sixteenth century.

4028 HORTON-SMITH, L. G. H. Dr. Walter Baily (or Bayley), *c.* 1529–1592, physician to Queen Elizabeth, his parentage, his life, and his relatives and decendents. Lond. 1952.
Cf. idem, *Notes and Queries*, cxcvi (1951), 178–80.

4029 JAMES, P. R. The Baths of Bath in the sixteenth and seventeenth centuries. Lond. 1938.
Excellent.

4030 JAMES, R. R. Thomas Huys, M.D., physician to Mary Tudor. *Janus*, xl (1936), 171–7.

4031 JAMES, R. R. William Goodorus: serjeant surgeon to Queen Elizabeth. *Lancet*, ccxxxi (1936), 1018.

4032 JAMES, R. R. The earliest list of surgeons to be licensed by the Bishop of London under the Act of 3 Henry VIII, c. ii. *Janus*, xli (1937), 97–106.

4033 JOHNSON, J. N. The life of Linacre. . . . By R. Graves. Lond. 1835.
Cf. W. Osler, *Linacre memorial lecture*, Cambr. 1908; and R. J. Mitchell, *Thomas Linacre, E.H.R.* l (1935), 696–8.

4034 KOCHER, P. H. The physician as atheist in Elizabethan England. *Hunt. Lib. Quar.* x (1947), 229–49.

4035 KOCHER, P. H. The idea of God in Elizabethan medicine. *Jour. Hist. Ideas*, xi (1950), 3–29.

4036 LANGDON-BROWN, WALTER. The background to Harvey. *Lancet*, ccxxxi (1936), 961–7.

4037 LARKEY, S. V. Public health in Tudor England. *Amer. Jour. Public Health*, xxiv (1935), 1099–1102.

4038 LARKEY, S. V. The hippocratic oath in Elizabethan England. *Bull. Inst. Hist. Med.* iv (1936), 201–19.

4039 MULLETT, C. F. Public baths and health in England, 16th–18th century. *Supplements to Bull. of Hist. of Med.*, no. 5. Baltimore, 1946.

4040 MULLETT, C. F. Some neglected aspects of plague medicine in sixteenth century England. *Scientific Monthly*, xliv (1937), 325–37.

4041 MULLETT, C. F. The plague of 1603 in England. *Annals Med. Hist.*, n.s., ix (1937), 230–47.

4042 MUNK, W. R. Roll of the College of Physicians, 1518–1700. 3 vols. Lond. 1878.

4043 OSLER, W. Evolution of modern medicine. Oxf. 1913; 1921.

4044 PILCHER, L. S. List of works by old masters of medicine and surgery. Philadelphia, 1918.

4045 POMERANZ, HERMAN. Medicine in the Shakespearean plays and era. *Medical Life*, xli (1934), 351–76, 479–532.

4046 RADBILL, SAMUEL. John Jones, phisition. The second writer on pediatrics in English. *Bull. Inst. Hist. Med.* vi (1938), 145–62.

4047 SALTMARSH, JOHN. Plague and economic decline in England in the later Middle Ages. *Cambr. Hist. Jour.* vii (1941), 23–41.

4048 SOUTH, J. F. Memorials of the craft of surgery in England. By D'A. Power. Lond. 1886.
Rich on Tudor period. Well documented text and app.

4049 TIBBITS, E. G. The hospital of Robert, earl of Leicester, in Warwick. *Trans. and Proc. Birm., Arch. Soc.* lx (1940), 112–44.

4050 TURNER, WILLIAM. A book of the natures and properties as well of the bathes in England as of other bathes in Germany and Italy, 1562. By J. Giesen. Württemberg, 1938.
Originally published as part ii of Turner's *Herbal*.

4051 VICARY, THOMAS. A profitable treatise of the anatomy of man's body. Lond. 1577; by F. J. Furnivall and Percy Furnivall, *E.E.T.S.*, extra ser., liii (1888).
Probably nothing more than a transcript of a fourteenth-century MS. Cf. *D.N.B.* (9), art. Vicary.

4052 WILSON, F. P. The plague in Shakespeare's London. Oxf. 1927.
Cf. idem, *The plague pamphlets of Thos. Dekker*, Oxf. 1925.

ii. SOCIAL AND DOMESTIC LIFE

A. General

It would be impossible to cite here all the contemporary pamphlet literature, poems, plays, essays, &c., that throw light on social conditions. There are good chapters on Tudor social literature in *Cambr. Hist.* (6), iii, ch. 5; iv, ch. 16. Reference should be made particularly to the works of Crowley, Latimer,

Greene, Lodge, Gascoigne, Nashe, Dekker, Deloney, Churchyard, and to Hall's *Satires*, Marston's *Scourge of Villanie*, and Stubbs's *Anatomy of Abuses*. All these are discussed with ample bibliographies in *Cambr. Hist.* (6).

A good deal of correspondence on domestic affairs is included in the *Reports of the Hist. MSS. Comm.* (pp. 10–22 *supra*). The observations of visiting foreigners are given in Rye (4157).

Wills and testaments are often valuable for social history. A great many of them have been printed. Cf. on this subject Gross (1), 604–6. In addition to the references cited there, cf. also *Wills from doctor's commons . . . 1495–1695*, by J. G. Nichols and J. Bruce, *Camden Soc.* lxxxiii (1863), and *Index of Wills . . . in the probation registry at Canterbury, 1396–1558 and 1640–50*, by H. R. Plomer, *Brit. Rec. Soc. Index Library* (1920); vol. ii, *1558–1577*, by C. H. Ridge, ibid. lxv (1940); vol. iii, *1581–1595*, by C. H. Ridge, ibid. lxxvi (1954). Cf. also *Norwich consistory court depositions, 1499–1512 and 1518–1530*, by E. D. Stone and B. Cozens-Hardy, *Norfolk Rec. Soc.* x (1930); *Index to wills proved in the consistory court of Norwich . . . 1370–1550 and wills among the Norwich enrolled deeds, 1286–1508*, by M. A. Farrow, *Brit. Rec. Soc. Index Library*, lxix (1945); vol. ii, *1550–1603*, by M. A. Farrow, ibid. lxxiii (1950); and *Administrations in the consistory court of Chichester 1555–1800 . . .*, by E. A. Fry, *Brit. Rec. Soc. Index Library*, lxiv (1940). Also *Index of the wills and administrations entered in the registers of the archbishops at York being consistory wills A.D. 1316 to A.D. 1822 known as Archbishop's wills*, by J. Charlesworth and A. V. Hudson, *Yorks. Arch. Soc.* rec. ser., xciii for 1936 (1937). Many other wills are scattered through the publications of local historical societies.

Reference should be made in general to 2573, 2574, 3574, 3577, 3590, and to the further references there cited.

4053 ARENTS, GEORGE. Tobacco: its history illustrated by books, manuscripts and engravings in the library of George Arents, Jr.; vol. i, 1507–1615; ii, 1615–1698. By J. E. Brooks. 2 vols. New York, 1937.
Cf. also S. A. Dickson, *Panacea or precious bane: tobacco in sixteenth century literature*, *Bull. New York Pub. Lib.* lvii (1953), 367–81, 419–32, 471–96, 544–66, 580–97

4054 CAMDEN, CARROLL. The Elizabethan woman. Lond. 1952.

4055 CASTIGLIONE, BALDASSARE. Il cortegiano. Venice, 1528; trans. Thos. Hoby (*The courtyer of Count Baldessar Castilio . . . very necessary and profitable for yonge gentilmen and gentilwomen . . .*), Lond. 1561; same trans. by W. Raleigh, Lond. 1900.

4056 CHILD MARRIAGES, DIVORCES and ratifications . . . 1561–6. By F. J. Furnivall. *E.E.T.S.*, cviii (1897).

4057 DIARY OF MARGARET, LADY HOBY, 1599–1605. By D. M. Meads, Lond. 1930. Extracts from the same diary are printed in *Trans. R.H. Soc.*, 3rd ser., ii (1908), 153–74.

4058 EARLY ENGLISH TREATISES and poems on education, precedence and manners in olden time. By F. J. Furnivall, *et al. E.E.T.S.*, extra ser., viii (1869).
Contains: Sir Humphrey Gilbert, *Queene Elizabeth's achademy . . for education of her*

majestie's wardes (also printed in *Arch.* xxi (1827), 506–20); tracts on precedence, funerals, manners, and instructions to children, noblemen, fools, and governors; essays on early Italian and German books of courtesy.

4059 FUSSELL, G. E. and K. R. The English countrywoman: a farmhouse social history, A.D. 1500–1900. Lond. 1953

4060 FUSSELL, G. E. and K. R. The English countryman: his life and work, A.D. 1500–1900. Lond. 1955.

4061 HARDING, D. P. Elizabethan betrothals and 'Measure for Measure'. *Jour. of Eng. German. Philol.* xlix (1950), 139–58.

4062 HARRIS, GEORGE. Domestic everyday life, manners, and customs in this country . . . to the end of the eighteenth century. *Trans. R.H. Soc.,* ix (1881), 224–53.
Covers the sixteenth and seventeenth centuries.

4063 HOLLES, GERVAISE. Memorials of the Holles family, 1493–1656. By A. C. Wood. Camden Soc., 3rd ser., lv (1937).
Edited from MSS. at Longleat and Welbeck.

4064 HYAMSON, A. M. The sephardim of England: a history of a Spanish and Portuguese Jewish community, 1492–1951. Lond. 1951.

4065 INEDITED TRACTS; illustrating the manners, opinions, and occupations of Englishmen during the sixteenth and seventeenth centuries. By W. C. Hazlitt. *Roxburghe Club* (1868).
Contains: *Cyvile and uncivyle life. A discourse very profitable, Where is disputed what order of lyfe best beseemeth a gentleman. . . .* 1579. (Also printed in 1586 under the title, *The English courtier and the country-gentleman.*) J. M., *A health to the gentlemanly profession of servingmen,* or, *The servingman's comfort,* 1598.

4066 KELSO, RUTH. The doctrine of the English gentleman in the sixteenth century. Urbana, 1929.

4067 KELSO, RUTH. Doctrine for a lady of the renaissance. Urbana, 1956.

4068 LEMONNIER, LÉON. La vie quotidienne en Angleterre sous Élisabeth. Paris, 1950.

4069 MANNERS AND MEALS in olden time. By F. J. Furnivall. *E.E.T.S.,* xxxii (1868).
Contains a number of fifteenth- and sixteenth-century books on behaviour, including: *The Babees Book* (c. 1475); Hugh Rhodes, *The boke of nurture . . . for men, servants and children* (1st ed. 1545); John Russell, *The boke of nurture folowyng Englandis gise* (c. 1540); *Boke of Kervynge* (1st ed. 1508); Francis Seager, *The schoole of vertue* (1st ed. 1557).

4070 MURRAY, L. H. The ideal of the court lady, 1561–1625. Chicago, 1938.

4071 NICHOLS, JOHN. Illustrations of the manners and expences of antient times in England . . . from the accompts of churchwardens. Lond. 1797.
A valuable collection of items.

4072 NOTESTEIN, WALLACE. The English woman, 1580–1625. *Studies in Social History. A tribute to G. M. Trevelyan.* By J. H. Plumb. Lond. 1955. pp. 69–107.

4073 POWELL, C. L. English domestic relations, 1487–1653.... New York, 1917.
Chiefly useful as a guide to the material which the author has used.

4074 RICH, E. E. The population of Elizabethan England. *Econ. Hist. Rev.,* 2nd ser., ii (1949), 247–65.
Based upon the muster rolls.

4075 VATKE, E. F. T. Culturbilder aus Alt-England. Berlin, 1887.
A mass of quotations from literary sources describing the household economy and social practices of the Tudor period.

4076 WENHAM, EDWARD. Pomanders. *Connoisseur,* xciii (1934), 228–32.

4077 WOLF, LUCIEN. Jews in Tudor England. *Essays in Jewish History,* *Jew. Hist. Soc.* (1934), 73–90.

4078 WOODWARD, W. A. The countryman's jewel: days in the life of a sixteenth century squire. By Marcus Woodward. Lond. 1934. Compiled from Leonard Mascall's version of Charles Estienne's *Praedium Rusticum.*

B. The Social Order

The basic statement on the social concept is in Lovejoy (4081). An excellent short account of its application to sixteenth-century England is in Tillyard (3646), 10–20. Cf. Rowse (765), Hexter (3759).

4079 CAMPBELL, MILDRED. The English yeoman under Elizabeth and early Stuarts. New Haven, 1942.

4080 COOPER, J. P. The counting of manors. *Econ. Hist. Rev.,* 2nd ser., viii (1955–6), 377–89.
Valuable. Questions the statistical methods of Tawney (4085), and Stone (4084). Statistics on Elizabethan peerages in an app.

4081 LOVEJOY, A. O. The great chain of being. Cambr., U.S.A., 1936.
Traces historically the concept of social order in sixteenth-century England.

4082 NOTESTEIN, WALLACE. The English people on the eve of colonization, 1603–1630. *New American Nation Series.* New York, 1954.
Valuable chapters on social classes.

4083 SIEGEL, P. N. English humanism and the new Tudor aristocracy *Jour. Hist. Ideas,* xiii (1952), 450–68.

4084 STONE, LAWRENCE. The anatomy of the Elizabethan aristocracy. *Econ. Hist. Rev.* xviii (1948), 1–53.
Cf. idem, *The Elizabethan aristocracy—a restatement, Econ. Hist. Rev.,* 2nd ser., iv (1952), 302–21. A reply to Trevor-Roper (4086).

4085 TAWNEY, R. H. The rise of the gentry, 1558–1640. *Econ. Hist. Rev.* xi (1941), 1–38.
Cf. idem, *The rise of the gentry: a postscript, Econ Hist. Rev.,* 2nd ser., vii (1954), 91–98. A reply to Trevor-Roper (4086).

4086 TREVOR-ROPER, H. R. The Elizabethan aristocracy: an anatomy anatomized. *Econ. Hist. Rev.,* 2nd ser., iii (1951), 279–98.

4087 TREVOR-ROPER, H. R. The Gentry, 1540–1660. *Econ. Hist. Rev. Supplement* (1953).

C. HOUSEHOLD MANAGEMENT

(a) *General*

4088 A BREVIATE touching the order and government of a nobleman's house. By Jos. Banks. *Arch.* xiii (1800), 315–89.

4089 JONES, P. VAN B. The household of a Tudor nobleman. *Univ. of Illinois Studies*, vi (1917).
Contains a good bibliography. Cf. also 4655.

(b) *Household Books*

For bibliography, cf. Jones (4089). The volumes listed below are the most complete household books for the sixteenth century in print. Extracts from many others, however, will be found scattered through the reports of *Hist. MSS. Comm.* (pp. 10–22 *supra*), particularly the Hastings MSS. (146), i. 354–417, and Northumberland MSS. (172), app. 226–31, and in family histories. For the royal household, cf. nos. 1240–53. Cf. also manorial accounts, ch. vii *supra* (pp. 218–20).

4090 LORD BURGHLEY'S HOUSEHOLD ACCOUNTS. By Conyers Read. *Econ. Hist. Rev.*, 2nd ser., ix (1956), 343–8.

4091 ESTATE ACCOUNTS OF THE EARLS OF NORTHUMBERLAND, 1562–1637. By M. E. James. *Surtees Soc.* cxliii (1948). Durham, 1955.
Cf. A. R. Batho, *The finances of an Elizabethan nobleman* [Henry Percy, 9th earl of Northumberland], *Econ. Hist. Rev.*, 2nd ser., ix (1957), 433–50.

4092 EXTRACTS FROM THE HOUSEHOLD ACCOUNTS of Sir Thos. Lovel and of the earls of Rutland. By H. M. Lyte and W. H. Stevenson, in *Rutland MSS.* (161), iv, pp. viii–xi, 260–573.

4093 EXTRACTS FROM THE HOUSEHOLD AND PRIVY PURSE EXPENDITURE of Le Strange of Hunstanton, 1519–78. By D. Gurney. *Arch.* xxv (1834), 411–569.

4094 EXTRACTS FROM THE BOOKE OF THE HOWSHOLD charges and other paiments laid out by the L. North and at his commandement, &c. By William Stevenson. *Arch.* xix (1821), 283–301.

4095 EXTRACTS FROM THE HOUSEHOLD ACCOUNT of Sir Henry Willoughby, executors' accounts during minority of his children, and accounts of Sir Francis Willoughby. By W. H. Stevenson, in *Middleton MSS.* (163), pp. xiii–xiv, 327–464.

4096 FFARINGTON, WILLIAM. The Derby household books. By F. R. Raines. *Chetham Soc.* xxxi (1853).
Forms pt. ii of *The Stanley Papers*. Contains household expenses, &c., 1561 and 1586–90.

4097 THE HOUSE AND FARM ACCOUNTS of the Shuttleworths . . . co. Lancaster . . . from September 1582 to October 1621. By J. Harland. 4 vols. *Chetham Soc.* xxxv, xli, xliii, xlvi (1856–8).

4098 HOUSEHOLD BOOKS of John, duke of Norfolk, and Thomas, earl of Surrey, 1481–90. By J. P. Collier. *Roxburghe Club*, 1844.
Contains valuable agricultural accounts, accounts of entertainments, journeys, and household expenses.

4099 THE HOUSEHOLD EXPENSES FOR ONE YEAR OF PHILIP, 3rd earl of Wharton, 1585–6. By W. C. Trevelyan. Newcastle, 1899.

4100 INVENTORIES OF THE WARDROBES, plate, chapel stuff, &c. of Henry Fitzroy, duke of Richmond and Katherine, princess dowager. By J. G. Nichols. *Camden Soc. Misc.* iii (1855).
Inventories made in 1526 and 1534–5.

4101 PERCY, HENRY, 9th earl of Northumberland. Instructions to his son Algernon Percy touching the management of his estates. By J. H. Markland. *Arch.* xxvii (1838), 306–58; by G. B. Harrison. Lond. 1930.
Neither edition complete. Harrison printed the first two books from a copy of *c.* 1625; Markland an expurgated text of the second part. A third part is printed by F. Grose in the *Antiq. Repertory*, iv (1809), 374–80.

4102 THE NORTHUMBERLAND HOUSEHOLD BOOK. The regulations and establishment of the household of Henry Algernon Percy, 5th earl of Northumberland, begun A.D. 1512. By Thomas Percy. Lond. 1770; 1827; repr. in Grose, *Antiq. Repertory*, iv, Lond. 1809.
One of the best extant household books of the period.

4103 SELECTIONS FROM THE HOUSEHOLD BOOKS OF EDWARD, duke of Buckingham, 1507–8. By John Gage. *Arch.* xxv (1834), 311–41.

4104 SELECTIONS FROM THE HOUSEHOLD BOOKS of Sir William Fairfax. By S. C. Lomas in *Wombwell MSS.* (211), 67–86.

4105 SELECTIONS FROM THE HOUSEHOLD ACCOUNTS of Richard Bertie and his lady. . . . By S. C. Lomas in *Ancaster MSS.* (97), 459–72.

4106 THE SPENDING OF THE MONEY of Robert Nowell of Reade Hall, Lancaster, 1568–80. By A. B. Grosart. In *The Towneley Hall MSS.*, i. s.l. 1877.
Valuable.

4107 WOLSEY, THOMAS. An order . . . to lymitt John, earle of Oxenford, in the orderinge of his expenses of household, &c. By Henry Ellis. *Arch.* xix (1821), 62–65.

D. Food

There is a chapter on food in Harrison (615).

4108 HAZLITT, W. C. Old cookery books and ancient cuisine. Lond. 1886; 1902.

4109 OXFORD, A. W. English cookery books to the year 1850. Oxf. 1913.

4110   A PROPER NEWE BOOKE OF COOKERYE. Lond. 1558; by F. Frere, Cambr. 1913.
The 1913 ed. contains an account of domestic life in the Tudor period.

4111   WALFORD, CORNELIUS. Early laws and customs in Great Britain regarding food. *Trans. R.H. Soc.* viii (1880), 70–162.
Summarizes various types of laws dealing with food.

E. Dress

The best extant collections of historic English dress are in the Victoria and Albert Museum, London. The Isham collection there contains examples of costume from 1555 through Charles II. The museum publishes valuable illustrated catalogues.
There is a chapter on dress in Harrison (615).

4112   BROOKE, I. English costume in the age of Elizabeth. 2nd ed. Lond. 1950.

4113   CALTHROP, D. C. English costume. 4 vols. Lond. 1906; 1 vol. Lond. 1923.

4114   CUNNINGTON, C. W. and P. E. W. Handbook of English costume in the sixteenth century. Philadelphia, 1954.

4115   FAIRHOLT, F. W. Costume in England. Lond. 1862; 4th ed. rev. by H. A. Dillon. 2 vols. *Bohn's Artists' Library*, Lond. 1896.
The standard work of reference.

4116   LAVER, JAMES. Early Tudor, 1485–1558. *Costume of the Western World Ser*. Lond. 1951.

4117   LINTHICUM, M. C. Costume in the drama of Shakespeare and his contemporaries. Oxf. 1936.
Excellent.

4118   MORSE, H. K. Elizabethan pageantry. A pictorial survey of costume and its commentators from 1560–1620. Lond. 1934.

4119   REYNOLDS, GRAHAM. Elizabethan and Jacobean, 1558–1625. *Costumes of the Western World Ser*. Lond. 1951.

F. Amusements

An excellent chapter with full bibliographies on the various sports and pastimes is in 2573, ii, 344–483. The subjects there included are: hunting, falconry, coursing, fowling, angling, archery, fencing and duelling, horsemanship, bear baiting, bull baiting, cock fighting, dancing, games. Cf. *Cambr. Hist.* (6), iv, ch. xvii, for a discussion of writers on country pastimes. Cf. also 3596. For further bibliographies, see W. Gerrare, *Bibliography of guns and shooting* (from 1450), Lond. 1841; R. B. Marston, *Walton and some early writers on fish and fishing*, Lond. 1894; 1905; R. Souhart, *Bibliographies des ouvrages sur la chasse, la vénerie, la fauconnerie*, Paris, 1886; Oxf. 1908.

4120   SILVER, GEORGE. Paradoxes of defence, 1599. Lond. 1933.
On fencing.

4121　STRUTT, JOSEPH. Glig-gamena angel-deod. Or, the sports and pastimes of the people of England. Lond. 1810; enlarged, by J. C. Cox, Lond. 1903.
The standard work.

12. TRAVEL

A. ROADS

Cf. in general Webb (1316). Harrison (615) has a chapter (bk. 2, ch. ii) on English inns and thoroughfares. Reference should also be made to Leland (4197) and to Camden's *Britannia* (4190), particularly to the maps in Holland's translation.

4122　BALLEN, DOROTHY. Bibliography of road making and roads in the United Kingdom. Lond. 1914.

4123　BATES, E. S. Touring in 1600. A study in the development of travel as a means of education. Boston, 1911.

4124　BERNARD, JEAN. Le guide des chemins d'Angleterre. Paris, 1579.

4125　EMMISON, F. G. 1555 and all that: a milestone in the history of the English road. *Essex Rev.* lxiv (1955), 15–25; 'The very naughty ways' of Elizabethan Essex, ibid. 85–91; Highways act of 1555 a success? ibid. 221–34.

4126　FORDHAM, H. G. The road books and itineraries of Great Britain, 1570–1850. Cambr. 1924.
Cf. idem, in *Bibliog. Soc. Trans.* xiii (1916), 38–68.

4127　THOMSON, G. SCOTT. Roads in England and Wales in 1603. *E.H.R.* xxxiii (1918), 234–43.

B. ENGLISH TRAVELLERS

A good deal was written in the sixteenth century in the way of general advice to travellers and particular instructions for young men about to travel. There is a convenient list of these in Howard (4134), 205 ff.; cf. for one not listed there Read (759), i, 18–20. Cf. also 3279–80. On voyages of commerce and discovery, and on travellers to Russia and the Near and Far East, cf. chs. vii and viii *supra* (pp. 249–79). Coryat's *Crudities* (Davies (9), no. 3488) and Moryson's *Itinerary* (5810), though written in the reign of James I, are characteristic of the sixteenth century. There are some interesting accounts of foreign travel in the correspondence and reports of English agents overseas, cf., for example, 948b.

4128　BORDE, ANDREW. The fyrst boke of the introduction of knowledge. Lond. 1542; by F. J. Furnivall, *E.E.T.S.*, extra ser., x (1870).
A collection of essays on the chief nationalities and kingdoms of Europe.

4129　BOROWY, WACLAW. Angielska relacja o Polsce z r. 1598. *Przeglad Wspólczesny*, lviii (1936), 1–16.
Relative to Fynes Moryson's visit to Poland. Note on Moryson by the same author in *Bakalarz z Cambridge w Polsce xvi w, Drodza* (1936), 573.

4130 MR. HARRIE CAVENDISH his journey to and from Constantinople 1589. By Fox, his servant. By A. C. Wood. *Camden Misc.* xvii, 3rd ser., lxiv (1940).

4131 ECCLES, MARK. Samuel Daniel in France and Italy. *Studies in Philol.* xxxiv (1937), 148–67.

4132 FERRIS, RICHARD. The most dangerous and memorable adventure of R. Ferris, who undertoke to rowe by sea to Bristowe. Lond. 1590; repr. in *Eng. Garner* (279), vi, 154–66.

4133 HOBY, SIR THOMAS. The travels and life of. By E. Powell. *Camden Soc. Misc.* x (1902).

4134 HOWARD, CLARE. English travellers of the renaissance. Lond. 1913. Useful biliographies.

4135 LEES-MILNE, JAMES. Tudor travellers in Italy. *The Month*, n.s., v (1951), 15–23.

4136 McLEAN, DAVID. Three gentlemen adventurers. The story of the Sherley brothers. *Sussex County Mag.* viii (1934), 29–35, 101–6, 180–8, 236–44, 326–31, 360–6, 435–41, 500–4, 576–81, 613–16, 679–83, 734–41; ix (1935), 38–44, 118–23, 173–5, 246–50, 316–20, 375–7, 434–6, 507–12, 563–8, 652–8, 704–8, 785–6.

4137 PARKS, G. B. The English traveller to Italy: the Middle Ages (to 1525). Stanford, 1954.

4137a PENROSE, BOIES. The Sherleian Odyssey. Taunton, 1938.

4138 PENROSE, BOIES. Urbane travellers, 1591–1635. Philadelphia, 1942. Deals with Fynes Morison, Thomas Coryate, Lithgow, Sandys, Thos. Herbert, and Henry Blunt.

4139 ROSS, E. D. Sir Anthony Sherley and his Persian adventure. Lond. 1933.

4140 SHERLEY, THOMAS. Discours of the Turkes. By E. D. Ross. *Camden Misc.* xvi, 3rd ser., lii (1936).

4141 SMITH, WILLIAM. The particular description of England. By H. B. Wheatley and E. W. Ashbee. Lond. 1879. Written about 1588 but not printed before 1879.

4142 TURLERUS, HIERONYMUS. De perigrenatione. . . . Strassburg, 1574; Eng. trans. (*The traveller of Jerome Turler*), Lond. 1575. Probably the first book devoted to the praise of travel. Extracts are printed in 4157.

4143 WEBBE, EDWARD. The rare and most wonderful thinges which Edward Webbe . . . hath seene. Lond. 1590; by E. Arber (*English reprints*), Lond. 1868.

C. FOREIGN TRAVELLERS IN ENGLAND

There is a certain amount of pertinent material scattered through the dispatches of foreign ambassadors in England; cf. ch. ii *supra* (pp. 65–85).

4144 BELL, JAMES. A narrative of the journey of Cecilia, princess of Sweden to the court of queen Elizabeth. By M. Morison. *Trans. R.H. Soc.,* 2nd ser., xii (1898), 181–224; *Haslewood Books,* Lond. 1926.
The 1898 ed. contains in an app. a number of pertinent state papers.

4145 BREUNINGS VON BUCHENBACH, H. J. Relation über seine Sendung nach England im Jahr 1595. By A. Schlossberger. *Bibliothek des litterarischen Vereins in Stuttgart,* lxxxi (1863).

4146 BUTLER, K. T. Giacopo Castelvetro, 1546–1616. *Italian Studies,* v (1950), 1–42.

4147 DIARY OF THE JOURNEY of Philip Julius, duke of Stettin-Pomerania through England in the year 1602. By G. von Bülow and W. Powell. *Trans. R.H. Soc.,* 2nd ser., vi (1892), 1–67.

4148 HAY, DENYS. Pietro Griffo, an Italian in England, 1506–1512. *Italian Studies,* ii (1939), 118–28.

4149 HENTZNER, PAUL. Itinerarium Germaniae, Galliae, Angliae, Italiae. Nuremberg, 1612.
The passages relating to England were repr. by Horace Walpole at Strawberry Hill, 1757. Extracts also are printed in Rye (4157). Cf. W. D. Robson-Scott, *Some notes on Hentzner's Itinerarium, Mod. Lang. Rev.* xlvi (1951), 458–61.

4150 JOURNEY THROUGH ENGLAND and Scotland made by Liupold von Wedel in the years 1584 and 1585. By G. von Bülow. *Trans. R.H. Soc.* 2nd ser., ix (1895), 223–70.

4151 NUCIUS, NICANDER. The second book of the travels of Nicander Nucius of Corcyra. By J. A. Cranmer. *Camden Soc.* xvii (1841).
Describes England and Ireland at the end of Henry VIII's reign. Cf. D. E. Eicholz, *A Greek traveler in Tudor England, Greece and Rome,* xvi (1947), 76–84.

4152 ODLOZILÍK, OTAKAR. Cesty z Čech a Moravy do Velké Britanie v letech 1563–1620. *Časopis Matice Moravské,* xli (1935), 241–320.
Journeys from Bohemia and Moravia to Britain.

4153 PLATTER, THOMAS. Thomas Platter's travels in England, 1599. By Clare Williams. Lond. 1937.

4154 A RELATION . . . OF THE ISLAND OF ENGLAND about the year 1500, with particulars of the customs of these people and of the royal revenues under . . . Henry VII. By C. A. Sneyd. *Camden Soc.* xxxvii (1847).
A brilliant description of England by an anon. Italian.

4155 ROBSON-SCOTT, W. D. German travellers in England, 1400–1800. Oxf. 1953.

4156 ROBSON-SCOTT, W. D. Josua Maler's visit to England in 1551. *Mod. Lang. Rev.* xlv (1950), 346–51.

4157 RYE, W. B. England as seen by foreigners in the days of Elizabeth and James I. Lond. 1865.
Contains extracts from narratives of some fifteen foreign visitors to England, with valuable introduction and notes. For additional extracts from the journal of Samuel Kiechel, 1585, parts of which Rye translates, cf. *Archiv für Geographie, Historie, Staats- und Kriegs-Kunst,* Vienna, 1820, 267 ff.

4158 SMITH, EDWARD. Foreign visitors in England and what they have thought of us. Lond. 1889.

4159 TWO ITALIAN ACCOUNTS OF TUDOR ENGLAND: A journey to London in 1497: a picture of English life under Queen Mary. By C. V. Malfatti. Barcelona, 1953; Oxf. 1954.

4160 WEISS, ROBERT. Cornelio Vitelli in France and England. *Jour. Warburg and Court. Inst.* ii (1939), 219–26.

D. Rogues and Vagabonds

The pamphlet literature on roguery is voluminous. The following are the more important texts and the standard modern works. Cf. also Tawney and Power (2539), ii, iii, and Ribton (2926).

For laws against rogues and beggars, see Nicholls (2925).

4161 AWDELEY, JOHN. The fraternitye of vacabondes. Lond. 1575; by Viles and Furnivall in 4169.

4162 AYDELOTTE, FRANK. Elizabethan rogues and vagabonds. Oxf. 1913.
The standard work.

4163 CHANDLER, F. W. The literature of roguery. 2 vols. Boston, 1907.
Of great bibliographical value.

4164 DEKKER, THOMAS. The belman of London . . . Lanthorne and candlelight, or the second part of the Belman. Lond. 1608; by A. B. Grosart, in *Non-dramatic works of Dekker* (Lond. 1884–6), iii.
Cf. also Kate Gregg, Thomas Dekker, a study in economic and social background, *Univ. of Washington Pub.* ii (1924), 55–112.

4165 THE ELIZABETHAN UNDERWORLD. By A. V. Judges. Lond. 1930.
Reprints tracts and ballads, with an introduction.

4166 GREENE, ROBERT. A notable discouery of coosenage. (The art of conny-catching.) Lond. 1591; the second and third parts of conny-catching, Lond. 1591–2; by A. B. Grosart, in *Complete works of Greene* (1881–6), x.
Cf. also R. Greene, *The blacke bookes messenger* (Lond. 1592) and *The defence of conny-catching* (Lond. 1592), both repr. in *Bodley Head Quartos*, Lond. 1924. Cf. J. L. Lievsay, *Newgate penitents: further aspects of Elizabethan pamphlet sensationalism*, *Hunt. Lib. Quar.* vii (1943), 47–69.

4167 HARMAN, THOMAS. A caveat or warening for commen cursetors vulgarly called vagabones. Lond. 1567; by Viles and Furnivall in 4169.

4168 NASH, THOMAS. Pierce Penilesse . . . his supplication to the divell. Lond. 1592; by R. B. McKerrow, in *Works*, i (1904).
Cf. also his picaresque novel, *Jack Wilton*.

4169 THE ROGUES AND VAGABONDS OF SHAKESPEARE'S YOUTH. By E. Viles and F. J. Furnivall. *New Shakespeare Soc.*, 6th ser., vii (1880).
Prints 4161, 4167, and other texts

XI

LOCAL HISTORY

No attempt is made in this chapter to cover completely the vast field of local history, and much which perhaps belongs here has been included in other chapters. All English ecclesiastical history, general and local, is dealt with on pp. 151–212 *supra*; local government on pp. 108–17 *supra*; manorial courts on pp. 217–24 *supra*; local musters on pp. 289–90 *supra*; local subsidy rolls on pp. 101–5 *supra*; local industries on pp. 228–32 *supra*. Churchwardens' accounts (cf. 1715 *supra*) and parish registers (cf. 1716 *supra*) have not been considered in detail, studies of place-names have been ignored (cf. *Public. of English Place-Name Soc.*, Cambr. 1924 ff., together with many separate publications).

The local history of Scotland is considered in ch. xii *infra*, of Ireland in ch. xiii *infra*, and of Wales in ch. xiv *infra*.

A. GENERAL BIBLIOGRAPHIES

For a short bibliography of local history, cf. 4183. Still valuable are Upcott (4187) and Anderson (4170) for lists of special collections, Gross (4176) on municipal history, and Humphreys (4180) for lists of bibliographies of separate counties and towns. Thompson (4185) is a brief but useful guide. Lancaster (3a) is excellent for local history.

The *Reports of the Hist. MSS. Comm.* covering local archives are considered on pp. 10–22 *supra*, and are indexed as far as the year 1914 in 4177 *infra*. The guides published by the *Institute of Historical Research* (Lond.) (4178) are useful, as is the *Bulletin* (45). For a list of the yearly publications of the local records societies, cf. *Archives*, a bi-yearly publication of the *British Records Association* (Lond. 1948 ff.). Local source material is also described in the *Bulletins of the National Register of Archives* (Lond. 1948 ff.).

Vol. iii of the *Reports of the Royal Comm. on Pub. Records* (81) is the fullest guide to the various classes of official local records. Cf. also *Reports of the Committee appointed to inquire as to the custody of local records*, Lond. 1902.

Many of the various local record societies have published guides to local records, cf. *infra*.

4170 ANDERSON, J. P. The book of British topography; a classified catalogue of the topographical works in the library of the British Museum relating to Great Britain and Ireland. Lond. 1881.
The most generally useful list of books on local history published before 1881.

4171 ANTIQUARIES JOURNAL. Lond. 1922 ff.
Published quarterly, contains lists of articles in current archaeological journals.

4172 COLLECTANEA TOPOGRAPHICA ET GENEALOGICA. [By J. G. Nichols.] 8 vols. Lond. 1834–43.

4173 COX, J. C. How to write the history of a parish. 5th ed. Lond. 1909.
Describes the various classes of local records.

4174 DANVILLE, W. V., and FIELD, F. J. A manual of British topography; a catalogue of county and local histories, pamphlets, &c. Lond. 1909.
A booksellers' catalogue, but published in book form and very full.

4175 GOMME, G. L. Index of archaeological papers, 1665–1890 [with annual supplements to 1908]. Lond. 1907.
Valuable, but not exhaustive.

4176 GROSS, CHARLES. A bibliography of British municipal history. *Harvard Hist. Studies*, v (1897).
Much the best work for the cities, towns, and gilds to 1897. Contains also useful lists of county and other local histories.

4177 A GUIDE TO THE REPORTS issued by the royal commission for historical MSS. Topographical. Lond. 1914; Persons, 2 vols. Lond. 1935–8.
Index volumes to the *Hist. MSS. Comm. Reports*.

4178 GUIDE TO THE ACCESSIBILITY OF LOCAL RECORDS of England and Wales. *Bull. Inst. Hist. Research*, spec. suppl. i (1932); ii (1934).

4179 HEARNSHAW, F. J. C. Municipal records. *Helps for Students of History*, ii. Lond. 1918.

4180 HUMPHREYS, A. L. A handbook of county bibliography; being a bibliography of bibliographies relating to the counties and towns of Great Britain and Ireland. Lond. 1917.
This is a detailed and useful guide to all bibliographies of counties and towns before 1917 but gives no direct information on county or town histories.

4181 INDEX OF INQUISITIONS preserved in the Public Record Office. *Lists and Indexes*, xxiii (1907) and xxvi (1909).
Covers the period Henry VIII to Elizabeth.

4182 A LIST OF WORKS relating to British general and local history. *Bull. of the New York Public Lib.* xiv (1910).
A useful list.

4183 LOCAL HISTORY HANDLIST: a short bibliography and list of sources for the study of local history and antiquities. *Hist. Assoc.*, spec. ser., ii. Lond. 1947.
Cf. also *Subject index to periodicals: Regional lists, 1954*, Library Assoc., Lond. 1954–6.

4184 MEADS, D. M. Searching local records. *Rev. Eng. Studies*, iv (1928), 173–90, 301–22.
A useful description of various kinds of local material.

4185 THOMPSON, A. H. A short bibliography of local history. *Hist. Assoc. Leaflet*, no. 72. Lond. 1928.
Small but helpful. Cf. also ibid., *Parish history and records*, Helps for Students of History, no. 15, Lond. 1919.

4186 TOPOGRAPHER AND GENEALOGIST. [By J. G. Nichols.] 3 vols. Lond. 1846–58.

4187 UPCOTT, WILLIAM. A bibliographical account of the principal works relating to English topography. 3 vols. Lond. 1818.
An excellent work, still valuable, notwithstanding its early date.

B. GENERAL WORKS

The more important English periodicals devoted to local history are listed in Gross (1), 20 ff.; the publications of local societies in Gross (1), 100 ff. Gross lists also (149 ff.) most of the important general books on local English history printed prior to 1914. Reference should also be made to Davies (8), 272–88.

The Victoria County Histories (4203) are easily the best of all the local histories, but many of the older county histories are valuable. A selected list of these is printed in Thompson (4185), 4–5. Cf. Rowse (765), ch. v.

4188 BIBLIOTHECA TOPOGRAPHICA BRITANNICA. By John Nichols *et al.* 8 vols. Lond. 1780–90. Continued in *Miscellaneous Antiquities*, 2 vols. Lond. 1791–1800.

Contains histories of various manors, parishes, palaces, abbeys, &c.

4189 BRITISH BOROUGH CHARTERS, 1307–1660. By Martin Weinbaum. Cambr. 1943.

4190 CAMDEN, WILLIAM. Britannia, sive florentissimorum regnorum Angliae, Scotiae, Hiberniae chorographica descriptio. Lond. 1586; 6th ed. (enlarged) 1606; first Eng. trans. by Philemon Holland, Lond. 1610; trans. (enlarged) by Richard Gough, 3 vols. Lond. 1789.

Includes a valuable account of the O'Neills in Ireland under Elizabeth. Holland's trans. contains contemporary maps by Norden and Saxton.

4191 CHUBB, THOMAS. The printed maps in the atlases of Great Britain and Ireland. A bibliography, 1579–1870. Lond. 1927.

4192 FORDHAM, H. G. Some notable surveyors and map makers of the sixteenth–eighteenth centuries and their work. Cambr. 1929.

4193 GENTLEMAN'S MAGAZINE LIBRARY, English topography. By G. L. Gomme, 17 vols. Lond. 1891–1905.

A classified collection of the important articles relevant to English topography printed in the *Gent. Mag.*, 1731–1868, arranged alphabetically by counties. Valuable.

4194 GREEN, M. A. E. W. Town life in the fifteenth century. 2 vols. Lond. 1894; 1 vol. Lond. 1907.

Contains much of value for the sixteenth century.

4195 HISTORICAL MONUMENTS of Great Britain. By the earl of Crawford and Balcarres. Lond. (in progress).

A careful survey of all extant buildings in Great Britain of any archaeological or historical significance. Excellent illustrations. The following volumes have appeared (to 1955): *Buckinghamshire*, 2 vols.; *Dorset*, 1 vol.; *Essex*, 4 vols.; *Herefordshire*; *Hertfordshire*; *Huntingdonshire*; *London*, 5 vols.; *Middlesex*; *City of Cambridge*; *City of Oxford*. For a complete list cf. *Sectional list, no. 27, Ancient monuments and historic buildings in England, Wales and Scotland*, rev. to 31 Jan. 1956; *List of publications issued by the Ministry of Works and the Royal Commissions on Ancient and Historical Monuments of England, Wales, and Monmouthshire, and Scotland*, Lond. 1956.

4196 HOSKINS, W. G. English provincial towns in the early sixteenth century. *Trans. R.H. Soc.*, 5th ser., vi (1956), 1–19.

4197 LELAND, JOHN. Itinerary. By Thos. Hearne. 9 vols. Oxf. 1710–12;
1745–7; 1770; by L. T. Smith, 5 vols. Lond. 1906–8.
This material, with that in 4198, was collected by Leland between 1535 and 1543, but
was not printed before the eighteenth century. Cf., however, *The Laboryouse journey
and serche of Johan Leylande for Englande's antiquities*, by Johan Ball, Lond. 1549.
For full bibliography of Leland, cf. [Edward Burton?], *Life of John Leland . . .*, Lond.
1896.

4198 LELAND, JOHN. De rebus britannicis collectanea. By Thomas
Hearne. 6 vols. Oxf. 1715.

4199 LEWIS, S. A topographical dictionary of England, with atlas. 5 vols.
Lond. 1831; 7th ed. Lond. 1849.
The standard book of reference. Valuable.

4200 MEREWETHER, H. A., and STEPHENS, A. J. The history of the
boroughs and municipal corporations of the United Kingdom. 3 vols. Lond.
1835.
Valuable material, badly arranged and often incorrectly interpreted.

4201 NORDEN, JOHN. Speculum Britanniae. Lond. 1593–8.
Only two parts, *Middlesex* and *Hertfords.*, published by Norden. Three other counties,
Cornwall, *Essex*, and *Northants.*, were published later from his MSS. (cf. nos. 4285,
4366, 4449, 4584, 4648 *infra*). Cf. also *Library*, 4th ser., vii (1926), 233–52.

4202 REPORT OF THE COMMISSIONERS appointed to inquire into the
municipal corporations in England and Wales. *Parl. papers*, 1835, xxiii–xxviii;
1836, xxiv; 1837, xxv; 1838, xxxv; Index, 1839, xviii.
Covers Ireland as well, but not Scotland.

4203 VICTORIA HISTORY of the counties of England. By William Page
et al. Westminster, 1900 (in progress).
This great work is complete for the following counties: Bedfordshire, Berkshire,
Buckinghamshire, Hampshire, Hertfordshire, Huntingdonshire, Lancashire, Rutland-
shire, Surrey, Warwickshire, Worcestershire, Yorkshire (North Riding). Portions of
the history of London and of 22 other counties have been published.
  Of less value for the sixteenth century than for earlier periods, but indispensable on all
aspects of local history, cf. *Guide to the Victoria history of the Counties of England*, Lond.
1912.

C. INDIVIDUAL COUNTIES, CITIES, BOROUGHS, PARISHES AND OTHER LOCAL DIVISIONS

The material in this section, which does not pretend to be exhaustive, is arranged
under counties as follows:
  1. Local bibliographical guides.
  2. Publications of local historical or partly historical societies.
  3. County histories and collections of county records, excepting governmental
and legal records given in ch. iii *supra* (pp. 108–17).
  4. Town histories and collections of town documents of importance for the
Tudor period, excepting legal and governmental records given in ch. iii *supra*
(pp. 108–17), and industrial and commercial records given in ch. vii *supra*
(pp. 226–32).
  Histories and records of smaller local divisions of special value for the Tudor
period. On the records of the manorial courts, &c., cf. pp. 113–14, 217–49 *supra*.

1. BEDFORDSHIRE

(1) *Bibliographies*

4204 GUIDE TO THE BEDFORDSHIRE RECORD OFFICE. By Richard Turner. Bedford, 1957.

(2) *Local Societies*

4205 BEDFORDSHIRE HISTORICAL RECORD SOCIETY. Publications. Aspley Guise, 1913 ff.

4206 BEDFORDSHIRE NOTES AND QUERIES. 3 vols. Bedford, 1886–93.

(3) *County Histories and Records*

Cf. also Gross (1), nos. 841–2, 2268–70. *V.C.H. Bedfordshire* is complete in 3 vols. and index (Lond. 1904–14).

4208 FISHER, THOMAS. Collections historical, genealogical, and topographical for Bedfordshire. Lond. 1812–36.

4209 PARRY, J. D. Select illustrations, historical and topographical, of Bedfordshire. Lond. 1827.
Deals with Bedford, Ampthill, Houghton, Luton, and Chicksands.

(4) *Other Works*

4210 DICKENS, A. G. Estate and household managements in Bedfordshire, *c*. 1540. *Bedford. Hist. Rec. Soc.* xxxvi (1956), 38–45.

4211 NEWNHAM PRIORY: a Bedford rental 1506–7. By W. N. Henman. *Bedford. Hist. Rec. Soc.* xxv (1947), 15–81.
Cf. also Barbara Crook, *Newnham Priory: rental of manor at Biddenham, 1505–6*, ibid. 82–103.

2. BERKSHIRE

(1) *Bibliographies*

There is none of importance. A MS. collection for the history of Berkshire, left by John Warburton, Somerset herald, in 1759 is preserved in the library of the *Society of Antiquaries*. Cf. also *Guide to the Berkshire record office.* By Felix Hull. Reading, 1952.

(2) *Local Societies*

Cf. also 4564.

4212 BERKSHIRE NOTES AND QUERIES, i, pts. 1–3. Lond. [1890–1].

4213 NEWBURY DISTRICT FIELD CLUB. Transactions. Newbury, 1871 ff.

4214 QUARTERLY JOURNAL of the Berkshire archaeological and architectural society. 3 vols. Reading [1889–95].
Continued as *Berks., Bucks., and Oxon. Archaeological Journal*, Reading, 1895–1930; then as the *Berks. Archaeological Journal*, Reading, 1930 ff.

(3) *County Histories and Records*

Cf. Gross (1), nos. 2272, 2274. *V.C.H. Berkshire* is complete in 4 vols. and index (Lond. 1906–24).

4215 ASHMOLE, ELIAS. The history and antiquities of Berkshire, with a description of Windsor. 3 vols. Lond. 1719.

(4) *Town Histories and Records*

Cf. Gross (1), nos. 842a–9.
The records of the following Berkshire towns are described in *Hist. MSS. Comm. Reports*: Abingdon (Reports i, ii), Reading (Report xi, app. vii), Wallingford (Report vi).

4216 COATES, CHARLES. History and antiquities of Reading. Reading, 1802; supplement, 1810.

4217 CLARKE, W. N. Parochial topography of the hundred of Wanting [Wantage]. Oxf. 1924.

4218 HISTORY AND ANTIQUITIES of Newbury and environs, including 28 parishes in . . . Berks. Speenhamland, 1839.

4219 READING RECORDS; diary of the corporation . . . 1431–1654. By J. M. Guilding. 4 vols. Lond. 1892–6.
Vol. i covers period to 1603.

4220 TIGHE, R. R., and DAVIS, J. E. Annals of Windsor. 2 vols. Lond. 1858.
The best history of Windsor. Contains many sixteenth-century documents.

4221 THE UNTON INVENTORIES, relating to Wadley and Faringdon in the years 1596 and 1620, with a memoir of the family of Unton. By J. G. Nichols. *Ashmolean Soc.* Lond. 1841.

(5) *Other Works*

4222 COOKE, A. H. A rent roll of the suppressed priory of Goring, 1546. *Berks. Arch. Jour.*, n.s., xxxv (1931), 120–3.

4223 PRESTON, A. E. The demolition of Reading Abbey. *Berks. Arch. Jour.*, n.s., xxxix (1935), 107–44.
Contains demolition account of 1549.

4224 SANDHURST MANOR; crown survey. By G. A. Kempthorne. *Berks. Arch. Jour.*, n.s., xxxix (1935), 192–7.
Made 14 Nov. 1950.

4225 SPOKES, P. S. Some notes on the domestic architecture of Wallingford, Berkshire. *Berks. Arch. Jour.*, n.s. l (1947), 30–48.

3. BUCKINGHAMSHIRE

(1) *Bibliographies*

4226 BIBLIOTHECA BUCKINGHAMENSIS. [By Henry Gough.] *Architect. and Arch. Soc. for the co. of Bucks.* Aylesbury, 1890.

(2) *Local Societies*

Cf. also 4214, 4564.

4227 ARCHITECTURAL AND ARCHAEOLOGICAL SOCIETY FOR THE COUNTY OF BUCKINGHAM. Records of Buckinghamshire. Aylesbury, 1858 ff.

4228 RECORDS BRANCH OF THE BUCKINGHAMSHIRE ARCHAEO-LOGICAL SOCIETY. Aylesbury, i–vi, 1937–41; *Bucks. Record Soc.* vii–, 1942 ff.

(3) *County Histories and Records*

Cf. Gross (1), nos. 849a–51, 1058, 2278–9. The *Verney papers* (284) throw light upon Bucks. county history under the Tudors. *V.C.H. Bucks.* is complete in 4 vols. and index (Lond. 1905–27). For historical monuments, cf. 4195.

4229 GIBBS, ROBERT. Buckinghamshire, a record of local occurrences, A.D. 1400–1800. 4 vols. Aylesbury, 1878–82.

4230 LIPSCOMB, GEORGE. The history and antiquities of the county of Buckingham. 4 vols. Lond. 1831–47.
One of the better older county histories.

4231 SHEAHAN, J. J. History and topography of Buckingham. Lond. 1862.
A useful book, arranged by hundreds.

(4) *Town Histories and Records*

Records of Great Wycombe are described in *Hist. MSS. Comm. Reports*, v.

4232 GIBBS, ROBERT. Buckinghamshire, a history of Aylesbury with its borough and hundreds. Aylesbury, 1885.
Good.

4233 RATCLIFFE, OLIVER. History and antiquities of the hundred of Newport Pagnell. Olney, 1900.

4234 WILLIS, BROWNE. The history and antiquities of the town, hundred and deanery of Buckingham. Lond. 1755.

(5) *Other Works*

Cf. 1207, 4693, and 4813.

4235 BROWNE, A. L. Wills of Buckinghamshire clergy in the sixteenth century. *Rec. of Bucks.* xiii (1936), 195–204.

4237 A DOCUMENT RELATING TO WHADDON CHASE in the sixteenth century. *Rec. of Bucks.* xiii (1937), 281–4.

4238 SCHULZ, H. C. An Elizabethan map of Wotton Underwood, Buckinghamshire. *Hunt. Lib. Quar.* iii (1939), 43–46.

4. CAMBRIDGESHIRE

(1) *Bibliographies*

4239 BAKER MSS. Baker, Thomas (1656–1740), made an extensive collection of MS. materials for the university, county, and town, of which 23 vols. are in the British Museum, 19 in the Cambridge University Library. An index was published for the *Cambridgeshire Antiquarian Society* in 1848.

4240 A CATALOGUE OF BOOKS printed at or relating to the university, town and county of Cambridge from 1521 to 1893. By Robert Bowes. Cambr. 1894.

4241 CATALOGUE . . . of the books and papers bequeathed to the university by J. W. Clark. By A. T. Bartholomew. Cambr. 1912.

(2) *Local Societies*

Cf. also 4459 and 4753.

4242 CAMBRIDGE ANTIQUARIAN SOCIETY publications. Cambr. 1859 ff.

4243 CAMBRIDGE AND HUNTINGDONSHIRE ARCHAEOLOGICAL SOCIETY. Transactions. Ely, 1904 ff.

(3) *County Histories and Records*

Vols. i, ii, iv of *V.C.H. Cambridge, Isle of Ely*, have appeared. Lond. 1938–53.

4244 BLOMEFIELD, FRANCIS. Collectanea Cantabrigiensia, or collections relating to Cambridge university, town and county. Norwich, 1750.

4245 CARTER, EDMUND. The history of the county of Cambridge. Cambr. 1753.

4246 CONYBEARE, E. A history of Cambridgeshire. *Popular County Histories*. Lond. 1897.

4247 CUNNINGHAM, WILLIAM. The story of Cambridgeshire as told by itself. Cambr. 1928.

4248 PALMER, W. M. Cambridge subsidy rolls, 1250–1695. Norwich, 1912.

(4) *Town Histories and Records*

Cf. Gross (1), nos. 852–8, 2284. For the university of Cambridge, cf. 3761a–5.

4249 CAMBRIDGE BOROUGH DOCUMENTS. By W. M. Palmer. Cambr. 1931.

4250 CHARTERS OF THE BOROUGH OF CAMBRIDGE. By F. W. Maitland and Mary Bateson. Cambr. 1901.
Contains a valuable introduction, and charters of Henry VIII, Edward VI, Philip and Mary, and Elizabeth.

4251 COOPER, C. H. Annals of Cambridge. 5 vols. Cambr. 1842–1908.
The best history of the town of Cambridge. Vols. i and ii cover the sixteenth century.

4252 WATSON, W. Historical account of Wisbech and . . . towns and villages, drainage of the fens, &c. Wisbech, 1827.
Cf. *Hist. MSS. Comm. Reports*, ix.

5. CHESHIRE

(1) *Bibliographies*

4253 COOKE, J. H. Bibliotheca Cestriensis, a biographical account of books relating to, published in or written by authors resident in Cheshire. Warrington, 1904.

4254 A LIST OF BOOKS relating to Cheshire history. Lond. 1853–5.

(2) *Local Societies*

Cf. also 4487–92.

4255 ADVERTISER NOTES AND QUERIES, reprinted from *The Stockport Advertiser*. 5 vols. Stockport, 1881–5.
Continued in 4259.

4256 ARCHITECTURAL, ARCHAEOLOGICAL AND HISTORICAL SOCIETY for the county, city and neighbourhood of Chester. *Jour. Chester*, 1849–85, 1887 ff.
For the varying names of this publication, cf. *British Union-Catalogue* (38), 187.

4257 CHESHIRE AND LANCASHIRE historical collector. 2 vols. Manchester, 1853–4.

4258 THE CHESHIRE SHEAF, published quarterly for the *Cheshire Courant*. Chester, 1880–91.

4259 CHESHIRE NOTES AND QUERIES. Stockport, 1886–1912.
Continues 4255.

(3) *County Histories and Records*

Cf. Gross (1), nos. 2288, 2291, 2294–6. Erdeswicke's MSS. collections for the history of Cheshire are in B.M. *Harl. MSS.* 473, 506, 1990. For quarter sessions, cf. 1298; for farming, cf. 2629.

4260 AXON, W. E. A. Cheshire gleanings. Manchester, 1884.

4261 A DESCRIPTIVE LIST of the printed maps of Cheshire, 1577–1900. By Harold Whitaker. *Chetham Soc.*, n.s., ci (1943).

4262 EARWAKER, J. P. East Cheshire, or a history of the hundred of Macclesfield. 2 vols. Lond. 1877–80.

4263 HANSHALL, J. H. History of the county palatine of Chester. Chester, 1817.

4264 KING, DANIEL. The vale royal of England or the county palatine of Chester illustrated. Originally 'performed' by William Smith, Rouge Dragon Herald in 1585. Lond. 1656; rev. by Thomas Hughes, Lond. 1852; repr. in Ormerod (4265), 2nd ed.

4265 ORMEROD, GEORGE. History of the county palatine and city of
Chester. 3 vols. Lond. 1819; by Thos. Helsby, 3 vols. Lond. 1875–82.
The best history of Chester.

4266 YATES, J. B. The rights and jurisdiction of the county palatine of
Cheshire. *Chetham Soc. Misc.* ii (1855).

(4) *Town Histories and Records*

Cf. Gross (1), nos. 861–4a. The town records of Chester are described in *Hist.
MSS. Comm. Reports*, viii (118).

4267 HEMINGWAY, JOSEPH. History of the city of Chester, from its
foundation to the present time. 2 vols. Chester, 1831.
Good.

4268 MORRIS, R. H. Chester in the Plantagenet and Tudor reigns. [Chester,
1893.]
The best history for this period, with many documents.

4269 HEAD, ROBERT. Congleton, past and present. . . . Congleton, 1887.

4270 SELECTED ROLLS OF THE CHESTER CITY COURTS. By A.
Hopkins. Manchester, 1951.

4271 SULLEY, PHILIP. The hundred of Wirral. Birkenhead, 1889.
Cf. also Ronald Stewart-Brown, *The wapentake of Wirral . . .*, Liverpool, 1907.

(5) *Other Works*

4272 BAILEY, F. A. Some memoranda by William Moore, Esq., concerning
Liverpool and Walton, 1510–12. *Hist. Soc. Lancs. and Ches.* c (1949), 33–44.

4273 BROWNE, A. L. Sir John Throckmorton, chief justice of Chester.
Jour. Chester and North Wales Archit. Soc., n.s., xxxi (1935), 55–71.

4274 A MIDDLEWICH [Cheshire] CHARTULARY compiled by William
Vernon in the seventeenth century. Pt. i, by Joan Varley, *Chetham Soc.*, n.s.,
cv (1941), pt. ii by Joan Varley and James Tait, cviii (1944).

4275 STEWART-BROWN, R. The Cheshire writs of *Quo Warranto* in 1499.
E.H.R. xlix (1934), 676–84.

6. CORNWALL

(1) *Bibliographies*

4276 BIBLIOTHECA CORNUBIENSIS, a catalogue . . . of works relating
to the county of Cornwall. By G. C. Boase and W. P. Courtney. 3 vols.
Lond. 1874–82.

(2) *Local Societies*

Cf. also 4309–12.

4277 JOURNAL OF THE ROYAL INSTITUTION of Cornwall. Truro,
1864 ff.

4278 THE CORNISH MAGAZINE. By H. T. Quiller-Couch. 2 vols. Truro, 1898–9.

(3) *County Histories and Records*

On the stanneries, cf. 1325, 2806–7. Cf. Gross (1), no. 2300. Vol. i and pts. of ii of *V.C.H. Cornwall* have appeared. Lond. 1906–56.

4279 CAREW, RICHARD. The survey of Cornwall. Lond. 1602; by Thomas Tonkin, Lond. 1811.
The ed. of 1811 includes a life of Carew by Pierre de Maizeaux.

4280 COLLECTANEA CORNUBIENSIA: a collection of biographical and topographical notes relating to Cornwall. By G. C. Boase. Truro, 1890.

4281 ESSAYS IN CORNISH HISTORY. By A. L. Rowse and M. I. Henderson. Oxf. 1935.

4282 GILBERT, C. S. An historical and topographical survey of Cornwall. 2 vols. Plymouth, 1817–20.

4283 GILBERT, DAVIES. The parochial history of Cornwall. 4 vols. Lond. 1838.

4284 HITCHINS, FORTESCUE. The history of Cornwall. Helstone, 1824.

4285 NORDEN, JOHN. Speculi Britanniae pars, a topographical and historical description of Cornwall. Lond. 1728.
One of the valuable sections of this contemporary work, written in 1610 but not published until 1728.

4286 POLWHELE, RICHARD. History of Cornwall, civil, military, &c. 7 vols. Falmouth and Lond. 1805–16.
The best of the older histories of Cornwall.

4287 ROWSE, A. L. Tudor Cornwall: portrait of a society. Lond. 1941.

4288 A COMPLETE PAROCHIAL HISTORY of the county of Cornwall. 4 vols. Truro, 1867–72.
Cf. also *The Cornish church guide*, Truro, 1925.

(4) *Town Histories and Records*

Cf. Gross (1), nos. 865–7.

4289 MACLEAN, JOHN. The parochial and family history of the deanery of Trigg Minor. 3 vols. Bodmin, 1868–79.
Valuable because of its detail.

7. CUMBERLAND

(1) *Bibliographies*

There is none of importance.

(2) *Local Societies*

Cf. also 4658.

4290 CUMBERLAND AND WESTMORELAND antiquarian and archaeological society. Transactions. Kendal, 1866–1900, 1901 ff. Publications, Kendal, 1877 ff.

(3) *County Histories and Records*

Reference should also be made to histories of the Scottish border (1356–63, 5068, 5075, 5089). The best complete history of the county is 4817. Vols. i, ii of *V.C.H. Cumberland* have appeared. Lond. 1901–5.

4291 FERGUSON, R. S. History of Cumberland. Lond. 1893.

4292 HUTCHINSON, WILLIAM. The history of the county of Cumberland and some places adjacent. 2 vols. Carlisle, 1794.

(4) *Town Histories and Records*

Cf. Gross (1), nos. 870, 870a.

4293 CHIPPINDALL, W. H. History of the township of Ireby. *Chetham Soc.*, n.s., xcv (1935).

4294 CREIGHTON, MANDELL. Carlisle. *Historic Towns Series.* Lond. 1889.

4295 FERGUSON, R. S., and NANSON, W. Some municipal records of the city of Carlisle. Lond. and Carlisle, 1887.
Contains many documents of the sixteenth century and later. See *Royal Charters of the city of Carlisle*, by R. S. Ferguson, Carlisle, 1894.

8. DERBYSHIRE

(1) *Bibliographies*

There is none of importance.

(2) *Local Societies*

Cf. also 4669.

4296 DERBYSHIRE ARCHAEOLOGICAL and natural history society. Journal. Lond. 1879 ff.

(3) *County Histories and Records*

For quarter session records, cf. 1297. Vols. i, ii of *V.C.H. Derbyshire* have appeared, Lond. 1905–7. On farming, cf. 2631.

4297 CALENDAR OF THE RECORDS of the county of Derby. By J. C. Cox. Lond. 1899.

4298 A DESCRIPTIVE CATALOGUE of Derbyshire charters. By I. H. Jeayes. Lond. 1906.
Useful.

4299 GLOVER, STEPHEN. History of the county of Derby. By Thomas Noble. 2 vols. Derby, 1829; 2 vols. Derby, 1831–2.
See also his *History of the borough of Derby*, 1843.

4300 PILKINGTON, JAMES. A view of the present state of Derbyshire with an account of its antiquities. 2 vols. Lond. 1789.

(4) *Town Histories and Records*

Cf. Gross (1), nos. 872–6, 2307–9.

4301 HUTTON, WILLIAM. History of Derby. Lond. 1791; 2 vols. Lond. 1817.

4302 SMITH, G. LE B. Haddon, the manor, the hall, its lords and traditions. Lond. 1906.

(5) *Other Works*

4303 DERBY BOROUGH RENTAL, 1540. By F. Williamson. *Jour. Derby. Arch. and Nat. Hist. Soc.*, n.s., ix (1935), 71–79.

4304 AN INVENTORY OF THE CONTENTS OF MARKEATON HALL made by Vincent Mundy, Esq. in the year 1545. By W. G. Clark-Maxwell. *Jour. Derby. Arch. and Nat. Hist. Soc.*, li (1930), 117–40.

9. DEVONSHIRE

(1) *Bibliographies*

4305 BRUSHFIELD, T. N. The literature of Devonshire. Plymouth, 1893.

4306 DAVIDSON, JAMES. Bibliotheca Devoniensis, a catalogue of the printed books relating to the county of Devon. Exeter, 1852; supplement, Exeter, 1861.

4307 DREDGE, J. I. A few sheaves of Devon bibliography. Plymouth, 1889.

(2) *Local Societies*

4308 DEVONSHIRE ASSOCIATION FOR THE ADVANCEMENT OF SCIENCE, literature and art. Transactions. Plymouth, 1863 ff.

4309 DEVON AND CORNWALL RECORD SOCIETY. Publications. Exeter, 1905 ff.

4310 DEVON NOTES AND QUERIES. Exeter, 1901–9; continued as *Devon and Cornwall Notes and Queries*, Exeter, 1909 ff.

4311 NOTES AND GLEANINGS: a monthly magazine for Devon and Cornwall. 5 vols. Exeter, 1888–92.

4312 THE WESTERN ANTIQUARY, or note-book for Devon, Cornwall and Somerset. 12 vols. and supplement. Plymouth, 1882–95.

(3) *County Histories and Records*

The *Somerset papers* (193) contain much material on Devonshire history. Reference should be made also to the section on naval history (pp. 295–305 *supra*). For Devonshire quarter sessions, cf. 1307; for farming, cf. 2630 and 2649. Vol. i of *V.C.H. Devon* has appeared. Lond. 1906.

4313 HOSKINS, W. G., and FINBERG, H. P. R. Devonshire studies. Lond. 1952.
Chiefly agrarian.

4314 MOORE, S. A. A short history of the rights of common upon the forest of Dartmoor and the commons of Devon. Plymouth, 1890.
Valuable.

4315 POLWHELE, RICHARD. A history of Devonshire. 3 vols. Exeter, 1797.
The best of the older histories of Devon.

4316 RISDON, TRISTRAM. The chorographical description . . . of Devon . . . and Exeter. 2 vols. Lond. 1714; enlarged by Richard Rawlinson, Lond. 1811.
A survey made at the beginning of the seventeenth century.

4317 WORTH, R. N. A history of Devonshire. Lond. 1886.

(4) *Town Histories and Records*

Cf. Gross (1), nos. 877–85, 2312, 2320, 2322–3.

4318 ALEXANDER, J. J. The earliest sheriffs of Exeter, 1537–53. *Devon and Cornwall Notes and Queries*, xix (1937), 297–9.

4319 CHANTER, J. R. Sketches of the literary history of Barnstaple. Barnstaple, 1866.
Contains the interesting diary of Philip Wyot, town clerk, 1586–1608.

4320 CHANTER, J. R. Barnstaple records. *North Devon Journal* and *North Devon Herald*, Jan. 1879–May 1881; repr., 2 vols., Barnstaple, 1900.
A description of the town archives with translations of important documents.

4321 COTTON, WILLIAM. A graphic and historical sketch of the antiquities of Totnes. Lond. 1850.
The best history of the town. Its records are described in *Hist. MSS. Comm. Reports*, iii.

4322 COTTON, WILLIAM, and WOOLCOMBE, HENRY. Gleanings from the municipal and cathedral records relating to the city of Exeter. Exeter, 1877.
Contains materials for the insurrection of 1549 and other important events of the sixteenth century. Cf. also *Exeter city muniments* in *Notes and Gleanings* (4311), ii–v passim.

4323 GRIBBLE, J. B. Memorials of Barnstaple. Lond. 1830.
The best history of the town.

4324 HENDERSON, C. G. The clergy of the diocese of Exeter at the Reformation. *Essays in Cornish history*. By A. L. Rowse and M. I. Henderson. Oxf. 1935. pp. 215–18.

4325 THE LIGHTING OF EXETER, 1561. *Devon and Cornwall Notes and Queries*, xix (1936), 148–52.
Extract from the *Act Book*, iv, 146.

4325a MACCAFFREY, W. T. Exeter, 1540–1640. Cambr. U.S.A., 1958.

4326 OLIVER, GEORGE. The history of the city of Exeter. . . . Exeter, 1821; later ed. with documents, 1861.
The best history of Exeter, but contains little concerning the sixteenth century. Cf. also 3045.

4327 VOWELL (alias HOOKER), JOHN. The description of the citie of Excester. [Lond. 1575?]; Exeter, 1765; parts 2 and 3, by W. J. Harte, J. W. Schopp, and H. Tapley-Soper, 2 vols. *Devon and Cornwall Record Society*, 1919.
This is a series of extracts from the mass of unpublished records of the city collected by the sixteenth-century chamberlain. See also his *Pamphlet of the offices . . . of the citie of Excester*, Lond. 1584.

4328 MEN AND MANNERS IN TUDOR PLYMOUTH. *Trans. Devon. Assoc. for the Advancement of Science*, xiv (1882), 603–30, xv (1883), 455–75.

4329 WORTH, R. N. A history of Plymouth. Plymouth, 1872; 1890.
Cf. also idem, *Calendar of the Plymouth municipal records*, Plymouth, 1893.
On Plymouth and the Spanish armada, cf. 3526.

4330 HARDING, WILLIAM. A history of Tiverton. 2 vols. Tiverton and Lond. 1845–7.
The best history of Tiverton.

4331 WORTHY, CHARLES. Devonshire parishes. 2 vols. Exeter and Lond. 1887–9.

(5) *Other Works*

Cf. 26, 49.

4332 CRUWYS MORCHARD MANOR COURT ROLL. *Devon and Cornwall Notes and Queries*, xx (1939), 237–40.
Transcript of a roll of 1511.

4333 DEVON MONASTIC LANDS: Calendars of particulars for grants, 1536–1558. By Joyce Youings. *Devon and Cornwall Rec. Soc.*, n.s., i (1955).

4334 DRAKE, DAPHNE. Old maps of Devon. *Devon and Cornwall Notes and Queries*, xx (1938), 21–27.
Sixteenth- and seventeenth-centuries maps.

4335 HOSKINS, W. G. Cadbury and Thorverton subsidies. *Devon and Cornwall Notes and Queries*, xx (1938), 74–76.
Lay subsidy of 4 Oct. 1591. Cf. also idem, *Farway subsidies*, ibid. 32–34.

4336 POWLEY, E. S. The house of de la Pomerai. Lond. 1944.
Excellent study of an important Devon house, the Pomerays of Berry Pomeroy. Cf. also A. W. Everett, *Berry Pomeroy, Devon and Cornwall Notes and Queries*, xx (1939), 295–7.

10. DORSETSHIRE

(1) *Bibliographies*

4337 MAYO, C. H. Bibliotheca Dorsetiensis, being a carefully compiled account of printed books relating to the county of Dorset. Lond. 1885.

4338 DORSET RECORDS, indexes, calendars, and abstracts of records. By E. A. Fry and G. S. Fry. [Lond.] 1894 ff.

4339 REPORT OF THE COUNTY RECORDS COMMITTEE for the county of Dorset. Dorchester, 1878.

(2) *Local Societies*

Cf. 4721.

4340 DORSET NATURAL HISTORY AND ANTIQUARIAN field club
Proceedings. Sherborne, 1877–1927.
Becomes *Dorset Natural History and Archaeological Society*, 1928 ff.

(3) *County Histories and Records*

Vol. ii of *V.C.H. Dorset* has appeared. Lond. 1908.

4341 DORSET INQUISITIONS POST MORTEM. By C. S. Frey.
Somerset and Dorset Notes and Queries, xxii (1937), 92, 133–5.

4342 HUTCHINS, JOHN. History and antiquities of the county of Dorset.
2 vols. Lond. 1774; best ed. by W. Shipp and J. W. Hodgson, 4 vols. Westminster, 1861–70.

4343 INSTITUTIONS OF SOME DORSET CLERGY in the sixteenth
century. *Somerset and Dorset Notes and Queries*, xxi (1934), 115–16, 128–37.

4344 INVENTORY OF THE HISTORICAL MONUMENTS in Dorset.
Vol. 1. West Dorset. Lond. 1952.

4345 SQUIBB, G. D. Dorset incumbents, 1542–1731. *Proc. Dorset Nat. Hist.
and Arch. Soc.*, pt. i, lxx (1949), 99–117; pt. ii, lxxi (1950), 110–32; pt. iii,
lxxii (1951), 111–28; pt. iv, lxxviii (1952), 141–62; pt. v, lxxiv (1953), 60–78;
pt. vi, lxxv (1955), 115–32.

4346 SQUIBB, G. D. A calendar of XVIth century Dorset deeds. *Proc.
Dorset Nat. Hist. and Arch. Soc.* lxix (1948), 68–107.

(4) *Town Histories and Records*

Cf. Gross (1), nos. 887–91, 2327.

4347 MOULE, H. J. A descriptive catalogue of the charters, minute books
. . . of Weymouth and Melcombe Regis, 1252–1800. Weymouth, 1883.
Cf. *Hist. MSS. Comm. Reports*, xix.

11. DURHAM

(1) *Bibliographies*

There is no good county bibliography. On the records of the palatinate of
Durham, see 1327 and 1343 and Gross (1), nos. 2338–9.

4348 HANDLIST OF HALMOTE COURT BOOKS, palatinate of Durham
and bishopric estates. Durham, 1956.

4349 HANDLIST OF RENTALS OF WARDS and townships among the
Halmote Court records of the palatinate of Durham and bishopric estates.
Durham, 1956.

(2) *Local Societies*

4350 DURHAM AND NORTHUMBERLAND architectural and archaeological society. Transactions. Sunderland, 1863 ff.

4351 SURTEES SOCIETY. Publications. Lond. [1835] ff.
Publishes material relating to the history of north England, chiefly Durham, Northumberland, and Yorkshire.

(3) *County Histories and Records*

Cf. 1343, and Gross (1) nos. 895, 2333, 2336–7, 2340, 2345, 2348, 2351. Vols.
i–iii of *V.C.H. Durham* have appeared. Lond. 1905–28. Cf. 4659.

4352 BLAIR, C. H. H. The renaissance heraldry of the county palatine of
Durham. *Arch. Aeliana*, 4th ser., xii (1935), xvii–xx, 1–81.

4353 HUTCHINSON, WILLIAM. The history and antiquities of the county
palatine of Durham. 3 vols. Newcastle, 1785–94; 3 vols. Durham, 1823.

4354 RAINE, JAMES. The history and antiquities of North Durham . . .
now united to the county of Northumberland. Lond. 1852.

4355 SURTEES, ROBERT. The history and antiquities of the county palatine of Durham. 4 vols. Lond. 1816–40; new ed. in progress, Sunderland,
1908 ff.

4356 SYKES, JOHN. Local records or historical register of remarkable events
in the counties of Durham and Northumberland. Newcastle, 1824; 1833;
continued to 1857 by John Latimer, Newcastle, 1857.

(4) *Town Histories and Records*

Cf. also Gross (1), nos. 896–7, 2349, 2351–4.

4357 WELFORD, RICHARD. History of Newcastle and Gateshead. 3 vols.
Lond. 1884–7.
Vol. ii is devoted to the sixteenth century. Cf. also 1725, 3027, 3044, 4662.

12. ESSEX

(1) *Bibliographies*

Extensive MS. collections for a history of Essex made by William Holman
(ob. 1730) are preserved in the Bodleian library, *Rawlinson MSS.* B 305, 314,
315. Cf. also *Hist. MSS. Comm. Report*, x, app. 4. Cf. Edwards (73) and 4359.

4358 CUNNINGHAM, A. Catalogue of books . . . relating to . . . the county
of Essex. Braintree, 1902.

4359 ESSEX LOCAL HISTORY: a short guide to books and manuscripts.
By G. A. Ward. Chelmsford, 1950.

4360 GUIDE TO THE ESSEX RECORD OFFICE. By F. G. Emmison.
2 vols. *Essex Record Office*, i–ii (1947–8).

(2) *Local Societies*

Cf. also 4564 and 4753.

4361 ESSEX ARCHAEOLOGICAL SOCIETY. Transactions. Colchester, 1858 ff.

4362 ESSEX REVIEW. Chelmsford, 1892 ff.

(3) *County Histories and Records*

Cf. also 4195 and Gross (1), no. 2355. Vols. i, ii, iv of *V.C.H. Essex* have appeared. Lond. 1903–56. Cf. 1111 and 2205.

4363 CHARNOCK, R. S. Ancient manorial customs in the county of Essex, Lond. 1870.

4364 COUNTY MAPS OF ESSEX, 1576–1852. *Essex Record Office*, xxv (1955).

4365 MORANT, PHILIP. History and antiquities of the county of Essex. 2 vols. Lond. 1768; 2 vols. Chelmsford, 1816.
The best of the older histories of Essex.

4366 NORDEN, JOHN. Speculi Britanniae pars, an historical and chorographical description of Essex. By H. Ellis, *Camden Soc.* ix (1840).
Written c. 1600, but not printed before 1840.

4367 OGBORNE, ELIZABETH. A history of Essex. Lond. 1814.

4368 SUCKLING, A. I. Memorials of the antiquities and architecture, family history and heraldry of the county of Essex. Lond. 1845.

4369 WRIGHT, THOMAS. The history and topography of the county of Essex. 2 vols. Lond. 1831–5.

(4) *Town Histories and Records*

Cf. also Gross (1), nos. 901–3, 2357–9, 2361, 2368–8a.

4370 BENHAM, W. G. Essex sokens and other parishes in the Tendring hundred. Colchester, 1928.

4371 BENTON, P. History of Rochford hundred. Rochford, 1867.

4372 BERRIDGE, JESSE. Little Baddow in the sixteenth century. *Essex Rev.* xlv (1936), 194–200; xlvi (1937), 103–9.

4373 BRAND, F. J. Some early Essex grants and charters, c. 1150–1537. By W. J. Pressey and J. E. Oxley. Ilford, 1937.

4374 CROMWELL, THOMAS. History and description of the ancient town and borough of Colchester. 2 vols. Lond. 1825.
There are numerous publications of the records of Colchester; cf. Gross (1), nos. 2357–9, 2361, 2368a.

4375 CUTTS, E. L. Colchester. . . . *Historic Towns Series*. Lond. 1888.
A small but valuable book.

4376 EMMISON, F. G. A survey of Chelmsford, 1591. *Trans. Essex Arch. Soc.*, n.s., xxiii (1942), 133–40.

4377 FARMER, J. A history of the ancient town and abbey of Waltham. Lond. 1735.

4378 FISHER, W. R. The forest of Essex. Lond. 1887.

4379 PETCHEY, W. J. Maldon, 1558–1574. *Essex Rev.* lxii (1953), 47–58; lxiii (1954), 24–32.

4380 RENDALL, G. H. Dedham in history, feudal, industrial and ecclesiastical. Colchester, 1937.

(5) *Other Works*

On Essex trade, cf. 2977.

4381 AUSTEN, F. W. Rectors of two Essex parishes and their times from the thirteenth to the twentieth centuries. Colchester, 1943.

4382 BENHAM, W. G. Manorial rolls of Fingringhoe, West Mersea, and Pete Hall, 1547–58. *Essex Rev.* l (1941), 189–200; li (1942), 32–42, 88–97.

4383 BENHAM, W. G. 'The spacious times of Great Elizabeth.' Some court records. *Essex Rev.* li (1942), 177–83; lii (1943), 31–37, 89–95, 116–22.
Describes the keeping of local records.

4384 BENHAM, W. G. Notes from Colchester court rolls of 1527–8. Some curious words. *Essex Rev.* xlvii (1938), 91–93.

4385 DOYLE, A. I. Borley and the Waldegraves in the sixteenth century. *Trans. Essex Arch. Soc.*, n.s., xxiv (1951), 17–31.
Inherited by Sir Edward Waldegrave (1517?–61), 1543.

4386 EDWARDS, A. C. Sir John Petre and his household, 1576–7. *Essex Rev.* (1954), 189–204.

4387 EMMISON, F. G. Survey of Manor of Woodham Ferrers, 1582. *Trans. Essex. Arch. Soc.*, n.s., xxiv (1951), 6–16.

4388 ERITH, E. J. The Scotts of Woolston Hall, Chigwell. *Essex Rev.* lxii, no. 245 (1953), 39–51; no. 246, 47–55; no. 247, 34–40.

4389 GRIEVE, H. E. P. The deprived married clergy in Essex, 1553–61. *Trans. R.H. Soc.*, 4th ser., xxii (1940), 141–69.

4390 STEER, F. W. Essex lady who was a queen's favourite. *Essex Rev.* l (1941), 94–99.
Susan Tonge.

13. GLOUCESTERSHIRE

(1) *Bibliographies*

4391 AUSTIN, ROLAND. Catalogue of the Gloucestershire collection, books, pamphlets, and documents in the Gloucester public library relating to the county of Gloucester. Gloucester, 1928.

4392 HYETT, F. A., and BAZELEY, W. Bibliographer's manual of Gloucestershire literature. 3 vols. Gloucester, 1895–7; supplement by F. A. Hyett and R. Austin, 3 vols. Gloucester, 1915–16.

(2) *Local Societies*

4393 BRISTOL AND GLOUCESTERSHIRE archaeological society. Transactions. [Bistol, 1876] ff.

4394 BRISTOL RECORD SOCIETY. Bristol, 1930 ff.

4395 GLOUCESTERSHIRE NOTES AND QUERIES. Lond. [1879] ff.
Discontinued in 1905, resumed in 1913.

(3) *County Histories and Records*

Cf. Gross (1), nos. 905, 906a, 907, 909–12, 2369. On the forest of Dean, cf. Nisbet (1347), Nicholls (2796), and Gross (1), no. 913. Vol. ii of *V.C.H. Glos.* has appeared. Lond. 1907. Cf. 2207.

4396 ATKYNS, ROBERT. The ancient and present state of Gloucestershire. Lond. 1712; 1768.

4397 BIGLAND, R. Historical collections relative to the county of Gloucester. 2 vols. Lond. 1786–92.

4398 [RUDDER, SAMUEL.] A new history of Gloucestershire. Cirencester, 1779.
The parts referring to the city of Gloucester were repr. at Cirencester, 1781.

4399 SMYTH, JOHN. The Berkeley MSS. By John Maclean. 3 vols. *Bristol and Glos. Arch. Soc.* Gloucester, 1883–5.
Vols. i and ii contain the lives of the Berkeleys, lords of the manor of Berkeley 1066–1608, vol. iii a description of the hundred of Berkeley. Prints much documentary material.

4400 WILLCOX, W. B. Gloucestershire, a study in local government, 1590–1640. New Haven, U.S.A., 1940.

(4) *Town Histories and Records*

Cf. Gross (1), nos. 914, 2370, 2372–3, 2376, 2382, 2385a. Cf. also 3035. On the merchant adventurers of Bristol, cf. Latimer (3053).

4401 BARRETT, W. History and antiquities of the city of Bristol. Bristol, 1789.

4402 BRISTOL CHARTERS, 1378–1499. By H. A. Cronne. *Bristol Rec. Soc.* xi (1946); 1509–1899 by R. C. Latham, xii (1947).

4403 BRISTOL WILLS AND DOCUMENTS. Trans. by Arthur Sabin. *Trans. Bristol and Glos. Arch. Soc.* lxiv (1944), 118–47.

4404 BRISTOL REFERENCE LIBRARY. A catalogue of books . . . printed in England and Ireland up to the year 1640 and of English books printed abroad. Bristol, 1954.

4405 CALENDAR OF RECORDS of the corporation of Gloucester. By W. H. Stevenson. Gloucester, 1893.
Valuable.

4406 FULLER, E. A. Cirencester; the manor and town. *Bristol and Glos. Arch. Soc. Trans.* ix (1885), 298–344.

4407   FOSBROKE, T. D. An original history of the city of Gloucester. Lond. 1819.

4408   THE GREAT RED BOOK OF BRISTOL. By E. W. W. Veale. Pt. iii, *Bristol Rec. Soc.* xvi (1951); pt. iv, xviii (1953).
Little on the Tudor period.

4409   LOBEL, M. D. The history of Dean and Chalford. *Oxf. Rec. Soc.* xvii (1935).

4410   RICART, ROBERT. The maire of Bristowe is kalendar. By L. T. Smith. *Camden Soc.*, 2nd ser., v (1872).
Valuable; cf. Gross (1), no. 2375.

4411   SEYER, SAMUEL. Memorials historical and topographical of Bristol and its neighbourhood. 2 vols. Bristol, 1821–3.
The best history of Bristol.

(5) *Other Works*

Cf. 2345.

4412   BROWNE, A. L. The Bray family in Gloucestershire. *Trans. Bristol and Glos. Arch. Soc.* lv (1934), 293–315.

4413   HILL, M. C. Dowdeswell Court book, 1577–1673. *Trans. Bristol and Glos. Arch. Soc.* lxvii (1949), 119–216.

4416   TWO COMPOTUS ROLLS of Saint Augustine's Abbey, Bristol, 1491–2 and 1511–12. By Gwen Beachcroft and Arthur Sabin. *Bristol Rec. Soc.* ix (1938).

14. HAMPSHIRE

(1) *Bibliographies*

4417   GILBERT, H. M. Bibliotheca hantoniensis, an attempt at a bibliography of Hampshire. Southampton, 1872; by H. M. Gilbert and G. N. Godwin, Southampton, 1891.

(2) *Local Societies*

4418   HAMPSHIRE FIELD CLUB and archaeological society. Papers and proceedings. Southampton, 1890 ff.
Simply called *Hampshire Field Club* until 1899.

4419   HAMPSHIRE RECORD SOCIETY. Publications. 12 vols. Lond. 1889–99.

4420   SOUTHAMPTON RECORD SOCIETY. Publications. Southampton, 1905–41; n.s. 1951 ff.

(3) *County Histories and Records*

MS. collections for the history of Hampshire by John Warburton (*ob.* 1759) are preserved in the library of the Society of Antiquaries. *V.C.H. Hampshire* is complete in 5 vols. and index. Lond. 1900–14.

4421 BOX, E. G. Hampshire in early maps and early road books. *Hampshire Field Club and Arch. Soc. Papers and Proc.* xiii (1935), 61–68.

4422 COX, J. C. Hampshire. Lond. 1905.

4423 SHORE, T. W. A history of Hampshire including the Isle of Wight. Lond. 1892.

4424 WOODWARD, B. B., WILKS, T. C., and LOCKHART, C. S. M. A general history of Hampshire, including the Isle of Wight. 3 vols. Lond. 1861–9.
The best of the older histories of Hampshire.

(4) *Town Histories and Records*

Cf. also Gross (1), nos. 920–7, 2387–9, 2390a–1b. For the records of Southampton, cf. *Hist. MSS. Comm. Reports*, xi, app. iii.

4425 BLACK BOOK OF SOUTHAMPTON. By A. B. W. Chapman. Vol. iii, 1497–1620. *Southampton Rec. Soc.* xvii (1915).
Contains ordinances, leases, &c.

4426 BOOK OF EXAMINATIONS, 1601–2, with a list of ships belonging to Southampton, 1570–1603. By R. C. Anderson. *Southampton Rec. Soc.* xxvi (1926).

4427 BOOK OF REMEMBRANCE OF SOUTHAMPTON, 1440–1620. By H. W. Gidden. 3 vols. *Southampton Rec. Soc.* xxvii, xxviii, xxx (1927–8, 1930). The third book of remembrances of Southampton 1514–1602. By A. L. Merson. Ibid. n.s. i, 1514–40; ii, 1540–73; iii, 1573–1602. 1952–55.

4428 COLLECTION OF RECORDS AND DOCUMENTS relating to the hundred and manor of Crondal. By F. J. Baigent. *Hampshire Rec. Soc.* iii (1891).

4429 DAVIES, J. S. A history of Southampton. Southampton, 1883.
The best history of Southampton. Cf. also F. J. C. Hearnshaw and F. Clarke, *A short history of Southampton*, Oxf. 1910.

4430 KITCHIN, G. W. Winchester. *Historic Towns Series*. Lond. 1890.

4431 MILNER, JOHN. A history and survey of the antiquities of Winchester. Winchester, [1798]; 3rd ed., 2 vols. [1839].
A good town history.

4432 OGLANDER MEMOIRS, extracts from the MSS. of Sir John Oglander . . . deputy governor of Portsmouth and deputy lieutenant of the Isle of Wight, 1595–1648. Lond. 1888.

4433 SAUNDERS, W. H. Annals of Portsmouth, 1545–1865. Lond. 1880.

4434 WORSLEY, RICHARD. History of the Isle of Wight. Lond. 1781.

(5) *Other Works*

Cf. 4798.

4435 THE MISCELLANEOUS PAPERS of Captain Thomas Stockwell, 1590–1614. By J. Rutherford. Vol. i, 1590–1611, ii, 1597–1614 (1934). *Southampton Rec. Soc.* (1932–3).

15. HEREFORDSHIRE

(1) *Bibliographies*

4436 ALLEN, J. Bibliotheca Herefordiensis; or a descriptive catalogue of books . . relating to the county of Hereford. Hereford, 1821.

(2) *Local Societies*

4437 CANTILUPE SOCIETY. [Publications.] Hereford, 1906 ff.
Devoted to the purpose of printing the episcopal registers of Hereford.

(3) *County Histories and Records*

The records of the county are described in *Hist. MSS. Comm. Reports*, xiii, app. 4. Vol. i of *V.C.H. Hereford* has appeared. Lond. 1908.

4438 DUNCUMB, J., COOKE, W. H., and others. Collections toward the history and antiquities of the county of Hereford. 6 vols. Hereford, 1804–1912 (in progress).
The best complete history of the county.

4439 AN INVENTORY OF THE HISTORICAL MONUMENTS of Herefordshire. *Roy. Comm. on Hist. Mon.* Lond. 1930.

4440 LODGE, JOHN. History of the county of Hereford. Kingston, 1793.

(4) *Town Histories and Records*

Cf. Gross (1), nos. 928a, 928b, 930. Cf. also 2846.

4441 CATALOGUE OF AND INDEX TO MSS. PAPERS . . . from the municipal archives of the city of Hereford. Hereford, 1894.
Cf. *Hist. MSS. Comm. Reports*, xiii.

4442 JOHNSON, RICHARD. The ancient customs of the city of Hereford . . . also some account of the trades of the city. Lond. 1868; 1882.

4443 TOWNSEND, G. F. The town and borough of Leominster. . . . Lond. 1863.
Contains many sixteenth-century documents.

16. HERTFORDSHIRE

(1) *Bibliographies*

There is none of importance.

(2) *Local Societies*

Cf. also 4564.

4444 EAST HERTFORDSHIRE ARCHAEOLOGICAL SOCIETY. Transactions. Hertford, 1901 ff.

4445 ST. ALBANS ARCHITECTURAL AND ARCHAEOLOGICAL SOCIETY. Transactions. St. Albans, 1885 ff.
Called since 1895 *St. Albans and Hertfordshire Architectural and Archaeological Society.*

(3) *County Histories and Records*

In the Public Record Office, Augmentation Office, Misc. Books, no. 391, is a survey of the county of Hertfordshire, 1556–7. For the quarter session records of the county, cf. 1300. *V.C.H. Hertford* is complete in 4 vols. and index. Lond. 1902–14. Cf. also 4195.

4446 CHAUNCY, HENRY. Historical antiquities of Hertfordshire. Lond. 1700; 2 vols. Lond. 1826.
A valuable description of the county and all its subdivisions.

4447 CLUTTERBUCK, ROBERT. History and antiquities of the county of Hertford. 3 vols. Lond. 1815–27.

4448 CUSSANS, J. E. History of Hertfordshire. 3 vols. Lond. 1870–81.
The best of the older histories of the county.

4449 NORDEN, JOHN. Speculi Britanniae pars. The description of Hertfordshire. Lond. 1598.

(4) *Town Histories and Records*

Cf. Gross (1), nos. 934–34a, 2403–4.

4450 BREWER, J. S. Hatfield house. Lond. 1881.
Refers chiefly to its Tudor associations.

4451 TURNER, LEWIS. History of the ancient town and borough of Hertford. Hertford, 1830.
Cf. *Hist. MSS. Comm. Reports*, xiv.

4452 HINE, R. L. The history of Hitchin. 2 vols. Lond. 1927–9.
Valuable.

4453 GIBBS, A. E. The corporation records of St. Albans. St. Albans, 1890.
Contains extracts from municipal records, beginning 1588.

(5) *Other Works*

4454 ANDREWS, H. C. The Knighton family of Bayford, Herts. and little Bradley, Suffolk. *Trans. East Herts. Arch. Soc.* viii (1931), 43–55.

4455 KERR, P. W. The Leventhorpes of Sawbridgeworth. *Trans. East. Herts. Arch. Soc.* ix (1936), 129–51.

4456 RICKMAN, L. L. Brief studies on the manorial and economic history of Much Hadham. *Trans. East. Herts. Arch. Soc.* viii (1934), 288–312.
Based upon court rolls, 19 to 27 Eliz. 1577–85.

4457 SIDELIGHTS ON BRASSES IN HERTFORDSHIRE CHURCHES. By H. C. Andrews. *Trans. East Herts. Arch. Soc.* viii 1930–1 (1933), 155–75; viii 1932–3 (1934), 313–32; ix 1934 (1935), 38–66; ix 1935 (1936), 178–211; ix 1936 (1937), 284–315; x 1937 (1938), 20–56; x 1938 (1939), 183–98; x 1939 (1940), 265–83; xi 1940 (1941), 26–49; xi 1941 (1942), 113–27; xi 1942 (1943), 177–96; xi 1943–4; (1945), 237–46; xii 1945–6 (1947), 9–17; xii 1947–9 (1950), 85–95.

17. HUNTINGDONSHIRE

(1) *Bibliographies*

4458 NORRIS, H. E. Catalogue of the Huntingdonshire books collected by H. E. Norris. Cirencester, 1895.

(2) *Local Societies*

Cf. 4243.

4459 FENLAND NOTES AND QUERIES. A quarterly antiquarian journal for the Fenland in the counties of Huntingdon, Cambridge, Lincoln, Northampton, Norfolk, and Suffolk. Peterborough, 1889–1909.

(3) *County Histories and Records*

The *V.C.H. Huntingdon* is complete in 3 vols. and index. Lond. 1926–32. Cf. also 4195. On the Spanish armada and Huntingdonshire, cf. 3390.

(4) *Town Histories and Records*

Cf. Gross (1), nos. 935, 937, 2406a, 2407.

18. KENT

(1) *Bibliographies*

4460 CHURCHILL, I. J. A handbook to Kent records. *Kent Arch. Soc.,* Rec. Branch, ii (1914).

4461 SMITH, J. R. Bibliotheca cantiana; a bibliographical account of what has been published on the history, topography, antiquities . . . of the county of Kent. Lond. 1837; 1851.
Ed. of 1851 includes Surrey and Sussex.

(2) *Local Societies*

Cf. also 4564.

4462 KENT ARCHAEOLOGICAL SOCIETY. Archaeologia Cantiana. Lond. 1858 ff.; Kent Records. Lond. 1912 ff.
Archaeologia Cantiana is one of the best series of local publications.

4463 KENTISH NOTE BOOK. 2 vols. Gravesend, 1891–4.

(3) *County Histories and Records*

Cf. Gross (1), nos. 2428–9. Vols. i–iii of *V.C.H. Kent* have appeared. Lond. 1908–32.

4464 BOX, E. G. Two sixteenth century maps of Kent, with further notes on early road-books. *Arch. Cantiana,* xlv (1935), 48–59.
Cf. also G. M. Livett, *Early Kent maps (sixteenth century), Arch. Cant.* xlix (1938), 247–7.

4465 DUNKIN, A. J. A history of the county of Kent. 2 vols. Lond. 1852–6.

4466 FURLEY, ROBERT. A history of the weald of Kent. 2 vols. in 3 pts. Lond. 1871–4.
Very full on the Cinque ports.

4467 HASTED, EDWARD. A history and topographical survey of the county of Kent. 4 vols. Canterbury, 1778–99; 12 vols. 1797–1801; new ed. of pt. i by H. H. Drake, 1886.
The best of the older histories of the county. Ed. of 1797–1801 contains Hasted's *History of Canterbury.*

4468 WELAND, W. H. England's topographer or a new and complete history of the county of Kent. 4 vols. Lond. 1828–30.

4469 LAMBARD, WILLIAM. A perambulation of Kent. Lond. 1576; 1596; 1656; 1826, &c.
One of the earliest and most famous of county histories.

4470 [PHILIPOT, JOHN]. Villare Cantianum or Kent surveyed and illustrated. Lond. 1659; 1664; 2nd ed. (rev.) 1776.
This work published by Thomas Philipot under his own name, though written by his father, John.

(4) *Town Histories and Records*

Cf. Gross (1), nos. 968–72, 977, 981, 2427, 2429a, 2433, 2437, 2444a. For the Cinque ports, see Gross (4176), nos. 671–705, and Gross (1), no. 2640. S.P. Domestic, Eliz. cxxviii (in P.R.O., calendared in 86 *supra*), is entirely devoted to the Cinque ports, notably Rye, in 1578. Cf. also 1336, 1345–6, 4466.

Records of various Kentish towns are described in *Hist. MSS. Comm. Reports,* iv–vi, ix.

4471 BOYS, WILLIAM. Collections for an history of Sandwich in Kent. With notices of the other Cinque Ports and members, and of Richborough. Canterbury, 1792.
A valuable book.

4472 BRIDGMAN, JOHN. An historical and topographical sketch of Knole. Lond. 1817; 1821.
Knole was the residence of the Sackvilles, earls of Dorset.

4473 LYON, JOHN. History of the town and port of Dover and Dover castle, with some account of the Cinque ports. 2 vols. Dover, 1813–14.
The best history of Dover.

4474 SOMNER, WILLIAM. Antiquities of Canterbury. Canterbury, 1640; 1703.
The most elaborate history of Canterbury.

4475 STATHAM, S. P. H. The history of the castle, town and port of Dover. Lond. 1899.
Cf. also idem, *Dover charters and other documents* . . . [1227–1569], Lond. [1902].

4476 WEBB, E. A., MILLER, G. W., and BECKWITH, J. History of Chislehurst. Lond. 1899.
Scholarly. Valuable for the history of the Walsingham family.

(5) *Other Works*

Cf. 4798.

4477 FORSETT, JOHN. The customal of New Romney written in 1554. *Kent. Arch. Soc.* Rec. Branch, xvi (1945), supplement.
Cf. William Cook, *Arch. Cant.* li (1939), 188–90.

4478 HARRISON, EDWARD. The court rolls and other records of the Manor of Ightham as a contribution to local history. *Arch. Cant.* xlviii (1936), 169–218; xlix (1937), 1–95.
Entirely on the Tudor period.

4479 HULL, FELIX. The lathe in the early sixteenth century. *Arch. Cant.* lxvii (1954), 97–100.
An administrative district of Kent containing several hundreds.

4480 KENT OBIT AND LAMP RENTS. By Arthur Hussey. *Kent Rec.* xiv (1937).

4481 MACDONALD, ALEC. Plans of Dover harbour in the sixteenth century. *Arch. Cant.* xlix (1938), 108–26.

4482 WOODRUFF, C. E. The sacrist's roll of Christ Church, Canterbury. *Arch. Cant.* xlviii (1937), 38–80.
Extracts for the years 1431–1533.

19. LANCASHIRE

(1) *Bibliographies*

4483 FISHWICK, HENRY. The Lancashire library, a bibliographical account . . . up to 1720. Lond. 1875.

4484 HAWKER, A. J. Lancashire printed books . . . to 1800. Wigan, 1925.

4485 THE MANCHESTER PUBLIC LIBRARIES. Reference library subject catalogue. Sect. 929: Genealogy. Pt. ii, Parish registers, wills. Manchester, 1957.

4486 SUTTON, A. Bibliotheca Lancastrensis. Manchester, 1898.

(2) *Local Societies*

4487 CHETHAM SOCIETY. Remains historical and literary . . . of Lancaster and Chester. [Manchester], 1844 ff.

4488 HISTORIC SOCIETY OF LANCASHIRE and Cheshire. Proceedings (called after 1855 Transactions). Liverpool, 1849 ff.

4489 LANCASHIRE AND CHESHIRE ANTIQUARIAN SOCIETY. Transactions. Manchester, 1884 ff.

4490 LANCASHIRE AND CHESHIRE historical and genealogical notes. 3 vols. Leigh, 1879–83.

4491 LOCAL GLEANINGS RELATING TO LANCASHIRE and Cheshire. By J. P. Earwaker. 1 vol. (all printed). Manchester, 1889–90.

4492 RECORD SOCIETY FOR . . . LANCASHIRE and Cheshire. Publications. [Lond.], 1879 ff.

(3) *County Histories and Records*

For the records of the Duchy of Lancaster, cf. 1326–7, 1330, and Gross (1),
nos. 2450–60; for Lancashire quarter session records, cf. 1301; for the lord-
lieutenancy of Lancashire, 1275; for the history of the Duchy of Lancaster, cf.
1349; for justices of peace, cf. 1296; for parliament, cf. 1121. See also in general
Gross (1), nos. 2448–9. *V.C.H. Lancashire* is complete in 8 vols. Lond. 1906–14.

4493 A DESCRIPTIVE LIST OF THE PRINTED MAPS OF LAN-
CASHIRE, 1577–1900. By Harold Whitaker. *Chetham Soc.*, n.s., ci (1938).

4494 BAINES, EDWARD. A history of the county palatine and duchy of
Lancashire. 2 vols. Manchester and Lond. 1824; best ed. by James Croston,
5 vols. Manchester, 1888–93.
The best of the older histories of the county.

4495 FISHWICK, HENRY. Lancashire in the time of Elizabeth. *Trans.*
R.H. Soc. vi (1877), 183–202.

4496 GREGSON, MATTHEW. Portfolio of fragments relative to the History and Antiquities of the County Palatine and Duchy of Lancaster. Liverpool, 1817.

4497 LANCASHIRE DEEDS. Vol. i, Shuttleworth deeds. Pt. i by John
Parker. *Chetham Soc.* xci (1935).

4498 WILMORE, ALBERT. South Lancashire. Cambr. 1928.

(4) *Town Histories and Records*

Cf. also Gross (1), nos. 984b, 984c, 986, 989–90, 2473, 2473a.

4499 ANCIENT CHARTERS . . . of the borough of Clitheroe [1283–1674].
By John Harland. Manchester, 1851.
Cf. also *Court rolls of the honour of Clitheroe*, by William Farrer, 3 vols., Manchester,
1897–1913.

4500 ABRAM, W. A. Memorials of the Preston guilds. Preston, 1882.

4501 BECK, T. A. Annales Furnesienses. . . . Lond. 1844.

4502 BEAUMONT, WILLIAM. Annals of the lords of Warrington, 1587–
1853. 2 vols. *Chetham Soc.* lxxxvi–lxxxvii (1872–3).

4503 CHIPPINDALL, W. H. The history of the township of Arkholme in
the county of Lancaster. *Chetham Soc.*, n.s., xc (1931), 1–65.

4504 CLEMESHA, H. W. A history of Preston in Amounderness. Man-
chester, 1912.
Cf. also Chas. Hardwick, *A history of the borough of Preston*, Preston, 1857, and
Gross (1), nos. 2474–7.

4505 THE COURT LEET OR PORTMOOT RECORDS of Salford, 1735–8. With a transcript of a roll of 1559. By James Tait. *Chetham Misc.*, n.s., vi (1935).

Cf. also R. S. France, *Sixteenth century Salford Portmoot records*, *Trans. Hist. Soc. Lancs. and Ches.* xcv (1944), 118–22.

4506 FISHWICK, HENRY. The history of the parish of Rochdale. Rochdale, 1889.

Cf. also his *Bibliography of Rochdale*, Manchester, 1880.

4507 HARLAND, JOHN. Mamecestre: chapters from the early history of . . . Manchester. 3 vols. *Chetham Soc.* liii, lvi, lviii (1861–2).

Chiefly documents. Cf. also W. E. A. Axon, *Annals of Manchester*, Lond. 1886, and John Reilly, *The history of Manchester*, Manchester, 1861.

4508 LIVERPOOL TOWN BOOKS. Proceedings of assemblies, common councils, portmoot courts, &c., 1550–1862. By J. A. Twemlow. 2 vols. Liverpool, 1918, 1936.

Unfinished, vol. 2 ends at 1603.

4509 MUIR, R., and PLATT, E. M. A history of municipal government in Liverpool to 1835. Lond. 1906.

Cf. also R. Muir, *A history of Liverpool*, Lond. 1907.

4510 PICTON, J. A. Memorials of Liverpool. 2 vols. Lond. 1873; 1875; rev. 1907.

For collections of Liverpool documents edited by Picton, cf. Gross (1), nos. 2469–70.

4511 PORTEUS, T. C. The hundred of Leyland in Lancashire. *Chetham Soc.*, n.s., xc (1931), 1–119.

4512 REDFORD, ARTHUR. The history of local government in Manchester. 3 vols. Lond. 1939–40.

4513 A SELECTION FROM THE PRESCOT COURT LEET and other records, 1447–1600. By F. A. Bailey. *Rec. Soc. of Lancs. and Ches.* lxxxix (1937), 1–59.

4514 SIMPSON, ROBERT. History and antiquities of the town of Lancaster. Lond. 1852.

The best history of Lancaster. For source material relating to the town, cf. Gross (1), nos. 2472, 2472a.

4515 SINCLAIR, DAVID. The history of Wigan. 2 vols. Wigan, 1882–[3].

Valuable. Cf. also Gross (1), no. 2478.

4516 TUPLING, G. H. The economic history of Rossendale. Manchester, 1917.

Good.

4517 WHITAKER, T. D. A history of the original parish of Whalley and honour of Clitheroe. Blackburn, 1801; best ed. by J. G. Nichols and P. A. Lyons, 2 vols. Lond. 1872–6.

(5) *Other Works*

4518 AXON, ERNEST. The King's preachers in Lancashire, 1599–1845. *Trans. Lancs. and Ches. Antiq. Soc.* lvi (1944), 67–104.

4519 BAILEY, F. A. The Elizabethan playhouse at Prescot, Lancashire. *Trans. Hist. Soc. Lancs. and Ches.* ciii (1952), 69–81.

4520 BANKES, J. M. H. James Bankes and the Manor of Winstanley, 1596–1617. *Trans. Hist. Soc. Lancs. and Ches.* xciv (1943), 56–93.

4521 CHIPPINDALL, W. H. A sixteenth century survey and year's account of the estates of Hornby Castle, Lancashire. *Remains Hist. and Lit. . . . Lancaster and Chester*, n.s., cii (1939).

4522 FRANCE, R. S. A rental of the S. Lancashire lands of St. John of Jerusalem circa 1540. *Trans. Lancs. and Ches. Antiq. Soc.* lviii (1947), 57–70.

4523 THE NARRATIVE OF THE INDICTMENT of the traitors of Whalley and Cartmell, 1536–7. By J. E. W. Wallis. *Chetham Soc.*, n.s., xc (1931).

4524 A XVITH CENTURY RENTAL of Sir Richard Molyneux of Sefton. *The Clifton Papers.* By R. C. Shaw. Preston, 1935.

20. LEICESTERSHIRE

(1) *Bibliographies*

There is none of importance.

(2) *Local Societies*

4525 LEICESTERSHIRE ARCHAEOLOGICAL SOCIETY. Transactions. Leicester, 1855 ff. From 1855 to 1917 called *Leicestershire Architectural and Archaeological Soc.* In 1955 became *Leicestershire Archaeological and Historical Soc.* Has printed accounts of many Leicestershire manors.

4526 LEICESTER LITERARY AND PHILOSOPHICAL SOCIETY. Transactions. Leicester, 1835; 1879–80; 1884–5; 1886 ff.

4527 LEICESTERSHIRE AND RUTLAND NOTES AND QUERIES. 3 vols. Leicester, 1891–5.

(3) *County Histories and Records*

Some Leicester county records are described in *Hist. MSS. Comm. Reports*, viii. Vols. i–iii of *V.C.H. Leicester* have appeared. Lond. 1907–55. On farming, cf. 2639, 2650, and 2662.

4528 GIMSON, B. L., and RUSSELL, P. Leicestershire maps: a brief survey. Leicester, 1947.

4529 HOSKINS, W. G. Essays in Leicestershire history. Liverpool, 1950. The Midland peasant. The economic and social history of a Leicestershire village. Lond. 1957.

4530 NICHOLS, JOHN. History and antiquities of the county of Leicester. 4 vols. (in 8 pts.). Lond. 1795–1815.
The best complete history of the county.

4531 THROSBY, JOHN. Memoirs of the town and county of Leicester. 6 vols. Leicester, 1777.
Cf. idem, *Hist. and antiq. of the ancient town of Leicester*, 1791.

(4) *Town Histories and Records*

4532 CHARMAN, DEREK. Wealth and trade in Leicester in the early sixteenth century. *Trans. Leics. Arch. Soc.* xxv (1949), 67–97.

4532a HOSKINS, W. G. An Elizabethan provincial town: Leicester. *Studies in Social History. A tribute to G. M. Trevelyan.* By J. H. Plumb, Lond. 1955. pp. 33–67.

4533 AN INDEX TO THE ANCIENT MANUSCRIPTS of the borough of Leicester. By J. C. Jeaffreson. Westminster, [1878].

4534 MARKET HARBOROUGH PARISH RECORDS to A.D. 1530. By J. E. Stocks and W. B. Bragg. Lond. 1890.

4535 NOTICES . . . extracted from the chamberlains' accounts of Leicester. By William Kelly. Lond. 1865.

4536 RECORDS OF THE BOROUGH OF LEICESTER . . . from the archives of the corporation. By Mary Bateson. 3 vols. Cambr. 1899–1905.
Goes to 1603. One of the best collections of local records.

4537 THOMPSON, JAMES. History of Leicester to the end of the seventeenth century. Lond. 1849.
The best history of the town. For a collection of the town charters, cf. Gross (1), no. 2482. Cf. also 4531.

(5) *Other Works*

4538 HORTON-SMITH, L. G. H. The Hortons of Leicestershire. Lond. 1943.

4539 HOSKINS, W. G. Leicestershire yeoman families and their pedigrees. *Trans. Leics. Arch. Soc.* xxiii (1947), 30–62.

4540 MELTON MOWBRAY LAY SUBSIDY, 1543. By A. B. Clarke. *Trans. Leics. Arch. Soc.* xviii (1935), 196–201.

4541 SKILLINGTON, F. E. Post-medieval Cossington. *Trans. Leics. Arch. Soc.* xix (1938), 293–345; xx (1938), 1–53.

21. LINCOLNSHIRE

(1) *Bibliographies*

4542 CORNS, A. R. Bibliotheca Lincolniensis. A catalogue of the books . . . relating to the city and county of Lincoln. Lincoln, 1904.

(2) *Local Societies*

4543 LINCOLN RECORDS SOCIETY. Publications, Lincoln, 1911 ff.
An older, extinct society of the same name published 1 vol., Horncastle, 1889.

4544 LINCOLNSHIRE ARCHITECTURAL AND ARCHAEOLOGY SOCIETY. Papers. Lincoln, 1850–1937, n.s., 1938 ff.
Became in 1935 *Lincolnshire Associated Architectural Societies.*

4545 LINCOLNSHIRE HISTORIAN. Lincolnshire local history society. Lincoln, 1947 ff.
Supersedes *Lincolnshire Magazine.*

4546 LINCOLNSHIRE MAGAZINE. Lindsey local history society. Lincoln, 1932–9.

4547 LINCOLNSHIRE NOTES AND QUERIES. Horncastle, 1888–1936.

(3) *County Histories and Records*

For Lincolnshire court rolls, cf. Gross (1), no. 2487b. Vol. ii of *V.C.H. Lincoln* has appeared. Lond. 1906. Cf. 1988.

4548 ALLEN, THOMAS. History of the county of Lincoln. 2 vols. Lond. 1834.

4549 FOSTER, C. W. Calendar of administration in Lincoln, 1540–1659. Horncastle, 1921.

4550 A HANDLIST OF THE RECORDS OF THE BISHOPS OF LINCOLN and of the archdeacons of Lincoln and Stow. By Kathleen Major. Lond. 1953.
Cf. also 1859.

4551 MARRAT, WILLIAM. A history of Lincolnshire. 3 vols. Boston, 1814–16.

4552 THIRSK, JOAN. English peasant farming. The agrarian history of Lincolnshire from Tudor times. Lond. 1957.

4553 WALSHAW, G. R. An ancient Lincolnshire map. *Lincoln Mag.* ii (1935), 196–206.
Made by William Hausarde, 1595.

4554 WHEELER, W. H. History of the fens of south Lincolnshire. Boston, 1896.

(4) *Town Histories and Records*

Cf. Gross (1), nos. 999, 1000–1, 2488, 2489, 2491, 2493, 2497, 2512. Records of the town of Great Grimsby are described in *Hist. MSS. Comm. Reports,* xiv

4555 DRAKARD, JOHN. History of Stamford. Stamford, 1822.

4556 HARROD, W. Antiquities of Stamford and St. Martin's compiled . . . for Rev. Francis Peck. 2 vols. Stamford, 1785.

4557 HILL, J. W. F. Tudor and Stuart Lincoln. Cambr. 1956.
Valuable.

4558 MOOR, C. History of Gainsborough. Lincoln, 1904.

4559 THOMPSON, PISHEY. History and antiquities of Boston and the hundred of Skirbeck. Boston (Eng.), 1856.
The best history of Boston, Eng. See also his *Collections, &c.,* Boston, 1820.

22. LONDON AND MIDDLESEX

(1) *Bibliographies*

Davies (8), pp. 280–1, has a useful note on this subject. Cf. 70.

4560 CATALOGUE OF THE GUILDHALL LIBRARY of the city of London with additions to June 1889. Lond. 1889.

4561 A CATALOGUE OF WESTMINSTER RECORDS deposited at the town hall. . . . By J. E. Smith. Lond. 1900.

4562 COUNTY OF MIDDLESEX, CALENDAR to the sessions records. By W. L. Hardy. New series. Lond. 1935 ff.

4563 A DISCOURSE ON SOME UNPUBLISHED RECORDS of the city of London. By E. Freshfield. Lond. 1887.

(2) *Local Societies*

4564 HOME COUNTIES MAGAZINE: devoted to the topography of London, Middx., Essex, Herts., Bucks., Berks., Surrey, and Kent. Lond. 1899–1912.

4565 LONDON AND MIDDLESEX ARCHAEOLOGICAL SOCIETY. Transactions. Lond. 1860 ff.

4566 LONDON TOPOGRAPHICAL SOCIETY. Publications. Lond. 1911 ff.

4567 MIDDLESEX AND HERTFORDSHIRE NOTES AND QUERIES. 4 vols. Lond. 1895–8.
Continued in 4564.

4568 MIDDLESEX COUNTY RECORDS SOCIETY. Lond. 1886–1892.

(3) *County Histories and Records*

For Middlesex quarter sessions, cf. 1302. For London parish records, cf. Davies (8), nos. 2885, 2886, 2891–3, 2900. For London livery companies, cf. nos. 2695–2753, for aliens in London, no. 1887. The older histories of London are given in Gross (1), nos. 176–9. Cf. also Gross (1), nos. 2504, 2515. For historical monuments, cf. 4195. Vol. ii of the *V.C.H. Middlesex* has appeared, Lond. 1911, and vol. i of London, Lond. 1909.

4569 ANALYTICAL INDEX to the . . . remembrancia preserved among the archives of . . . London. By W. H. and H. C. Overall. Lond. 1878.
The remembrancia books contain copies of correspondence between the civic authorities and the court, &c. The index is really a brief calendar.

4570 BEAVEN, A. B. The aldermen of the city of London. 2 vols. Lond. 1908–13.

4570a BESANT, WALTER. London in the time of the Tudors. Lond. 1904. Vol. ii of Besant's *History and Survey of London*. 8 vols.
Excellent plans, maps, and illustrations, but text must be used with caution.

4571 BRAYLEY, E. W. The history of the abbey church of St. Peter, Westminster. 2 vols. Lond. 1818–23.

4572 BRAYLEY, E. W., and BRITTON, J. History of the ancient palaces and later houses of parliament. Lond. 1836.

4573 BRIGGS, M. S. Middlesex old and new. Lond. 1935.

4574 BROADBANK, J. G. History of the port of London. 2 vols. Lond. 1921.

4576 A CALENDAR OF THE MARRIAGE LICENCE ALLEGATIONS in the registry of the Bishop of London. Vol. i, 1597–1648. By R. M. Glencross. *Brit. Rec. Soc. Index Lib.* lxii (1937).

4577 CALENDAR OF WILLS proved and enrolled in the court of Hustings. By R. R. Sharpe. 2 vols. Lond. 1889–90.

4578 A CATALOGUE OF MAPS, plans and views of London . . . collected by F. Crace. By J. G. Crace. Lond. 1878.
The best bibliography of London maps. Cf. Davies (8), no. 2883; cf. also G. E. Mitton, *Maps of old London*, Lond. 1908.

4579 DAVIS, E. J. The transformation of London. In *Tudor Studies* (324), 287–314.
Confined to Tudor period. Contains a valuable bibliographical note.

4579a DAVIS, E. J. The goldsmiths in 'La Strada', 1497, *History*, xvii (1932), 47–48.
A Venetian account of England.

4579b DAVIS, E. J. The university site, Bloomsbury. *London Topog. Rec.* xvii (1936), 19–139.

4579c EKWALL, EILERT. Street names of the city of London. Oxf. 1954.

4580 FRESHFIELD, E. A discourse on some unpublished records of the city of London. Lond. 1887.
Indicates the general contents of London parochial records.

4580a GRAHAM, ROSE. A plan of the site and buildings of St. Anthony's Hospital, Threadneedle Street, *c.* 1530. *London Topog. Rec.* xvi (1932), 1–8.

4580b HENDON SURVEY of A.D. 1574. By N. G. Brett-James. *Trans. London and Middx. Arch. Soc.*, n.s., vii (1934), 33–70.
3 Elizabethan maps of Hendon.

4581 HOME, GORDON. Old London bridge. Lond. 1931.

4581a HONEYBOURNE, M. B. The precincts of the Grey Friars. *London Topog. Rec.* xvi (1932), 9–51.

4581b JAMISON, C. The history of the Royal hospital of St. Katherine by the Tower of London. Oxf. 1952.

4582 AN INVENTORY OF THE HISTORICAL MONUMENTS of Middlesex. Lond. 1937.

4583 MACHYN, HENRY. Diary, 1550–63. By J. G. Nichols. *Camden Soc.* xlii (1844).
The diary of a London citizen.

4584 NORDEN, JOHN. Speculum Britanniae: the first parte, an historical and chorographical description of Middlesex. Lond. 1598.
Later eds. include Hertfordshire (4449).

4585 NORTON, GEORGE. Commentaries on the history, constitution, &c. ... of London. Lond. 1829; 3rd ed. 1869.
The best constitutional history of London.

4586 PINKS, W. J. A history of Clerkenwell. Lond. 1865.

4587 ROBBINS, MICHAEL. Middlesex. *New Survey of England Ser.* xi. Lond. 1953.

4587a ROGERS, KENNETH. Bread street, its ancient signs and houses. *London Topog. Rec.* xvi (1932), 52–81.

4587b SAMUEL, W. S. Some notes on 16th century London Jews. Lond. 1937. Cf. also C. J. Sisson, *A colony of Jews in Shakespeare's London, Essays and Studies,* xxiii (1938), 38–51.

4587c SCOULOUDI, IRENE. Alien immigration into and alien communities in London, 1558–1640. *Hug. Soc. Lond. Proc.* xvi (1938), 27–49.

4588 SHARPE, R. R. London and the kingdom. 3 vols. Lond. 1894–9.

4589 SIMPSON, W. S. St. Paul's and old city life from the thirteenth to the sixteenth centuries. Lond. 1894.

4590 SMYTH, CHARLES. Church and parish: studies in church problems illustrated from the parochial history of St. Margaret's Westminster. Lond. 1955.

4591 STOW, JOHN. A survey of London. Lond. 1598; by John Strype, 2 vols. Lond. 1720; by C. L. Kingsford, 2 vols. Oxf. 1908.
Kingsford's ed. is the standard for Stow's original work. It contains valuable bibliographical material in the introduction. Strype's notes (ed. 1720) contain much additional matter. Cf. also Arthur Bonner, *John Stow and his survey, Trans. London and Middx. Arch. Soc.,* n.s., viii (1938), 70–74. Cf. also nos. 301, 304, 310, 315, 319.

4592 SURVEY OF LONDON issued by ... the London county council. Lond. 1900 (in progress).
Deals with buildings and antiquities grouped by parishes. Valuable. Cf. 4195.

4592a WALTERS, H. B. London churches at the reformation, with an account of their contents. *Church Hist. Soc. Pub.,* n.s., xxxvii (1939).

4593 WILEY, W. E. The parish of St. Giles in the fields. By G. L. Gomme. 2 vols. Lond. 1912–14.

4594 WILLIAMS, N. J. Sessions of the clerk of the market of the household of Middlesex. *Trans. Lond. and Middlesex Arch. Soc.* xix, pt. 2 (1957), 1–14.

23. NORFOLK

(1) *Bibliographies*

4605 BIBLIOTHECA NORFOLCIENSIS: A catalogue of ... works relating to Norfolk in the library of J. J. Colman. ... By [John Quinton]. Norwich, 1896.

4606 RYE, WALTER. An index to Norfolk topography. *Index Soc.* x (1881); supplementary vol. Norwich, 1896.
Cf. also idem, *An index rerum to Norfolk antiquities*, Norwich, 1899.

4607 WOODWARD, SAMUEL. The Norfolk topographer's manual. Lond. 1842.

(2) *Local Societies*

4608 NORFOLK AND NORWICH ARCHAEOLOGICAL SOCIETY. Norfolk archaeology. Norwich, 1847 ff.

4609 NORFOLK ANTIQUARIAN MISCELLANY. 3 vols. Norwich, 1877–87; 2nd ser., pts. 1–3, by Walter Rye, Norwich, 1906–8.

4610 NORFOLK RECORD SOCIETY. s.l. 1931 ff.

(3) *County Histories and Records*

Cf. Gross (1), nos. 1029, 1032, 1037. The *Stiffkey papers* (1287), the *Gawdy papers* (612), and the *Paston letters* (292) are all of Norfolk families. Vols. i, ii of *V.C.H. Norfolk* have appeared. Lond. 1901–6.

4611 BLOMEFIELD, FRANCIS, and PARKIN, C. Topographical history of . . . Norfolk. 5 vols. Fersfield, 1739–75; 11 vols. Lond. 1805–10; index, by J. N. Chadwick, King's Lynn, 1862.
The best complete history of the county. Vol. x (ed. 1805) contains an excellent history of Norwich.

4612 NORFOLK RECORDS: a collection of record references derived from indexes in the Public Record Office, London. By W. D. Selby and Walter Rye. *Norfolk and Norwich Arch. Soc.* 2 vols. 1886–92.

4613 RYE, WALTER. A history of Norfolk. *Popular County Histories.* Lond. 1885.
Brief but good. Cf. also idem, *Historical essays chiefly relating to Norfolk*, Norwich, 1928.

(4) *Town Histories and Records*

Cf. also Gross (1), nos. 1028, 1028a, 1031, 1033, 1035, 1035a, 2534, 2538–41, 2543, 2545, 2547–8. Cf. 2995.

4614 CALENDAR OF FRERE MSS.: Hundred of Holt. *Norfolk Rec. Soc.* i (1931), 5–40. Cf. 142.

4615 CARTHEW, G. A. The hundred of Launditch and deanery of Brisley: evidences and notes from public records. 3 parts. Norwich, 1877–9.
A valuable collection, but with many errors in transcription.

4616 HILLEN, H. J. The borough of King's Lynn. Norwich, [1907].
The best history of Lynn.

4617 MANSHIP, HENRY. History of Great Yarmouth. By C. J. Palmer. 2 vols. Great Yarmouth, 1854–6.
Written in the time of Queen Elizabeth, but first published in 1854–6.

4618 NASH, THOMAS. Nashes Lenten stuff . . . of Great Yarmouth in Norfolk. Lond. 1599; repr. in *Harl. Mis.* (281), vi, 143–81.
Relates to the herring fishing.

4619 RECORDS OF THE CITY OF NORWICH. By William Hudson and J. C. Tingey. 2 vols. Norwich, 1906–[10].
Valuable, but chiefly medieval. Cf. also *Catalogue of the records of the city of Norwich*, by W. Hudson and J. C. Tingey, Norwich, 1898; and W. Hudson, *Sketch of the commercial history of Norwich till . . . the time of Q. Elizabeth*, *Proc. Hug. Soc. of London*, ii (1887–8), 519–24.

4620 RECORDS OF THE GILD OF ST. GEORGE in Norwich, 1389–1547: a transcript. By Mary Grace. *Norfolk Rec. Soc.* ix (1937).
Tudor period is covered pp. 78–157.

4621 A REGISTER OF THE FREEMEN OF NORWICH, 1548–1713. By Percy Millican. Norwich, 1934.
A register devoted to obscure names.

4622 RICHARDS, WILLIAM. The history of Lynn. 2 vols. Lynn, 1812.

4623 RYE, WALTER. Depositions taken before the mayor and aldermen of Norwich. Norwich, 1905.
Cf. also idem, *Extracts concerning musters in the sixteenth century*, *Norfolk and Norwich Arch. Soc.*, 1847; *Norwich pageants, extracts from the grocer's book*, Norwich, 1856.

4624 PALMER, C. J. The history of Great Yarmouth. Great Yarmouth, 1856.
Valuable.

4625 SWINDEN, HENRY. History and antiquities of Great Yarmouth. Norwich, 1772.
The best history of Yarmouth.

(5) Other Works

4626 BURSTALL, E. B. The Pastons and their manor of Binham. *Norfolk Arch.* xxx (1952), 101–29.

4627 COZENS-HARDY, B. The Norwich Chapelfield house estate since 1545 and some of its owners and occupiers. *Norfolk Arch.* xxvii (1941), 351–84.

4628 COZENS-HARDY, B. Presents to the Sheriff of Norfolk, 1600–1603. *Norfolk Arch.* xxvi (1941), 52–58.

4629 EXTRACTS FROM THE TWO EARLIEST MINUTE BOOKS of the Dean and chapter of Norwich cathedral, 1566–1649. By J. F. Williams and B. Cozens-Hardy. *Norfolk Rec. Soc.* xxiv (1953).

4630 GRACE, MARY. The chamberlains and treasurers of the city of Norwich, 1293–1835. *Norfolk Arch.* xxv (1935), 181–201.

4631 INVENTORIES OF NORFOLK CHURCH GOODS (1552). By H. B. Walters. *Norfolk Arch.* xxvi, 1938 (1938), 245–70; xxvii, 1939 (1941), 97–144; xxvii, 1940 (1941), 263–89; xxvii, 1941 (1941), 385–416; xxviii, 1942

(1945), 7–22; xxviii, 1943 (1945), 89–106; xxviii, 1944 (1945), 133–80; xxviii, 1945 (1945), 217–18; xxx, 1947 (1952), 75–87; xxx, 1950 (1952), 160–7; xxx, 1951 (195?), 213–19; xxx, 1952 (1952), 370–8.

4632   KENT, E. A. Some notes on the desecrated church of St. Cuthbert, Norwich. *Norfolk Arch.* xxvii (1941), 94–96.

4633   THE LAY SUBSIDY OF 1581 assessors' certificates for the Norfolk hundreds of Depwadem, South Greenhoe, Henstead, Mitford, and Shropham. By E. D. Stone and Percy Millican. *Norfolk Rec. Soc.* xvii (1944), 95–127.

4634   MARTIN, A. R. The Greyfriars of Walsingham. *Norfolk Arch.* (1935), 227–71.
The excavation of the buildings.

4635   MILLICAN, PERCY. The rebuilding of Wroxham bridge in 1576: a transcript of the account book. *Norfolk Arch.* xxvi (1938), 281–95.

4636   MILLICAN, PERCY. The Gawdys of Norfolk and Suffolk. *Norfolk Arch.* xxvi (1938), 335–90; xxvii (1941), 31–93. Cf. 142–3, 612.

4637   A PLAN FOR THE FORTIFICATION OF YARMOUTH in 1588. By B. H. St. J. O'Neill and W. E. Stephens. *Norfolk Arch.* xxviii (1945), 1–6.

4638   STEER, F. W. The Butts family of Norfolk. *Norfolk Arch.* xxix (1946), 181–200.

4639   THREE CARROW ACCOUNT ROLLS. By J. Redstone. *Norfolk Arch.* xxix (1946), 41–88.

4640   WYNDHAM, H. A. A family history, 1410–1688. The Wyndhams of Norfolk and Somerset. Oxf. 1939.
Cf. also R. W. Ketton-Cremer, *Thomas Windham of Felbrigg, Norfolk Arch.* xxvii (1941), 417–28.

24. NORTHAMPTONSHIRE

(1) *Bibliographies*

4641   TAYLOR, J. Bibliotheca Northantoniensis. Northampton, s.a.
A bibliographical account of what has been written or printed relating to Northamptonshire (25,000 references). Only six copies seem to have been printed, apparently about 1869.

(2) *Local Societies*

4642   NORTHAMPTONSHIRE NOTES AND QUERIES. Northampton, 1884 ff. Discontinued 1895; revived 1906–31.

4643   NORTHAMPTONSHIRE RECORD SOCIETY. Publications. Hereford, 1924 ff. *Northamptonshire past and present.* Northampton, 1948 ff.

(3) *County Histories and Records*

There is some material of value in *Montague papers* (167). Vols. i–iv of *V.C.H. Northants.* have appeared, Lond. 1902–37, together with a valuable supplementary volume by Oswald Barron, *Northamptonshire families.* 1906.

4644 BAKER, GEORGE. History and antiquities of the county of Northampton. 2 vols. Lond. 1822–41.
Although not completed, this is the best of the older histories of the county.

4645 BRIDGES, JOHN. History and antiquities of Northamptonshire, compiled from the manuscript collections of Sir Peter Whalley. 2 vols. Lond. 1791.

4646 A DESCRIPTIVE LIST OF THE PRINTED MAPS OF NORTHAMPTONSHIRE, 1576–1900. By Harold Whitaker. *Northampton Rec. Soc.* xiv (1948).

4647 HARTSHORNE, C. H. Historical memorials of Northamptonshire. Northampton, 1848.

4648 NORDEN, JOHN. Speculi Britanniae pars altera, or a delineation of Northamptonshire in the year 1610. Lond. 1720.

4649 NORTHAMPTON AND RUTLAND CLERGY FROM 1500. By H. I. Longden. 16 vols. Northampton, 1939–52.
Complete indexes of persons, places, subject and biographies of over 14,000 clergy.

(4) *Town Histories and Records*

For a series of valuable parish histories, cf. Thompson (4185), 15. Cf. also Gross (1), nos. 1038a, 1039, 1040a, 2553. For valuable books on Peterborough cathedral, 1980, 2047.

4650 ELIZABETHAN PETERBOROUGH. By W. T. Mellows and D. H. Gifford. *Northampton Rec. Soc.* xviii.
In the press.

4651 RECORDS OF THE BOROUGH OF NORTHAMPTON. By C. A. Markham and J. C. Cox. 2 vols. Northampton, 1898.

4652 PETERBOROUGH LOCAL ADMINISTRATION. Parochial government before the Reformation. Churchwardens' accounts 1467–1573, with supplementary documents 1107–1488. By W. T. Mellows. *Northampton Rec. Soc.* ix (1939).

4653 PETERBOROUGH LOCAL ADMINISTRATION. Parochial government from the reformation to the revolution, 1541–1689. Minutes and accounts of the feoffees and governors of the city lands with supplementary documents. By W. T. Mellows. *Northampton Rec. Soc.* x (1937).

(5) *Other Works*

4654 HORTON-SMITH, L. G. H. The later Lumleys of Harlestone in the county of Northampton, circa 1545 onwards. Northampton, 1944.

4655 KENNEDY, P. A. A gentleman's home in the reign of Henry VII. *Northampton past and present*, ii (1954), 17–28.
The home of Henry de Vere of Addington. Inventory (from Drayton house) made in 1493.

4656 WAKE, JOAN. The Brudenells of Deene. Lond. 1953.

4657 THE WEALTH OF FIVE NORTHAMPTONSHIRE FAMILIES, 1540–1640. By M. E. Finch. *Northampton Rec. Soc.* xix (1955).

25. NORTHUMBERLAND

(1) *Bibliographies*

There is none of importance.

(2) *Local Societies*

Cf. 4350–1.

4658 SOCIETY OF ANTIQUARIES OF NEWCASTLE-ON-TYNE. Archaeologia Aeliana. Newcastle, 1822 ff.

(3) *County Histories and Records*

On parliament, cf. 1112, 1113. Cf. also 4354, 4356.

4659 FEET OF FINES, Northumberland and Durham. *Newcastle-on-Tyne Rec. Comm. Pub.* x (1933).

4660 A HISTORY OF NORTHUMBERLAND ... issued under the direction of the Northumberland county history committees. 15 vols. Newcastle, 1893–1940 (in progress).
Valuable.

4661 HODGSON, JOHN, and HINDE, J. H. A history of Northumberland. 7 vols. Newcastle, 1820–58.

(4) *Town Histories and Records*

Cf. also Gross (1), nos. 1041a, 1043, 1045–7, 2559. On Berwick, cf. 1362 *supra*.

4662 BRAND, JOHN. The history and antiquities of Newcastle-upon-Tyne. 2 vols. Lond. 1789.
The best history of Newcastle. Cf. also 1725, 3027, 3044, and 4357.

4663 THE CARR MANUSCRIPT, 1432–1634. A catheloge of all the maiores and sherifs of his maiestye towne and countye of Newcastle upon Tyne ... with sarton briefes of cronicles that hapned in theyr several reignes sence anno domo 1432. By C. H. H. Blair. *Arch. Aeliana*, xviii (1940), 15–63.

4664 THE MAYORS AND LORD MAYORS of Newcastle-upon-Tyne, 1216–1940, and the sheriffs of the county of Newcastle-upon-Tyne, 1399–1940. By C. H. H. Blair. *Soc. Antiq. Newcastle Pub.* xvii (1940).

4665 SHERIFFS OF NORTHUMBERLAND, pt. i, 1076–1602. By C. H. H. Blair. *Arch. Aeliana*, xx (1942), 11–89; xxii (1944), 22–82.

(5) *Other Works*

4666 BLAIR, C. H. H. The castle of Wark-upon-Tweed. *Hist. Berwick Nat. Club*, xxix (1936), 76–103.

4667 HEDLEY, W. P. The Ridleys of Ridley and Willemontswick. *Arch. Aeliana*, xxxii (1954), 160–75.

26. NOTTINGHAMSHIRE

(1) *Bibliographies*

There is none of importance.

(2) *Local Societies*

4669 NOTTINGHAMSHIRE AND DERBYSHIRE NOTES and queries. 6 vols. Derby, 1892–8.

4670 THOROTON SOCIETY. Transactions. Nottingham, 1898 ff.; Record series, Nottingham, 1903–14.

(3) *County Histories and Records*

Vols. i, ii of *V.C.H. Notts.* have appeared. Lond. 1906–10.

4671 ABSTRACT OF NOTTS. INQUISITIONES POST MORTEM, 1242–1321 and 1485–1546. 2 vols. (in 6 pts.). By W. P. W. Phillimore and J. Standish. Nottingham, 1898–1914.

4672 ABSTRACTS OF NOTTINGHAMSHIRE MARRIAGE LICENCES. Vol. i, Archdeaconry court, 1577–1700; peculiar of Southwell, 1588–1754. By T. M. Blagg and F. A. Wadsworth. *Brit. Rec. Soc. Index Lib.* lvii (1930).

4673 BAILEY, THOMAS. Annals of Nottinghamshire . . . including the borough. 4 vols. Nottingham, 1852–6.

4674 DOMESDAY OF INCLOSURES FOR NOTTINGHAM, 1517. By I. S. Leadam. *Thoroton Soc., Rec. Ser.*, ii (1904).

4675 THE NOTTINGHAMSHIRE PRESENTMENT BILL OF 1587. By A. C. Wood. *Thorot. Soc. Rec. Ser. Misc.* xi (1943).

4676 THOROTON, ROBERT. The antiquities of Nottinghamshire. Lond. 1677; 3 vols. Lond. 1790; with additions by John Throsby, 3 vols. Lond. 1797.
The best complete history of the county.

4677 WOOD, A. C. A history of Nottinghamshire. Nottingham, 1947.

(4) *Town Histories and Records*

Cf. also Gross (1), nos. 1050a, 1051.

4678 BARKLEY, M. W. Newark in the sixteenth century. *Trans. Thorot. Soc.* liii (1950), 15–25.

4679 BROWN, CORNELIUS. A history of Newark-on-Trent. 2 vols. Newark, 1904–7.
Cf. also Gross (1), no. 1049a.

4680 GRAY, DUNCAN. Nottingham through 500 years—a short history of town government. Nottingham, 1949.

4681 NORTH COLLINGHAM CUSTOMARY AGREEMENT TO EN-
CLOSE, 1567. *Thorot. Soc. Rec. Ser. Misc.* xi (1944–5), 111–34.

4682 PARSLOE, C. G. The growth of a borough constitution: Newark-on-
Trent, 1549–1688. *Trans. R.H. Soc.*, 4th ser., xxii (1940), 171–98.

4683 RECORDS OF THE BOROUGH OF NOTTINGHAM. By W. H.
Stevenson and others. 6 vols. Nottingham, 1882–1914.
Well edited. For older histories of the town, cf. Gross (1), nos. 1049–50.

(5) *Other Works*

4684 TURBERVILLE, A. S. A history of Welbeck Abbey and its owners.
Vol. i 1539–1755. Lond. 1938.

27. OXFORDSHIRE

(1) *Bibliographies*

4685 BIBLIOGRAPHY OF PRINTED WORKS RELATING TO
OXFORDSHIRE (excluding the university and the city of Oxford). By
E. H. Cordeaux and D. R. Merry. Oxf. 1955.

4686 OXFORD BOOKS: a bibliography of printed works relating to Oxford.
By Falconer Madan. 2 vols. Oxf. 1895–1912.

(2) *Local Societies*

Cf. also 4214.

4687 NORTH OXFORDSHIRE archaeological and natural history society.
Banbury, [1856] ff.
Called since 1888 *Oxfordshire Archaeological Society.*

4688 OXFORD ARCHITECTURAL AND HISTORICAL SOCIETY.
Oxf. 1835–1900.

4688a OXONIENSIA, Oxf. 1936 ff.

4689 OXFORD HISTORICAL SOCIETY. Publications. Oxf. 1885 ff.

4690 OXFORD RECORD SOCIETY. Oxford record series. Oxf. 1919 ff.
Has published many valuable manorial and parochial records.

(3) *County Histories and Records*

Vols. i–iii, v of *V.C.H. Oxford* have appeared. Lond. 1907–57.

4691 FALKNER, J. M. A history of Oxfordshire. Lond. 1899.

4692 PLOT, ROBERT. The natural history of Oxfordshire. Oxf. 1677; by
J. Burman, Oxf. 1705.
A curious collection by the first keeper of the Ashmolean museum.

4693 KENNETT, WHITE. Parochial antiquities . . . in the counties of
Oxford and Bucks. Oxf. 1685; enlarged ed., 2 vols. Oxf. 1818.

(4) *Town Histories and Records*

Cf. also Gross (1), nos. 1052–5, 1057, 1058a, 1061–4, 2570. For Oxford University, cf. nos. 3766–70 *supra*.

4694 ELIZABETHAN OXFORD. By Chas. Plummer. *Oxford Hist. Soc.* viii (1887).
Reprs. rare contemporary tracts.

4695 GRETTON, R. H. The Burford records. Oxf. 1922.

4696 OXFORD CITY DOCUMENTS, financial and judicial, 1268–1665. By J. E. T. Rogers. *Oxford Hist. Soc.* xviii (1891).

4696a OXFORD COUNCIL ACTS, 1583–1626. By H. E. Salter, Oxf. 1928; also in *Oxf. Hist. Soc.* lxxxvii (1928).

4697 OXFORD MARKET. By Octavius Ogle. *Oxford Hist. Soc. Collectanea*, ii (1890), 1–135.

4698 PONSONBY, CHARLES. Wotton: the history of an Oxfordshire parish. Oxf. 1947.

4699 ROYAL LETTERS ADDRESSED TO OXFORD. . . . By Octavius Ogle. Oxf. 1892.

4700 SELECTIONS FROM THE RECORDS of the city of Oxford, 1509–1583. By W. H. Turner. Oxf. 1880.

4701 WOOD, ANTHONY À. The ancient and present state of the city of Oxford. With additions by John Peshall. Lond. 1773.
Cf. also idem, *Survey of the city of Oxford*, by Andrew Clark, *Oxford Hist. Soc.*, 3 vols., 1889–99.

(5) *Other Works*

4702 CHAMBERS, EDMUND. Eynsham under the monks. *Oxf. Rec. Soc.* xviii (1936).

4703 GEE, E. A. Oxford carpenters, 1370–1530. *Oxoniensia*, xvii–xviii (1952–3), 112–53.

4704 O'CONOR, N. J. Godes peace and the Queenes. Vicissitudes of a house, 1539–1615. Oxf. 1934.
Rycote and Weston manors.

4705 PHILIP, I. A. The court leet of the university of Oxford. *Oxoniensia*, xv (1950), 81–91.

28. RUTLANDSHIRE
(1) *Bibliographies*
There is none of importance.

(2) *Local Societies*
Cf. 4527.

(3) *County Histories and Records*
V.C.H. Rutland is complete in 2 vols. and index. Lond. 1908–35. Cf. 4649.

4706 BLORE, THOMAS. History and antiquities of the county of Rutland.
Vol. i. Stamford, 1811.
Only 1 vol. printed.

4707 WRIGHT, JAMES. History and antiquities of the county of Rutland.
Lond. 1684.

29. SHROPSHIRE

(1) *Bibliographies*

There is none of importance.

(2) *Local Societies*

4708 SHROPSHIRE ARCHAEOLOGICAL and natural history society.
Transactions. Shrewsbury, 1878 ff.

4709 SHROPSHIRE NOTES AND QUERIES. 3 vols. Shrewsbury,
1886–7; another series, 8 vols. Shrewsbury, 1892–9.

(3) *County Histories and Records*

Vol. i of *V.C.H. Shropshire* has appeared. Lond. 1908. On farming, cf. 2633.

4710 BLAKEWAY, J. B. Sheriffs of Shropshire. Shrewsbury, 1831.

4711 EYTON, R. W. Antiquities of Shropshire. 12 vols. Lond. 1854–60.
The best history of the county, but relatively weak on the Tudors.

4712 HURLBURT, CHARLES. History and description of the county of
Salop. 2 vols. Shrewsbury, 1837.

(4) *Town Histories and Records*

Cf. Gross (1), p. 567 and nos. 1068, 1068a, 1068b, 2574, 2578–80a, 2583, 2586,
2588.

4713 HOBBS, J. L. Three borough rentals of Shrewsbury, 1521, 1580, 1610.
Trans. Shrop. Arch. Soc. liii (1950), 212–41.

4714 LETTER FROM GEORGE, EARL OF SHREWSBURY, concerning
the countess of Shrewsbury, 15th June, 1586. *Thorot. Soc. Rec. Ser. 2nd Misc.*
xiv (1951), 21–25.

4715 OWEN, H., and BLAKEWAY, J. B. A history of Shrewsbury. 2 vols.
Lond. 1825.
Valuable.

4716 SHREWSBURY BURGESSES, 16th–17th centuries. By Michael
Peele. *Trans. Shrop. Arch. Soc.* xlviii (1937), 213–32.

(5) *Other Works*

4717 HILL, M. C. The Wealdmoors, 1560–1660. *Trans. Shrop. Arch. Soc.* liv
(1953), 255–326.

4718 THE LORDSHIP OF CUASE, 1540–1. *Trans. Shrop. Arch. Soc.* liv (1951–2), 45–68, 327–37.

30. SOMERSETSHIRE

(1) *Bibliographies*

4719 GREEN, EMANUEL. Bibliotheca Somersetensis. 3 vols. Taunton, 1902.

4720 HUMPHREYS, A. L. Somersetshire parishes. 2 vols. Lond. 1906.
Contains much bibliographical material.

(2) *Local Societies*

Cf. also 4312.

4721 NOTES AND QUERIES FOR SOMERSET AND DORSET. Sherborne, 1890 ff.

4722 SOMERSET ARCHAEOLOGICAL and natural history society. Transactions. Shrewsbury, 1878 ff.

4723 SOMERSET RECORD SOCIETY. Publications. Lond. 1887 ff.

(3) *County Histories and Records*

Cf. Gross (1), nos. 1069a, 1072b, 1077. On the Spanish armada and Somerset, cf. 3386. Vols. i, ii of *V.C.H. Somerset* have appeared. Lond. 1906–11.

4724 COLLINSON, JOHN. History and antiquities of the county of Somerset. 3 vols. Bath, 1791.

4725 PHELPS, WILLIAM. History and antiquities of Somersetshire. 2 vols. Lond. 1836–9.

(4) *Town Histories and Records*

Cf. Gross (1), nos. 1072c, 1073, 1073a, 1075, p. 569 and nos. 2591–2, 2607a, 2608. Cf. 4029.

4726 DEAN COSYN AND WELLS CATHEDRAL MISCELLANEA. By Aelred Watkin. *Somerset Rec. Soc.* lvi (1941).

4727 A HANDLIST OF THE HORNER MSS. at Wells (to the end of the reign of Henry VII). By Aelred Watkin. *Somerset Rec. Soc.* lviii (1942), 104–13.

4728 AN INVENTORY OF PAROCHIAL DOCUMENTS in the diocese of Bath and Wells and the county of Somerset. By J. E. King. Taunton, 1938.

4729 A LIST OF PRECENTORS: chancellors and treasurers of Wells Cathedral. By Aelred Watkin. *Somerset Rec. Soc.* lvii (1942), 51–103.

4730 LYTE, H. C. M. A history of Dunster. 2 vols. Lond. 1909.

4731 MUNICIPAL RECORDS OF BATH, 1189–1604. By A. J. King and B. H. Watts. Lond. 1885.

4732 ROBINSON, J. A. Somerset historical essays. Lond. 1921.

4733 SAVAGE, JAMES. History of the hundred of Corhampton. Bristol, 1830.

4734 SOMERSET ENROLLED DEEDS. By S. W. Bates-Harbin. *Somerset Rec. Soc.* li (1937).

4735 SOMERSET WILLS FROM EXETER. By S. W. Rawlins and I. Jones. *Somerset Rec. Soc.* lxii (1952).
Covering the years 1529–1600.

4736 TOULMIN, JOSHUA. History of the town of Taunton. Taunton, 1791; by James Savage, Taunton, 1822.

4737 WARDLE, T. D. The accounts of the chamberlains of the city of Bath, 1568–1602. Lond. 1923.

4738 WARNER, RICHARD. The history of Bath. Bath, 1801.
The best history of Bath.

4739 WELLS CITY CHARTERS. By D. O. Shelton and Richard Halworthy. *Somerset Rec. Soc.* xlvi (1932).

4740 WHITTY, R. G. H. The court of Taunton in the sixteenth and seventeenth centuries. Taunton, 1934.
A study in the legal and social history of Taunton under the Tudors and Stuarts.

4741 WIVELISCOMBE COURT ROLL, 1580. *Somerset and Dorset Notes and Queries*, xxi (1935), 223–7.

(5) *Other Works*

Cf. 4640.

31. STAFFORDSHIRE

(1) *Bibliographies*

4742 SIMMS, RUPERT. Bibliotheca Staffordiensis; or a bibliographical account of books relating to the county of Stafford. Lichfield, 1894.

(2) *Local Societies*

4743 WILLIAM SALT ARCHAEOLOGICAL SOCIETY: Collections for a history of Staffordshire. Birmingham, 1881 ff.
In 1935 became *Staffordshire Record Society*.

(3) *County Histories and Records*

Vol. i of *V.C.H. Stafford* has appeared. Lond. 1908. For quarter sessions cf. 1303, for chancery proceedings, cf. 1661.

4744 ERDESWICKE, SAMPSON. A survey of Staffordshire. By Richard Rawlinson. Lond. 1717; by Thomas Harwood, 1844.
The author of this survey died in 1603; his original MS. is in B.M. Harl. MSS., no. 1990.

4745 PLOT, ROBERT. The natural history of Staffordshire. Oxf. 1686.

4746 SHAW, S. History and antiquities of Staffordshire. 2 vols. Lond. 1798–1801.
The best history of the county.

(4) *Town Histories and Records*

Cf. Gross (1), nos. 1082a–7, 2609–b, 2622, 2624a.

4747 CHERRY, J. L. and KARL. Historical studies relating chiefly to Staffordshire. Stafford, 1908.

4748 PALMER, C. J. History of the town and castle of Tamworth. Tamworth, 1845.

4749 PAPE, THOMAS. Newcastle-under-Lyme in Tudor and early Stuart times. *Manchester Univ. Pub. Hist.* lxxv. Manchester, 1938.

4750 THORPE, HARRY. Lichfield: a study of its growth and function. *Staff. Rec. Soc. 1950–1* (1954), 139–211.

(5) *Other Works*

4751 A ROWLEY REGIS ROLL, 1556. By J. T. Homer. *Staff. Rec. Soc.* 1936 (1936), 207–27.

4752 TWEMLOW, F. R. The Manor of Tyrley. *Staff. Rec. Soc.* 1945–46 (1948).
Pp. 67 ff. on Tudor period.

32. SUFFOLK

(1) *Bibliographies*

There is none of importance, but much bibliographical material will be found in 4757.

(2) *Local Societies*

4753 THE EAST ANGLIAN, or notes and queries connected with . . . Suffolk, Cambridge, Essex, and Norfolk. Lowestoft, 1864–1910.

4754 SUFFOLK INSTITUTE of archaeological and natural history. Proceedings. Bury St. Edmunds, 1853 ff.
The 1st vol. is called *Proceedings of the Bury and West Suffolk Archaeological Institute*.

4755 SUFFOLK GREEN BOOKS. Wells, 1894–1929.
Especially valuable for the sixteenth century.

(3) *County Histories and Records*

Vols. i, ii of *V.C.H. Suffolk* have appeared. Lond. 1907–11. Cf. 2046.

4756 CATALOGUE OF BENEFICED CLERGY OF SUFFOLK, 1086–1550. By Claude Morley. *Proc. Suffolk Inst. Arch. and Nat. Hist.* xxii (1934), 29–85; pt. ii, 1551–1631, by R. F. Butler, ibid. xxii (1936), 294–320.

4757 COUNTY OF SUFFOLK. Its history as disclosed by existing records. . . . By W. A. Copinger. 5 vols. Lond 1904–6.

4758   COPINGER, W. A. The manors of Suffolk. . . . 7 vols. Lond. 1905–11.

4759   CAGE, JOHN. History and antiquities of Suffolk: Thingoe hundred. Lond. 1838.

4760   SUCKLING, A. I. History and antiquities of . . . Suffolk. 2 vols. Lond. 1846–8.
The best of the older histories of the county. Cf. idem, *An index to the history and antiquities of the county of Suffolk*, Ipswich, 1952.

(4) *Town Histories and Records*

Cf. Gross (1), nos. 1090a, 1091, 1093, 2629–30, 2632, 2632a.

4762   ROBERTS, R. A. The borough business of a Suffolk town (Orford), 1559–1660. *Trans. R.H. Soc.*, 4th ser., xiv (1931), 95–120.

4763   WODDERSPOON, JOHN. Memorials of Ipswich. Ipswich, 1850.
The best history of Ipswich. Cf. also Gross (1), no. 1089.

4764   YATES, RICHARD. An illustration of the monastic history of the town and abbey of St. Edmund's Bury. 2 pts. Lond. 1805; 1843.
The best history of the town and abbey.

(5) *Other Works*

Cf. 4454, 4636.

4765   RYAN, G. H., and REDSTONE, L. J. Timperly of Hintlesham. Lond. 1931.

33. SURREY

(1) *Bibliographies*

Cf. 1299, 4461.

4766   A CATALOGUE OF BOOKS in the library of the Surrey archaeological society. By Mill Stephenson. *Surrey Arch. Soc. Trans.* x (1891).

4767   A CATALOGUE OF WORKS relating to Surrey in the Minet library, Camberwell. Lond. 1901; supplement, 1923.
A valuable bibliography.

4768   GUIDE TO THE ARCHIVES . . . relating to Surrey. By C. H. Jenkinson, M. S. Giuseppi, and D. L. Powell. *Surrey Rec. Soc.* xxiii (1925), xxiv (1926), xxvi (1927), xxviii (1928), xxix (1929).
Deals with Surrey records in P.R.O.; also local parish, manor, and borough records. Scholarly.

(2) *Local Societies*

Cf. 4564.

4769   SURREY ARCHAEOLOGICAL SOCIETY. Collections. Lond. 1858 ff.

4770   SURREY RECORD SOCIETY. Publications. Lond. 1913 ff.

(3) *County Histories and Records*

For a very valuable collection of papers relating to the administration of Surrey under the Tudors, cf. 165. The *V.C.H. Surrey* is complete in 4 vols. and index. Lond. 1902–14.

4771 ABSTRACTS OF SURREY FEET OF FINES, 1509–1558. By C. A. F. Meekings. *Surrey Rec. Soc.* xix (1946).

4772 AUBREY, JOHN. The natural history and antiquities of the county of Surrey. By Richard Rawlins. 5 vols. Lond. 1718–19.

A valuable description of the county, parish by parish, made from actual observations by the author who lived in the middle of the seventeenth century. Contains many inscriptions, &c., since destroyed.

4773 BASKERVILLE, G., and GOODMAN, A. W. Surrey incumbents in 1562. *Surrey Arch. Coll.* xlv (1937), 97–115.

4774 BRAYLEY, E. W. A topographical history of Surrey. 5 vols. Dorking, 1841–8; by Edward Walford, 4 vols. Lond. [1878–81].

4775 HEARNSHAW, F. J. C. The place of Surrey in the history of England. Lond. 1934.

4776 MALDEN, H. E. A history of Surrey. Lond. 1900.

4777 MANNING, OWEN, and BRAY, WILLIAM. History and antiquities of the county of Surrey. 3 vols. Lond. 1804–14.

(4) *Town Histories and Records*

Cf. Gross (1), nos. 1096a, 1097–9, 1100a–c, 2634–8, and Thompson (4185), 15–16.

4778 GUILDFORD BOROUGH RECORDS, 1514–1546. By E. M. Dance. *Surrey Rec. Soc.* (In the press.)

4779 THE HISTORY OF GUILDFORD, the county town of Surrey . . . with some account of the country three miles round. Guildford, 1777; 1801.

4780 HARRISON, FREDERIC. Annals of an old manor house, Sutton Place, Guildford. Lond. 1893; condensed ed. Lond. 1899.

A model account of the history of a great house from the time of Henry VIII onwards.

4781 KINGSTON-UPON-THAMES Bridgewardens' accounts, 1526–7. By N. J. Williams. *Surrey Rec. Soc.* xxii (1955).

4782 RENDLE, WILLIAM. Old Southwark and its people. Southwark, 1878.

4783 SHEARMAN, PHILIP. Ewell in 1577. *Surrey Arch. Coll.* liv (1955), 102–7.

34. SUSSEX

(1) *Bibliographies*

Cf. 4461.

4784 BUTLER, G. S. Topographica Sussexiana; an attempt towards forming a list of the various publications relating to the county of Sussex. *Sussex Arch.*

Soc. Coll. xv–xviii (1863–6); continued to 1882 by F. E. Sawyer, *Sussex Arch. Soc. Coll.* xxxii–xxxiii (1882–3).

(2) *Local Societies*

4785 SUSSEX ARCHAEOLOGICAL SOCIETY. Collections. Lond. 1848 ff.

4786 SUSSEX RECORD SOCIETY. Publications. Lewes, 1902 ff.
One of the best county publishing societies.

(3) *County Histories and Records*

Vols. i–iv, vii, ix of *V.C.H. Sussex* have appeared. Lond. 1905–53. Cf. 2632.

4787 DALLAWAY, JAMES. History of the western division of the county of Sussex. 2 vols. (in 3 pts.). Lond. 1815–30; 2nd ed. of pt. 3, by Edmund Cartwright, Lond. 1832.

4788 HORSFIELD, T. W. History, antiquities and topography of the county of Sussex. 2 vols. Lewes, 1835.

4789 LOWER, M. A. A compendious history of Sussex, with an index to the first 20 vols. of the *Sussex Arch. Soc. Coll.* 2 vols. Lewes, 1870.
Cf. also idem, *Worthies of Sussex*, Lewes, 1865; and *A survey of the coast of Sussex made in 1587 by Thomas Palmer and Walter Coverte, deputy lieutenants*, Lewes, 1870.

(4) *Town Histories and Records*

Cf. Gross (1), nos. 1120a, 1105, 1111, 2646, 2647a.

4790 THE ACTS OF THE DEAN AND CHAPTER of the cathedral church of Chichester, 1472–1544. By W. D. Peckham. *Sussex Rec. Soc.* lii (1951–2).

4791 FLEMING, LINDSAY. History of Pagham in Sussex. 3 vols. Sussex, 1949–50.

4792 GODFREY, W. H. Legh Manor, Cuckfield. *Sussex Arch. Coll.* lxxviii (1937), 16–76.

4793 HAY, ALEXANDER. History of Chichester. Chichester, 1804.

4794 HOLLOWAY, WILLIAM. History and antiquities of the ancient town and port of Rye, with incidental notices of the Cinque ports. Lond. 1847.
The best history of Rye. Contains a sixteenth-century version of the custumal of Rye.

4795 THE MANOR OF ETCHINGHAM CUM SALEHURST. By S. P. Vivian. *Sussex Rec. Soc.* liii (1953).

4796 MOSS, W. G. History and antiquities of the town and port of Hastings. Hastings, 1824.
The best history of Hastings. The records of the town are described in *Hist. MSS. Comm. Reports*, xiii.

4797 SALZMAN, L. F. The borough of Lewes in 1498. *Sussex Notes and Queries*, v (1934), 65–70, 97–101.

4798 SURVEYS OF THE MANORS OF ROBERTSBRIDGE, SUSSEX, AND MICHELMARSH, HAMPSHIRE, and of the demesne lands of Halden in Rolvenden, Kent, 1567–70. By R. H. D'Elboux. *Sussex Rec. Soc.* xlvii (1944).

4799 THE TOWN BOOK OF LEWES, 1542–1701. By L. F. Salzman. *Sussex Rec. Soc. Pubs.* xlviii (1947).
pp. 1–47 cover Tudor period.

4800 TRANSCRIPT OF SUSSEX WILLS as far as they relate to ecclesiological and parochial subjects, up to the year 1560. By R. G. Rice and W. H. Godfrey. *Sussex Rec. Soc.* 4 vols., xli, xlii, xliii, xlv (1935–41).

35. WARWICKSHIRE

(1) *Bibliographies*

There is none of importance.

(2) *Local Societies*

4801 BIRMINGHAM AND MIDLAND INSTITUTE. Archaeological section. Transactions. Birmingham, 1871 ff. *Midland Record Society*. Transactions. 6 vols. [Birmingham], 1897–1902.

4802 DUGDALE SOCIETY. Publications. Oxf. 1921 ff.
Devoted to the history of Warwickshire, notably to Stratford-on-Avon.

4803 THE MIDLAND ANTIQUARY, 4 vols. Birmingham, 1882–7.

4804 WARWICKSHIRE ANTIQUARIAN MAGAZINE. 8 pts. Warwick, 1859–77.

(3) *County Histories and Records*

V.C.H. Warwick has been completed in 7 vols. and index. Lond. 1904–51.

4805 ECCLESIASTICAL TERRIERS OF WARWICKSHIRE PARISHES. Vol. i A–Li. By D. M. Barratt. *Dugdale Soc.* xxii (1955).
Elizabethan and Stuart terriers.

4806 DUGDALE, WILLIAM. The antiquities of Warwickshire. Lond. 1656; by William Thomas, 2 vols. Lond. 1730.

4807 WARWICKSHIRE FEET OF FINES. Vol. iii 19 Edw. III (1345)–24 Hen. VII (1509). By Lucy Drucker. *Dugdale Soc.* xviii (1943).

(4) *Town Histories and Records*

Cf. also Gross (1), nos. 1139, 1141–4, 2683–6.

4808 BLACK BOOK OF WARWICK. By Thos. Kemp. Warwick, 1898.
Contains extracts from corporation books 1–27 Eliz. See also, by the same editor, *The book of John Fisher, town clerk and deputy recorder*, 1580–8, Warwick, 1900.

4809 FOX, L. Some new evidences of leet activity in Coventry, 1540–1. *E.H.R.* lxi (1946), 235–43.

4810 HARRIS, M. D. Life in an old English town: a history of Coventry. Lond. 1898.
Valuable. See also her *Story of Coventry,* Lond. 1911.
There are older histories of Coventry by Benj. Poole, Lond. 1870; and by Thomas Sharpe, Lond. 1871. For the records of the town, cf. *A calendar of the books, charters, &c. of the city of Coventry,* by J. C. Jeaffreson, Coventry, 1896; M. D. Harris, *Unpublished documents relating to town life in Coventry, Trans. R.H. Soc.,* 4th ser., iii (1920). 103–24; idem, *Coventry leet books,* 4 vols., Coventry, 1907–13.

4811 LEE, SIDNEY. Stratford upon Avon, from the earliest times to the death of Shakespeare. Lond. 1885; 1907.
There is a good bibliography of the histories and records of the town in Chambers, *Shakespeare* (3643), i, 1–2.

4812 THE RECORDS OF THE GUILD OF HOLY TRINITY. St. Mary, St. John the Baptist, and St. Katherine of Coventry. By Mary Harris. *Dugdale Soc.* xiii (1935); vol. ii by Geoffrey Templeman, ibid. xix (1944).

(5) *Other Works*

Cf. 4839.

4813 GAY, E. F. The rise of an English country family, Peter and John Temple, to 1603. *Hunt. Lib. Quar.* i (1938), 367–90.
At Burton Dasset in Warwickshire and Stowe in Buckinghamshire. Cf. *Handlist of the Stowe collection in the Hunt. Lib., California,* by J. G. Jenkins, *Buck. Rec. Soc. List and Index,* vol. i (1956).

36. WESTMORLAND

(1) *Bibliographies*

There is none of importance.

(2) *Local Societies*

Cf. 4290.

(3) *County Histories and Records*

4814 FERGUSON, R. S. A history of Westmorland. 2 vols. Lond. 1894.

4815 FLEMING, D. A description of the county of Westmorland. By G. F. Duckett. Lond. 1882.
A seventeenth-century work of special value for the Tudor period.

4816 AN INVENTORY OF THE HISTORICAL MONUMENTS IN WESTMORLAND. Lond. 1936.

4817 NICOLSON, JOSEPH, and BURN, R. History and antiquities of the counties of Westmorland and Cumberland. 2 vols. Lond. 1777.

37. WILTSHIRE

(1) *Bibliographies*

There is none of importance.

(2) *Local Societies*

4818 WILTSHIRE ARCHAEOLOGICAL AND NATURAL HISTORY Society. Magazine. Devizes, 1854 ff.

4819 WILTSHIRE NOTES AND QUERIES. Lond. 1893–1916.

4820 WILTS. RECORD SOCIETY. Publications. Salisbury, 1896–1903, 1939 ff.

(3) *County Histories and Records*

For county records, cf. 1305; for quarter session records, cf. 208. On taxation, cf. 1211. Vols. i (pt. i), ii, iii, v, vii of *V.C.H. Wilts.* have been published. Lond. 1953–7.

4821 AUBREY, JOHN. Collections for the natural and topographical history of Wiltshire. By Thomas Phillips. 2 vols. Lond. 1821–38; with extensions by John Britton, Lond. 1847; further extended by J. E. Jackson, Devises, 1862.

4822 HOARE, R. C., and others. Modern history of Wiltshire. 6 vols. Lond. 1822–45.
Vol. vi contains a good history of Salisbury.

4823 MEMOIRS ILLUSTRATIVE of the history and antiquities of Wiltshire and the city of Salisbury. *Arch. Soc. of Great Britain* (1851).

(4) *Town Histories and Records*

Cf. Gross (1), nos. 1146–8, 1151–2, 2688–9, 2695–8. Cf. also no. 4822 *supra*.

4824 BENSON, ROBERT, and HATCHER, HENRY. Old and new Sarum or Salisbury. Lond. 1843.
The best history of Salisbury.

4825 GUILD STEWARD'S BOOK of the borough of Calne, 1561–1688. By A. W. Mabbs. *Wilts. Arch. and Nat. Hist. Soc.*, Rec. Branch, vii (1953).

4826 LIST OF WILTSHIRE BOROUGH RECORDS earlier in date than 1836. By Maurice Rathbone. *Wilts. Arch. and Nat. Hist. Soc.*, Rec. Branch, v (1951).

4827 MASTERS, G. J. E. Collections for a history of West Dean. Devizes, 1885.

4828 SCROPE, G. J. P. History of the manor and ancient barony of Castle Combe. [Lond.] 1852.

38. WORCESTERSHIRE

(1) *Bibliographies*

4829 BURTON, J. R., and PEARSON, F. S. Bibliography of Worcestershire. 2 vols. *Worcs. Hist. Soc.* ix (1898–1903).

4830 NICHOLS, C. L. A bibliography of Worcestershire. Worcester, 1899.

(2) *Local Societies*

4831 WORCESTERSHIRE ARCHAEOLOGICAL SOCIETY. Transactions. Worcester, 1923 ff.

4832 WORCESTERSHIRE HISTORICAL SOCIETY. Publications. Worcester, 1893 ff. Suspended 1916–26.

(3) *County Histories and Records*

For quarter session records, cf. 1306. *V.C.H. Worcs.* is complete in 4 vols. and index. Lond. 1901–24.

4833 ANDREWS, T. B. Memorials of old Worcestershire. Lond. 1911 ff.

4834 GAUT, R. C. A history of Worcestershire agriculture and rural evolution. Worcester, 1939.

4835 HABINGTON, THOMAS. A survey of Worcestershire. By John Amphlett. 2 vols. *Worcs. Hist. Soc.* ii, iii (1895–9).
A survey, parish by parish, made between 1560 and 1647.

4836 [NASH, T. R.] Collections for the history of Worcestershire. 2 vols. and suppl. Lond. 1781–99; index by John Amphlett, *Worcs. Hist. Soc.* v (1894–5).

4837 WALTERS, H. B. Inventories of Worcestershire church goods (1552). *Trans. Worcs. Arch. Soc.*, n.s., xvii (1941), 11–21; n.s., xxvii (1951), 47–62; n.s., xxix (1953), 38–49; n.s., xxx (1954), 54–71; n.s., xxxi (1955), 20–38; n.s., xxxii (1956), 38–64.

(4) *Town Histories and Records*

Cf. Gross (1), nos. 1154–9b, 2701, 2702a–b, 2703, 2705, 2705a, 2706a.

4838 THE RED BOOK OF WORCESTER, pt. iii. By M. Hollings. *Worcs. Hist. Soc.* (1939).

(5) *Other Works*

4839 BARNARD, E. A. B. The Sheldons: being some account of the Sheldon family of Worcestershire and Warwickshire. Cambr. 1936.

4840 WILSON, R. A. Canon Davenport's note book on Worcester clergy from the reformation to the restoration. *Trans. Worcs. Arch. Soc.*, n.s., xi (1935), 106–18.

39. YORKSHIRE

(1) *Bibliographies*

4841 BOYNE, WILLIAM. The Yorkshire library: a bibliographical account of books on topography relating to the county of York. Lond. 1869.

4842 CATALOGUE OF THE PUBLICATIONS OF THE RECORDS SERIES, 1885–1946. By C. T. Clay. *Yorks. Arch. Soc.* (1948).

4843   FREEMANTLE, W. T. A bibliography of Sheffield and vicinity to . . . 1700. Sheffield, 1911.

(2) *Local Societies*

Cf. also 4351.

4844   BRADFORD HISTORICAL and antiquarian society. The antiquary. Bradford, 1881 ff.

4845   HALIFAX ANTIQUARIAN SOCIETY. Papers. Halifax, 1901 ff.

4846   EAST RIDING ANTIQUARIAN SOCIETY. Transactions. Hull, 1873 ff.

4847   NORTH RIDING RECORD SOCIETY. Publications. 13 vols. Lond. 1884–97.

4848   THORESBY SOCIETY. Publications. Leeds, 1889 ff.

4849   YORKSHIRE ARCHAEOLOGICAL AND TOPOGRAPHICAL association. Yorkshire Archaeological and Topographical Journal, Lond. 1870 ff.; Record Series, Lond. 1885 ff.; a series of extra vols. 1892 ff.; extra series, 1935 ff.
Known after 1893 as *Yorkshire Archaeological and Topographical Society*.

4849a   YORKSHIRE COUNTY MAGAZINE. Bingley, 1891–4. Continuing 4849b.

4849b   YORKSHIRE NOTES AND QUERIES and folklore journal. Bingley, 1885–90.
Continued in 4849a.

(3) *County Histories and Records*

For quarter session records of the West Riding, cf. 1304. Vols. i–iii and index of *V.C.H. Yorks.* have appeared, Lond. 1907–13, and *V.C.H. Yorks., North Riding*, is complete in 2 vols. and index. Lond. 1914–23. On agriculture, cf. 2640; on markets, cf. 2994; on parliament, cf. 1118. Cf. also 2324.

4850   ALLEN, THOMAS. A new and complete history of the county of York. 3 vols. Lond. 1828–31.

4851   BAINES, THOMAS. Yorkshire past and present. 2 vols. (in 4 pts.). Lond. 1871–7.

4852   BROOKS, F. W. Yorkshire and the Star Chamber. *East Yorks. Local Hist. Soc. Ser.* iv. (1954).

4853   CARTRIGHT, J. J. Chapters in the history of Yorkshire . . . in the reigns of Elizabeth, James I, and Charles I. Wakefield, 1872.

4854   A DESCRIPTIVE LIST OF THE PRINTED MAPS of Yorkshire and its ridings, 1577–1900. By Harold Whitaker. *Yorks. Arch. Soc.*, rec. ser., lxxxvi (1933).

4855   EARLY YORKSHIRE CHARTERS. Vol. vii. By C. T. Clay. *Yorks. Arch. Soc.*, extra ser., v (1947).

4856 HUNTER, J. South Yorkshire. 2 vols. Lond. 1828–31.
Cf. idem, *Hallamshire*, by A. Gatty, Lond. 1869.

4857 MONASTIC CHANCERY PROCEEDINGS (Yorkshire). By J. S.
Purvis. *Yorks. Arch. Soc.*, rec. ser., lxxxviii (1934).

4858 PARK, G. R. Parliamentary representation of Yorkshire, 1290–1886.
Hull, 1886.

4859 PAROCHIAL DOCUMENTS OF THE ARCHDEACONRY OF
THE EAST RIDING. An inventory. By M. W. Barley. *Yorks. Arch. Soc.*,
rec. ser., xcix (1931).
Sixteenth and seventeenth centuries.

4860 SMITH, WILLIAM. Old Yorkshire. 5 vols. Lond. 1881–4.

4861 TUDOR PARISH DOCUMENTS OF THE DIOCESE OF YORK.
By J. S. Purvis. Cambr. 1948.

4862 WHITAKER, T. D. A history of Richmondshire in the North Riding
of the county of York. 2 vols. Lond. 1823.
Cf. idem, *History and antiquities of the deanery of Craven*, 3rd ed., by A. W. Morant,
Leeds, 1878.

4863 YORKSHIRE CLERICAL DOCUMENTS, 1554–6. By A. G.
Dickens. *Bodleian Lib. Rec.* iii (1950), 34–40.

4864 YORKSHIRE DEEDS. Vol. viii, by C. T. Clay. *Yorks. Arch. Soc.*,
rec. ser., cii (1940); ix, by M. J. Hebditch, cxi (1948); x, by J. S. Price, cxx
(1955).

(4) *Town Histories and Records*

Cf. also Gross (1), nos. 1160–71, 1173–5, 1176–7b, 1182–7, 1191, 2709–18,
2720–4, 2729–30, 2733, 2735–6, 2740–a, 2743, 2744, 2746–7.

4865 ATKINSON, W. A. The castle and the tolbooth, a sixteenth century
dispute in Knaresborough. *Yorks. Arch. Jour.* xxxiii (1937), 175–95.

4866 BENSON, GEORGE. Later medieval York . . . 1100 to 1603. York,
1919.

4867 BEVERLEY BOROUGH RECORDS, 1575–1821. By J. Dennett.
Yorks. Arch. Soc., rec. ser., lxxxiv (1933).

4868 BROOKS, F. W. A calendar of the early judgments of the Hull Trinity
House, *Yorks. Arch. Soc.*, rec. ser., *Miscellanea*, cxvi (1951), 1–46.
Home for distressed mariners at Hull.

4869 DARBYSHIRE, H. S., and LUMB, G. D. The history of Methley.
Thoresby Soc. xxxv (1937). Cf. also W. B. Crump, *Methley Hall and its
builders. Thoresby Misc.* xi, *Thoresby Soc.* xxxvii (1945), 313–32.

4870 DRAKE, FRANCIS. Eboracum; or the history and antiquities of the
city of York. Lond. 1736.
Valuable.

4871 FASTI PAROCHIALES. Vol. i, Being notes on the advowsons and pre-reformation incumbents of the parishes in the deanery of Doncaster. By A. H. Thompson and C. T. Clay. *Yorks. Arch. Soc.*, rec. ser., lxxxv (1933); ii, cvii (1943).

4872 FROM AN OLD YORK CHRONICLE. *Yorks. Archit. and Arch. Soc. Proc.* i (1935), 36–41.
Extracts, 1578–1709.

4873 HALL, T. W. Sheffield, Hallamshire. Sheffield, 1934.
A descriptive catalogue (3rd vol.) of Sheffield manorial records from the court-roll, 1427 to 1597, also diverse ancient charters and instruments as to Sheffield, notes on Owlerton Hall and index to Liber Finium.

4874 THE RENTAL OF THE FREEHOLDERS and copy-holders of Halifax, 1587–8. By H. P. Kendall. *Trans. Halifax Antiq. Soc.* (1930), 9–45.

4875 SELLERS, MAUD. York in the sixteenth and seventeenth centuries. *E.H.R.* xii (1897), 275–304.
Mainly about the cloth trade.

4876 SHEPPARD, T. The lost towns of the Yorkshire coast. Lond. 1912.

4877 WATERS, S. H. Wakefield in the seventeenth century: a social history of the town and neighbourhood from 1550 to 1710. Wakefield, 1933.

4878 YORK CIVIC RECORDS. By Angelo Raine. Vol. i, *Yorks. Arch. Soc.*, rec. ser., xcviii (1939); ii, ciii (1941); iii, cvi (1942); iv, cviii (1945); v, cx (1946); vi, cxii (1948); vii, cxv (1950); viii, cxix (1953).
Covers the period 1487–1588.

(5) *Other Works*

4879 AVELING, HUGH. The Catholic recusancy of the Yorkshire Fairfaxes. Pt. i. *Biog. Studies*, iii (1955), 69–114.

4880 HORNSEY, MARGARET. John Harrison, the Leeds benefactor and his times. *Thoresby Soc. Misc.* xxxiii (1935), 103–47.

4881 LAWSON-TANCRED, THOMAS. Records of a Yorkshire Manor. Lond. 1937.

4882 LYTHE, S. G. E. The Court of Sewers for the east parts of the East Riding. *Yorks. Arch. Jour.* xxxiv (1938), 11–24.

4883 A RENTAL OF THE BAILIWICK of Whitkirk. By G. E. Kirk. *Thoresby Soc. Misc.* xxxiii (1935), 71–82.
Renewal of rental, 1523.

4884 RUSTON, A. G., and WITNEY, DEVIN. Hooton Pagnell—the agricultural evolution of a Yorkshire village. New York, 1934.

4885 A SIXTEENTH CENTURY RENTAL OF THE MANOR OF TEMPLE NEWSAM and its appurtenances. By G. E. Kirk. *Thoresby Soc. Misc.* xxxiii (1935), 61–70.

4886   WHONE, CLIFFORD. The Paslew estate in Harden and Exley. *Brad. Antiq.*, n.s., viii (1952), 39–67.
During the sixteenth and part of the seventeenth centuries.

4887   WHONE, CLIFFORD. Christopher Danby of Masham and Farnley. *Thoresby Soc. Misc.* xxxvii (1945), 1–28.

XII

SCOTLAND

A. GENERAL

I. BIBLIOGRAPHY

There is no adequate bibliography of Scotland for the Tudor period. Useful lists are found in (4909) and in Brown (4996), vols. i and ii, and attached to the chaps. relating to Scotland in *Cambr. Mod. Hist.* (20), ii and iii. Particularly valuable are the lists and indexes of the publications of Scottish historical Societies begun by Terry (4915–16), and continued by Matheson (4903). The indexes to the *Scottish Historical Review* (discontinued 1928, resumed 1947) are also serviceable. Mitchell and Cash (4904) print in vol. ii, 483–8, a list of Scottish bibliographies, and in vol. i an extensive (uncritical) bibliography of Scottish local history, arranged by counties.

Thomson's discussion of the Scottish public records (4917) is indispensable to the research student, though virtually confined to Scottish records preserved in Scotland.

4888   ALDIS, H. G. A list of books printed in Scotland before 1700, including those printed forth of the realm for Scottish booksellers, with brief notes on the printers and stationers. *Edin. Bibliog. Soc.*, no. 6 (1904).

4889   ANDERSON, P. J. Collections towards a bibliography of the universities of Aberdeen. *Edin. Bibliog. Soc.*, no. 8 (1907).

4890   ANDERSON, P. J. A concise bibliography of the printed and MS. material on the history . . . of the burgh, parish and shire of Inverness. *Aberdeen Univ. Studies*, no. 73 (1917).

4891   BAXTER, J. H. Collections towards a bibliography of St. Andrews. St. Andrews, 1926.

4892   BEVERIDGE, ERSKINE. A bibliography of works relating to Dunfermline and the west of Fife. . . . *Edin. Bibliog. Soc.*, no. 5 (1901).

4893   BLACK, G. F. List of works relating to Scotland. New York, 1916.
A list of works in the New York Public Library. Valuable.

4894   BULLOCH, J. M. Bibliography of the Gordons. *Aberdeen Univ. Studies*, no. 94 (1924).

4895   DICKSON, ROBERT, and EDMOND, J. P. Annals of Scottish printing from the introduction of the art in 1507 to the beginning of the seventeenth century. Cambr. 1890.
Useful bibliography.

4896   HANCOCK, PHILIP. A bibliography of books on Scotland, 1916–50. (In the press.)
Designed as a continuation of Mitchell and Cash (4904).

4897 HAND LIST OF SCOTTISH AND WELSH RECORD PUBLICA-
TIONS. By Peter Gouldesbrough, A. P. Kup, and Idwal Lewis. *Brit. Rec. Assoc. Pub.* Lond. 1954.
Excludes official publications, otherwise comprehensive.

4898 INGLIS, H. R. G., MATHIESON, JOHN, and WATSON, C. B. The early maps of Scotland. Edin., 2nd ed., 1936.

4899 JOHNSTONE, J. F. K. A concise bibliography of the history . . . of Aberdeen, Banff and Kincardine. Aberdeen, 1914.

4900 JOHNSTONE, J. F. K. A concise bibliography of the city of Aberdeen. *Pub. Hist. Assoc. of Scotland*, iii, 1913.

4901 KIPKA, KARL. Maria Stuart in Drama der Weltliteratur. 2 vols. Leipzig, 1905–7.
Covers literature of the seventeenth and eighteenth centuries, with bibliography.

4902 LIVINGSTONE, M. A guide to the public records of Scotland deposited in his majesty's general register house, Edinburgh. Edin. 1905.
Contains valuable explanations. Cf. also *Accessions of public records to the register house since 1905, Scot. Hist. Rev.* xxvi (1947), 26–46.

4903 MATHESON, CYRIL. A catalogue of the publications of Scottish historical and kindred clubs and societies . . . papers relative to Scottish history issued by H.M. stationery office, including the reports of the royal commission on historical mss., 1908–27. Aberdeen, 1928.
Continues 4915–16. Valuable.

4904 MITCHELL, A., and CASH, C. G. Contribution to the bibliography of Scottish topography. 2 vols. *Scot. Hist. Soc.*, 2nd ser., xiv–xv (1917).
Vol. i, topographical; ii, topical: industries, maps, travellers, &c.

4905 MOWAT, JOHN. A new bibliography of Caithness. Wick, 1940.

4906 NATIONAL LIBRARY OF SCOTLAND. Catalogue of MSS. acquired since 1925. Vol. i. Edin. 1938.

4907 NICOLSON, WILLIAM. The Scottish historical library, containing a short view and character of most of the writers, records, registers, law-books, &c. . . . down to the union of the two kingdoms in James I. Lond. 1702; 1776.
A learned and still useful work.

4908 ROBERTSON, A. W. Hand list of bibliography of the shires of Aberdeen, Banff and Kincardine. *New Spalding Club*, no. 11a (1893).

4909 SCOTLAND—A SELECT BIBLIOGRAPHY. By H. W. Meikle, W. Beattie, and H. H. Wood. Cambr. 1950.
The most comprehensive of the short bibliographies; but J. D. Mackie, *Scottish History* (Reader's Guide), Cambr. 1956, contains valuable comments on the books listed.

4910 SCOTT, JOHN. Bibliography of works relating to Mary, queen of Scots, 1544–1700. *Edin. Bibliog. Soc.*, no. 2 (1896).
Describes contents of all works listed, mentions reprs., and tells where copies of 1st eds. can be found. Cf. also J. Scott, *Mary, queen of Scots: an extensive and interesting collection of books and manuscripts for the sixteenth and seventeenth centuries*, Lond. 1905. This is an auction catalogue of the library of John Scott and contains 24 titles not given in the above.

4911 SCOTT, W. R. Scottish economic literature to 1800. Glasgow, 1911. Cf. also T. Keith, *Bibliography of Scottish economic history, Pub. Hist. Assoc. of Scotland,* v (1914), and W. H. Marwick, *A Bibliography of Scottish economic history, Econ. Hist. Rev.* iii (1931), 117–37, and *A bibliography of works on Scottish economic history published during the last twenty years,* ibid., 2nd ser., iv (1952), 376–82.

4913 SOURCES AND LITERATURE OF SCOTS LAW. *Stair Soc.,* i (1936).
Sections contributed by experts. Indispensable for every branch of Scottish history.

4914 STUART, MARGARET, and PAUL, J. B. Scottish family history. Edin. 1929.
The essential guide to writings on Scottish families. *Scottish family histories: a list of books for consultation in the reference library,* George IV Bridge, Edin. 1951, is highly selective, but includes more recent books.

4915 TERRY, C. S. An index to the papers relating to Scotland in the Historical MSS. Commission reports. Aberdeen, 1908.
Covers the publications to 1907 inclusive. Continued to 1927 in Matheson (4903). Does not take the place of the indexes to the reports.

4916 TERRY, C. S. A catalogue of the publications of Scottish historical and kindred clubs and societies, and of the volume relating to Scottish history issued by H.M. stationery office, 1780–1908. Glasgow, 1909.
Indispensable as far as it goes; continued to the end of 1927 in Matheson (4903).

4917 THOMSON, J. M. The public records of Scotland. Glasgow, 1922.
A valuable discussion of types of records and their present state of preservation, with mention of those available in print. Confines itself, however, to records preserved in Scotland.

2. Sources

(a) *Public Records*

Almost all the collections of source materials relating to the history of England in the sixteenth century contain material for the history of Scotland. The English P.R.O., the British Museum, and the libraries of Oxford and Cambridge are all rich in Scottish material. There is much also about Scotland in *Letters and Papers, Henry VIII* (91), in *State Papers, Henry VIII* (92), and in the *Cal. S.P., Foreign* (87), where fuller abstracts are to be found of some items calendared in 4924, down to 1577, *Domestic* (86), *Spanish* (867–8), *Venetian* (992), and *Roman* (991). The dispatches of French ambassadors in England (pp. 66–69 *supra*) are particularly valuable. For materials printed and unprinted, preserved in Scotland, cf. 4902 and 4917; for materials in private collections, cf. 4903 and 4915. The *Salisbury papers* (185) are indispensable for Anglo-Scottish relations; Scottish proclamations are calendared in Steele (1017), vol. ii.

4918 ACCOUNTS OF THE MASTER OF WORKS, Vol. I, 1529–1616. Lond. (In the press.)

4919 ACTA DOMINORUM CONCILII, acts of the lords of council in civil
causes, 1478–1503. By Thos. Thomson (i), Geo. Neilson and Henry Paton
(ii), J. A. Crawford (iii). 3 vols. Edin. 1839–1943; selections, 1501–54, by
R. K. Hannay, Edin. 1932.
Records of judicial proceedings of the council, with which records of other council
business were sometimes intermingled. Valuable for early Scottish legal system.
Vol. ii contains also some *Acta auditorum et dominorum concilii*, 1469–83, and an excellent introduction discussing committees of Scottish parliament and origins of Scottish
law. Vol. iii is published by the *Stair Soc.* viii (1943).
Cf. also A. A. M. Duncan and M. P. McDiarmid, *Scot. Hist. Rev.* xxxiii (1954), 86–88.

4920 ACTA DOMINORUM AUDITORUM, acts of the lords auditors of
causes and complaints, 1466–94. By Thos. Thomson. Edin. 1839.
Proceedings of parliamentary judicial committee in civil causes prior to the evolution
of the Court of Session; cf. 4919, vol. ii, app., for supplementary records. Others are
printed in W. Robertson, *The records of the parliament of Scotland*, i, Edin. 1804.

4922 THE ACTS OF THE PARLIAMENTS OF SCOTLAND. By Thos.
Thomson and Cosmo Innes. 12 vols. Edin. 1814–75.
Vols. ii–iv cover the period 1424–1625. Vol. xii contains the invaluable index and some
supplementary matter.

4923 CALENDAR OF DOCUMENTS RELATING TO SCOTLAND
preserved in the P.R.O., London. By Jos. Bain. 4 vols. Edin. 1881–8.
Extends to 1509. Patent, charter, close, and plea rolls. Omits *Rotuli Scotiae* printed
in 4934.

4924 CALENDAR OF STATE PAPERS RELATING TO SCOTLAND
and Mary, queen of Scots, 1547–1603. By Jos. Bain (vols. i, ii), W. K. Boyd
(vols. iii–ix), W. K. Boyd and H. W Meikle (x), A. I. Cameron (xi), M. S.
Giuseppi (xii), (xiii in press). 12 vols. Edin. and Glasgow, 1898–1952 (in
progress).
Prints very fully, but not always accurately, pertinent material in P.R.O. Undertakes
to include material in B.M. and elsewhere and becomes more complete in this regard
as it proceeds. Completed to the year 1597. A final vol. (xiii) is in the press. With
Letters and Papers, Henry VIII (91), supersedes M. J. Thorpe, *Calendar of the state
papers relating to Scotland*, 2 vols. Edin. 1858.

4925 COMPOTA THESAURARIORUM REGUM SCOTORUM: accounts
of the lord high treasurer of Scotland. By Thos. Dickson (vol. i) and J. B.
Paul (ii–xi). 11 vols. Edin. 1877–1916.
Accounts of casual revenue and of royal expenditure. Selections printed *in extenso*.
Covers period 1473–1566. There is a gap in the records from May 1498 to Feb. 1501.
Valuable prefaces, particularly in vol. i.

4926 THE HAMILTON PAPERS, letters and papers illustrating the political
relations of England and Scotland in the sixteenth century. By Jos. Bain.
2 vols. Edin. 1890–2.
Papers originally in archives of the Council of the North, now in B.M. Consist chiefly
of diplomatic correspondence between England and Scotland. Papers printed in full.
Valuable. Vol. i contains app. of material taken from MSS. at Longleat relative to
Hertford's expeditions, 1542. Cf. 235 for other Hamilton papers.

4927 INQUISITIONUM AD CAPELLAM DOMINI REGIS RETORNA-
TARUM, quae in publicis archivis Scotiae adhuc servantur, abbreviatio. By
Thos. Thomson. 3 vols. Edin. 1811–16.

Records of *retours*, the findings of local juries concerning the transfer of land by
inheritance, and generally the service of heirs, 1547–1699. Entries abridged, very few
before 1603.

4928 INVENTAIRE CHRONOLOGIQUE DES DOCUMENTS relatifs
à l'histoire de l'Écosse conservés aux archives du royaume à Paris. By Alexandre
Teulet. *Abbotsford Club*, no. 14 (1839).

From Alexander III through Mary Stuart. Documents calendared.

4929 PAPIERS D'ÉTAT, pièces et documents inédits ou peu connus relatifs
à l'histoire de l'Écosse au 16ᵉ siècle. By A. Teulet. 3 vols. *Bannatyne Club
pub.*, no. 107 (Paris, 1852–60); later ed. *Relations politiques de la France et de
l'Espagne avec l'Écosse au XVIᵉ siècle*, 5 vols., Paris, 1862.

Eds. substantially the same except for some rearrangement of order of documents and
omission from 2nd ed. of letters printed in facsimile in 1st. In 2nd ed. vols. i–iv contain extracts from French papers covering the period 1515–1603, chiefly from dispatches
of French ambassadors in England; vol. v, Spanish papers printed in full, chiefly from
correspondence of Spanish ambassadors at Paris. Includes much Spanish material of
value for Anglo-Scottish affairs not given in *Cal. S.P., Spanish* (867–8). For additional
French material relating to Scotland, cf. Paul Destray, *Un diplomate français du XVIᵉ
siècle, Philipert du Croc*, Nevers, 1924, which prints forty documents from Du Croc's
papers. Du Croc went on missions to Scotland 1566, 1567, and 1572.

4930 THE REGISTER OF THE PRIVY COUNCIL OF SCOTLAND
(1545–1625). By J. H. Burton (vols. i and ii) and David Masson (iii–xiv).
14 vols. Edin. 1877–98.

Vols. i–iv cover the period 1545–1604, and there is addenda material in vol. xiv (1545–
1625). There is further addenda material (1544–1660) in vol. viii of the 2nd ser. of
privy council registers (cf. Davies (8), no. 3008).

   Minutes of Scottish privy council, printed for the most part in full. Throw light upon
Scottish administrative system as well as upon political affairs.

   Cf. also *Extracts from the registers of the privy council of Scotland and other papers
connected with the method and manner of ryding the Scottish parliament*, 1600–1703, by
James Dennistoun and Alexander Macdonald, *Maitland Club Misc.* (4950) iii, pt. 1.

4931 REGISTRUM MAGNI SIGILLI REGUM SCOTORUM, the register
of the great seal of Scotland. By Thos. Thomson (vol. i), J. B. Paul (ii and
iii), J. M. Thomson (iii–ix), *et al.* 12 vols. Edin. 1814–1914.

Vol. i has been revised by J. M. Thomson, vols. ii–vi cover the period 1424–1608.
Royal charters and grants, printed in abridged form.

4932 REGISTRUM SECRETI SIGILLI REGUM SCOTORUM: the
register of the privy seal of Scotland (1488–1567). By Matthew Livingstone
and D. H. Fleming (i–ii), D. H. Fleming and James Beveridge (iii), James
Beveridge (iv), Gordon Donaldson (v). 5 vols. Edin. 1908–57 (In progress).

Register of writs for which privy seal sufficed and those for which privy seal was on
warrant and great seal necessary. Items before 1497 few and miscellaneous. Some
entries in full, others abridged, especially where corresponding entry appears in register
of great seal (4931).

4933 ROTULI SCACCARII REGUM SCOTORUM, the exchequer rolls
of Scotland (1264–1600). By John Stuart (vol. i), George Burnett (i–xiv),

Æ. J. G. Mackay (xiii–xiv), G. P. McNeill (xv–xxiii). 23 vols. Edin. 1878–
1908.
Vols. ix–xxiii cover the period 1480–1600. Printed in full. Appendixes contain some
land accounts, rentals of crown lands, and responde books. Excellent introduction.

4934 ROTULI SCOTIAE IN TURRI LONDINIENSI et in domo capitulari
Westmonasteriensi asservati (1291–1516). By D. Macpherson, J. Caley,
W. Illingworth, T. H. Horne. 2 vols. Edin. 1814–19.
Cover instructions to border wardens, licences to Scottish students, merchants, &c.,
grants for services in Scotch wars, &c., military instructions. Printed in full.

4935 SELECTED CASES FROM ACTA DOMINORUM CONCILII ET
SESSIONIS, 1532–3. By I. H. Shearer. *Stair Soc.* xiv. 1951.
Has been severely criticized.

(b) *Other Source Collections*

In addition to those cited below, Wright (626), Ellis (290), Lodge (283), and
Hardwicke (280) contain much Scottish material. For material in *Hist. MSS.
Comm. Reports*, cf. 214–61, 4903, and 4915 *supra*.

4936 ANALECTA SCOTICA. By James Maidment. 2 vols. Edin. 1834–7.
Very miscellaneous. No systematic arrangement, but most of sixteenth-century
material in vol. i.

4937 BANNATYNE MISCELLANY. By Walter Scott (vol. i) and David
Laing (vols. ii, iii). 3 vols. Edin. 1827–55.
Miscellaneous sixteenth-century documents.

4938 THE BINNS PAPERS, 1320–1864. *Scot. Rec. Soc.* lxx (1936).

4939 BRILL, E. V. K. A sixteenth century complaint against the Scots. *Scot.
Hist. Rev.* xxvii (1948), 187–91.

4940 CALENDAR OF WRITS PRESERVED AT YESTER HOUSE, 1166–
1625. By C. C. H. Harvey and John MacLeod. *Scot. Rec. Soc.* lx (1930).

4940a CORRESPONDENCE OF SIR PATRICK WAUS of Barnbarroch,
knight, parson of Wigtown; first almoner to the queen; senator of the College
of Justice; Lord of Council and ambassador to Denmark (1540–97). By R. V.
Agnew. 2 vols. *Pub. of Ayrshire and Galloway Arch. Assoc.* xiv (1887).

4941 DOCUMENTS relative to the reception at Edinburgh of the kings and
queens of Scotland, 1561–1650. Edin. 1832.
Selections illustrative of ceremonies and officials' duties printed *in extenso* from register
of privy council and records of Edinburgh.

4942 THE CLAN CAMPBELL: ABSTRACTS OF ENTRIES relating to
the Campbells in the sheriff court books of Argyle, Perth, &c. By H. Paton.
8 vols. Edin. 1913–22.

4943 EARLY TRAVELLERS IN SCOTLAND. By P. H. Brown. Edin.
1891.
Contains translations of the accounts of: Pedro de Ayala, 1498; Andrea Trevisano,
1498; Peder Swave, 1535; Nicander Nucius, 1545; Jean de Beaugue, 1548; Estienne
Perlin, 1551; Fynes Moryson, 1598; Henri, duc de Rohan, 1600; map of Scotland
from Mercator's atlas, 1595.

4944 EXCERPTA SCOTICA. By James Maidment. Edin. 1825.
Contains miscellaneous papers of the sixteenth century.

4945 THE GORDON LETTERS. By John Stuart. *Spalding Club Misc.* iii (1846).
Few sixteenth-century royal letters to the earl of Huntly. Articles of agreement between the earl of Huntly and the Regent Murray.

4946 LETTERS TO THE ARGYLL FAMILY from Elizabeth, queen of England, Mary, queen of Scots, King James VI, King Charles I, King Charles II and others. By Alexander Macdonald. *Maitland Club Pub.*, no. 50 (1839).
Includes 24 letters 1520–1600 from MSS. in general register house given in facsimile or printed *in extenso*. App. of charters and commissions.

4947 MISCELLANEA SCOTICA, 4 vols. Glasgow, 1818–20.
Reprs.: Monipennie (4991); Buchanan's *Chamaeleon* (4973); Monro's *Western Isles* (5026); *Navigation of King James V round Scotland*, by Nicholas d'Arfeville; *History of life and death of King James V*, Paris, 1612.

4948 MISCELLANEOUS PAPERS principally illustrative of events in the reigns of Queen Mary and King James VI. By W. J. Duncan. *Maitland Club Pub.*, nol 26 (1834).
Largely ecclesiastical, from MSS. in the Scots College at Paris.

4949 MISCELLANY OF THE ABBOTSFORD CLUB. By James Maidment. Edin. 1837.
Miscellaneous documents of the reign of James VI.

4950 MISCELLANY OF THE MAITLAND CLUB. By Alexander Macdonald, James Dennistoun, Joseph Robertson. 4 vols. Edin. 1833–47.
Vol. i (pts. 1 and 2), ii (pt. 2), and iii (pt. 1) are specially important for the sixteenth century. Only pt. 1 of vol. iv was published.

4951 NUGAE DERELICTAE. By James Maidment and Robert Pitcairn. Edin. 1822; repr. with introductory note by Thomas G. Stevenson, Edin. 1888.
Miscellaneous tracts, notes, &c., printed or repr. in very limited ed. Includes contemporary account, probably by an eye-witness, of battle of Flodden.

4952 NUGAE SCOTICAE. Miscellaneous papers illustrative of Scottish affairs 1535–1781. By James Maidment, G. R. Kinloch, and Charles Baxter. Edin. 1829.
Includes notices regarding early drama in Scotland, sixteenth and seventeenth centuries.

4953 PAPERS FROM THE CHARTER CHEST AT DUN. By John Stuart. *Spalding Club Misc.* iv (1849).
Chiefly the papers of John Erskine, laird of Dun, who took part in the reformation.

4954 PAPERS FROM THE CHARTER CHEST AT GORDON CASTLE. By John Stuart. *Spalding Club Misc.* iv (1849).
Chiefly bonds of manrent, friendship, &c.; rentals and other miscellaneous papers of the sixteenth century.

4955 PAPERS from the collection of Sir William Fraser. By J. R. N. Macphail. *Scot. Hist. Soc.*, 3rd ser., v (1924).
Includes materials relating to Paldy fair, 1599–1641, and to fishing in the Ithan, 1534–67.

4956 THE PITTODRIE PAPERS, 1524–1628. By John Stuart. *Spalding Club Misc.* ii (1842).
Chiefly papers of Thomas Erskine, secretary to James V

4957 REGISTRUM HONORIS DE MORTON. By Thomas Thomson, Alexander Macdonald, Cosmo Innes. 2 vols. *Bannatyne Club*, no. 94 (1853).
Vol. i, papers, 1529–1607; ii, charters. Many royal letters and other correspondence of interest from the charter rooms of Morton and Lochleven. Especially valuable for Regent Morton.

4958 SADLER, SIR RALPH. The state papers and letters of. By Arthur Clifford. 2 vols. Edin. 1809.
Valuable for Anglo-Scottish relations 1539–47, the rising in the north 1569, and Mary Stuart's imprisonment in England. An earlier ed. of Sadler's papers (Edin. 1720) covers simply his Scottish negotiations temp. Henry VIII.

4959 SCOTIA REDIVIVA, a collection of tracts illustrative of the history and antiquities of Scotland. Vol. i (all published). Edin. 1826; later ed. (*Tracts illustrative of the . . . antiquities of Scotland*), Edin. 1836.
Reprs. among other tracts Johnston's history (4982) and a tract on the baptism of son of James VI, 1594.

4960 SCOTLAND BEFORE 1700 from contemporary documents. By P. H. Brown. Edin. 1893.
Contains: Descriptions of country from Major (4986), Boece (4969), Buchanan (4972), and Leslie (4983); proceedings of the justice-aire of Jedburgh, 1510; extracts from lord high treasurer's accounts, 1515–42; descriptions of Edinburgh by Dunbar (*c.* 1500) and Alexander Alesius, 1529 (also in 4937); statutes concerning sports, 1440–1565 (also in 4936); trade regulations, 1529–31 (also in 4950); progress of Regent Moray, 1568 (also in 4937); witchcraft trial, 1576 (also in 5415); Monro's *Western Isles* (5026); Leslie's map of Scotland, 1578; Munster's map of Edinburgh, 1559.

4961 SELECTION from the papers of the family of Boyd of Kilmarnock, 1468–1590. *Abbotsford Club Misc.* (1837).

4962 THE SPOTTISWOODE MISCELLANY. 2 vols. Edin. 1844–5.
Vol. i contains: account of the battle of Balrinnes, 3 Oct. 1594; letter addressed to James VI by Johne Harisone, giving an account of his visit to Barbary to liberate slaves; documents relative to the palace of Linlithgow, 1540–1648. Vol. ii contains: charter of possessions of templars and hospitallers, 1563; kirk sessions of Perth, extracts, 1577–1634; papers relative to the submission of Angus Macdonald of Isla to James VI, 1596 (from Balcarres papers).

4963 WARRENDER PAPERS. By A. I. Cameron. 2 vols. *Scot. Hist. Soc.*, 3rd ser., xviii–xix (1931–2).
Miscellaneous papers, printed *in extenso*, 1527–1603. Vol. i covers period 1542–87. Valuable, particularly for Anglo-Scottish relations. Many ecclesiastical papers in this collection (in Register House) remain unprinted.

(c) *Chronicles and Diaries (covering all or most of the period)*

The histories of Buchanan (4972), Leslie (4983), and Lindsay of Pitscottie (4984), the Diurnal (4979) and the memoirs of Sir James Melville (4989) are particularly valuable. Reference should also be made to the three great church historians of the period, Knox (5449), Calderwood (5482), and Spottiswoode (5530). The English chronicles of Hall (312), Grafton (306), Holinshed (314), and Camden (302) contain much on Scotland.

4964 [AYSCU, EDWARD.] A historie contayning the warres, treaties, marriages, and other occurrences betweene England and Scotland, from King

William the conqueror untill the happy union of them both in our gratious King James. Lond. 1607.

Abridgement of previous histories, set out to glorify James VI and justify his claim to the English throne and sustain the religious settlement.

4965 BANNATYNE, GEORGE. Memorials, 1545–1608. By David Laing. *Bannatyne Club*, no. 35 (1829); *Hunterian Club*, no. 1 (11 pts.) (1873–1901).

The *Bannatyne Club* ed. contains a memoir of Bannatyne by Sir Walter Scott, repr. in *Hunterian Club* ed., pt. viii.

4966 BANNATYNE, GEORGE. The Bannatyne manuscript. Written in tyme of pest, 1568. By W. Tod Ritchie. Vol. i. *Scot. Text Soc.*, 3rd ser., v (1934).

4967 BANNATYNE, RICHARD. Memorials of transactions in Scotland, 1549–73. By J. G. Dalyell. Edin. 1806; by Robert Pitcairn, *Bannatyne Club*, no. 51 (1836).

1806 ed. from MS. in Advocates' library; 1836 ed. from university of Edinburgh MS. Author secretary to John Knox. Memorials largely composed or enlarged by Knox. Compiled in form of a diary of occurrences. Knox left Bannatyne his notes for the continuation of his history of the reformation to be edited by him. 1806 ed. confined to 1570–3.

4968 BIRREL, ROBERT. Diary, 1532–1605. In *Fragments of Scottish History*. By J. G. Dalyell. Edin. 1798.

Diary of an Edinburgh burgess of no apparent party. Touches briefly and without comment on all important events and some minor ones.

4969 BOECE, HECTOR. Historia gentis Scotorum a prima gentis origine. Paris, 1527; trans. into Scotch by John Bellenden (*Hystory and cronikles of Scotland*). Edin. 1531; rep. Edin. 1821.

A new ed. of Bellenden's trans. in 2 vols. by R. W. Chambers, E. C. Batho, and H. W. Husbands, has been published by the *Scot. Text Soc.*, 3rd ser., x and xv (1938, 1941). Cf. also George Watson, *The Mar Lodge translation of the history of Scotland, Scot. Text Soc.*, 3rd ser., xvii (1946). An English version of Boece's description of Scotland, but not his whole history, by Wm. Harrison, forms an introduction to the sect. on Scotland in Holinshed (314). A metrical version of the history by Wm. Stewart made c. 1530 was first printed in *Rolls Series*, 3 vols., 1858 (ed. by W. B. Turnbull) under title *The Buik of the Croniclis of Scotland*. Boece goes only to the accession of James III (1460) but his description of Scotland is valuable for the sixteenth century.

Later chronicles incorporate much of this history, notably Buchanan (4972) and Chalmers (4975). On Bellenden's trans. cf. *Scot. Hist. Rev.* xvii (1919), 5–15; xix (1921), 196. Cf. also J. B. Black, *Aberdeen Univ. Studies* (1937).

4970 BRANTÔME, P. DE BOURDEILLE, SEIGNEUR DE. Œuvres. By M. L. C. Lalanne. 12 vols. Paris, 1864–96.

Vol. iii (*Recueil des dames*) contains valuable comments on Scottish situation.

4971 BUCHANAN, GEORGE. Opera omnia. By Thomas Ruddiman. 2 vols. Edin. 1715; 1725.

4972 BUCHANAN, GEORGE. Rerum Scoticarum historia. Edin. 1582; Geneva, 1583; English trans., Lond. 1690; 2 vols. Edin. 1762; by James Aikman, 4 vols. Glasgow, 1827.

The important Protestant history.

4973 BUCHANAN, GEORGE. Vernacular writings. By P. H. Brown.
Scot. Text Soc. xxvi (1892).
Most important is the *Opinion anent the reformation of the universitie of Saint Andros.*
Contain also *Ane admonition to the trew lordis mantenaris*; *Chamaeleon*; two letters from
Buchanan to Sir Thomas Randolph.

4974 CHAMBERS (or CHALMERS), DAVID. Discours de la légitime succession des femmes aux possessions de leurs parens: et de gouvernement des
princesses aux empires et royaumes. Paris, 1579.
Author a senator of the college of justice and an ardent partisan of Mary Stuart.

4975 CHAMBERS (or CHALMERS), David. Histoire abbregée de tous les
roys de France, Angleterre et Escosse, mise en ordre par forme d'harmonie:
contenant aussi un brief discours de l'ancienne alliance, & mutuel secours
entre la France et l'Escosse. Paris, 1579.

4976 CHAMBERS (or CHALMERS), DAVID. La recherche des singularitez
plus remarquables, concernant l'estat d'Escosse. . . . Paris, 1579.
Sometimes issued with 4975 under that title.

4977 THE CHRONICLE OF HOLYROOD. By M. O. Anderson and A. O.
Anderson. *Scot. Hist. Soc.*, 3rd ser., xxx (1938).

4978 A CHRONICLE OF THE KINGS OF SCOTLAND from Fergus the
first to James the sixth in the year 1611. By J. W. Mackenzie. *Maitland Club*,
no. 8 (1830).
First part trans. from French of David Chambers (4975); continuation to 1573 apparently trans. from Buchanan (4972); continuation 1573–1611 written after 1603 by
unknown contemporary.

4979 A DIURNAL OF REMARKABLE OCCURRENTS that have passed
within the country of Scotland since the death of King James IV till the year
1575. By Thomas Thomson. *Bannatyne Club*, no. 43; *Maitland Club*, no. 23
(1833); repr. *Book of the old Edinburgh club*, xvi (1928).
Author apparently a minor official in Edinburgh writing contemporaneously 1557–72.
Valuable chiefly for local affairs.

4980 HERRIES, LORD (Sir John Maxwell). Historical memoirs of the reign
of Mary, queen of Scots, and a portion of the reign of King James the sixth.
By Robert Pitcairn. *Abbotsford Club*, no. 6 (1836).
Covers period 1542–71. From a transcript in Advocates library (216) of the original
at Scots college, Douai, destroyed in French revolution. Author staunch adherent of
Mary, queen of Scots, died 1583. Continued by 8th Lord Herries, a Stuart adherent,
c. 1667.

4981 INNES OF LEARNEY, THOMAS. Sir David Lindsay of the Mount,
Lord Lyon king of arms, 1538–55. *Scot. Notes and Queries*, 3rd ser., xiii
(1935), 145–8, 170–3, 181–3.

4982 JOHNSTON, ROBERT. Roberti Johnstoni, Scoto-Britanni, historiarum
libri duo, continentes rerum Britannicarum vicinarumque regionum historias
maxime memorabiles. Amsterdam, 1642.
An English trans. by T. Middleton of the part relating to Scotland was published in
Lond. 1646 under the title *The history of Scotland during the minority of King James*,
repr. in 4959, *supra*. The complete work of which the above formed only a part

published in Amsterdam, 1655, under title *Historia rerum Britannicarum et multarum Gallicarum Belgicarum et Germanicarum politicarum quam ecclesiasticarum ... 1572 ... 1628*. The author, an Edinburgh burgess, died 1639.

4983 LESLEY, JOHN. De origine, moribus et rebus gestis Scotorum, libri decem. Rome, 1578; [Rome?], 1675; repr. (in part) in Jebb (5186), i, 148–236.
Engl. trans.: (1) *The history of Scotland from the death of James I, 1436 to ... 1561*, by T. Thomson, *Bannatyne Club*, no. 38 (1830); (2) *The history of Scotland wrytten first in latin by ... Jhone Leslie ... and translated in Scottish by father James Dalrymple ... 1596*, by E. G. Cody and W. Murison, 2 vols., *Scot. Text Soc.* v, vi (1888–95). Thomson's ed. is printed from a MS. made for presentation to Mary, queen of Scots; Cody and Murison collate this text with that of Dalrymple. A Latin MS. of Leslie in the Vatican containing a meagre account of the period 1562–71 is printed in Eng. trans. by Forbes-Leith (5460), pp. 84–126. Leslie (bp. of Ross) was a partisan of Queen Mary and a Roman Catholic.

4984 LINDSAY, ROBERT, of Pitscottie. The history of Scotland from 21 February, 1436 to March 1565. To which is added a continuation by another hand till August, 1604. By Robt. Freebairn. Edin. 1728; by J. G. Dalyell, 2 vols., Edin., 1814; by Æ. J. G. Mackay, 3 vols., *Scot. Text Soc.* xlii, xliii, lx (1899–1911).
Written between 1576 and 1579, author a Protestant Fifeshire farmer. First part a trans. of the 18th book of Boece (4969). Lindsay's narrative from 1565 to 1575 printed for first time in Mackay's ed.

4985 LYNDSAY, DAVID. Collected works. By H. Charteris. Edin. 1568; by G. Chalmers, 3 vols. 1806; by John Small, 5 vols. (in progress). *E.E.T.S.* xi, xix, xxxv, xxxvii, xlvii (1865–71); by David Laing, 3 vols., Edin. 1879; by Douglas Hamer, 4 vols., *Scot. Text Soc.*, 3rd ser., i, ii, vi, viii (1931–6).
Lyndsay's writings are satirical of political and social conditions, especially of the king and the church. At least 12 eds. of his collected works were published before 1640. Laing's and Hamer's eds. contain full bibliographies.

4986 MAJOR, JOHN. De gestis Scotorum. Paris, 1521; Edin. 1740; Eng. trans. by A. Constable, *Scot. Hist. Soc.* x (1892).
Events narrated of earlier date, but description of country valuable for sixteenth century. Constable's ed. contains a life of Major by Æ. J. G. Mackay and a bibliography of Major and his disciples by T. G. Law.

4987 MARJOREYBANKS, GEORGE. Annals of Scotland, 1514–91. By J. G. Dalyell. Edin. 1814.
Author an Edinburgh burgess.

4988 MAITLAND, RICHARD, and KINGSTON, VISCOUNT. The history of the house of Seytoun ... to the year 1687.... By J. Fullarton. *Bannatyne Club*, no. 31; *Maitland Club*, no. i (1829).

4989 MELVILLE, SIR JAMES, of Halhill. Memoirs of his own life, 1549–93. By George Scott. Lond. 1683; best ed. by Thomas Thomson, *Bannatyne Club*, no. 18; *Maitland Club*, no. 21 (1827); by A. F. Steuart, Lond. 1929.
Author at Scottish court of Mary and James VI, sympathetic with Mary.

4990 MELVILLE, JAMES. Diary, 1556–1601. By G. R. Kinloch. *Bannatyne Club*, no. 34 (1829); by Robert Pitcairn, *Wodrow Soc.*, no. 3 (1842).
By the nephew of the presbyterian leader, Andrew Melville. Useful for ecclesiastical and political affairs. Written in form of autobiography rather than as diary. Not to be confused with 4989.

4991 MONIPENNIE, JOHN. The abridgement or summarie of the Scots chronicles ... from Fergus I to James VI. [Lond.], 1612; 1633; 1820; repr. in *Miscellanea* (4947).
Very brief.

4992 MOYSIE, DAVID. Memoirs of the affairs of Scotland ... from 1577 ... to ... 1603. Together with a discourse of the conspiracy of the earl of Gowry. By Walter Ruddiman. Edin. 1755; best ed. by James Dennistoun, *Bannatyne Club*, no. 39; *Maitland Club*, no. 3 (1830).
Discourse of the conspiracy of Gowrie not in *Maitland* and *Bannatyne Club* ed. Valuable for chronicle of court, military, and other public affairs.

4993 SATIRICAL POEMS of the time of the reformation. By James Cranstoun. 2 vols. *Scot. Text Soc.*, xx, xxiv, xxviii, xxx (1891–3).
Fullest collection of contemporary ballads and broadsides.

4994 UBALDINO, PETRUCCIO. Descrittione del regno di Scotia. Antwerp, 1588; by Andrew Coventry, *Bannatyne Club*, no. 32 (1829).
Relation of a Florentine miniature painter residing in England at the time of Edward VI and Elizabeth. Drawn very largely from Boece (4969).

3. LATER WORKS

Tytler (5019) and Burton (4999) are the best of the earlier general histories of Scotland. Brown (4996) and Lang (5007) the best of the more recent works.

4995 BARBÉ, L. A. Sidelights on the history, industries, and social life of Scotland. Lond. 1919.
Interesting information and comment on Perkin Warbeck in Scotland, food control, fisheries and mines, and various items which appear in lord high treasurer's accounts.

4996 BROWN, P. H. History of Scotland. 3 vols. Cambr. 1908–1909.
Not yet superseded though out of date in its approach and emphasis.

4997 BROWN, P. H. Surveys of Scottish history. Glasgow, 1919.
Includes: Intellectual influences of Scotland on the continent; a forgotten scholar of the sixteenth century; the Scottish nobility and their part in national history.

4998 BURNS, J. H. John Irland and 'The Meroure of Wyssdome'. *Innes Rev.* vi (1955), 77–98.
Scottish diplomatist.

4999 BURTON, J. H. History of Scotland. 7 vols. Edin. 1853; 1867–70; 8 vols. and index. Edin. 1873–4.
One of the good older histories; best on legal aspects.

5000 COWAN, SAMUEL. The lord chancellors of Scotland from the institution of the office to the treaty of Union. 2 vols. Lond. 1911.
Several, particularly of the earlier notices, are brief owing to scanty material.

5001 CUNNINGHAM, AUDREY. The loyal clans. Cambr. 1932.
An important study of highland history in relation to government policy.

5002 A DICTIONARY OF THE OLDER SCOTTISH TONGUE. By W. A. Craigie. Pts. i–xvii. Oxf. 1933–57 (in progress).

5003 DUNBAR, ARCHIBALD. Scottish kings. Edin. 2nd ed. 1906.
Useful for chronology and as a guide to sources.

5004 DURKAN, JOHN. The beginnings of humanism in Scotland. *Innes Rev.* iv (1953), 5–24.

5005 ELDER, J. R. Spanish influences in Scottish history. Glasgow, 1920.
A convenient collection of information, but presentation not altogether critical, consistent, or reliable.

5006 KEITH, ROBERT. The history of the affairs of church and state in Scotland from the beginning of the reformation . . . to the retreat of Queen Mary into England, anno 1568. Edin. 1734; best ed. by J. P. Lawson (vols. i and ii) and J. C. Lyon (vol. iii), 3 vols. *Spottiswoode Soc.* 1844–50.
The earliest history of the period based on laborious original research. Prints many documents, augmented in *Spottiswoode Soc.* ed.

5007 LANG, ANDREW. A history of Scotland. 4 vols. Edin. 1900–7; 2nd (corrected) ed. vols. i and ii (1900–3).
Able, but not dispassionate.

5008 LEE, MAURICE. James Stewart, earl of Moray: a political study of the Reformation in Scotland. New York, 1953.

5009 MACGREGOR, ALASDAIR. The sea-dogs of Scotland. *Quar. Rev.* cclxix (1937), 329–40.

5010 MACKENZIE, A. M. The rise of the Stewarts (to 1513). Lond. 1935.

5011 MACKENZIE, A. M. The Scotland of Queen Mary and the religious wars, 1513–1628. Lond. 1936.
This and 5010 form a general history of the period. 'Nationalist' and anti-presbyterian in tone.

5012 MACKENZIE, W. C. The highlands and isles of Scotland. Edin. 1937; rev. ed. 1949.
Three chapters on relations between west highlands and Ireland.

5013 MATHIESON, W. L. Politics and religion. A study in Scottish history from the reformation to the revolution (1550–1695). 2 vols. Glasgow, 1902.
A suggestive essay.

5014 MENZIES, W. B. Robert Wedderburn, notary and poet. *Scot. Text Soc.*, 3rd ser., iv (1933), 81–87.

5015 OMOND, G. W. T. The lords advocates of Scotland from the close of the fifteenth century to the passing of the reform bill. 2 vols. Edin. 1883.
Contains some general matter of interest in addition to the lives. About 100 pages are devoted to the period before 1600.

5016 ROBERTSON, WILLIAM. History of Scotland during the reigns of Queen Mary and King James VI till his accession to the throne of England. 2 vols. Lond. 1759; 1787.
Contains an app. of original documents and a dissertation on the Darnley murder and the casket letters. The 11th ed. (1787) was the last corrected by the author.

5017 SCOT, JOHN, of Scotstarvet. The staggering state of the Scots statesmen for one hundred years, 1550–1650. By Walter Goodall. Edin. 1754.
Brief biographies. Author a prominent Scottish lawyer, died 1670.

5018   A SOURCE BOOK OF SCOTTISH HISTORY. By W. Croft Dickinson, Gordon Donaldson, and I. A. Milne. Vol. ii (1424-1567), iii (1567-1707). Edin. 1953-4.
Very useful.

5019   TYTLER, P. F. History of Scotland. 9 vols. Edin. 1828-43; 5th ed., 4 vols. Lond. 1873-7.
Best of older histories. Emphasizes political narrative rather than social conditions.

B. LOCAL HISTORY

The best bibliography is 4904. For bibliographies of particular towns, counties, and regions, cf. 4889-92, 4899-4900, 4908, and the bibliographies in 5075, 5079, 5081, 5084, 5087, and 5093. For the history of the English border reference should be made to ch. iii *supra* (pp. 116-17). The publications of the *Spalding Club* are useful for the history of the north-east. Cf. also local court records (5373-4). Also valuable are the inventories of the *Royal Commission on the Ancient Monuments of Scotland*.

1. Sources for Regional History

5020   ANCIENT MONUMENTS IN SCOTLAND: a list corrected to 31 December, 1954. Edin. 1955.
Cf. also V. G. Childe and W. D. Simpson, *Scotland, Illustrated guide to ancient monuments . . .*, vol. vi, Edin. 1955.

5021   COLLECTANEA DE REBUS ALBANICIS, consisting of original papers and documents relating to the history of the highlands and islands of Scotland. *Iona Club*, no. 1 (1847).
Miscellaneous papers, many in the sixteenth century; notably on the history of the fisheries in the Isles (1566-1635), on trade between the Highlands and the Lowlands (1565-1622), on the preservation of game (1584-1628), on Highland dress, &c.

5022   DOCUMENTS RELATING TO ORKNEY AND SHETLAND, 1438-1563. By John Stuart. *Spalding Club Misc.* v (1852).

5023   HIGHLAND PAPERS. By J. R. N. Macphail. 4 vols. *Scot. Hist. Soc.*, 2nd ser., v, xii, xx; 3rd ser. xxii (1914-34).
Papers from Gregory's collection for his *History of the western isles* (5077). Vol. i includes papers relating to the murder of the laird of Calder, 1591-6; vol. ii includes documents relating to *The ewill trowbles of the Lewes*, 1566-76.

5024   AN INVENTORY OF LAMONT PAPERS, 1231-1897. By Norman Lamont. *Scot. Rec. Soc.* liv (1914).
Calendar of papers of clan Lamont. Useful for west highlands. Pt. i, inventory, 1231-1599.
   Further additions (1442-1859) and corrections by the same editor were published by *Scot. Rec. Soc.*, 1918.

5025   JOHNSTON, A. W., and JOHNSTON, AMY. Orkney and Shetland records. Vol. i. *Viking Soc. for Northern Research Pub.* (1907-13).

5026 MONRO, DONALD. Description of the western isles of Scotland, called Hybrides, in 1549. Edin. 1774; 1884.
Also printed in 4947 and 4960 and with M. Martin, *Description of the western islands of Scotland*, Stirling, 1934.

5027 OBSERVATIONS OF MR. DIONESS CAMPBELL, deane of Limerick, on the west isles of Scotland, 1596. By Joseph Robertson. *Maitland Club Misc.* (4950) iv, pt. i.
Report to inform Robert Cecil with a view to the employment of clans against Tyrone in Ireland.

5028 OPPRESSIONS OF THE SIXTEENTH CENTURY in the islands of Orkney and Zetland from original documents. By David Balfour. *Maitland Club*, no. 75; *Abbotsford Club*, no. 31 (1859).
Prints *in extenso* complaints of inhabitants of islands against the oppression of Lord Robert Stuart, 1575–6, and commission of James VI to try him for oppression; also similar supplication to parliament, 1592.

5029 RECORDS OF THE EARLDOM OF ORKNEY, 1299–1614. By J. S. Clouston. *Scot. Hist. Soc.*, 2nd ser., vii (1914).
Chiefly charters, deeds, &c.

2. Town Records

For lists of burgh records cf. 4913 and also 4897.

(a) *Edinburgh*

5030 ACTS, STATUTES AND OTHER PROCEEDINGS of the provost, bailies, and council of the burgh of Edinburgh, 1529–31. By James Dennistoun and Alexander Macdonald. *Maitland Club Misc.* (4950), ii, pt. i.

5031 CHARTERS AND OTHER DOCUMENTS relating to the city of Edinburgh. By J. D. Marwick. *Scot. Burgh Rec. Soc.* vii (1871).

5032 EDINBURGH RECORDS. By Robert Adam. 2 vols. Edin. 1899.
Vol. i contains bailies' accounts 1544–66 and town treasurers' accounts 1552–67. Vol. ii contains dean of guild's accounts 1552–67.

5033 EXTRACTS FROM THE RECORDS of the burgh of Edinburgh (1403–1603). By J. D. Marwick (vols. i–v) and Marguerite Wood (vi). 6 vols. *Scot. Burgh Rec. Soc.* ii–vi (1869–92), extra vol. 1927.

5034 EXTRACTS FROM THE RECORDS of the burgh of the Canongate near Edinburgh, 1561–88. By James Dennistoun and Alexander Macdonald. *Maitland Club Misc.* (4950), ii, pt. ii.

5036 PROTOCOL BOOK OF JOHN FOULAR 1500–28. By Walter MacLeod and M. Wood. 5 vols. *Scot. Rec. Soc.* (1930–53).

5037 PROTOCOL BOOK OF JAMES YOUNG, 1485–1515. By H. M. Paton and Gordon Donaldson. *Scot. Rec. Soc.*, pts. i–viii (1941–52).

5038 REGISTER OF APPRENTICES of the city of Edinburgh, 1583–1666.
By F. J. Grant. *Scot. Rec. Soc.* xxviii (1906).

5038a ROLL OF EDINBURGH BURGESSES and guild brethren, 1406–
1700. By C. B. Watson. *Scot. Rec. Soc.*, ix (1929).

5039 WOOD, MARGUERITE. The lord provosts of Edinburgh, 1296–
1932. Edin. 1931.

(b) *Glasgow*

5040 ABSTRACTS OF PROTOCOLS of the town clerks of Glasgow to
1600. By Robert Renwick. 11 vols. Glasgow, 1894–1900.

5041 BURGH RECORDS OF THE CITY OF GLASGOW, 1573–81. By
John Smith. *Maitland Club*, no. 16 (1832); index, 1834.
Selections from the earliest extant vol. of Glasgow records, especially court records,
ordinances, treasurers' accounts.

5042 THE BURGESSES AND GUILD BRETHREN of Glasgow, 1573–
1750. By J. R. Anderson. *Scot. Rec. Soc.* lvi (1925).

5043 CHARTERS AND OTHER DOCUMENTS relating to the city of
Glasgow. By J. D. Marwick and Robert Renwick. 2 vols. *Scot. Burgh Rec.
Soc.* xiv, xvii (1894–1906).
Vol. i, covering 1175–1649, was published in two parts, pt. ii in 1894, and pt. i in 1897.
An app. to vol. ii relates to the years 1434–1648.

5044 EXTRACTS FROM THE RECORDS of the burgh of Glasgow. By
J. D. Marwick and Robert Renwick. 12 vols. *Scot. Burgh Rec. Soc.* xi ff.
(1876–1927).
Vol. i covers period 1573–1642.

(c) *Other towns*
Aberdeen

5045 ABERDEEN COUNCIL LETTERS (1552–1633). By L. B. Taylor.
Lond. 1943; 1950.

5046 EXTRACTS FROM THE COUNCIL REGISTER of the burgh of
Aberdeen, 1398–1625. By John Stuart. 2 vols. *Spalding Club*, nos. 12, 19
(1844–8).

5047 RECORDS OF OLD ABERDEEN, 1157–1903. By A. M. Munro.
2 vols. *New Spalding Club*, nos. 20, 36 (1899, 1909).
Extracts from the Council, Convener Court, Hammermen, trade, &c.

5048 REGISTER OF BURGESSES of guild and trade of the burgh of Aberdeen, 1399–1631. *New Spalding Club Misc.* i (1890).

5049 TESTIMONIAL BOOK OF ABERDEEN. Testimoniales gratit be ye
Baillies sen ye last day of Merche, 1589. By L. B. Taylor. *The Miscellany of
the Third Spalding Club*, vol. ii (1940), 1–85.

Ayr

5050 AYR BURGH ACCOUNTS, 1534–1624. Trans. by G. S. Pryde. *Scot.
Hist. Soc. Pub. for 1935–6*, 3rd ser., xxviii (1937).

Banff

5051 THE ANNALS OF BANFF. By William Cramond. 2 vols. *New Spalding Club*, nos. 8, 10 (1891, 3).
Vol. i contains extracts from court book, 1546–53 and church accounts, 1547–52.

Dundee

5052 CHARTERS, WRITS, AND PUBLIC DOCUMENTS of the royal burgh of Dundee, 1292–1880. By William Hay. Dundee, 1880.
Cf. also 5611.

Dunfermline

5053 THE BURGH RECORDS OF DUNFERMLINE . . . courts, sasines, &c., 1488–1584. By E. Beveridge. Edin. 1917.

5054 EXTRACTS FROM THE BURGH RECORDS OF DUNFERMLINE in the 16th and the 17th centuries. By Andrew Shearer. Dunfermline, 1951.

Elgin

5055 THE RECORDS OF ELGIN, 1234–1800. By William Cramond and Stephen Ree. 2 vols. *New Spalding Club*, nos. 27, 35 (1903, 8).
Vol. i includes extracts from burgh court book, 1540–85; ii, extracts from church records, 1584 ff.

Haddington

5056 CHARTERS AND WRITS concerning the royal burgh of Haddington, 1318–1543. By J. G. Wallace-James. Haddington, 1895.

Inverness

5057 RECORDS OF INVERNESS. By William Mackay, H. C. Boyd, and G. S. Laing. 2 vols. *New Spalding Club*, nos. 38, 43 (1911, 24).
Vol. i, extracts from burgh court books, 1556–86; ii, 1602–88.

Kirkcaldy

5058 KIRKCALDY BURGH RECORDS, 1562–1907. By L. MacBean. Kirkcaldy, 1908.

Lanark

5059 EXTRACTS FROM THE RECORDS of the royal burgh of Lanark, 1150–1722. By Robert Renwick. Glasgow, 1893.
Contains also charters and other documents.

Paisley

5060 CHARTERS AND DOCUMENTS relating to the burgh of Paisley 1163–1665 and extracts from the records of the town council, 1594–1620. By W. M. Metcalfe. Paisley, 1902.

Peebles

5061 CHARTERS AND DOCUMENTS relating to the burgh of Peebles, 1165–1710. By William Chambers and Robert Renwick. 2 vols. *Scot. Burgh Rec. Soc.* x, xxiv (1872, 1910).
Vol. ii (1652–1714) includes an app. (1367–1665).

Perth

5062 THE CHRONICLE OF PERTH: a register of remarkable occurrences
chiefly connected with that city from the year 1210 to 1668. By James Maidment. *Maitland Club*, no. 10 (1831).
Meagre until after 1600.

Stirling

5063 CHARTERS AND OTHER DOCUMENTS relating to the royal burgh
of Stirling, 1124–1705. By Robert Renwick. Glasgow, 1884.

5064 EXTRACTS FROM THE RECORDS of the royal burgh of Stirling.
By Robert Renwick. 2 vols. Glasgow, 1887–9.
Vol. i covers 1295–1666, and app. to vol. ii covers 1471–1752.

3. LATER WORKS

(a) *General*

It is impossible to include the many valuable parish histories. For guides to them,
cf. Mitchell and Cash (4904) and Hancock (4896). There is a useful alphabetical
list of parishes, showing the county, diocese, presbytery, and commissariot in
which each lay, in Keith, *Scottish bishops*, 1824 ed.

5065 CHALMERS, GEORGE. Caledonia. 8 vols. Paisley, 1887–1902.

5066 THE ORDNANCE GAZETTEER OF SCOTLAND: a graphic and
accurate description of every place in Scotland. By F. H. Groome. 6 vols.
Glasgow, 1901.
Still a most useful work of reference. Has bibliographies.

5067 ORIGINES PAROCHIALES SCOTIAE: the antiquities . . . of the
parishes of Scotland. By Cosmo Innes. 2 vols. (3 pts.) *Bannatyne Club*,
no. 97 (1851–5).
Covers only dioceses of Glasgow, Argyll, the Isles, Ross, and Caithness. Invaluable
as far as it goes.

(b) *Districts and Counties*

5068 ARMSTRONG, R. B. The history of Liddesdale, Eskdale, Ewesdale,
Wauchopdale and the Debatable Land. Vol. i (all published). Edin. 1883.

5069 BAIN, R. History of the ancient province of Ross, the county palatine
of Scotland. . . . Dingwall, 1899.

5070 BARRY, GEORGE. History of the Orkney Islands. Edin. 1805; 2nd
ed. by James Headrick, Lond. 1908.

5071 BROWNE, J. A history of the highlands and of the highland clans.
4 vols. Glasgow, 1838; Lond. 1849.

5072 BUCHAN, J. W., and PATON, HENRY. A history of Peeblesshire.
3 vols. Glasgow, 1925–7.

5073 CLOUSTON, J. S. A history of Orkney. Kirkwall, 1932.
Cf. 5070.

5074 KELTIE, J. S. A history of the Scottish highlands. 2 vols. Edin. 1875.
Is virtually an enlarged ed. of 5071.

5075 DOUGLAS, G. A history of the border counties: Roxburgh, Selkirk and Peebles. *County Histories of Scotland Series.* Edin. 1899.
Bibliography.

5076 GILLIES, W. A. In famed Breadalbane. Perth, 1938.

5077 GREGORY, DONALD. History of the western highlands and isles of Scotland from . . . 1493 to . . . 1625. Edin. 1836; 1881.
Useful.

5078 IRVING, JOHN. History of Dumbartonshire. Dumbarton, rev. ed. 1917–24.

5079 LEES, J. C. A history of the county of Inverness. *County Histories of Scotland Series.* Edin. 1897.
Bibliography.

5080 MACKAY, A. The history of the province of Cat [Caithness and Sutherland] . . . to the year 1615. By D. Beaton. Wick, 1914.

5081 MACKAY, Æ. J. G. A history of Fife and Kinross. *County Histories of Scotland Series.* Edin. 1896.
Bibliography.

5082 MACKERLIE, P. H. History of the lands and their owners in Galloway. 5 vols. Edin. 1870–8; 2 vols. Paisley, 1906.

5083 MARWICK, H. Ancient monuments in Orkney. *Ancient Monuments and historic buildings.* Edin. 1952.

5084 MAXWELL, H. A history of Galloway and Dumfries. *County Histories of Scotland Series.* Edin. 1896; 1900.
Bibliography.

5085 METCALFE, W. M. History of the county of Renfrew. . . . Paisley, 1905.

5086 MILLER, J. The lamp of Lothian, or the history of Haddington. . . . Haddington, 1844; 1900.

5087 PATERSON, J. History of the counties of Ayr and Wigtown. 5 vols. Edin. 1863–6.

5088 RAMPINI, C. A history of Moray and Nairn. *County Histories of Scotland Series.* Edin. 1897.
Bibliography.

5089 RIDPATH, G. The border history of England and Scotland. . . . Lond. 1776; rev. by P. Ridpath, Berwick, 1848.

5090 SHAW, LACHLAN. The history of the province of Moray. 3 vols. Glasgow, 1882.

5091 WARDEN, A. J. Angus or Forfarshire. 5 vols. Dundee, 1880.

5092 WATT, J. C. The Mearns of old, a history of Kincardineshire . . . to the seventeenth century. Edin. 1914.

5093 WATT, W. A history of Aberdeen and Banff. *County Histories of Scotland Series.* Edin. 1900.
Bibliography.

(c) *Towns*

5094 CRAMOND, W. Municipal life in Elgin in the sixteenth century; being extracts from the Burgh and Head Court Book of . . . Elgin, 1570–85. Elgin, 1898.

5095 DICKIE, W. Scottish burghal life in the sixteenth and seventeenth centuries, illustrated by extracts from Kirkcudbright records. *Trans. Dumfries and Galloway Nat. Hist. and Antiq. Soc.* xxiv (1906).

5096 AN INVENTORY OF THE ANCIENT AND HISTORICAL MONUMENTS OF THE CITY OF EDINBURGH. *Royal Comm. on the Anc. Mons. of Scot.* Edin. 1951.

5097 KEITH, THEODORA. Municipal elections in the royal burghs of Scotland prior to the union. *Scot. Hist. Rev.* xiii (1916), 111–25.

5098 MACLEOD, D. History of the castle and town of Dumbarton. Dumbarton, 1877; 1878.

5099 MARWICK, J. D. Early Glasgow; a history . . . to the year 1611. By Robert Renwick. Glasgow, 1911.

5100 M'DOWALL, W. History of the burgh of Dumfries, with notices of Nithsdale, Annandale and the western border. Edin. 1867; revd. ed. 1873; 1887; 1906.

5101 MAXWELL, A. The history of old Dundee. . . . Dundee, 1884.

5102 MUNRO, A. M. The common good of the city of Aberdeen, 1319–1887. Aberdeen, 1888.

5103 MURRAY, DAVID. Early burgh organization in Scotland as illustrated in the history of Glasgow and of some neighbouring burghs. Vols. i, ii. Glasgow, 1924–32.
Excellent, both on political and economic organization, vol. i deals with Glasgow; vol. ii with Rutherglen, Lanark, Prestwick, Newton-upon-Ayr, Ayr.

5104 RENWICK, R. Peebles during the reign of Queen Mary. Peebles, 1903.

5105 RENWICK, ROBERT, LINDSAY, JOHN, and TODD, G. E. History of Glasgow. 3 vols. Glasgow, 1921–34.

5106 ROYAL BURGH OF AYR. By A. I. Dunlop. Edin. 1953.
Articles by various contributors.

5107 WILSON, D. Memorials of Edinburgh in the olden time. 2 vols. Edin. 1848; rev. and enlarged, 1891.

(d) *Families and clans*

For bibliography see Stuart and Paul (4914). There are a number of notes on Highland families published in *Trans. of the Gaelic Soc. of Inverness,* cf. Terry (4916), pp. 70 ff. For the Campbells, cf. 4942. The publications of the *Spalding Club* are especially valuable for the families of the north-east. In 4913 there is a list of the most important family histories and collections, pp. 262–3. Among the MS. sources, the records of testaments are especially valuable (cf. *The Commissary courts*, p. 461). Few parish registers are extant for this period: cf. *Detailed list of the old parochial registers of Scotland*, Edin. 1872. The testaments are with the national records in the [old] Register House, the parish registers in the custody of the Registrar General in the New Register House.

5108 ADAM, FRANK. The clans, septs and regiments of the Scottish highlands. Edin. 3rd ed. 1935.

5109 BLACK, G. F. The surnames of Scotland. New York, 1946.

5110 ELLIOTT, G. F. S. The border Elliotts and the family of Minto. Edin. 1897.

5111 FOSTER, J. J. The Stuarts: being illustrations of the personal history of the family . . . in the sixteenth, seventeenth, and eighteenth centuries. 2 vols. Lond. 1902.

5112 FRASER, J. Chronicles of the Frasers . . . 916–1674. By W. Mackay. *Scot. Hist. Soc.* xlvii (1905).

5113 FRASER, WILLIAM. His memorials of various Scottish noble families contain much useful material on the history of Scotland in the sixteenth century. All of them were published in Edinburgh between 1859 and 1897, as follows: Montgomeries, earls of Eglinton, 2 vols. 1859; Maxwells of Pollok, 2 vols. 1863; chiefs of Colquhoun, 2 vols. 1869; The Lennox, 2 vols. 1874; earls of Cromartie, 2 vols. 1876; The Douglas book, 4 vols. 1885; Family of Wemyss, 3 vols. 1888; earls of Haddington, 2 vols. 1889, The Melvilles, earls of Melville, and the Leslies, earls of Leven, 3 vols. 1890; earls, &c., of Annandale, 2 vols. 1894; Lords Elphinstone, Balmerino, Coupar, 2 vols. 1897.
For a complete list of Fraser's publ. cf. *D.N.B.* (9), Supplement vol., art. W. Fraser

5114 LINDSAY, LORD. Lives of the Lindsays, or a memoir of the house of Crawford and Balcarres, &c. 4 vols. Wigan, 1840; 3 vols. Lond. 1849; 1858.

5115 MACDONALD, A., and MACDONALD, A. The clan Donald. 3 vols. Inverness, 1896–1904.

5116 MACKECHNIE, HECTOR. The Lamont clan. Edin. 1938.

5117 MACKINTOSH, A. M. Historical memoirs of the house and clan of Mackintosh and of the clan Chattan. 2 vols. Lond. 1880.
Cf. also idem, *The Mackintoshes and clan Chattan*, Edin. 1903.

5117a THE SCOTS PEERAGE. By J. B. Paul. 9 vols. Edin. 1904–14.
The standard Scottish peerage, based upon Wood's ed. of Douglas's *Peerage of Scotland*.

5117b RENILSON, JOHN. Ferniehirst castle and the Kers. *Hist. Berwick Nat. Club*, xxxi (1950), 208–20.

5118 SKENE, W. F. The highlanders of Scotland. 2 vols. Lond. 1837; by A. MacBain, Stirling, 1902.

5119 TAYLER, HENRIETTA. History of the family of Urquhart. Aberdeen, 1946.

5120 THE WEDDERBURN BOOK. 2 vols. s.l. 1898.
Valuable for the Wedderburns, sixteenth-century poets and reformers.

C. POLITICAL HISTORY

1. PERIOD 1485-1561

(a) *Sources*

In addition to the works cited below, reference should be made to the Acts of Parliament (4922), Acts of the Lords of the Council in Civil Causes (4919), Acts of the Lords Auditors (4920), Register of the Privy Council (4930), the registers of the great seal (4931) and the privy seal (4932), the exchequer rolls (4933), and the lord high treasurer accounts (4925). Proclamations covering the period are in Steele (1017), ii.

The best contemporary or nearly contemporary accounts are in Buchanan (4972) and Leslie (4983), Lindsay of Pitscottie (4984) and *A Diurnal* (4979). For Anglo-Scottish relations most of the sources are given in 87, 91, 1352, 4924, and 4926. For Franco-Scottish relations, cf. 4929 and the correspondence of French ambassadors in England given in ch. ii *supra* (pp. 66–69). There is a considerable amount of important material in the *Spanish* (867) and *Venetian* (992) *Calendars*.

5121 BEAUGUE, JEAN DE. L'histoire de la guerre d'Escosse; traitant comme le royaume fut assaily, et en grand partie occupé par les Anglois, et depuis rendu paisable à sa reyne, et reduit en son ancien estat et dignité. Paris, 1556; by comte de Montalembert, Bordeaux, 1862. Trans. *The martial achievements of the Scots nation.* By Patrick Abercromby. 2 vols. Edin. 1711–15; best ed. by Joseph Bain, *Maitland Club*, no. 2 (1830).
Record of expedition sent to Scotland by Henry II of France. Author accompanied expedition as personal friend of commander. Extract describing country printed in 4943.

5122 BERTEVILLE, LE SIEUR. Récit de l'expedition en Écosse l'an 1546 [*sic*], et de la battayle de Muscleburgh . . . au roy Edouard VI. By David Constable. *Bannatyne Club*, no. 10 (1825).
Berteville, a retainer of Warwick, took part in expedition. Prints facsimile of contemporary plan of the battle of Pinkie. The date, of course, should be 1547.

5123 BODRUGAN, NICHOLAS, alias ADAMS. An epitome of the title that the kynges maiestie of Englande hath to the sovereigntie of Scotland. . . . Lond. 1548; later ed. in 5124, app.
Written after battle of Pinkie. Addressed to Edward VI.

5124 THE COMPLAYNT OF SCOTLAND wyth ane exortatione to the thre estaits to be vigilante in the deffens of their public veil. s.l. 1549. By John Leyden. Edin. 1801; best ed. by J. A. H. Murray, 2 vols. *E.E.T.S.*, extra ser., xvii, xviii (1872–3).
Appeal to Scots to drive out English with help of French alliance. Author a partisan of French, a churchman still Catholic, probably a native of the border. Murray's ed. includes app. of tracts which preceded *Complaynt* and to which latter was probably an answer; cf. 5123, 5126, 5127, 5133.

5125 A CONTEMPORARY ACCOUNT of the battle of Flodden. . . . *Soc. of Antiq. of Scot. Proc.* vii (1870), 141–52.

5126 A DECLARATION, conteynyng the just causes and consyderations, of this present warre with the Scottis, wherin also appereth the trewe and right title that the kinges most royall maiesty hath to the soverayntie of Scotlande. Lond. 1542; later ed. in 5124, app.
Henry VIII's vindication of his declaration of war on the Scots and reassertion of his title to Scottish throne.

5127 AN EPISTLE or exhortation to unitie and peace sent from the lorde protector and others the kynges most honorable counsaill of England to the nobilitie, gentlemen, and commons, and al others the inhabitauntes of Scotlande. Lond. 1548; later ed. in 5124, app.
Conciliatory tract issued by Somerset after the battle of Pinkie. A Latin ed. was issued simultaneously in 1548.

5128 EPISTOLAE Jacobi quarti, Jacobi quinti et Mariae, regum Scotorum ... 1505–45. By Thomas Ruddiman. 2 vols. Edin. 1722–4.
Miscellaneous selection from the Balfour (Denmilne) MSS. in the Advocates' library (216). Many of the letters are calendared in 5136 and 5137.

5129 EXCERPTA E LIBRIS DOMICILII domini Jacobi quinti regis Scotorum 1525–33. By J. H. Mackenzie, James Mackenzie, and Robert Graham. *Bannatyne Club*, no. 54 (1836).
Extracts from household books.

5130 THE FLODDEN DEATH ROLL. *Scot. Antiq.* xiii (1899), 101–11, 168–72.
A list compiled from various sources of important people slain at Flodden.

5131 FLODDEN PAPERS: diplomatic correspondence between the courts of Scotland and France, 1507–17. By Marguerite Wood. *Scot. Hist. Soc.*, 3rd ser., xx (1933).

5132 FOREIGN CORRESPONDENCE with Marie de Lorraine, queen of Scotland. By Marguerite Wood. 2 vols. *Scot. Hist. Soc.*, 3rd ser., iv, vii (1923–5).
Papers from Balcarres collection, 1537–57. To the year 1542 these letters contain chiefly family news and discussions of French affairs. Those of the years 1542–57 very valuable for Scottish affairs. French letters printed in full, others summarized. Most papers in collection of the time of Henry VIII are calendared in *Letters and papers* (91); some from Henry II of France (1545–54) were printed in *Maitland Club Misc.* (4950), i, pt. 2. For the Balcarres papers, cf. 216; for Mary of Lorraine's Scottish correspondence, cf. 5141.

5133 [HARRYSONE, JAMES.] An exhortacion to the Scottes, to conforme them selfes to the honorable, expedient and godly union betwene the two realmes of Englande and Scotlande. Lond. 1547; later ed., in 5124 app.
Author a Scot who appeals to Scots to accept English claims.

5134 INSTRUCTIONS TO THE FRENCH AMBASSADOR, 30 March 1550. By Gladys Dickinson. *Scot. Hist. Rev.* xxvi (1947), 154–67.

5135 THE LATE EXPEDICION IN SCOTLANDE ... of ... the erle of Hertforde ... 1544. Lond. 1544; by J. G. Dalyell (*Fragments of Scottish*

History), Edin. 1798; in *Rare and curious collection of historical tracts and pamphlets*, Edin. 1886.

'Sent to Lord Russel, lord privie seal, from the kynges armye there, by a frende of hys.' This narrative largely incorporated in Grafton's *Chronicle* (306). Cf. also *A diary of the expedition of 1544*, by W. A. J. Archbold, *E.H.R.* xvi (1901), 503–7.

5136 THE LETTERS OF JAMES THE FOURTH, 1505–13. Calendared by R. K. Hannay, edited by R. L. Mackie and Anne Spilman. *Scot. Hist. Soc.*, 3rd ser., xlv (1953).

5137 THE LETTERS OF JAMES V. By R. K. Hannay and Denys Hay. Edin. 1954.

5138 LETTERS OF PATRICK, EARL OF BOTHWELL, and articles which he undertook to maintain at the appointment of the king of France, 1548–9. By David Laing. *Bannatyne Club Misc.* (4937), iii, 403–16.

5139 MISSION BE BECCARIE DE PAVIE, BARON DE FOURQUE-VAUX, en Écosse, 1543: documents originaux du fonds Fourquevaux. By Gladys Dickinson. Oxf. 1948.

5140 PATTEN, WILLIAM, Londoner. The expedicion into Scotlande of ... Edward, duke of Soomerset ... set out by way of diarie. Lond. 1548; by J. G. Dalyell (*Fragments of Scottish History*), Edin. 1798; in *Eng. Garner* (279), iii, 51–155.

Exhorts Scots to join with English in allegiance. Largely quoted by Holinshed (314). Used by Hayward for his *Reign of Edward VI* (562).

5141 THE SCOTTISH CORRESPONDENCE of Mary of Lorraine ... 1543–60. By A. I. Cameron. *Scot. Hist. Soc.*, 3rd ser., x (1927).

For Mary of Lorraine's foreign correspondence, see 5132.

5142 SCOTISH FFEILDE. By J. P. Oakden. *Chetham Soc.*, n.s., xciv (1935). On Flodden.

5143 TWO MISSIONS OF JACQUES DE LA BROSSE: an account of the affair of Scotland in the year 1543 and the journal of the siege of Leith, 1550. By Gladys Dickinson. *Scot. Hist. Soc.*, 3rd ser., xxvi (1942).

Cf. also 5148.

(b) *Later Works*

Keith (5006), Pinkerton (5167), Brown (4996), and Mathieson (5013) are the best general accounts. For the history of the reformation in Scotland, cf. sect. E *infra* (pp. 461–70). Laing's ed. of Knox's history and Dickinson's (5449) are particularly valuable. The best life of Cardinal Beaton is in 5502.

On Anglo-Scottish relations during the period Froude (340), Fisher (339), Pollard (363), and Mackie (354) should be consulted. Cf. also 5168 and 5174.

5144 BAPST, EDMOND. Les mariages de Jacques V. Paris, 1889.

5145 BAXTER, J. W. William Dunbar, a biographical study. Edin. 1952.

Cf. also M. P. McDiarmid, William Dunbar, *Scot. Hist. Rev.* xxxiii (1954), 46–52.

5146 BECKER, P. W. De rebus inter Joannem et Christianum II Daniae reges, ac Ludovicum XII et Jacobum IV, Galliae Scotiaeque reges, a 1511–14 actis. Copenhagen, 1835.

App. of documents.

5147 BRUCE, GAINSFORD. The English expedition into Scotland in 1542. *Arch. Aeliana*, 3rd ser., iii (1907), 191–212.

5148 BRYCE, W. M. A French mission to Scotland in 1543. *Soc. of Antiq. of Scot. Proc.* xlii (1908), 243–52.

5149 BUTLER, L. W. G. Battle of Flodden, 1513. *United Service Mag.* (Lond.) cxxiv (1899), 399–413.
Military account of battle.

5150 CAW, J. L. Portraits of the first five Jameses. *Scot. Hist. Rev.* vii (1909), 113–18.

5151 CONWAY, AGNES. Henry VII's relations with Scotland and Ireland, 1485–98. Cambr. 1932.
Documents in app. particularly valuable for royal finances in Ireland.

5152 DICKINSON, GLADYS. Some notes on the Scottish army in the first half of the sixteenth century. *Scot. Hist. Rev.* xxviii (1949), 133–45.

5153 DRUMMOND, WILLIAM. The history of Scotland from the year 1423 until the year 1542. Lond. 1655; Edin. 1711.
The 1711 ed. is in his *Works*, pp. 1–116. Cf. Conway (5151), p. xxiii.

5154 ELLIS, HENRY. Observations upon a household book of King James the fifth of Scotland, preserved in the library of the . . . earl of Aberdeen . . . containing the accompt of one year from September 4th, 1538 to September 13th, 1539. *Arch.* xxii (1829), 1–12.

5155 FERGUSSON, JAMES. 1547: The Rough wooing. *Blackwood's Mag.* cclxii (1947), 183–94.
Discusses Somerset's campaign and the fight at Pinkie. Cf. 5122.

5156 HODGKIN, THOMAS. The battle of Flodden. *Arch. Aeliana*, n.s., xvi (1894), 1–45.
Cf. also C. J. Bates, *Flodden Field*, *Arch. Aeliana*, n.s., xvi (1894), 351–72.

5157 INGLIS, J. A. Sir Adam Otterburn of Redhall, king's advocate, 1524–38. Glasgow, 1935.

5158 JERNINGHAM, H. E. H. An affray at Norham Castle and its influence on Scotch and English history. *Scot. Antiq. Soc.* xv (1901), 179–88.
Event occurred 1499.

5159 KENNETH, BROTHER. Sir David Lindsay, reformer. *Innes Rev.* i (1950), 79–91.

5160 LANG, ANDREW. The cardinal and the king's will. *Scot. Hist. Rev.* iii (1906), 410–22.
Cf. Simpson in *E.H.R.* xxi (1906), 112–18, and Lang, ibid., 317–19.

5161 LEATHER, G. F. T. New light on Floddon [*sic*]. Berwick upon Tweed, 1937.

5162 LETTERS OF THE PAPAL LEGATE in Scotland, 1543. By R. K. Hannay. *Scot. Hist. Rev.* xi (1911), 1–26.
Six letters from the Vatican archives printed *in extenso* with introductory note.

5163 MACKENZIE, W. M. The secret of Flodden. Edin. 1931.
Prints translation of contemporary Italian poem *La Rotta de Scocesi*.

5164 M'KERLIE, E. M. H. Mary of Guise-Lorraine, queen of Scotland. Lond. 1931.

5165 MACKIE, J. D. The English army at Flodden: the armies compared—a victory of organization; the secret of Flodden. *Misc. of the Scot. Hist. Soc.* viii (1951).

5165a MACKIE, R. L. King James IV of Scotland. Edin. 1958.

5166 PAUL, J. B. Edinburgh in 1544 and Hertford's invasion. *Scot. Hist. Rev.* viii (1910), 113–31.

5167 PINKERTON, JOHN. The history of Scotland from the accession of the house of Stuart to that of Mary. 2 vols. Lond. 1797.
App. to vol. ii contains correspondence. Valuable for the period it covers.

5169 SETON, BRUCE. The distaff side: a study in matrimonial adventure in the fifteenth and sixteenth centuries. *Scot. Hist. Rev.* xvii (1919), 272–87.
Cf. *Queen Margaret Tudor, Scot. Hist. Rev.* xviii (1920), 155.

5170 SMITH, G. G. The two chancellors: James Betoun and Thomas Wolsey. *Scot. Rev.* x (1887), 337–68.
A good analysis of Beaton's position.

5171 SINCLAIR, G. A. The Scots at Solway Moss. *Scot. Hist. Rev.* ii (1904), 372–7.

5172 STUART, M. W. The Scot who was a Frenchman. Lond. 1940.
John Stewart, duke of Albany (1481–1536).

5174 TUDOR INTRIGUES IN SCOTLAND. *Scot. Rev.* xxiv (1894), 225–52.
Relates chiefly to the activities of Margaret Tudor.

2. MARY STUART

(a) *Sources*

(1) *General*

Most of the documentary material about Mary is printed in *Cal. S.P., Scotland* (4924). The *Spanish Calendar* (868) and the correspondence of the French ambassadors in England (ch. ii *supra*, pp. 66 ff.) are also of first-rate importance, as is Teulet's collection (4929). The standard ed. of her correspondence is in Labanoff (5181), though he omits the Casket letters as forgeries. Among private collections the *Salisbury MSS.* (185) are very important. Much documentary material is printed in the appendixes to Keith (5006). The Acts of Parliament (4922), the registers of the privy council (4930), of the great seal (4931), and of the privy seal (4932), the exchequer rolls (4933), and the lord treasurer's accounts (4925) are all important. Mary's extant proclamations are given in Steele (1017), ii.

Of the contemporary chroniclers Buchanan (4972) and Knox (5449) her enemies, and Leslie (4983) her friend, are the most valuable. Melville's memoirs (4989) are also important.

The voluminous contemporary controversial literature associated with every important event in her career is adequately treated in Scott (4910). Only a few of the more important pamphlets are included below. Many are reprinted in Anderson (5177) and Jebb (5186).

5175 [BUCHANAN, GEORGE.] De Maria Scotorum regina, totaque eius contra regem coniuratione, foedo cum Bothuelio adulterio, nefaria in maritum crudelitate & rabie, horrendo insuper & deterrimo eiusdem parricidio: plena & tragica plane historia. s.l. 1571.
Trans. into Scotch (s.l. 1571) under the title *Ane detectioun of the doinges of Marie quene of Scottes.* . . . Subsequent eds. appeared at St. Andrews 1572, and at Lond. 1572. A French trans. with a supplement on the duke of Norfolk was published in 1572 nominally at Edin., but probably at La Rochelle. Later English eds. 1651, 1689. Repr. in *Buchanan's Works* (4971) and in Jebb (5186). A bitter attack on Mary. The second part was probably not by Buchanan.

5176 COLLECTION DE MANUSCRIPTS, LIVRES, ESTAMPES ET OBJETS D'ART RELATIFS À MARIE STUART, reine de France et d'Écosse. By Mrs. G. T. Bliss. Paris, 1931.

5177 COLLECTIONS RELATING TO MARY, queen of Scots. By James Anderson. 4 vols. Edin. 1727-8.
Important collection of contemporary pamphlets with a few documents.

5178 [ELDER, JOHN.] The copie of a letter sent into Scotlande, of the arivall and landynge, and moste noble marryage of the most illustre Prynce Philippe, prynce of Spaine, to the most excellente Princes Marye, quene of England. . . . Lond. 1555.
Written by tutor of Darnley Contains a description of Darnley.

5178a GATHERER, W. A. The tyrannous reign of Mary Stuart. Edin. 1958.

5179 INUENTAIRES DE LA ROYNE DESCOSSE douairière de France. By Joseph Robertson. *Bannatyne Club*, no. 111 (1863).
Catalogues of the jewels, dresses, furniture, books, and paintings of Mary, queen of Scots, 1556-69.

5180 LESLIE, JOHN. A defence of the honour of the right highe, mightye and noble Princesse Marie, queene of Scotlande and dowager of France, with a declaration as well of her right, title and intereste to the succession of the crowne of Englande, as that the regimente of women is conformable to the lawe of God and nature. Lond. 1569.
Later eds. of all or part of this tract appeared at Liège, 1571, in English; at Rheims, 1580, in Latin; at Rheims, 1584, in English; at Rouen, 1587, in French and in Spanish. The first book of the Liège ed. is repr. in Anderson (5177). The Liège ed., in which Leslie assumes the pseudonym of Philippes Morgan, differs from the 1st ed. in emphasizing Mary's English claims.

5181 LETTRES, INSTRUCTIONS ET MÉMOIRES de Marie Stuart. By Alexandre Labanoff. 7 vols. Paris, 1844.
Omits Casket letters as forgeries and denies integrity of Babington correspondence. Does not include all extant letters of Mary. For earlier collections of her correspondence, cf. vol. vii. Cf. 5218.

5182 LETTRES DE MARIE STUART. By Alexandre Teulet. Paris, 1859.
Supplementary to Labanoff (5181). Includes Casket letters, documents relative to the murder of Darnley and accounts of Mary's execution. Cf. 5218.

5183 LETTERS OF MARY QUEEN OF SCOTS. By Agnes Strickland. 2 vols. Lond. 1842; vol. iii, Lond. 1843; vols. i–iii in 2 vols. Lond. 1843.
Vols. i and ii are English trans. of Labanoff's *Lettres inédites de Marie Stuart*, Paris, 1839.

5184 LETTERS OF MARY STUART. Ed. and trans. William B. Turnbull. Lond. 1845.
Selected and trans. from Labanoff (5181).

5185 MAITLAND'S NARRATIVE of the principal acts of the regency, during the minority, and other papers relating to the history of Mary, queen of Scots. (By W. S. Fitch.) Ipswich, 1833.
Written by son of Mary's secretary, Maitland of Lethington, to justify his father. Only 50 copies, privately printed. Cf. also *The apology for William Maitland of Lethington*, by the same author, in *Scot. Hist. Soc. Misc.* ii (1904), 133–228.

5186 DE VITA ET REBUS GESTIS MARIAE . . . quas scriptis tradidere auctores. By S. Jebb. 2 vols. Lond. 1725.
Important collection of contemporary pamphlets.

(2) *Mary before her flight into England*

For Mary's early career in France and in Scotland the correspondence of her mother, Mary of Lorraine (5132 and 5141), is of first-rate importance. For the Casket letters and the murder of Darnley, cf. pp. 444–6 *infra*.

5187 LES AFFAIRES DU CONTE DE BODUEL, 1568. By Henry Cockburn and Thomas Maitland. *Bannatyne Club*, no. 29 (1829).
Bothwell's justification of his conduct, addressed to the king of Denmark, 1568. App. contains papers relating to Bothwell, repr.

5188 DISCOURS du grand et magnifique triumphe. Paris, 1558; by William Bentham, *Roxburghe Club* (1818).
For other pamphlets and broadsides about Mary's marriage with Francis, cf. Scott (4910), nos. 10–19.

5189 A HISTORIE OF THE ESTATE OF SCOTLAND 1558–60. By David Laing. *Wodrow Soc. Misc.* i (1844), 51–85.
Author unknown, MS. a transcription, 1663.

5190 KNOX, JOHN. The first blast of the trumpet against the monstrous regiment of women. (Geneva), 1558.
Many times repr.; cf. Laing's ed. of Knox's works (5450), iii, 349–422.

5191 A LETTER FROM MARY, queen of Scots to the duke of Guise, Jan. 1562. By J. H. Pollen. *Scot. Hist. Soc.* xliii (1904).
Letter reproduced in facsimile with translation. Introduction discusses Mary's relation to the Guises; prints other letters *in extenso*.

5192 LETTERS FROM MARY, queen of Scots, to Sir Robert Melvill; and other papers from the archives of the earl of Leven and Melville. 1565–8. By James Dennistoun and Alexander Macdonald. *Maitland Club Misc.* (4950), iii, pt. I.
Four letters. One receipt for jewels. Band between Darnley and the protestant lords in 1565.

5193 MAKGILL, JACQUES, and BELLENDEN, JEAN. Discours particulier d'Écosse: escrit par commandement et ordonnance de la royne dovairière et régente . . . 1559. By Thomas Thomson. *Bannatyne Club*, no. 5 (1824).
Official report on state of Scotland transmitted to Mary Stuart in France. Authors clerk-register and justice-clerk.

5194 NAU, CLAUDE. History of Mary Stuart from the murder of Riccio to her flight into England. By Joseph Stevenson. Edin. 1883.
Nau, one of Mary's French secretaries, wrote while in her service. Narrative a fragment, 1566–71. Here printed in French with trans. App. contains Jesuit reports to Rome of Mary's actions.

5195 PAPAL NEGOTIATIONS WITH MARY queen of Scots during her reign in Scotland 1561–7. By J. H. Pollen. *Scot. Hist. Soc.* xxxvii (1901).
Papers from Vatican archives and elsewhere, mostly given *in extenso* with trans.

5196 PARK, W. Letter of Thomas Randolph to the earl of Leicester, 14 February, 1566. *Scot. Hist. Rev.* xxxiv (1955), 135–9.

5197 RUTHVEN, PATRICK. A relation of the death of David Rizzi. . . . Lond. 1699; Edin. 1890.
Written at Berwick, 28 March 1565, by one of the principals of the murder.

5198 SELECTIONS FROM UNPUBLISHED MANUSCRIPTS in the College of Arms and the B.M. illustrating the reign of Mary, queen of Scotland, 1543–68. By Joseph Stevenson. *Maitland Club*, no. 41 (1837).

5199 [SEMPILL, ROBERT.] The complaynt of Scotland. [Edin. 1567]; by James Maidment (in *Scottish Ballads and Songs*), Edin. 1859; by T. G. Stevenson (in *Sempill Ballates*), Edin. 1872.
A ballad by Sempill on Darnley's murder, not to be confused with 5124. For other contemporary ballads and broadsides on the murder, cf. Scott (4910), nos. 49–55.

(3) *Mary in England*

Almost all the important documentary material on Mary's imprisonment and death is given in the *Scottish Calendar* (4924). The *Spanish Calendars* (868) and the correspondence of the French ambassadors in England, together with Teulet's collection (4929), are important. There is much of value in the *Foreign* Calendars (87) and in the *Salisbury MSS.* (185), and one very important account of her trial in the *Hardwicke Papers* (280). The *Sadler Papers* (4958) and Poulet's *Letter-book* (5210) are full of pertinent material. Cf. also the documents printed in 5226 and, for the Babington plot, those in 5212. Because of Mary's complicity in various Roman Catholic plots against Elizabeth, much relevant material will be found in ch. vi *supra* (pp. 189–200).

5200 ACCOUNTS AND PAPERS relating to Mary, queen of Scots. By A. J. Crosby and John Bruce. *Camden Soc.* xciii (1867).
Expenses of Mary Stuart's maintenance in England and of her funeral, from wardrobe miscellaneous accounts, P.R.O.

5201 THE BARDON PAPERS: documents relating to the imprisonment and trial of Mary, queen of Scots. By Conyers Read. *Camden Soc.*, 3rd ser., xvii (1909).
App. iii discusses the genuineness of Mary's letter endorsing the Babington Plot.

5202 [BELLEFOREST, F. DE (?).] L'innocence de la trés-illustre, trés-chaste, et debonnaire princesse, Madame Marie, royne d'Escosse. s.l. 1572; repr. by Jebb (5186).
Largely a French trans. of *A treatise of treasons* (5219).

5203 BIRCH, W. DE G. Original documents relating to Sheffield, principally in connection with Mary, queen of Scots. *Brit. Arch. Assoc. Jour.* xxx (1874), 308–24.

5204 BLACKWOOD, ADAM. Martyre de la royne d'Escosse. Edin. (probably Paris), 1587; 1588; 1589; repr. in Jebb (5186).

5205 THE COPY OF A LETTER to . . . the earle of Leycester . . . with a report of certain petitions made to the queene's majesty . . . from all the lords and commons. . . . [Lond.?], 1586; in *Somers Tracts* (296), i, 224–36.
This is the official account of the petitions of parliament for the execution of Mary Stuart and of Elizabeth's answers.

5206 COLLECTIONS RELATIVE TO THE FUNERALS of Mary, queen of Scots. By Robert Pitcairn. Edin. 1822; by R. Prescott-Innes, Edin. 1890.
Reprs. 11 accounts of Mary's funeral from tracts and other printed sources; cf. also *A remembrance of the order and manner of the burial of Mary, queen of Scots* in *Arch.* i (1770), 355–60; repr. in *Eng. Garner* (279), viii, 341–50.

5207 CROMPTON, RICHARD. A short declaration of the ende of traytors, and false conspirators against the state. . . . Lond. 1587.
Legal justification of Mary's sentence. A Dutch trans. was printed (in Middleburg) 1587.

5208 THE DIARY OF JOHN LESLIE, bishop of Ross, April 11–October 16, 1571. By David Laing. *Bannatyne Misc.* (4937), iii, 111–57.
Details his embassy to England in Mary's behalf. Cf. *Discourse . . . of his whole . . . proceedings during the time of his ambassage,* in Anderson (5177), iii.

5209 [KYFFIN, M.] Defense of the honourable sentence and execution of the queen of Scots. Lond. 1587. French trans., s.l., 1588.
Legal considerations. Prints Mary's correspondence with Babington.

5210 THE LETTER-BOOKS OF SIR AMIAS POULET, keeper of Mary queen of Scots. By John Morris. Lond. 1874.
Based upon an original letter-book of Poulet now in the Bodleian library. Valuable. On the proposal to Poulet to assassinate Mary, cf. C. Read in *E.H.R.* xl (1926), 234–5.

5211 MARIAE STUARTAE REGINAE principis Catholicae, nuper ab Elizabetha regina et ordinibus Angliae, post novendecim annorum captivitatem in arce Fodringhaye interfectae supplicium & mors pro fide Catholica constantissima. Cologne, 1587.
First publication about Mary's death issued by Catholic party, incorporated in *Summarium rationum* (5216).

5212 MARY QUEEN OF SCOTS and the Babington plot. By J. H. Pollen. *Scot. Hist. Soc.,* 3rd ser., iii (1922).
Prints *in extenso* virtually all the pertinent documents on the subject. Valuable introduction. Cf. also J. B. Bury, *Note on Pollen's Babington plot, Hist.* xxii (1937), 88–89.

5213 LA MORT DE LA ROYNE D'ÉCOSSE. s.l., s.a. [1588?]; 1589;
repr. by Jebb (5186).
Written by some Marian sympathizer from information furnished by Bourgoing, Mary's
physician.

5214 NEALE, J. E. Proceedings in parliament relative to the sentence on
Mary, queen of Scots. *E.H.R.* xxxv (1920), 103–13.
Proceedings printed *in extenso* with introductory note. Repr. in Steuart (5220).

5215 SALUTEM IN CHRISTO. Lond. 1571.
The case against Norfolk in the Ridolfi Plot. For another pamphlet on the same
subject, probably by Sir Francis Walsingham, cf. Read, *Walsingham* (759), i, 63 n. and
68–74.

5216 [SCOTUS, ROMOALDUS.] Summarium rationum, quibus cancel-
larius Angliae et prolocutor Puckeringius Elizabethae Angliae reginae per-
suaserunt occidendam esse serenissimam Mariam. Ingolstad, 1588; s.l., 1628;
repr. by Jebb (5186).
Catholic analysis of the case against Mary.

5217 SEPP, B. Maria Stuarts Briefwechsel mit Antony Babington. Munich,
1886.
Correspondence here printed; cf. also *Bardon papers* (5201), 26–40, and particularly
Pollen (5212), 1–48.

5218 SOME UNPUBLISHED LETTERS OF MARY, QUEEN OF
SCOTS. By S. L. England. *E.H.R.* lii (1937), 77–87.
Letters to La Mothe Fénélon, 1571–2, from the John Murray collection.

5219 A TREATISE OF TREASONS against Queen Elizabeth, the croune of
England. . . . [Paris or Antwerp], 1572.
Author Scotch or French. Pt. 1 a reply to *Salutem in Christo* (5215); pt. 2 attack on
Cecil and Bacon, accusing them of conspiring against Mary, James, and Elizabeth
herself.

5220 TRIAL OF MARY, queen of Scots. By A. F. Steuart. Edin. 1923;
1951.
Prints inaccurately much pertinent material, cf. J. E. Neale in *E.H.R.* xxxviii (1923),
445–6.

5221 TWO LISTS of supposed adherents of Mary, queen of Scots, 1574 and
1582. By J. B. Wainwright. *Cath. Rec. Soc. Misc.* viii (1913), 86–142.

5222 [WHETSTONE, GEORGE.] The censure of a loyal subiect: upon
certaine noted speach and behaviours of those fourteen notable traitors. . . .
By Thomas Churchyard. Lond. 1587.
On the Babington plot.

(b) *Later Works*

(1) *General*

Of Mary's many biographies, by no means all of which are here listed, the best is
Henderson (5243), and for her early life, Fleming (5237). Froude's account of
her (340), though brilliant, is strongly biased. A scholarly and sympathetic
presentation of her connexion with the Babington plot is in Pollen's introduction
to his collection of sources on the subject (5212). Read (759) presents the official

case against her. For Elizabeth's attitude towards Mary's execution cf. Neale (1067), ii, 103–44.

5223 ANTHEUNIS, LOUIS. Le secretaire de Marie Stuart, Gilbert Curle, 1549–1609, et sa famille. *Rev. Questions Hist.* cxxxiii (1939), 58–85.

5224 BARBÉ, L. A. Kirkaldy of Grange. Edin. 1897.
A rather eulogistic biography.

5225 BRYCE, W. M. Mary Stuart's voyage to France in 1548. *E.H.R.* xxii (1907), 43–50.

5226 CHANTELAUZE, REGIS. Marie Stuart, son procès et son exécution d'après le journal de Bourgoing, son médecin, la correspondancc d'Amyas Paulet, son geôlier, et autres documents nouveaux. Paris, 1876.
Prints the jour. of Bourgoing, Mary's physician, printed in trans. in Cowan (5230).

5227 CHAUVIRÉ, ROGER. Le secret de Marie Stuart. Paris, 1937.

5228 CHAUVIRÉ, ROGER. Le secret de Marie Stuart. *Rev. travaux acad. sciences morales et politiques,* 3rd ser., xcviii (1938), 388–401.
Her guilt in view of recent studies.

5229 CHERUEL, P. A. Marie Stuart et Catherine de Médicis. Étude historique sur les relations de la France et de l'Écosse dans la seconde moitié du xvie siècle. Paris, 1858.

5230 COWAN, SAMUEL. The last days of Mary Stuart and the journal of Bourgoyne her physician. Lond. 1907.
Uncritical; cf. 5226.

5231 CUST, L. H. Notes on the authentic portraits of Mary queen of Scots. Lond. 1903.
Based on the researches of the late Sir George Scharf, rewritten in the light of new information. Cf. also *Scot. Hist. Rev.* iv (1906), 135–43; xvii (1919), 32–36, 152, 234–5.

5232 DAVISON, M. H. A. The maladies of Mary, queen of Scots, and her husbands. *Proc. Scot. Soc. of Hist. of Med. for 1955–6* (1956), 20–34.
Cf. Dan McKenzie, *The obstetric history of Mary, queen of Scots, at Lochleven. Caledonian Medical Jour.* xv (1932), 2–6.

5233 DE KALB, EUGENIE. Robert Poley's movements as a messenger of the court, 1588–1601. *Rev. Eng. Studies,* ix (1933), 13–18.

5234 DOUBLEDAY, H. A. The Mar Case. *Complete Peerage,* vol. ix. Lond. 1936.

5235 DUNCAN, THOMAS. Mary Stuart and the house of Huntly. *Scot. Hist. Rev.* iv (1906), 365–73.

5236 DUNCAN, THOMAS. The queen's Maries. *Scot. Hist. Rev.* ii (1904), 363–71.

5237 FLEMING, D. H. Mary, queen of Scots from her birth to her flight into England. Lond. 1897; 1898.
The best biography of Mary's early life. Notes and references very extensive. Valuable guide to and commentary on sources.

5238 GATHERER, W. A. Queen Mary's journey from Aberdeen to Inverness, 1562. *Scot. Hist. Rev.* xxxiii (1954), 19–21.

5239　GENT, FRANK. The coffin in the wall. Edin. [1944].

Reprinted from *Chamber's Jour*. Disposes of the recurrent suggestion that remains found in Edinburgh castle in 1830 may have been those of the son born to Queen Mary in June 1566. Cf. *Scot. Hist. Rev.* xv (1917), 146–55, 155–8.

5240　GORE-BROWN, R. F. Lord Bothwell. A study of the life, character, and times of James Hepburn, 4th earl of Bothwell. Lond. 1937.

A spirited defence.

5241　HAMER, DOUGLAS. The marriage of Mary, queen of Scots to the Dauphin: a Scottish printed fragment. *Library*, n.s., xii (1932) 420–8.

5242　HANNAY, R. K. The earl of Arran and Queen Mary. *Scot. Hist. Rev.* xviii (1920), 258–77.

5243　HENDERSON, T. F. Mary, queen of Scots. 2 vols. Lond. 1905.

Best complete biography, though less valuable for last part of her life.

5244　HOLT, H. F. On the great seal of Francis II of France and Mary, queen of Scots, as king and queen of France, Scotland, England & Ireland. *Brit. Arch. Assoc. Jour.* xxiv (1868), 343–51.

5245　HOLT, H. F. Observations upon a 'shilling' of Francis the Dauphin and Mary Stuart, representing them as 'king and queen of Scotland, England & Ireland', dated 1558: with notes regarding the assumption by Queen Mary of the arms and crown of England. *Proc. Soc. Antiq. Scot.* vii (1870), 279–87.

5246　HOSACK, J. Mary, queen of Scots, and her accusers. Edin. 1869; 2 vols. Edin. 1870–4.

1st ed. ends 1570; 2nd ed. complete biography. Prints documents in app. The best statement of the case for Mary in the Casket letter controversy.

5247　HUME, M. A. S. The love affairs of Mary, queen of Scots: a political history. Lond. 1903.

Uses material in Spanish archives to show Casket letters not forgeries.

5248　KERVYN DE LETTENHOVE, J. M. B. C. BARON. Marie Stuart: l'œuvre puritaine — le procès, — le supplice, 1585–7. 2 vols. Paris, 1889.

Treats of efforts of French and Scottish kings on Mary's behalf in the last phase of her life.

5249　LANG, ANDREW. Portraits and jewels of Mary Stuart. Glasgow, 1906.

Repr. with enlargements from *Scot. Hist. Rev.* iii (1905), 129–56, 274–300; cf. also on jewels, ibid. xviii (1920), 83–99.

5250　LANG, ANDREW. The household of Mary, queen of Scots, in 1573. *Scot. Hist. Rev.* ii (1904), 345–55.

5251　LANG, ANDREW. The mystery of the queen's Marie. *Blackwood's Mag.* clviii (1895), 381–90.

Cf. idem, *The queen's Marie* in *The valet's tragedy and other studies*, Lond. 1903.

5252　LEADER, J. D. Mary, queen of Scots, in captivity: a narrative of events 1569–84. Sheffield, 1880.

Prints many extracts from MSS. and printed sources for period 1569–84. Useful for detailed account of Mary's imprisonment.

5254 LOCKIE, D. M. The political career of the bishop of Ross, 1568–80. The background to a contemporary life of Mary Stuart. *Univ. of Birm. Hist. Jour.* iv (1953), 98–145.
John Lesley, the historian and apologist for Mary.

5255 MAXWELL, HERBERT. Tour of Mary, queen of Scots, through south-western Scotland, 1563. *Scot. Hist. Rev.* xviii (1920), 1–14.
Prints roll of expenses; cf. ibid. xx, 171–2.

5256 MIGNET, F. A. M. Histoire de Marie Stuart, 1851; 1854; Eng. trans. by A. R. Scoble, Lond. 1851.
Scholarly biography, using materials in Spanish archives. Also prints some French letters.

5257 MUMBY, F. A. Elizabeth and Mary Stuart. The beginning of the feud. Boston, 1914.
Reprs. original letters pertaining to Mary's relations with Elizabeth prior to the Darnley marriage.

5258 MUMBY, F. A. The fall of Mary Stuart. Lond. 1921.
Covers years from marriage with Darnley to flight to England by selected letters, printed *in extenso.*

5259 NEILL, KERRY. Spenser's *Arcadia* and Mary, queen of Scots. *P.M.L.A.* lx (1945), 582–8.

5260 NYS, ERNEST. The trial of Mary, queen of Scots, from the point of view of public international law. *Juridical Rev.* xvii (1905), 50–53.

5261 PEARSON, KARL. The skull and portraits of Henry Stewart, Lord Darnley. *Biometrika,* xx (1928), 1–104.
Makes important suggestions about Darnley's intellect and his medical history.

5262 POLLEN, J. H. Studies on the history of Mary Stuart. *The Month,* xci (1898), 342–55, 575–91; xcvi (1900), 167–76, 241–55, 392–402; xcvii (1901), 258–71; cii (1903), 430–3; cix (1907), 356–65; cx (1907), 240–53, 363–74; cxvii (1911), 11–24, 136–49.
Scholarly and valuable.

5263 POLLEN, J. H. The dispensation for the marriage of Mary Stuart with Darnley, and its date. *Scot. Hist. Rev.* iv (1906), 241–8.

5264 RAIT, R. S., and CAMERON, A. I. King James's secret. Lond. 1927.
An account of James's attitude towards the trial and execution of Mary Stuart, with illustrative documents from the Warrender papers (4963).

5265 RUBLE, J. E. A. DE. La première jeunesse de Marie Stuart. Paris, 1891.

5266 RUSSELL, E. Maitland of Lethington, the minister of Mary Stuart, a study of his life and times. Lond. 1912.
Based almost exclusively on the state papers. Valuable.

5267 SAMUEL, J. S. Mary Stuart and Eric XIV of Sweden, a postscript to Scottish history. *Glasgow Arch. Soc. Trans.,* n.s., vi (1910), 131–47.

5268 SCOTT, A. M. The battle of Langside. *Brit. Arch. Assoc. Jour.* xlv (1889), 22–24.
Cf. also idem, *Notes on the battle of Langside,* in *Trans. Glasgow Arch. Soc.,* n.s., i (1890), 281–300.

5269 SCHIERN, FREDERIK, Life of James Hepburn, earl of Bothwell. [Copenhagen?], 1860–3; [Copenhagen?], 1875; trans. from Danish by David Berry, Edin. 1880.
Deals especially with Bothwell's detention in Norway and imprisonment in Denmark.

5270 SKELTON, JOHN. Maitland of Lethington, and the Scotland of Mary Stuart. 2 vols. Edin. 1887–8.
Inaccurate.

5271 SMALL, JOHN. Queen Mary at Jedburgh in 1566. *Proc. Soc. Antiq. Scot.*, n.s., iii (1881), 210–33.
Prints *in extenso* a will made by Mary and dictated to bishop of Ross when Mary was ill at Jedburgh.

5272 STRICKLAND, AGNES. Lives of the queens of Scotland. 8 vols. Edin. 1850–9.
Includes a life of Mary Stuart, published separately, 2 vols. Lond. 1873.

5273 STUART, JOHN. A lost chapter in the history of Mary, queen of Scots, recovered. Edin. 1874.
Account of Bothwell's marriage with Lady Jane Gordon and their divorce. Dispensation printed in app.

5274 TAYLER, A. N. Queen Mary in the north in 1562 and 1564. *Banff Field Club Trans. for 1935* (1935), 43–68.

5275 VAN SCOY, HERBERT, and WEBER, B. C. The marriage of Mary, queen of Scots and the Dauphin. *Scot. Hist. Rev.* xxxi (1952), 41–48.

5276 WIESENER, L. Marie Stuart et le comte de Bothwell. Paris, 1863.

5278 ZWEIG, STEFAN. Maria Stuart. Vienna, 1935. Eng. trans. Lond. 1935.

(2) *The Casket Letters*

Of the voluminous controversial literature on this subject only the important contributions are here given. The question at issue is as to whether the letters were of Mary's own composing or whether they were forged in whole or in part by her enemies. Henderson (5287, to be supplemented by 5243, vol. ii, app. A) gives the best statement in support of the genuineness of the letters, Goodall (5286), Skelton (5298), and Hosack (5246) are the ablest exponents of the forgery theory. Lang's position (5290) varies in different eds. Froude's account (340) is brilliant but strongly biased against Mary. The first published ed. of the letters is in Buchanan (5175). Henderson (5287) prints in an app. the various extant versions. Mahon (5292) prints some material from Cambr. Univ. library.

5279 BEKKER, E. Maria Stuart, Darnley, Bothwell. *Giessener Studien aus dem Gebiet der Geschichte*, no. i (1881).
Pro-Marian. Cf. *Cambr. Mod. Hist.* iii.

5280 BRESSLAU, HARRY. Die Kassettenbriefe der Königin Maria Stuart. *Historisches Taschenbuch*, 6th ser., i (1882).
Prints first 6 letters in app. Analyses argument of Kervyn de Lettenhove (5289). Anti-Marian.

5281 CAMPBELL, H. The love letters of Mary, queen of Scots, with her love sonnets. . . . Lond. 1824; Lond. 1825, with app.
Anti-Marian.

5282 CHALMERS, GEORGE. A detection of the love letters lately attributed to Mary. Lond. 1825.
Pro-Marian (a counter to 5281).

5283 CHAUVIRÉ, ROGER. État present de la controverse sur les lettres de la cassette. *Rev. Hist.* clxxiv (1934), 429–66; clxxv (1935), 41–82.

5284 FORST, H. Maria Stuart und der Tod Darnleys. Bonn, 1894.

5285 FORST, H. Über Buchanans Darstellung der Geschichte Maria Stuarts. Bonn, 1882.

5286 GOODALL, WALTER. An examination of the letters said to be written by Mary, queen of Scots, to James, earl of Bothwell; shewing by intrinsick and extrinsick evidence that they are forgeries. 2 vols. Edin. 1754.
Vol. ii contains the letters and other pertinent source material.

5287 HENDERSON, T. F. The casket letters. Edin. 1889; 2nd ed. with reply to objections, Edin. 1890.
Best statement of the case for the authenticity of the Casket letters. Cf. also *Scot. Hist. Rev.* v (1907), 161–74, and M. Philippson in *Revue historique*, xlvi (1891), 161–7.

5288 HOSACK, J. Mary Stewart: a brief statement of the principal charges brought against her. . . . Edin. 1888.

5289 KERVYN DE LETTENHOVE, J. M. B. C. BARON. Marie Stuart d'après les documents conservés au château d'Hatfield. *Bulletin de l'académie royale de Belgique*, 2nd scr., xxxiv (1872), 80–111.
Deals with copy of letter 3 at Hatfield; cf. Bresslau (5280).

5290 LANG, ANDREW. The mystery of Mary Stuart. Lond. 1901; 1904; 1912.
Valuable discussion of Casket letters. Cf., for Lang's controversy with Henderson on the subject, *Scot. Hist. Rev.* v (1907), 1–13, 161–74; and Henderson (5243), ii, app. A. In the ed. of 1912 Lang announced his conversion to Henderson's views. Cf. also J. B. Black, *The Casket letter controversy* (the Andrew Lang lecture for 1949), Edin. 1951.

5291 MAHON, R. H. The indictment of Mary, queen of Scots. Cambr. 1923.
New light on proceedings against Mary in 1568, prints Buchanan's indictment from Cambr. Univ. library.

5292 MAHON, R. H. Mary, queen of Scots: a study of the Lennox narrative in the university library at Cambridge. Cambr. 1924.
A re-examination of the Casket letters. Pro-Marian. Cf. also idem, *The Tragedy of Kirk o' Field*, Cambr. 1930.

5293 RIESS, LUDWIG. Die Lösung des Maria Stuart-Problems. *Historische Z.* cx (1913), 237–91.

5294 ROBERTSON, W. A critical dissertation concerning . . . the genuineness of the queen's letters to Bothwell. In vol. ii of *History of Scotland*. Lond. 1759.
Anti-Marian. Cf. Tytler (5299) for criticism of Robertson's view.

5295 ROMANE, A., and VERDAL, G. Darnley ou le roi fantôme. Paris, 1938.

5296 SEPP, B. Tagebuch der unglücklichen Schotten-Königin zu Glasgow (Jan. 1567). Munich, 1882.
Pro-Marian.

5297 SEPP, B. Maria Stuart und ihre Ankläger zu York, Westminster und Hampton Court (1568-9). Munich, 1884.
Pro-Marian.

5298 SKELTON, JOHN. The impeachment of Mary Stuart. Edin. 1876.
Attacks authenticity of Casket letters. Cf. also Skelton's article in *Blackwood's Mag.* cxlvi (1889), 790-807, and his *Essays in history and biography* (Edin. 1883).

5299 TYTLER, WILLIAM. The inquiry historical and critical into the evidence against Mary, queen of Scots, and an examination of the histories of Dr. Robertson and David Hume. Edin. 1759; 1790.
Apologist for Mary.

3. James VI

(a) *Sources*

(1) *General*

The acts of parliament (4922), the registers of the privy council (4930), of the great seal (4931) and the privy seal (4932), the exchequer rolls (4933), and the lord treasurer's accounts (4925) are all important. James's proclamations are given in Steele (1017), ii. For James's relations with England, the *Scottish calendar* (4924), the *Hamilton papers* (4926), and the *Border papers* (1352) are the chief sources; there is a good deal of material also in the *Salisbury MSS.* (185). Cf. as well 5302, 5303, 5318, 5320, and 5322, *infra*.

The *Spanish Calendar* (868), the dispatches of French ambassadors in England (ch. ii *supra*, pp. 66 ff.), and Teulet's collections (4929) should be consulted.

Among contemporary chroniclers Buchanan (4972), Knox (5449), Calderwood (5482), and 5308, *infra*, are the best for James's reign. Reference should also be made to Melville (4990) and Moysie (4992).

For the political works of James cf. 1425, for his other writings cf. *D.N.B.* (9), art. James I.

5300 THE APOLOGY FOR WILLIAM MAITLAND of Lethington, 1610. By Andrew Lang. *Scot. Hist. Soc. Misc.* ii (1904), 133-228.

5301 THE APOLOGY OF MR. PATRICK GALLOWAY, minister of Perth, when he fled to England, 1585. By Walter Scott and David Laing. *Bannatyne Misc.* (4937), i, 107-29.
Author expelled from pulpit for criticisms of court.

5302 CORRESPONDENCE OF KING JAMES VI of Scotland with Sir Robert Cecil and others in England during the reign of Queen Elizabeth. By John Bruce. *Camden Soc.* lxxviii (1861).
App. contains papers illustrative of transactions between King James and Robert, earl of Essex. Chiefly from *Salisbury MSS.* (185). Cf. 5322.

5303 THE CORRESPONDENCE OF ROBERT BOWES of Aske, esq.,
ambassador of Queen Elizabeth to the court of Scotland. By Joseph Stevenson.
Surtees Soc. xiv (1842).
Letters from B.M. and from Bowes' letter-book at Streatlam castle. Covers the years
1577–83. Valuable.

5304 DOCUMENTS ILLUSTRATING CATHOLIC POLICY in the
reign of James VI, 1596–8. By T. G. Law. *Scot. Hist. Soc. Misc.* i (1893),
1–73.
Includes *Memorials of John Ogilvy*, who purported to be agent of James VI to king of
Spain, 1596, and W. Creighton's *Apology and defence of the king of Scotland*, 1598.

5305 AN ESTIMATE OF THE SCOTTISH NOBILITY during the
minority of James VI and subsequently. By Charles Rogers. *Trans. R.H.
Soc.* ii (1872), 222–96.
Prints Alexander Hay's list, 1577, and other lists, 1583–1602. Also printed as *Grampian
Club*, no. 6 (1873).

5306 EXTRACTS FROM THE DESPATCHES OF M. COURCELLES,
French ambassador at the court of Scotland, 1586–7. By Robert Bell. *Banna-
tyne Club*, no. 22 (1828).
Valuable.

5307 FOWLER, WILLIAM. The works of William Fowler, secretary to
Queen Anne, wife of James VI. Vol. ii by H. W. Meikle, iii by H. W. Meikle,
James Craigie, John Purves, *Scot. Text Soc.*, 3rd ser., vii (1936), xiii (1940).

5308 THE HISTORIE AND LIFE OF KING JAMES THE SEXT: being
an account of the affairs of Scotland, from the year 1566, to the year 1596;
with a short continuation to the year 1617. By Thomas Thomson. *Bannatyne
Club*, no. 13 (1825).
MS. from marquis of Lothian's library. Authorship unknown, but attributed to John
Colville. Written between 1588 and 1597. Crawford's *Memoirs of affairs of Scotland*,
Lond. 1706, prints the MS. with omissions and interpolations. Malcolm Laing pub-
lished part of it (1566–82) in 1804.

5309 LAING, JAMES. De vita et moribus atque rebus gestis haereticorum
nostri temporis. . . . Paris, 1581.
Dedicated to Queen Mary and James VI. Author Scottish doctor at the Sorbonne.

5310 LETTERS AND STATE PAPERS during the reign of James the VI,
1578–1625. By James Maidment. *Abbotsford Club*, no. 13 (1838).
Miscellaneous; valuable; *in extenso*. From the Balfour MSS. and the Balcarres papers
in the Advocates' library (216).

5311 LETTERS OF QUEEN ELIZABETH AND KING JAMES VI of
Scotland. By John Bruce. *Camden Soc.* xlvi (1849).
Letters chiefly 1582.

5312 LETTERS TO KING JAMES VI: from the queen, Prince Henry,
Prince Charles, the Princess Elizabeth and her husband Frederick, king of
Bohemia, and from their son Prince Frederick Henry. By Alexander Mac-
donald. *Maitland Club*, no. 35 (1835).
Facsimiles, with introduction which prints *in extenso* several letters relating to the
private life of the king.

5313 THE LIBRARY OF JAMES VI in the hand of Peter Young, his tutor, 1573–83. By T. G. Law. *Scot. Hist. Soc. Misc.* i (1893), pp. xi–lxxv.

5314 THE MANNER AND FORM OF THE EXAMINATION and death of William, earl of Gowrye, May 1584. By Walter Scott and David Laing. *Bannatyne Misc.* (4937), i, 91–107.

5315 MONIPENNIE, JOHN. Certain matters concerning the realme of Scotland, composed together . . . as they were A.D. 1597. Lond. 1603; repr. in *Somers Tracts* (296), iii, 344–403.

5316 NEGOTIATIONS BETWEEN JAMES VI AND I AND FERDINAND I, grand duke of Tuscany. By J. D. Mackie. *St. Andrews Univ. Pub.* xxv (1927).

5317 NEWES FROM SCOTLAND, declaring the damnable life of Doctor Fian, a notable sorcerer, who was burned at Edenbrough in Januarie last. s.l. 1591; *Roxburghe Club*, 1816.
Account of trial in which accused confessed to trying to drown James VI on his return from Denmark.

5318 ORIGINAL LETTERS OF MR. JOHN COLVILLE, 1582–1603. To which is added his Palinode, 1600. By David Laing. *Bannatyne Club*, no. 104 (1858).
Colville the paid agent of English government in Scotland.

5319 PAPERS RELATIVE TO THE MARRIAGE OF KING JAMES VI of Scotland, with the Princess Anna of Denmark, 1589. And the form and manner of her majesty's coronation at Holyrood House, 1590. By J. T. G. Craig. *Bannatyne Club*, no. 26 (1828).
From register of the privy council and other papers in the register house. Includes Andrew Melville's *Stephaniskion*, John Russell's *Verba*, and John Burel's verses describing the queen's entry into Edinburgh.

5320 PATRICK, MASTER OF GRAY. Letters and papers. By Thos. Thomson. *Bannatyne Club*, no. 48 (1835).
Letters, 1584–1608, with app. of documents, 1515–1606. Valuable.

5321 RELATION BY THE MASTER OF GRAY, concerning the surprise of the king at Stirling Nov. 1585. By Walter Scott and David Laing. *Bannatyne Misc.* (4937), i, 129–41.
Account of Arran's fall written by one of his rivals for the favour of James VI.

5322 THE SECRET CORRESPONDENCE OF SIR ROBERT CECIL with James I. By Lord Hailes. Edin. 1766.
Papers from the *Salisbury MSS.* (185), but not the same as those in 5302.

5323 WILLIAM SEMPLE'S REPORTS ON SCOTLAND in 1588 and 1610. By David and Anthony Mathew. *E.H.R.* xli (1926), 579–83.
From Scots College, Valladolid. Lists of lords with political connexions.

5324 THE STRALOCH PAPERS. By John Stuart. *Spalding Club Misc.* i (1841).
1585–1665, contains a few letters of James VI.

5325   A SURVEY of the castle and town of Edinburgh, Jan. 1573. Journal
of the siege of the castle of Edinburgh, April and May, 1573. By David Laing.
Bannatyne Misc. (4937), ii, 65–80.
Survey taken for English before the siege, jour. from 1577 ed. of Holinshed (314),
(possibly by Thomas Churchyard). Jour. repr. in *Book of the old Edinburgh Club*, xvi
(1928).

(2) *The Gowrie Conspiracy*

In addition to the works given below reference should be made to Calderwood
(5482), Moysie (4992), the privy council registers (4930), the acts of parliament
(4922), the *Scottish Calendar* (4924), Winwood (832), and documents printed in
Pitcairn (5415) and Tytler (5019). Cf. also bibliography in *D.N.B.* (9), arts.
Alexander and John Ruthven.

5326   THE APPLICATION OF THREE SEVERAL DISCOURSES delivered on occasion of the Gowrye conspiracy. By Walter Scott and David
Laing. *Bannatyne Misc.* (4937), i, 141–61.

5327   A DISCOURSE of the unnatural and vile conspiracie attempted by John
earl of Gowrye and his brother against his majestie's person at St. Johnstown
upon the 5th of August, 1600. Edin. 1600; repr. in *Somers Tracts* (296), i,
508–32; *Harleian Misc.* (281), ii, 334–52.
Official account of the conspiracy.

5328   THE GOWRIE CONSPIRACY. Confessions of George Sprott. By
Andrew Lang. *Roxburghe Club*, 1902.
Papers among MSS. of the earl of Haddington and summarized in Fraser, *Memorials
of the earls of Haddington*, Edin. 1889. Sprott's claim to have forged Logan letters
substantiated by handwriting and evidence of these papers.

5329   LETTERS OF JOHN, EARL OF GOWRIE, 1595. By Walter Scott
and David Laing. *Bannatyne Misc.* (4937), i, pt. 2, 349–56.
Two letters, only ones known to be extant.

5330   NARRATIVE BY MR. ROBERT BRUCE, one of the ministers of
Edinburgh, concerning his troubles in the year 1600. By Walter Scott and
David Laing. *Bannatyne Misc.* (4937), i, 161–77.
Account of Gowrie conspiracy.

5331   PAPERS RELATING TO WILLIAM, first earl of Gowrie and Patrick
Ruthven, his fifth and last surviving son. By John Bruce. Lond. 1867.
Papers from B.M. and P.R.O. printed *in extenso* with commentary.

(b) *Later Works*

(1) *General*

The best general account of the reign is in Brown (4996). For James's struggle
with the church and his intrigues for the English throne, cf. S. R. Gardiner
(Davies (8), no. 219), i, ch. 2. Cf. also 775.

5332   AITKEN, J. M. The trial of George Buchanan before the Lisbon inquisition. Edin. 1939.

5333   BROWN, P. H. George Buchanan. Edin. 1890.

5334 BUCHANAN, GEORGE. *Glasgow Quatercentenary Studies*, 1906.
Valuable collection of essays on Buchanan's life and writing.

5335 LEE, MAURICE. The fall of the regent Morton: a problem in satellite diplomacy. *Jour. Mod. Hist.* xxviii (1956), 111–29.

5336 McKECHNIE, W. S. Thomas Maitland. *Scot. Hist. Rev.* iv (1906), 274–93.

5337 MACKIE, J. D. Scotland and the Spanish armada. *Scot. Hist. Rev.* xii (1914), 1–23.

5338 MACKIE, J. D. The secret diplomacy of King James VI in Italy prior to his accession to the English throne. *Scot. Hist. Rev.* xxi (1923), 267–83. Cf. 5316.

5339 MILLAR, A. H. The wedding of James VI in Norway. *Scot. Rev.* xxi (1893), 142–61.

5340 NEILSON, GEORGE. Rob Stene: a court satirist under James VI. *Scot. Hist. Rev.* ii (1904), 253–9.

5341 PHILLIPS, J. E. George Buchanan and the Sidney circle. *Hunt. Lib. Quar.* xii (1948), 23–55.

5342 SETON, BRUCE. The vice admiral and the quest of the 'Golden Pennie'. *Scot. Hist. Rev.* xx (1922), 122–9.

5343 SETON, W. W. The early years of Henry Frederick, prince of Wales and Charles, duke of Albany, 1593–1605. *Scot. Hist. Rev.* xiii (1915), 366–79.

5344 SHEARMAN, FRANCIS. 'The Spanish Blanks.' *Innes Rev.* iii (1952), 81–103.
Suggests that the affair was engineered by the kirk. Cf. *Scot. Hist. Rev.* xxxii (1953), 195–6. Cf. also *Scot. Rev.* xxii (1893), 1–22.

5345 SINCLAIR, G. A. The Scottish progress of James VI. *Scot. Hist. Rev.* x (1912), 21–28.

5346 STÄHLIN, KARL. Der Kampf um Schottland und die Gesandtschaftsreise Sir Francis Walsinghams im Jahre 1583. *Leipziger Studien aus dem Gebiet der Gesch.* ix, pt. 1 (1902).
Excellent on conditions in Scotland and on Anglo-Scottish relations, 1583. Prints important documents in the appendixes.

5348 WILLSON, D. H. King James VI and I. New York, 1956.
The best biography of James VI.

(2) *The Gowrie Conspiracy*

The latest review of the evidence is by W. F. Arbuckle (5349).

5349 ARBUCKLE, W. F. The 'Gowrie Conspiracy'. *Scot. Hist. Rev.* xxxvi (1957), 1–24, 89–110.
To be cont.

5350 BARBÉ, L. A. The tragedy of Gowrie house. Paisley, 1887.

5351 BRUCE, JOHN. Observations on the trial and death of William, earl of Gowrie, A.D. 1584, and on their connection with the Gowrie conspiracy, A.D. 1600. *Arch.* xxxiii (1849), 143–73.

5352 BRUCE, JOHN. Observations upon certain documents relating to William, first earl of Gowrie and Patrick Ruthven, his fifth and last surviving son. *Arch.* xxxiv (1852), 190–224.
Cf. 5331.

5353 COWAN, SAMUEL. The Ruthven family papers; the Ruthven version of the conspiracy and assassination at Gowrie house, Perth, 5 August, 1600. Lond. 1912.
Very badly edited. No light on conspiracy.

5354 COWAN, SAMUEL. The Gowrie conspiracy and its official narrative. Lond. 1902.

5355 LANG, ANDREW. James VI and the Gowrie mystery. Lond. 1902.
Exonerates James; introduces some new material.

5356 MACKIE, J. D. A secret agent of James VI. *Scot. Hist. Rev.* ix (1911), 376–86.

5357 ROUGHEAD, WILLIAM. The riddle of the Ruthvens and other studies. Edin. 1919; rev. ed. Edin. 1936.
Several brilliant essays.

D. CONSTITUTIONAL AND LEGAL HISTORY AND POLITICAL THEORY

1. GENERAL

(a) *Sources*

The sources for the constitutional history of Scotland in this period are far scantier than those for England. Most of them are preserved in the Register House, Edinburgh (4902). For an excellent discussion of their general character cf. Thomson (4917). Those in print are arranged under the appropriate sections following. A good deal of illuminating comment on the actual workings of the Scottish government will be found in the dispatches of resident foreign agents, notably those of Thomas Randolph (4924) and those of Pedro de Ayala (868). A contemporary English analysis of the defects of the Scottish government is printed in Stählin (5346), 133 ff.

The works of Scottish political theorists are included in ch. iv *supra*. Reference should be made particularly to Buchanan (1409), Knox (1394), James VI (1425), Barclay (1426), and Craig (1424).

(b) *Later Works*

There is no adequate constitutional history of Scotland. A useful survey of Scottish political theorists is given in McIlwain (1425). Reference should also be made to the appropriate sections in Allen (1432), Figgis (1447–8), and Gooch (1455).

5358 ERSKINE, JOHN. An institute of the law of Scotland. Edin. 1773.

5359 INNES, COSMO. Lectures on Scotch legal antiquities. Edin. 1872.
Deals with antiquaries, charters, parliament, the old church, old forms of law, rural occupations, and books.

5360 MACKENZIE, GEORGE. The institutions of the law of Scotland. Edin. 1684; 8th ed. 1758.
An old, inaccurate, but still useful survey.

5361 MACKINNON, JAMES. The constitutional history of Scotland from the early times to the reformation. Lond. 1924.
Inadequate.

5362 ROBERTSON, ALEXANDER. A course of lectures on the government, constitution, and law of Scotland, from the earliest to the present time. Lond. 1878.

5363 SMITH, D. B. John Barclay. *Scot. Hist. Rev.* xii (1914), 37–59.

5364 SMITH, D. B. William Barclay. *Scot. Hist. Rev.* xi (1913), 136–63.

5365 SMITH, D. B. Sir Thomas Craig, feudalist. *Scot. Hist. Rev.* xii (1914), 217–302.

5366 WALLACE, GEORGE. The nature and descent of ancient peerages connected with the state of Scotland . . . and the constitution of parliament in that country. Edin. 1783; 1785.

2. THE CROWN

(a) *Sources*

Scottish proclamations are calendared in Steele (1017), ii. For those preserved in the original printed form, cf. *S.T.C.* (35), nos. 21930 ff. For the theoretical position of the crown in the state reference should be made to the works of Buchanan, Knox, and James VI (ch. iv *supra*). For records of the regalia and the royal household, cf. Livingstone (4902), 7–8.

(b) *Later Works*

5367 LOVAT-FRASER, J. A. Constitutional position of the Scottish monarch prior to the union. *Law Quar. Rev.* xvii (1901), 252–62.

3. OFFICERS OF THE ROYAL HOUSEHOLD

Of these the chancellor and the secretary were the most important administrative officials. The Scottish chancellor had extensive administrative as well as judicial duties. The secretary's position was closely analogous to that of the principal secretary in England. He was particularly active in foreign affairs. The constable had lost most of his significance by the sixteenth century and the steward had given place to the master of the household. The lord chamberlain had lost his original functions as collector and dispenser of the royal revenues to the treasurer and comptroller, who are considered in sect. 8 *infra*. The chamberlain retained, however, some judicial functions, considered in sect. 9 (b) (7) *infra*. For the king's advocate, cf. 5396, 5403; for the keeper of the privy seal, cf. 4932, introduction, and Thomson (4917), p. 66; for the lord clerk register, cf. Thomson (4917), pp. 23–24.

(a) *Sources*

For the register of the great seal, cf. 4931, 4932. On the use of the great seal, privy seal, and signature (sign manual), cf. Livingstone (4902), 155 ff., and Thomson (4917), 62 ff. There are virtually no surviving records of the secretary's office for this period, but several volumes of the official correspondence have been published in Ruddiman (5128), and in 5136 and 5137.

(b) *Later Works*

There is no adequate study of the officers of the royal household. Cowan (5000) deals with the lives of the lord chancellors. For cardinal Beaton, the greatest of them, cf. 5502. For the greatest of the secretaries, Maitland of Lethington, cf. 5266 and 5270, and for Patrick Panter, secretary to James IV, cf. 5136, xxviii–xxxiv. For some papers of Erskine, secretary to James V, cf. 4956.

5368 CRAWFURD, GEORGE. Lives and characters of the crown officers of Scotland from . . . David I to the union. Vol. i (no more published). Edin. 1726.

4. THE PRIVY COUNCIL

(a) *Sources*

For the MS. records of the privy council, cf. Livingstone (4902), 17–23. The council register has been printed (4930) for the period 1545–1604 ff. The records of the judicial proceedings of the council have been printed for the years 1478–1503 and selections from its proceedings in public affairs from 1501 to 1554.

(b) *Later Works*

The best, in fact the only, adequate account is in Burton's introduction to the register (4930).

5. PARLIAMENT

(a) *Sources*

The official records, apart from a little scattered earlier material, commence in 1466 and run with some gaps to 1707. These are in print (4922). For material not in print, cf. Livingstone (4902), 15. The surviving records are little more than acts. There is nothing like a journal of proceedings surviving, nor any writs of summons. Reference should be made to the dispatches of foreign agents in Scotland for the workings of parliament, particularly to those of Randolph (4924) and of Pedro de Ayala (868). The proceedings of the judicial committee of parliament (the lords auditors) have been printed in part (4919 and 4920). The lords of the articles kept no records.

(b) *Later Works*

The best account is in Rait (5372). There is a good account of the committees of parliament in 4919, ii, intro. Reference should also be made to Porritt (1133), ii, chs. 33–35.

5369 FOSTER, J. Members of parliament, Scotland, 1357–1882. Lond. 1882; 2nd ed. rev. and corrected, 1882.
Repr. from *Collectanea Genealogica*. A new work, containing biographies of all members of the Scottish parliaments, is in preparation.

5370 MACKIE, J. D., and PRYDE, G. S. The estate of burgesses in the Scots parliament and its relation to the convention of royal burghs . . . with an inventory of the MS. records of the older royal burghs of Scotland. By A. J. Mill. St. Andrews, 1923.
Valuable review of Scottish burgh representation.

5371 MATHIESON, W. L. The Scottish parliament, 1560–1707. *Scot. Hist. Rev.* iv (1906), 49–62.

5372 RAIT, R. S. The parliaments of Scotland. Glasgow, 1924.
Excellent, especially on sixteenth and seventeenth centuries.

6. THE CONVENTION OF ESTATES

(a) *Sources*

The proceedings of the convention of estates are sometimes recorded in the Privy Council Register (4930). The only separate extant records, those of the conventions of 1598–9, 1643–4, 1665, 1667, and 1678, are not printed.

(b) *Later Works*

There is no separate study. Reference should be made to 5372.

7. THE CONVENTION OF ROYAL BURGHS

(a) *Sources*

5373 RECORDS OF THE CONVENTION OF ROYAL BURGHS of Scotland and extracts from other records relating to the affairs of the burghs of Scotland, 1295–1738. By J. D. Marwick. 6 vols. Edin. 1866–90.
Vols. i and ii cover the period 1295–1614; vi (by David Donaldson) contains the index and a glossary. The preface to vol. i is useful.

(b) *Later Works*

Reference should also be made to 5370 and to the preface of 5373.

5374 PAGAN, THEODORA. The convention of the royal burghs of Scotland. Glasgow, 1926.
Scholarly. Valuable chapters on finance, trade, and industry.

8. PUBLIC FINANCE

(a) *General*

The *Acts of Parliament* (4922) give the details of taxes granted by parliament and sometimes indicate the method of assessing and collecting them. The only sources in print are the exchequer rolls (4933) and the lord treasurer's accounts (4925). There is a good deal of unprinted material, particularly on the customs revenue, in the General Register House at Edinburgh; cf. Livingstone (4902), 28–52.

On local finance, particularly on the local collection of customs and on the 'Common Good' of the burghs, there is a considerable body of material preserved in local records, some of which are in the General Register House; cf. Livingstone (4902), 48–52. Local financial records are often to be found incorporated in the printed local source material listed in sect. B 2 *supra* (pp. 424–7), cf. particularly 5032, 5044, and 5055.

Dues payable to the crown by crown vassals upon entry or infeftment in their lands are recorded in the *Responde Books*. These are unprinted, but cf. 4933, appendixes. For those preserved in MS., cf. Livingstone (4902), 33 and Thomson (4917), 74. A few of the account books of the royal household survive; cf. Thomson (4917), 84. Extracts from some of these are printed in 5129.

The history of the levy and collection of the revenues in sixteenth-century Scotland is yet to be written. Excellent brief accounts of the administrative machinery are in Livingstone (4902), 28–31, and in Thomson (4917), 76–84. There is a good deal of information on the subject in the prefaces to the published volumes of the exchequer rolls (4933) and the lord treasurer's accounts (4925), particularly the prefaces to vol. i of each series. On the assessment of national taxes in the towns, cf. Pagan (5374), 52 ff. For local town taxes, cf. sect. B 3 (c) *supra* (p. 429), notably 5102.

5375 PURVES, W. Revenue of the Scottish crown, 1681. By D. M. Rose. Edin. 1897.
    Comparison of crown rentals of 1681 with those of 1603, by the king's solicitor.

(b) *The Coinage*

(1) *Sources*

The chief sources are the *Acts of Parliament* (4922) and the royal proclamations in Steele (1017), ii.

(2) *Later Works*

Reference should be made to Grueber (1254) and Ruding (1265).

5376 BURNS, EDWARD. The coinage of Scotland from David I to Queen Anne. 3 vols. Edin. 1887.

5377 CATALOGUE OF THE SCOTTISH COINS in the national museum of antiquities, Edinburgh. By A. B. Richardson. Edin. 1901.

5378 COCHRAN-PATRICK, R. W. Records of the coinage of Scotland from the earliest period to the union. 2 vols. Edin. 1876.

5379 CLOUSTON, J. S. Coins in use in Scotland in the sixteenth century. *Scot. Hist. Rev.* xvii (1919), 156–7.

5380 STEWART, I. H. The Scottish coinage. Lond. 1955.

9. THE HISTORY OF SCOTTISH LAW

(a) *General*

(1) *Sources*

The statutes are given in the acts (4922). For contemporary editions of the statutes, cf. *S.T.C.* (35), 21875–91. Balfour (5382) is the earliest textbook of

Scottish law. Bisset (5383) gives a contemporary account of legal procedure. For court records see the sections dealing with the various courts below.

5381 ANCIENT LAWS AND CUSTOMS of the burghs of Scotland. By Cosmo Innes. 2 vols. *Scot. Burgh Rec. Soc.* i and ii (1868–9).

5382 BALFOUR, JAMES. Practicks. By W. Goodall. Edin. 1754.
The first textbook on Scottish law, written *c.* 1580, probably only in part by Balfour. Goodall's introduction contains a life of Balfour. Cf. Heaton McKechnie, in *Jurid. Rev.* xliii (1931), 179–92.

5383 BISSET, HABUKKUK. Rolment of courtis. By P. J. Hamilton-Grierson. 3 vols. *Scot. Text Soc.*, n.s., x, xiii, xviii (1920–6).
A compilation of the forms of civil action, compiled 1609–22. Contains a biographical sketch of Bisset (vol. i) and a learned introduction (vol. iii) on Scottish legal procedure.

5384 CRAIG, THOMAS. Jus feodale. Edin. 1603; Leipzig, 1716; by James Baillie, Edin. 1732; trans. by J. A. Clyde, 2 vols., Edin.–Lond. 1934.
A learned work, still the standard authority on Scottish feudal land law.

5385 REGIAM MAJESTATEM: veteres leges et constitutiones. . . . By John Skene. Edin. 1609; 1774.
An English as well as a Latin version appeared in 1609. The book contains, besides the medieval collections of royal and feudal laws known as *Regiam majestatem* and *Quoniam attachiamenta*, a sixteenth-century treatise entitled *The form and maner of court baron, Ane short forme of process to be used before the lords of council and session,* a treatise on criminal law, on the justiciar and his ayre court, on the sheriff, the chamberlain, and the lords of regality. Cf. *Regiam Majestatem* and *Quoniam attachiamenta,* trans. by Lord Cooper, *Stair Soc.* xi (1947).
One of the most valuable contemporary sources on Scottish legal procedure. Cf. G. Neilson, *Sir John Skene's MS. Memorabilia Scotica, 1475–1612, and revisals of Regiam Majestatem* in *Trans. Glasgow Arch. Soc.* vii (1924).

5386 SKENE, JOHN. De verborum significatione. Edin. 1597; 1681.
An early Scottish law dictionary, still useful.

(2) *Later Works*

The *Stair Soc.* has in active preparation an introductory history of Scots law containing contributions from various exports. For an excellent account of legal procedure in the sixteenth century, cf. Hamilton-Grierson (5383), iii, intro. There is a good account of the origins of Scottish law by Neilson (4919), ii, intro. Green (5393) contains learned articles on different phases of the subject. The writings of the great Scottish jurists of the seventeenth and eighteenth centuries, notably Stair (5389) and, despite his obvious bias, Mackenzie (5360) are still valuable. Cf. also 5359.

5387 ANDERSON, A. M. The criminal law of Scotland. 7th ed. Edin. 1904.

5388 BELL, ROBERT. Dictionary and digest of the law of Scotland. Edin. 1890.

5389 DALRYMPLE, JAMES, LORD STAIR. Institutions of the law of Scotland. Edin. 1681; 1693.
Cf. A. H. Campbell, *The structure of Stair's Institutions, Glasgow Univ. Pub.* xcviii (1954).

5390 DICKINSON, W. C. The administration of justice in medieval Scotland. *Aberdeen Univ. Rev.* xxxiv (1952), 338–51.

5391 CLOUSTON, J. S. The lawthing and early officials of Orkney. *Scot. Hist. Rev.* xxi (1923), 101–15.

5392 COOPER, LORD The dark age of Scottish legal history, 1350–1650. Glasgow, 1952.

5393 ENCYCLOPAEDIA OF THE LAWS OF SCOTLAND. By John Chisholm. 14 vols. Edin. 1896–1904; by J. L. Wark, 16 vols. and index, with 3 supp. vols., Edin. 1926–52.
Generally known as *Green's Encyclopaedia*. Learned articles on legal history.

5394 GLASSFORD, J. Remarks on the constitution and procedure of the Scottish courts of law. Edin. 1812.

5395 HANNAY, R. K. Some questions regarding Scotland and the canon law. *Juridical Rev.* xliv (1937), 25–34.

5396 HENDERSON, J. A. History of the society of advocates in Aberdeen (1549–1912). *New Spalding Club*, no. 40, and *Aberdeen Univ. Studies*, no. 12 (1912).

5397 HISTORY OF THE SOCIETY of writers to H.M. Signet. Edin. 1890; continued, Edin. 1936.
Includes lists of members and abstracts of the minutes, beginning 1594. The 1936 ed. contains an article by R. K. Hannay on the early history of the signet.

5398 [HOME, HENRY, LORD KAMES.] Historical law tracts. 2 vols. Edin. 1758; 3rd ed. corrected and enlarged, Edin. 1776; 4th ed. enlarged, Edin. 1792.

5399 HUME, DAVID. Commentaries on the law of Scotland respecting the description and punishment of crimes. 2 vols. Edin. 1797.
The standard work on Scottish criminal law.

5400 McKECHNIE, HECTOR. Judicial process upon brieves, 1219–1532. Glasgow, 1956.

5400a McMILLAN, A. R. G. The evolution of the Scottish judiciary. Edin. 1941.
Repr. from the *Juridical Rev.*

5401 MELVILLE, R. D. The use and forms of judicial torture in England and Scotland. *Scot. Hist. Rev.* ii (1904), 225–49.

5402 MURRAY, DAVID. Legal practice in Ayr and the west of Scotland in the fifteenth and sixteenth centuries. *Proc. Inc. Soc. Law Agents in Scotland.* Glasgow, 1910.

5403 OMOND, G. W. T. The lord advocates of Scotland from the close of the fifteenth century to the reform bill. 2 vols. Edin. 1883.

5404 RANKINE, JOHN. The law of land ownership in Scotland. Edin. 4th ed. 1909.

5405 ROSS, WALTER. Lectures on the law of Scotland. Edin. 1792; 1822.

5406 STARKE, JAMES. Circuit court held at Dumfries . . . 1504. *Trans. Dumfriesshire and Galloway Nat. Hist. and Antiq. Soc.* iv (1868).

5407 WILSON, J. D. The reception of the Roman law in Scotland. *Juridical Rev.* ix (1897), 361–94.
Cf. also H. Goudy, *Inaugural lecture on the fate of the Roman law north and south of the Tweed*, Lond. 1894.

(b) *The Courts of Law*

(1) *Parliament*

(a) Sources

For the sources on the judicial committee of parliament, cf. 4919, 4920.

(b) Later Works

Cf. Neilson's introduction to vol. ii of 4919. On the relation of the lords auditors to the privy council and the court of session, cf. Hannay (5413).

5408 HAMILTON-GRIERSON, P. J. Appellate jurisdiction of the Scottish parliament. *Scot. Hist. Rev.* xv (1918), 205–22.

5409 HAMILTON-GRIERSON, P. J. The judicial committees of the Scottish parliament, 1369–70 to 1544. *Scot. Hist. Rev.* xxii (1924), 1–14.

(2) *Council*

(a) Sources

The records of the judicial acts of the council from 1478 are preserved in the Register House, Edinburgh. For those in print, cf. pp. 412 ff. The series continues without a break as the proceedings of the Court of Session after 1532.

(b) Later Works

Cf. introductions to 4919 and 4930, and above all Hannay (5413).

(3) *The Court of Session and the College of Justice*

(a) Sources

For the unprinted sources, cf. Livingstone (4902), 81–97. Cf. also 5385 and the works of Chambers (nos. 4974–6 *supra*), who was a senator of the college.

5410 THE ACTS OF SEDERUNT of the lords of council and session from 15 January 1553 to 11 July 1790. By Alexander Tait. Edin. 1790.

5411 THE ACTS OF SEDERUNT of the lords of council and session, May 1532–January 1553. By Ilay Campbell. Edin. 1811.
The acts of sederunt are concerned principally with the rules of the court. The court's proceedings, known as the Acts and Decreets, are unprinted except for selected items reproduced in Balfour's *Practicks* (5382) and W. M. Morison, *Dictionary of decisions*, 38 vols., 1801–4.

(b) Later Works

The best account of the origins is in Hannay (5413).

5412 BRUNTON, GEORGE, and HAIG, DAVID. Historical account of the senators of the college of justice from its institution in 1532. Edin. 1832.

5413 HANNAY, R. K. The college of justice; essays on the institution and development of the court of session. Edin. 1933.
The authoritative work, incorporating the substance of earlier articles by the author.

5414 MACKAY, Æ. J. G. The practice of the court of session. 2 vols. Edin. 1877–9.

(4) The Justiciar and the Ayre Courts and the Criminal Law

(a) Sources

The existing justiciary records begin in 1488. Formerly preserved in the Justiciary Office, Edinburgh, they are now in the Register House. Selections of them to the year 1624 are printed in Pitcairn (5415) with valuable illustrative material. Cf. Scott, *The archives of the high court of justiciary*, in *Juridical Rev.* iii (1891), 197–212; iv (1892), 32–43, 105–18. Reference should also be made to (5385) and to (4913), 370–7, 406–10.

5415 ANCIENT CRIMINAL TRIALS IN SCOTLAND. By Robert Pitcairn. 3 vols. *Bannatyne Club*, no. 42, and *Maitland Club*, no 19 (1829–33).
Covers the period 1488–1624.

(b) Later Works

There is no adequate modern study. Reference should be made to Anderson (5387) and to Thomson (4917), 137 ff.

(5) The Court of Exchequer and the Court of the Lord Lyon

Reference should be made to Livingstone (4902), 28 ff., 104–6, 214–15. For the Lyon court, cf. (4913), 379–95.

(6) High Court of Admiralty

(a) Sources

5416 ACTA CURIAE ADMIRALLATUS SCOTIAE, Sept. 6, 1557–March 11, 1561. T. C. Wade. *Stair Soc.* xliv (1937).

(b) Later Works

5417 THE SEA LAW OF SCOTLAND. By T. C. Wade. *Scot. Text Soc.* 3rd ser., iv (1933) 25–79.

(7) The Court of the Four Burghs

A court of appeals from burgh courts, presided over by the chamberlain. Scattered references will be found in 5373 and 5381, passim. Cf. Thomson (4917), 137.
There is no adequate modern account. Reference should be made to 5373 and 5374, intro.

(8) Local Courts

In the local courts, notably the sheriff's courts, the burgh courts, and the regality courts, registers were set up by law in the sixteenth century for recording land transfers, letters of horning (outlawry), and letters of inhibition (designed to prevent the alienation of the heritable property of delinquent debtors). The function of recording conveyances of land did not remain with the sheriff courts, and an independent *Register of sasines* was established, at first under the jurisdiction of the secretary (1599) and from 1617 under that of the lord clerk register. For the general character of these records and for lists of those preserved at the Register House, Edinburgh, cf. Livingstone (4902), 140–51, 166–81, 215–17.

(a) The Sheriff Courts

(1) Sources

For a list of the extant records of sheriff, regality and baron courts, cf. 4913, 117–29, and for a list of published records, ibid. 130–2. Cf. also Livingstone (4902), 131 ff., and *Report of the committee appointed to inquire as to . . . the custody and preservation of sheriff court records*, Edin. 1926.

5418 THE RECORDS OF THE SHERIFF COURT of Aberdeenshire. By David Littlejohn. 3 vols. *The New Spalding Club*, xxviii, xxxi, xxxii (1904–7).
Aberdeen has the earliest extant book of record of any Scottish sheriffdom. It begins 1503. Records printed to 1660. The best source on the sheriff's court, but suffers from its abridgement. Useful introduction.

5419 THE SHERIFF COURT BOOK OF FIFE, 1515–22. By W. C. Dickinson. *Scot. Hist. Soc.*, 3rd ser., xii (1928).
Contains an excellent introduction and valuable appendices.

5420 SHERIFF COURT BOOK of the sheriffdom of Dumfries, 1537–8, 1577–83. By P. J. Hamilton-Grierson. *Trans. Dumfries and Galloway Nat. Hist. and Antiq. Soc.*, 3rd ser., v (1918), xii (1926).

5421 HAMILTON-GRIERSON, P. J. The suitors of the sheriff court. *Scot. Hist. Rev.* xiv (1916), 1–19.
Excerpts from the Linlithgow sheriff court book.

(2) Later Works

The best accounts are in the introductions to 5418 and 5419.

(b) The Regality Courts and Baron Courts

Feudal courts corresponding to the court baron and the court leet in England. Cf. in general Livingstone (4902), 129–30, and Green (5393), art. Regality. For unprinted records preserved at the Register House, Edinburgh, cf. Livingstone (4902), 131 ff. and 4913.

5422 COURT BOOK OF REGALITY OF BROUGHTON AND BURGH OF CANONGATE, 1569–1573. Trans. by Marguerite Wood. Edin. 1937.

5423 THE COURT BOOK OF THE BARONY OF CARNWATH, 1523–1542. By W. C. Dickinson. *Scot. Hist. Soc. Pub. for 1935–36* (1937), 3rd ser., xxix.

5424 EXTRACTS FROM THE REGISTER OF THE REGALITY COURT OF SPYNIE, 1592–1601. *Spalding Club Misc.* ii (1842).

5425 REGALITY OF DUNFERMLINE COURT BOOK, 1531–1538. By J. M. Webster and A. A. M. Duncan, Dunfermline, 1953.

5426 SELECTIONS FROM THE RECORDS OF THE REGALITY of
    Melrose . . . By C. S. Romanes. 3 vols. *Scot. Hist. Soc.*, 2nd ser., vi, viii, xiii
    (1914–17).
    Vol. iii is the only one on the sixteenth century.

(c) The Burgh Courts

For the unprinted sources preserved at the Register House, cf. Livingstone
(4902), 131 ff.; for material in print, cf. 5381 and section B 2 *supra* (pp. 424 ff.).
Cf. especially the introduction to *Early Records of the Burgh of Aberdeen*, by
W. C. Dickinson, *Scot. Hist. Soc.*, 3rd ser., xlix (1957). Cf. 4913, 99–103. There
is much material in town histories listed in sect. B *supra* (pp. 423 ff.) particularly
5103, and in the introductions to collections of town records in sect. B 2 *supra*,
pp. 424–7.

(d) The Notary Public

For the nature of this office and for the notarial records or protocol books in
general, cf. Thomson (4917), ch. iv, and (4913), 290–300. For protocol books
preserved at the Register House, Edinburgh, cf. Livingstone (4902), 183 ff., and
4913, 289–90. These records are of greatest value for every branch of history.

Of those preserved for the sixteenth century, twelve have been edited for the
Scot. Rec. Soc. Abstracts from another are printed in vol. vi of *Publications of
the Ayrshire and Galloway Arch. Assoc.*; abstracts of the protocol book of Herbert
Anderson, 1541–69, by the *Trans. Dumfries and Galloway Nat. Hist. and Antiq.
Soc.*, 3rd ser., ii, iii (1914–15); and abstract of *Protocol book of burgh of Stirling,
1469–84*, Edin. 1896. Cf. 5035–7, 5040, 5431.

(e) The Commissary Courts

The extensive jurisdiction of the pre-reformation ecclesiastical courts held by
officials and commissaries was, from 1564, transferred to commissary courts
authorized by the crown, which dealt with confirmation of testaments and with
matrimonial and slander cases. Cf. in general (4913), 135–48, Thomson (4917),
117 ff., and Livingstone (4902), 106 ff. For printed selections from the proceedings of an official's court, cf. 5432, and for lists of records preserved in the
Register House, cf. Livingstone (4902), 109–29. All the extant records of
testaments for the sixteenth century have been indexed by the *Scot. Rec. Soc.*

5427 MUIRHEAD, J. S. The old minute book of the faculty of procurators
    in Glasgow, 1668–1758. Glasgow, 1948.
    Introduction deals with consistorial courts of Glasgow before the reformation.

E. ECCLESIASTICAL HISTORY

1. SOURCES

(a) *The Pre-reformation Church*

The 'registers' of Scottish bishoprics, religious houses, and other ecclesiastical
foundations are in the main in the nature of cartularies rather than ecclesiastical
registers. As most of them are relatively unimportant for sixteenth-century
church history they are not included in this bibliography. For a list of the
printed 'registers' and cartularies, cf. (4913), 260–1.

5428 BOETHIUS, HECTOR. (Boece, Hector.) Murthlacensium et Aberdonensium episcoporum vitae. Paris, 1522. *Bannatyne Club*, no. 11 (1825); later ed. and trans. by James Moir, *New Spalding Club*, no. 12 (1894).

5429 CONCILIA SCOTIAE ECCLESIAE SCOTICANAE statuta tam provincialia quam synodalia quae supersunt, 1225–1559. By Joseph Robertson. 2 vols. *Bannatyne Club*, no. 113 (1866); trans. by David Patrick, *Scot. Hist. Soc.* liv (1907).
Statutes of the Scottish church, 1225–1559.

5430 JOHN (HAMILTON), Archbishop of Saint Andrews. The catechisme set furth be. St. Andrews, 1552; by T. G. Law, Oxf. 1884.
A definition of a moderately conservative position, promulgated by the Scottish synod of 1552.

5431 LIBER PROTOCOLLORUM 1499–1513. Rental book of diocese of Glasgow, 1509–1570. By Joseph Bain and Charles Rogers. 2 vols. *Grampian Club*, no. 8 (1875).

5432 LIBER OFFICIALIS SANCTI ANDREE: curie metropolitane Sancti Andree in Scotia sententiarum in causis consistorialibus que extant. *Abbotsford Club*, no. 25 (1845).
A very small selection of the sentences of the consistorial court of the diocese, 1541–54.

5433 OBITUARY FROM THE RENTAL BOOK of the preceptory of St. Anthony near Leith, 1526. By David Laing, *Bannatyne Club Misc.* (4937), ii, 297 ff.

5434 RENTALE DUNKELDENSE: being the accounts of the chamberlain of the bishopric of Dunkeld, 1506–1517. By R. K. Hannay. *Scot. Hist. Soc.*, 2nd ser., x (1915).
Includes trans. of part of Myln's *Lives of the bishops of Dunkeld, Bannatyne Club*, i (1823) and a note on the cathedral church by F. C. Eeles.

5435 RENTALE SANCTI ANDREE; being chamberlain and granitar accounts of the archbishopric in the time of cardinal Betoun, 1538–1546. By R. K. Hannay. *Scot. Hist. Soc.*, 2nd ser., iv (1911).

5436 RICHARDSON, ROBERT. Commentary on the rule of St. Augustine. By G. G. Coulton. *Scot. Hist. Soc.*, 3rd ser., xxvi (1935).
By a canon of Cambuskenneth, 1530.

5437 SOME PROCESSES BELONGING TO GLENLUCE ABBEY. By R. C. Reid. *Trans. Dumfries and Galloway Nat. Hist. and Antiq. Soc.*, 3rd ser., xxi (1939), 290–309.

5438 ST. ANDREWS FORMULARE, 1514–1546. By Gordon Donaldson and C. Macrae. 2 vols. *Stair Soc.* (1942–4).
Style book (containing many genuine documents) of a notary who served archbishops of St. Andrews and Glasgow.

5439 VETERA MONUMENTA HIBERNORUM ET SCOTORUM historiam illustrantia. By A. Theiner. Rome, 1864.
Documents from the papal registers to 1547.

(b) *The Reformed Church*

Reference should also be made to the works of Buchanan, and other Scottish reformers, in ch. iv and ch. xii, sects. A and C *supra*, and to Foxe (1726). The position of the Scottish protestant church in matters of liturgy and discipline is defined in 5442, 5443 and 5445. A great deal of pertinent material is printed in Calderwood (5482) and in Laing's ed. of Knox's works (5450).

5440 ACCOUNTS OF THE COLLECTORS OF THIRDS OF BENE-FICES, 1561–1572. By Gordon Donaldson. *Scot. Hist. Soc.*, 3rd ser., xlii (1949).
For supplementary information, cf. *The 'new enterit' benefices, 1573–1586, Scot. Hist. Rev.* xxxii (1952), 93–96.

5441 ACTS AND PROCEEDINGS of the general assemblies of the kirk of Scotland from the year 1560 (1560–1618). By Thomas Thomson. 3 vols. *Bannatyne Club*, no. 81; *Maitland Club*, no. 49 (1839–45).
Commonly referred to as *The booke of the universall kirk of Scotland*. Not official records, for originals were burned in 1834, but a partial reconstruction from transcripts and extracts in print.

5442 [THE BOOK OF COMMON ORDER]: The forme of prayers and ministration of the sacraments, &c. . . . approved and received by the churche of Scotland. . . . Edin. 1564; repr. in 5450, vi, 275 ff.
For other sixteenth-century ed., cf. *S.T.C.* (35), 16577 ff., also Maxwell (5451).

5443 THE FIRST AND SECONDE BOOKE OF DISCIPLINE. [Leyden?] 1621.
This is the first separately printed ed. The 1st book was, however, added by Knox to the 3rd book of his *History of the Reformation in Scotland* and printed in part in the ed. of 1586 or 1587 of that work. It is repr. in 5450, ii, 183 ff. and in Dickinson's ed. (5449), ii, 280 ff. The 2nd book appears in 5482 and 5441. For bibliographical information, cf. 5450, i, pp. xxix–xliv, ii, 181 n.

5444 COCKBURN, PATRICK. In dominicam orationem pia meditatio. . . . St. Andrews, 1555. Repr. privately, 1908.
Early tract by an active reformer.

5445 THE CONFESSIOUN OF FAITH profesit and belevit be the protestantes within the realme of Scotland. [Edin.], 1561.
Incorporated by Knox in his history (5449) and repr. in 5450, ii, 95 ff., also in Dickinson's ed. (5449), ii, 257 ff. The confession also appears in the *Acts of the parliaments of Scotland*, ii, 526 ff., and iii, 14 ff.
A new ed. of the confession by G. D. Henderson appeared in 1937.

5446 FERGUSSON, DAVID. Tracts, 1563–1572. *Bannatyne Club*, no. 110 (1860).
Author minister of Dunfermline. Contains Réné Benoist's epistle to John Knox, 1561; Fergusson's answer to same, 1563; sermon by Fergusson, 1571.

5447 GAU, JOHN. The richt way to the kingdome of heuine. . . . Malmoe, 1533; by A. F. Mitchell, *Scot. Text Soc.* xii (1888).
One of the earliest expressions of Scottish Protestantism, but apparently a literal trans. of a Danish book. Cf. 5450, i, 503, 528; vi, 665; and also Mitchell's introduction and notes.

5448 [GUDE AND GODLIE BALLATIS]: The haill hundreth and fyftie psalmes of David . . . wyth utheris diversis poyetis. . . . Edin. 1567; best ed. by A. F. Mitchell, *Scot. Text Soc.* xxxix (1897).
The notes to Mitchell's ed. give full bibliographical data.

5449 KNOX, JOHN. The history of the reformation in Scotland, 1st ed. unfinished, suppressed, by T. Vautrollier, Lond. 1587; 1st accurate ed. by M. Crawford, Edin. 1732; best eds. by D. Laing, Edin. 1846–8, vols. i, ii and vi of *Works* (5450) and W. C. Dickinson, 2 vols., Edin. 1949.
One of the most important sources for the history of the reformation in Scotland. Laing's notes and appendixes are very valuable. In the introduction to vol. i he discusses MSS. and early eds. of the work. Dickinson's ed. has the complete text in English, admirably edited with introductory essay and a very full index.

5450 KNOX, JOHN. The works of. By David Laing. 6 vols. Edin. 1846–64.
Vols. i–ii include the history of the reformation. Vols. iii–vi all the miscellaneous writings of Knox and most of his extant correspondence. Laing gives full bibliographical data for all he prints.

5451 KNOX, JOHN. John Knox's Genevan service book (1556). By W. D. Maxwell. Edin. 1931.
The liturgical portions of the Genevan service book used by Knox while a minister of the English congregation of Marian exiles at Geneva, 1556–9.

5452 THE MISCELLANY OF THE WODROW SOCIETY. Vol. i by David Laing. Edin. 1844.
Reprints of several sixteenth-century tracts relative to the Scottish church, and a few letters of the period relating to ecclesiastical affairs.

5453 REGISTERS OF MINISTERS, exhorters, and readers, and of their stipends, after the period of the reformation. *Maitland Club*, no. 5 (1830).
Register of stipends, 1567–73. Extracts from book of assignations, 1576. There is similar matter for 1574 in 5452.

5454 SCOT, WILLIAM. Apologetical narration of the state of the kirk of Scotland, 1558–1633. By David Laing. *Wodrow Soc.* no. 10 (1846).
Author an ardent Presbyterian minister.

5455 SOURCES FOR SCOTTISH ECCLESIASTICAL ORGANIZA-TION AND PERSONNEL, 1560–1600. By Gordon Donaldson. *Bull. Inst. Hist. Research*, xix (1943), 188–203.

(c) *Post-reformation Roman Catholicism*

5456 THE ANTIQUITY OF THE CHRISTIAN RELIGION among the Scots, 1594. By H. D. G. Law. *Scot. Hist. Soc. Misc.* ii (1904), 115–32.
An appeal to Catholics to support the Scots college recently moved from Pont-à-Moussin to Douai, trans. from a Latin MS. by Geo. Thomson.

5457 CATHOLIC TRACTATES of the sixteenth century, 1573–1600. By T. G. Law. *Scot. Text Soc.* (1901).

5458 CHADWICK, HUBERT. Father William Creichton, S. J. and a recently discovered letter, 1589. *Arch. Hist. Soc. Iesu*, vi (1937), 259–86.

5459 CHADWICK, HUBERT. A memoir of Father Edmund Hay, S. J. *Arch. Hist. Soc. Iesu*, viii (1939), 66–85.

5460 NARRATIVES OF SCOTTISH CATHOLICS under Mary Stuart
and James VI. By William Forbes-Leith. Edin. 1885; Lond. 1889.
Correspondence chiefly from Vatican and Jesuit archives; includes also continuation of
Leslie's history (4983).

5461 NARRATIVES OF THE SCOTTISH REFORMATION. i, Report
of Father Robert Abercrombie, S J. in the year 1580. *Innes Rev.* vii (1956),
27–59; ii, Thomas Innes on catholicism, 1560–1653. *Ibid.* 112–21.

5463 RECORDS OF THE SCOTS COLLEGES at Douai, Rome, Madrid,
Valladolid, and Ratisbon. Vol. i, register of students. *New Spalding Club*,
no. 30 (1906).
Catholic colleges.

5464 RELACIÓN DEL ESTADO DEL REYNO de Escocia, en lo tocante
a nuestra religión Católica. s.l., 1594.
Account of persecution of Catholic party under James VI.

5465 WINZET, NINIAN. Certaine tractatis for reformatioun of doctryne
and maneris, set furth at the desyre and in the name of afflictit catholikis. . . .
Edin. 1562; by David Laing, *Maitland Club*, no. 33 (1835); by J. K. Hewison,
2 vols., *Scot. Text Soc.* xv, xxii (1888–90).
Written by a Linlithgow schoolmaster who was ejected from his office for refusal to
sign the confession of faith in 1561.

(d) *Local*

Reference should be made also to sect. B *supra* (pp. 423–31), and 4897. Cf.
(4913), 156–62 (for lists of MS. and printed records of courts of reformed
church) and Thomas Burns, *The Benefice Lectures*, Edin. 1905, for a complete
inventory of records of general assembly, synods, presbyteries, and kirk sessions.

5466 ECCLESIASTICAL RECORDS OF ABERDEEN. Selections from
the records of the kirk session, presbytery and synod of Aberdeen. *Spalding
Club*, no. 15 (1846).
Kirk session from 1562, presbytery from 1598.

5467 EXTRACTS FROM THE KIRK SESSION records of Kinghorn
(1581–1659). Kirkaldy, 1863.

5467a EXTRACTS FROM THE KIRK SESSION records of Perth, 1577–
1634. *Spottiswoode Misc.* (4962), ii, 225 ff.

5468 EXTRACTS FROM THE REGISTERS of the presbytery of Glasgow
and of the kirk sessions of Edinburgh and Stirling prior to the year 1601.
By Alexander Macdonald and James Dennistoun. *Maitland Club Misc.* (4950),
i, pt. 1.
Those of Glasgow cover the years 1592–1601, those of Edinburgh, 1574–5, those of
Stirling, 1597–1600.

5469 RECORDS OF THE DIOCESES OF ARGYLL and the Isles, 1560–
1860. By J. B. Craven. Kirkwall, 1907.

5470 RECORDS OF THE KIRK SESSION OF ELGIN, 1584–1779. By
W. Cramond. Elgin, 1897.

5471 REGISTER OF THE MINISTERS, elders and deacons of . . . St. Andrews, 1559–1600. By D. H. Fleming. 2 vols. *Scot. Hist. Soc.* iv, vii (1889–90).
Incorporates proceedings of court of superintendent of Fife. The earliest and most important kirk session record. Extracts were printed in *Bannatyne Misc.* (4937), i, pt. 2, 251–65 and *Maitland Club Misc.* (4950), iii, pt. 2.

2. LATER WORKS

The general histories of Scotland, particularly those of Brown (4996) and Lang (5007) and Mathieson (5013), should be consulted. Mathieson emphasizes particularly the interaction of religion and politics. Keith (5006) is important. Useful notes on many of the early Scottish reformers will be found in the app. to vol. i of Laing's ed. of the works of Knox (5450). Laing's footnotes (ibid.) to Knox's *History of the Reformation* are a mine of information. For Scottish divines overseas, the lives of Alexander Aless (Alesius) and of John Macalpine (Maccabeus) in the *D.N.B.* should be consulted, together with the references there cited.

5472 ADAMSON, M. R., BURNS, J. H., ANDERSON, W. J., and McLAREN, ROBERT. The ordination of John Knox, a symposium. *Innes Rev.* vi (1955), 99–106.

5473 BELLESHEIM, A. Geschichte der katholischen Kirche in Schottland. 2 vols. Mainz, 1883; English trans. with additions by Hunter Blair, 4 vols. Edin. 1887–90.
Standard Catholic history. Blair's version is not always a close translation.

5474 BIRNIE, A. A short history of the Scottish teinds. Edin. 1928.

5475 BROWN, P. H. George Buchanan, humanist and reformer. Edin. 1890.

5476 BROWN, P. H. George Buchanan and the inquisition from newly discovered documents. *Scot. Rev.* xxi (1891), 296–315.

5477 BROWN, P. H. John Knox: a biography. Edin. 1895.

5478 BROWN, W. E. John Ogilvie. Lond. 1925.
Jesuit executed for treason in 1615. Cf. Thomas Collins, *Martyr in Scotland*, Lond. 1955.

5479 BRYCE, W. M. The Scottish grey friars. 2 vols. Edin. 1909.
A substantial work, printing many documents.

5480 BRYCE, W. M. The black friars of Edinburgh. Edin. 1911.
Repr. from *Book of Old Edin. Club*.

5481 BURNS, J. H. New light on John Major. *Innes Rev.* v (1954), 83–100.
Suggests that Major was a Protestant.

5482 CALDERWOOD, DAVID. The true history of the church of Scotland from the beginning of the reformation unto the end of the reign of King James VI . . . [Rotterdam], 1678; best ed. by T. Thomson and D. Laing, 8 vols., *Wodrow Soc.*, no. 7 (1842–9).
1st ed. a condensed history printed from a MS. prepared by the author. *Wodrow Soc.* ed. is from a MS. in B.M.; cf. vol. viii for comparison of two eds. The most important of the Scottish church histories except that of Knox. Indispensable for the documents it prints, but the commentary of Calderwood (1575–1650), a prominent Presbyterian minister, is strongly partisan.

5483 CHADWICK, HUBERT. The Scots College, Douai, 1580–1613. *E.H.R.* lvi (1941), 571–85.

5484 CORMACK, A. A. Teinds and agriculture. Oxf. 1930.

5485 COULTON, G. G. Scottish abbeys and social life. Cambr. 1933.

5486 COUPER, W. J. The Levitical family of Simpson. *Rec. of Scot. Church Hist. Soc.* iv, v (1933–4).

5487 CRAVEN, J. B. History of the church in Orkney, vol. i (to 1558), ii (1558–1662). Kirkwall, 1897–1901.
Outstanding among local church histories.

5488 DONALDSON, GORDON. 'The Example of Denmark' in the Scottish Reformation. *Scot. Hist. Rev.* xxvii (1948), 57–64.

5489 DONALDSON, GORDON. The Scottish episcopate at the Reformation. *E.H.R.* lx (1945), 349–64.

5490 DONALDSON, GORDON. The making of the Scottish prayer book of 1637. Edin. 1954.
Contains a chapter on the prayer book in Scotland before 1600.

5491 DONALDSON, GORDON. The polity of the Scottish church, 1560–1600. *Rec. of Scot. Church Hist. Soc.* xi (1953), 212–26.

5492 DONALDSON, GORDON. The Galloway clergy at the Reformation. *Trans. Dumfries and Galloway Nat. Hist. and Antiq. Soc.*, 3rd ser., xxx (1953), 38–60.

5493 DOWDEN, JOHN. The bishops of Scotland, being notes on the lives of all the bishops . . . prior to the reformation. By J. M. Thomson, Glasgow, 1912.
Requires correction; cf. list of bishops in (78).

5494 EASSON, D. E. The reformation and the monasteries in Scotland and England: some comparisons. *Scot. Eccles. Soc. Trans.* xv, pt. i (1957), 7–23.

5495 EASSON, D. E. Gavin Dunbar, Lond. 1947.

5496 EELES, F. C. King's College chapel, Aberdeen: its fittings, ornaments, and ceremonial in the sixteenth century. Edin. 1956.

5497 FLEMING, D. H. The reformation in Scotland. Lond. 1910.
Discussion of the 'causes, characteristics, consequences' of the reformation rather than a narrative of events. Strongly Protestant in opinion, but scholarly and accurate.

5498 GILLON, R. M. John Davidson of Prestonpans, reformer, preacher and poet in the generation after Knox. Lond. 1936.

5499 [GUNN, C. B.] The book of Peebles church, St. Andrews collegiate parish church, 1195–1560. . . . Peebles, 1908.
Cf. idem, *The church and monastery of the Holy Cross of Peebles . . . 1261–1560*, Peebles, 1909, and *The book of the Cross kirk, 1560–1690 . . .*, Peebles, 1912.

5500 GRUB, GEORGE. An ecclesiastical history of Scotland . . . to the present time. 4 vols. Edin. 1861.
Standard church history; episcopal viewpoint.

5501 HANNAY, R. K. The church lands at the reformation. *Scot. Hist. Rev.* xvi (1918), 52–89.

5502 HERKLESS, JOHN, and HANNAY, R. K. The archbishops of St. Andrew, 5 vols. Edin. 1907–15.
Scholarly and substantial, a vol. each to Andrew Forman, James Beaton, David Beaton, and John Hamilton.

5503 LANG, ANDREW. John Knox and the reformation. Edin. 1905.
Cf. W. C. Dickinson, *Andrew Lang, John Knox, and Scottish presbyterianism* (Andrew Lang lecture for 1951), Edin. 1952.

5504 LAW, T. G. Collected essays. By P. H. Brown. Edin. 1904.
Includes: John Major, Scottish scholastic, 1470–1550; Letters and memorials of cardinal Allen; English Jesuits and Scottish intrigues, 1581–2; The Spanish blanks and Catholic earls, 1592–4; Father William Crichton, S.J.

5505 LORIMER, PETER. John Knox and the church of England. Lond. 1875.

5506 LORIMER, PETER. Precursors of Knox; or memoirs of Patrick Hamilton, the first preacher and martyr of the Scottish reformation. Edin. 1857.

5507 McCRIE, THOMAS. Life of John Knox. Edin. 1811; 2 vols. Edin. 1831.
Largely superseded by later research, but not to be ignored.

5508 McCRIE, THOMAS. Life of Andrew Melville. 2 vols. Edin. 1819; 1899.
Contains a wide range of information, much of it from MS. sources, on ecclesiastical and educational history. The author a strong Presbyterian partisan.

5509 McMILLAN, WILLIAM. The worship of the Scottish reformed church, 1550–1638. Lond. 1931.
Brings together much important information.

5510 McMILLAN, WILLIAM. The Lord high commissioner to the general assembly. *Rec. of the Scot. Church Hist. Soc.* vi (1936), 36–45; vi (1937), 96–114.

5511 MACEWEN, A. R. A history of the church in Scotland. Vol. i to 1546. Lond. 1913; vol. ii, 1546–60, Lond. 1918.
Good. Covers material thoroughly. Protestant viewpoint, but not strongly partisan.

5512 MACGREGOR, J. G. The Scottish Presbyterian polity in the sixteenth century. Edin. 1926.
Inadequate.

5513 MACPHAIL, J. R. N. Hamilton of Kincavil and the general assembly of 1563. *Scot. Hist. Rev.* x (1912), 156–61.

5514 MAURY, G. B. John Cameron: a Scottish protestant theologian in France; 1579–1625. *Scot. Hist. Rev.* vii (1909), 325–45.

5515 MORRIS, D. B. The story of a Cambuskenneth monk. *Trans. Stirling Nat. Hist. and Arch. Soc. for 1936–7*, lix (1937), 41–48.

5516 MORTIMER, C. G. The Scottish hierarchy in 1560. *Clergy Rev.* xii (1936), 442–50.

5517   PATRICK, MILLAR. Four centuries of Scottish psalmody. Oxf. 1949.

5518   PAUL, J. B. Clerical life in Scotland in the sixteenth century. *Scot. Hist. Rev.* xvii (1919), 177–90.

5519   PERCY, EUSTACE. John Knox. Lond. 1937.

5520   RANKIN, W. E. K. The parish church of the Holy Trinity, St. Andrews: pre-reformation. *St. Andrews Pub.* lii (1955).

5521   REID, W. S. Clerical taxation: the Scottish alternative to dissolution of the monasteries, 1530–1560. *Cath. Hist. Rev.* xxxiv (1948), 129–53.

5522   REID, W. S. The middle class factor in the Scottish reformation. *Church Hist.* xvi (1947), 137–53.

5523   REID, W. S. The Scottish counter-reformation before 1560. *Church Hist.* xiv (1945), 104–25.

5524   ROBERTSON, J. History of the reformation in Aberdeen. Aberdeen, 1887.

5525   ROGERS, CHARLES. Memoir of George Wishart, the Scottish martyr. *Trans. R.H. Soc.* iv (1876), 260–363.
Foxe (1726) and Knox (5449) are the primary authorities for Wishart's martyrdom, but are both strongly biased in his favour.

5526   ROW, JOHN. The history of the kirk of Scotland 1558–1637 with a continuation to July 1639 by his son John Row. By D. Laing. *Wodrow Soc.* no. 4 (1842); 2 vols., *Maitland Club*, no. 55 (1842).
First publication of the history as revised and amplified by the author during the latter period of his life (d. 1646). MS. in handwriting of his son, John Row. Author a prominent member of anti-episcopal party. The *Wodrow Soc.* ed. has the better text.

5527   SCOTT, HEW. Fasti ecclesiae Scoticanae. The succession of ministers in the parish churches of Scotland from the reformation, 1560, to the present time. 6 vols. *Bannatyne Club*, c (1866–71).
New and enl. ed., 7 vols., Edin. 1915–28; vol. viii, Edin. 1950, contains *addenda* and *corrigenda* especially important for sixteenth century.

5528   SHEARMAN, FRANCIS. James Wood of Boniton. *Innes Rev.* v (1954), 28–32.

5529   SMITH, D. B. The reformers and divorce. *Scot. Hist. Rev.* ix (1913), 10–36.

5530   SPOTSWOOD (or Spotiswood, or Spottiswoode), JOHN. History of the church of Scotland . . . to the end of the reign of James the VI. Lond. 1655; by M. Russell and Mark Napier, 3 vols. *Spottiswoode Soc.* no. 6; *Bannatyne Club*, no. 93 (1847–51).
Written at the request of James VI; presents the official, episcopal version. Prints a number of valuable documents but is much less important than Calderwood.

5531   THREE SCOTTISH REFORMERS, Alexander Cunningham, fifth earl of Glencairn, Henry Balnaves of Halhill, John Davidson, minister of Prestonpans, with their poetical remains. By Charles Rogers. Lond. 1874.

5532   WARNER, G. F. James VI and Rome. *E.H.R.* xx (1905), 124–7.
Letters of James VI *in extenso*.

5533 WATT, HUGH. John Knox in controversy. Edin. 1950.

5534 WODROW, ROBERT. Collections upon the lives of the reformers and
the most eminent ministers of the church of Scotland. By W. J. Duncan.
2 vols. (4 parts). *Maitland Club*, no. 32 (1834–48).
Author a minister at Eastwood, 1679–1734. For other selections from Wodrow's
collections, cf. *Selections from Robert Wodrow's biographical collections; divines of north-
east Scotland*, by Robert Lippe, *New Spalding Club*, no. 5 (1890).

5535 WRIGHT, R. S. The kirk in the Canongate. Edin. 1956.
Includes extracts from kirk session minutes, 1564–7.

F. ECONOMIC AND SOCIAL HISTORY

1. Sources

(a) *General*

For bibliographies of Scottish economic history, cf. 4911. A good deal of material
pertinent to Scottish commercial and industrial life will be found in the published
records of the Scottish burghs, notably those of Edinburgh (5031–4). Much
material for economic and social history will be found in notaries' protocol books
and collections of family papers.

5536 THE BLACK BOOK OF TAYMOUTH, with other papers from the
Breadalbane charter room. By Cosmo Innes. *Bannatyne Club*, no. 100
(1855).

5537 FEUING OF DRYGRANGE, from the monastery of Melrose. By G.
Neilson. *Scot. Hist. Rev.* vii (1909–10), 355–63.
An illustration of the process of feuing.

5538 THE ROYAL HOUSEHOLD BOOKS AND PAPERS. By William
Angus. *Scot. Hist. Rev.* xxxi (1952), 192–3.

5539 TRIALS FOR WITCHCRAFT, 1596–97. By John Stuart. *Spalding
Club Misc.* i (1841).
Accounts of trials from Aberdeen court records. Cf. 5317. Cf. also G. F. Black, *A
Calendar of cases of witchcraft in Scotland, 1510–1727*, *Bull. New York Pub. Lib.* xli
(1937), 811–47, and H. G. Stafford, *Notes on Scottish witchcraft cases*, in *Essays in honor
of Conyers Read*, Chicago, 1953, pp. 96–118.

(b) *Industry and Trade*

Cf. Town records 424–7 *supra*, pp. 424–7.

5540 ARMSTRONG, W. B. Two papers relating to the export of coals from
Scotland, 1596 and 1614. *Proc. Soc. Antiq. Scot.* xxiv (1890), 474–7.

5541 ATKINSON, STEPHEN. The discoverie and historie of the gold
mynes in Scotland. *Bannatyne Club*, no. 14 (1825).
Written 1619 by a silver refiner who had engaged in mining undertakings.

5542 BOOK OF THE PERTH HAMMERMEN, 1518 to 1568. . . . By
C. A. Hunt. Perth, 1889.

5543 THE COMPT BUIK OF DAVID WEDDERBURNE, merchant of
Dundee, 1587–1630; together with the shipping lists of Dundee, 1580–1618.
By A. H. Millar. *Scot. Hist. Soc.* xxviii (1898).
Printed *in extenso*. Earliest Dundee shipping list known to be extant. Valuable.

5544 EXTRACTS FROM THE MINUTE BOOKS of the weavers corporation of Galashiels, 1574–1692. *Hawick Arch. Soc.*, no. 8 (1869).

5545 THE HAMMERMEN OF EDINBURGH . . . extracts from the original
records, 1494 to 1558. By J. Smith. Edin. 1905.
Cf. also W. C. Little, *An historical account of the hammermen of Edinburgh, Trans. Soc.
Antiq. of Scot.* i (1792), 170 ff.

5546 LEDGER OF ANDREW HALYBURTON, conservator of the privi-
leges of the Scotch nation in the Netherlands, 1492–1503. Together with the
book of customs and valuation of merchandises in Scotland, 1612. By Cosmo
Innes. Edin. 1867.
Oldest extant Scottish merchant's account book and earliest complete tariff of customs.
Prints in full accounts with individuals. Introduction valuable.

5547 THE STIRLING GUILDRY BOOK: extracts from the records of the
merchant guild of Stirling, 1592–1846. By W. B. Cook and D. B. Morris.
Scot. Burgh Rec. Soc., extra vol., 1916.

(c) *Education*

Cf. the publications of the Spalding Clubs for records, lists of officers and
graduates of Aberdeen University, *Spalding Club*, no. 26 (1854); *New Spalding
Club*, nos. 4, 11, 18, 19 (1893–8). Cf. also 5496.

5548 ACTS OF THE PARLIAMENT and of the privy council of Scotland,
relative to the establishing and maintaining of schools from the year 1496 to
the year 1696. By James Dennistoun and Alexander Macdonald. *Maitland
Club Misc.* ii, pt. 1 (4950).

5549 EDINBURGH UNIVERSITY: Catalogue of graduates of the university of Edinburgh. Edin. 1858.

5550 EXTRACTS FROM ACCOUNTS OF THE COMMON GOOD of
various burghs relating to payments for schools and schoolmasters between
the years 1557 and 1634. By James Dennistoun and Alexander Macdonald.
Maitland Club Misc. ii, pt. 1 (4950).

5551 GLASGOW UNIVERSITY: Munimenta alme universitatis Glasguen-
sis, records of the university of Glasgow from its foundation till 1727. By
Cosmo Innes and Joseph Robertson. 4 vols. *Maitland Club*, no. 69 (1854).

5552 ROBERTSON, GEORGE, and CHARTERIS, HENRY. De vita et
morte Roberti Rollok, academiae Edinburgenae primarii, narrationes. Edin.
1599; by John Lee. *Bannatyne Club*, no. 16 (1826).
Contemporary biography of principal of university of Edinburgh, 1583–99.

5553 ST. ANDREWS UNIVERSITY: early records of the university of St.
Andrews, to 1579. By J. M. Anderson. *Scot. Hist. Soc.*, 3rd ser., viii (1926).
Matriculation and graduate lists.

5554 THE SCOTTISH NATION in the university of Orleans, 1336–1538. By John Kirkpatrick. *Scot. Hist. Soc. Misc.* ii (1904), 47–105.

(d) *Scots Abroad*

5555 PAPERS illustrating the history of the Scots brigade in the service of the United Netherlands, 1572–1782. By James Ferguson. 3 vols. *Scot. Hist. Soc.* xxxii, xxxv, xxxviii (1899–1901).

Vol. i, 1572–1697. Scots brigade commissions, claims, petitions, requests; reports of Dutch ambassadors to Scotland. Papers chiefly from Hague archives, printed *in extenso*.

5556 PAPERS RELATING TO THE SCOTS IN POLAND, 1576–1793. By Francis Steuart. *Scot. Hist. Soc.* lix (1915).

A few papers printed *in extenso* relating to the privileges and activities of Scotch merchants in Poland in the sixteenth century. For further literature on the Scot abroad, cf. Davies (8), no. 3062.

2. LATER WORKS

(a) *General*

On industrial organization and trade, reference should be made to the town histories *supra* (pp. 429 ff.); on Scottish mining, cf. 5584; on Scottish handicraft, 3923, 5645; on the relief of the poor in Scotland, 5586; on the Scottish herring fisheries, 2821, 2824. The best general account is in Grant (5562). Cf. 2926.

5557 BROWN, P. H. Scotland in the time of Queen Mary. Lond. 1904.

A survey of physical, economic, and social aspects of the country based largely on the material published by him in 4943 and 4960, and on burgh records.

5558 BURNS, JAMES. The Scotland of John Major. *Innes Rev.* ii (1951), 65–76.

5559 CHAMBERS, ROBERT. Domestic annals of Scotland. 3 vols. Edin. 1858–61; abr. ed., Edin. 1885.

5560 FLEMING, D. H. The influence of the reformation on social and cultural life in Scotland. *Scot. Hist. Rev.* xv (1917), 1–30.

5561 FRANKLIN, T. B. A history of Scottish farming. Edin. 1952.

5562 GRANT, I. F. Social and economic development of Scotland before 1603. Edin. 1930.

The best general account.

5563 GUTHRIE, DOUGLAS. King James the fourth of Scotland: his influence on medicine and science. *Bull. of the Hist. of Med.* xxi (1947), 173–92.

5564 INNES, COSMO. Sketches of early Scotch history and social progress. Edin. 1861.

Social and economic.

5565 JOHNSTON, T. History of the working classes in Scotland. Glasgow, 1923.

Socialist propaganda, but contains valuable material.

5566 MACDONALD, C. M. The struggle . . . for the preceptory of Tor-phichen. *Scot. Hist. Rev.* xiv (1916), 19–49.

5567 MACKENZIE, W. M. The Scottish burghs, Edin. 1949.
A general survey, meagre on the sixteenth century.

5568 MACKIE, J. D. Scotland and the renaissance. *Proc. Roy. Philos. Soc. Glasgow for 1932–4*, (1934), lxi, 74–89.

5569 MACKINNON, JAMES. The social and industrial history of Scotland from the earliest times to the union. 2 vols. Lond. 1920–1.
Good brief review.

5570 MACKINTOSH, J. History of civilization in Scotland. 4 vols. Aberdeen, 1878–88; Paisley, 1896.
The most comprehensive account of the subject, but lacking in scholarship.

5571 MULLET, C. F. Plague policy in Scotland, 16th and 17th centuries. *Osiris*, ix (1950) 435–56.
Cf. also John Ritchie, *The plague in Dumfries*, *Trans. Dumfries and Galloway Nat. Hist. and Antiq. Soc.*, 3rd ser., xxi (1939), 90–105.

5572 MURRAY, M. A. The 'devil' of North Berwick. *Scot. Hist. Rev.* xv (1917), 310–22.
Concerns witch trials, 1590–1.

5573 PATON, JAMES. Scottish history and life. Glasgow, 1902.
Contains several authoritative articles on economic topics.

5574 PAUL, J. B. Social life in Scotland in the sixteenth century. *Scot. Hist. Rev.* xvii (1919), 296–310.

5575 READ, JOHN. Alchemy under James IV of Scotland. *Ambix.* ii (1938–9), 60–67.

5576 ROGERS, C. Social life in Scotland from early to recent times. 3 vols. *Grampian Club*. Edin. 1884–6.

5577 RORIE, DAVID. George Boswell-chirurgeon to King James VI. *Scots Mag.*, n.s., xxix (1938), 348–56.

5578 STEWART, T. G. Notes on Scottish medicine in the days of Queen Mary. *Blackwood's Mag.*, cliii (1893), 885–902.
Gives an account of the various illnesses from which Mary and her contemporaries suffered.

5579 WARRACK, JOHN. Domestic life in Scotland, 1488–1688. *The Rhind lectures in archaeology*. Lond. 1920.

(b) *Industry and Trade*

5580 ANGUS, W. The incorporated trade of the skinners of Edinburgh, with extracts from their minutes, 1549–1603. *Book of the old Edin. Club*. vi (1913).

5581 BAIN, E. Merchant and craft guilds, a history of the Aberdeen incorporated trades. Aberdeen, 1887.

5582 BREMNER, D. The industries of Scotland. . . . Edin. 1869.
Newspaper articles repr. and extended.

5583 CARSTAIRS, A. M. The Convener's court book of the seven incorporated trades in St. Andrews. *Scot. Hist. Rev.* xxxiv (1955), 32–43.

5584 COCHRAN-PATRICK, R. W. Early records relating to mining in Scotland. Edin. 1878.
Deals mainly with the mining of precious metals. On coal mining, cf. 2785.

5585 COOK, W. B. The oldest minute book of Stirling incorporation of hammermen. *Trans. Stirling Nat. Hist. and Arch. Soc.* xxiv (1902), 18–34.

5586 CORMACK, ALEXANDER. Poor relief in Scotland. Aberdeen, 1923.
For further reference to poor relief in Scotland, cf. Webb (2928), 8, n. 2.

5587 CUNNINGHAM, WILLIAM. Differences in economic development in England and Scotland: (1) Burgh life, (2) Tillage. *Scot. Hist. Rev.* xiii (1915), 168–88.

5587a DAVIDSON, JOHN, and GRAY, ALEXANDER. The Scottish staple at Veere. Lond. 1909.
Valuable discussion of sixteenth-century Scottish trade in general as well as description of staple.

5587b EDINBURGH GUILDS AND CRAFTS (1616–1872). By J. D. Marwick. *Scot. Burgh Rec. Soc.* xxi (1909).
The introduction is valuable for the sixteenth century.

5588 FAIRWEATHER, W. C., and MELDAU, R. The men of Noroway contra the men of Orkney. *Viking Soc. Old Lore Misc.* x (1936), 36–42.

5589 FLEMING, D. H. Ye doingis of ane antient craft; being an account of the hammermen of St. Andrews from pre-reformation times until the end of the last (eighteenth) century. Cupar Fife, 1884.
Paper read before *The Lit. and Philos. Soc. of St. Andrews.*

5590 GRAY, W. F. The incorporation of candle-makers of Edinburgh, 1517–1884. *Book of the old Edin. Club*, xvii (1930), 91–146.

5591 HANNAY, R. H. Shipping and the staple, 1515–31. *Book of the old Edin. Club*, ix (1916), 49–78.

5592 KEITH, THEODORA. Influence of the convention of the royal burghs of Scotland on the economic development of Scotland before 1707. *Scot. Hist. Rev.* x (1912), 250–71.
Cf. idem, *Trading privileges of the royal burghs of Scotland*, E.H.R. xxviii (1913), 454–71, 678–90.

5593 KNOOP, DOUGLAS, and JONES, G. P. The Scottish mason and the mason work. Manchester, 1939.

5594 LAMOND, ROBERT. The Scottish craft gild as a religious fraternity. *Scot. Hist. Rev.* xvi (1916), 191–212.

5595 LUMSDEN, H., and AITKEN, P. H. History of the hammermen of Glasgow. . . . Paisley, 1912; 1915.
For the history of other crafts in Glasgow, cf. 4904, pp. 326–8.

5596 LUMSDEN, H. History of the skinners, furriers and glovers of Glasgow. Glasgow, 1937.

5597 MACADAM, W. I. Notes on the ancient iron industry of Scotland. *Proc. Soc. Antiq. Scot.*, n.s., ix (1886–7), 89–131.

5598 MACADAM, W. I. The ancient iron industry in Scotland. *Inverness Scien. Soc. and Field Club*, iii (1883–8).

5599 MALCOLM, C. A. Incorporation of cordiners of Canongate, 1538–1773. *Book of Old Edin. Club*, xviii (1932), 100–50.

5600 MARWICK, W. H. The incorporation of tailors of Canongate. *Book of Old Edin. Club*, xxii (1938), 91–131.

5601 MORRIS, D. B. Stirling merchant gild and life of John Cowane. Edin. 1919.

5602 NEVISON, J. L. Late sixteenth century applique work in Scotland. *Burl. Mag.* lxviii (1936), 170–6.

5603 PERRELS, J. W. Bijdragen tot de Geschiedenis van den Schotschen staple te Vere. 1903–5.
    Repr. from the proceedings of the *Zeeuwsch Genootschap der Wetenschappen*.

5604 PORTEOUS, J. M. God's treasure house in Scotland, a history of times, mines [gold, silver, and lead] and lands in the southern highlands. Lond. 1876.

5605 REID, W. S. Robert Barton of Ovir Barnton. A Scottish merchant of the sixteenth century. *Med. et Hum.* v (1948), 46–61.

5606 ROOSEBOOM, M. P. The Scottish staple in the Netherlands. The Hague, 1910.
    Confined strictly to subject of Scottish negotiations for staple privileges. App. contains 231 pages of documents *in extenso*.

5607 SCOTT, W. R. The fiscal policy of Scotland before the union. *Scot. Hist. Rev.* i (1903), 173–90.
    Cf. idem, *Scottish industrial undertakings before the union*, ibid. i, ii, iii.

5608 [STUART, CHAS.] The staple contract betwixt the royal burrows of Scotland and the city of Campvere in Holland, with an historical account of the staple . . . 1749; repr. in Maitland, *History of Edinburgh*, 1754.

5609 THOMSON, D. The weaver's craft, being a history of the weaver's incorporation of Dunfermline. Paisley, 1903.

5610 TURNER, G. The Scottish iron industry from the fifteenth to the seventeenth century. *Scotia*, i (1907).

5611 WARDEN, A. J. Burgh laws of Dundee with the history . . . of the guild of merchants and fraternities of craftsmen. Lond. 1872.

5612 WOOD, MARGUERITE. Hammermen of Canongate. *Book of Old Edin. Club.* xix (1933), 1–30; xx (1935), 78–110.

5613 YAIR, JAMES. An account of the Scotch trade in the Netherlands and of the staple port in Campvere. Lond. 1776.
    Author had access to records now lost. Yair's account used extensively by Davidson and Gray (5587a).

(c) *Education*

5614 ANDERSON, J. M. The university of St. Andrews. Cupar, 1878, supplement, 1883.

5615 BROWN, P. H. A forgotten scholar of the sixteenth century. *Scot. Hist. Rev.* x (1912), 122–38; repr. in *Surveys* (4997).
Florence Wilson.

5616 CANT, R. G. The university of St. Andrews. Edin. 1946.
Brief.

5617 CANT, R. G. The college of St. Salvator. Edin. 1950.
Includes inventory of furnishings of the collegiate church; edited by F. C. Eeles.

5618 COUTTS, JAMES. A history of the university of Glasgow . . . (1451–1909). Glasgow, 1909.

5619 FORBES-LEITH, W. S. Pre-reformation scholars in Scotland in the sixteenth century. Glasgow, 1915.
Inadequate. Bibliography.

5620 GRANT, ALEXANDER. The university of Edinburgh during its first three hundred years. 2 vols. Edin. 1884.

5621 GRANT, J. History of the burgh and parish schools of Scotland. Glasgow, 1876.
Deals only with the burgh schools.

5622 KERR, J. Scottish education, school and university, from early times to 1908. Cambr. 1910; 1913 with addendum, 1908–13.

5623 MACDONALD, C. M. John Major and humanism. *Scot. Hist. Rev.* xiii (1915), 149–58.

5624 MACKIE, J. D. The university of Glasgow. Glasgow, 1954.
Comprehensive.

5625 MORGAN, ALEXANDER. The rise and progress of Scottish education. Edin. 1927.

5626 PLATTARD, JEAN. Scottish masters and students at Poitiers in the second half of the sixteenth century. *Scot. Hist. Rev.* xxi (1923), 82–86, 168.

5627 RAIT, R. S. Andrew Melville and the revolt against Aristotle in Scotland. *E.H.R.* xiv (1899), 250–60.

5628 RAIT, R. S. The universities of Aberdeen. Aberdeen, 1895.

5629 STRONG, J. A history of secondary education in Scotland (to 1908). Oxf. 1909.

(d) *Scots Abroad*

5630 DYER, F. E. Scottish travellers and English pirates. *S.M.T. Mag.*, n.s., xiii (1934), 62–64.

5631 FISCHER, T. A. The Scots in Germany. Edin. 1902.

5632 FISCHER, T. A. The Scots in eastern and western Russia and hinterland. Edin. 1903.

5633 FISCHER, T. A. The Scots in Sweden. Edin. 1907.

5634 FORBES-LEITH, WILLIAM. The Scots men-at-arms and life-guards in France 1418–1830. 2 vols. Edin. 1882.

5635 MICHEL, FRANCISQUE. Les Écossais en France; les Français en Écosse. 2 vols. Lond. 1862.
Scholarly.

(e) *Art and Architecture*

5636 CAW, J. L. Scottish portraits. 5 vols. Edin. 1902–3.
Cf. also for portraits of Mary, queen of Scots, nos. 5231, 5249.

5637 FINLAY, IAN. Scottish crafts, Lond. 1948.

5638 FINLAY, IAN. Art in Scotland, Oxf. 1948.

5639 FINLAY, IAN. Scottish gold and silver work. Lond. 1956.
Cf. 3917, 3923.

5640 MACGIBBON, D., and ROSS, T. Castellated and domestic architecture of Scotland. 5 vols. Edin. 1887–92.

5641 MACGIBBON, D., and ROSS, T. Ecclesiastical architecture of Scotland. 3 vols. Edin. 1896–7.

5642 MAXWELL, J. S. Shrines and homes of Scotland. Glasgow, 1937.

5643 MILL, A. J. Medieval plays in Scotland. Oxf. 1927.
Prints many extracts from sixteenth-century records.

5643a MITCHELL, W. S. History of Scottish bookbinding. Edin. 1955.

5644 SIMPSON, W. D. Tolquhon Castle and its builders. *Proc. Soc. Antiq. Scot. for 1937–8*, lxxii (1938), 248–72.

5645 SMALL, J. W. Scottish woodwork of the sixteenth and seventeenth centuries. Edin. 1878.

XIII

IRELAND

A. BIBLIOGRAPHY

Dunlop's bibliography in *Cambr. Mod. Hist.* (20), iii, 852–9, is the pioneer work in Irish sixteenth-century bibliography; Maxwell (5707), though brief, is serviceable. For pertinent works, cf. Gross (1), nos. 50–52, 84a, 361, 938a. On local Irish history, cf. 4180.

The following periodicals print much valuable Irish material:

5646 ANALECTA HIBERNICA. Including the reports of the Irish Manuscripts Commission, Dublin, 1930 ff.

5647 ARCHIVIUM HIBERNICUM or Irish historical records. Dublin, 1912 ff.
Published by *Catholic Record Society of Ireland*. Prints transcripts from Vatican archives.

5648 ARDAGH AND CLONMACNOISE ANTIQUARIAN SOCIETY. Journal. Dublin, 1926 ff.

5649 BELFAST NATURAL HISTORY AND PHILOSOPHICAL SOCIETY. Proceedings and reports. Belfast, 1873 ff.

5650 BREIFFNE ANTIQUARIAN SOCIETY. Journal. Cavan, 1920–34.

5651 CLOGHER RECORD. Clonmel, 1953 ff.

5652 CORK HISTORICAL AND ARCHAEOLOGICAL SOCIETY. Journal. Cork, 1892 ff. Index to 1940, by D. J. O'Donahue (1943).

5653 COUNTY KILDARE ARCHAEOLOGICAL SOCIETY. Journal. Dublin, 1891 ff.

5654 DOWN AND CONNOR HISTORICAL SOCIETY. Journal. Belfast, 1928 ff.

5655 ÉIGSE: A journal of Irish Studies. Dublin, 1939 ff.

5656 ÉRIU. Founded as the Journal of the school of Irish learning. Dublin, 1904 ff.

5657 GALWAY ARCHAEOLOGICAL AND HISTORICAL SOCIETY. Journal. Galway, 1900 ff., Index, i–vii (1900–12), Galway, 1913.

5658 HERMATHENA: A series of papers . . . by members of Trinity college, Dublin. Dublin, 1874 ff. Index to 1943 by J. G. Smyly (1944).

5659 IRISH ARCHAEOLOGICAL AND CELTIC SOCIETY. Publications. Dublin, 1853–80.
Continuation of *Irish Archaeological Society*, Dublin, 1840–53, and *Celtic Society*, 1847–53. Cf. Gross (1), nos. 555–6.

5660 IRISH CATHOLIC HISTORICAL COMMITTEE. Proceedings. Dublin, 1955 ff.

5661 IRISH COMMITTEE OF HISTORICAL SCIENCES. Bulletin. Dublin, 1939 ff.

5662 IRISH ECCLESIASTICAL RECORD. Dublin, 1864–76, 1880 ff.
Index, 1864–1922.

5663 IRISH HISTORICAL STUDIES. Dublin, 1938 ff.

5664 THE IRISH SWORD. Journal of the military history society of Ireland. Dublin, 1952 ff.

5665 IRISH TEXTS SOCIETY. Publications. Lond. 1899 ff.

5666 IRISH THEOLOGICAL QUARTERLY. Dublin, 1906–22; 1951 ff.

5667 REPORTORIUM NOVUM. Dublin diocesan historical record. Dublin, 1955 ff.

5668 REVUE CELTIQUE. Paris, 1870–1934.
Continued as *Études Celtiques*, Paris, 1936 ff.

5669 ROYAL IRISH ACADEMY. Transactions, Dublin, 1786–1906; Proceedings, Dublin, 1836 ff.; Index to the serial publications, 1786–1906, Dublin, 1912; Index 1907–32, Dublin, 1934.

5670 ROYAL SOCIETY OF ANTIQUARIES of Ireland. Transactions and journal. Dublin, 1849 ff.
Originally called the *Kilkenny and South-east of Ireland Archaeological Society*; still later (1896) the *Royal Historical and Archaeological Association of Ireland*. Index published after every 20 years. Cf. Gross (1), no. 141.

5671 SEANCHAS ARDMHACHA. Journal of the Armagh diocesan historical society. Armagh, 1954 ff.

5672 STUDIES. An Irish quarterly review. Dublin, 1912 ff.

5673 ULSTER JOURNAL OF ARCHAEOLOGY. Belfast, 1853 ff.
1st ser. 1853–62; 2nd ser. 1894–1911; 3rd ser. 1938 ff.

5674 WATERFORD AND SOUTH-EAST OF IRELAND Archaeological Society. Journal. Waterford, 1894–1920.

Other guides and catalogues include:

5675 ABBOTT, T. K. Catalogue of the manuscripts in the library of Trinity College, Dublin. Dublin, 1900; Catalogue of Irish MSS. by T. K. Abbott and E. J. Gwynn, Dublin, 1921.
Cf. also R. H. Murray, *Short guide to some MSS. in the Library of Trinity College, Dublin* (*Helps for Students of History*, no. 32), Lond. 1920.

5676 BEST, R. I. Bibliography of Irish philology and of printed Irish literature. Dublin, 1913. Bibliography of Irish philology and manuscript literature: publications, 1913–41, Dublin, 1942.

5678 BURKE, J. B. Genealogical and heraldic history of the landed gentry in Ireland. By A. C. Fox-Davies. Lond. 1912.

5678a CATALOGUE OF THE BRADSHAW COLLECTION of Irish Books in Univ. Library, Cambridge. 3 vols. Cambr. 1910.

5679 CATALOGUE OF IRISH MSS. In the British Museum. Vol. i by S. H. O'Grady; ii by S. H. O'Grady and R. Flower; iii by R. Flower and Myles Dillon. 3 vols. Lond. 1909–53. Cf. 5798.

5680 CLARKE, D. J., and MADDEN, P. J. Printing in Ireland. *An Leabharlann*, xii (1954), 113–30.

5681 CORISH, P. J. Irish history and the papal archives. *Irish Theol. Quar.* xxi (1954), 375–81.

5682 DEAN, JAMES. Catalogue of Manuscripts in the Public Library of Armagh. Armagh, 1928.

5683 DIX, E. R. McC. The earliest Dublin printing with list of books, proclamations, &c., printed in Dublin prior to 1601. Dublin, 1901.

5684 DUNLOP, ROBERT. Sixteenth century maps of Ireland. *E.H.R.* xx (1905), 309–37.
Maps described. Cf. also T. J. Westropp, *Brazil and the legendary islands of the North Atlantic, Proc. R.I.A.* xxx, sect. c (1912), 223–60. Cf. 5702.

5685 ELLESMERE COLLECTION in the Huntington Library, list of documents of Irish interest in *Anal. Hiber.* viii (1938), 431–42.

5686 ELMES, R. M. Catalogue of Irish topographical prints and original drawings. *Nat. Lib. of Ire.* Dublin, 1945.

5687 FITZWILLIAM MSS. at Milton, England. By Charles McNeill. *Anal. Hiber.* iv (1932), 287–326.

5688 GIBLIN, CATHALDUS. Vatican library MSS. Barberini Latini: guide to the material of Irish interest on microfilm in the National Library, Dublin. *Archiv. Hiber.* xviii (1955), 67–144.

5689 GILBERT, J. T. Irish bibliography. By E. R. McC. Dix. *Proc. R.I.A.* xxv, sect. c, no. 5 (1904), 117–42.
Illustrated.

5690 GILBERT, J. T. Irish bibliography. By D. J. Clarke. *An Leabharlann*, xii (1954), 37–41.

5691 GRIFFITH, MARGARET. A short guide to the Public Record Office of Dublin. *Irish Hist. Stud.* viii (1952), 45–58.

5692 GUIDE TO ENGLISH FINANCIAL RECORDS FOR IRISH HISTORY, 1461–1588, with illustrative extracts, 1461–1509. By D. B. Quinn. *Anal. Hiber.* x (1941), 1–69.

5693 A GUIDE TO GENEALOGICAL COLLECTIONS. By Séamus Pender. *Anal. Hiber.* vii (1934).

5694 HAYES, R. J. List of manuscripts relating to Ireland in the Bibliotheque Nationale, Paris. *Nat. Lib. Ire. Report of the Council . . . 1949–50* (1951), 9–100.

5695 HAYES, R. J. List of manuscripts relating to Ireland copied on microfilm and 'photostat'. *Nat. Lib. Ire. Report of the Council . . . 1950–51* (1952), 10–124; *1951–52* (1953), 10–103.

5696 HISTORICAL MSS. COMMISSION. Guide to the reports or collections of MSS. part 1, topographical. Lond. 1914.
Cf. for Ireland, nos. 262–71 *supra*. Cf. 5705.

5697 HOGAN, JAMES. The Irish manuscripts commission: work in progress. Cork, 1954.

5699 KENNEY, J. F. The sources for the early history of Ireland: an introduction and guide. Vol. i, ecclesiastical. New York, 1929.

5700 KING, J. Subject index of Irish bibliography. Lond. 1903.

5701 LESLIE, J. B. Catalogue of manuscripts in possession of the Representative church body, Dublin, collected by the Ecclesiastical Records Committee. Dublin, 1938.

5702 LYNAM, E. W. O'F. English map-makers of the sixteenth century. *Geog. Jour.* cxvi (1950), 7–28.

5703 MACARTHUR, WM. Bibliography of histories of Irish counties and towns.
Fourteen articles in *Notes and Queries* (61) 6 Feb. 1915, to 30 Dec. 1916. See also his *List of Irish Annals*, ibid., 12 June 1915.

5705 MACLYSAGHT, EDWARD. Survey of documents in private keeping, first series. *Anal. Hiber.* xv (1944), 1–459; second ser. Ibid. xx (1958), 311–18.

5706 McNEILL, CHARLES. Publications of Irish interest . . . by Irish authors on the continent . . . prior to the eighteenth century. *Bibliog. Soc. Ire.* iv (1930), 3–42.

5706a MARSH'S LIBRARY, DUBLIN, Catalogue of MSS. By J. R. Scott and N. J. D. White. Dublin, 1913.

5707 MAXWELL, CONSTANTIA. A short bibliography of Irish history. *Historical Assoc.*, leaflet no. 23. Lond. 1921.
Useful.

5708 MEEHAN, PATRICK. Dublin records, the local officer. A short account of records in the corporation archives. *Dublin Hist. Rec.* ii (1939–40), 119–20.

5710 NATIONAL LIBRARY OF IRELAND. Handlist of MSS. in the Library. *Report of the Council of Trustees 1932–3* (1933).

5711 NEW YORK PUBLIC LIBRARY. Bulletin. List of works relating to Ireland, the Irish language and literature. New York, 1905.

5712 O'CURRY, EUGENE. Lectures on the manuscript material of ancient Irish history. Dublin, 1861.
Valuable account of sources of various annals and other sources to the seventeenth century.

5713 O'HANLON, JOHN. Ordnance survey records. *Jour. R.S.I.A.* (1856–67), iv–ix.

5714 O'RAHILLY, T. F., and others. Catalogue of Irish manuscripts in the Royal Irish Academy. Dublin, 1926–.

5715 O'REILLY, EDWARD. A chronological account of nearly four hundred Irish writers . . . to the year 1750. *Iberno-Celtic Soc. Trans.* i. Dublin, 1820.

5716 QUINN, D. B. Agenda for Irish history: i, Ireland 1461–1603. *Irish Hist. Stud.* iv (1945), 254–69.
Mostly Tudor period.

5717 QUINN, D. B. Information about Dublin printers, 1556–73, in English financial records. *Irish Book Lover*, xxviii (1942), 112–15.

5718 QUINN, D. B. Irish records, 1920–1933: a survey. *Bull. Inst. Hist. Research*, xi (1933), 99–104.

5719 RAWLINSON COLLECTION in the Bodleian, Irish material in. By Charles McNeill. *Anal. Hiber.* i, ii (1930–1), pp. 1–178; 1–291.

5720 REPORTS OF THE DEPUTY KEEPER of the public records, Ireland. Dublin, 1869 ff.
The apps. contain many lists and calendars of records. The first report gives an account of the contents of the principal repositories of Irish public records.

5721 REPORT OF THE DEPUTY KEEPER OF THE RECORDS OF NORTHERN IRELAND, 1924 ff. Belfast, 1925 ff.

5722 REPORTS . . . respecting the public records of Ireland. 3 vols. [Lond. 1815–25.]
These 3 vols. contain the first 15 annual reports. For subsequent reports, cf. Gross (1), no. 490. Superseded by 5720. Cf. M. Griffith, *Irish Hist. Studies*, vii (1950), 17–38.

5723 REPORT . . . UPON THE CARTE AND CAREW PAPERS in the Bodleian and Lambeth libraries. By T. D. Hardy and J. S. Brewer. Lond. 1864.
Catalogue of Carte MSS. in Bodleian, including Lord Dep. Fitzwilliam's correspondence, 1560–95. Superseded by reports of C. W. Russell and J. P. Prendergast in *30th report* (app. 504–29, 1868), and *32nd report* (app. 1–236, 1871) of the deputy keeper of the Public Records of England. List of Carew MSS. volumes catalogued at Lambeth but preserved elsewhere or missing.

5724 SADLEIR, T. U. Ulster Office records. *Genealogists' Mag.* vi (1934), 434–8.
Ulster office now genealogical office, Nat. library of Ireland.

5725 SHIRLEY, E. P. Catalogue of the library at Lough Fea in illustration of the history and antiquities of Ireland. Lond. 1872.
Contains notices of political tracts. For editorial help, cf. W. Reeves, *Irish Book Lover*, ii (1911), 99.

5726 WALSH, PAUL. Catalogue of Irish manuscripts in Maynooth college library. Pt. i, Contents of Murphy MSS. 1–10. Maynooth, 1943.

5728 WOOD, HERBERT. A guide to the records deposited in the public record office of Ireland. Dublin, 1919.
Cf. also R. H. Murray, *A short guide to the principal classes of documents preserved in the Public Record Office, Dublin.* Lond. 1919. Most of these records were destroyed by fire in 1922; cf. Herbert Wood, *The public records of Ireland before and after 1922, Trans. R.H. Soc.*, 4th ser., xiii (1930), 17–49. Surviving and substitute material noted in 5720 (*Reports*, 55, 56).

B. POLITICAL HISTORY, 1485–1603

1. SOURCES

(a) *General*

The P.R.O. in London, the B.M., and the Lambeth Palace library are all rich in Irish material. Much of this material is available in microfilm in the Nat. library of Ireland which is now the main repository which receives substantial accessions. There is much material in the library of Trinity College, Dublin, not catalogued, and in Marsh's library, Dublin. The official Irish records formerly preserved in the P.R.O., Dublin, were mostly destroyed in the destruction of the Four Courts in 1922.

The chief printed sources are the *Cal. S.P., Ireland, 1509–1603* (5736), *Letters and Papers, Henry VIII* (91), *Calendar of Carew MSS., 1515–1624* (5733), *Acts of the Privy Council, Ireland* (5729), and the private collections calendared in *Hist. MSS. Comm. Reports* (262–71). Irish proclamations are calendared in Steele (1017), ii. There is also much material on Ireland in the *Cal. S.P., Domestic* (86), *Foreign* (87), *Venetian* (992), and especially *Spanish* (867–8), *Rome* (991), and *Milan* (990); in the *Cal. S.P., Scotland* (4924), in the *Acts of Privy Council* (1152), and in the *Hamilton Papers* (4926). The *Salisbury MSS.* (185) are rich in Irish material. Collins, *Sidney Papers* (629), and *MSS. of Lord de L'Isle and Dudley* (124) are valuable for Sir Henry Sidney's administration in Ireland. Wright (626) prints some of Sussex's correspondence from Ireland *c.* 1561. Devereux (608) contains Irish letters of Walter and Robert, earls of Essex. Birch (601) prints a number of letters pertinent to the Irish career of Robert, earl of Essex. Pollard (400), iii, prints a useful selection of sources on Irish history under Henry VII.

Some general information on the sources of Irish history is to be found in C. P. Cooper, *Report on Rymer's Foedera*, 1869 (unpublished), app. A–E, cf. Gross (1), no. 2099.

5729 ACTS OF THE PRIVY COUNCIL in Ireland. By J. T. Gilbert. *Hist. MSS. Comm.*, 15th report (264).

5730 BOAZIO, BAPTISTA. Map of Ireland, about 1600. Lond. 1938.
Cf. also E. W. O'F. Lynam, *Boazio's map of Ireland, circa 1600*, Brit. Mus. Quar. xi (1937), 92–95. Cf. 3873b.

5731 BUTLER, T. B. King Henry VIII's Irish army list. *Irish Genealogist*, i (1937), 3–13, 36–38.

5732 CALENDAR OF ORMOND DEEDS. By Edmund Curtis. Vol. i, 1172–1350; ii, 1350–1413; iii, 1413–1509; iv, 1509–47; v, 1547–84; vi, 1584–1603. *Ir. MSS. Comm.* Dublin, 1932–43.
Cf. article on Edmund Curtis, *Irish Hist. Stud.* i (1938), 81–85. Cf. article by the same author on the seals out of the Ormond archives, *Jour. R.S.A.I.* lxvi (1936), 1–8; lxvii (1937), 72–76.

5733 CALENDAR OF THE CAREW MSS. preserved in the archiepiscopal library at Lambeth, 1515–1624. By J. S. Brewer and William Bullen. 6 vols. Lond. 1867–73.
Miscellaneous collection of documents and notes relating to affairs of state and history

of Ireland. Vols. i–iv (1515–1603) arranged chronologically; vol. v contains the *Book of Howth*, Bray's *Conquest of Ireland*, and miscellanea; vol. vi (1603–24). Carew collected chiefly copies and notes rather than original documents. Calendared fully. Much printed *in extenso*. On the history of the Carew MSS. cf. *E.H.R.* xlii (1927), 261–7.

5734 CALENDAR TO FIANTS of the reigns of Henry VIII . . . Elizabeth. *Reports of deputy keeper of the public records in Ireland.* Dublin, 1875–90.
Henry VIII (1521–46), report 7; Edward VI, report 8, app. 9; Philip and Mary, report 9, app. 4; Elizabeth (1558–70), report 11, app. 3; Elizabeth (1570–6), report 12, app. 5; Elizabeth (1576–83), report 13, app. 4; Elizabeth (1583–6), report 15, app. 1; Elizabeth (1586–95), report 16, app. 2; Elizabeth (1596–1601), report 17, app. 4; Elizabeth (1601–3), and addenda, Henry VIII to Mary, report 18, app. 1. Index to Henry VIII in 7th, Edward VI in 8th, Mary in 9th, Elizabeth in 21st and 22nd reports.

5735 CALENDAR OF PATENT and CLOSE ROLLS of chancery in Ireland. Henry VIII–Eliz.; 1–8 Charles I. By J. Morrin. 3 vols. Dublin, 1861–3.
Very brief summaries. Preface to vol. i contains an account of history of Irish records, and the Irish Record Commission. Severely criticized in *Record Revelations* by an Irish archivist [J. T. Gilbert], Lond. 1863. The revised ed., Lond. 1864, is entitled *On the history and treatment of the Public Records of Ireland*.

5736 CALENDAR OF STATE PAPERS, IRELAND. Vols. i–v, 1509–1596. By H. C. Hamilton. Lond. 1860–1890; vols. vi–x, 1596–1601, by E. G. Atkinson, Lond. 1893–1905; vol. xi, 1601–3; addenda, 1565–1654, with Hanmer papers, by R. P. Mahaffy, Lond. 1912.
Vols. i, ii, 1509–85, little more than a catalogue. Later vols. edited by Hamilton and Atkinson much fuller. Vol. xi, edited by Mahaffy, not carefully edited. Material calendared all preserved in P.R.O. London. Some state papers copied in Carew MSS. (5733).

5737 A CLASSIFIED SCHEDULE and inventory of the (Irish) memoranda rolls (6 Ed. I–50 Geo. III). *Irish record commissioners*, 8th report, 522–58. [Lond. 1819.]

5738 CLASSIFIED SCHEDULE and general inventory of the (Irish) plea rolls (36 Hen. III–25 Chas. II). *Irish record commissioners*, 8th report, 79–125. [Lond. 1819.]
Cf. also *Early rolls of judicial proceedings* (lists of Irish plea rolls, 36 Henry III–16 Chas. I) in *Deputy keeper's reports, Ireland*, xxvi, 52–68; xxviii, 39–56, Dublin, 1894–6.

5739 STATE PAPERS, HENRY VIII. Vols. ii, iii. Correspondence between the governments of England and Ireland, 1515–1546. Vol. ii, 1515–38; iii, 1538–46. 2 vols. Lond. 1834.
These are vols. ii and iii of no. 92 *supra*. Documents are printed *in extenso* and maps are included.

5740 DESIDERATA CURIOSA HIBERNICA, or a select collection of state papers. By [John Lodge]. 2 vols. Dublin, 1772.
Useful for the reigns of Elizabeth, James I, and Charles I.

5741 EXTRACTS FROM IRISH ORDNANCE ACCOUNTS, 1537–9. By Brian Trainor. *Irish Sword*, i (1953), 324–34.

5742 EXTRACTS OUT OF HERALD'S BOOK in Trinity College, Dublin relating to Ireland in the 16th century. By Edmund Curtis. *Jour. R.S.A.I.* lxii (1932), 28–49.

5743 FIANTS OF QUEEN ELIZABETH relating to the county of Cork. Extracted from the reports of the Deputy-Keeper of public records in Ireland. By J. T. Collins. *Jour. Cork. Hist. Soc.*, 2nd ser., xl (1935), 29–36, 74–81; xli (1936), 29–36, 66–77; xliii (1937), 25–34, 84–91; xliii (1938), 12–20, 113–20; xliv (1939), 50–58, 120–6; xlv (1940), 38–46, 127–34; xlvii (1942), 34–42.

5744 GILBERT, J. T. Facsimiles of national MSS. of Ireland. 4 vols. Dublin, 1874–84.
Important.

5745 GILBERT, J. T. Account of facsimiles of national manuscripts of Ireland . . . Lond. 1884.
Description and calendar of a miscellaneous collection of Irish documents (5744) selected for their representative character. Very useful.

5746 HARRIS, WALTER. Collectanea de rebus Hibernicis. By Charles McNeill. *Anal. Hiber.* vi (1934), 248–450.

5747 HENRY FITZROY, Duke of Richmond, and his connexion with Ireland 1529–30. By D. B. Quinn. *Bull. Inst. Hist. Research*, xii (1935), 175–7.
A pertinent document.

5748 HISTORICAL COLLECTANEA by Thaddaeus Dowling. By S. H. O'Grady. *Cat. Irish MSS. in Brit. Mus.* i (1909), 61.

5749 INQUISITIONUM in officio rotulorum cancellariae Hiberniae asservatarum repertorium. By J. Hardiman. 2 vols. Dublin, 1826–9.
Mostly inquisitions post mortem and inquisitions of attainder, a few before Elizabeth, arranged by counties, but only those of Leinster and Ulster published.

5750 IRISH ANNALS [1567–1651], by H. Morris. *County Louth Arch. Jour.* iv (1917), 202–4.

5751 THE IRISH CORRESPONDENCE of James FitzMaurice of Desmond. By John O'Donovan. *R.S.A.I.*, 2nd ser., ii (1859), 354–69.
Irish text with trans.

5752 IRISH HISTORY from contemporary sources (1509–1610). By Constantia Maxwell. Lond. 1923.
Cf. also by the same editor, *The foundations of modern Ireland, Texts for Students of History*, no. 27, Lond., 1921.

5753 THE 'JORNEY' OF THE BLACKWATER: from the state papers of Queen Elizabeth, 1598. By Daniel MacCarthy. *R.S.A.I.*, 2nd ser., i (1858), 256–82.
In extenso, with introduction.

5754 JOURNAL OF THE IRISH HOUSE OF LORDS in Sir John Perrot's parliament (3 May 1585–13 May 1586). By F. J. Routledge. *E.H.R.* xxix (1914), 104–17.
Earliest extant fragment of official journal of Irish parliament, printed *in extenso* from Carte MSS., vol. 61 (5723).

5755 LETTER OF QUEEN ELIZABETH on the murder of Robert Browne of Mulrancan, 1572. *R.S.A.I.*, 3rd ser., i (1868), 17.
From Carte MSS., vol. 57.

5756 LETTER FROM ANTONIO DE GUARAS to the Irish rebels, 1573. By R. Garnett, *E.H.R.* viii (1893), 91–92.
In extenso. Shows intrigue against Elizabeth.

5757 A LETTER FROM SIR CHARLES O'CARROLL to Lord Mountjoy, lord lieutenant of Ireland. By John O'Donovan. *R.S.A.I.*, 2nd ser., i (1858), 311–14.

5758 LETTERS FROM SIR ROBERT CECIL to Sir George Carew. By John Maclean. *Camden Soc.* lxxxviii (1864).
Valuable letters on Ireland, 1601–3, from Carew MSS. (5733), Lambeth 604.

5759 LORD CHANCELLOR GERRARD'S notes of his report on Ireland. By Charles McNeill. *Anal. Hiber.* ii (1931), 93–291.

5760 MACCARTHY, DANIEL. The life and letters of Florence MacCarthy Reagh. Lond. 1867.
Much material *in extenso.* Originally published in *R.S.A.I.*, 2nd ser. ii–v (1858–64), *passim.*

5761 LIBER MUNERUM PUBLICORUM HIBERNIAE. By Rowley Lascelles. 2 vols. Lond. 1852; index, *Deputy keeper reports, Ireland,* ix (1877), 21–58.
Contains patents of office, letters patent and close, &c. (1181–1653).

5762 NOTES ON MSS. OF EARL ANNESLEY at Castlewellen, county Down. *Deputy keeper reports, Ireland,* no. 33, app. i, in *Parl. papers,* 1901, vol. xxxiii.
Contains note of a vol. on the revenue of Ireland for 1560. Cf. *Anal. Hiber.* xvi (1946), 346.

5763 O'DONNELL LETTERS TO LORD LIEUTENANT SUSSEX, 1562. By S. H. O'Grady. *Cat. Irish MSS. in Brit. Mus.* i (1909), 57.

5764 THE O'KANE PAPERS. By A. F. O'D. Alexander. *Anal. Hiber.* xii (1943), 69–127.

5765 O'RAHILLY, T. F. Irish poets, historians and judges in English documents, 1538–1615. *Proc. R.I.A.* xxxvi, sect. C (1923), 86–120.

5766 ORIGINAL LETTERS OF SHAN O'NEILL in Irish and Latin. Trans. J. O'Donovan. *Ulster Jour. of Arch.* v (1857), 259–74.

5767 O'SULLIVAN-BEARE TO PHILIP III, 20 Feb. 1602. By R. B. Breathach. *Éigse.* vi (1948–52), 314–25.
From Archivos de Simancas.

5768 THE PERROT PAPERS. By Charles McNeill. *Anal. Hiber.* xii (1943), 3–65.

5769 THE PLAN OF THE GOLDEN FORT AT SMERWICK, 1580. By Frederick Jones. *Irish Sword,* i (1954), 41–42.

5770 THE RED BOOK OF ORMOND. By N. B. White. *Irish MSS. Comm.* Dublin, 1932.

5771 SHORT ANNALS of Tirconaill [1540–1642], of Fir Manach [1566–1625]. By Paul Walsh (Pol Breathnach). *Irish Book Lover,* xxii (1934), 104–9; xxiii (1935), 7–10; xxiv (1936), 13.

5772 THE SOCIAL STATE of the southern and eastern counties of Ireland in the sixteenth century: being the presentments of the gentlemen, commonalty and citizens of Carlow, Cork, Kilkenny, Tipperary, Waterford, and Wexford, made in the reigns of Henry VIII and Elizabeth. By H. F. Hore and James Graves. *Kilkenny Arch. Soc.* 1868–9.
Throws light on the state of affairs in the marches. Extracts illustrating Brehon law operating in sixteenth century are edited by E. MacNeill and others in *Gaelic Jour.* viii (1897), 74–75, 86–90, 99–100, 114–15.

5773 SOME MEDIEVAL DOCUMENTS. By M. V. Ronan. *Jour. R.S.A.I.* lxviii (1937), 229–41.
Includes a text of indenture, 1544, and a pension list, 1555.

5775 OF THE TAKING AWAIE OF A GENTLEWOMAN, the youngest daughter of Sir Nicholas Bagenall, late marshall of her majestie's armie, by the erle of Tirowen. By Daniel MacCarthy. *R.S.A.I.*, 2nd ser., i (1858), 298–311.
From P.R.O. *in extenso.*

5776 THE TAKING OF THE EARL OF ORMONDE, A.D. 1600. By James Graves. *R.S.A.I.*, 2nd ser., iii (1861), 388–432.
Correspondence and papers *in extenso.*

5777 THE TANNER LETTERS, original documents and notices of Irish affairs in the sixteenth and seventeenth centuries. By Charles McNeill. Dublin, 1943.

5778 TREATY BETWEEN ARGYLL AND O'DONNELL [1560]. By John Mackechnie. *Scot. Gaelic Stud.* vii (1951), 94–102; Eng. trans. in 5023, iv, 212 ff.

5779 UNPUBLISHED GERALDINE DOCUMENTS. Pt. i by Samuel Hayman, *R.S.A.I.*, 3rd ser., i (1868), 356–416; pt. ii by James Graves, ibid. 459–559, 4th ser., i (1870), 591–640, iv (1879), 14–52, 157–66; pt. iii, by H. Fitzgibbon, ibid., 4th ser., iv (1879), 246–64. Repr., 4 vols., Dublin, 1870–81.
These documents concerned only with the Munster branch of the family. Pt. i contains Russell's *Relation of the Fitzgeralds of Ireland* written c. 1638; pt. ii, *The pedigree of the Geraldines of Desmond*; pt. iii, *The Whyte Knight.* Pt. i, is particularly valuable. Cf. also *The Geraldines of Desmond*, from Michael O'Clery's book of pedigrees, by S. Hayman, *R.S.A.I.*, 4th ser., v (1880), 211–35, 411–40; vii, 66–92.

5780 UNPUBLISHED LETTERS OF JAMES V OF SCOTLAND relating to Ireland. Trans. by G. A. Hayes-McCoy. *Anal. Hiber.* xii (1943), 179–91.

(b) *Chronicles, Diaries, and Contemporary Narratives*

The chronicles of greatest value are the *Annals of the Four Masters* (5783) and the *Annals of Loch Cé* (5782).

Holinshed's *Chronicles* (314) contain valuable sections on Ireland by Hooker and Stanihurst. Camden's *Britannia* (4190) is useful for the rebellion of the O'Neills. Wilbraham's *Journal* (638) contains information on English law officials in Ireland. *Hooker's life of Carew* (636) includes a daily record of proceedings in the Irish parliament of 1569–71 of which Hooker was a member. For contemporary material on the Spanish Armada and Ireland, cf. nos. 3505–6 *supra*.

5781 ANNALA CONNACHT, The Annals of Connacht (A.D. 1224–1544). By A. M. Freeman. Dublin, 1944.
From *R.I.A.*, MS. 1219 (Stowe C. III, 1). Cf. 5782.

5782 ANNALS OF LOCH CÉ, 1014–1590. By W. M. Hennessy. *Rolls Series*. 2 vols. Lond. 1871; trans. by W. M. Hennessy, 2 vols., Dublin, 1940.
Originally ran to 1571. Brian McDermott, the owner and restorer of the MS., continued it to 1590. Especially valuable for Connaught, 1577–90. Cf. article by Paul Walsh, *Irish Eccles. Rec.* (1941), which shows the sources from which Hennessy took entires. Cf. also (5679), i, 21.

5783 ANNALA RIOGHACHTA EIREANN. Annals of the kingdom of Ireland by the Four Masters, from the earliest period to the year 1616. By John O'Donovan. 7 vols. Dublin, 1851; 7 vols., Dublin, 1856.
Earlier eds. by Chas. O'Conor [vol. iii of *Rerum hibernicarum scriptores veteres*, 4 vols., Buckingham, 1814–26], and by Owen O'Clery, Dublin, 1846, are superseded by O'Donovan's ed. These annals are a digest of older annals compiled by the O'Clearys between 1632 and 1636 in the Franciscan monastery of Donegal. They constitute with (5782) the most important of Irish chronicles for the sixteenth century. O'Donovan's notes are valuable.
   Cf. Colm O Lochlainn, *Annals of the Four Masters, Irish Book Lover*, xxxi (1951), 126–8 which contains a bibliographical note on O'Donovan's ed. Cf. ibid. xxix (1943), 4–8; xxv (1937), 75–76, 100–2 for biographical and philological errata. Cf. Paul Walsh, *Slips in O'Donovan's Four Masters, Irish Book Lover*, xxv (1937), 75–76, 100–2.

5784 ANNALS OF ULSTER, otherwise annals of Senat: a chronicle of Irish affairs, 431–1541. By W. M. Hennessy and B. MacCarthy. 4 vols. Dublin, 1887–1901.
Vol. iv contains introduction and index. Compiled on island in Loch Erne by Cathal Maguire (*ob.* 1498); continued to 1540 by Rory O'Cassidy and afterwards by unknown writer to 1604. Relates chiefly to Ulster. Valuable, but ed. inaccurate. Cf. W. Stokes, *The annals of Ulster, Revue Celtique*, xviii (1897), 74–86.

5785 BAGENAL, SIR HENRY. Description of Ulster, 1586. *Ulster Jour. of Arch.* ii (1854), 137–60.

5786 BODLEY, JOSIAS. Descriptio itineris d. Josias Bodleii ad Lecaliam in Ultonia, anno 1602; trans. in *Ulster Jour. of Arch.* ii (1854), 73–99.
A description in doggerel Latin of a journey from Armagh to Downpatrick. Printed also in Falkiner, *Illustrations*, &c. (5850).

5787 CAMPION, EDMUND. A history of Ireland. By James Ware. In 5913 *infra*; in *Ancient Irish Histories*. 2 vols. Dublin, 1809; repr. New York, 1940.
Preface dated 27 May 1571. Dedicated to the earl of Leicester but no evidence that it was published before Ware's edition. The basis for the account of Ireland in Holinshed (314). On Campion and his career, cf. Simpson (2376) and Waugh (2386).

5788 CHURCHYARD, THOMAS. The misery of Flanders . . . the unquietness of Ireland. Lond. 1579.
Cf. also idem, *A scourge for rebels . . . as farre as the painfull and dutiful service of the earle of Ormond . . . is known*, Lond. 1584. This book gives eye-witness accounts of the death of the earl of Desmond in 1583. *The fortunate farewell to the . . . earl of Essex.* Lond. 1599.

5789 DAVIES, JOHN. A discoverie of the true causes why Ireland was never entirely subdued, nor brought under obedience of the crowne of England, untill the beginning of his majestics happie raigne. [Lond.], 1612.
Many times repr. (cf. 5805), a good ed. being in *Works of Sir John Davies*, by A. B. Grosart, 3 vols., Lond. 1869–79.

5790 THE DESCRIPTION OF IRELAND . . . in anno 1598. By Edmund Hogan. Lond. 1878.
Author probably an English official, possibly S. Haynes. Cf. p. xi for a list of descriptions of Ireland, and of parts of Ireland and maps.

5791 DERRICKE, JOHN. The image of Irelande. Lond. 1581; in *Somers Tracts* (296), i, 558–621; by John Small, Edin. 1883.
Description in verse of native Irish temp. Elizabeth with remarkable illustrations.

5792 DOCWRA, HENRY. A narration of the services done by the army ymployed to Lough-Foyle under the leading of me, Sr Henry Docwra, knight. By J. O'Donovan. *Celtic Soc. Misc.* Dublin, 1849.
Written in 1614. Author one of leaders of English forces against Tyrone. Valuable. In same volume: *Relation of services done in Ireland* [by Sir Richd. Bingham].

5793 DOWLING, THADDAEUS. Annales Breves Hiberniae. Annals of Ireland. By Richard Butler. *Irish Arch. Soc.* Dublin, 1849.
Annals extend to 1600. Brief, though fuller on sixteenth century than earlier. Author Irish protestant clergyman, chancellor of diocese of Leighlin, d. 1628.
Useful on Surrey in Ireland. From Trin. Col. Dub. MS. E. 3. 20.

5794 DYMMOK, JOHN. A treatice of Ireland. By Richard Butler. *Tracts relating to Ireland*, ii, *Irish Arch. Soc.* Dublin, 1843.
Journal of principal events May–September 1599. Author probably with Essex. From B.M. Harl. 1291. Written *c.* 1600. The editor prints in app. 'The rate of wages of the galloglass after their own confession before Sir T. Cusack and Mr. Secretary [Challoner?], 15 Nov. 1568'.

5795 THE EXPEDITION OF THOMAS STUKELEY in 1578. By Z. N. Brooke. *E.H.R.* xxviii (1913), 330–7.
Account from Vatican Latin MSS. 5385, of invasion of Ireland planned with sanction of Pope Gregory XIII.

5796 F., G. Hiberniae Vindiciae adversus Dempsteri. Antwerp, 1621.

5797 FARMER, WILLIAM. Chronicles of Ireland from 1594 to 1613. By C. L. Falkiner. *E.H.R.* xxii (1907), 104–30, 527–52.
Author a friend of Chichester, lord deputy of Ireland (1605–16).

5798 FLOWER, ROBIN. Histories and annals. Manuscripts in the British Museum. *Anal. Hiber.* ii (1931), 310–29.
On the interrelations of Irish annals.

5800 GAINSFORDE, THOMAS. The true and exemplary and remarkable history of the earl of Tyrone. Lond. 1619.
Author was in the Elizabethan force against O'Neill.

5801 GRACE, JAMES. Annales hiberniae [1074–1515]. By Richard Butler. *Irish Arch. Soc.* Dublin, 1842.
From Trin. Col. Dub. MS. E. 3. 20. Entries correspond with Pembridge Annals in Camden (4190). Preceding and subsequent entries brief. Latter part very brief, consisting chiefly of deaths of Lacys, Burkes, Butlers, Fitzgeralds. Author, a native of Kilkenny, probably compiled these annals between 1537 and 1539.

5802 HARINGTON, JOHN. A short view of the state of Ireland in 1605.
By W. D. Macray (in *Anecdota Bodleiana*), Oxf. 1879.
From an original MS. in Rawlinson MSS. Bodleian library (Rawl. B. 162). For other
MSS. cf. *Hist. MSS. Comm., 3rd report*, Eaton Hall, p. 212, Cecil, p. 159.

5803 HIBERNICA: or some ancient pieces relating to Ireland. By Walter
Harris. Dublin, 1747; 1770.
Contains: (1) *The voyage of Sir Richard Edgecombe into Ireland, 1488, to take new oaths
of allegiance*; (2) *Breviat of the getting of Ireland*, by Patrick Finglas, chief justice of
Ireland, temp. Henry VIII.

5804 THE JOURNAL OF SIR PETER LEWYS, 1564–5. By James Mills.
R.S.A.I., 5th ser., vi (1896), 136–41.
Lewys, proctor of Christ Church, Dublin.

5805 IRELAND UNDER ELIZABETH & JAMES I described by Spenser,
Davies and Moryson. By Henry Morley. *Carisbrooke Library*, ser. x. Lond.
1890.
Cf. 5789, 5810, 5822.

5805a KEATING, GEOFFREY (Seathrún Ceitinn). Forus feasa ar Eirinn.
(A history of Ireland). By D. O'Connor. Dublin, 1723; 1725; by W. Halliday,
1811; best ed. by David Comyn and P. S. Dinneen, 4 vols., Lond. 1902–14.
Criticizes historical methods of Cambrensis in Camden (Gross (1), no. 576), Spenser in
Ware (5822), Stanihurst (5823), Hanmer in Ware (5913), Camden (4190), Moryson
(5810), Davies (5789), Campion in Ware (5787). Cf. also Anne Cronin, *Sources for
Keating's Ireland, Éigse*, iv, v (1944–47), 235–79, 122–35.

5806 LEE, THOMAS. A brief declaration of the government of Ireland . . .
in the government of Sir William Fitz-Williams (1588–94). Printed in *Desiderata Curiosa Hibernica* (5740), i, 87–150; by J. Curry (in *Civil Wars in
Ireland*, 587–600). Dublin, 1810.
An unpublished tract by the same writer entitled *The discoverye and recoverye of Ireland*
is in B.M., Add. MS. 33743.

5807 LOMBARD, PETER. De regno hiberniae . . . commentarius. By P. F.
Moran. Dublin, 1868.
Written by the archbishop of Armagh in 1600. Contains useful documentary material.
Cf. M. J. Byrne, *The Irish war of defence, 1598–1600*, Lond. 1930, which is a translation
of part of *De regno*.

5808 LOFTUS, DUDLEY, ANNALS OF. By N. B. White. *Anal. Hiber.* x
(1941), 223–38.
Description with extracts of Marsh's library, MS. 211. 34. 2. 7. Cf. Edwards (6020),
p. 175 n.

5809 MAG CARTHAIGH, FINGHIN. (Florence MacCarthy.) A concise
sketch for antiquarian studies of the earl of Thomond, *c.* 1610, of Irish history.
By S. H. O'Grady. *Cat. Irish MSS. in B.M.* i (1926), 61–67.
Written in the Tower of London after 1601. Description of B.M. Add. MS. 4793. Text
in Gilbert (5744).

5810 MORYSON, FYNES. An itinerary containing his ten years' travel. . . .
Lond. 1617; 4 vols. Glasgow, 1907–8.
The 2nd pt. with part of the 3rd pt. was repr. as *An history of Ireland, 1599 to 1603*,
2 vols., Dublin, 1735. Repr. in part in 5805. Unpublished chapters of the *Itinerary*

taken from a supplementary MS. of Moryson's were edited by Chas. Hughes in *Shakespeare's Europe*, Lond. 1903.
Apart from Moryson's description of Ireland his book is important for Tyrone's rebellion, during which Moryson served four years under Mountjoy.

5811	O'CLERY (O'CLEIRIGH), LUGHAIDH. Life of Hugh Roe O'Don-nell (Aodh Ruadh O Domhnaill). By Denis Murphy. Dublin, 1893; by Paul Walsh, *Archivium hibernicum*, vii (1908–22); *Irish Texts Soc*. xlii (1948).
Author uncle of one of compilers of *Annals of the Four Masters* (5783), Walsh's ed. contains Irish text, translation, and annotations from material not accessible to editor of 1893 ed. 1948 ed. contains text and translation. Cf. *Irish Hist. Stud*. i, 229–50.

5812	O'FERRALL, R. B., and O'CONNELL, R. D. Commentarius Rinuc-cinianus de Sedis Apostolicae legatione ad foederatos Hiberniae Catholicos per annos 1645–9. By Stanislaus J. Kavanagh. *Irish MSS. Comm*. Dublin, 1932.
Introductory survey by Irish Capuchins since the reformation. Original MS. destroyed in 1943 at Milan.

5813	PAYNE, ROBERT. A briefe description of Ireland. . . . Lond. 1589; 1590; by Aquilla Smith in *Tracts relating to Ireland*, i. *Irish Arch. Soc*. Dublin, 1841.
Made by a resident manager in Ireland for his partners. Chiefly concerns agriculture.

5814	PERROT, SIR JOHN. The history of that most eminent statesman. By Richard Rawlinson. Lond. 1727.
From a MS. of latter end of reign of Elizabeth. The unknown author claims to have been an eye-witness to much which he records.

5815	PERROTT, SIR JAMES. The Chronicle of Ireland 1584–1608. By Herbert Wood. *Irish MSS. Comm*. Dublin, 1933.
Chronicle proposed to carry on Hooker's and Holinshed's chronicle. Chronicle begins with an administrative map since 1584 and explains the policy of four governors.

5816	QUINN, D. B. 'A discourse of Ireland' (circa 1599): a sidelight on Eng-lish colonial policy. *Proc. R.I.A.* xlvii, sect. C. (1942), 151–66.

5817	RICH, BARNABE. A short survey of Ireland. Lond. 1609.
For a biography of Rich, cf. 3326.

5818	RICH, BARNABE. Allarme to England, foreshewing what perilles are precured when the people live without regarde of martialle lawe. Lond. 1578.
Shows wretched state of Ireland. Author resident in Dublin, 1573–c. 1620. Served under Essex. Cf. also idem, . . . *The Irish hubbub or the English hue and crie*, Lond. 1622.

5819	RICH, BARNABE. A new description of Ireland. . . . Lond. 1610; later ed. entitled *A new Irish prognostication . . .*, Lond. 1624.
Cf. also idem, *A true and kinde excuse, in defence of that booke intituled a newe description of Irelande*, Lond. 1612.

5820	RIDER, JOHN. The copie of a letter concerning the newes out of Ireland. Lond. 1601.

5821	S., E. C. The government of Ireland under Sir John Perrot, 1584–8. Lond. 1626.
Prints Perrot's plan for suppressing the rebellion in Munster. There are no solid grounds for the identification of E. C. S. with Sir Ed. Cecil, Viscount Wimbledon.

5822   SPENSER, EDMUND. A view of the state of Ireland . . . in 1596.
First printed by Ware (5913); best ed. by W. L. Renwick, *Complete works of Spenser*, iv, Lond. 1934.

On Spenser's Irish career, cf. 3647 and 3648. Cf. articles by Ray Heffner, *Spenser's view of Ireland: some observations, Mod. Lang. Quar.* iii (1942), 507–15; R. B. Gottfried, *Spenser's view and Essex, P.M.L.A.* lii (1937), 645–51; R. M. Smith, *More Irish words in Spenser, Mod. Lang. Notes,* lix (1944), 472–7; R. M. Smith, *Spenser, Holinshed, and the Leabhar Gabhála, Jour. of Eng. German Philol.* xliii (1944), 390–401; and R. M. Smith, *The Irish backgrounds of Spenser's view, Jour. of Eng. German Philol.* xlii (1943), 499–515.

5823   STANIHURST, RICHARD. De rebus in Hibernia gestis, libri iv.
Antwerp, 1584; in Holinshed (314), ed. 1587, ii, 9–45, 82–106.

Contains a view of the ancient and present state of Ireland, the manners, rites, and customs of the old Irish inhabitants and of those within the English Pale.

5824   [STAFFORD, THOMAS.] Pacata Hibernia; Ireland appeased and reduced, or an historie of the late warres of Ireland, especially within the province of Mounster under the government of Sir George Carew. Lond. 1633; 2 vols., Dublin, 1810; by S. H. O'Grady, 2 vols., Lond. 1896.

Relates chiefly to Tyrone's rebellion. Valuable. Prints number of letters *in extenso*. Account attributed to Stafford, a lieutenant under and reputed son of Sir George Carew.

5825   A VICE-REGAL [SIR H. SIDNEY'S] PROGRESS through the south west of Ireland in 1567. By James Buckley. *Jour. of Waterford and SE. Ire. Arch. Soc.* xii (1909), 61–76, 132–46, 174–84.

Printed from the original in S.P., Ire., Eliz. xx.

2. LATER WORKS

Cf. Gross (1), p. 168. The standard modern account is Bagwell (5827). Richey's history (5907), Dunlop's articles (5842–8), his Irish biographies contributed to the *D.N.B.* (9), and his chapters on Ireland in the *Cambr. Mod. Hist.* (20) are valuable. Conway (5151) is important for the administration of Henry VII in Ireland. Cf. also Mackie (354) and Black (671). Cf. Rowse (766) on Elizabethan expansion. Mathew (355) is very valuable. Froude's (340) account should be consulted, and Pollard's (363). Gregory's *History of the Western Highlands* (5077) will be found useful for Scottish dealings with Irish rebels under Elizabeth. The meteoric career of Essex in Ireland can be followed in Cheyney (690), Devereux (608), Abbott (653), and Mathew (355). Hume's *Treason and plot* (711) contains information regarding Irish intrigues with Spain; cf. also on this subject Binchy (880). Strype's *Smith* (570) is important for Smith's attempt to plant the Ardes, and Edwards's *Ralegh* (609) for Ralegh's Irish career. Wiffen's *House of Russell* (382), ii, should be consulted for Sir William Russell, lord deputy of Ireland, 1594–7. On military operations in Ireland, cf. chap. ix, A 3 (d) *supra* (pp. 287 ff.), especially Falls (3366–7). For the wrecks of the Spanish Armada on the Irish coast, cf. nos. 3525, 3529, 3540.

5826   A GEOGRAPHICAL DESCRIPTION of the kingdom of Ireland . . . likewise setting down a brief relation of the former rebellions . . . especially that in Q. Elizabeth's time to Tyrone. Lond. 1642.

Address to the reader signed 'G. N.'

5827 BAGWELL, RICHARD. Ireland under the Tudors. 3 vols. Lond.
1885–90.
Standard work on subject.

5828 BARRETT, E. J. B. The Great O'Neill. Boston, 1939.
Shane O'Neill, lord of Tyrone, 1530?–1567. Cf. articles by M. F. Alvarez, *La Suble-
vación de Shane O'Neil contra Isabel de Inglaterra, Simancas*, i (1950), 327–33; and
J. Hogan, *Shane O'Neill comes to the court of [Queen] Elizabeth [1562], Essays and
studies presented to Tadhg Ua Donnchadha*, Cork, 1947, pp. 154–70.

5829 BECKETT, J. C. A short history of Ireland. Lond. 1952.

5830 BONN, MORITZ. Die englische Kolonisation in Irland. 2 vols. Stuttgart, 1906.
Valuable discussion of English colonial policy in Ireland with emphasis on colonial
theory. Well documented.

5831 BROOKS, E. ST. J. The death of Alice Draycott. *County Louth Arch.
Jour.* (1955), 179–89.
A. Draycott was associated in the death of the 1st earl of Essex.

5832 BRYAN, DONOUGH. Gerald Fitzgerald, the great earl of Kildare.
Dublin, 1933.
Gerald Fitzgerald, 8th earl of Kildare, 1456–1513, deputy-governor in Ireland. Cf.
G. O. Sayles, *The vindication of the earl of Kildare from treason, 1495, Irish Hist. Stud.*
vii (1950), 39–47.

5833 BUTLER, W. F. T. Confiscation in Irish history. Dublin, 1917.
Ch. i, The Tudor confiscations.

5834 CARVE (CARUE or CAREW), THOMAS de Mobernon, Tipperary.
Lyra seu anacephalaeosis Hibernica, in qua de exordio seu origine, nomine,
moribus, ritibusque gentis Hibernicae succincte tractatur; cui quoque acces-
sere annales ejusdem Hiberniae . . . ab anno 1148 usque ad annum 1650.
Vienna [1651]; 2nd ed., with many alterations, Sulzbach, 1666. Cf. 6085a.

5835 CHAUVIRÉ, ROGER. History of Ireland. Trans. by the earl of Wicklow. Dublin, 1952.

5836 COX, RICHARD. Hibernia Anglicana. 2 vols. Lond. 1689; 1690.

5837 CUNNINGHAME, RICHARD. The broken sword of Ulster. Dublin,
1904.
Describes events 1585–1616.

5838 CURTIS, EDMUND. A history of medieval Ireland from 1110 to 1513.
Dublin, 1923.
Valuable on medieval period. For sixteenth century contains chapter on Kildare
ascendancy, 1477–1513.

5839 CURTIS, EDMUND. A history of Ireland. Lond. 1936: rev. ed. 1938.

5840 CURTIS, EDMUND, and MCDOWELL, R. B. Irish historical
documents, 1172–1922. Lond. 1943.

5842 DUNLOP, ROBERT. Ireland from the earliest times to the present day.
London, 1922.
One of the best short accounts of Irish history.

5844 DUNLOP, ROBERT. The plantation of Leix and Offaly 1556–1622. *E.H.R.* vi (1891), 61–96.

5845 DUNLOP, ROBERT. The plantation of Munster, 1584–9. *E.H.R.* iii (1888), 250–69.
Cf. also idem, *An unpublished survey of the plantation of Munster, R.S.A.I.*, 6th ser., xvi (1924), 128–46.

5846 DUNLOP, ROBERT. Some aspects of Henry VIII's Irish policy. In *Owens College Historical Essays*, 279–306. Lond. 1902; Manchester, 1907.
Valuable. Emphasizes slight actual effect of Henry's legislation.

5847 DUNLOP, ROBERT. Sixteenth century schemes for the plantation of Ulster. *Scot. Hist. Rev.* xxii (1924), 51–60, 115–26, 199–212.

5848 DUNLOP, ROBERT. Ireland under the Commonwealth. 2 vols. Manchester, 1913.
Introductory chapter 1541–1651.

5849 EDWARDS, R. D. Venerable John Travers and the rebellion of Silken Thomas. *Studies*, xxiii (1934), 687–99.

5850 FALKINER, C. L. Illustrations of Irish history and topography, mainly of the seventeenth century. Lond. 1904.
Includes parts of Fynes Moryson's *Itinerary* (5810), and a trans. of Bodley's *Visit to Lecale* (5786).

5851 FALKINER, C. L. Essays relating to Ireland, biographical, historical, topographical. Lond. 1909.
Includes essays on Spenser in Ireland, on Sir John Davies, and on parliamentary antiquities. App. contains lists of speakers in the Irish house of commons, and of lords in the parliament of 1569–71, and Hooker's *Journal* (Jan.–Feb. 1568/9) when he was a member of the Irish house of commons.

5852 GILBERT, J. T. History of the viceroys of Ireland. Dublin, 1865.
Feudal establishments to the accession of Henry VIII. Contains useful biographical and historical data, but should be used with care.

5854 GREEN, A. S. Henry VIII, 'King of Ireland'. In *Miscellany presented to Kuno Meyer*, 278–85. Halle, 1912.
Discusses Henry VIII's title.

5855 GWYNN, STEPHEN. The history of Ireland. New York, 1923.
A rather detailed political narrative, moderate and well written, but not based upon research.

5856 HAMILTON, E. W. L. Elizabethan Ulster. Lond. 1919.
Good narrative of events based on sources.

5857 HASSENCAMP, R. Geschichte Irlands. Leipzig, 1887; Eng. trans. by E. A. Robinson (*History of Ireland from the Reformation to the Union*), Lond. 1888.
Good. The original German ed. lacks footnote references inserted in the English trans. by the author.

5859 HAYDEN, MARY. Lambert Simnel in Ireland. *Studies*, iv (1915), 622–38.
Impostor. Impersonated Edward, earl of Warwick (1475–1499).

5860 HAYES-McCOY, G. A. Strategy and tactics in Irish warfare, 1593–
1601. *Irish Hist. Stud.* ii (1941), 255–79.
Cf. also idem, *The army of Ulster, 1593–1601, Irish Sword,* i (1950–1), 105–17.

5861 HAYES-McCOY, G. A. Scots mercenary forces in Ireland (1563–
1603), Lond. 1937.

5862 HAYES-McCOY, G. A. The battle of Kinsale, 1601. *Studies,* xxxviii
(1949), 307–17.

5863 HAYES-McCOY, G. A. Ballyshannon, its strategic importance in the
wars in Connacht, 1550–1602. *Jour. Galway Arch. and Hist. Soc.* xv (1934),
141–59.

5864 HAYES-McCOY, G. A. The battle of Clontibret, 1595. *Studies,* xxxviii
(1949), 307–17.

5865 HAYES-McCOY, G. A. The early history of guns in Ireland. *Jour.
Galway Arch. and Hist. Soc.* xviii (1938), 43–65.

5866 HAYES-McCOY, G. A. The Gallóglach Axe. *Jour. Galway Arch. and
Hist. Soc.* xvii (1937), 101–21.
On the Irish sword, cf. ibid. xxiii (1948), 14–18.

5867 HAYES-McCOY, G. A. Sixteenth-century coastal patrol. *An Cosantóir,*
x (1949), 16–25.

5868 HAVERTY, MARTIN. The history of Ireland ancient and modern.
Dublin, 1860.

5869 HENLEY, PAULINE. Spenser in Ireland. Cork, 1928.
Cf. Falkiner, *Spenser in Ireland* in *Essays* (5851), 3–31.

5870 HENNESSY, J. P. Sir Walter Ralegh in Ireland. Lond. 1883.
Prints *in extenso* Raleigh's letters from Ireland, and those bearing on Irish affairs, his
accounts, muster rolls, and other pertinent documents.

5871 HINTON, E. M. Ireland through Tudor eyes. Philadelphia, 1935.
Prints extracts from contemporary writers.

5872 HOGAN, EDMUND. Distinguished Irishmen of the sixteenth century. 1st ser. Lond. 1894.
Largely based on 5975.

5873 HOGAN, JAMES. Ireland in the European system. Vol. i, 1500–57
(no more published). Lond. 1920.
Examines Irish intrigues on the continent against England. Occasionally inaccurate.

5874 HUGHES, JAMES. Sir Edmund Butler of the Dullogh, knight.
R.S.A.I., 4th ser., i (1870), 153–92, 211–31.
Recounts chiefly Butler's conduct in parliament, 1569, his rebellion, 1569, his sub-
mission, and his pardon, 1573. Prints selections from documents.

5876 HULL, ELEANOR. History of Ireland. Lond. 1926, 1931.

5877 JONES, F. M. James Blake of Galway and the death of Red Hugh O'Donnell. *Irish Eccles. Rec.*, 5th ser., lxxv (1951), 30–38.
On James Blake cf. also article by Paul Walsh, *James Blake of Galway, Irish Eccles. Rec.*, 5th ser., i (1937), 382–97. On the death of O'Donnell, cf. Canice Mooney, *The death of Red Hugh O'Donnell, Irish Eccles. Rec.*, 5th ser., lxxxi (1954), 328–45.

5878 JONES, F. M. The Spaniards and Kinsale, 1601. *Jour. Galway Arch. and Hist. Soc.* xxi (1944), 1–43.

5879 JOYCE, P. W. A short history of Ireland from the earliest times to 1608. Lond. 1893.
Good on internal history of Ireland, but pays little attention to Ireland's international position.

5880 KELSO, J. B. Die Spanier in Irland, 1588–1603. Leipzig, 1902.
Scholarly.

5881 LAMBERT, G. W. Sir Nicholas Malby and his associates. *Jour. Galway Arch. and Hist. Soc.* (1948), 1–13.
Military governor and president of Connaught.

5882 LELAND, THOMAS. A history of Ireland from the invasion of Henry II. 3 vols. Dublin, 2nd ed., 1814.

5883 MACCARTHY, DANIEL. The disaster of Wicklow. *R.S.A.I.*, 2nd ser., ii (1859), 428–40.
Several papers *in extenso*, 1599.

5884 McCLINTOCK, H. F. A sixteenth century Dutch 'account of Ireland'. *Jour. R.S.A.I.* lxix, 7th ser., ix (1939), 223–5.
From Lucas de Heere. *Beschrijving der Britische Eilande.* By T. M. Clotzen and A. M. Draak. Antwerp, 1937.

5886 McKERRAL, ANDREW. West Highland mercenaries in Ireland. *Scot. Hist. Rev.* xxx (1951), 1–14.

5887 MACNEILL, EOIN. Military service in medieval Ireland. *Jour. Cork Hist. and Arch. Soc.* xlvi (1941), 6–15.
Cf. Falls (3366–7) and Mathew (355).

5888 MEEHAN, C. P. Fate and fortunes of Hugh O'Neill, earl of Tyrone, and Rory O'Donnell, earl of Tyrconnel. Dublin, 1868; 1870; rev. ed. 1886.
Identifies catholic and nationalist causes. App. of useful documents from Carew MSS. and archives of the Irish college at Salamanca.

5889 MITCHEL, JOHN. Life and times of Aodh (Hugh) O'Neill . . . with some account of Con, Shane and Tirlough. Dublin, 1845; *Duffy's Library of Ireland*, no. 5, New York, 1868.
Based on sources but uncritical. Aims at impartiality but unsuccessful from British standpoint.

5892 O'CONNOR, G. B. Elizabethan Ireland. Dublin, 1906.

5893 O'DOMHNAILL, SEAN. Warfare in sixteenth century Ireland. *Irish Hist. Stud.* v (1946), 29–54.

5894 O'DONNELL, TERENCE. Franciscan Donegal. Ros Nuala, 1952.

5895 O'FAOLAIN, S. The Great O'Neill. Lond. 1943.
Hugh O'Neill, 2nd earl of Tyrone, 1540?–1616. Cf. J. K. Graham, *The birth date of Hugh O'Neill, 2nd earl of Tyrone, Irish Hist. Studies*, i (1938), 58–59.

5896 O'GORMAN, THOMAS. A notice of the career of Shane O'Neill (surnamed An Diomais, or 'The proud'), prince of Tirowen, 1520–67. *R.S.A.I.*, 4th ser., viii (1887–8), 449–62; ix (1889), 53–58.
Largely based on *Annals of the Four Masters* (5783), supplemented by state papers.

5897 O'RAHILLY, ALFRED. The Massacre of Smerwick (1580). *Jour. Cork Hist. and Arch. Soc.* xlii (1937), 1–15, 65–83; *Cork Univ. Hist. and Arch. Papers*, i (1938).

5898 O'SULLIVAN BEARE, PHILIP. Historiae Catholicae Iberniae compendium. [Lisbon], 1621; by Matthew Kelly, Dublin, 1850; trans. by M. J. Byrne (*Ireland under Elizabeth*), Dublin, 1903.
Of value for incidents whose records have been lost, but unreliable. Author emigrated to Spain in 1602 at age of 10. Educated by Jesuits, served in Spanish army and navy. Trans. includes Elizabethan part of original work.

5899 O'SULLIVAN BEARE, PHILIP. Zoilomastix: vindiciae Hiberniae. By A. Gwynn. *Anal. Hiber.* vi (1934), 1–11.
Description of MS. in Upsala Univ. library.

5900 O'SULLIVAN, M. D. The fortification of Galway in the sixteenth and early seventeenth centuries. *Jour. Galway Arch. and Hist. Soc.* xvi (1934), 1–47.

5901 O'SULLIVAN, M. D. Barnabe Googe, Provost-Marshal of Connaught, 1582–5. *Jour. Galway Arch. and Hist. Soc.* xviii (1938), 1–39.

5902 PLOWDEN, FRANCIS. Historical review of the state of Ireland, from the invasion of Henry II. 2 vols. Lond. 1803.

5903 POLLEN, J. H. The Irish expedition of 1579. *The Month*, ci (1903), 69–85.
Utilizes unpublished material in the Vatican archives. Particularly valuable for the career of Sir Thomas Stukely.

5904 PRENDERGAST, J. P. The plantation of the barony of Idrone, in the county of Carlow. *R.S.A.I.*, 2nd ser., ii (1859), 400–28; iii (1861), 20–44, 69–80, 144–64, 171–88, 196–208.
Pts. i and ii only on sixteenth century.

5905 QUINN, D. B. Edward Walsh's 'Conjectures' concerning the state of Ireland [1552]. *Irish Hist. Studies* (1947), 303–22.

5906 QUINN, D. B. Anglo-Irish Ulster in the early sixteenth century. *Proc. Belfast Nat. Hist. and Philos. Soc. for 1933–4* (1935), 56–78.

5907 RICHEY, A. G. A short history of the Irish people to the date of the plantation of Ulster. By R. R. Kane. Dublin, 1887.
Previously published in 2 vols.: (1) *Lectures on the history of Ireland to 1534*, Dublin, 1869; (2) *Lectures on the history of Ireland from 1534 to the plantation of Ulster*, Dublin, 1870.
Excellent, especially for Henry VIII's policy, but out of print.

5908 SAINTHILL, RICHARD. The old countess of Desmond. Dublin, 1861; 2nd pt., 1863.

5909 STRICKLAND, W. G. Irish soldiers in the service of Henry VIII. *R.S.A.I.*, 6th ser., xiii (1923), 94–97.

5910 WALSH, PAUL. Sir Mulmory M'Swiney, chieftain, 1596–1630. *Irish Eccles. Rec.* li (1938), 181–202.

5911 WALSH, PAUL. Historical criticism of the life of Hugh Roe O'Donnell. *Irish Hist. Studies*, i (1939), 229–50.

5912 WALSH, PAUL. Captain Green O'Molloy [fl. 1580–1602], *Irish Book Lover*, xxv (1937), 26–31.
Cf. also ibid. xxiii (1935), 134–41.

5913 WARE, JAMES. The historie of Ireland, collected by . . . M. Hanmer, E. Campion, and E. Spencer. Dublin, 1633; 2 vols. (*Ancient Irish Histories*), Dublin, 1809.

5914 WARE, JAMES. De Hibernia et antiquitatibus ejus disquisitiones. Lond. 1654; 2nd ed. (enl.), Lond. 1658.
Cf. for trans. 5915, for later ed. 5916.

5915 WARE, JAMES. Rerum hibernicarum annales regnantibus Henrico VII–Elizabetha. Dublin, 1664.
The part covering Henry VII was included in the 2nd ed. of 5914. A trans. of this work and of 5914 from the MS. by Robert Ware was published posthumously under the title *The antiquities and history of Ireland* . . ., Dublin, 1704. Cf. 5974. For the forgeries interpolated by his son in Ware's works, cf. *Bull. Inst. Hist. Research*, xi (1933), 54–56.

5916 WARE, JAMES. De praesulibus hiberniae commentarius. Dublin, 1665.
An incomplete and amended ed. entitled *The whole works of Sir James Ware* . . ., ed. by Walter Harris, was published in 3 vols., Dublin, 1739–46; 2 vols., Dublin, 1764. It included 5914 and 5916 with Ware's list of Irish writers.
Sir James Ware (1594–1660) laid the foundations for the modern study of Irish history and literature. His historical work is inaccurate but still valuable, especially his annals for the reign of Henry VII. Cf. J. Lynch, *De praesuli. bus. Hiberniae* . . . Hist. MSS. Comm. Dublin, 1944.

5917 WELPLY, W. H. Seven Anglo-Irishmen of the Tudor times. *Notes and Queries*, clxxxvii (1944), 90–95.
Henry Draycott; Edward, George, Owen and Thomas Moore; Robert Pipho; Barnaby Rich.

5918 WELPLY, W. H. Edmund Spenser's brother-in-law, John Travers. *Notes and Queries*, clxxix (1940), 74–78, 92–96, 112–15.
Master of the ordnance in Ireland (1533–58). Cf. also W. H. Welply, *Sir John Travers, Kt., and his brothers-in-law, Sir William Fitzwilliam(s), Kt., and Anthony Fortescue, Notes and Queries*, cxc (1946), 2–5, 25–28.

5919 WILSON, PHILIP. The beginnings of modern Ireland. Dublin, 1912.
Covers period 1500–58. Based on sources. Good

C. CONSTITUTIONAL AND LEGAL HISTORY

1. SOURCES

The sources on constitutional and legal history are included in sect. B 1 *supra*; cf. particularly 5729, 5733, 5736–8, 5739, 5754, 5774. Sir John Davies's speech of 1613 (in 5789) should be consulted on the Irish parliament. For the Irish house of commons, Hooker's journals, printed in 636 and 5851 are valuable. With these compare his English parliamentary works (1100). Steele (1017), ii, calendars the Irish proclamations and in i, pp. clxxxviii–cxcii, prints *in extenso* the *Modus tenendi parliamenta et concilia in Hibernia*, dated 11 Jan. 1418/19.

5920 COURT OF CASTLE CHAMBER. Records, i, 1573–1620, in possession of earl of Egmont. Cf. 262.
A vol. in Trinity College library entitled *Dublin Star Chamber trials* contains transcript of the above with some other decrees. Cf. on this subject Wood (5951).

5921 THE STATUTES AT LARGE, passed in the parliaments held in Ireland: from the third year of Edward the second, A.D. 1310, to the [fortieth year of George the third, A.D. 1800]. 20 vols. Dublin, 1786–1801.
Cf. also *Statutes 10 Henry VI to 14 Elizabeth established in Ireland*, Lond., 1572; *Statutes within Ireland (proclamation and abridgement of)*, Lond., 1576; and *Statuta, ordinationes, acta edit. in parliamenti apud Dublin 27 Elizabeth*, Lond. 1586. Cf. 5947.

2. LATER WORKS

A general account of the old Irish house of commons is in Porritt (1133). Steele's Introduction to the Proclamations (1017), pp. cxvii ff., contains useful notes on the Irish administrative system; cf. 5846, 5851, 5854, 5907, 5919. Earlier work on Tudor government has been largely superseded by Quinn (5942–7), Falkiner (5929), and Wood (5951–4).

Conflicting Irish and English legal and constitutional concepts played a dramatic part in the climax of the Tudor wars. Irish usages, geared to a war economy, are analysed in Butler (5925, 6073).

5922 BALL, F. E. The judges of Ireland, 1221–1921. 2 vols. Lond. 1926.
Biographical sketches and a survey of their work and of legal development during the centuries.

5923 BEATSON, ROBERT. Political index to the histories of Great Britain and Ireland (vol. iii). Lond. 1806.
Hereditary honours, public offices, persons in office.

5924 BURTCHAELL, G. D. Genealogical memoirs of the members of parliament for the county and city of Kilkenny. Dublin, 1888.

5925 BUTLER, W. F. T. Irish land tenures, celtic and foreign. *Studies*, xiii (1924), 291–305, 524–40.

5926 CARNEY, MAURA. Agreement between Ó Domhnaill and Tadhg Ó Conchobhair concerning Sligo Castle (23 June 1539). *Irish Hist. Studies*, iii (1943), 283–96.

5927 CLARKE, M. V. Medieval representation and consent. Lond. 1936.
Ch. iii on Henry VIII and the proctors of the Irish parliament.

5928 EDWARDS, R. D., and MOODY, T. W. The history of Poynings' Law, 1495–1615. *Irish Hist. Studies*, ii (1941), 415–24.

5929 FALKINER, C. L. The parliament of Ireland under the Tudors. *Proc. R.I.A.* xxv, sect. C, no. 10 (1905), 508–41, 553–66.
Valuable. Prints list of speakers, also of lords from B.M. Egerton MSS. 2642 and Hooker diary from Cambr. Univ. library Mm 1/32. Reprinted in 5851.

5930 HAMMOND, J. W. The King's printers in Ireland, 1551–1919. *Dublin Hist. Rec.* xi (1949), 29–31, 58–64, 88–96.

5931 HARDIMAN, JAMES. Ancient Irish deeds to the seventeenth century. *Trans. R.I.A.* xv (1828), 3–96.

5932 HOGAN, JAMES. The Irish law of kingship. *Proc. R.I.A.* xl, sect. C (1932), 186–254.

5933 HOGAN, JAMES. The tricha cét and related land measures. *Proc. R.I.A.* xxxviii, sect. C (1929), 148–235.

5934 HUGHES, J. L. J. The chief secretaries in Ireland, 1566–1921. *Irish Hist. Studies,* viii (1952), 59–72.

5935 LYNCH, WILLIAM. View of legal institutions, offices, and baronies in Ireland. Lond. 1830.
Contains parliamentary records of the sixteenth century no longer extant.

5936 MACNEILL, EOIN. Early Irish laws and institutions. *New York Univ. Law Quar. Rev.* vii (1930), 149–265; viii (1931), 81–108; 271–84.
Published separately with introduction, criticizing Butler and Mathew, Dublin, 1935.

5937 MACNEILL, EOIN. Ireland and Wales in the history of jurisprudence. *Studies,* xvi (1927), 254–8, 605–15.
Cf. also idem, *Jour. R.S.A.I.* lvii (1927), 154–5.

5938 MOODY, T. W. The Irish parliament under Elizabeth and James I: a general survey. *Proc. R.I.A.* xlv, sect. C (1939), 41–81.

5939 O'DONOVAN, J. Covenant between the Mageoghegan and the Fox, 20 August 1526. *Irish Arch. Soc. Misc.* (1846), 179–97.
Misdated. Probably 1566, cf. 6087.

5940 OLDFIELD, T. H. B. Representative history of Great Britain and Ireland, being a history of the house of commons and of the counties, cities and boroughs of the United Kingdom from the earliest period. 6 vols. Lond. 1816.
Vol. vi deals with Irish boroughs.

5941 O'SULLIVAN, M. D. Irish lawyers in Tudor Ireland. *Dublin Rev.* clxxix (1926), 1–11.

5942 QUINN, D. B. The Irish parliamentary subsidy in the fifteenth and sixteenth centuries. *Proc. R.I.A.* xlii, sect. C (1935), 215–46.

5943 QUINN, D. B. Anglo-Irish local government, 1485–1534. *Irish Hist. Studies,* i (1939), 354–81.

5944 QUINN, D. B. The bills and statutes of the Irish parliaments of Henry VII and Henry VIII. *Anal. Hiber.* x (1941), 71–169.

5945 QUINN, D. B. The early interpretation of Poynings' law, 1494–1534. *Irish Hist. Studies,* ii (1941), 241–54.

5946 QUINN, D. B. Parliaments and great councils in Ireland, 1461–1586. *Irish Hist. Studies,* iii (1942), 60–77.

5947 QUINN, D. B. Government printing and the publication of the Irish statutes in the sixteenth century. *Proc. R.I.A.* xlix, sect. C (1943), 45–129.

5948	RICHARDSON, H. G., and SAYLES, G. O. The Irish parliament in the Middle Ages. Phila. 1952.
Ch. xvii is on Poynings' law.

5949	RICHARDSON, H. G. The Irish parliament rolls of the fifteenth century. *E.H.R.* lviii (1943), 448–61.

5950	SMYTH, C. J. Chronicle of the law officers of Ireland, containing lists of the lord chancellors and keepers of the great seal, masters of the rolls, chief justices and judges. . . . . Lond. 1839.
Index useful.

5951	WOOD, HERBERT. The court of Castle chamber, or star chamber of Ireland. *Proc. R.I.A.* xxxii, sect. C, no. 10 (1914), 152–70.

5952	WOOD, HERBERT. The office of chief governor of Ireland, 1172–1509. *Proc. R.I.A.* xxxvi, sect. C (1923), 206–38.

5953	WOOD, HERBERT. The offices of secretary of state and keeper of the signet or privy seal. *Proc. R.I.A.* xxxviii, sect. C (1928), 51–68.

5954	WOOD, HERBERT. The titles of the chief governor of Ireland. *Bull. Inst. Hist. Research*, xiii (1935), 1–8.

D. ECCLESIASTICAL HISTORY

I. SOURCES

Edwards (6020) contains an excellent bibliography; cf. bibliography of Bellesheim (6001) on the Catholics. Pollen (1740) is brief but useful. Sanders (1748) gives some information about Irish church affairs from the Roman Catholic point of view. Verstegen (2280) includes material on persecutions of Catholics in Ireland under Elizabeth.

5955	ACCOUNTS OF SUMS REALISED by sales of chattels of some suppressed Irish monasteries. By Charles McNeill. *R.S.A.I.*, 6th ser., xii (1922), 11–37.

5956	ANCIENT DEEDS in parishes of Dublin. St. Anne's gild in St. Audoen's, 1430–1740. By H. F. Berry. *Proc. R.I.A.* xxv (1904–5), sect. C 21–106.
Cf. also for *St. Catherine's and St. James's, 1296–1743*, by H. F. Twiss [née Berry], *Proc. R.I.A.* xxxv (1918–20), sect. C, 265–81; for *St. Werburgh's, 1243–1676*, ibid. 282–315; for *St. John's*, by J. L. Robinson, ibid. xxxiii (1916–17), sect. C, 175–224.

5957	ANNALES ECCLESIASTICI, 1572–85. By Augustin Theiner. Rome, 1856.
Useful documents. Cf. also 5439.

5958	ARCHBISHOP CROMER'S REGISTER. By L. P. Murray. *County Louth Arch. Jour.* vii (1933), 516–24; viii (1934), 38–49; viii (1935), 169–77; viii (1936), 257–74; viii (1937), 322–51; ix (1939), 36–41; ix (1940), 124–30; by A. Gwynn, x (1943), 116–27; x (1944), 165–78.
George Cromer, d. 1543, archbishop of Armagh, 1521.

5959 BALE, JOHN. The vocacyon of Johan Bale to the bishoprick of Ossorie in Ireland. Rome [*recte* Lond.], 1553; repr. in *Harl. Misc.* (281), vi, 437.
Valuable. Author a zealous Protestant bishop of Ossory, temp. Edward VI ff.

5960 BOOK OF OBITS AND MARTYROLOGY of Christ Church, Dublin. By J. C. Crosthwaite and J. H. Todd. *Irish Arch. Soc.* Dublin, 1844.

5961 BOOK OUT OF IRELAND IN LATTEN, 1551. By M. V. Ronan. *Irish Eccles. Rec.*, 5th ser., xxv (1925), 501–13, 606–22.

5962 CALENDAR OF ARCHBISHOP ALEN'S REGISTER, *c.* 1172–1534. By Charles McNeill. *Roy. Soc. Antiq. of Ire. for 1949*, extra vol. Dublin, 1950.
John Alen, 1476–1534, archbishop of Dublin. Register is sole authority for many important documents from twelfth to sixteenth century.

5963 CALENDAR OF THE LIBER RUBER of the diocese of Ossory. By H. J. Lawlor. *Proc. R.I.A.* xxvii, sect. C (1908), 159–208.

5964 THE CHARTERS OF THE CISTERCIAN ABBEY OF DUISKE, CO. KILKENNY. By C. M. Butler and J. H. Bernard. *Proc. R.I.A.* xxxv, sect. C (1918), 1–188.

5965 CORRESPONDENCE OF FATHER LUDOVICO MANSONI, S.J., papal nuncio to Ireland. By F. M. Jones. *Archiv. Hiber.* xvii (1953), 1–68.

5966 COSTELLO, M. A. De annatis Hiberniae. Calendar of first fruits, &c. Vol. i, Ulster, 1400–1535. By Ambrose Coleman. Dublin 1912.
Cf. also for non-Ulster dioceses, *Obligationes pro Annatis*, all published in the *Archiv. Hiber.* from the transcripts of M. A. Costello for individual dioceses: *Dublin, 1421–1520*, by Ambrose Coleman, *Archiv. Hiber.* ii (1913), supp. 1–37; *Kildare, 1413–1521*, by Ambrose Coleman, ibid. 39–72; *Killaloe, 1421–1535*, by Dermot Gleason, ibid. x (1943), 1–103; *Limerick, 1421–1511*, by Michael Moloney, ibid. x (1943), 104–62; *Waterford, 1421–1507*, by Patrick Power, ibid. xii (1946), 1–14; *Lismore, 1426–1529*, by Patrick Power, xii (1946), 15–61; *Ferns, 1413–1524*, by Joseph Ranson, ibid. xviii (1955), 1–15.

5967 DOCUMENTS CONCERNING PRIMATE DOWDALL. By Thomas Gogarty. *Archiv. Hiber.*, i (1912), 248–76; ii (1913), 242–55.
These papers illustrate Dowdall's career (1487–1558) as a churchman. Cf. *Louth Arch. Jour.* ii, no. 2 (1909), 149–64, for his career as a statesman.

5968 EUBEL, CONRAD. Hierarchia Catholica Medii Aevi, 1198–1667. 4 vols. Münster, 1898–1935.

5969 EXTENTS OF IRISH MONASTIC POSSESSIONS, 1540–1. By N. B. White. *Irish MSS. Comm.* Dublin, 1943.
From MSS. in the P.R.O.

5970 FASTI ECCLESIAE HIBERNICAE. By Henry Cotton. 6 vols. Dublin, 1847–78; rev. ed., vol. i, 1851.
Gives brief biographies and details of official appointment of prelates of the Anglican church in Ireland. Vol. v consists of addenda, corrigenda, and index by J. R. Garstin; vol. vi is supplementary by C. P. Cotton.

5971 FITZSIMON, H. Words of comfort to persecuted Catholics. By E. Hogan. Dublin, 1881.

5972 GWYNN, AUBREY. The antiphonary of Armagh. *County Louth Arch. Soc.* xi (1945), 1–14.

5973   HARTRY, J. M. Triumphalia Chronologica Monasterii Sanctae Crucis in Hibernia. By Denis Murphy. Dublin, 1891.

5974   HISTORICAL COLLECTIONS of the church in Ireland . . . set forth in the life and death of Geo. Browne. By Robert Ware. Lond. 1681; repr. in Ware's *Antiquities* (5915) and in *Harl. Misc.* (281), v, 595–606.
Browne was a Catholic priest turned Protestant. This purports to be his letters to lord privy seal. These letters were forgeries. Cf. P. Wilson, in *Trans. Biblio. Soc.* xv (1920), and T. E. Bridgett, *Blunders and Forgeries*, Lond. 1890.

5975   IBERNIA IGNATIANA, seu Ibernorum societatis Jesu patrum monumenta collecta, &c. (1540–1607). By Edmund Hogan. Dublin, 1880.
Letters and papers in Jesuit archives on the activities of the Jesuits in Ireland. Valuable. Includes account of first Jesuit missions to Ireland, 1542.

5976   IRISH MONASTIC AND EPISCOPAL DEEDS, A.D. 1200–1600 Trans. from originals preserved at Kilkenny Castle. With an appendix of documents of the sixteenth and seventeenth centuries relating to monastic property after the dissolution. By N. B. White. *Irish MSS. Comm.* Dublin, 1936.

5977   JENNINGS, BRENDAN. Brevis synopsis provinciae Hiberniae FF. minorum. *Anal. Hiber.* vi (1934), 139–91.
Text of oldest manuscript of the Brevis written by Fr. Francis Matthews and copied early seventeenth century by Fr. Anthony Haly. It covers mostly the sixteenth century.

5978   LAEMMER, HUGO. Monumenta Vaticana historiae ecclesiasticae saeculi xvi. Freiburg, 1861.

5979   LESLIE, J. B. Ardfert and Aghadoe clergy and parishes. Dublin, 1940.

5980   LESLIE, J. B. Raphoe clergy and parishes. Enniskillen, 1940.

5981   LESLIE, J. B. Armagh clergy and parishes. Dundalk, 1911; suppl. 1948.

5983   MACBRIDE, P. Some unpublished letters of Mateo de Oviedo, archbishop of Dublin [1599–1602]. *Reportorium Novum*, i (1955), 91–117.

5984   MAGRATH, MEILER. Visitation of Waterford and Lismore, 1588. By P. Power. *Waterford and SE. Ire. Arch. Soc. Jour.* xii (1909), 155–61, xiii (1910), 8–16.
From Trin. Col., Dub., MS. E. 3. 14.

5985   MEMORIALS of those who suffered for the Catholic faith in Ireland in the sixteenth, seventeenth, and eighteenth centuries. By M. W. P. O'Reilly. Lond. 1868.
Collected and edited from original sources.

5986   MISCELLANEA VATICANO-HIBERNICA. By J. Hagan. *Archiv. Hiber.* ii, 274–320; iii, 227–365; iv, 215–318; v, 157–85; vii, 67–356 (1914–22).
Papers from Vatican archives printed *in extenso* in Latin or Italian with accompanying brief calendars in English.

5987   MONUMENTA HIST. SOC. JESU. Mon. Ignatiana, epistolae, xxix. Madrid, 1909.

5988 O'HEYN, JOHN. Epilogus chronologicus exponens succinte conventus et foundationes Ord. Praedicatorum in Regno Hyberniae. Louvain, 1706.
Rev. ed. by A. Coleman is titled *Irish Dominicans of the 17th century*, Dundalk, 1902.

5989 ORIGINAL LETTERS AND PAPERS in illustration of the history of the church in Ireland during the reigns of Edward VI, Mary and Elizabeth. By E. P. Shirley. Lond. 1851.
From P.R.O., S.P., Ireland.

5990 COLLECTIONS OF IRISH CHURCH HISTORY, from the MSS. of the late Laurence F. Renehan. Vol. i, archbishops; ii, bishops of Fern and Limerick, by Daniel MacCarthy. Dublin, 1861–74.
Contains much miscellaneous documentary material *in extenso*.

5991 REGESTRUM MONASTERII FRATRUM PRAEDICATORUM DE ATHENRY. By A. Coleman. *Archiv. Hiber.* i (1912), 201–21.

5992 REPORT ON DOCUMENTS relating to the wardenship of Galway. By Edward MacLysaght. *Anal. Hiber.* xiv (1944).

5993 THE REPORTORIUM VIRIDE of John Alen, archbishop of Dublin, 1533. By N. B. White. *Anal. Hiber.* x (1941), 173–222.

5994 RICH, BARNABE. A Catholic conference between Syr Tady Mac-Mareall a popish priest of Waterforde, and Patricke Plaine a young student in Trinity College. . . . Lond. 1612.

5995 ROTHE, DAVID. Analecta sacra nova et mira de rebus Catholicorum in Hibernia . . . gestis. Pt. i, Cologne, 1616; pts. i and ii, Cologne, 1617; pt. iii, entitled *De processu Martyriali*, Cologne, 1619; by P. F. Moran, Dublin, 1884.
Author Roman Catholic bishop of Ossory. An impeachment of the Irish ecclesiastical policy of Elizabeth and James I. Cardinal Moran's introduction to the ed. of 1884 deals chiefly with the lives of Creagh, O'Hurley, and O'Devany.

5996 SPICILEGIUM OSSORIENSE: being a collection of original letters and papers illustrative of the history of the Irish church from the reformation to the year 1800. 3 vols. By P. F. Moran. Dublin, 1874–84.
Valuable for dealings of Irish Catholics with Spain and Holy See in reign of Elizabeth. Prints *in extenso* letters of Irish Catholics to Philip, and other important Catholic papers.

5997 STATE PAPERS concerning the Irish church in the time of Queen Elizabeth. By W. M. Brady. Lond. 1868.

2. LATER WORKS

The best work on the Irish church in the Tudor period is by Edwards (6020). Cf. *Handlist of Irish diocesan histories*, in *Pro. I.C.H.C.* (5660), 1957, pp. 31–37.

5998 ARCHDALL, MERVYN. Monasticon Hibernicum. Lond. 1786; best ed. by P. F. Moran *et al.*, 2 vols. Dublin, 1873–6.
History of abbeys, and other religious houses in Ireland to the reformation. Moran's ed. is still unfinished. Important.

5999 BALL, J. T. The reformed church of Ireland, 1537–1886. Lond. 1886; rev. ed., Lond. 1889.
Chiefly from point of view of ecclesiastical legislation. Good.

6000   BEGLEY, JOHN. Diocese of Limerick in the sixteenth and seventeenth centuries. Dublin, 1927.

6001   BELLESHEIM, ALPHONS. Geschichte der katholischen Kirche in Irland von der Einführung des Christenthums bis auf die Gegenwart. 3 vols. Mainz, 1890–1.
Best modern discussion from Catholic viewpoint. Vol. ii, 1509–1690. Good bibliography.

6002   BOERO, GIUSEPPE. Vita del servo di Dio, P. Pascasio Broet. Florence, 1877.
Life of a Jesuit missionary to Ireland, 1542. Written as pious propaganda and not as history. Cf. *Epistolae P. Broeti*, Madrid, 1903.

6003   BOERO, GIUSEPPE. Vita del servo di Dio, P. Alfonso Salmerone. Florence, 1880.
Jesuit missionary to Ireland, 1542. Cf. *Epistolae A. Salmeronis*, Madrid, 1906.

6004   BOYLE, PATRICK. The Irish college in Paris, 1578–1901. Dublin, 1901.
Contains accounts also of other Irish colleges in France, and of Scotch and English colleges in Paris. Extensive app. of documents. Cf. James O'Boyle, *Irish colleges on the Continent*. Dublin, 1935.

6005   BRADY, W. M. The episcopal succession in England, Scotland, and Ireland, 1400–1875. 3 vols. Rome, 1876–7.
Vol. ii Ireland. Details of official appointments in the Roman Catholic church. Cf. 6038.

6007   BRADY, W. M. The alleged conversion of the Irish bishops to the reformed religion . . . disproved. Lond. [Dublin], 1866; 5th ed. Lond. 1867.
The 5th ed. is entitled *The Irish Reformation or the alleged conversion of the Irish bishops at the accession of Queen Elizabeth . . . disproved*.
Useful biographical information about Irish bishops, temp. Elizabeth.

6008   BURKE (seu DE BURGO), THOMAS. Hibernia dominicana. Cologne [Kilkenny?], 1762; supplement, 1772.
The title-page gives Colonia Agrippina (Cologne) as the place of publication, but a copy in the Vatican bears the imprint Kilkenniae.
A history of the Dominican order in Ireland.

6009   C., J. Theatre of the Catholique and Protestant religion. . . . s.l. 1620.
By a student of divinity [John Copinger].

6011   CONYNGHAM, D. P. Lives of the Irish martyrs. New York, 1878.
Cf. also *The church of Erin, her saints, her martyrs, her monasteries, and her shrines*, by J. Walsh and D. P. Conyngham, New York, 1885.

6012   CORBOY, JAMES. Father David Galway. S.J. 1579–1634. *Irish Monthly*, lxii (1944), 58–67.

6013   CORBOY, JAMES. Father James Archer, 1550–1625 (?), Father Henry Fitzsimon, 1566–1643, and Father Christopher Holywood, 1559–1626. *Studies*, xxxii (1943), 260–6; xxxiii (1944), 99–107, 543–9.

6014   CORBOY, JAMES. The Irish college at Salamanca. *Irish Eccles. Rec.*, 5th ser., lxiii (1944), 247–53.

6015   D'ALTON, JOHN. Memoirs of the archbishops of Dublin. Dublin, 1838.
Useful personal accounts.

6016 D'ALTON, E. A. History of the archdiocese of Tuam. 2 vols. Dublin, 1928.

6017 DE PROVINCIA HIBERNIAE S. FRANCISCI. By Brendan Jennings. *Anal. Hiber.* vi (1934), 12–138.

6018 DURKAN, JOHN. Robert Wauchope, archbishop of Armagh. *Innes Rev. i* (1950), 48–65.

6019 DWYER, PHILIP. Diocese of Killaloe. . . . Dublin, 1878.

6020 EDWARDS, R. D. Church and state in Tudor Ireland. A history of penal laws against Irish catholics, 1534–1603. Dublin, 1935.
The standard work. Useful bibliography.

6021 EDWARDS, R. D. The Irish bishops and the Anglican schism, 1534–47. *Irish Eccles. Rec.*, 5th ser., xlv (1935), 39–60, 196–205.

6024 GARVEY, J. The conversion of P. Corwine . . . anno 1589. [By Robert Ware.] Dublin, 1681.
Contains letters purporting to be composed by a Protestant primate and by a Franciscan friar of whom nothing is known, except through R. Ware, for whose implication in forgeries cf. 5915, 5974.

6025 GLEESON, D. F. The episcopal succession of Killaloe, A.D. 1317–1616. *N. Munster Antiq. Jour.* ii (1940), 51–62.

6027 GROVES, H. C. The titular archbishops of Ireland in the reign of Queen Elizabeth. Dublin, 1897.
Contains a bibliography.

6028 GWYNN, AUBREY. The medieval province of Armagh, 1470–1545. Dundalk, 1946.

6029 GWYNN, AUBREY. The Irish monastery of Bangor. *Irish Eccles. Rec.*, 5th ser., lxxiv (1950), 388–97.

6031 HOLLAND, WILLIAM. History of west Cork and the diocese of Ross. Skibbereen, 2nd ed. 1950.

6032 HOLLOWAY, HENRY. The reformation in Ireland. A study of ecclesiastical legislation. Lond. 1919.
Unsound on Poynings' law and inaccurate on Henry VIII's legislation.

6033 JONES, F. M. Canonical faculties on the Irish mission in the reign of Queen Elizabeth, 1558–1603. *Irish Theol. Quar.* xx (1953), 152–71.

6034 JOURDAN, G. V. The breach with Rome, &c. *History of the church of Ireland.* By W. A. Phillips. Vol. ii. Oxf. 1934.
Cf. M. J. Hynes, *The Church of Ireland, Cath. Hist. Rev.* xxi (1936), 400–28.

6035 KING, ROBERT. Primer of the history of the holy Catholic church in Ireland. . . . 3rd ed. 2 vols. Dublin, 1845–6; supplementary vol., Dublin, 1851.
Supplementary vol. contains app. of useful documents collected from printed sources. Text documented. Church of Ireland viewpoint.

6036 KINGSTON, JOHN. William Bathe, S.J., 1564–1614. *Irish Eccles. Rec.*, 5th ser., lxxxii (1954), 179–82.

6038 LAWLOR, H. J. The reformation and the Irish episcopate. *Church Hist. Soc.*, no. 93 (1906), rev. ed. 1932.
Takes issue with Brady (6005).

6039 LAWLOR, H. J. Fasti of St. Patrick's Dublin. Dundalk, 1930.

6040 MACNAMEE, J. J. History of the diocese of Ardagh. Dublin, 1954.

6041 MANT, RICHARD. History of the church of Ireland from the reformation to the revolution. 2 vols. Lond. 1840.
Anglican viewpoint. The author Anglican bishop of Down and Conor. Documented.

6042 MAHAFFY, J. P. An epoch in Irish history: Trinity College, Dublin, its foundation and early fortunes, 1591–1660. Lond. 1903; 1906.
Ch. i deals with Jesuits in Ireland.

6043 MASON, W. M. History and antiquities of the . . . cathedral church of St. Patrick, 1190–1819. Dublin, 1820.

6044 MEEHAN, C. P. Rise and fall of the Irish Franciscan monasteries. Dublin, 1867.
Inexact.

6045 MILLETT, BENIGNUS. The pastoral zeal of Robert Wauchope. *Seanchas Ardmhacha*, ii (1956), 32–60.

6046 MORAN, P. F. History of the Catholic archbishops of Dublin since the reformation. Dublin, 1864.
App. of documents.

6047 MORAN, P. F. The episcopal succession in Ireland during the reign of Elizabeth. . . . Dublin, 1866.
Details of appointments of Catholic prelates.

6049 MURRAY, L. P. The last abbot of Mellifont. *County Louth Arch. Soc. Jour.* viii (1936), 223–33.

6050 MURRAY, L. P. The Franciscan monasteries after the dissolution. *County Louth Arch. Soc. Jour.* viii (1936), 275–82.

6051 O'DUFFY, E. The apostasy of Meiler Magrath . . . about 1577. Cashel, 1864.
Refers to the notorious archbishop of Cashel. Contains documents.

6052 OLDEN, THOMAS. The church of Ireland. Lond. 1902.

6054 REID, J. S. History of the Presbyterian church in Ireland. By W. D. Killen. 3 vols. Belfast, 1867.
Introductory chapter deals with period before 1603.

6055 ROGERS, PATRICK. The suppression of the monasteries in Antrim and Down. *Down and Connor Hist. Soc. Jour.* ix (1938), 25–38.

6056 ROGERS, PATRICK. Henry VIII and the Irish monasteries. *Bonaventura*, i, no. 2 (1937), 115–27; no. 3 (1937), 123–35; no. 4 (1938), 122–30; ii, no. 1 (1938), 128–45.

6057 ROGERS, PATRICK. The Irish Franciscan observants and the royal supremacy. *Capuchin Annual*, 1935 (1935), 203–14.

6058 RONAN, M. V. The reformation in Dublin, 1536–58. Lond. 1926.
Prints some documents in text inexactly. Roman catholic viewpoint.

6059 RONAN, M. V. The reformation in Ireland under Elizabeth, 1558–80. Lond. 1930.
A sequel to 6058.

6060 RONAN, M. V. The Irish martyrs of the penal laws. Lond. 1935.

6061 RONAN, M. V. Cardinal Pole's absolution of George Browne. *Irish Eccles. Rec.*, 5th ser., lxxii (1949), 193–206.
George Browne, archbishop of Dublin, 1536.

6062 ROTHE, DAVID. De Processu Martyriali. Cologne, 1619.

6063 SEYMOUR, ST. J. D. Diocese of Emly. Dublin, 1913.

6064 SILKE, J. J. Later relations between Primate Peter Lombard and Hugh O'Neill. *Irish Theol. Quar.* xxii (1955), 15–30.

6065 SILKE, J. J. Peter Lombard and James I. *Irish Theol. Quar.* xxii (1955), 124–49.

6066 TWIGG, O. M. Richard Creagh, archbishop of Armagh, 1515–85. *Dublin Rev.* cxci (1932), 71–79.

6067 WADDING, LUKE. Annales Minorum. Vols. xvi, xvii–xxiv. Florence, 1933–4.

6068 WEBSTER, A. Diocese of Cork. Dublin, 1920.

6069 [ZIMMERMAN, A.] Die irischen Märtyrer unter Königin Elisabeth. *Der Katholik,* neue Folge, lx (1888), 179–200.

E. SOCIAL AND ECONOMIC HISTORY

1. GENERAL

Social history must be approached through the study of the learned families and the literary history of the rival Gaelic and English civilizations on the eve of their transformation in the struggle of the Tudor conquests and the continental-trained missionaries of the counter-reformation. Writers like Keating (5805a) concentrated on earlier history to avoid current war issues and their work is essential for the study of social history. Cf. Kenney (5699), pp. 24–26 for a sixteenth-century list of Gaelic bibliothecae, and Flower (5798), for Anglo-Irish annals, in addition to Seymour (6085).

A good bibliography of Irish economic history by P. L. Prendeville is in *Econ. Hist. Rev.* iii, no. 2 (1931), 27–92.

(a) Sources

Source material in print is included in sect. B 1 *supra* (pp. 483 ff.). The *Statutes* (5921) and the *Proclamations* (1017) are valuable. Among contemporary descriptions of Ireland, Camden (4190), Stanihurst (5823), Davies (5789), and Spenser (5822) are important. Cf. also 5772, 5786, 5790, 5791, 5805, 5805a, and 5813.

6070 CHIERICATI, FRANCESCO, a Isabella d'Este Gonzaga, 1517. In *Portioli Quattro documenti d'Inghilterra*, &c. Mantua, 1868; repr. by B. Morsolin in *Atti dell' accademia Olimpica de Vicenza*, Vicenza, 1873.
Describes Chiericati's visit to St. Patrick's purgatory with an interesting account of the state of Ulster, *c.* 1520. C. was a papal emissary to Ireland, temp. Henry VIII. Cf. J. P. Mahaffy on two early tours in Ireland, *Hermathena*, no. 40 (1914), 1–16.

6071 O HUIGINN, TADHG DALL. The bardic poems of [1550–91]. By Eleanor Knott. 2 vols. *Irish Texts Soc.* xxii, xxiii (1922, 1926).
Text, trans., and notes.

(b) *Later Works*

An economic history of Ireland in the sixteenth century is a *desideratum*. Butler's work (6073) is important. Cf. also 5892 and 5914. On the English colonizing projects in Ireland, cf. 5830, 5833, 5844–5, 5847. Cf. also 2926.

6072 BOOK OF FENAGH. By W. M. Hennessy and D. H. Kelly. Dublin, 1875, repr. 1939. Supp. vol. by R. A. S. Macalister. *Irish MSS. Comm.* Dublin, 1939.
Cf. P. Walsh, *Irish Eccles. Rec.*, 5th ser., lv (1939), 561–81; lvi (1940), 56–72.

6073 BUTLER, W. F. Gleanings from Irish history. Lond. 1925.
Includes: (1) *The lordship of MacCarthy Mor*, valuable for Irish social arrangements in sixteenth century; (2) *The policy of surrender and regrant*, dealing with land policy temp. Elizabeth. Scholarly.

6074 GANNON, J. P. A review of Irish history in relation to the social development of Ireland. Lond. 1900.
Suggestive on sixteenth-century social development and on Ireland in relation to rest of Europe.

6075 GREEN, A. S. The making of Ireland and its undoing, 1200–1600. Lond. 1908; 1909.
Essays on trade and industries, education and learning. Controversial. Uncritical on Gaelic culture.

6076 HULL, ELEANOR. A textbook of Irish literature. 2 vols. Dublin, 1906–8.

6077 HYDE, DOUGLAS. A literary history of Ireland. Lond. 1899.

6078 JOPE, E. M. Scottish influence in the north of Ireland: castles with Scottish features, 1580–1640. *Ulster Jour. of Arch.*, 3rd ser., xiv (1952), 31–47.

6079 LYNAM, E. W. O'. F. The end of the clan system. *Studies*, iii (1914), 553–66.

6080 MACCARTHY, DANIEL. Notes on Irish dress and armour in the sixteenth century. *R.S.A.I.*, 2nd ser., i (1856–7), 364–70.
Cf. also J. C. Walker, *Historical essay on the dress of the ancient Irish*, Dublin, 1788.
For Irish dress, methods of warfare, &c., reference should be made to illustrations in Derrick (5791) and Stafford (5824).

6081 MCCLINTOCK, H. F. Some hitherto unpublished pictures of sixteenth century Irish people, and the costumes appearing in them. *Jour. R.S.A.I.* lxxxiii (1953), 150–5.

6082 MAGEOGHEGAN, CONELL. The annals of Clonmacnoise. By Denis Murphy. Dublin, 1896.
For the registry of Clonmacnoise, by John O'Donovan, cf. *Kilkenny Arch. Soc. Jour.*, n.s., i (1858), 444–60.

6083 MOONEY, CANICE. Franciscan architecture in pre-reformation Ireland. *Jour. R.S.A.I.* lxxxv (1955), 133–73.

6084 MURPHY, GERARD. Folksong traceable to Elizabethan times. *Éigse*, vii (1953–5), 117–30.

6085 SEYMOUR, ST. J. D. Anglo-Irish literature, 1200–1582. Cambr. 1929.

6086 WALSH, PAUL. The Ó Cléirigh family of Tir Conaill. Dublin, 1938.

6087 WALSH, PAUL. Irish men of learning. By Colm O Lochlainn. Dublin, 1947.
Includes studies of sixteenth-century learned families: O Duigenan, O Maelconaire, O Huiginn, MacFirbhisigh, O Cuirnín, Mac an Bhaird.

6088 WEBB, J. J. The guilds of Dublin. Lond. 1929.

2. INDUSTRY AND COMMERCE

Much useful information on Irish industry will be found in *Cal. Ancient Rec. Dublin* (6121) and in local histories given in sect. F *infra* (pp. 512 ff.). For trade between Chester and Ireland, cf. Morris (4268). Useful brief contemporary notes on Irish trade are included in 2963. Ruding (1265) is the best book on the Irish coinage.

6089 BERRY, H. F. The records of the Dublin gild of merchants, known as the gild of the Holy Trinity, 1438–1671. *R.S.A.I.*, 5th ser., x (1900), 44–68.
Description of records with a few extracts.

6090 BERRY, H. F. The merchant tailors' gild—that of St. John the Baptist, Dublin, 1418–1841. *R.S.A.I.*, 6th ser., xxiii (1918), 19–64.
Prints extracts from the sources, several of the sixteenth century.

6091 DIX, E. R. McC. Humfrey Powell, the first Dublin printer. *Proc. R.I.A.* xxvii, sect. C (1908), 213–16.

6092 CURTIS, E. The court book of Esker and Crumlin, 1592–1600. *R.S.A.I.*, 6th ser., lix (1929), 45–64, 128–48; lx (1930), 38–51, 137–49.
Important for manorial organization and land tenure in the Pale.

6093 GREEN, A. S. Irish land in the sixteenth century. *Ériu*, iii (1907), 174–85.

6094 GUINNESS, H. S. Dublin trade gilds. *R.S.A.I.*, 6th ser., xii (1922), 143–63.
Catalogue of extant gild records.

6095 LONGFIELD, A. K. Anglo-Irish trade in the sixteenth century. Lond. 1929.
Scholarly. Cf. also idem, *Anglo-Irish trade in the sixteenth century as illustrated by the English custom accounts and port books, Proc. R.I.A.* xxxvi, sect. C (1924), 317–32.

6096 LOUGH, S. M. Trade and industry in Ireland in the sixteenth century. *Jour. Pol. Econ.* xxiv (1916), 713–30.
Slight but useful.

6097 McNEILL, W. H. The introduction of the potato into Ireland. *Jour. Mod. Hist.* xxi (1949), 218–22.

6098 O'DONOVAN, JOHN. The economic history of live stock in Ireland. Cork, 1940.

6099 O'SULLIVAN, M. D. The exploitation of the mines of Ireland in the sixteenth century. *Studies*, xxiv (1935), 442–52.

6100 O'SULLIVAN, WILLIAM. The economic history of Cork city from the earliest times of the act of union. Cork, 1937.

6101 STUBBS, W. C. The weavers' guild, the guild of the blessed virgin Mary, Dublin, 1446–1840. *R.S.A.I.*, 6th ser., ix (1919), 60–88.

6102 VICARS, ARTHUR. Index to the prerogative wills of Ireland, 1536–1810. Dublin, 1897.

6103 WENT, A. E. J. The Galway fishery: an account of the ownership of the fishery. *Proc. R.I.A.* xlviii (1942), 233–53; xlix (1944), 187–219.

6104 WENT, A. E. J. Fisheries of the river Liffey: notes on the corporation fisheries up to the dissolution of the monasteries. *Jour. R.S.A.I.* lxxxiii (1953), 163–73; lxxxiv (1954), 41–58.

6105 WESTROPP, M. S. D. Irish glass; . . . from the sixteenth century. . . . Lond. 1920.

3. EDUCATION

6106 BRADY, JOHN. Some Irish scholars of the xvith century. *Studies*, xxvii (1948), 226–31.

6107 BURTCHAELL, G. D., and SADLEIR, T. U. Alumni Dublinensis, 1593–1846. Lond. 1924. New ed. with suppl. (1593–1860), Dublin, 1935.

6108 CORCORAN, TIMOTHY. Studies in the history of classical teaching, Irish and continental, 1500–1700. Dublin, 1911.
Contains: *Wm. Bathe, S.J., of Dublin (1564–1614) and his method of language teaching.*

6109 CORCORAN, TIMOTHY. Early Irish Jesuit educators: I. Thomas White of Clonmel (1556–1622). *Studies*, xxix (1940), 545–69, xxx (1941), 59–74.

6110 O'DOHERTY, D. J. Students of the Irish college, Salamanca, 1595–1619. *Archiv. Hibern.*, ii (1913), 1–36.
Lists of students from oaths of each student, giving details of his place of birth and education.

6111 PETITIONS OF IRISH STUDENTS in the university of Salamanca, 1574–91. By Amalio Huarte. *Archiv. Hibern.*, iv (1915), 96–130.
From acts of senate of University. Printed *in extenso* in Spanish with English summary.

6112 STATE POLICY IN IRISH EDUCATION, A.D. 1536–1816, exemplified in documents collected for lectures to post-graduate classes. By Timothy Corcoran, Dublin, 1916.
Documents from state papers well edited and indexed with valuable introduction.

6113 STUBBS, J. W. History of the university of Dublin from its foundation to the end of the eighteenth century, with original documents preserved in the college. Dublin, 1889.
Cf. on the same subject, W. Urwick, *Early history of Trinity College, Dublin, 1591–1600*, Lond. 1892, and Mahaffy (6042).

F. LOCAL HISTORY

For this subject in general, cf. *Cambr. Mod. Hist.* (20), iii, 852 ff., Maxwell (5707), 24–25 and T. P. O'Neill, *Sources of Irish local history*, Dublin, 1958.

Local and family history in sixteenth-century Ireland necessitates the treatment of many regions as autonomous states until the extension of Tudor rule. Cf. Quinn (5716).

Maps are important in the development of Irish local history. The Trinity College, Dublin, collection is listed in Abbott (5675). For early Italian maps of Ireland cf. Westropp (6179). Other early maps are printed in 316, 5824 (ed. 1633), 5855, 5892. A map *c.* 1560, attributed to L. Nowell, has been printed by the Ordnance Commissioners. Lyman's note on Irish maps (5702) is valuable. Useful modern maps of sixteenth-century Ireland, by R. Dunlop, are in Lane-Poole, Historical Atlas of Modern Europe, Oxf. 1902, maps 30, 31. Cf. also 5684, 5739, 5790, 5846, 6144.

For Irish fortified places *c.* 1600, cf. *Cal. S.P. Ireland, James I*, ii, pp. xxxix ff.

6115 BERRY, H. F. Friday book of Dublin corporation, 1567–1611. *Proc. R.I.A.* xxx, sect. C (1913), 477–514.

6116 BERRY, H. F. Mallow manor and castle. *Jour. Cork Arch. Soc.* ii (1893), 21–25, 41–45.

6117 BOUCH, J. J. Select bibliography of Dublin. *Lord Mayor's handbook. Dublin Municipal Annual* (1942), 79–89.

6118 BROWNE, NICHOLAS. Munster in 1597. By James Buckley. *Jour. of Cork Hist. and Arch. Soc.*, 2nd ser., xii (1906), 53–68.

6119 BUTLER, W. F. T. Division of S. Munster. *Jour. Cork Arch. Soc.* iii (1897), 121–36, 233–46.

6120 BUTLER, W. F. T. Two Kerry baronies. *Jour. Cork Arch. Soc.* xxxiii (1928), 1–10; xxiv (1929), 15–21.

6121 CALENDAR OF ANCIENT RECORDS OF DUBLIN. Vols. i, ii. By J. T. Gilbert. Dublin, 1889–91.
In the possession of the municipal corporation. Vol. i includes charters, the Liber Albus, the Chain Book, and assembly rolls since 1443.

6122 CARNEY, JAMES. Poems on the Butlers of Ormond, Cahir, and Dunboyne (A.D. 1400–1600). Dublin, 1945.

6123 CARNEY, JAMES. Thomas Costello and O'Rourke's wife. *Celtica*, i (1950), 238–79.

6124 CLARKE, D. Dublin Society's statistical surveys. *An Leabharlann* (1957).

6125 COGAN, A. Diocese of Meath, ancient and modern. 3 vols. Dublin, 1862–70.
Does not use material in P.R.O., S.P., Ireland.

6126 COLEMAN, J. Bibliographia Conaciensis. *Jour. Galway Arch. and Hist. Soc.* v (1908), 28–34, 239.

6127 THE COMPOSSICION BOOK OF CONOUGHT [1585]. By A. M. Freeman. *Irish MSS. Comm.* Dublin, 1936.
Cf. *Index*, by G. A. Hayes-McCoy, *Irish MSS. Comm.*, Dublin, 1942.

6128 COWLEY, WALTER. Survey of Offaly (1550). By E. Curtis. *Hermathena*, xlv (1930), 312–52.
Valuable description of an Irish lordship. From P.R.O., S.P., Ireland. Edward VI, vol. ii.

6129 CURTIS, EDMUND. Butler lordship of Achill, Burrishoole and Aughrim (1236–1640). *Jour. Galway Arch. and Hist. Soc.* xv (1933), 121–8.

6130 CURTIS, EDMUND. Documents relating to Aran. *Jour. Galway Arch. and Hist. Soc.* xvi (1934), 48–56.

6132 CURTIS, EDMUND. Medieval earldom of Ulster, 1333–1603. *Proc. Belfast Nat. Hist. Soc.* (1930–1), 62–80.

6133 FALKINER, C. L. The counties of Ireland. *Proc. R.I.A.* xxiv, sect. C, no. 11 (1903), 169–74.

6134 FERRAR, J. History of Limerick. Dublin, 1787.

6135 FROST, JAMES. History and topography of the County Clare. Dublin, 1893.

6137 'GEOGHEGAN, A. G. A notice of the early settlement, in A.D. 1596, of the city of Derry, by the English, to its burning by Sir Cahir O'Doherty, in A.D. 1608. *R.S.A.I.*, 2nd ser., iv (1862–3), 386–404; v (1864–5), 153–72.
Cf. T. W. Moody, *The Londonderry Plantation*, 1609–41. Belfast, 1939.

6138 GIBSON, C. B. The history of the county and city of Cork. 2 vols. Lond. 1861.

6139 GILBERT, J. T. History of the city of Dublin. 3 vols. Dublin, 1854–9.
Abridged ed. by R. M. Gilbert, 1903.

6140 GLEESON, D. F. Roscrea: a history of the Catholic parish of Roscrea from the earliest times to the present day with some account of the territories of Uí Cairin and Éile Uí Cearbhaill. Dublin, 1947.

6141 GLEESON, J. History of the Ely O'Carroll territory, or ancient Ormonde situated in north Tipperary and northwestern King's county, Ireland. Dublin, 1915.

6143 HARRIS, W. The history and antiquities of the city of Dublin. Dublin, 1766.

6144 HICKSON, M. A. Selections from old Kerry records. Lond. 1872. 2nd ser., Lond. 1874.
1874 series has maps from Carew MSS.

6145 HITCHCOCK, F. R. The midland septs and the Pale. Dublin, 1908.

6146 HORE, P. H. History of the town and county of Wexford. 6 vols. Lond. 1900–11.
Valuable. Based on local records, &c.

6147 KELLY, R. J. The wardens of Galway. *R.S.A.I.*, 5th ser., vi (1896), 70–80.

6148 LENIHAN, MAURICE. Limerick; its history and antiquities. Dublin, 1866.

6149 LIBER PRIMUS KILKENNIENSIS. By Charles McNeill. Dublin, 1931.

6150 MACAIRT, SEAN. Leabhar Branach: the book of the O'Byrnes. Dublin, 1944.

6151 MACALISTER, R. A. S. The Book of MacCarthaigh Riabhach, otherwise the book of Lismore. *Irish MSS. Comm. Facs. in collotype of Irish MSS.* v. Dublin, 1950.

6152 MACALISTER, R. A. S. The book of Uí Maine, otherwise called 'The book of the O'Kellys'. *Irish MSS. Comm. Facs. in collotype of Irish MSS.* iv. Dublin, 1942.

6153 MACGRATH, CUTHBERT. Material for a history of Clann Bhruaidheadha (Brodys). *Éigse*, iv (1943), 48–66.

6154 MACLEOD, IONA. Bibliography of articles relating to Carlow and district. *Carloviana*, i (1947), 33–36.

6155 M'SKIMIN, SAMUEL. History and antiquities of the county of the town of Carrickfergus. Belfast, 1811; 1823; by E. J. McCrum, Belfast, 1909.

6156 O'BYRNE, D. History of the queen's county. Dublin, 1856.

6157 O'FLAHERTY, RODERIC. Chorographical description of west or H-Iar Connaught (1684). By James Hardiman, *Irish Arch. Soc.* Dublin, 1846.
Contains copies of indentures in *Composition of Connacht*, 6127. Valuable.

6158 O'FLYNN, T. M. History of Leitrim. Dublin, 1937.

6159 O'HANLON, J. C., O'LEARY, EDWARD, and LALOR, MATTHEW. History of the queen's county. 2 vols. Dublin, 1907–14.

6160 O'KEEFFE, J. G. Ancient territory of Fermoy. *Ériu*, x (1928), 170–89.

6161 O'RORKE, T. History of Sligo, town and county. 2 vols. Dublin, 1889.
Contains a useful account of the activities of Hugh Roe O'Donnell before Tyrone's rebellion.

6162 O'SULLIVAN, M. D. Old Galway, the history of a Norman colony in Ireland. Cambr. 1942.

6163 O TUATHAIL, EAMONN. Farney men of 1592. *Clogher Rec.* i (1955), 140–53.

6164 PENDER, SEAMUS. Studies in Waterford history. *Jour. Cork Hist. and Arch. Soc.* lvi (1951), 120–2; lvii (1952), 14–19.

6165 POWER, P. Chrichad an Chaoilli: the topography of Fermoy. Cork, 1932.

6166 POWER, P. Waterford and Lismore: a compendious history of the united dioceses. Cork, 1937.

6167 PRICE, LIAM. The Byrnes' country in county Wicklow in the sixteenth century. *Jour. R.S.A.I.* lxiii (1933), 224–42; lxvi (1936), 41–66.

6168 REPORT ON THE MUNICIPAL CORPORATIONS in Ireland. *Parl. papers*, 1835, vols. xxvii–xxviii; 1836, vol. xxiv.

6169 RYLAND, R. H. History, topography and antiquities of the county and city of Waterford. Dublin, 1824.

6170 SHIRLEY, E. P. Some account of the territory or dominion of Farney. Lond. 1845.
Several sixteenth-century letters *in extenso*.

6171 SHIRLEY, E. P. The history of the county of Monaghan. Lond. 1879.
Some sixteenth-century material *in extenso*.

6172 SMITH, CHAS. The ancient and present state of the county and city of Cork. 2 vols. Dublin, 1750; repr. as a supplement to *Jour. of Cork Hist. and Arch. Soc.*, Cork, 1893–4.

6173 SMITH, CHAS. Ancient and present state of the county of Kerry. Dublin, 1756.

6174 SMITH, CHAS. Ancient and present state of the county and city of Waterford. Dublin, 1746; rev. ed. 1774.

6175 STUART, JAMES. Historical memoirs of the city of Armagh. Newry, 1819; rev. ed. by A. Coleman, Dublin, 1900.

6176 WALSH, PAUL. Origins of King's County. *Irish Book Lover*, xxvi (1938), 50–56.

6177 WALSH, PAUL. Parish annals. Stamullen, Moorechurch, Ballygarth, Julianstown. In *Leaves of History*, pp. 53–103. Drogheda, 1930.

6178 WESTROPP, T. J. Notes on the sheriffs of county Clare, 1570–1700. *R.S.A.I.*, 5th ser., i (1890–1), 68–80.
Brief mention of each. Cf. also idem, *Principal books and papers relating to Co. Clare*, *R.S.A.I.*, 5th ser., x (1900), 449–50.

6179 WESTROPP, T. J. Early Italian maps of Ireland, 1300–1600, with notes on foreign settlers and trade. *Proc. R.I.A.* xxx (1913), 361–428.

6180 WOOD-MARTIN, W. G. History of the county and town of Sligo. 3 vols. Dublin, 1882–92.

G. FAMILY HISTORY

For a bibliography on family history, cf. E. MacLysaght (6192a). Between this work which necessarily concerns itself with present-day families, and the medieval genealogies noted in *Analecta Hibernica*, nos. 7 and 18, there exists a chasm. The latter were formal genealogical title-deeds of the Irish gentry most of whom were expropriated in the Tudor and Stuart conquest. The former largely depends upon the official pedigrees approved and sometimes concocted by the Dublin heraldic office of the Ulster king at arms. Few sixteenth-century families have been the subject of serious historical study, and the works denoted below are included for their critical value rather than for their comprehensiveness.

Reference should be made for Irish biography in general to *D.N.B.* (9). The lives of those prominent in Ireland in the sixteenth century, written by Robert Dunlop, are particularly valuable. Note especially those on the earl of Sussex, Sir Henry Sidney, Sir John Perrot, Shane O'Neill, Tyrone, O'Donnell. Cf. also J. Wills, *Lives of illustrious and distinguished Irishmen*, 6 vols., Dublin, 1840–7.

6181　BAGENAL, P. H. Vicissitudes of an Anglo-Irish family, 1530–1800. Lond. 1925.

6182　BLAKE, M. J. Blake family records. 1st ser., 1300–1600. Lond. 1902; index in 2nd ser., Lond. 1905.
Calendar of papers. Valuable on social changes in the west of Ireland.

6183　BUTLER, W. F. The descendants of James, ninth earl of Ormond. *Jour. R.S.A.I.* lix (1929), 29–44.

6184　CURTIS, E. The MacQuillan or Mandeville lords of the Route. *Proc. R.A.I.* xliv, sect. C (1938), 99–113.

6185　CURTIS, E. The barons of Norragh, 1171–1660. *Jour. R.S.A.I.* lxv (1935), 84–101.

6186　FITZGERALD, C. W. The earls of Kildare and their ancestors from 1057 to 1773 with addenda. 2 vols. Dublin, 1858–62; 2nd addenda, Dublin, 1866.
Especially full on sixteenth century. Drawn chiefly from printed sources. Quotes from state papers, chronicles, and some few manuscripts sources.
Inaccurate.

6187　GILLMAN, H. W. Sir Cormac McTeige MacCarthy of Muskerry. *Jour. Cork Hist. and Arch. Soc.* i (1892), 193–200.

6188　HILL, GEORGE. An historical account of the MacDonnells of Antrim, including notices of some other septs, Irish and Scottish. Belfast, 1873.
Important.

6189　HORE, H. F. The clan Kavanagh, *temp.* Henry VIII. *R.S.A.I.*, 2nd ser., ii (1858–9), 73–92.
Prints a few illustrative papers.

6190　LEABHAR CHLAINNE SUIBHNE, an account of the MacSweeney families in Ireland. By Paul Walsh. Dublin, 1920.
With pedigrees. From *R.I.A.* MS. 24 P. 25.

6191   LODGE, JOHN. The peerage of Ireland. . . . By Mervyn Archdall. 7 vols. Dublin, 1789.
Valuable.

6192   MACDUINNSHLEIBHE, PEADAR. The legal murder of Aodh Rua MacMahon, 1590. *Clogher Rec.* i (1955), 39–52.

6192a   MACLYSAGHT, EDWARD. Irish families, their names, arms and origins. Dublin, 1957.

6193   [MADDEN, T. M.] Genealogical historical and family records of the O'Maddens of Hy-Many and their descendants. Dublin, 1894.

6194   MATHEWS, THOS. An account of the O'Dempseys of clan Malierc. Dublin, 1903.

6195   O'CONOR DON, C. O. The O'Conors of Connaught. Dublin, 1891.
Mostly genealogical, but shows slowness of Tudor conquest over O'Conors. Many letters, several sixteenth century, *in extenso*.

6196   O'DALY, DANIEL or DOMINIC. Initium, incrementa et exitus familiae Geraldinorum, Desmoniae . . . ac persecutionis haereticorum descriptio. [Lisbon], 1655; French trans. by l'Abbé Joubert, Dunkirk, 1697; Eng. trans. by C. P. Meehan, Dublin, 1847; 1878.
English title *The Geraldines, earls of Desmond, and the persecutions of the Irish Catholics.* Author a Dominican and censor of the supreme court of the Inquisition in Portugal.

6197   O'DONOGHUE, J. Historical memoirs of the O'Briens . . . compiled from the Irish annalists. Dublin, 1860.

6198   O'HART, JOHN. Irish and Anglo-Irish gentry when Cromwell came to Ireland. Dublin, 1884–92.
Valuable. A supplement to 6199.

6199   O'HART, JOHN. Irish pedigrees: or the origin and stem of the Irish nation. Dublin, 1876; 2nd ser. 1878.

6200   O'TOOLE, P. L. History of the clan O'Toole . . . and other Leinster septs. Dublin, 1890.

6201   PENDER, SEAMUS. The O'Clery book of genealogies. *Anal. Hiber.* xviii (1951).

6201a   RANGER, T. O. Richard Boyle and the making of an Irish fortune, 1588–1614. *Irish Hist. Studies* ix (1957), 257–97.

6202   REDMOND, G. O'C. An historical memoir of the family of Poher, Poer or Power. Dublin, 1891 (repr. from *The Irish Builder*).

6203   THE RENTAL BOOK OF GERALD FITZGERALD, ninth earl of Kildare. Begun in the year 1518. By H. F. Hore. *R.S.A.I.*, 2nd ser., ii (1858–9), 266–80, 301–10; iv (1862–3), 110–37; v (1864–5), 501–18, 525–46.

6204   S[AVAGE]-A[RMSTRONG], G. F. The ancient and noble family of the Savages of the Ards. Lond. 1888; rev. and enl. Lond. 1906.
1906 ed. is entitled *A genealogical history of the Savage family in Ulster.*

6205   WALSH, PAUL. Gaelic genealogies of the Plunkets. *Irish Book Lover*, xxv (1937), 50–57.

6206 WALSH, PAUL. The O Cleirigh family of Tir Conaill, an essay, with the O Cleirigh genealogies. Dublin, 1938.

6207 WALSH, PAUL. O'Donnell genealogies. *Anal. Hiber.* viii (1938), 373–418.

6208 WALSH, PAUL. Scots Clan Domhnaill in Ireland. *Irish Eccles. Rec.*, 5th ser., xlviii (1936), 23–42.

6209 WALSH, PAUL. Septs of Muinntear Gallchubhair. *Irish Book Lover*, xxvii (1940), 194–200.

6209a WEBB, ALFRED. Compendium of Irish biography, comprising sketches of distinguished Irishmen. . . . Dublin, 1878.
Good documentation.

6210 THE WILL AND FAMILY of Hugh O'Neill, earl of Tyrone. By Paul Walsh. Dublin, 1930; 1939.

XIV

WALES

A. GENERAL

1. BIBLIOGRAPHY

The best bibliography of Welsh history is 6211. For MS. material relating to Wales in the P.R.O., cf. in general *Giuseppi* (74), i, index, Wales; *P.R.O. Lists and indexes*, xl (1914), and *Deputy Keepers' Reports*, i (1840), 78–122. On MSS. subsequently removed to National library of Wales, cf. W. Ll. Davies, *The National Library of Wales*, Aberystwyth, 1937, 83. Descriptive accounts of important private and other collections in N.L.W. are given periodically in *Journal of the National Library of Wales* (1939 ff.). Welsh MS. material in the B.M. is listed in 6223. For general surveys of Welsh records, cf. 6216, 6218, 6225. Rowlands (6227) is valuable for printed books, 6212 for the bibliography of Welsh local history, and 4897 for a list of record publications. Bibliographies are appended to the articles in 6258. For county bibliographies, cf. sect. C *infra*. Current contributions to Welsh history can be followed in 6213.

6211 A BIBLIOGRAPHY OF THE HISTORY OF WALES. By R. T. Jenkins, William Rees *et al.* Cardiff, 1931. (Revised edition in active preparation.)

6212 A BIBLIOGRAPHY OF PUBLISHED WORKS on the municipal history of Wales and the border, with special reference to published records. By William Rees. *Bull. of Board of Celtic Studies* (Univ. of Wales), ii, pt. iv (1925), with addendum, iii, pt. i.

6213 BIBLIOTHECA CELTICA. A register of publications relating to Wales and the Celtic peoples and languages, published by the National Library of Wales. Aberystwyth, 1909–28 (1910–34), 9 vols.; n.s., 1929–38 (1939, 1952), 2 vols.; 3rd ser., 1953– (1954–).

6214 DAVIES, J. H. Early Welsh bibliography. *Trans. Cymmrod. Soc.* (1897–8).
For Tudor printed books in Welsh, cf. 2–10.

6215 DAVIES, W. LL. Welsh books entered in the Stationers' company's registers. Pt. i, 1554–1660. *Jour. Welsh Biblio. Soc.* ii, no. 5 (1921), 167–74.

6216 HALL, HUBERT. The diplomatics of Welsh records. *Trans. Cymmrod. Soc.*, session 1900–1, 40–52.
App. contains list of repositories of Welsh records and classification.

6217 HALL, HUBERT. The foreign aspect of the Welsh records. *Y Cymmrodor*, xxii (1910), 1–21.

6218 HALL, HUBERT. Welsh local records: details, and classified topographical list. *Trans. Cymmrod. Soc.*, session 1914–15, 16–42.

6219 HUGHES, W. J. Wales and the Welsh in English literature. Wrexham, 1924.

6220 JONES, IFANO. A history of printing and printers in Wales to 1810. Cardiff, 1925.

6221 LLOYD, H. W. Welsh books printed abroad in the sixteenth and seventeenth centuries and their authors. *Y Cymmrodor*, iv (1881), 25–69.

6222 OWEN, B. Llyfryddiaeth morwyr Cymru. *Jour. Welsh Biblio. Soc.* iii (1927), nos. 3 and 4, pp. 99–104, 180–5.
A bibliography of Welsh seamen.

6223 OWEN, EDWARD. A catalogue of the manuscripts relating to Wales in the British Museum. 4 parts. *Cymmrod. Rec. Series*, no. 4. Lond. 1900–22.
Valuable. Manuscripts described fully and calendared.

6224 PHILLIMORE, EGERTON. The publication of Welsh historical records. *Y Cymmrodor*, xi (1892), 133–75.

6225 ROBERTS, R. A. The public records relating to Wales. *Y Cymmrodor*, x (1890), 157–206.

6226 ROBERTS, R. A. Welsh records and a record office for Wales. *Trans. Cymmrod. Soc.*, session 1915–16, 225–53.

6227 ROWLANDS, W. Llyfryddiaeth y Cymry: Cambrian bibliography, containing an account of the books printed in the Welsh language or relating to Wales, from 1546 to 1800. By D. Silvan Evans. Llanidloes, 1869.
Written in Welsh. A continuation to 1810 by C. Ashton, also in Welsh, *Llyfryddiaeth Gymreig*, vol. i (all published), Oswestry, 1908.

The following periodical publications are devoted in whole or in part to Welsh history. Cf. also sect. C, and for periodicals published between 1931 and 1945, cf. A. ap Gwynn and I. Lewis, *Subject index to Welsh periodicals*, i–vi, 1931–5 (Cardiff, Swansea), 1934–57.

6228 ARCHAEOLOGIA CAMBRENSIS. Lond. 1846 ff. Published by the Cambrian Archaeological Assoc. Index to first four series, 1846–84, by D. R. Thomas, Lond. 1892. Index to 5th series, 1884–1900, by F. Green, Lond. 1902.

6229 BULLETIN OF THE BOARD OF CELTIC STUDIES of the university of Wales. Cardiff, 1923 ff.

6230 CYMMRODORION SOCIETY. *Y Cymmrodor*. Lond. 1877 ff.; *Transactions*. Lond. 1892 ff.
An index to these publications to 1912, by G. O. Williams, appeared in the *Transactions*, session 1911–12, supplement.

6231 LIVERPOOL WELSH NATIONAL SOCIETY. *Transactions*. Liverpool, 1885–1912.

6232 WELSH BIBLIOGRAPHICAL SOCIETY. *Journal*. Carmarthen, 1910 ff.

2. SOURCES

Cf. *supra* p. 22.

A good deal of material on Wales is to be found in the printed sources for the reign of Henry VII (396–7), in the *Letters and Papers, Henry VIII* (91), *Cal. S.P., Domestic* (86), *Proceedings and Ordinances of the Privy Council* (1153), and *Acts of Privy Council* (1152).

Proclamations relating to Wales are calendared in Steele (1117). Collins's *Sidney Papers* (629) and *MSS. of Lord De L'Isle and Dudley* (124) are valuable for Sir Henry Sidney's government of Wales under Elizabeth. Cf. also 634.

Smith's ed. of Leland's *Itinerary* (4197) includes Leland's Welsh notes and gives a valuable survey of Tudor Wales.

6233   CHURCHYARD, THOMAS. The worthiness of Wales. . . . Lond.
1587; repr. in facsimile, *Spenser Soc.* 1876.
A long chorographical poem full of historical and antiquarian interest.

6234   DRAYTON, MICHAEL. Poly-Olbion, or a chorographical description of Great Britain. 1st part, Lond. [1612]; 2nd part, Lond. 1622.
Although not published until the next century, the poems dealing with 'My friends the Cambro-Britans' (iv–x) are based on Elizabethan sources, especially Camden (4190) and Llwyd (6235–6). Cf. notes by K. Tillotson and B. H. Newdigate in vol. v of Hebel ed. of the *Complete works* (Oxf. 1931); and cf. also I. Gourvitch in *Rev. Eng. Studies*, iv (1928), 69–77, 394–403.

6235   LLOYD (or LLWYD), HUMPHREY. Commentarioli descriptionis Britannicae fragmentum. Cologne, 1572; trans. by T. Twyne, *The breviary of Britayne*, Lond. 1573.

6236   LLOYD (or LLWYD), HUMPHREY. The historie of Cambria. . . . By David Powel. Lond. 1584; by W. Wynne (augmented), Lond. 1697; by R. Llwyd, Shrewsbury, 1832.
Lloyd (ob. 1568) originally compiled the work, based on *Brut y Tywysogion*, erroneously attributed to Caradoc of Llancarvan. Powell published it with large additions, including *A description of Cambria* by Sir John Price, and dedicated it to Sir Philip Sidney. Re-issued in 1697 by William Wynne with further additions. Several eds. of Wynne's version appeared, the last in 1832. The 1584 ed. was repr. Lond. 1811. Cf. also J. E. Lloyd, *Powel's Historie* (1584), *Arch. Camb.* xcvii (1942–3), 96–97. Cf. J. E. Lloyd and V. Scholderer, *Jour. Nat. Lib. Wales*, iii (1943–4), 15–18.

6237   MATTHEWS, J. H. Welsh materials for English history. *Arch. Camb.*, 6th ser., xiv (1914), 309–22.
Edits Phillips MSS. 13720 (Cardiff), a chronicle temp. Henry VIII to Mary.

6238   NATIONAL LIBRARY OF WALES: (a) Calendars of deeds and documents. Vols. i, *The Coleman deeds*, by Francis Green (1921); ii, *The Crosswood deeds*, by Francis Green (1927); iii, *The Hawarden deeds*, by Francis Green (1931). (b) *Catalogue of MSS.*, vol. i Add. MSS. in the collection of Sir John Williams (1921). (c) *Calendar of Wynn (of Gwydir) papers, 1515–1690* by J. Ballinger (1926). (d) *Handlist of manuscripts in the Nat. Lib. of Wales*, 2 vols. and index (1943–51), in progress. (e) *Clenennau letters and papers in the Brogyntyn collection*, by T. J. Pierce; pt. i (1947), in progress.

6239 OWEN, GEORGE. The taylor's cussion. By E. M. Pritchard. Lond. 1906.
The commonplace book of Geo. Owen (1552?–1613); printed in facsimile.

6240 PARRY, ROBERT. Diary (1539–1613). *Arch. Camb.*, 6th ser., xv (1915), 109–39.

6241 ROBERTS, PETER. Y cwtta cyfarwydd. By D. R. Thomas. Lond. 1883.
Notebook of Thos. Rowlands, 1595–1607.

6242 THE STATUTES OF WALES. By Ivor Bowen. Lond. 1908.
A valuable compilation. Acts relating to Wales printed in full with analytical intro.

6243 WYNN, JOHN. The history of the Gwydir family. Lond. 1770; 1781; 1827; 1878; best text by J. Ballinger, Cardiff, 1927.
The ed. of 1878 contains notes by W. W. E. Wynne; the ed. of 1927 is edited from the autograph MS. of Sir John Wynn.
Written by first baronet of Gwydir (1553–1628). Gives best contemporary account of social conditions in North Wales.

6244 EVANS, E. V. Andrew Boorde and the Welsh people. *Y Cymmrodor* (1919), 44–55.
A valuable contemporary description by an English doctor.

3. LATER WORKS

There is no complete history of sixteenth-century Wales. D. Williams (6306) has important chapters on Tudor Wales, and Mathew (355) is very valuable for Welsh connexions. The contributions of Skeel, H. Owen, and W. Ll. Williams are still very important. Cf. also J. F. Rees (6252), Wm. Rees (6253) and Dodd (6280–3) for specialized topics on sixteenth-century Wales. The Welsh biographical dictionary (6258) is indispensable. For a standard history of Welsh literature, cf. 6251.

6245 DAVIES, MARGARET. Wales in maps. Cardiff, 1951.

6246 JONES, FRANCIS. An approach to Welsh genealogy. *Trans. Cymmrod. Soc. for 1948* (1949), 303–466.

6247 JONES, J. I. Atlas hanesyddol o Cymru. Cardiff, 1952.

6248 NEVINS, J. B. Picture of Wales during the Tudor period. Liverpool, 1893.
Quotes at length from contemporary sources.

6249 NORTH, F. J. Humphrey Llwyd's maps of England and Wales. *Arch. Camb.* xcii (1937), 11–63.
Published also as *National Museum of Wales Handbook*, 1937.

6250 NORTH, F. J. The map of Wales. *Arch. Camb.* xc (1935), 1–69.
An historical survey of Welsh cartography. Fully illustrated.

6251 PARRY, THOMAS. Hanes llenddiaeth Gymraeg hyd 1900. Cardiff, 1944.
The standard history of Welsh literature. Trans. into English by H. I. Bell as *A History of Welsh literature*, Oxf. 1955.

6252   REES, J. F. Tudor policy in Wales. *Hist. Assoc. Leaflet,* ci (1935).
Also published in *Studies in Welsh History,* Cardiff, 1947.

6253   REES, WILLIAM. The union of England and Wales. *Trans. Cymmrod. Soc. for 1937* (1938), 27–100.

6254   REES, WILLIAM. An historical atlas of Wales. Cardiff, 1951.

6255   RHYS, JOHN, and BRYNMOR-JONES, D. The Welsh people; their origin, history, laws, language, &c. Lond. 1900; 4th ed. 1906.
An expansion of sections written for the reports of the Welsh Land Commission (*Parl. papers,* 1896, xxxiii, xxxv). Lacks unity of plan but useful for the transition in land system temp. Elizabeth.

6256   WILLIAMS, E. R. Some studies in Elizabethan Wales. Newtown, [1924?].
Popular, much on the sea and piracy.

6257   WILLIAMS, JANE. A history of Wales (to 1603). Lond. 1869.

6258   Y BYWGRAFFIADUR CYMREIG HYD 1940. By J. E. Lloyd, R. T. Jenkins, and W. Ll. Davies. Lond. 1953.
Welsh biographical dictionary. Indispensable. English version in course of printing.

B. POLITICAL, LEGAL, AND ADMINISTRATIVE HISTORY

1. SOURCES

Cf. 608, 629, and 634.

6259   AN 'ELECTIONEERING' LEASE OF 1585. By A. H. Dodd. *E.H.R.* lxv (1950), 221–2.

6260   BREESE, E. Kalendars of Gwynedd: lists of lords-lieutenant, custodes rotulorum, sheriffs, and knights of the shire for Anglesey, Carnarvon, and Merioneth, Lond. 1873.
Notes by W. W. E. Wynne. To be used with caution.

6261   CALENDAR OF SALUSBURY CORRESPONDENCE. By W. J. Smith. *Univ. of Wales, Board of Celtic Studies, History and Law,* ser. xiv. Cardiff, 1954.

6262   CALENDAR OF THE REGISTER of the queen's majesty's council in . . . Wales and the Marches. . . . By R. Flenley. *Cymmrod. Rec. Ser.,* no. 8 (1916).
Valuable text and a useful introduction on the workings of the council.

6263   CATALOGUE OF STAR CHAMBER PROCEEDINGS relating to Wales. By I. ab O. Edwards. *Univ. of Wales, Board of Celtic Studies, History and Law Ser.,* i. Cardiff, 1929.
Unindexed and not always reliable, but indispensable.

6264 CHARTER OF HENRY VII to the bondmen and other inhabitants of North Wales. *Arch. Camb.*, 1st ser., ii (1847), 215–22.
Similar charters to other crown lordships in North Wales in *Cal. Patent Rolls, 1494–1509* (391) ii, 434, 464, 471, 586; trans. by A. N. Palmer in *Y Cymmrodor*, xix (1906), 51–67.

6265 EXCHEQUER PROCEEDINGS (EQUITY) CONCERNING WALES: Henry VII–Elizabeth. Abstracts of bills and inventory of further proceedings. By E. G. Jones. *Univ. of Wales, Board of Celtic Studies, History and Law Ser.*, iv. Cardiff, 1939.

6266 INVENTORY OF THE EARLY CHANCERY PROCEEDINGS CONCERNING WALES. By E. A. Lewis. *Univ. of Wales, Board of Celtic Studies, History and Law Ser.*, iii. Cardiff, 1937.

6267 RECORDS OF THE COURT OF AUGMENTATIONS relating to Wales and Monmouthshire. By E. A. Lewis and J. C. Davies. *Univ. of Wales, Board of Celtic Studies, History and Law Ser.*, xiii. Cardiff, 1954.

6268 SECOND EARL OF PEMBROKE (Henry Herbert). Letter on the Council of Wales, 1586. By William Phillips. *Shrop. Arch. and Nat. Hist. Soc.*, 2nd ser., i (1888–9), 431–4.
Letter to Lord Burghley, B.M. Lansdowne MS. 53.

6269 SOME ELIZABETHAN DOCUMENTS and further Elizabethan documents. By David Mathew. *Bull. Board Celt. Studies*, vi (1932), 70–78, 159–71.
State papers relating to appointment of councillors and sheriffs and possible invasion points in Wales. Cf. also 355.

6270 THE SALUSBURIES AS MAINTAINERS of murderers: a Chirk castle view, 1599. By W. J. Smith. *Jour. Nat. Lib. Wales*, vii (1952), 235–8.
Documents giving list of murders in Denbighshire, 1591–9.

6271 THREE LEGAL TRACTS concerning the courts leet in Wales after the Act of Union. By E. A. Lewis. *Bull. Board Celt. Studies*, ix (1937–9), 345–56.

6272 WELSH ADVENTURERS TO THE WEST INDIES IN THE 16th CENTURY. By J. H. Davies and J. G. Davies. *Y Cymmrodor*, xxvi (1916), 215–41.
Two versions of 'karol' by William Peilyn on Welsh seamen in Preston and Somers' expedition of 1595. With genealogical notes by F. M. K. Bulkeley-Owen.

2. LATER WORKS

No history of modern Wales has been attempted on the scale of Sir John Lloyd's classic *History of Wales*, which ends 1282. David Williams's *Modern Wales* (6306) is a useful but undocumented survey, best on later centuries. There is no history in English of Tudor Wales, but every aspect of the period has been covered in monographs in learned journals. The best available account of the working of Tudor government in Wales is in the introduction to *Cal. of Caernarvonshire, quarter sessions records* (6319), xxvii–cix. Cf. 5937.

6273 BALLINGER, JOHN. Katheryn of Berain. *Y Cymmrodor*, xl (1929), 1–42.

6274 BEBB, W. AMBROSE. Cyfnod y Tuduriaid. Wrexham, 1939.
A popular sketch of Tudor Wales, based mainly on literary sources.

6275 BOWEN, IVOR. Grand juries, justices of the peace, and quarter sessions in Wales. *Trans. Cymmrod. Soc. for 1933–5* (1936), 51–104.

6276 BUSHELL, W. D. The Lady Margaret Beaufort and King Henry VII. *Arch. Camb.*, 6th ser., xvi (1916), 189–221, 301–40.

6277 CHOTZEN, T. M. Some sidelights on Cambro-Dutch relations. With a special reference to Humphrey Llwyd and Abrahamus Ortelius. *Trans. Cymmrod. Soc. for 1937* (1938), 101–44.

6278 CHURTON, RALPH, bishop of Lincoln. The lives of Wm. Smyth and Sir Richard Sutton. . . . Oxf. 1800.
App. of letters. William Smyth (or Smith) was lord president of Wales 1501–12.

6279 DAVIES, A. S. Aberdovey and the Spanish invasion in 1597. *Arch. Camb.* lxxxvii (1932), 386–92.

6280 DODD, A. H. Wales and Ireland from reformation to revolution. *Studies in Stuart Wales.* Cardiff, 1952. pp. 76–109.

6281 DODD, A. H. Wales and the Scottish succession, 1570–1605. *Trans. Cymmrod. Soc. for 1937* (1938), 201–25.

6282 DODD, A. H. Wales's parliamentary apprenticeship, 1536–1625. *Trans. Cymmrod. Soc. for 1942* (1944), 8–72.

6283 DODD, A. H. North Wales in the Essex revolt of 1601. *E.H.R.* lix (1944), 348–70.

6284 DODERIDGE, JOHN. The history of the ancient and modern estate of the principality of Wales. . . . Lond. 1630; 1714.
Doderidge (1553–1628), a judge, wrote early in the reign of James I.

6285 DUCKETT, G. F. The marches of Wales. *Arch. Camb.*, 4th ser., xii (1881), 137–50, 186–202.

6286 JENKINS, R. T. Y newid yng Nghymru yng nghyfnod y Tuduriaid *Yr Apêl at hanes.* Wrexham, 1930. pp. 9–34.
Important essay on Tudor Wales reprinted from *Y Berniad*, vi.

6287 JERMAN, H. N. A map showing the territorial divisions of Wales before the Act of Union, 1536. *Arch. Camb.* xcii (1937), 170–2.

6288 JONES, DAVID. Sir Rhys ap Thomas: a study in family history and Tudor politics. *Arch. Camb.*, 5th ser., ix (1892), 81–101, 192–214.
Cf. also *A short view of the long life of that ever wise valiaunt and fortunat commander Rice ap Thomas, Knight.* A seventeenth-century biography of value, printed in *Cambrian Register*, 1795 (Lond. 1796), 49–144.

6289 JONES, FRANCIS. Sir Rhys ap Thomas: the Blood of the Raven. *Trans. Carmarthen. Antiq. Soc. and Field Club*, xxix (1939), 29–33. Cf. also idem, *Sir Rhys ap Thomas and the knights of St. John, Carmarthen. Antiq.* ii (1951), 70–74.

6290 JONES, IFANO. Sir Matthew Cradock and some of his contemporaries. *Arch. Camb.*, 6th ser., xix (1919), 393–458.

6291 JONES, W. G. Welsh nationalism and Henry Tudor. *Trans. Cymmrod. Soc.*, session 1917–18, 1–59.
Throws important light on Tudor influence in Wales by reference to bardic literature.

6292 LEWIS, D. The court of the president and council in Wales and the marches from 1478 to 1575. *Y Cymmrodor*, xii (1897), 1–16.

6293 LEWIS, T. H. The justice of the peace in Wales. *Trans. Cymmrod. Soc. for 1943–4* (1946), 120–32.

6294 LEWIS, T. H. Attendances of justices and grand jurors at the courts of quarter sessions in Wales, 16–18th centuries. *Trans. Cymmrod. Soc. for 1942* (1944), 108–22.

6295 LEWIS, T. H. The administration of justice in the Welsh county in its relation to other organs of justice, higher and lower. *Trans. Cymmrod. Soc. for 1945* (1946), 151–66.

6296 OWEN, HENRY. English law in Wales and the marches. *Y Cymmrodor*, xiv (1901), 1–41.
Prints as app. the crown case in privy council proceedings, 1603.

6297 OWEN, HENRY. The administration of English law in Wales and the marches. Lond. 1900.
A good sketch with bibliography.

6298 ROBERTS, GLYN. Parliamentary representation of the Welsh boroughs. *Bull. Board of Celtic Studies*, iv, pt. iv (1929), 352–8.

6299 ROWE, V. A. The influence of the earls of Pembroke on Parliamentary elections. *E.H.R.* l (1935), 242–56.

6300 SKEEL, C. A. J. The council in the marches of Wales. Lond. 1904.
Full bibliography. For details of administration of the Council of Wales there is a good deal of information in local sources. Cf. in this connexion Gross (1), nos. 1067, 1069, 2578; also T. Wright, *History of Ludlow*, Lond. 1841–3; 1852. Cf. R. H. Clive, *Documents connected with the history of Ludlow and the lords marcher*. Lond. 1841; also A. H. Dodd, *A lost capital, Studies in Stuart Wales*, Cardiff, 1952, pp. 49–75.

6301 SKEEL, C. A. J. Wales under Henry VII. In *Tudor Studies* (379), 1–25.

6302 THOMAS, D. LL. Further notes on the court of the marches. *Y Cymmrodor*, xiii (1900), 97–163.
Prints sixteenth-century documents.

6303 THOMAS, D. LL. Welsh lawyers of the Tudor and Stuart period.
Trans. Liverpool Welsh Nat. Soc. 1899–1900, pp. 65–95.

6304 TOUT, T. F. The Welsh shires: a study in constitutional history.
Y Cymmrodor, ix (1888), 201–26.
Deals with the shiring of Wales.

6305 VAUGHAN, RICE. Practica Walliae. Lond. 1672.
For legal procedure in the court of Great Sessions.

6306 WILLIAMS, DAVID. Modern Wales. Lond. 1950.
Chs. ii–vi especially useful on sixteenth century; ch. i gives a useful introductory sketch.

6308 WILLIAMS, W. T. Henry of Richmond's itinerary to Bosworth. *Y Cymmrodor*, xxix (1919), 33–43.
Cf. also H. N. Jerman, *A map of the routes of Henry Tudor and Rhys ap Thomas through Wales in 1485*, Arch. Camb. xcii (1937), 167–70.

6309 WILLIAMS, W. LL. A Welsh insurrection. *Y Cymmrodor*, xvi (1902), 1–93.
Deals with conspiracy of Rhys ap Griffith, 1531.

6310 WILLIAMS, W. LL. Making of modern Wales: studies in the Tudor settlement of Wales. Lond. 1919.
Scholarly. Especially full on court of Great Sessions and on decay of Catholicism.

6311 WILLIAMS, W. LL. The king's court of great session in Wales. *Y Cymmrod.*, xxvi (1916), 1–87.
A careful and detailed study.

6312 WILLIAMS, W. LL. The union of England and Wales. *Trans. Cymmrod Soc.*, session 1907–8, 47–117.
Analysis of method of annexation of Wales.

6313 WILLIAMS, W. R. The parliamentary history of the principality of Wales, 1541–1895. Brecknock, 1895.
Names and pedigrees of all members from Wales, accounts of contested elections, petitions, &c. To be used with great caution. Cf. also Porritt (1133).

6314 WILLIAMS, W. R. The history of the great sessions in Wales, 1542–1830, together with the lives of the Welsh judges. Brecknock, 1899.

C. LOCAL HISTORY

1. SOURCES

For printed collections of local Welsh records, cf. Gross (1), nos. 2658, 2665, 2668–9, 2671–2, 2676–8; for *Inquisitiones post mortem* for Flintshire and Montgomeryshire, ibid., nos. 2162, 2180b. Much material for Welsh local history is to be found in the National library of Wales and in county record offices. On the former see W. Ll. Davies, *The National Library of Wales*, Aberystwyth, 1937, ch. viii, supplemented by *Handlist of MSS.* (6238, pt. d); on the latter see publications of county record offices, e.g. W. O. Williams, *An introduction to the county records*, Caernarvon, 1950; *The Glamorgan county record office (Local archives of Great Britain*), *Archives*, iii (1950); and reports of county archivists and record committees from the various shires, e.g. Carmarthen (1953), Flintshire (1952 ff.), Glamorgan (1947 ff.), Merioneth (1954 ff.), and Monmouth (1905, 1939 ff.). Cf. also 6212.

6315 AN ANGLESEY CROWN RENTAL of the sixteenth century. By T. Jones Pierce. *Bull. Board Celt. Studies*, x (1940), 156–76.

6316 AN ANGLESEY MUSTER BOOK. By E. G. Jones. *Trans. Anglesey Antiq. Soc.* (1946), 26–36.

6317 CAERNARVONSHIRE SUBSIDY ROLL, 1597–8. By E. G. Jones. *Bull. Board Celt. Studies*, viii (1937), 336–44.

6318 CALENDAR OF THE CAERNARVONSHIRE quarter sessions records. By W. O. Williams. Vol. i, 1541–58. *Caernarvon. Hist. Soc.* (1956).
The introduction is indispensable.

6319 CALENDAR OF THE PUBLIC RECORDS relating to Pembrokeshire. By Henry Owen. *Cymmrod. Rec. Ser.*, no. 7. Pt. i, Haverford (1911); pt. ii, Cilgerran and Narberth (1914); pt. iii, Pembroke and Tenby (1918).
Calendars documents through reign of Henry VIII.

6320 CAMDEN, VAUGHAN and LHWYD, and MERIONETHSHIRE. By E. D. Jones, *Merioneth Hist. Rec. Soc.* ii (1956), 209–22.
Contemporary descriptions of shire transcribed and annotated.

6321 CARDIFF RECORDS. By J. H. Matthews. 6 vols. Cardiff, 1898–1911.

6322 CLARK, G. T. Cartae et alia munimenta quae ad dominium de Glamorgan pertinent. 4 vols. Dowlais (vol. i), Cardiff (vols. ii–iv), 1885–93; 6 vols. Cardiff, 1910.
Chiefly land records. Vols. v and vi (ed. 1910) contain sixteenth-century material. Cf. also idem, *Manorial particulars of the county of Glamorgan, Arch. Camb.*, 4th ser., viii (1877), 349–69; ix (1878), 1–21, 114–34.

6323 A COLLECTION OF HISTORICAL DOCUMENTS relating to Carmarthen castle to the close of the reign of Henry VIII. By E. A. Lewis. *West Wales Hist. Rec.* iii (1913), 1–72; iv (1914), 1–72.

6324 COURT LEET of the Manor of Llanwddyn (1579–98). By E. A. Lewis. *Montgomery Coll.* xliv (1936), 1–31.

6325 DWNN, LEWYS. Heraldic visitations of Wales and part of the Marches. By S. R. Meyrick. 2 vols. Llandovery, 1846.
Collections of pedigrees made by Dwnn, deputy-herald, 1586–1613.

6326 EVANS, ELWYN. Arwystli and Cyfeiliog in the sixteenth century. An Elizabethan inquisition. *Montgomery Coll.* li, pt. i (1949–50).

6327 FLINTSHIRE SUBSIDY ROLL, 1592. *Arch. Camb.*, 6th ser., ii (1902), 141–50.

6328 HISTORICAL MEMORANDA of Breconshire. By John Lloyd. Brecon, 1886.
Miscellaneous documents transcribed or translated.

6329 JONES, E. G., and ROBERTS, B. D. History of the Bulkeley family.
Trans. Anglesey Antiq. Soc. (1948), 1–99.
Transcript of seventeenth-century document.

6330 LEWIS, RICE. A Breviat of Glamorgan, 1596–1600. By William Rees.
S. Wales and Monmouth Rec. Soc. iii (1954), 92–150.

6331 MATERIALS ILLUSTRATING THE HISTORY OF DYNEVOR
AND NEWTON from the earliest times to the close of the reign of Henry VIII.
By E. A. Lewis. *West Wales Hist. Rec.* i (1911), 145–224; ii (1912), 105–33.

6332 A MERIONETH GRIEVANCE remedied by special act of parliament.
By E. D. Jones. *Jour. Merioneth Hist. Soc.* ii (1953–6), 149–50.

6333 A MERIONETH SUBSIDY ROLL, 42 Eliz., 1599/1600. By Bob Owen.
Jour. Merioneth Hist. Soc. ii (1953–6), 151–6.

6334 MERRICK, RICE. A book of Glamorganshire antiquities. Middlehill,
1825; by J. A. Corbett, Lond. 1887.
Merrick was clerk of the peace of Glamorgan (*c.* 1580). Valuable information upon
administration in Wales. Corbett's ed. gives a list of sheriffs to 1584 and reprs. part
of Leland's *Itinerary* (4197) relating to Glamorganshire.

6335 OWEN, GEORGE. The description of Pembrokeshire. By Henry
Owen. 4 pts. *Cymmrod. Rec. Ser.,* i (1892–1936).
Pt. iii contains *The dialogue of the government of Wales, Cruell laws against Welshmen,
A treatise of Lordshipps marchers in Wales,* and *The description of Wales.* This ed. supersedes all earlier eds. of Owen's works. Fragments of pt. ii (never completed) are printed
by B. G. Charles (from MSS. in Nat. Lib. Wales) in *Jour. Nat. Lib. Wales,* v (1947–8),
179–285.

6336 PHILLIPS, J. Glimpses of Elizabethan Pembrokeshire. *Arch. Camb.,*
5th ser., xiv (1897), 308–23; xiv (1899), 269–83; 6th ser., iv (1904), 253–74.
Extracts from local records.

6337 PIERCE, T. J. Early Caernarvonshire seamen. *Trans. Caernarvon. Hist.
Soc.* vi (1945), 58–63.

6338 THE PLEA ROLLS of Anglesey (1509–16). By Hugh Owen. *Trans.
Anglesey Antiq. Soc. Suppl.* (1947).

6339 ROLLS OF WARDS of the Lords Marcher of Kemes, Pembrokeshire.
By Francis Jones. *Bull. Board of Celt. Studies,* x (1939), 83–94.

6340 ROYAL COMMISSION ON ANCIENT MONUMENTS in Wales
and Monmouthshire. *Inventories.* Lond. 1911 ff.
Montgomery (1911), Flint (1912), Radnor (1913), Denbigh (1914), Carmarthen (1917),
Merioneth (1921), Pembroke (1925), Anglesey (1937), Caernarvon east (1956). All
published before 1937 need revision. On background of the Commission, cf. Gross (1),
p. 67.

6341 SELECT MONTGOMERYSHIRE DEEDS, i, 1579–98. By E. A.
Lewis and J. C. Davies. *Montgomery. Coll.* xlix (1945–6), 12–36.

6342 SOME RECORDS of a sixteenth century Pembrokeshire estate. By
Francis Jones. *Bull. Board of Celt. Studies,* xiii (1949), 92–104.

6343 STRADLING, JOHN. The storie of the lower borowes of Merthyr mawr. By H. J. Randall and William Rees. *S. Wales and Monmouth Rec. Soc. Pub.* i (1933).

6344 A SURVEY OF THE LORDSHIP OF HAVERFORD in 1577. By Henry Owen. *Arch. Camb.*, 6th ser., iii (1903), 39–55.

2. HISTORICAL AND ANTIQUARIAN JOURNALS

There are many transactions and journals of local historical and antiquarian societies of which those listed below are the principal. Cf. also 4256, 4258, 4259, 4487–9, 4492, 4708, which are similar publications issued in border shires and contain Welsh material.

6345 ANGLESEY ANTIQUARIAN SOCIETY and Field Club, *Transactions*. Llangefni, 1913 ff.

6346 BRECKNOCK SOCIETY. *Transactions . . .* and *Records*. Cardiff, 1928–9.
Revived as *Brycheiniog*, Cardiff, 1955 ff.

6347 CAERNARVONSHIRE HISTORICAL SOCIETY. *Transactions*. Caernarvon, 1939 ff.

6348 CARDIGANSHIRE ANTIQUARIAN SOCIETY. *Transactions and Archaeological Record*. Aberystwyth, 1909–39. Revived as *Ceredigion*, Llandyssul, 1950 ff.

6349 CARMARTHENSHIRE ANTIQUARIAN SOCIETY AND FIELD CLUB. *Transactions*. Carmarthen, 1905 ff.

6350 COLLECTIONS, HISTORICAL AND ARCHAEOLOGICAL, RELATING TO MONTGOMERYSHIRE, published by the Powysland club. Lond. 1868 ff. Since 1946 (xlix) called *Montgomery. Coll.* No imprint since 1948.
Vols. xxix–xl (1896–1928) included supplements, separately paged (1–648 continuously), containing much valuable source material for county history.

6351 DENBIGHSHIRE HISTORICAL SOCIETY. *Transactions*. Conway, 1952 ff., Denbigh, 1957 ff.

6352 FLINTSHIRE HISTORICAL SOCIETY PUBLICATIONS. Prestatyn, 1911–25; Caernarvon, 1951 ff.
Vols. v–vii bore the title *Journal*.

6353 MERIONETH HISTORICAL AND RECORD SOCIETY. *Journal*. Bala, 1950 ff.

6354 RADNORSHIRE SOCIETY. *Transactions*. Llandrindod Wells, 1931 ff.

6355 WEST WALES HISTORICAL RECORDS published annually by the Historical Society of West Wales. Carmarthen, 1910–29.

3. LATER WORKS

For local histories of Welsh towns, cf. Gross (1), nos. 1132a (West Gower, Glamorgan); 1133 (Swansea); 1133b (Kidwelly); 1136 (Flint); 1137 (Denbigh); 1134a (boroughs of North Wales). Cf. also no. 4202 *supra*. For county bibliographies cf. Owen Williams, *Bibliography of the county* [Denbigh]: pt. ii, historical and topographical sources. Wrexham, 1937; new and enl. ed. Ruthin, 1951; and E. R. Harries, *Bibliography of the county of Flint*: pt. i, biographical sources, Mold, 1953.

6356 ALLEN, JAMES. Notes on the sheriffs of Pembrokeshire, 1541–1899. Tenby, 1900.

6357 BRADNEY, J. A. A history of Monmouthshire from the coming of the Normans into Wales down to the present time. 4 vols. Lond. 1904–32.
The county is surveyed in great detail parish by parish, but Bradney died before completing the 4th vol. as he planned it, and with further intended vols. unwritten.

6358 BUCKLEY, J. Genealogies of the Carmarthenshire sheriffs from 1539 to 1759. 2 vols. Carmarthen, 1910–13.

6359 DODD, A. H. Welsh and English in east Denbighshire. *Trans. Cymmrod. Soc. for 1940* (1941), 34–65.

6360 EVANS, C. J. O. Glamorgan, its history and topography. Cardiff, 1938.

6361 EVANS, C. J. O. Monmouthshire, its history and topography. Cardiff [1954?].

6362 FENTON, R. A historical tour through Pembrokeshire. Lond. 1811; Brecon, 1903.
Index by Henry Owen, Lond. 1894.

6363 GLENN, T. A. The family of Griffith of Garn and Plasnewydd in the county of Denbigh. Lond. 1934. pp. 81–111.

6364 HANMER, LORD. Memorials of the parish and family of Hanmer. Lond. 1876.

6365 JONES, E. G. Some notes on the principal county families of Anglesey in the sixteenth and early seventeenth centuries. *Trans. Anglesey Antiq. Soc.* (1939), 61–75; (1940), 46–61.

6366 JONES, E. G. County politics and electioneering, 1558–1625. *Trans. Caernarvon. Hist. Soc.* i (1939), 37–46.

6367 JONES, E. G. Anglesey and invasion, 1539–1603. *Trans. Anglesey Antiq. Soc.* (1946), 26–37.

6368 JONES, E. S. (Lady Clement). Trevors of Trevalyn and their descendants. Privately printed, 1955.

6369 JONES, THEOPHILUS. A history of the county of Brecknock. 2 vols. Brecknock, 1805–9; 1 vol. Brecon, 1898; enlarged by J. R. Bailey, 4 vols. Brecon, 1909–30.

6370 LAWS, EDWARD. The history of little England beyond Wales and the non-Kymric colony settled in Pembrokeshire. Lond. 1888.

6371 LEWIS, T. H. Carmarthenshire under the Tudors. *W. Wales Hist. Rec.*, viii (1919–20).

6372 LLOYD, J. E. A history of Carmarthenshire. Vol. ii. Cardiff, 1939.

6373 LLOYD, J. Y. W. The sheriffs of Denbighshire (1541–1700). *Arch. Camb.*, 3rd ser., xv (1869), 1–29, 97–117; 4th ser., i (1870), 169–92.

6374 LLOYD, J. Y. W. The history of the princes, the lords marchers, and the ancient nobility of Powys Fadog, and the ancient lords of Arwystle, Cedewen, and Meirionydd. 6 vols. Lond. 1881–7.
Much information on personal and family history of princes and lords from MS. sources. Ill-arranged.

6375 LLOYD, W. V. The sheriffs of Montgomeryshire . . . from 1540–1639. Lond. 1876.
The series was first published in *Montgomery. Coll.* ii–vi, ix (1869–73, 1876), and was continued to 1658 in ibid. xvii (1893).

6376 LLWYD, ANGHARAD. A history of the island of Anglesey. Ruthin, 1832.
Unreliable.

6377 MEYRICK, S. R. The history and antiquities of the county of Cardigan. Lond. 1808; Brecon, 1907.

6378 MOSTYN, LORD, and GLENN, T. A. A history of the family of Mostyn of Mostyn. Lond. 1925.

6379 NICHOLAS, T. Annals and antiquities of the counties and county families of Wales. 2 vols. Lond. 1872.

6380 OWEN, EDWARD. The decline of the Tudors of Penmynydd. *Trans. Anglesey Antiq. Soc.* (1934), 48–60; (1935), 80–89.

6381 OWEN, HENRY. Old Pembroke families. Lond. 1902.

6382 PHILLIPS, JAMES. The history of Pembrokeshire. Lond. 1909.

6383 PHILLIPS, J. R. Memoirs of the ancient family of Owen of Orielton, Co. Pembroke. Lond. 1886. pp. 1–26.

6384 RECORDS OF DENBIGH AND ITS LORDSHIP. By John Williams. Vol. i (all published). Wrexham, 1860.
Valuable material of more than local interest but often unreliable. Cf. also J. Williams, *Ancient and modern Denbigh*, Denbigh, 1856.

6385 WILLIAMS, DAVID. History of Monmouthshire, Lond. 1796.

6386 WILLIAMS, JONATHAN. The history of Radnorshire. Tenby, 1859; Brecknock, 1905.
Cf. also W. H. Howes, *Radnorshire*, Hereford, 1949, ch. vi.

D. ECCLESIASTICAL HISTORY

1. SOURCES

For Roman Catholicism in Wales, the publications of the *Catholic Record Society*, Foley (2328), and Knox (2254) are indispensable. *Efrydiau Catholig* (Aberystwyth, 1946 ff.) also contains many valuable articles on Welsh catholic history. For the church in Wales, cf. Parker's *Correspondence* (1737) and the *Journal of the Historical Society of the Church in Wales* (Cardiff, 1949 ff.). The records of the church in Wales have been deposited by the governing body in the National library of Wales, and a survey of them is given by J. C. Davies in *Jour. Nat. Lib. Wales*, iv (1945–6). They are not abundant for the sixteenth century. Cf. also 634. For parish registers, cf. 1716, 6407a, 6408a.

6387 BISHOP SULIEN, BISHOP RICHARD DAVIES, and ARCH-
BISHOP PARKER. By Glanmor Williams. *Jour. Nat. Lib. Wales*, v (1948),
215-19.

6388 CAROLAU RICHARD WHITE. By T. H. Parry-Williams. Cardiff,
1931.
Satirical poems by a Catholic martyr. Cf. also *Cath. Rec. Soc.* v (1905), 90-99, and
A true account of the life and martyrdom of Mr. Richard White, contemporary tract
printed in Lloyd, *Powys Fadog* (6374), iii, 128-64.

6389 CHANTRY REPORTS, 2nd Edward VI, on the parish of Clyro. *Radnor
Soc. Trans.* ix (1939), 44.

6390 CLYNNOG, MORYS. Athravaeth Gristnogavl. Milan, 1568; repr. in
fac., *Cymmrod. Soc.*, Lond. 1880.
A catechism of Catholic doctrine.

6391 CORRESPONDENCE OF THE OWENS OF PLAS DU, 1573-1604.
By A. H. Dodd. *Trans. Carnarvon. Hist. Soc.* i (1939), 47-54.
Carnarvonshire recusant refugees.

6392 DAU LYTHYR GAN OWEN LEWIS. By Geraint Gruffyd Gruffydd.
Llên Cymry, ii (1952-3), 36-45.
Two letters by the bishop of Cassano, a Welsh Catholic refugee in Italy.

6393 DETHOLIAD O ENGLYNION HIRAETH AM YR HEN FFYDD.
By D. J. Bowen. *Efrydiau Cath.* vi (1954), 5-12.
Recusant verse.

6394 THE DIOCESE OF BANGOR in the sixteenth century. By A. I. Pryce.
Bangor, 1923.
A digest of episcopal registers, 1512-1646.

6395 DOCUMENTS RELATING TO THE DISSOLVED MONASTERY
OF GRACE DIEU. By Edward Owen. *S. Wales and Monmouth. Rec. Soc.*
ii (1950), 189-99.

6396 ELY, HUMPHREY. Certaine briefe notes upon a briefe apologie set
out under the name of the priests. Paris, [1603].
For Welsh Catholicism.

6397 EPISCOPAL REGISTERS OF ST. DAVID'S, 1397-1518. By R. F.
Isaacson and R. A. Roberts. 3 vols. *Cymmrod. Rec. Ser.*, no. 6 (1917-20).

6398 GLAMORGAN RECUSANTS, 1577-1611. A selection from the
returns in the P.R.O. By F. H. Pugh. *S. Wales and Monmouth. Rec. Soc.* iii
(1954), 49-67.

6399 INJUNCTIONS OF THE ROYAL VISITATION OF 1559 for the
diocese of Llandaff. By Glanmor Williams. *Jour. Nat. Lib. Wales.* iv (1946),
189-97.

6400 KYFFIN, MORYS. Deffyniad ffydd eglwys Loegr (1595). By W.
Williams. Cardiff, 1908.
Trans. of Jewel's *Apologia* (1395).

6401 LEWYS, HUGH. Perl mewn adfyd (1595). By W. J. Gruffydd. Carfidd,
1929.
Trans. of Coverdale's *Spiritual and most precious pearl* (1714).

6402 LLANDAFF RECORDS. By J. A. Bradney and R. Rickards. 5 vols. Cardiff and Lond. 1903–14.

6403 THE LLEYN RECUSANCY CASE, 1578–81. By E. G. Jones. *Trans. Cymmrod. Soc. for 1936* (1937), 97–123.

6404 MEMORIALS OF FATHER AUGUSTINE BAKER. By J. McCann and H. Connolly. *Cath. Rec. Soc.* xxxiii (1933).
Includes his autobiography and contemporary life by Leander Prichard. Valuable for religious conditions in Monmouthshire under Elizabeth.

6405 PENRY, JOHN. An exhortation unto the governors and people of . . . Wales to labour earnestly to have the preaching of the gospell planted among them. s.l. 1588.
For other religious writings of Penry, cf. 2470.

6406 PENRY, JOHN. A viewe of some part of such publicke wants and disorders as are in the service of God within her majestie's countrie of Wales, together with an humble petition to the high court of parliament for their speedy redress. [Coventry? 1589]; by J. O. Halliwell, Lond. 1861.

6407 [PENRY, JOHN.] A treatise containing the aequity of an humble suplication which is to be exhibited to her gracious majesty, and the high court of parliament in behalf of the county of Wales, that some order may be taken for the preaching of the gospel among those people. . . . Oxf. 1587; by G. A. J. Grieve, *Congregational Hist. Soc.*, Lond. 1905.

6407a PHILLIPS, J. The oldest parish registers in Pembrokeshire. *Arch. Camb.*, 6th ser., ii (1902), 115–27; iii (1903), 298–318; v (1905), 38–61.

6408 [PRICE, JOHN.] Yny lhyvyr hwnn. . . . Lond. 1546; by J. H. Davies, Bangor, 1902.
The first printed Welsh book (but cf. 6498) containing the Creed, Paternoster, Ave Maria, &c.

6408a REGISTRA ANTIQUA de Llantilio Cresseney et Penrhos in comitatu Monumethensi, 1547–1644. By J. A. Bradney. Lond. 1916.
Copy of the original parish registers made by W. Powell (1603–34). Bradney also published the registers of three other parishes in Monmouthshire.

6409 ROBERT, GRUFFYDD (GRIFFITH ROBERTS) Y drych cristiano-gawl. Milan, 1585.
A Catholic manual. Introduction on the religious condition of Wales.

6410 [SALESBURY, WILLIAM.] Testament Newydd. Lond. 1567; reprs. Bala, 1819 (pt. i only); Carnarvon, 1850.
The first Welsh trans. of the New Testament. Contains Salesbury's dedicatory letter to Queen Elizabeth and Bishop Richard Davies's *Epistol at y Cembru.* On the history of this trans. cf. *D.N.B.* (9), art. W. Salesbury. Cf. also T. C. Edwards, *William Salesbury's translation of the New Testament into Welsh, Trans. Liverpool Welsh Nat. Soc.* (1885–6), 51–81.
Cf. J. H. Davies, *Llyfryddiaeth y Bibl Cymraeg,* ibid. (1897–8), 1–22; R. T. Jenkins, *William Salesbury yn y llannau, Y Traethodydd,* 3rd ser., xv (1946), 87–91. Cf. also 6482.

6411 SALESBURY, WILLIAM. Ban wedy i dynny air yngair allan a ben gyfreith Howel da. Lond. 1550.
An attempt to prove the validity of clerical marriage under Welsh law.

6412 SALESBURY, WILLIAM. The baterie of the popes botereulx, commonlye called the high altare. Lond. 1550.
Cf. Glanmor Williams in *Bull. Board of Celt. Studies*, xiii (1949), 146–50.

6413 THE SECOND VOLUME OF ST. DAVID'S REGISTERS, 1554–64. By Glanmor Williams. *Bull. Board of Celt. Studies*, xiv (1950), 45–54, 125–38.

6414 A ST. ASAPH 'REGISTER' OF EPISCOPAL ACTS, 1506–71. By G. Milwyn Griffiths. *Jour. Hist. Soc. Church Wales*, vi (1956), 25–49.

6414a THE SPEECH OF WILLIAM BLETHIN, bishop of Llandaff and the customs and ordinances of the church of Llandaff. 1575. By J. A. Bradney. *Y Cymmrodor*, xxxi (1921), 240–69.

2. LATER WORKS

On the Welsh factions among the English Roman Catholics, see 2240, 2273, 2311, 2347, 2356, 2357. On John Penry, cf. 2470, 2486, and 2493. On the reformation in Wales, cf. Dodd (6431), and T. C. Edwards (6434). On Welsh monasteries cf. Tanner (2094) and Jones (6448–9). The articles of Glanmor Williams (6399, 6412–3, 6456, 6478–81) and of J. M. Cleary (6426–8) are valuable.

6415 ASHTON, C. Bywyd ac amserau yr Esgob Morgan. Treherbert, 1891.
The best biography of Bishop William Morgan of St. Asaph (1540?–1604), translator of the Bible into Welsh.

6416 ATKINS, IVOR. The authorship of the XVI century description of St. David's printed in Browne Willis's *Survey* (Lond. 1717). *Jour. Nat. Lib. Wales*, iv (1945–6), 115–22.

6417 ATTWATER, D. The catholic church in modern Wales. Lond. 1935.

6418 BALLINGER, J. The bible in Wales. Lond. 1906.
An historical treatment with full bibliography. Cf. J. Lloyd Jones, *The Bible in Wales*, Cardiff, 1938.

6419 BALLINGER, J. The first Welsh prayer book. *Jour. Welsh Biblio. Soc.* ii, no. 7 (1922), 238–43.

6421 BEBB, W. A. Machlud y mynachlogydd. Aberystwyth, 1937.
Popular work on the fall of the Welsh monasteries.

6422 BEVAN, W. L. St. Davids. *Diocesan Histories*, S.P.C.K. Lond. 1888.

6423 BIRCH, W. DE GRAY. Memoirs of the see and cathedral of Llandaff. Neath, 1912.

6424 BREESE, E. Dervel Gadarn. *Arch. Camb.*, 4th ser., v (1874), 152–6.
An object of Welsh veneration destroyed on Cromwell's order; cf. Froude (340), ch. xv (1879 ed.), iii, 108–9. For another pilgrims' resort in South Wales, cf. 6435.

6425 CAMM, BEDE. A Benedictine martyr in England. Lond. 1897.
Cf. also idem, *Le vénérable Jean Roberts, La revue bénédictine* (1895–6); and 'Talnant', *John Roberts, priest, Jour. Welsh Biblio. Soc.* i (1910–15), 197–8.

6426 CLEARY, J. M. The catholic resistance in Wales, 1568–1678. *Blackfriars*, xxxviii (1957), 111–25.

6427 CLEARY, J. M. The catholic recusancy of the Barlow family of Slebech in Pembrokeshire in the XVI and XVII centuries. *The Newman Assoc., Cardiff Circle, Paper* i (1956).

6428 CLEARY, J. M. Sir Edward Carne. *The Illtydian*, xix (1947), 186–92.

6429 CRONIN, J. M. Various papers on Welsh Catholicism in the sixteenth century. *St. Peter's Mag.* Cardiff.
The series includes the following: Sir William Guy of Penrhyn, *c.* 1590 (*St. Peter's Mag.* 1924, pp. 178 ff.); the martyrdom of Mr. Day (or Davis), 1593 (ibid. 1924, pp. 258 ff.); Jane Vaughan (ibid. 1925, pp. 15 ff.); Catholic clergy in South Wales, 1560–80 (ibid. 1925, pp. 98 ff.); the old English college (at Rome) and its Welsh associations (ibid. 1926, pp. 43 ff.); Ven. J. Jones (or Buckley) (ibid. 1926, pp. 130 ff.); Catholicism in Glamorgan (ibid. 1927, pp. 300 ff., 330 ff., 364 ff.); South Wales chantries (ibid. 1928, pp. 162 ff., 197 ff., 299 ff., 327 ff.).

6430 DAVIES, E. T. An ecclesiastical history of Monmouthshire. Pt. i, Risca, Monmouth, 1953.
Ch. v is especially relevant.

6431 DODD, A. H. The church in Wales in the age of the reformation. *Welsh Church Congress Handbook* (Cardiff, 1953), 18–41.

6432 EDWARDS, A. G. Landmarks in the history of the Welsh church. Lond. 1912.

6433 EDWARDS, H. W. J. The reformation in Wales. *Clergy Rev.* (1949), 105–14.
Roman Catholic point of view.

6434 EDWARDS, T. C. Wales and the reformation. *Blackfriars*, xv (1934), 259–67.

6435 EDWARDS, T. C., and WILLIAMS, G. J. Penrice: y cefndir hanesyddol. *Efrydiau Cath.* v (1951), 24–45.
With an app. of poems connected with the shrine.

6436 ELLIS, T. P. The Welsh Benedictines of the terror. Newtown, 1936.

6437 ELLIS, T. P. The Catholic martyrs of Wales, 1535–1680. Lond. 1933.

6438 EVANS, A.O. Edmund Prys. *Trans. Cymmrod. Soc. for 1922–3*, 112–68.
Prints original documents. Prys (1541?–1624) trans. the psalms into Welsh verse. Cf. also T. R. Roberts, *Edmund Prys* (Caernarvon, 1899). Cf. also T. G. Jones, *Y Llenor*, ii (1923), 245–64; iii (1924), 19–31; W. Ll. Davies, *Jour. Welsh Biblio. Soc.* ii (1916–23), 276–301.

6439 EVANS, A. O. Nicholas Robinson (1530?–85). *Y Cymmrodor*, xxxix (1928), 149–99.
Life of Robinson, bishop of Bangor. Prints some original documents.

6440 EVANS, A. O. A memorandum on the legality of the Welsh prayer book. Bangor, 1925.

6441 FLOWER, ROBIN. Richard Davies, William Cecil, and Giraldus Cambrensis. *Jour. Nat. Lib. Wales*, iii (1943), 11–14.

6442 FLOWER, ROBIN. William Salesbury, Richard Davies, and Archbishop Parker. *Jour. Nat. Lib. Wales*, ii (1941), 7–16.
With a documentary app. by D. M. Lloyd.

6443 GREEN, C. A. H. The chapter of Llandaff cathedral, 1561–1668.
Y Cymmrodor, xxxi (1921), 217–39.

6444 GRUFFYDD, GERAINT. Catecism y deon Nowell yn Gymraeg.
Jour. Welsh Biblio. Soc. vii (1951–2), 114–15, 203–7.
Welsh trans. (1578) of Latin catechism by dean of St. Paul's (1570–2).

6445 HIRSCH-DAVIES, J. E. DE. A popular history of the church in Wales.
Lond. 1911.
Chs. xv–xvii give a popular and undocumented but reasonably well-balanced account
of the reformation in Wales.

6446 HUGHES, W. Bangor. *Diocesan Histories, S.P.C.K.* Lond. 1911.

6447 JAMES, J. W. Welsh church history. Lond. 1945.
Scholarly.

6448 JONES, ARTHUR. The property of the Welsh friaries at the dissolution.
Arch. Camb. xci (1936), 30–50.

6449 JONES, ARTHUR. The estates of the Welsh abbeys at the dissolution.
Arch. Camb. xcii (1937), 259–86.

6450 JONES, A. S. D. (dean of Chichester). The prayer-book in the Welsh
church. *Church Quar. Rev.* cxlix (1950), 186–95.

6451 JONES, D. H. The Neath Chantry: a contribution to local ecclesiastical
history. *Trans. Neath Antiq. Soc. for 1934–6*, 2nd ser., v (1936), 25–29.

6452 JONES, E. D. Survey of South Wales Chantries, 1546. *Arch. Camb.*
lxxxix (1934), 135–55.

6453 JONES, E. G. Cymru a'r hen ffydd. Cardiff, 1951.
A short history of Welsh recusancy. Cf. also idem, *Catholic recusancy in the counties of
Denbigh, Flint, and Montgomery, Trans. Cymmrod. Soc. for 1945* (1946), 114–33.

6454 JONES, G. H. Celtic Britain and the pilgrim movement. *Y Cymmrodor*,
xxiii (1912), 1–581.

6455 JONES, J. J. A Welsh catholic controversialist. *Jour. Welsh Biblio. Soc.*
ii (1938), 90–92.
John Gwynedd.

6456 LEWIS, SAUNDERS. Damcaniaeth eglwsig brostestanaidd. *Efrydiau
Cath.* ii (1947), 36–55.
Cf. also Glanmor Williams, *Cipdrem arall ar y ddamcaniaeth brotestanaidd, Y Traethodydd*, 3rd ser., xvi (1948), 49–57, and R. O. F. Wynne in *Efrydiau Cath.* vi (1954),
17–27; vii (1955), 13–20. Catholic and Protestant interpretations of the Welsh reformation.

6457 LEWIS, T. H. Carmarthenshire and the reformation movement. *Trans.
Carmarthen Antiq. Soc.* xiv (1919–21), 33–37.

6458 LLEWELYN, T. An historical account of the British or Welsh versions
of the bible. Lond. 1768; 1793.

6459 MATHEW, D. and A. The survival of the dissolved monasteries in
Wales. *Dublin Rev.* clxxxiv (1929), 70–81.

6460 MATHIAS, W. A. Rhai sylwadau ar Robert Gwyn. *Llên Cymru*, iii
(1954–5), 63–73.
Notes on a Welsh Catholic missionary priest and writer.

6461 NEWELL, E. J. A history of the Welsh church to the dissolution of the monasteries. Lond. 1895.

6462 NEWELL, E. J. Llandaff. *Diocesan Histories, S.P.C.K.* Lond. 1902

6463 OWEN, EDWARD. The spoils of the Welsh religious houses. *Arch. Camb.*, 5th ser., xiv (1897), 285–93.
Cf. also idem, *The bells of the Welsh dissolved monasteries, Arch. Camb.*, 6th ser., xiii (1896), 262–5.

6464 OWEN, EDWARD. The fate of the structures of Conway abbey and Bangor and Beaumaris friaries. *Y Cymmrodor*, xxvii (1917), 70–114.
Prints original documents.

6465 OWEN, EDWARD. The monastery of Basingwerk at the period of its dissolution. *Flints. Hist. Soc.* vii (1920), 47–89.
Cf. also Glyn Roberts, *The Dominican friary of Bangor, The Dominican*, 4th centenary no., Bangor, 1957, pp. 5–25.

6466 OWEN, EDWARD. Strata Marcella abbey immediately before and after its dissolution. *Y Cymmrodor*, xxix (1919), 1–32.
Prints several documents.

6467 PRYCE, A. I. The reformation in the diocese of Bangor, as illustrated by the records. *Trans. Anglesey Antiq. Soc.* (1939), 43–60.

6468 RANDOLPH, J. A. Welsh abbeys: being short accounts of their abbots, lands, buildings and churches and their values at the dissolution. Carmarthen, 1905.
Slight, but useful.

6469 REES, J. R. Slebech commandery and the knights of St. John. *Arch. Camb.*, 5th ser., xiv–xvi (1897–9).
Disposal of estates at dissolution, ibid. xvi (1899), 283–98.

6470 REES, THOMAS. History of Protestant non-conformity in Wales. Lond. 1883.
The standard history, but slight on the sixteenth century.

6471 ROGERS, D. M. 'Popishe Thackwell' and early Catholic printing in Wales. *Biog. Studies*, ii (1953), 37–54.

6472 THOMAS, LAWRENCE. The reformation in the old diocese of Llandaff. Cardiff, 1930.

6473 THOMAS, D. R. The history of the diocese of St. Asaph. Lond. 1874; 3 vols. Oswestry, 1908–13.
Cf. also idem, *St. Asaph*, in *Diocesan Histories, S.P.C.K.*, Lond. 1888.

6474 THOMAS, D. R. The life and works of Davies and Salesbury. Oswestry, 1902.
Cf. idem, *Some early Welsh translations of Holy Scriptures, Trans. Liverpool Welsh Nat. Soc.* 1898–9, pp. 17–32. Cf. also Thomas Jones, *Pre-reformation Welsh versions of the scriptures, Jour. Nat. Lib. Wales*, iv (1946), 97–114, and E. D. Jones, *William Salesbury a'i deulu, 1546, Bull. Board of Celt. Studies*, vii (1934), 137–41.

6475 WHITEBROOK, J. C. Hugh Jones, bishop of Llandaff. *Notes and Queries*, clxxvii (1939), 290.

6476 WILLIAMS, DAVID. The miracle of St. Donat's. *The Welsh Rev.* vi (1947), 33–38.

6477 WILLIAMS, D. D. Hanes mynachdai Gogledd Cymru. Liverpool, 1914.
Short history of North Wales monasteries.

6478 WILLIAMS, GLANMOR. Bywyd ac amserau'r esgob Richard Davies. Cardiff, 1953.
Cf. idem, *Richard Davies, bishop of St. David's, 1561–81, Trans. Cymmrod. Soc.* xlix (1948), 215–19, and also idem, *The deprivation and exile of Richard Davies under Mary, Jour. Hist. Soc. of Church of Wales,* i (1947), 81–90.

6479 WILLIAMS, GLANMOR. The protestant experiment in the diocese of St. David's, 1534–55. *Bull. Board of Celt. Studies,* xv (1953), 212–24; xvi (1955), 38–48.

6480 WILLIAMS, GLANMOR. The Elizabethan settlement of religion in Wales and the Marches, 1559–60. *Jour. Hist. Soc. of Church in Wales,* ii (1950), 61–71.
With documentary app.

6481 WILLIAMS, GLANMOR. Some protestant views of early British church history. *History,* xxxviii (1953), 219–33.

6482 WILLIAMS, H. Testament Cymraeg cyntaf y Cymry. *Y Drysorfa,* 1888, 126–30, 163–8.
A valuable critical examination of Salesbury's New Testament.

6483 WILLIAMS, W. LL. Welsh Catholics on the continent. *Trans. Cymmrod. Soc. for 1901–2,* 46–144.
Contains app. of sixteenth-century documents.

6484 WILSON-REID, D. William Glyn, bishop of Bangor, 1555–8. *Trans. Anglesey. Antiq. Soc.* (1950), 87–90.
Founder of Friars School. Cf. 5672.

E. ECONOMIC, SOCIAL, AND CULTURAL HISTORY

1. SOURCES

The best sources for social life are the family correspondence and the Welsh poetry of the age; for economic life, collections of estate, farming, and business records. All are well represented in the National library of Wales, on which cf. 6238. For pertinent Welsh bardic poetry, cf. 6251.

6485 AN ACCOUNT BOOK of Sir Thomas Myddleton for the years 1583–1603. By E. D. Jones. *Jour. Nat. Lib. Wales,* i (1939), 83–88.

6486 ANGLIA WALLIA. *Arch. Camb.,* 6th ser., xi (1911), 421–32.
A contemporary description of havens, roads, &c., of Wales from *Q. Rembr. Roll,* 4th Eliz.

6487 THE BROGYNTYN WELSH MANUSCRIPTS. By E. D. Jones. *Jour. Nat. Lib. Wales,* v (1948), 233–64; vi (1949), 1–42, 149–61.
Excerpts, with translations, illustrating social life of the age.

6488 A CONTRIBUTION TO THE COMMERCIAL HISTORY of medieval Wales with tabulated accounts from 1301 to 1547. By E. A. Lewis. *Y Cymmrodor,* xxiv (1913), 86–188.

6489 ELLIS, MEGAN. Dress and materials for a 'serving maid' circa 1600. *Jour. Nat. Lib. Wales*, i (1939), 76–82.

6490 FISHER, JOHN. The Cefn Coch MSS. Liverpool, 1899.
Containing much of the work of the Elizabethan bard and buccaneer, Thomas Prys, and an account of the Caerwys eisteddfod of 1523 and 1568.

6491 A LETTER FROM DR. JOHN DEE to a Radnorshire cousin, 1577. By F. Noble. *Trans. Radnor Soc.* xxi (1955), 15–16.
Cf. ibid. xxvi (1956), 40–42, for Dee's Radnorshire connexions.

6492 PRICE, JOHN. Historiae Brytannicae defensio. Lond. 1573.
Cf. 6236, cf. also N. R. Ker, *Sir John Prise, Library*, 5th ser., x (1955), 1–24.

6493 THE REGISTER OF THE CORVISORS OF RUTHIN, 1570–1671. By E. D. Jones. *Jour. Nat. Lib. Wales*, vii (1952), 239–45.

6494 RHANNU TIR RHYS AP ELISE. By E. D. Jones. *Jour. Nat. Lib. Wales*, iii (1953–4), 23–28.
Devolution of a Denbighshire estate, with facsimile of document from Bagot collection. (99).

6495 ROBERT, GRUFFYDD (GRIFFITH ROBERTS). Dosparth byrr. . . [Milan], repr. (inaccurate), Carmarthen, 1857. Republished as supplements to *Revue Celtique* (Paris, 1870–3) with title *A Welsh grammar and other tracts by Griffith Roberts*; standard ed. by G. J. Williams, *Gramadeg Cymraeg Gruffydd Robert*, Cardiff, 1939.
Gruffydd Robert was a religious refugee. His preface throws light on linguistic conditions and aims, and editorial introduction of 1939 ed. surveys the field of Tudor scholarship in Wales. Other contemporary works on the Welsh language are listed in Parry (6251), 157–8.

6496 SALESBURY, WILLIAM. Llysieulyfr meddiginiaethol. By E. S. Roberts. Cardiff, 1916.
Herbal, trans. from Latin and English, with valuable introduction. Cf. also *Catalogue of MSS. . . . illustrating the history of medicine in Wales*, Brit. Medical Assoc., Aberystwyth, 1928, pp. 21–22.

6497 SALESBURY, WILLIAM. A dictionary in Englyshe and Welshe, Lond. 1547; fac. repr., 4 pts., *Cymmrod. Soc.*, 1877–8.
Contains dedication to Henry VIII showing Salesbury's attitude toward the language problem. Cf. also E. L. Evans, *William Salesbury, Y Llenor*, xii (1933), 106–18, 180–5; W. A. Mathias, *Gweithiau William Salesbury, Jour. Welsh Biblio. Soc.* vii (1951–2), 125–43; T. Parry, *Tri chyfeiriad at William Salesbury, Bull. Board Celt. Studies*, ix (1937–9), 108–12; and idem, *Siôn Dafydd Rhys, Y Llenor*, ix (1930), 157–65, 234–41; x (1931), 35–46. Cf. also 6410.

6498 [SALESBURY, WILLIAM.] Oll synnwyr pen kembero ygyd. Lond. [c. 1547–53]; repr., with intro., by J. G. Evans, Bangor, 1902.
A collection of Welsh proverbs. Disputes with 6408 the claim to be the first book printed in Welsh. On this cf. J. H. Davies (6214).

6500 THREE SALESBURY MANSIONS IN 1601. By W. J. Smith. *Bull. Board Celt. Studies*, xv (1952–4), 293–302.
Inventories of furniture.

6501 THE TOLL BOOKS OF SOME NORTH PEMBROKESHIRE
FAIRS (1599–1603). By E. A. Lewis. *Bull. Board Celt. Studies*, vii (1934),
283–318.

6502 TWO LETTERS . . . concerning the translation of certain books into
Welsh. By Geraint Gruffydd, *Jour. Welsh Biblio. Soc.* vii (1953), 114–15,
203–7.
Sidelights on religious and educational ideals, 1598–1602.

6503 WALES IN THE TIME OF QUEEN ELIZABETH. By J. Fisher.
Arch. Camb., 6th ser., xv (1915), 237–48.
Prints *in extenso* an anonymous tract *De presenti statu totius Walliae*.

6504 THE WELSH PORT BOOKS, 1550–1603. By E. A. Lewis, *Cymmrod.
Rec. Ser.* xii (1927).
Cf. also E. A. Lewis, *The port books of the port of Cardigan in Elizabethan and Stuart
times, Trans. Cardigan. Antiq. Soc.* vii (1930), 21–29.

6505 WILLIAMS, G. J. Llythyr Siôn Dafydd Rhys at y beirdd. *Efrydiau
Cath.* iv (1947), 5–11.
Illustrates the conflicts between tradition and contemporary ideas in scholarship,
religion and ethics.

2. LATER WORKS

(a) *General*

There is a useful analysis of Welsh society in Rowse (766), ch. ii; a brief working
survey of Welsh economic history in B. B. Thomas, *Braslun o hanes economaidd
Cymru*, Cardiff, 1941.

6506 DAVIES, D. J. The economic history of South Wales prior to 1800.
Cardiff, 1933.

6507 FOX, CYRIL. A country house of the Elizabethan period in Wales.
Cardiff, 1941.

6508 FOX, CYRIL, and RAGLAN, LORD. Monmouthshire houses: a study
of the building techniques and small house-plans in the fifteenth to the seventeenth centuries. Cardiff, 1951–4.
Pt. ii, *c.* 1550–1610.

6509 HARRIES, F. J. The Welsh Elizabethans. Pontypridd, 1924.
Popular and interesting on exploration and the sea. Cf. also 3489, 6256, and 6272.

6510 HARRIES, F. J. Shakespeare and the Welsh. Lond. 1919.
Cf. Hughes, A. E. *Shakespeare and his Welsh characters, Trans. Cymmrod. Soc.* (1917–
18) 659–88.

6511 LEE, SIDNEY. The autobiography of Edward, Lord Herbert of Cherbury. Lond. 1886.
Early pp. throw light on social condition in Elizabethan Wales. Cf. also R. I. Aaron,
Origin of the MSS. of Lord Herbert of Cherbury's Autobiography, Montgomery. Coll
xlvii (1942), 138–41.

6512   MENDENHALL, T. C. A Merioneth wage assessment of 1601. *Jour.
Merioneth Hist. Rec. Soc.* ii (1955), 204–8.
Cf. also W. Davies, *A general view of the agricultural and domestic economy of North
Wales*, Lond. 1810, 500–1.

6513   NEVINS, J. B. Picture of Wales during the Tudor period. Liverpool,
1893.

6514   PEATE, I. C. The Welsh house: a study in folk culture. *Y Cymmrodor*,
xlvii (1940); 3rd ed., Liverpool, 1946.

6515   WILLIAMS, D. A note on the population of Wales, 1536–1801. *Bull.
Board Celt. Studies*, viii (1937), 359–63.

(b) *Agriculture, industry, and trade*

Cf. 2766, 2785–6, 2794–5, 3017, 3489, 6256.

6516   CRONIN, J. M. A vanished Irish colony in South Wales (*c.* 1540–
1603). *St. Peter's Mag.* (Cardiff), 1925, pp. 81–82.

6518   JOHN, D. G. The organization and activities of the chartered companies
in South Wales in the sixteenth century. *Trans. Neath Antiq. Soc.*, n.s., iv
(1934), 67–71.

6519   JONES, T. I. J. A study of rents and fines in South Wales in the 16th
and early 17th centuries. *Harlech Studies: Essays presented to Dr. Thomas
Jones.* By B. B. Thomas. Cardiff, 1938, pp. 215–44.

6520   KNOOP, DOUGLAS, and JONES, G. P. The repair of Beaumaris
town wall, 1536–8. *Trans. Anglesey Antiq. Soc.* (1935), 59–79.

6521   LEWIS, W. J. A Welsh salt-mining venture of the sixteenth century.
Jour. Nat. Lib. Wales, viii (1953–4), 419–25.

6522   ROBERTS, GLYN. Piracy on the Welsh coast. *Trans. Neath Antiq.
Soc.*, 2nd ser., ii (1931–2), 77–87.

6523   SKEEL, C. A. J. The cattle trade between England and Wales from the
fifteenth to the nineteenth centuries. *Trans. R.H. Soc.*, 4th ser., ix (1926),
135–58.

6524   SKEEL, C. A. J. The Welsh woollen industry in the sixteenth and
seventeenth centuries. *Arch. Camb.*, 7th ser., iv (1924), 1–38.

6525   THOMAS, DAVID. Hen longau sir Caernarvon. *Caernarvon. Hist.
Soc.* (1952).
Ch. ii deals with sixteenth-century shipping, with a map and excerpts from con-
temporary verse. Cf. also idem, *Old ships and sailors of Wales*, Cardiff, 1949.

6526   WILLIAMS, W. O. The Anglesey gentry as business men in Tudor and
Stuart times. *Trans. Anglesey Antiq. Soc.* (1948), 100–14.

(c) *Learning and education*

The literary output of the age in Welsh is listed and evaluated in T. Parry (6251); cf. also critical articles of later date in *Llên Cymru*, 1950 ff. As religious propaganda and educational zeal were closely linked, many of the titles listed under sect. D are also appropriate here.

6527   BARBER, H. and L. H. The history of Friars' school, Bangor. Bangor, 1901.
Cf. W. O. Williams, *Friars' school from its foundation to the year 1789, The Dominican*, 4th centenary no., Bangor, 1957, pp. 27–50. Cf. also 6464, 6484.

6528   BOWEN, D. J. Ail eisteddfod Caerwys a chais 1594. *Llên Cymru*, iii (1954–5), 139–61.
The 2nd Tudor eisteddfod. Cf. J. H. Davies, *The roll of the Caerwys eisteddfod of 1523*, *Trans. Liverpool Welsh Nat. Soc.* (1904–9), 87–102; cf. 6490.

6529   BOWEN, D. J. Gruffydd Hiraethog ar argyfwng cerdd dafod. *Llên Cymru*, ii (1952–3), 147–60.
The last of the great Tudor bards and instructors in bardic lore.

6530   GRIFFITHS, G. M. Educational activity in the diocese of St. Asaph, 1500–1640. *Jour. Hist. Soc. of Church in Wales*, iii (1953), 64–77.

6531   JONES, J. H. John Owen, Cambro-Britannus. *Trans. Cymmrod. Soc. for 1940* (1941), 130–43.
Cf. also idem in *Greece and Rome*, x (1941), 65–73.

6532   JONES, T. G. Cultural bases: a study of the Tudor period in Wales. *Y Cymmrodor*, xxxi (1921), 161–92.

6533   JONES, T. G. Tudor Welshmen's English. *Y Cymmrodor*, xxix (1919), 56–69.

6534   KNIGHT, L. S. Welsh cathedral schools to 1600. *Y Cymmrodor*, xxix (1919), 76–104.

6535   KNIGHT, L. S. Welsh independent grammar schools to 1600. Newtown, 1926.
Based on original documents.

6536   LEWIS, SAUNDERS. Tudur Aled. *Efrydiau Cath.* i (1946), 32–46.
An influential bard critically discussed in the light of changing religious thought.

6537   MATHIAS, W. A. Lyfr rhetoreg William Salesbury. *Llên Cymru*, i (1950–1), 259–68; ii (1952–3), 71–81.
A treatise on rhetoric.

6538   MILLER, E. J. Wales and the Tudor drama. *Trans. Cymmrod. Soc. for 1948* (1949), 170–83.

6539   NEWCOMBE, RICHARD. Memoir of Dr. Gabriel Goodman, with some account of Ruthin school. Ruthin, 1825.

6540   ROBERTS, E. P. Siôn Tudur, *Llên Cymru*, ii (1952–3), 82–96.
A popular bard and his patrons.

6541 ROBERTS, R. E. Welsh music in the Tudor period. *Trans. Soc. Cymmrod.*, 1925–6, 1–24.

6542 WILLIAMS, I. M. Ysgolheictod hanesyddol yr unfed ganrif ar bymtheg. *Llên Cymru*, ii (1952–3), 111–24, 209–23.
On Welsh historical scholarship of the century, cf. 6235–6 and 6492.

6543 WILSON, W. G. Welshmen in Elizabethan London. *Life and letters today*, xli (1944), 77–86.

INDEX

THIS index is at once an author and a subject index. To economize space, titles of works are not given except when the author is unknown. In general, works written by an author are indicated by numerals following *auth.*, works edited by numerals following *ed.*, works translated by numerals following *trans.* All numerals refer to numbered titles except that where page references are cited they are enclosed in square brackets and where dates are cited they are enclosed in round brackets.

An exhaustive subject index would involve an analysis of the contents of every work cited and nothing of the sort has been attempted here. The subject entries in this index are no more than an attempt to classify the contents of entries so far as they are revealed in their titles. Though this is obviously inadequate it will probably be found helpful if used in conjunction with the rather elaborate table of contents and the prefatory notes to the different sections and subsections into which this book is divided.

Aaron, R. I.: *auth.* 6511.

Abbadessa, Giuseppe: *auth.* 1997.

Abbot, Charles, 1st baron Colchester: *ed.* 1120.

Abbott, E. A.: *auth.* 653, 3655.

Abbott, T. K.: *ed.* 5675.

Abbott, W. C.: *auth.* 3448.

Abell, John, Marian refugee: 2151.

Abell, Westcott: *auth.* 3298.

Aberdeen (Scot.), burgh of: 5045, 5047; biblio. of, 4900; burgesses of, 5048; common good of, 5102; records of, 214, 5046–7; Reformation in, 5524; trades of, 5047, 5582; universities of, 4889, 5628f.

Aberdeen (Scot.), diocese of: 5428, 5496.

Aberdeen (Scot.), shire of, 4899, 4908, 5093; court records of, 5418.

Aberdeen (Scot.), earl of, MSS. of: 215.

Aberdovey (Wales): 6279.

Abingdon, co. Berks.: [p. 357].

Abrahams, Israel: *auth.* 2808.

Abrahams, Phyllis: *ed.* 69.

Abram, W. A.: *auth.* 4500.

Abrams, Annie: *auth.* 3571.

Accounting, history of: 2863.

Acheley, Thomas: *auth.* 2946.

Acontius, Jacobus, jurist: 2904.

Acton, J. E. E. Dalberg, lord: *auth.* 322, 467, 1431.

Actors: *v.* play-actors.

Acworth, George, divine: 2232–3.

Adair, E. R.: *auth.* 379, 1020, 1048, 1152, 1154, 1168, 1586, 3299.

Adam, Frank: *auth.* 5108.

Adam, Robert: *ed.* 5032.

Adams, Arthur: *auth.* 2705.

Adams, E. N.: *auth.* 3720.

Adams, Robert: *trans.* 3519.

Adams-Acton, Murray: *auth.* 3869, 3925.

Adamson, M. R.: *auth.* 5472.

Additional MSS., B.M.: [p. 10].

Adelard, George: *auth.* 654.

Admiral, lord, the office of: 3551, 3555.

Admirals, British: lives of, 3466, 3485, 3497; lists of, 3542.

Admiralty: court of, 1544, [p. 138], 1568, 1570–2, 1574, 1576–7, 2529; law, influence of Roman law on, 1562; library of, 3437.

Admonition to parliament (Puritan tracts): 2391–2.

Advocates, society of, in Aberdeen: 5396.

Advocates' library, Edinburgh, MSS. of: 216.

Africa: English trade with, *v.* Commerce.

Aghadoe (Ire.) clergy: 5979.

Agnew, R. V.: *ed.* 4940.

Agricola (Bauer), George: *auth.* 2777.

Agriculture: [pp. 217–24]; in Eng. and Scot. compared, 5587; in Ire. 5813, 6092; in Wales, 6255; *v.* copyhold: enclosure; manor; serfdom; tenure.

Aiken, James: *ed.* 10.

Aikin, Lucy: *auth.* 655.

Aikman, James: *ed.* 4972.

Ailesbury, marquis of, MSS. of: 96.

Ailsa, marquis of, MSS. of: 217.

Ainslie, J. L.: *auth.* 1754.

Ainsworth, Henry: *auth.* 2454.

Ainsworth, John: *ed.* 2707.

Aird, Ian: *auth.* 654.

Aitken, J. M.: *auth.* 5332.

Aitkin, P. H.: *auth.* 5595.

Alba, duke of: *ed.* 870.

Alberi, Eugenio: *ed.* 889.

County palatine: *v.* Chester; Durham; of Scotland, *v.* Ross.

Coupar, lords: 5113.

Couper, W. J.: *auth.* 5486.

Courcelles, M. de, French ambassador to Scotland: dispatches of, 5306.

Coursing (sport): [p. 347].

Court baron (Eng.): [pp. 113–14].

Court baron (Scot.): 5385.

Court of Commonweal: [pp. 147–8].

Court of High Commission: 2208.

Court leet: [pp. 113–14], 4505, 4705, 6271, 6324.

Court of session (Scot.): [p. 458]; *v.* College of justice.

Courteault, Henri: *auth.* 616.

Courtesy, books of: 4058.

Courtney, W. P.: *ed.* 7.

Courts of law, English: [pp. 144–50].

Coutts, James: *auth.* 5618.

Coventry, co. Warw.: 122, 4809–10; fullers' gild of, 2761.

Coventry, Andrew: *ed.* 4994.

Coverdale, Miles: 6401: *auth.* 1714; *ed.* 1734; trans. of Bible, 1938, 1940.

Coveste, Walter, dep. lieut. of Sussex: 4789.

Cowan, Samuel: *auth.* 5000, 5230, 5353–4.

Cowane, John: 5601.

Cowell, H. J.: *auth.* 1873, 2009, 2139–41.

Cowell, John: *auth.* 1511, 1520.

Cowley, J. D.: *ed.* 1482.

Cowley, Walter: *auth.* 6128.

Cowling, G. H.: *auth.* 3841.

Cowper, earl, MSS. of: 123.

Cowper, Francis: *auth.* 1632.

Cowper, J. M.: *auth.* 2857; *ed.* 1719, 1974, 2098a, 2592.

Cox, J. C.: *auth.* 1297, 1715–16, 4422; *ed.* 4121, 4297, 4651.

Cox, J. E.: *ed.* 1718.

Cox, Richard: *auth.* 5836.

Cozens-Hardy, B.: *auth.* 2100, 3522, 4627–8; *ed.* 2502, 2995, [p. 342], 4629.

Crace, J. G.: *ed.* 4578.

Cradock, sir Matthew: 6290.

Craft gilds, England: 2564, 2683, 2685, 2689, 2689a, 2762; government attitude to, 2685, 2689a; in Hereford, 2846, 4442; in Kingston-upon-Hull, 2764; in London, 2847; in Preston, 4500; in Shrewsbury, 2762, 2765; in Southampton, 2834; *v.* livery companies.

Craft gilds, Scotland: 5580–1, 5585, 5587b, 5589–90, 5599–601, 5611; religious aspects of, 5594.

Craig, Hardin: *auth.* 2425, 3604.

Craig, John: *auth.* 1259.

Craig, J. T. C.: *ed.* 5319.

Craig, sir Thomas: 5365; *auth.* 1424, 5384.

Craigie, James: *ed.* 1425, 5307.

Craigie, W. A.: *auth.* 5002.

Cramond, William: *auth.* 5094; *ed.* 5051, 5055, 5470.

Cranfill, T. M.: *auth.* 3326, 3421.

Cranmer, J. A.: *ed.* 4151.

Cranmer, Thomas, archbp. of Canterbury: 1782, 1935; bible of, 1942; controversy with S. Gardiner, 2103; execution of, 2110; letters of, 1734; liturgy of, 1835, 1911; lives of, 1735, 1765, 1817, 1833, 1850, 2136; recantations of, 1717; visitations of, 1994; works of, 1718.

Cranstoun, James: *ed.* 4993.

Crapelet, G. A.: *ed.* 441.

Craster, Edmund: *auth.* 3292.

Craven, deanery of, co. York: 4862.

Craven, J. B.: *auth.* 5487; *ed.* 5469.

Crawford, earls of: *v.* Lindsay.

Crawford, George: *auth.* 5368.

Crawford, J. A.: *ed.* 4919.

Crawford, M.: *ed.* 5449.

Crawford, Robert: *trans.* 3505.

Creagh, Richard, archbp. of Armagh: 5995, 6066.

Creeds of Christendom: 1933.

Crehan, J. H.: *auth.* 1772–3.

Creighton, Charles: *auth.* 4020.

Creighton, Mandell, bp. of London: *auth.* 485, 693, 2259, 4294.

Creizenach, Wilhelm: *auth.* 3630.

Cremeans, C. D.: *auth.* 1774.

Crépy, treaty of: 863.

Crescentio, Bartholomeo: *auth.* 3563.

Cresswell, Joseph, S.J. (*alias* Jno. Philopatris, Jno. Perne): *auth.* 2249–50.

Crichton, Creighton, or Creitton, William, S.J.: 5304, 5458, 5504.

Crime, history of in Eng.: 1554.

Cripps, W. J.: *auth.* 3911.

Croft, H. H. S.: *ed.* 1371, 3783.

Crofton, R. C.: *auth.* 2784.

Croke, sir John, speaker of Commons: speeches of, 141.

Cromartie, earls of: 5113.

Crompton, Richard: *auth.* 1281–2, 1414, 1685.

Cromwell, Thomas, earl of Essex: 493–5, 526, 543; letters, 447, 452, 520; lives of, 520, 547.

PRINTED IN GREAT BRITAIN
AT THE UNIVERSITY PRESS, OXFORD
BY VIVIAN RIDLER
PRINTER TO THE UNIVERSITY